The Works of
William Wells Brown

Wm. W. Brown.

Eng'd. 66 State St. from a Dag'n of Chase.

The Works of
William Wells Brown

Using His "Strong, Manly Voice"

Edited by
Paula Garrett and Hollis Robbins

Foreword by
Henry Louis Gates Jr.

OXFORD
UNIVERSITY PRESS

OXFORD
UNIVERSITY PRESS

Oxford University Press, Inc., publishes works that further
Oxford University's objective of excellence
in research, scholarship, and education.

Oxford   New York
Auckland   Cape Town   Dar es Salaam   Hong Kong   Karachi
Kuala Lumpur   Madrid   Melbourne   Mexico City   Nairobi
New Delhi   Shanghai   Taipei   Toronto

With offices in
Argentina   Austria   Brazil   Chile   Czech Republic   France   Greece
Guatemala   Hungary   Italy   Japan   Poland   Portugal   Singapore
South Korea   Switzerland   Thailand   Turkey   Ukraine   Vietnam

Copyright © 2006 Oxford University Press

Published by Oxford University Press, Inc.
198 Madison Avenue, New York, New York, 10016
www.oup.com/us

Oxford is a registered trademark of Oxford University Press

Library of Congress Cataloging-in-Publication Data

Brown, William Wells, 1814?–1884
[Selections. 2006]
The works of William Wells Brown : using his "strong, manly voice" /
edited by Paula Garrett and Hollis Robbins.
p. cm.
ISBN-13: 978-0-19-530963-8
ISBN-10: 0-19-530963-4
1. African Americans—Fiction. 2. Brown, William Wells, 1814?–1884 3. African American
authors—Biography. I. Robbins, Hollis, 1963– II. Garrett, Paula. III. Title
PS1139.B9.A6   2006
818'.409—dc22   2006016676
ISBN: 9780195309638

Printing number: 9 8 7 6 5 4 3 2 1

Printed in the United States of America
on acid-free paper

To Donna

and

To Skip

Contents

Foreword

When I was an assistant professor of African American Studies and English at Yale in the late 1970s and early 1980s, I would meet the great historian John W. Blassingame Sr. every morning for breakfast at Naples Pizza. Situated near the geographical center of the Yale campus, Naples had become the actual center of African American intellectual life at Yale by the time that I arrived back there in 1975, after graduate school at the University of Cambridge—all because John Blassingame preferred Naples to every other "restaurant" (and I use that term loosely!) in New Haven, for reasons that he took to his grave. So if you wanted to talk to Blassingame, even during office hours, you would have to do so amid the aromas of burning crusts and savory toppings, hot pepper flakes, and grated Parmesan cheese. When he died a few years ago, the owners of Naples even erected a bronze plaque over John's favorite stall.

Every morning John and I would meet, sometimes alone, sometimes with other colleagues, such as the economists Donald Brown and Gerald Jaynes, the philosopher Anthony Appiah, the historian Peter Ripley, the sociologist Hardy Frye, and the anthropologist John Brown Childs—all regulars during their time at Yale. We talked about everything from last night's basketball game to contemporary politics to historical events. We argued as if our lives depended on it over questions such as whether Booker T. Washington and W. E. B. Du Bois could have forged a strategic alliance or whether "Booker T." was an Uncle Tom. When I was in the process of ascertaining the race of Harriet E. Wilson, African American literature's first woman novelist, it was to Blassingame, at Naples, every day, that I would bring the results of my research and seek his counsel about new leads to pursue. It was there that we celebrated with a piece of pepperoni pizza and a glass of beer when Blassingame became satisfied that Wilson was black.

Blassingame was the first African American scholar to write a full-length study of the history of slavery from the viewpoint of the slaves themselves. Using slave narratives, which at painstaking length he attempted to authenticate, "Blass" (as we called him, with enormous affection and respect) re-created the morals and manners and the life and times of what he termed, brilliantly, "the slave community." And it was at Naples that he and I would plot—fantasize, actually—about the future of the fledgling field of African American studies in the decades ahead.

Upon one thing we agreed early on: we had to find a way to map the field with reference works, sophisticated reference works such as biographical dictionaries; encyclopedias of history and culture; scholarly editions of texts; collected works of authors who had published essays primarily in periodicals; collected papers for canonical figures like Booker T. Washington, W. E. B. Du Bois, Marcus Garvey, and Frederick Douglass (whose papers Blassingame was in the process of editing); bibliographies; concordances—in short, all foundational reference works that, taken together, make a field of study, well, scholarly. It is upon reference works such as these that any discipline of study is constructed, and "Afro-Am" (as we called it) would be no exception. Indeed, we were determined that we would be part of the generation that eliminated forever the curse of scholars of African American studies: that each successive generation was forced to reinvent the proverbial wheel, repeating research undertaken by previous scholars of which we remained painfully unaware. It was nothing less than a textual legacy of memory that we hoped to leave to our colleagues and contemporaries, and to our intellectual heirs. So we embarked upon projects such as the Douglass Papers, the Black Periodical Literature Project, the *Norton Anthology of African American Literature*, the *Encyclopedia Africana*, and others, with alacrity and a sense of excitement that is difficult for our students, who now take reference works such as these for granted, even to begin to understand.

Of these various projects, collecting the occasional essays of nineteenth-century public intellectuals and creative writers intrigued me most. Blassingame's genius had been to understand the crucial role that black-edited newspapers and magazines had played in forging an African American intellectual community by the middle of the nineteenth century. Periodicals such as *Freedom's Journal*, Frederick Douglass's newspaper, the *Anglo-African Magazine*, and *The African Methodist Episcopal Church Review*, among many others, were often the sole venue for opinion and thought among an energetic and emerging class of African American intellectuals, scholars, and writers, who were all eager to express their ideas and feelings, and just as eager to reflect upon the ideas and feelings of their contemporaries.

The problem with choosing newspapers and magazines as the principal forum for black expression is their transience: newspapers, then as now, had a short shelf life. One black writer in the middle of the nineteenth century worried about this, calling these periodicals "ephemeral caskets" in which so much that was rich and vital in the thinking of African Americans would be buried, lost, and forgotten, tossed into the dustbin of history. Who keeps newspapers, and for how long? People, then as now, wrap garbage with newspapers. Can you imagine a more fragile, or perilous, repository for the first vital writings of the first generation of black intellectuals, the children of slaves hell-bent on gaining their freedom, literally and figuratively—on gaining a freedom of the mind, the freedom to embrace the republic of letters, a freedom larger than manumission?

It is not that these writers willingly chose to publish their thoughts in such fragile venues as newspapers and magazines directed primarily at a black readership. While they obviously relished the opportunity to speak to "the race" on behalf of themselves, they also knew that these publications were the only conduit available for their writing: other than the abolitionist press that flourished between 1831 and the end of the Civil War, few white publications opened their pages to African American authors. To publish, as a black writer, meant to publish primarily in the black press.

Fortunately, many of these periodicals survive today, against the greatest odds, because of efforts during the 1930s and beyond to microfilm and preserve them. Scholars such as James Danky have painstakingly documented the location of extant copies of the originals and library locations of microfilm editions. Using these tools, scholars are now able to piece together the collective "mind" of African American people as it manifested itself in print in the nineteenth century.

Of the several black writers whose occasional essays cry out to be collected and published, we have chosen to launch Oxford's Selected Black Writings series with the works of James McCune Smith, W. S. Scarborough, and William Wells Brown, all former slaves. James McCune Smith was one of the most highly educated human beings of any nationality or ethnicity, earning a B.A., an M.A., and an M.D. at the University of Glasgow in Scotland. W. S. Scarborough, like McCune Smith, was extremely well educated, earning his bachelor's and master's degrees at Oberlin College after graduating from Atlanta University. Scarborough became a classical scholar at precisely the time when an aptitude—or lack thereof—for mastery of Latin and Greek had become a curious touchstone through which the innate, or genetic, "capacity" of persons of African descent might be determined or measured. If W. E. B. Du Bois, the antecedent of today's black public intellectuals, himself has an antecedent, it is W. S. Scarborough, the black scholar's scholar. William Wells Brown certainly occupies an important position in the history of black intellectuals and reformers in the nineteenth century, but the uniqueness of his place in the tradition has often been overlooked. On the one hand, he was most typical of his black abolitionist peers: a bright and energetic former slave who published an engaging slave narrative (1847) and a popular novel (*Clotel*, 1853) and turned his considerable talents and personal appeal to extremely productive use in the antislavery cause. On the other hand, he used his urbane personal style and his broad appeal to generate for himself a large middle-class, largely female, following.

Brown's widely read novel, *Clotel*—the first novel published by an African American—clearly underscores his interest in appealing to a female readership; but so too, do his descriptive travel narratives and his deliberately inspirational biographical histories of the race. Brown's *Negro in the American Rebellion: His Heroism and His Fidelity* (1867) is an engaging compilation of stories about slaves and free blacks who fought in the American Revolution, the War of 1812, and in the Civil War. Some of these individuals' stories are well known, such as that of Crispus Attucks, but some stories would probably not be remembered, such as Peter Salem at the Battle of Bunker Hill, but for Brown's popular account.

Who among us does not want to have ancestors, real or imagined, who have achieved great things or displayed great valor? I recently discovered that one of my own forebears, John Redman, was a Revolutionary War veteran, serving in the First Virginia Regiment of the Light Dragoons from 1778 to 1782. On horseback with sabers and pistols, Redman's regiment chased and fought the British for three years in battles from South Carolina to Georgia, and later fought in court for recognition of his service and won a pension for his efforts. As Brown first demonstrated, these stories are important because they bear witness to the fact that Americans of all colors share a common past, as well as a common future.

The educator and university president William J. Simmons, D.D. (1849–1890), a former slave and the author of *Men of Mark: Eminent, Progressive and Rising* (Cleveland: Geo. M. Rewell & Co., 1887), included Brown among the most important black historical figures of the nineteenth century. Simmons clearly thought of Brown as a personality as well as a political reformer. Simmons devotes a page and a half of the three-page sketch of Brown to an account of him tricking a member of the Ku

Klux Klan. After holding a meeting in Louisville, Kentucky, Brown started on a trip to speak at Pleasureville; he was met by a black man who told him that the meeting was five miles in the country. The two men began walking and after some time they heard horses ahead of and behind them. Brown was captured by a number of klansmen and carried to a house where a man, presumably one of their party, was afflicted with the *delirium tremens.* The doctor's wit not forsaking him, he said he could cure the man—that he was a dealer in the black arts and was well acquainted with the devil. Having his doctor's case with him, Brown asked if he might be permitted to go into a room by himself for a while, which the klansmen allowed. While alone he charged his syringe with a solution of acetate of morphia, and put the instrument in his vest pocket. Returning to the room he requested the aid of his captors in holding the sick man while Brown made passes over him, as if mesmerizing him, during which he stealthily injected the morphine solution into the man's leg, after which he quickly quieted. The episode made a terrific impression upon the klansmen and quite literally saved Brown's neck.

In spite of William Wells Brown being in a subordinate position to Frederick Douglass in the canon of African American literature, Brown was both remarkably popular and well respected among the abolitionist elite. The eminent African American historian and librarian Dorothy B. Porter, reviewing a book about two nineteenth-century Rhode Island abolitionists, Elizabeth Buffum Chace and Lucy Buffum Lovell (*Two Quaker Sisters, Elizabeth Buffum Chace and Lucy Buffum Lovell,* introduction by Malcom R. Lovell, Liveright Publishing Company, 1937) in *The Journal of Negro History* (Vol. 22, No. 3. July 1937, pp. 358–361) noted in a long aside that Elizabeth Buffum Chace was highly protective of William Wells Brown's class status:

> Among the many Negro abolitionists who visited in Elizabeth's home was William Wells Brown, who during one of his visits fell in love with her sixteen-year-old Irish serving maid. Mrs. Chace relates how she helped to break up the affair not because she was unwilling for Brown to marry the girl but because she considered him a "gentleman" and felt the girl was much inferior to Brown. (360)

That the upstanding Elizabeth Buffum Chace would intervene in Brown's love life, and do so as a protective sister determined to prevent him from marrying outside his class, is a clear indication of how very far Brown had come from the plantation to the respectability of the highest abolitionist social circles.

Perhaps the final word on William Wells Brown is best left to the scholar John Ernest, who has done so much to elevate Brown's place in the canon. In his essay "The Reconstruction of Whiteness: William Wells Brown's *The Escape; Or, a Leap for Freedom*," Ernest writes:

> In Brown's large body of work one encounters striking representations of a number of literary, cultural, and historical concerns that are now at the center of the scholarly stage, including blackface minstrelsy, passing, racial mixing, sentimental culture, various modes of cultural memory, and narrative fragmentation and self-reflexivity. (1109)

It is difficult to imagine any of Brown's contemporaries who contributed as much or as richly to so many genres as did William Wells Brown. With this superbly edited edition of Brown's work—the first collection to reveal the sheer range and power of Brown's extraordinary imagination and impressive literary skills—Paula Garrett and Hollis Robbins have firmly secured Brown's place in the canons both of American literature and African American literature.

Henry Louis Gates, Jr.

Acknowledgments

We would like to thank Henry Louis Gates Jr. and our editors at Oxford University Press for bringing forth this series of volumes devoted to the works of African American writers and leaders. At Oxford, we would particularly like to thank Kim Robinson, Georgia Maas, and Anna Weichselbraun for their patience and goodwill. We would also like to thank the many kind colleagues and scholars on whom we have called for thoughts and advice over the past year, particularly James Bowley, Amy Forbes, Bill Gleason, Anne MacMaster, Carol Mattingly, Dana Nelson, Peggy Prenshaw, Elaine Showalter, Bill Storey, Elisa Tamarkin, and Sanford Zale. We also would like to acknowledge the importance of recent scholarship on William Wells Brown, especially the work of Robert Levine and John Ernest.

The librarians at Millsaps College were particularly helpful to us in securing texts and images; a special thanks to Tom Henderson and Larry Madison for not terminating our ILL privileges when we missed our return dates and for securing the cover image for us.

Likewise, our friend and dean, Richard Smith, encouraged this scholarship from the beginning and recognized the importance of this collaboration.

Our friends have also encouraged us in the process: Chip and Melba Bowman, Kelsey, Kim, and Rick Burke, Harvey Fiser, and Margie Schloesser maintained an interest in our project and cheered us to its completion.

Finally, our families were exceptionally supportive. As always, thank you to Herbert and Jane Garrett and Donna Read and to Michael, Ariel, and Asher Robbins-Rothman.

Introduction

Around the United States one finds scores of Frederick Douglass high schools, elementary schools, libraries, and institutes; it is rare, however, to find anything named for William Wells Brown. Yet Douglass and Brown were equally well known and respected during the second half of the nineteenth century; both men were celebrated as rousing orators, articulate spokesmen for the antislavery cause, and thoughtful cultural critics. So why has Douglass surpassed Brown in the public mind as an icon—*the* icon—of the antislavery movement, while Brown is known primarily for his melodramatic and untidy novel, *Clotel*? Why are fans of Brown's life and works limited to scholars and students of African American studies?

The answer seems to be a matter of target audience. Frederick Douglass presented himself as a man speaking to men on equal terms. Douglass's point was very simple: if all men are created equal, and I am a man, then I will speak to you equally. Douglass made this point over and over again. The bearded, physically imposing, and verbally gifted Douglass could easily pull this off. His modus operandi was to be a Great Man, a Colored Founding Father, and a Man of Letters. Evidently he succeeded.

By contrast, the refined and gentlemanly William Wells Brown presented himself as a man speaking to people—to women, fugitive slaves, and free blacks—who were not altogether sure that America's foundational documents included them in the category of "men." Reading his speeches and letters today, we see that Brown's rhetorical stance is designed to produce a sense of conversational familiarity in his auditors and readers. In the various narratives of his life and adventures he tells of finding himself in difficult situations where he must talk or con his way out. Brown appeals to those who might not live up to the masculine ideal that the eloquent Douglass favored—passionate defiance of unconstitutional oppression. "Compared to the highly self-conscious rhetorical flourishes of Frederick Douglass's narrative," William Andrews writes, "Brown's decidedly understated, restrained, almost deadpan, manner of recounting his life seems artless."[1]

Yet as anyone who reads his work will notice quickly, Brown's speeches, his fictional work, and, certainly, his humor are not artless by any means. Wilson Jeremiah Moses deems Brown a "trickster," noting with some reluctance his "clever opportunism and spirit of enterprise."[2] In nearly all of his writings and speeches, Brown positioned himself as an ironic observer of slavery's ills, as a wry pundit or commentator—personally familiar with the physical suffering and emotional anguish of slavery, but self-controlled and self-aware enough to step outside his suffering and speak directly to his audience. A reporter for the *New Lisbon (Ohio) Aurora*, reviewing Brown's lectures on September 9 and 10, 1844, noted that, "The audience was frequently in roars of laughter, and anon everything was quiet as the tomb, save for his strong manly voice."[3] Brown's mischievous and urbane anecdotes of life as a slave, as a fugitive, and as a free black man procured a wide following among the most powerful of disenfranchised insiders: educated women. These women thronged to his speeches and public addresses, often accompanied, of course, by husbands, brothers, and other male relatives. But the arc of Brown's career points to the pursuit of a female audience. After lecturing on the antislavery lecture circuit for a decade or so, Brown joined the lyceum circuit, where he spoke out powerfully on the subject of slavery's abuse of women.[4] Years later, after the Civil War, Brown dedicated himself to supporting the temperance cause, a decidedly female political movement.

Tactically, Brown's repeated introductions of himself as racially mixed—born of a slave mother and a white father—served to emphasize the impact of slavery on women. We see Brown's rhetoric returning again and again to images of his mother and of benevolent women as a primary motivation for his antislavery and pro-women position. Much of the recent scholarly work on Brown's pastiche novel, *Clotel; or, The President's Daughter* (1853), places the novel among important works by women about slavery, notably Harriet Beecher Stowe's *Uncle Tom's Cabin* (1852), Harriet Jacobs's *Incidents in the Life of a Slave Girl* (1861), and Frances Harper's *Iola Lero; or, Shadows Uplifted* (1892). That is, *Clotel* appears to be a women's novel—not just about a woman but also *by* a woman, by one who shares women's concerns.[5]

Even in texts featuring his own story or in narratives of famous men, such as are featured in *Rising Son* (1874), Brown does not write with the same masculine bravado that characterizes Douglass's work. "Brown seems to have almost deliberately refused to identify himself according to

Douglass's myth of the heroic resisters," Andrews argues in his important collection of Brown's autobiographies.[6] "From the outset of Brown's *Narrative*, the reader encounters admirable black men who pit themselves physically and morally against ruthless slaveowners in an effort to attain human dignity. Yet invariably they fail. The slaves who succeed against these overwhelming odds are those who learn how to use guile and deception to protect and advance their interests," Andrews adds. The tools of guile and deception are often the only tools available to the physically weaker or disempowered. Brown's work should be of particular interest to students of the late-twentieth-century critical school of subaltern studies who focus on the variety of rhetorical, attitudinal, and humor strategies adopted by individuals in subordinate positions to negotiate structures of power and to survive.

Of all of Brown's readers, it seems likely that women, who often shared this sense of civic inferiority, resonated with Brown's perspective even as they admired Douglass's strength and power. Brown, too, admired strength and power, as is obvious in his description of Douglass in *Rising Son*, though Brown spends much less time on Douglass's physical attributes than on his acting and "mimicking" abilities:

Mr. Douglass is tall and well made. His vast and fully-developed forehead shows at once that he is a superior man intellectually. He is polished in his language, and gentlemanly in his manners. His voice is full and sonorous. His attitude is dignified, and his gesticulation is full of noble simplicity. He is a man of lofty reason; natural, and without pretension; always master of himself; brilliant in the art of exposing and abstracting. Few persons can handle a subject, with which they are familiar, better than he. There is a kind of eloquence issuing from the depths of the soul as from a spring, rolling along its copious floods, sweeping all before it, overwhelming by its very force, carrying, upsetting, ingulfing its adversaries, and more dazzling and more thundering than the bolt which leaps from crag to crag. This is the eloquence of Frederick Douglass. One of the best mimics of the age, and possessing great dramatic powers; had he taken up the sock and buskin, instead of becoming a lecturer, he would have made as fine a Coriolanus as ever trod the stage. (*Rising Son*, pp. 437–438)

Brown repeats this turn from physical to literary in his description of another of his well-known black intellectual contemporaries, Alexander Crummell:

Blood unadulterated, a tall and manly figure, commanding in appearance, a full and musical voice, fluent in speech, a graduate of Cambridge University, England, a mind stored with the richness of the English literature, competently acquainted with the classical authors of Greece and Rome, from the grave Thucydides to the rhapsodical Lycophron, gentlemanly in all his movements, language chaste and refined, Dr. Crummell may well be put forward as one of the best and most favorable representatives of his race. (*Rising Son*, p. 456)

Inverting Douglass's hierarchies, Brown continually privileges eloquence over action, ironic detachment over suffering, the literary-intellectual over the heroic.

Reading William Wells Brown on his own terms, this selection of his works reconsiders Brown's traditional status in the African American literary canon as a kind of Douglass "Lite" and resituates him within the larger context of reform movements beyond the antislavery circuit. Brown, we argue, is a speaker who deliberately cultivated a low-key, educated, courteously ironic style to appeal to a female audience. As his writings demonstrate, Brown's rhetorical strategies include a coy modesty, a concern for female education, a facility for the melodramatic, a genteel humor, the avoidance of any specific mention of blackness or labor, and an unabashed enthusiasm for everything British—an awestruck Anglophilia.[7]

Targeting a largely female audience was a deliberate departure from both Frederick Douglass's and William Lloyd Garrison's antislavery script. Even before Douglass and Brown famously clashed over letters of introduction to ladies in the British antislavery movement, Douglass's annoyance at Brown's gushing style played out in the pages of Douglass's newspaper. Again and again Douglass attempted to place the mantle of "heroic resister" on Brown, and Brown continually shrugged it off. Brown's voice is pitched to a much different key than Douglass's is. Brown does not overpower his readers with logic and ratiocination; rather, he intends for his readers and listeners to recognize the irony if not the doublespeak of his texts. To put it bluntly, he asks his female readers to recognize themselves in this well-dressed, well-spoken, well-bred, but not quite fully free American "citizen." These readers, familiar as they would have been with the capacity of language to both establish and challenge the status quo, recognized in his seeming self-effacement and his focus on the sexual depravity caused by slavery a political figure who understood deeply their fears and struggles.

Life

William Wells Brown (c. 1814–1884) was born in Lexington, Kentucky, the son of a female slave and a white relative of her owner. In his *Narrative of William W. Brown* (1847; excerpted in this collection) and in many other of his writings, Brown tells the tale of his childhood, youth, and eventual escape to freedom in 1834. Two years later, he became active in the Western New York Anti-Slavery Society in Buffalo. There are few independent details about Brown's life during the next nine years beyond what he reveals in his work; William Farrison's 1969 biography, *William Wells Brown: Author and Reformer*, remains the best single source for information about these early years. According to Farrison and later biographers, the next nine years were spent working on steamships crossing Lake Erie (often carrying fugitive slaves), learning to read and write, traveling, and finding the voice that would be raised in a life of political action. Brown also married and fathered three daughters, the first of whom died as an infant.

In 1843, the National Convention of Colored Citizens and a national abolitionist meeting were held in Buffalo. At these meetings Brown met some of the nation's most prominent black abolitionists, including Frederick Douglass, who recognized in Brown a promising advocate for the antislavery cause. Like Douglass, Brown parted ways with Garrison's radical antislavery stance and embraced the policy of working within the existing political framework. Also like Douglass, particularly in these early years, Brown saw that words wielded well, one speech at a time, could change the minds of citizens in small towns across the North. With his early success in 1844 as a lively public orator, Brown was invited to lecture to the American Anti-Slavery Society at its annual meeting in New York City; he spent the next three years primarily lecturing, touring as far east as to lecture to the Massachusetts Anti-Slavery Society in 1847.

The same year, 1847, Brown's career as a writer began with the publication of the first of several versions of his *Narrative of William W. Brown*. Brown's *Lecture Delivered before the Female Anti-Slavery Society of Salem*, delivered and published just after his *Narrative*, is much less known but is a far more important text in understanding the direction of Brown's career. Not widely anthologized, the lecture is offered here in full. This early lecture is notable for its emphatic denunciation of slavery as a system of governing people, not simply because of the damage done to the participants' moral lives and the moral lives of bystanders, but also because the practices of slavery and subordination cause (and cannot help but cause) actual suffering in individuals. Slavery in America cannot help but be harmful, Brown argues; misery is the natural by-product of slavery.

For many northern women, the most persuasive argument against slavery was the specter of slavery's damage to white American morals. Brown certainly appealed to this moral outrage throughout his career, describing scenes of lascivious white auctioneers, groping white overseers, and insulted white wives. Indeed, Brown makes this point clearly in his Salem lecture. But rather curiously for a beginning writer and lecturer, Brown insists upon the inability of language to represent slavery, raising the concept of enslavement to an abstract level that cannot be captured by and limited to his words:

> I may try to represent to you Slavery as it is; another may follow me and try to represent the condition of the Slave; we may all represent it as we think it is; and yet we shall all fail to represent the real condition of the Slave. Your fastidiousness would not allow me to do it; and if it would, I, for one, should not be willing to do it;—at least to an audience. Were I about to tell you the evils of Slavery, to represent to you the Slave in his lowest degradation, I should wish to take you, one at a time, and whisper it to you.
>
> Slavery has never been represented; Slavery never can be represented. (*Lecture*, pp. 81–82)

Brown is presenting himself as a gentleman—too much of a gentleman to say ugly truths in front of ladies—even while he is claiming that his objective is to speak upsetting truths to women. On one level Brown is arguing that the effects of slavery are a function of the system and that the system needs to be torn down or everyone who is disempowered will be at risk. But on a second level Brown is emphasizing that there are other systems of slavery and other modes of disempowerment. Under this conceptual framework, women should begin to see themselves at risk:

> Where we find one man holding an unlimited power over another, I ask, what can we expect to find his condition? Give one man power *ad infinitum* over another, and he will abuse that power; no matter if there be law; no matter if there be public sentiment in favor of the oppressed. (*Lecture*, p. 82)

The message is both explicit in regard to southern slavery and implicit in regard to women across America.

Brown's lecture also uses popular Fourth of July orations as an opportunity to demonstrate the distance between the discourse of freedom in America and the practices of freedom in America. Read alongside Frederick Douglass's famous speech, "What to the Slave Is the Fourth of July?" given in Rochester, New York, four and a half years later, we can clearly see the differences in the two men's political-rhetorical strategies. Brown's lecture takes up the symbolism of Independence Day thus:

> I know that upon [the] 4th of July, our 4th of July orators talk of Liberty, Democracy, and Republicanism. They talk of liberty, while three millions of their own countrymen are groaning in abject Slavery. This is called the "land of the free, and the home of the brave;" it is called the "Asylum of the oppressed;" and some have been foolish enough to call it the "Cradle of Liberty." If it is the "cradle of liberty," they have rocked the child to death. (*Lecture*, p. 91)

Brown targets the nature of the metaphors of Independence Day. What are asylums and cradles but loci of disempowerment? One isn't free in a cradle, Brown astutely recognizes. And his quick turn of humor, thinking literally of a cradle—a decidedly feminine image—and adding that "they have rocked the child to death," delivers with skill the full impact of his message: slaves and white women have much in common.

Douglass's speech, given on July 5, 1852, soars in an entirely different direction, indicting patriotic revelers with denunciations of hypocrisy:[8]

> What, to the American slave, is your 4th of July? I answer; a day that reveals to him, more than all other days in the year, the gross injustice and cruelty to which he is the constant victim. To him, your celebration is a sham; your boasted liberty, an unholy license; your national greatness, swelling vanity; your sounds of rejoicing are empty and heartless; your denunciation of tyrants brass fronted impudence; your shout of liberty and equality, hollow mockery; your prayers and hymns, your sermons and thanks-givings, with all your religious parade and solemnity, are to him, mere bombast, fraud, deception, impiety, and hypocrisy—a thin veil to cover up crimes which would disgrace a nation of savages. There is not a nation on the earth guilty of practices more shocking and bloody than are the people of the United States, at this very hour.

Douglass's scorched-earth rhetoric is triumphant. No ironic detachment here. By contrast, Brown's mockery, though milder and replete with domestic references, resonates with the quick humor of many white women writers of the day, namely Grace Greenwood or, later, Marietta Holley. Brown's aim is a concept of liberty that could be claimed by all those who were not yet full citizens. Douglass's appeal, far loftier, is directed toward men and political hypocrisy—his subject is not Slavery but The Suffering Male Slave.

In 1850 the passage of the Fugitive Slave Laws changed the political landscape north and south. While there had been federal laws on the books since 1793 that provided for the return of escaped slaves and other fugitives across state lines, these laws were strengthened considerably under the Compromise of 1850 that required "all good citizens" "to aid and assist in the prompt and efficient execution of this law." The earlier laws were general and applied equally to criminals and indentured servants. But prior to 1850, nonslave states tended to ignore the laws as they applied to fugitive slaves on the basis that individuals in free states could not be legally bound to recognize slavery. Some northern states passed laws forbidding state officials from arresting or holding fugitive slaves; others adopted personal-liberty laws allowing fugitive slaves a trial by jury.

Many northerners opposed the 1850 Fugitive Slave Laws on the basis of overreaching by the federal government. Even those not fully on the antislavery bandwagon approved on principle the project of circumventing these laws. Even more personal-liberty laws were passed in protest. Even so, several well-known fugitive slaves such as Brown fled to Europe, fearful of capture and determined to continue with their antislavery work.[9] Brown was selected to attend the International Peace Conference in Paris in August 1849; he sailed from Boston in July.

Brown's voyage to Europe came in the midst of a personal crisis regarding his embarrassing separation from his wife, Elizabeth Schooner, whom he had married almost immediately upon his arrival in Buffalo in 1834. For years gossip had circulated in antislavery circles about Brown's life apart from his wife. Finally, Brown decided to squelch the talk by telling his side of the story. In a long and rambling public letter to *The Liberator*, published on July 12, 1850, Brown described the early years of his marriage, claimed that his wife was repeatedly unfaithful with a close friend of the family, claimed his own abiding love as the reason for not separating at the time of the infidelity, and claimed that her recent public criticism of him was because of his denial of financial support. The letter can be characterized as priggish and not particularly kind:

> In the summer of 1834, the same year in which I made my escape from slavery, I unfortunately became acquainted with Miss Betsey

Schooner, and after a very short acquaintance, we were married. Up to the time of our marriage, I was entirely unacquainted with the fact that Mrs. Brown's mother was living with a second husband, while her first was still alive, having never been divorced. Soon after, I was made acquainted with the fact that Mrs. Brown's only sister was a mother, without having been a wife. Still later, I learned that Mrs. Brown's eldest brother, John, was in the Auburn, N.Y. State prison, where he died.

Though thus mistaken in the character of the family from which I had selected a wife, still being devotedly attached to Mrs. Brown, and aware that one member of a family should not be blamed for the misconduct of the others, I loved my wife none the less for what I had learned in relation to her family.

By casting himself as a bewildered, tenderhearted victim of a bad woman, and as an honorable man and doting father, Brown successfully thwarted future criticism. His female admirers seem not to have noticed that he was able to retain his reputation as a gentleman by authoring a blatantly ungentlemanly letter. The crisis passed. (The full text of the letter is included in this volume.)

Two years later, the publication of *Three Years in Europe; or, Places I Have Seen and People I Have Met* (1852) established Brown solidly in the middle class, with middle-class virtues that appealed largely to women. *Three Years* is an epistolary journal of his travels through Britain and France in which he stargazes at the great sites of great men (and occasionally women) of both countries. Though he interweaves his awestruck and admiring travel reports with an antislavery argument, the latter is obviously secondary. However, the later letters in the volume are antislavery pleas that appeal to the Europeans' better natures in an attempt to urge them to convince their American counterparts to end the system of slavery.

With this turn to travel writing, Brown cemented his appeal to women; writers such as Catherine Maria Sedgwick, Caroline Kirkland, Harriet Beecher Stowe, and Margaret Fuller were widely known for their travel letters from Europe. These writers carved out new roles for women and new definitions of womanhood with the same forthrightness with which they offered advice and directions about travel. Sedgwick's *Letters from Abroad to Kindred at Home* (1841), Kirkland's *Holidays Abroad; or, Europe from the West* (1849), and Stowe's *Sunny Memories of Foreign Lands* (1854) were all published before the Civil War. While their tone is familiar and familial, the works demonstrate a will to challenge gender constraints and ideologies as they simultaneously admire and criticize the Old World and create an active role for woman as critic.[10]

During the early 1850s, Frederick Douglass was writing, speaking, and publishing in America. Brown, however, remained abroad until 1854. Douglass published Brown's letters from Europe in the pages of *The North Star* and *Frederick Douglass' Paper*, attempting to frame Brown within the "heroic resister" paradigm, emphasizing to Brown's readers that Brown had traveled far from slavery, literally. Here is Douglass writing on April 17, 1851:

> We have the pleasure to lay before our readers another interesting letter from W. Wells Brown. We rejoice to find our friend still persevering in the pursuit of knowledge, and still more do we rejoice to find such marked evidence of the rapid progress as his several letters afford. But a few years ago, he was a despised, degraded, whip-scarred slave, knowing nothing of letters; and now we find him writing accounts of his travels in a distant land, of which a man reared under the most favorable educational advantages might be proud. Would to God that the noble example of William Wells Brown were more widely copied among those who escape from slavery. His noble aim, his untiring industry, his unquenchable zeal, and his manly fortitude under afflicting trials, are worthy of all imitation. We have many private assurances from England of the value of Mr. Brown's labors in the cause of freedom and humanity, and are most happy to find that the weapons which have been used here for his destruction, have not prevailed there.

Brown's travel letters, such as the one published six months later, on October 2, 1851, continued to resist Douglass's characterization of Brown's mood as "zealous." Brown mentions slavery only in passing; rather, he makes observations on his surroundings in the customary hearty style of the nineteenth-century gentleman traveler abroad:

> DEAR DOUGLASS:—I have just finished a short visit to the far famed city of Oxford, which has not unaptly been styled, the city of palaces.
>
> Aside from this being one of the principal seats of learning in the world, it is distinguished alike for its religious, and political changes in times past. At one time it was the seat of popery; at another, the uncompromising enemy of Rome. Here the tyrant, Richard the Third, held his court, and when James the First, and his son Charles the First found their capital too hot to hold them, they removed to their loyal city of Oxford. . . .

It was a beautiful day on which I arrived at Oxford, and instead of remaining in my hotel, I sallied forth to take a survey of the beauties of the city. I strolled into Christ Church Meadows, and there spent the evening in viewing the numerous halls of learning, which surrounds that splendid promenade.

And fine old buildings they are; centuries have rolled over many of them, hallowing the old walls and making them gray with age. They have been for ages the chosen homes of piety, and philosophy. Heroes and scholars, have gone forth from their studies here, into the great field of the world, to seek their fortunes, and to conquer and be conquered. . . .

Had it not been for the possession of energy, I might now have been working as a servant for some brainless fellow who might be able to command my labour with his money, or I might have been yet toiling in chains and slavery. But thanks to energy, not only for my being to day in a land of freedom, but also for my dear girls being in one of the best Seminaries in France, instead of being in an American school, where the finger of scorn would be pointed at them, by those whose superiority rests entirely upon their having a whiter skin. . . .

Then again let me say to our young men, Take courage, "There is a good time coming." The darkness of the night appears greatest, just before the dawn of day.

Yours, right truly,

W.W. BROWN.

Quite obviously, Brown is less interested in a heroic stance than he is in a literary familiarity. The letter is remarkable for its startling interweaving of antislavery rhetoric with the tone of middle-class sentimental erudition, all the more remarkable for its appearing in Frederick Douglass's newspaper. Brown's tone seems as if it would be more at home in the pages of *Godey's Lady's Book* than in an antislavery publication. It is also difficult to distinguish the antislavery origins of this love of all things British from literary and class preoccupations. Elisa Tamarkin argues persuasively that the sort of Anglophilia that fugitive slaves such as Douglass and Brown evidenced "underwrote the American antislavery movement as both an ideological mission and a cultural project, and, at the same time, supplied abolitionists with an available symbology of a country worth emulating, far beyond the mere adoption of emancipationist politics."[11]

Brown's interest in the "fine old walls" of halls and castles also reveals an important tension at the heart of Brown's status as a slave turned gentleman.

As Eugene Genovese points out, Brown, like Douglass and others, served in the Big House under slavery, experiencing firsthand not only the trappings of wealth and power but also the manners and attitudes. More important, these men knew too well the gothic underside—and moral blackness—of life in the Big House, especially for women. As Genovese notes, "The Big House itself often resembled a battlefield. If closeness bred affection and warmth, it also bred hatred and violence; often it bred all at once, according to circumstances, moods, and momentary passions."[12] England, with its wealth of "big" houses—castles and palaces, with their drawing rooms, that Brown, Douglass, and others visited and described in enthusiastic detail, such as Kenilworth Castle, Windsor Palace, St. Paul's, Westminster Abbey, Holyrood House, Ludlow Castle, and Queen Victoria's Birthday Drawing Room—offered an aesthetic experience that allowed Brown and others to recall their memories of southern luxury without the attendant sexual-emotional turmoil.

Beyond Brown's interest in halls and castles, his focus on the domestic sphere and his attendant popularity among women did not go unremarked at the time. Horace Mann noted Brown's appeal in an antislavery speech to the U.S. House of Representatives in 1850:

> Frederick Douglass has just returned from England, where he has enjoyed the honors of an ovation. William Wells Brown, another fugitive slave, is now in England. His journeys from place to place are like the "Progresses" of one of the magnates of that land,—passing wherever he will with free tickets, and enjoying the hospitalities of the most refined and educated men. The very last steamer brought out an account of his public reception at Newcastle. An entertainment was given him which was attended by four hundred ladies and gentlemen. Men of high distinction and character adorned it by their presence. The ladies made up a purse of twenty sovereigns, which they gave him. It was presented in a beautiful purse that one of their number,—the successful competitor for the honor,—had wrought with her own hands. All their generosity and kindness they considered as repaid by hearing from his own lips the pathetic story of his captivity and the heroism of his escape.[13]

In the years following, Brown carefully nurtured his reputation as a gentleman tenderly concerned about women and family. He spoke publicly about the education of his daughters, as this review in the *Syracuse* (New York) *Chronicle* reprinted in the *Provincial Freeman* (Toronto) on October 21, 1854, attests:

Mr. Brown stated that he had two daughters, who were very desirous to be well educated. In this country he had tried, in vain, to get them in a good school. He was everywhere told that they could be received only in the schools for colored children, which were not of a character to answer their wants. When he was abroad, and found that he could not safely return on account of the passage of the Fugitive Slave Law, he sent for his family, and, to his surprise, found that the feeling against color did not exist in England. His daughters were admitted without question to the best schools of England, and were readily employed as teachers, in which business they were now engaged. One of these, who desired to perfect herself in the languages, went to Paris, and was admitted without question to the best schools of that city; and both were now leading teachers, by the side of native born Saxons, with white children of the middle classes for their pupils.

Brown's careful attention to the differences between the cultures of England and America, which he presents through the experiences of his daughters, points to one of the ironies of the European tour as an essential part of a nineteenth-century education: travelers will note that race is far less important than class in many circles. Clearly Brown's daughters are genteel enough to require good education. By European standards, moreover, their education is sufficient for both to be accepted as teachers of white children from good families. Brown's point, that his daughters have a future in Europe that is denied them in America, is about the collision of race with class.

For young men, too, particularly men of letters, England offered far richer soil in which to grow and thrive. Clearly, it was far easier for Brown to imagine himself to be a man of letters when he was actually dining with men of letters. "When Brown says, 'I had eaten at the same table as Sir Edward Bulwer-Lytton, Charles Dickens, Eliza Cook, Alfred Tennyson, and the son-in-law of Sir Walter Scott,'" Tamarkin notes, "[h]e is invoking an American dream of English civility and manners that has everything to do with class."[14] Brown, as well as Douglass and Crummell, she continues, subscribed to a "cosmopolitan universalism" that offered him a broader stage than simply the abolitionist movement.[15] For Tamarkin, these effusions suggest that writers thought of Britain "as just plain *better*—richer, smarter, more smartly dressed."[16]

This "broader stage" is crucial to understanding William Wells Brown's cultural importance in the late 1840s and 1850s and to understanding why he came to be less important than Douglass in the African American canon. It is important to note that an antislavery advocate did not just decide to speak or write publicly about abolition or any other cause, such as temperance, women's rights, or universal suffrage. Groups promoting these causes tended to be highly organized, particularly the various national and local antislavery, colonization, and temperance groups. Brown moved among several of these groups, choosing venues and audiences that responded to his appeal.[17]

Still, although Brown positioned himself as a doting father during these years, he did not like the disparaging term "patriarch," as Michael D. Pierson notes:

In the 1850s, African American authors used their status as eyewitnesses to slavery's practical workings in the vital nationwide battle to establish the correct meaning of the term "patriarchal institution." With proslavery writers claiming that the term was an accurate description for their harmonious society, black writers probed the inconsistencies between southern claims of benevolence and the actual treatment they had received as slaves. In Harriet Jacobs's autobiographical novel, she expresses dismay that visitors might misinterpret the sight of a white slaveowner crying at the funeral of a slave. Might this not be seen, she wonders, as "a beautiful feature in the 'patriarchal institution'"? Jacobs asserts a different view, however. The dead slave, Nancy, was killed by the same tearful woman, who then tried to have the woman buried at the foot of her own future grave. While the black community managed to secure the dead woman's burial "with all the rest of her family," Jacobs reasons that white gestures of patriarchal affection masked the harder reality that slavery divided the biological families of the enslaved, in this case in death as so often in life. Fugitive slave William Wells Brown likewise disavowed southern claims of generosity when he described a slaveholding character, the Reverend Peck, as "a kind of a patriarch in his own way" in *Clotel; or, the President's Daughter*.[18]

Indeed, Brown further clarifies the irony of his characterization of Reverend Peck through his introduction of Peck's daughter, Georgiana. Georgiana embodies sufficient feminine virtue, but also embodies a strength of character that her father does not. Upon her father's death, not only does she immediately plan to free the slaves, but also (unlike Augustine St. Clare of Stowe's *Uncle Tom's Cabin*), upon the likelihood of her own death, she frees the slaves and has them delivered safely to land that she has purchased for them in the North. In this strong and strong-minded female character, Brown draws a stark contrast to her father, the patriarch.

It seems clear to the twenty-first-century reader of Brown's autobiography and his novel, *Clotel*, that his intended audience is women. The selections included in this collection suggest that women were Brown's focus in nearly all of his writings. We see Brown's constant attention to the particular problems faced by women under slavery, his preoccupation with cleanliness, modesty, and virtue, his concern for his reputation, his embrace of chivalry past and present.

While abroad, Brown increasingly focused his attention on slavery's depravity, especially for women. In an early speech in Croydon, England—printed in full in this collection—Brown reminded his audience that he can give them only a cleaned-up version of slavery because the details of American slavery would be too much for their sensibilities. He did, however, resort to colorful and fantastic metaphors to inspire his listeners:

When the people in this country read of some slave having been whipped to death or hung, with only a sham trial before two or three slaveholders, they were horrified; and yet these were nothing more than the circumstances naturally incident to slavery. Instead of vainly seeking to better the condition of the slave, let them then seek to knock off the chains from his limbs, and not be content with anything short of that. . . . Were he (Mr. Brown) about to depict the true character of American slavery, if he could, he would pluck a feather from the wing of some fallen angel, dip it in the wailings of despair, and write upon the blackened walls of perdition in characters which would frighten the hyena out of his ferocity. . . .

It is hard to imagine that barbaric truths of slavery's cruelties would be less fantastic than the image of a feather from a fallen angel being dipped in "the wailings of despair," but perhaps the truths would be more astonishing— that is, more liable to turn the audience into unresponsive stone. Brown's rhetorical flights of fancy apparently succeeded, judging by his fundraising success.

Just three weeks after the speech in Croydon, in a speech in London— also printed in full in this collection—Brown delivered still more rousing rhetorical flourishes for his British audience:

Why I am more free here tonight, in monarchical England, than I should be in my own republican country! Whatever our friend from

Boston may do, I would that I could say with him, "I must, in honor, stand up in favor of America." And yet I love America as much as he does. I admire her enterprising and industrious people quite as ardently as he can; but I hate her hideous institution, which has robbed me of a dear mother, which has plundered me of a beloved sister and three dear brothers, and which institution has doomed them to suffer, as they are now suffering, in chains and slavery. Whatever else there may be to admire in the condition of America, at all events, I hate that portion of her Constitution. I hate, I fervently hate, those laws and institutions of America, which consign three millions of my brethren and sisters to chains for life.

Adding the humorous recollection that his own master had "very kindly offered to sell me to myself for half price," Brown's detachment from the "plunderings" of his family produces the air of courtliness that tempers his repetitions of the word "hate."

Some years later, the August 22, 1857, issue of the *Provincial Freeman* carried a story of Brown's urbane humor, turning whiteness on its head, under the headline "A Good Joke":

Wm. Wells Brown, the colored orator, who is not so black as some white men, told a very good story at the Abbington celebration on Saturday. On a steamboat on Cayuga Lake the other day he went to the breakfast table with the other passengers. Just as he took his seat, a dark colored white man called a waiter and asked if colored persons were admitted to the table with white folks. The waiter did not know exactly what to say, so he called the Captain, who on entering the cabin enquired who had called for him. "I, sir," said *Mr. Brown*, pointing to the dark stranger, "I desire to know if it is your custom to allow colored people at the regular table?" The captain replied that no objection had ever been made before, and seeing the dark white man evidently annoyed in spirit, appealed to the generosity of the colored orator, to allow him to remain. Mr. Brown finally consented, and at this turn of affairs the white man, who was so black as to be passed for a negro, left the table in utter disgust, and unable to speak his thoughts.

One of the things that strikes the reader of this text is Brown's comfort in being served by others. Brown's Big House origins bequeathed him an ease with finer things. In Europe, Brown could show himself to be on equal domestic footing with educated white readers. This fact had a certain appeal to women. Some of the more brutal cruelties were seen from afar; others of a domestic nature were witnessed firsthand. Brown's comfort level in the mansions of Europe was seen as one with his class, not as a distance traveled.

Back in America, Frederick Douglass continued to emphasize Brown's origins as a slave and the strength required to escape from slavery, reminding his readers that while Brown was happily touring England, thousands in America were suffering under the lash. Here is Douglass writing on November 19, 1852:

> The extracts, in another column, from English papers, on a book lately published in England by WM. WELLS BROWN, will be gratifying to his many friends in this country. A cordial welcome awaits the industrious and persevering fugitive on his return, (which we hope will not be much longer delayed) to the United States. We want to see him again in grappling distance of that power which is crushing our common people, especially since so many of our sable advocates have either left the field or are laying on their oars.

And why shouldn't Douglass be irked? Brown was enjoying himself and enjoying the cultural richness of Europe. To Douglass's mind, Brown remained seemingly indifferent to the plight of slaves trapped variously in the slave huts and Big Houses of southern plantations.

Brown himself seemed to hear the calls to return, though he clearly had mixed feelings about doing so. On August 1, 1854, in a speech delivered in Manchester, England—printed in full in this collection—Brown said:

> I have now been five years in this country. I have traveled through Great Britain, and am almost an Englishman. I think I know something of the public sentiment here; and I say, the people want to know the truth, and to know what they can do for us. I tell them, that those ultra abolitionists in America, to whom I have referred, are those who in America are considered to be the greatest foes of the fugitive slave law, and of all the acts of the pro-slavery party; those are the persons of whom slaveowners speak with most malignity, and who are more vilified by the American pro-slavery press than all other parties and associations put together. This may be, unless I can comply with an invitation to speak on Thursday (and I am afraid that I cannot do so), my last opportunity of speaking publicly in this country; but I shall return to the United States, after being five years in England, conscious that

I may safely give to the free coloured people of the north, and to the abolitionists of the United States, the assurance that something is being done here for their cause, and that the English people only want to know what they can do, and they will set about it and do it. (Cheers.) We do not ask you to take up arms; we do not ask you to do any act, or utter any language, unbecoming Christians; but we ask you to learn the facts and the truth of this matter, and honestly and strongly to speak out upon it.

Even upon Brown's return to America, audiences flocked to hear him lecture on topics other than abolition. On January 20, 1855, the *Provincial Freeman* applauded Brown for his breadth:

William Wells Brown has just concluded a series of lectures in Philadelphia. This, we believe, is the first attempt of a colored man to give a course of lectures, embracing other topics than the antislavery subject, and we are glad to learn that these lectures have been very successful. The first evening, Mr. Brown gave his audience an introduction to some of the great men and women of the Old World, and portrayed the beauties of several of the noted places in London and Paris. . . . "The Humble Origin of Great Men" was the third of the course, and was well attended. This subject was well chosen, as it was calculated to inspire the colored people with energy, and cause them to surmount difficulties to educate themselves. . . .

To reporters such as the one above, it is not that Brown was indifferent to slavery; rather, Brown saw himself—was presenting himself—as a gentleman. Moreover, he was participating in a cultural format in order to engage the support of cultured Americans to the antislavery cause, the same way he actively courted English men and women abroad. To do so, Brown carefully identified himself with their perspectives, practically claiming British citizenship to do so.

In 1855, Douglass and Brown, the two lions of the antislavery tour, had a public falling-out over what may have been a misunderstanding but was most likely an expected manifestation of a latent rivalry. On March 2, *Frederick Douglass' Paper* printed the following item under the headline "William Wells Brown":

While our distinguished brother, Brown was abroad, laboring, with admirable industry in the cause of human freedom, and adding to his stock of knowledge of men and things, we esteemed it not less a pleasure than a duty to commend him and his work. We rejoiced that so much of talent and industry could be pointed to, (in vindication of our common people,) as were exemplified in MR. Brown. We do *not* regret any kind word we then said of him; but we *do* regret that he should feel called upon, to show his faithfulness to the American Anti-Slavery Society, by covering us with reproach and dishonor. If Mr. Brown has aught against us, he need not retail his complaints to cliques, parties, and antislavery circles, or allow them to be so retailed for him. Put your charges against us, Mr. Brown, in a suitable shape, and they shall appear, not only in the antislavery office at Boston, in the private ear of prejudice, but we promise you to publish them to our readers. As an honest man, we hold it to be your duty to do this, or to cease circulation as facts, what we know can be shown to be the merest fictions. Come, Mr. Brown, let us have the facts.

Two weeks later, on March 16, the paper reprinted Brown's response (it is printed in full in this collection), which Brown had published in the *Anti-Slavery Standard*, above Douglass's subsequent reply:

. . . My charge against you is, that, just before I left the United States for England, you wrote a private letter to a distinguished Abolitionis[t] in Great Britain, injurious to me, and intended to forestall my movements there. In a note which I forwarded to you, to your address at Rochester on the 20th of January last, I gave you to understand that I had been made aware of your having acted in that underhand manner: ". . . I need not say that the very unfavorable position in which your letter placed me before your friend, secured me for a cold reception at her hands. I need not name the lady; you know to whom I refer unless you wrote to more than one." Your attack upon me, in your paper of the 2nd inst., in which you ask for "facts," when my note containing the above had been in your possession more than a month, shows too well your wish to make a sneaking fling at me, instead of seeking for "facts," and acting the part of an honorable man. . . .

WILLIAM WELLS BROWN.

REPLY TO MR. BROWN.
. . . The facts wanted are, in brief, these:

1st. Who is the "*distinguished abolitionist* to whom you allege I wrote a *private letter injurious*" to you? Give the name and the local habitation. Certainly one so prompt to have "justice" done, can have no objection to come before the world in defense of justice.

2nd. State precisely and if not precisely state the *substance* of what I said in that letter, that the public may judge, not only whether it was injurious to you, but, secondly, whether it was intentionally "*injurious.*" I admit that the charge is a serious one; and if it be established beyond contradiction or reasonable explanation, I am willing to fall not only beneath the contempt of my brother Brown, but that of all honorable men. I call for the "*facts,*" and should do so in the face of a dozen such letters as the above. . . .

Their differences do not appear to have been worked out further, but these letters make clear that the two men saw themselves and their roles quite differently. William Wells Brown's rhetorical strategy of evoking culture and addressing the concerns of women—in particular, grounding his arguments in good part upon his personal reputation and position as a gentleman—differs greatly from Frederick Douglass's strategy of muscular, fiery, public oratory. If Douglass represented a cognitive approach to the question of abolition by emphasizing a commitment to the founding principles of America and appealing to the mind, Brown represented the emotional approach by emphasizing his role as doting father and an urbane man of letters.

This single-volume collection presents a broad spectrum of Brown's works, contextualizing each within the political expectations of its audience. Brown's style is evident throughout his career, from drama, fiction, and personal narrative to lectures and letters. To view Brown solely as the first black novelist is to sell short the significance of his role as a public intellectual whose strategy of addressing a female audience limited his reach historically, because the decisions about anthologizing and canonicity have been the purview of men.

Works

The texts that follow not only demonstrate Brown's range but also reveal how his rhetorical strategy prevailed across his literary output. No matter the constellation of political and cultural questions that inform his work, Brown the public intellectual read how women as well as men saw the historical, cultural, philosophical, scientific, and geopolitical controversies of his era. This collection will reclaim Brown's most vital and provocative nonfiction work and, in so doing, will broaden perceptions of black participation in abolitionist arguments in the nineteenth century.

This collection runs from 1847, with *A Lecture Delivered before the Female Anti-Slavery Society of Salem*, Brown's most theoretical and startling text, through 1880, with *My Southern Home*, Brown's satiric portrayal of his personal experience. Throughout this collection, all modifications to the original texts are put in square brackets.

Notes

1 William L. Andrews, "Introduction," *Journeys in New Worlds: Early American Women's Narratives* (Madison: University of Wisconsin Press, 1990).

2 Wilson Jeremiah Moses, *Alexander Crummell: A Study of Civilization and Discontent* (Amherst: University of Massachusetts Press, 1992), pp. 4 and 48–49.

3 Quoted in William Farrison, *William Wells Brown: Author and Reformer* (Chicago: University of Chicago Press, 1969), p. 90.

4 See, for example, Angela G. Ray, *The Lyceum and Public Culture in the Nineteenth-Century United States* (East Lansing: Michigan State University Press, 2005).

5 Ironically, of course, much of *Clotel* was indeed written by a woman, as Robert S. Levine's thorough and thoroughly useful edition of *Clotel* makes clear (Bedford Cultural Edition; Boston: Bedford, 2000). Levine calls Brown "one of the most renowned antislavery lecturers and . . . reformers of the time" (p. 4). By bringing a wide variety of texts and discourses into *Clotel*, Levine argues, "Brown also makes use of the (post)modernistic technique of bricolage, a close cousin to pastiche, which involves taking bits and pieces of writings (sometimes long pieces) and (re)assembling those 'found' cultural materials into something new" (p. 7). "Is Brown a plagiarist?" Levine asks, "or are there more complex ways of understanding his authorial strategies and perspectives?" (p. vii).

6 William Andrews, *From Fugitive Slave to Free Man: The Autobiographies of William Wells Brown* (New York: New American Library, 1993).

7 See Elisa Tamarkin, "Black Anglophilia; or, The Sociability of Antislavery," *American Literary History* 14, no. 3 (2002): 444–478.

8 Douglass also said, "This 4th of July is *yours*, not *mine. You* may rejoice, I must mourn."

9 Douglass lived abroad from 1845 to 1847, by which time, through the aid of friends, he had raised enough money to purchase his freedom.

10 Many of these works, such as Greenwood's *Haps and Mishaps* (1853), still express an unflagging optimism for American reform, even in the wake of the Fugitive Slave Laws. Fuller's *At Home and Abroad; or, Things and Thoughts in America and Europe* (1856), a collection of her travel letters originally published in Horace Greeley's *New York Tribune* from 1847 to 1849, was published soon after her bold assessment of feminism in America, *Woman in the Nineteenth Century* (1845). These letters, concerned primarily with women's political activism, express serious social criticism from the point of view of a staunch Republican calling for reform, if not revolution, both at home and abroad. Of course men authored travel books, too; Washington Irving in his "Spanish Sketch Book" (in *The Alhambra*, 1832) and Herman Melville in *Typee* (1846) depicted an intrepid traveler, an "American Adam," exploring exotic locations. Nathaniel Hawthorne published *The Marble Faun*, a kind of travel fiction, in 1860, and Grace Greenwood's friend and correspondent

Bayard Taylor also published numerous travel volumes, establishing a reputation as the most popular travel writer of the century. Both Hawthorne and Taylor defended America's reputation abroad and imagined an even greater dominance worldwide. But in the closing decades of the century, Mark Twain offered a more sardonic view, marked by a darkly humorous consciousness of the tarnished postwar national identity.

11 Tamarkin, pp. 445–446.

12 Eugene D. Genovese, *Roll, Jordan, Roll: The World the Slaves Made* (New York: Vintage, 1974), p. 361. Elisa Tamarkin is surprised by "the extravagant fixation on aspects of British culture far removed from, and far surpassing, the political imperatives of abolition itself" (p. 446). Indeed, on one level the "preoccupation" of blacks with England is "bizarre," as Tamarkin puts it (p. 447). Tamarkin details the moments in *Frederick Douglass' Paper* where article writers swooned over Kenilworth Castle, Windsor Palace, St. Paul's, Westminster Abbey, Holyrood House, Ludlow Castle, and Queen Victoria's Birthday Drawing Room.

13 *Speech of Horace Mann, of Massachusetts, on the Subject of Slavery in the Territories, and the Consequences of a Dissolution of the Union: Delivered in the United States House of Representatives, February 15, 1850* (Boston: Redding and Company, 1850). Mann's testosterone-laden verbiage included this: "If agitation and instigation are evils now, woe to those who would seek to mitigate or to repress them by the remedies of disunion and civil war. Let men who live in a powder mill beware how they madden pyrotechnists."

14 Tamarkin, p. 462.

15 Tamarkin, p. 453. Robert Levine adds, "Tamarkin makes a powerful case for reading African Americans' attraction to England not simply as indicative of the politics of abolitionism but also as markers (or central constituents) of the development of a black intellectual cosmopolitan politics during the antebellum period. Central to that development, she persuasively argues, was an interest in the high sociability and 'eminently pleasurable activities' enabled by transatlantic abolitionist culture" ("Commentary: Critical Disruptions," *American Literary History* 14, no. 3 [2002]: 540–550).

16 Tamarkin, p. 453.

17 The daughter of Rhode Island abolitionist Elizabeth Buffum Chace recalled Brown, who was frequently a guest in their home, as "an agreeable and handsome man who enjoyed and added to the minor pleasantry of daily occurrence" (142). Mrs. Chace stepped in to break up a love affair between Brown and the family's sixteen-year-old Irish maid, not because of race but because she believed him to be socially superior to her. "It would not have been well for him," she apparently argued, "to marry M. She could not have associated with the people that he did" (143). Wyman, Lillie Buffum Chace, and Arthur Crawford Wyman. *Elizabeth Buffum Chace, 1806–1899: Her Life and Her Environment* (Boston: W. B. Clarke Co., 1914).

18 Michael D. Pierson, "'Slavery Cannot Be Covered Up with Broadcloth or a Bandanna': The Evolution of White Abolitionist Attacks on the 'Patriarchal Institution,'" *Journal of the Early Republic* 25, no. 3 (2005): 383–415.

Speeches

A Lecture Delivered before the Female Anti-Slavery Society of Salem

Lyceum Hall, Nov. 14, 1847 (Boston: Massachusetts Anti-Slavery Society, 1847)

Brown delivered and published this speech just after his Narrative. The speech is one of the most important texts of Brown's career, marking the beginning of Brown's appeal to a white female audience. Not widely anthologized, this lecture is offered here in full. The lecture clearly situates Brown's arguments against slavery in larger conversations about full citizenship in America. Brown argues not just about the corruption of the system of slavery but also about its cruelty, putting a human face on a subject that was too easily detached from real people by white abolitionist leaders of the time.

Mr. Chairman, and Ladies and Gentlemen:— In coming before you this evening to speak upon this all-important, this great and commanding subject of freedom, I do not appear without considerable embarrassment; nor am I embarrassed without a cause. I find myself standing before an audience whose opportunities for education may well be said to be without limit. I can scarcely walk through a street in your city, or through a city or a town in New England, but I see your common schools, your high schools, and your colleges. And when I recollect that but a few years since, I was upon a Southern plantation, that I was a Slave, a chattel, a thing, a piece of property,—when I recollect that at the age of twenty-one years I was entirely without education, this, every one will agree, is enough to embarrass me. But I do not come here for the purpose of making a grammatical speech, nor for the purpose of making a speech that shall receive applause from my hearers. I did not accept the invitation to lecture before this association, with the expectation or the hope that I should be able to present anything new. I accepted the invitation because I felt that I owed a duty to the cause of humanity; I felt that I owed a duty to three millions of my brethren and sisters, with some of whom I identified by the dearest ties of nature, and with most of whom I am identified by the scars which I carry upon my back. This, and this alone, induced me to accept the invitation to lecture here.

My subject for this evening is Slavery as it is, and its influence upon the morals and character of the American people.

I may try to represent to you Slavery as it is; another may follow me and try to represent the condition of the Slave; we may all represent it as we think it is; and yet we shall all fail to represent the real condition of the Slave. Your fastidiousness would not allow me to do it; and if it would, I, for one, should not be willing to do it;—at least to an audience. Were I about to tell you the evils of Slavery, to represent to you the Slave in his lowest degradation, I should wish to take you, one at a time, and whisper it to you.

Slavery has never been represented; Slavery never can be represented. What is a Slave? A Slave is one that is in the power of an owner. He is a chattel; he is a thing; he is a piece of property. A master can dispose of him, can dispose of his labor, can dispose of his wife, can dispose of his offspring, can dispose of everything that belongs to the Slave, and the Slave shall have no right to speak; he shall have nothing to say. The Slave cannot speak for himself; he cannot speak for his wife, or his children. He is a thing. He is a piece of property in the hands of a master, as much as is the horse that belongs to the individual that may ride him through your streets to-morrow. Where we find one man holding unlimited power over another, I ask, what can we expect to find his condition? Give one man power *ad infinitum* over another, and he will abuse that power; no matter if there be law; no matter if their be public sentiment in favor of the oppressed.

The system of Slavery, that I, in part, represent here this evening, is a system that strikes at the foundation of society, that strikes at the foundation of civil and political institutions. It is a system that takes man down from the lofty position which his God designed that he should occupy; that drags him down, places him upon a level with the beasts of the field, and there keeps him, that it may rob him of his liberty. Slavery is a system that tears the husband from the wife, and the wife from the husband; that tears the child from the mother, and the sister from the brother; that tears asunder the tenderest ties of nature. Slavery is a system that has its bloodhounds, its chains, its negro-whips, it dungeons, and almost every instrument of cruelty that the human eye can look at; and all this for the purpose of keeping the Slave in subjection; and all this for the purpose of obliterating the mind, of crushing the intellect, and of annihilating the soul.

I have read somewhere of an individual named Caspar Hauser, who made his appearance in Germany some time since, and represented that he had made his escape from certain persons who had been trying to obliterate his mind, and to annihilate his intellect. The representation of that single individual raised such an excitement in Germany, that law-makers took it in hand examined it, and made a law covering that particular case and all cases that should occur of that kind; and they denominated it the "murder of the soul." Now, I ask, what is Slavery doing in one half of the States of this Union, at the present time? The souls of three millions of American citizens are being murdered every day, under the blighting influence of American Slavery. Twenty thousand have made their escape from the prison-house; some have taken refuge in the Canadas, and others are lurking behind the stumps in the Slave-States. They are telling their tales, and representing that Slavery is not only trying to murder their souls, but the souls of three million of their countrymen at the present day; and the excitement that one individual raised in monarchical Germany, three million have failed to raise in democratic, Christian, republican America!

I ask, is not this a system we should examine! Ought we not to look at it? Ought we not to see what the cause is that keeps the people asleep upon the great subject of American Slavery? When I get to talking about Slavery as it is,—when I think of the three millions that are in chains at the present time, I am carried back to the days when I was a Slave upon a Southern plantation; I am carried back to the time when I saw dear relatives, with whom I am identified by the tenderest ties of nature, abused and ill-treated. I am carried back to the time when I saw hundreds of Slaves driven from the Slave-growing to the Slave-consuming States. When I begin to talk of Slavery, the sighs and the groans of three millions of my countrymen come to me upon the wings of every wind; and it causes me to feel sad, even when I think I am making a successful effort in representing the condition of the Slave.

What is the protection from the masters which Slaves receive? Some say, law; others, public sentiment. But, I ask, Where is the law; where is the public sentiment? If it is there, it is not effectual; it will not protect the Slave. Has the case ever occurred where the Slaveholder has been sent to the State's prison, or anything of the kind, for ill-treating, or for murdering a Slave? No such case is upon record; and it is because the Slave receives no protection and can expect no protection from the hands of the master. What has the brother not done, upon the Slave-plantation, for the purpose of protecting the chastity of a dearly beloved sister? What has the father not done to protect the chastity of his daughter? What has the husband not done to

protect his wife from the hands of the tyrant? They have committed murders. The mother has taken the life of her child, to preserve that child from
the hands of the Slave-trader. The brother has taken the life of his sister, to
protect her chastity. As the noble Virginius seized the dagger, and thrust it
to the heart of the gentle Virginia, to save her from the hands of Appius
Claudius of Rome, so has the father seized the deadly knife, and taken the
life of his daughter, to save her from the hands of the master or of the Negro-
driver. And yet we are told that the Slave is protected; that there is law and
public sentiment! It is all a dead letter to the Slave.

But why stand here and try to represent the condition of the Slave? My
whole subject must necessarily represent his condition, and I will therefore
pass to the second part,—the influence of Slavery upon the morals of the
people; not only upon the morals of the Slave-holding South, or of the
Slave, but upon the morals of the people of the United States of America.
I am not willing to draw a line between the people of the North and the
people of the South. So far as the people of the North are connected with
Slaveholding, they necessarily become contaminated by the evils that follow in the train of Slavery.

Let me look at the influence which Slavery has over the morals of the
people of the South. Three millions of Slaves unprotected! A million of
females that have no right to marriage! Among the three millions of
Slaves upon the Southern plantation, not a single lawful marriage can be
found! They are out of the pale of the law. They are herded together, so far
as the law is concerned, as so many beasts of burden are in the free States.

Talk about the influence of Slavery upon the morals of the people, when
the Slave is sold in the Slave-holding States for the benefit of the church?
when he is sold for the purpose of building churches? when he is sold for
the benefit of the minister?

I have before me a few advertisements, taken from public journals and
papers, published in the Slaveholding States of this Union. I have one or
two that I will read to the audience, for I am satisfied that no evidence is
so effectual for the purpose of convincing the people of the North of the
great evils of Slavery as is the evidence of the Slaveholders themselves. I
do not present to you the assertion of the North; I do not bring before you
the advertisement of the Abolitionists, or my own assertion; but I bring
before you the testimony of the Slaveholders themselves,—and by their
own testimony must they stand or fall.

The first is an advertisement from the columns of the New Orleans
Picayune, one of the most reputable papers published in the State of
Louisiana, and I may say one of the most reputable papers published South
of Mason and Dixon's line. If you take up the Boston Courier, or any other

reputable paper, you will probably find in it an extract from the New Orleans Picayune, whose editor is at the present time in Mexico, where our people are cutting the throats of their neighbors.

"Cock-pit—Benefit of Fire Company No. 1, Lafayette.—A cock-fight will take place on Sunday, the 17th inst., at the well-known house of the subscriber. As the entire proceeds are for the benefit of the Fire Company, a full attendance is respectfully solicited.

Adam Israng,
Corner of Josephine and Telaupitolas Streets, Lafayette."
[*N. O. Pic. Of Sunday, Dec. 17.*

"Turkey Shooting.—This day, Dec. 17, from 10 o'clock, A.M., until 6 o'clock, P.M., and the following Sundays, at M'Donoughville, opposite the Second Municipality Ferry."

[From the same paper.

The next is an advertisement from the New Orleans Bee, an equally popular paper.

"A Bull Fight, between a ferocious bull and a number of dogs, will take place on Sunday next, at 4¼ o'clock P.M., on the side of the river, at Algiers, opposite Canal Street. After the bull fight, a fight will take place between a bear and some dogs. The whole to conclude by a combat between an ass and several dogs.

"Amateurs bringing dogs to participate in the fight will be admitted gratis. Admittance—Boxes, 50 cts.; Pit, 30 cts. The spectacle will be repeated every Sunday, weather permitting.

Pepe Llulla.

Now these are not strange advertisements to be found in a Southern journal. They only show what Slavery has been doing there to contaminate the morals of people. Such advertisements can be found in numbers of the public journals that are published in the Slave-holding States of this Union. You would not find such an advertisement in a Boston or a Salem paper. Scarcely a paper in New England would permit such an advertisement; and why? Because you are not so closely connected with Slavery; you are not so much under its blighting influence as are the Slave-owners in the Slave-holding States of the Union.

I have another advertisement, taken from a Charleston paper, advertising the property of a deceased Doctor of Divinity, probably one of the most popular men of his denomination that ever resided in the United States of America. In that advertisement it says, that among the property are "twenty-seven Negroes, two mules, one horse, and an old wagon." That is the property of a Slave-holding Doctor of Divinity![1]

I have another advertisement before me, taken from an Alabama paper, in which eight Slaves are advertised to be sold for the benefit of an Old School Theological Seminary for the purpose of making ministers. I have another, where ten Slaves are advertised to be sold for the benefit of Christ Church Parish. I have another, where four Slaves are advertised to be sold for the benefit of the Missionary cause,—a very benevolent cause indeed. I might go on and present to you advertisement after advertisement representing the system of American Slavery, and its contaminating influence upon the morals of the people. I have an account, very recent, that a Slave-trader,—one of the meanest and most degrading positions in which a man can be found upon God's footstool,—buying and selling the bodies and souls of his fellow country-men, has joined the church, and was, probably, hopefully converted. It is only an evidence that when Wickedness, with a purse of gold, knocks at the door of the Church, she seldom, if ever, is refused admission.

This is not the case here; for, some forty years since, the Church was found repudiating Slavery; she was found condemning Slavery as man-stealing, and a sin of the deepest dye. The Methodists, Presbyterians, and other denominations, and some of the first men in the country, bore their testimony against it. But Slavery has gone into all the ramifications of society; it has taken root in almost every part of society, and now Slavery is popular. Slavery has become popular, because it has power.

Speak of the blighting influence of Slavery upon the morals of the people? Go into the Slaveholding States, and there you can see the master going into the church, on the Sabbath, with his Slave following him into the church, and waiting upon him,—both belonging to the same church. And the day following, the master puts his Slave upon the auction-stand, and sells him to the highest bidder. The Church does not condemn him; the law does not condemn him; public sentiment does not condemn him; but the Slaveholder walks through the community as much respected after he has sold a brother belonging to the same church as himself, as if he had not committed an offence against God.

Go into the Slaveholding States, and to-morrow you may see families of Slaves driven to the auction-stand, to be sold to the highest bidder; the husband to be sold in the presence of the wife, the wife in the presence of the husband, and the children in the presence of them both. All this is done under the sanction of law and order; all is done under the sanction of public sentiment, whether that public sentiment be found in Church or in State.

Leaving the Slaveholding States, let me ask what is the influence that Slavery has over the minds of the Northern people? What is its contaminating influence over the great mass of the people of the North? It must have an influence, either good or bad. People of the North, being connected with the Slaveholding States, must necessarily become contaminated. Look all around, and you see benevolent associations formed for the purpose of carrying out the principles of Christianity; but what have they been doing for Humanity? What have they ever done for the slave?

First, we see the great American Bible Society. It is sending bibles all over the world for the purpose of converting the heathen. Its agents are to be found in almost every country and climate. Yet three millions of Slaves have never received a single bible from the American Bible Society. A few years since, the American Anti-Slavery Society offered to the American Bible society a donation of $5,000 if they would send bibles to the Slaves, or make an effort to do it, and the American Bible Society refused even to *attempt* to send the bible to the Slaves!

A Bible Society, auxiliary to the American Bible Society, held a meeting a short time since, at Cincinnati, in the State of Ohio. One of its members brought forward a resolution that the Society should do its best to put the bible in the hands of every poor person in the country. As soon as that was disposed of, another member brought forward a resolution that the Society should do its best to put the bible into the hands of every Slave in the country. That subject was discussed for two days, and at the end of that time they threw the resolution under the table, virtually resolving that they would not make an attempt to send bibles to the Slaves.

Leaving the American Bible Society, the next is the American Tract Society. What have you to say against the American Tract Society? you may ask. I have nothing to say against any association that is formed for a benevolent purpose, if it will only carry out the purpose for which it was formed. Has the American Tract Society ever published a single line against the sin of Slaveholding? You have all, probably, read tracts treating against licentiousness, against intemperance, against gambling, against Sabbath-breaking, against dancing, against almost every sin that you could think of; but not a single syllable has ever been published by the American Tract Society against the sin of Slaveholding. Only a short time since they offered a reward of $500 for the best treatise against the sin of dancing. A gentleman wrote a treatise, they awarded him the $500, and the tract is now in the course of publication, if it is not already published. Go into a nice room, with fine music, and good company, and they will publish a tract against your dancing; while three millions are dancing every day at the end of the master's cowhide, and they cannot notice it! Oh no; it is too small fry for them! They cannot touch that, but they can spend their money in publishing tracts against your dancing here at the North, while the Slave at the South may dance until he dances into his grave, and they care nothing about him.

A friend of mine, residing at Amsterdam, N. Y., who had been accustomed every year to make a donation to the American Tract and Bible Societies, some two years since said to the Agent when he was called upon, "I will not give you anything now, but tell the Board at New York that if they will publish a tract against the sin of Slaveholding, they may draw on me for $50." The individual's name is Ellis Clisby, a member of the Presbyterian church, and a more reputable individual than he cannot be found. The next year when the Agent called upon him, he asked where was the tract. Said the Agent, "I laid it before the Committee and they said they dared not publish it. If they published it their Southern contributions would be cut off." So they were willing to sacrifice the right, the interest, and the welfare of the Slave for the "almighty dollar." They were ready to sacrifice humanity for the sake of receiving funds from the South. Has not Slavery an influence over the morals of the North?

I have before me an advertisement where some Slaves are advertised to be sold at the South for the benefit of merchants in the city of New York, and I will read it to you. It is taken from the Alabama Beacon.

"Public Sale of Negroes.—By virtue of a deed of trust made to me by Charles Whelan, for the benefit of J. W. & R. Leavitt, and of Lewis B. Brown, all of the city of New York, which deed is on record in Greene County, I shall sell at public auction, for cash, on Main Street, in the town of Greensborough, on Saturday, the 22d day of December next, a Negro Woman, about 30 years old, and her child, eleven months old, a Negro Girl about 10 years old, and a Negro Girl about 8 years old.

Wm. Trapp, *Trustee.*"

Now if I know anything about the history of this country, the 22d day of December is the anniversary of the landing of the Pilgrims; the anniversary of the day when those ambassadors, those leaders in religion, came to the American shore; when they landed within the encircling arms of Cape Cod and Cape Ann, fleeing from political and religious tyranny, seeking political and religious freedom in the New World. The anniversary of that day is selected for selling an American mother and her four children for the benefit of New York merchants.

I happen to know something of one of the parties. He is a member of Dr. Spring's church, and it is said that he gives more money to support that church than any other individual. And I should not wonder, when the bones, and muscles, and sinews, and hearts of human beings are put upon the auction-stand and sold for his benefit, if he could give a little to the church. I should not wonder if he could give a little to some institution that might throw a cloak over him, whitewash him, and make him appear reputable in the community. Has not Slavery an influence over the morals of the North, and of the whole community?

Now let us leave the morals of the American people and look at their character. When I speak of the character of the American people, I look at their nation. I place all together, and draw no mark between the people and the government. The government is the people, and the people are the government. You who are here, all who are to be found in New England, and throughout the United States of America, are the persons that make up the great American confederacy; and I ask, what is the influence that Slavery has had upon the character of the American people? But for the blighting influence of Slavery, the United States of America would have a character, would have a reputation, that would outshine the reputation of any other government that is to be found upon God's green earth.

Look at the struggle of the fathers of this country for liberty. What did they struggle for? What did they go upon the battle-field for, in 1776? They went there, it is said, for the purpose of obtaining liberty; for the purpose of instituting a democratic, republican government. What is Democracy? Solon, upon one occasion, while speaking to the Athenians said, "A democratic government is a government where an injury done to the least of its citizens is regarded as an insult and an injury to the whole commonwealth." That was the opinion of an old law-maker and statesman upon the subject of Democracy. But what says an American statesman? A South Carolina governor says that Slavery is the corner-stone of our Republic. Another eminent American statesman says that two hundred years have sanctioned and sanctified American Slavery, and that is property which the law declares to be property. Which shall we believe? One that is reared in republican America, or one that is brought up in the lap of aristocracy? Every one must admit that democracy is nothing more or less than genuine freedom and liberty, protecting every individual in the community.

I might carry the audience back to the time when your fathers were struggling for liberty in 1776. When they went forth upon the battle-field and laid down their bones, and moistened the soil with their blood, that their children might enjoy liberty. What was it for? Because a three-penny tax upon tea, a tax upon paper, or something else had been imposed upon them. We are not talking against such taxes upon the Slave. The Slave has no tea; he has no paper; he has not even himself; he has nothing at all.

When we examine the influence of Slavery upon the character of the American people, we are led to believe that if the American Government ever had a character, she has lost it. I know that upon [the] 4th of July, our 4th of July orators talk of Liberty, Democracy, and Republicanism. They talk of liberty, while three millions of their countrymen are groaning in abject Slavery. This is called the "land of the free, and the home of the brave;" it is called the "Asylum of the oppressed;" and some have been foolish enough to call it the "Cradle of Liberty." If it is the "cradle of liberty," they have rocked the child to death. It is dead long since, and yet we talk about democracy and republicanism, while one-sixth of our country-men are clanking their chains upon the very soil which our fathers mois-tened with their blood. They have such scenes even upon the holy Sabbath, and the American people are perfectly dead upon the subject. The cries, and shrieks, and groans of the Slave do not wake them.

It is deplorable to look at the character of the American people, the character that has been given to them by the institution of Slavery. The profession of the American people is far above the profession of the peo-ple of any other country. Here the people profess to carry out the princi-ples of Christianity. The American people are a sympathising people. They not only profess, but appear to be a sympathising people to the inhabitants of the whole world. They sympathise with everything else but the American Slave. When the Greeks were struggling for liberty, meet-ings were held to express sympathy. Now they are sympathising with the poor down-trodden serfs of Ireland, and are sending their sympathy across the ocean to them.

But what will the people of the Old World think? Will they not look upon the American people as hypocrites? Do they not look upon your professed sympathy as nothing more than hypocrisy? You may hold your meetings and send your words across the ocean; you may ask Nicholas of Russia to take the chains from his poor down-trodden serfs, but they look upon it all as nothing but hypocrisy. Look at our twenty thousand fugitive Slaves, running from under the stars and stripes, and taking refuge in the Canadas; *twenty thousand,* some leaving their wives, some their husbands, some leaving their children, some their brothers, and some their sisters,— fleeing to take refuge in the Canadas. Wherever the stars and stripes are seen flying in the United States of America, they point him out as a Slave.

If I wish to stand up and say, "I am a man," I must leave the land that gave me birth. If I wish to ask protection as a man, I must leave the American stars and stripes. Wherever the stars and stripes are seen flying upon American soil, I can receive no protection; I am a Slave, a chattel, a thing. I see your liberty-poles around your cities. If to-morrow morning you are hoisting the stars and stripes upon one of your liberty-poles, and I should see the man following me who claims my body and soul as his property, I might climb to the very top of your liberty-pole, I might cut the cord that held your stars and stripes and bind myself with it as closely as I could to your liberty-pole, I might talk of law and the Constitution, but nothing could save me unless there be public sentiment enough in Salem. I could not appeal to the law or the Constitution; I could only appeal to public sentiment; and if public sentiment would not protect me, I must be carried back to the plantations of the South, there to be lacerated, there to drag the chains that I left upon the Southern soil a few years since.

This is deplorable; and yet the American Slave *can* find a spot where he may be a man;—but it is not under the American flag. Fellow citizens, I am the last to eulogise any country where they oppress the poor. I have nothing to say in behalf of England or any other country, any further than as they extend protection to mankind. I say that I honor England for protecting the black man. I honor every country that shall receive the American Slave, that shall protect him, and that shall recognise him as a man.

I know that the United States will not do it; but I ask you to look at the efforts of other countries. Even the Bey of Tunis, a few years since, has decreed that there shall not be a slave in his dominions; and we see that the subject of liberty is being discussed throughout the world. People are looking at it; they are examining it; and it seems as though every country, and every people, and every government were doing something, excepting the United States. But Christian, democratic, republican America is doing nothing at all. It seems as though she would be the last. It seems as though she was determined to be the last to knock the chains from the limbs of the Slave. Shall the American people be behind the people of the Old World? Shall they be behind those who are represented as almost living in the dark ages?

> "Shall every flap of England's flag
> Proclaim that all around are free,
> From farthest Ind to each blue crag
> That beetles o'er the western sea?
> And shall we scoff at Europe's kings,
> When Freedom's fire is dimmed with us;
> And round our country's altar clings
> The damning shade of Slavery's curse?"

Shall we, I ask, shall the American people be the last? I am here, not for the purpose of condemning the character of the American people, but

13

for the purpose of trying to protect or vindicate their character. I would to God that there was some feature that I could vindicate. There is no liberty here for me; there is no liberty for those with whom I am associated; there is no liberty for the American Slave; and yet we hear a great deal about liberty! How do the people of the Old World regard the American people? Only a short time since, an American gentleman, in traveling through Germany, passed the window of a bookstore where he saw a number of pictures. One of whom was a cut representing an American Slave on his knees, with chains upon his limbs. Over him stood a white man, with a long whip; and underneath was written, "the latest specimen of American democracy." I ask my audience, who placed that in the hands of those that drew it? I was the people of the United States. Slavery, as it is to be found in this country, has given the serfs of the Old World an opportunity of branding the American people as the most tyrannical people upon God's footstool.

Only a short time since an American man-of-war was anchored in the bay opposite Liverpool. The English came down by the hundreds and thousands. The stars and stripes were flying; and there stood those poor persons that had never seen an American man-of-war, but had heard a great deal of American democracy. Some were eulogising the American people; some were calling it the "land of the free and the home of the brave." And while they stood there, one of their number rose up, and pointing his fingers to the American flag, said:

"United States, your banner wears
Two emblems,—one of fame;
Alas, the other that it bears,
Reminds us of your shame.
The white man's liberty entyped,
Stands blazoned by your stars;
But what's the meaning of your stripes?
They mean your Negro-scars."

What put that in the mouth of that individual? It was the system of American Slavery; it was the action of the American people; the inconsistency of the American people; their profession of liberty, and their practice in opposition to their profession.

I find that the time admonishes me that I am going on too far; but when I get upon this subject, and find myself surrounded by those who are willing to listen, and who seem to sympathise with my down-trodden countrymen, I feel that I have a great duty to discharge. No matter what the people may say upon this subject; no matter what they may say against the great Anti-Slavery movement of this country; I believe it is the Anti-Slavery movement that is calculated to redeem the character of the America people. Much as I have said against the character of the American people this evening, I believe that it is the Anti-Slavery movement of this country that is to redeem its character. Nothing can redeem it but the principles that are advocated by the friends of the Slave in this country.

I look upon this as one of the highest and noblest movements of the age. William Lloyd Garrison, a few years since, planted a tree of Liberty, and that tree has taken root in all branches of Government. That tree was not planted for a day, a week, a month, or a year; but to stand till the last chain should fall from the limbs of the last Slave in the United States of America, and in the world. It is a tree that will stand. Yes, it was planted of the best plant that could be found among the great plants in the world.

> "Our plant is of the cedar,
> That knoweth not decay;
> Its growth shall bless the mountains,
> Till mountains pass away;
> Its top shall greet the sunshine,
> Its leaves shall drink the rain,
> While on its lower branches
> The Slave shall hang his chain."

Yes, it is a plant that will stand. The living tree shall grow up and shall not only liberate the slave in this country, but shall redeem the character of the American people.

The efforts of the American people not only to keep the Slaves in Slavery, but to add new territory, and to spread the institution of Slavery all over Christendom,—their high professions and their inconsistency, have done more to sadden the hearts of reformers in the Old World than anything else that could have been thought of. The reformers and lovers of liberty in the Old World look to the American Government, look to the lovers of liberty in America, to aid them in knocking the chains from their own limbs in Europe, to aid them in elevating themselves; but instead of their receiving cooperation from the Government of the United States, instead of their being cheered on by the people of the United States, the people and the Government have done all that they could to oppose liberty, to oppose democracy, and to oppose reform.

Go to the capital of our country, the city of Washington; the capital of the freest government upon the face of the world. Only a few days since, an American mother and her daughter were sold upon the auction-block in that city, and the money was put into the Treasury of the United States of America. Go there and you can scarcely stand an hour but you will see caufles of Slaves driven past the Capitol, and likely as not you will see the foremost one with the stars and stripes in his hand; and yet the American Legislators, the people of the North and the people of the South, the "assembled wisdom" of the nation, look on and see such things and hold their peace; they say not a single word against such oppression, or in favor of liberty.

In conclusion let me say, that the character of the American people and the influence of Slavery upon the character have been blighting and withering the efforts of all those that favor liberty, reform, and progression. But it has not quite accomplished it. There are those who are willing to stand by the Slave. I look upon the great Anti-Slavery platform as one upon which those who stand, occupy the same position,—I would say, a higher position, than those who put forth their Declaration in 1776, in behalf of American liberty. Yes, the American Abolitionists now occupy a higher and holier position than those who carried on the American Revolution. They do not want that that husband should be any longer sold from his wife. They want that the husband should have a right to protect his wife; that the brother should have a right to protect his sister. They are tired and sick at heart in seeing human beings placed upon the auction-block and sold to the highest bidder. They want that man should be protected. They want that a stop should be put to this system of iniquity and bloodshed; and they are laboring for its overthrow.

I would that every one here could go into the Slave-States, could go where I have been, and see the workings of Slavery upon the Slave. When I get to talking upon this subject I am carried back to the day when I saw a dear mother chained and carried off in a Southern steamboat to supply the cotton, sugar, or rice plantations of the South. I am carried back to the day when a dear sister was sold and carried off in my presence. I stood and looked at her. I could not protect her. I could not offer to protect her. I was a Slave, and the only testimony I could give her that I sympathised with her, was to allow tears to flow freely down my cheeks; and the tears flowing freely down her cheeks told me that my affection was reciprocated. I am carried back to the day when I saw three dear brothers sold, and carried off.

When I speak of Slavery I am carried back to the time when I saw, day after day, my own fellow-countrymen placed upon the auction-stand; when I saw the bodies, and sinews, and hearts, and the souls of men sold to the highest bidder. I have with me an account of a Slave recently sold upon the auction-stand. The auctioneer could only get a bid of $400, but as he was about to knock her off, the owner of the Slave made his way through those that surrounded him and whispered to the auctioneer. As soon as the owner left, the auctioneer said, "I have failed to tell you all the good qualities of this Slave. I have told you that she was strong, healthy, and hearty, and now I have the pleasure to announce to you that she is very pious. She has got religion." And although, before that, he could only get $400, as soon as they found that she had got religion they commenced bidding upon her, and the bidding went up to $700. The writer says that her body and mind were sold for $400, and her religion was sold for $300. My friends, I am aware that there are people at the North who would sell their religion for a $5 bill, and make money on it; and that those who purchased it would get very much cheated in the end. But the piety of the Slave differs from the piety of the people in the nominally free States. The piety of the Slave is to be a good servant.

This is a subject in which I ask your cooperation. I hope that every individual here will take hold and help carry on the Anti-Slavery movement. We are not those who would ask the men to help us and leave the women at home. We want all to help us. A million of women are in Slavery, and as long as a single woman is in Slavery, every woman in the community should raise her voice against that sin, that crying evil that is degrading her sex. I look to the rising generation. I expect that the rising generation will liberate the Slave. I do not look to the older ones. I have sometimes thought that the sooner we got rid of the older ones the better it would be. The older ones have got their old prejudices, and their old associations, and they cling to them, and seem not to look at the Slave or to care anything about him.

Now, fellow-citizens, when you shall return home, and be scattered around your several firesides, and when you have an opportunity to make a remark about what I have said here this evening, all I ask of you is to give the cause, justice; to give what I have said, justice. Give it a fair investigation. If you have not liked my grammar, recollect that I was born and brought up under an institution, where, if an individual was found teaching me, he would have been sent to the State's Prison. Recollect that I was brought up where I had not the privilege of education. Recollect that you have come here to-night to hear a Slave, and not a man, according to the laws of the land; and if the Slave has failed to interest you, charge it not to the race, charge it not to the colored people, but charge it to the blighting influence of Slavery,—that institution that has made me property, and that is making property of three millions of my countrymen at the present day. Charge it upon that institution that is annihilating the minds of three millions of my countrymen. Charge it upon that institution, whether found in the political arena or in the American churches. Charge it upon that institution, cherished by the American people, and looked upon as the essence of Democracy,—upon *American Slavery.*

Note

1 Dr. Furman, of South Carolina.

Speech delivered at the Lecture Hall, Croydon, England, September 5, 1849

from C. Peter Ripley et al., editors, *The Black Abolitionist Papers*, vol. 1,
The British Isles, 1830–1865 (Chapel Hill: University of North Carolina Press,
1985; used by permission of the publisher); originally published in the
Standard of Freedom [London], September 8, 1849)

In what is among the first of his speeches delivered to a British abolitionist audience, Brown makes radical comparisons between the freedoms he finds in England and the threat of slavery or imprisonment in the United States. He carefully appeals to his audience by repeatedly recognizing that abolitionists in America appreciate the work of abolitionists in England and that the English abolitionists are, in fact, having great influence in the cause of emancipation in the United States.

Mr. Brown, in coming forward, was greeted with warm applause, which having subsided, he said, that, in coming before a British public as the advocate of the American slave, he had nothing to commend himself in the way of educational attainments, having been brought up under the institution of slavery, without schooling, or the opportunity of obtaining that which every good citizen should possess, and be desirous of attaining—education. When speaking in America of the friends of the slave in England, every heart that was capable of beating for freedom leapt for joy. There was in the United States a higher appreciation of the advocacy of the friends of freedom in this country than they themselves probably supposed. The people of Great Britain had already done a great deal for the cause of emancipation in America. Let even a small meeting of the friends of the slave be held in England and it was immediately published in America, and men who cared nothing about the cause of abolition there, would talk about such a meeting as a matter of consequence. But the people of this country had not only already accomplished much for the American slave, but they had it in their power to effect a great deal more. (Hear.) Let an American slaveholder be warmly received in any part of Europe, and the whole body immediately rejoice that one of their number had met with such an honourable reception; but let him be received here as every man should be who robbed a large portion of his countrymen of their liberties, and the Americans immediately take that reception to heart, and it exercises great influence upon them. No meeting could be held in this country, no matter for what purpose, but especially of a moral and religious character, to which the slaveholders of America were not anxious to send representatives. (Hear.) If a World's Evangelical Alliance was projected, or a World's Temperance Convention was held in England, slavery was sure to be represented. (Hear.) If a Peace Congress was called together in Paris, slavery was present. And why was that? Because the slaveholders wished to make slavery appear before the world as good and tolerable a thing as possible. Among the first persons whom he (Mr. Brown) saw upon the floor of the Paris Peace Congress were two slaveholders from America, who had come over to England in the same steam-vessel as himself. Whether they were or were not delegates he could not say; but they sat among, and had the same badge or card of admission as the delegates; and yet it was known to a number of the members of Congress that those men were slaveholders. (Hear, hear.) Now had those individuals been received in Paris as they should have been received consistently with their true characters—as men-stealers—it would have created a great stir in the United States. Had they been regarded in the same manner as people would unhesitatingly look upon a horse-thief, or one who committed a light-handed act of injustice against his fellowmen, they would not have dared to remain in the Congress; but, as it was, they continued there as any other member, until the close of the sitting. He (Mr. Brown), however, thanked God that the anti-slavery cause had made such progress within the last twenty years, that if slaveholders were sent over to represent the United States in a World's Evangelical Alliance, some Garrison would make his appearance on the outside when the meeting was adjourned, and let the friends of freedom throughout Europe know that slaveholders had been there; and thus they would be prevented accomplishing that which they had designed. (Hear, hear, and cheers.) If at a great Temperance Convention slaveholders were sent here to represent America, some Douglass would there make his appearance, and create such a stir as would defeat their purposes; and if they got up a World's Peace Congress, some fugitive slave, like himself, would break loose from his chains, make his appearance upon the platform, and let the people know that slavery was still in existence in the United States, and that it was not that respectable thing in reality which some American delegates would fain have it appear. (Cheers.) Although an American himself, he (Mr. Brown) received more protection in England than he should in the United States. The people of England had but a very faint idea of what slavery was. They had, no doubt, many of them heard and read a great deal about slavery in America; but when the friends of freedom came before a British audience they had to pick and cull from the mass of evidence the least disgusting details which the auditory would be willing to listen to. He dare not bring before them the horrors of the slave-trade in America, or what he himself had witnessed of slavery; their own moral feeling would not allow of the detail, or, if it would, he for one would not be willing to go into those revolting statements. But it was common in Europe to ask, "Were not the slaves in America better off in their supply of food and clothing than the poorer classes in Europe?" He (Mr. Brown) would not stop to inquire whether they were or were not better off as far as food and clothing were concerned; he protested against American slavery, because it enslaved man, and brought the human being down from the high position which God intended him to occupy, and placed him upon a lower level than the beast of the field. Suppose the slaves in America did in fact get enough to eat and wear—grant it all—what compensation was that for being robbed of every right as men? Look at the three millions of slaves in America; witness the slave-trade as carried on in the capital of the United States, in Virginia, Kentucky, Maryland, and those places where slaves were raised for the supply of the southern market: look at the internal slave-trade, and then ask whether food and clothing was any compensation whatever for the deprivation which the slaves underwent? He (Mr. Brown) had not seen a poor man, woman, or child since he landed upon the British soil who was worse off than the slaves in the United States. What was food and clothing to a man as long as he knew that he was a chattel slave—the property of another person? What was the utmost amount of food and clothing to a man when he knew that he might be placed upon an auction-stand, sold to the highest bidder, and torn from his wife and children and everything that was dear to him? Then look at the mental degradation of the slave. If a man handed a copy of the Bible to a slave, or taught him to read the truths it contained, he was severely punishable by law. Why, only a few weeks before he (Mr. Brown) left America, a clergyman thought he was doing service by establishing Sabbath schools in one of the northern slave States, by merely getting a dozen slaves together, and teaching them what he conceived to be the principles of Christianity; and yet that very minister of religion was taken up, and received for the Christian act thirty lashes upon his bare back under the sanction of the laws of the country. (Hear.) No, no, he (Mr. Brown) would rather be a beggar in England than the best conditioned slave in

America. (Cheers.) If he were to die of hunger, however, let him perish at least free, without manacles upon his limbs. "I," said Mr. Brown, "have felt the chains upon my own limbs, and I have never seen a single moment since I escaped from slavery in Missouri that I would exchange for the best portions of slavery which I have left behind. And yet, since I made my escape from slavery, I have had to struggle for existence as hard as the poorest man in England, having come out from under the institution of slavery destitute of education or friends, in the coldest winter season, without a penny in my pocket or any friend to appeal to. And yet I had rather grope my way along, and try to get my living under the most disadvantageous circumstances than serve a single moment under the institution that I have left behind me." (Cheers.) It was a principle in the slave-holding states that the negroes must be kept in degradation in order to be retained in slavery. In 1844 a clergyman from the North proposed to send a ship-load of Bibles, and missionaries to teach the slaves to read them, but he was told that if he did so he must send with them another vessel freighted with soldiers, muskets, and bayonets, for the purpose of protecting the planters, for if the slaves had education they would no longer be retained in subjection—(hear)—as it wanted nothing but the power of knowledge to liberate them. When the people in this country read of some slave having been whipped to death or hung, with only a sham trial before two or three slaveholders, they were horrified; and yet these were nothing more than the circumstances naturally incident to slavery. Instead of vainly seeking to better the condition of the slave, let them then seek to knock off the chains from his limbs, and not be content with anything short of that. The government of the United States was on the side of slavery instead of being the friend of freedom. In its very capital men could obtain the privilege of buying and selling human beings, and of trading in human flesh, for the sum of 400 dols. per annum; and right in sight of the capital might be seen negro-pens and warehouses where slaves were kept for sale. And yet the men who practised that traffic were the professed followers of the meek and lowly JESUS! Christians in good and regular standing in some of the churches of America! (Hear.) Within the last twenty years the American government had used its influence for the spread of American slavery; and even where it was abolished in Mexico it had been reinstated by the United States. If a negro made his escape from a slave to a free State, and a Christian man gave him a crust of bread and a cup of cold water, that good man was for that very act subject to a fine of 500 dollars. When he (Mr. Brown) was making his escape he had nothing whatever to eat, except a few ears of corn which he plucked by the way; and yet, sick and weary as he was at last, and almost ready to die, he dared not ask relief until he saw a Quaker come by. (Cheers.) Some of the most heroic attempts had recently been made by slaves to obtain their freedom. One man, to gain his liberty, had travelled in a railway carriage upwards of 300 miles, packed in a little box, breathing God's air only through small gimlet holes. Were he (Mr. Brown) about to depict the true character of American slavery, if he could, he would pluck a feather from the wing of some fallen angel, dip it in the wailings of despair, and write upon the blackened walls of perdition in characters which would frighten the hyena out of his ferocity. What justice was there in America for the slave? A woman was recently tried for causing the death of a negro girl; she was acquitted, on the ground that it was her slave-woman who actually committed the deed. The slave-woman was afterwards tried and acquitted, on the ground that she committed the murder on the authority of her mistress! (Hear.) If a coloured man went to Washington without free papers, he would be thrown into gaol, there to remain until he had paid the gaol fees; if unable to do so, he was sold, to raise the amount of such fees, and the balance of the produce of sale actually went to swell the treasury of the United States government. He (Mr. Brown) thanked God, however, that there was an asylum still left for the slave, and that the Canadas, at the present moment, was the land of refuge for more than 20,000 escaped bondmen. (Cheers.) Nor could he convey to that meeting the feelings which came over him when he landed at Liverpool and felt that he was really free. Then he could indeed adopt the language of the poet, and say—

> Old England! old England! thrice blessed and free,
> The poor hunted slave finds a shelter in thee;
> Where no blood-thirsty hound ever dares on his track:
> At thy voice, old England, the monster falls back.
> Go back, then, ye blood-hounds, that howl in my path;
> In the land of old England I'm free from your wrath.
> And the sons of Great Britain my deep scars shall see.
> Till they cry, with one voice, "Let the bondman be free!"

Mr. Brown concluded a long and eloquent speech amidst loud applause.

Speech delivered at the Concert Rooms, Store Street, London, September 27, 1849

from C. Peter Ripley et al., editors, *The Black Abolitionist Papers*, vol. 1, *The British Isles, 1830–1865* (Chapel Hill: University of North Carolina Press, 1985; used by permission of the publisher); originally published in *The Liberator*, November 2, 1849

This speech, which Brown delivered shortly after he delivered his speech in Croydon, appeals more strongly to his British abolitionist audience to influence the cause of emancipation in the United States. Skillfully using American anti-British sentiment to rouse the support of his British audience, he calls for America to follow the lead of England in ending slavery. Brown's skillful appeal to his audience is as keen in this speech as anywhere in his work.

Sir, I wish to make a remark or two in seconding the resolution which is now before the meeting. I am really glad that this meeting has produced this discussion, for I think it will all do good; in fact, I know it will, for the cause of truth. Reference has been made to slavery having been carried to America by the sanction of this country. Now, that is an argument generally used in America by slaveholders themselves. (Hear, hear.) Go to the United States; talk to slaveholders about the disgrace of slavery being found in a professedly Christian republic, and they will immediately reply, "England imposed it upon us; Great Britain was the cause of it, for she established slavery in America, and we are only reaping the fruits of her act." Now, gentlemen, I would reply to our friend here, as I have replied to Americans again and again—If you have followed England in the bad example of the institution of slavery, now follow her in the good example of the abolition of slavery. (Cheers.) Some remarks were also made by that gentleman respecting the Americans having abolished the slave trade. It is true that they did pass a law, but not in 1808, that the slave trade should be abolished: they passed a law in 1788 that they would only continue the slave trade for twenty years longer, and at the end of that period there should not be any more slaves imported into the United States. They said, "We will rob Africa of her sons and daughters for twenty years longer, and then stop." (Hear and laughter.) But why did they determine that the slave trade should be put an end to? The honorable gentleman has not told you that. Why, it was to give to Virginia, Kentucky and Maryland a monopoly in the trade of raising slaves to supply the Southern market. (Cheers.) That was the reason, and the only reason, why they abolished the foreign slave trade in America. They allowed the foreign slave trade to be carried on for twenty years from that time, and during the whole of that period made those who were engaged in the internal slave traffic pay a duty of ten dollars for every slave brought into the country, the whole of the money going into the exchequer of the United States. The Government said, "We will have a tariff of so much per head upon God's children that are stolen from Africa, and the revenue derived therefrom shall be the support of the republican institutions of the United States." (Hear, hear.) Do the Americans claim credit for an act like that? Claim credit for abolishing the foreign slave trade, in order that they might make a lucrative domestic slave trade! (Cheers.) Why, ladies and gentlemen, only a few years since, 40,000 slaves were carried out of the single State of Virginia, in one year, and driven off to the far South, to supply the market there. Claim credit for abolishing the slave trade! Claim credit for husbands torn from their wives, and children from their parents! Claim credit for herds of human beings carried off in coffle gangs, and to be worked to death in the rice and cotton fields! That is the character of the domestic slave trade now carried on, even in the capital of America. No, no; the people of the United States can claim no credit on that score. They can find no apology in the fact of slavery being a domestic institution. A pretty "domestic institution," truly! (Hear, hear.) Why, in 1847, only two years since, a woman and her daughter were sold in the very capital of America, in the very city of Washington, by the U.S. marshal, on the 3d day of July, the day before the national anniversary of the glorious Declaration of Independence, by which all men were declared free and equal, and the product of the sale of these immortal beings was put into the treasury of the United States. That is one specimen among many of the working of the "domestic institution" of America. (Cheers.) It dooms me, for example, to be a slave as soon as I shall touch any part of the United States. (Hear, hear.) Yes, Sir, it is indeed domestic enough; it is domesticated all over the country; it extends from one end of America to the other, and is as domesticated as is the

Constitution of the United States itself; it is just as domesticated as is the territory over which the United States Government have jurisdiction. Wherever the Constitution proclaims a bit of soil to belong to the United States, there it dooms me to be a slave the moment I set my foot upon it; and all the 20,000 or 30,000 of my brethren who have made their escape from the Southern States, and taken refuge in Canada or the Northern States, are in the same condition. And yet this American slavery is apologized for as a "domestic institution"! I am glad that our eloquent friend, Mr. Thompson, has impressed the fact upon your minds, that slavery is a *national institution*, and that the guilt of maintaining it is *national guilt*. I am anxious that that circumstance should be understood, and that Englishmen should know, that the slave is just as much a slave in the city of Boston; of which this gentleman is just as much a citizen as he is in Charleston, South Carolina: he is just as much a slave in any of the Eastern States as he is in the Southern States. If I am protected in my person in the city of Boston, and if I have been protected there for the last two or three years, and the slaveholder has not been able to catch me and carry me back again into slavery, I am not at all indebted for that privilege to the Constitution of the United States, but I owe it entirely to that public sentiment which my friend Mr. Thompson, at the peril of his life, so nobly helped to create in America. (Loud cheers.) I am indebted to the anti-slavery sentiment, and that alone, when I am in Boston itself, for the personal protection I enjoy. I cannot look at the Constitution or laws of America as a protection to me; in fact, I have no Constitution, and no country. I cannot, like the eloquent gentleman who last addressed you, say—"I am bound to stand up in favor of America." (Hear.) I would to God that I could; but how can I! America has disfranchised me, driven me off, and declared that I am not a citizen, and never shall be, upon the soil of the United States. Can I, then, gentlemen, stand up for such a country as that? Can I have any thing to say in favor of a country that makes me a chattel, that renders me a saleable commodity, that converts me into a piece of property? Can I say any thing in favor of a country, or its institutions, that will give me up to the slaveholder, if he can only find out where I am, in any part of America? Why I am more free here tonight, in monarchical England, than I should be in my own republican country! Whatever our friend from Boston may do, I would that I could say with him, "I must, in honor, stand up in favor of America." And yet I love America as much as he does. I admire her enterprising and industrious people quite as ardently as he can; but I hate her hideous institution, which has robbed me of a dear mother, which has plundered me of a beloved sister and three dear brothers, and which institution has doomed them to suffer, as they are now suffering, in chains and slavery. Whatever else there may be to admire in the condition of America, at all events, I hate that portion of her Constitution. I hate, I fervently hate, those laws and institutions of America, which consign three millions of my brethren and sisters to chains for life. Talk about going to the slaveholders with money! Talk about recognizing their right to property in human beings! What! property in man! property in God's children! I will not acknowledge that any man has a right to hold me as property, till he can show his right to supersede the prerogative of that Creator whose alone I am. (Cheers.) Just read the letter which you will find in the preface to my narrative, where my own master has very kindly offered to sell me to myself for half price. (Laughter.) He imagines that the anti-slavery movement has depreciated his property in me, and therefore he offers to take half price for his runaway property. (Renewed laughter.) My answer to him was, that he should never receive a single dollar from me, or any one else in my behalf, with my consent. (Cheers.) I said so, because I am not willing to acknowledge the right of property in man under any circumstances. I believe that the same God who made the slaveholder made the slave (hear, hear) and that the one is just as free as the other.

Before resuming my seat, I would say to our friend from Boston, as I said to another gentleman a short time before I left America, who talked in a similar manner about the slave States, and the good treatment the slaves received, and so forth. At the close of a meeting, that gentleman rose, and requested permission to ask me some simple questions, which were as follows: Had I not enough to eat when I was in slavery? Was I not well clothed while in the Southern States? Was I ever whipped? and so forth. I saw that he only wanted a peg on which to hang a pro-slavery speech, but I answered his questions in the affirmative. He immediately rose and made a speech, in which he endeavored to make his audience believe that I had run away from a very good place indeed. (Laughter.) He asked them if they did not know hundreds and thousands of poor people in America and England, who would be willing to go into the State of Missouri and there fill the situation I had run away from. (Cries of Oh, Oh!) A portion of the assembly for a moment really thought his plea for slavery was a good one. I saw that the meeting was anxious to break up, in consequence of the lateness of the hour, and therefore that it would not do for me to reply at any length, and I accordingly rose and made a single remark in answer to this pro-slavery speech. I said, the gentleman has praised up the situation I left, and made it appear quite another thing to what it ever appeared to me when I was there; but however that may be, I have to inform him that that situation is still vacant, and as far as [I] have

27

any thing voluntary to do with it, it shall remain so; but, nevertheless, if that gentleman likes to go into Missouri and fill it, I will give him a recommendation to my old master, and I doubt not that he would receive him with open arms, and give him enough to eat, enough to wear, and flog him when ever he thought he required it. (Loud cheers and laughter.) So I say to our friend from Boston, to-night, if he is so charmed with slavery, he shall have the same recommendation to my old master. (Loud cheers.)

Speech delivered at the Hall of Commerce, London, August 1, 1851

from C. Peter Ripley et al., editors, *The Black Abolitionist Papers*, vol. 1,
The British Isles, 1830–1865 (Chapel Hill: University of North Carolina Press,
1985; used by permission of the publisher); originally published in *The Liberator*,
September 5, 1851

*This speech is Brown's most direct repudiation of the Fugitive Slave Law.
it is, therefore, one of the most overtly political documents of Brown's
career. Unlike his earlier speeches in England, this speech includes direct
mockery of Americans' "boasting of their liberty, their humanity. . . ." Also
of note in this speech is Brown's mention of William and Ellen Craft,
about whom he writes in both* Clotel *and* The Escape.

The Chairman (who upon taking the chair was received with loud
applause), in opening the proceedings, remarked that, although the
metropolis had of late been inundated with meetings of various characters,
having reference to almost every variety of subject, yet that the subject
they were called upon that evening to discuss differed from them all.
Many of those by whom he was surrounded, like himself, had been victims
to the inhuman institution of slavery, and were in consequence exiled from
the land of their birth. They were fugitives from their native land, but not
fugitives from justice, and they had not fled from a monarchical, but from
a so-called republican government. They came from amongst a people
who declared, as a part of their creed, that all men were born free, but who,
while they did so, made slaves of every sixth man, woman and child in the
country. (Hear, hear.) He must not, however, forget that one of the purposes for which they were met tonight was to commemorate the emancipation of their brethren and sisters in the isles of the sea. That act of the
British Parliament, and he might add in this case with peculiar emphasis,

of the British nation, passed on the 12th day of August, 1833, to take effect on the 1st day of August, 1834, and which enfranchised 800,000 West Indian slaves, was an event sublime in its nature, comprehensive and mighty in its immediate influences and remote consequences, precious beyond expression to the cause of freedom, and encouraging beyond the measure of any government on earth to the hearts of all enlightened and just men. This act was the commencement of a long course of philanthropic and Christian efforts on the part of some of the best men that the world ever produced. It was not his intention to go into a discussion or a calculation of the rise and fall of property, or whether sugar was worth more or less by the act of emancipation. But the emancipation of slavery in the West Indies was a blow struck in the right direction at that most inhuman of all trafficks, the slave trade—a trade which would never cease so long as slavery existed, for where there was a market there would be merchandise; where there was demand there would be a supply; where there were carcasses there would be vultures; and they might as well attempt to turn the water, and make it run up the Niagara River as to change this law. It was often said by the Americans, that England was responsible for the existence of slavery there, because it was introduced into the country while the colonies were under the British Crown. If that was so, they must come to the conclusion that, as England abolished slavery in the West Indies, she would have done the same for the American States, if she had had the power to do so; and if that was so, they might safely say that the separation of the United States from the mother country was (to say the least) a great misfortune to one-sixth of the population of that land. England had set a noble example to America, and he would to Heaven that his countrymen would follow the example. The Americans boasted of their superior knowledge, but they need not boast of their superior guilt, for that was set upon a hilltop, and that, too, so high that it required not the lantern of Diogenes to find it out. Every breeze from the western world brought upon its wings the groans and cries of the victims of this guilt. Nearly all countries had fixed the seal of disapprobation to slavery, and when, at some future age, this stain upon the page of history shall be pointed at, posterity will blush at the discrepancy between American profession and American practice. What was to be thought of a people boasting of their liberty, their humanity, their Christianity, their love of justice, and at the same time keeping in slavery more than three millions of God's children, and shutting out from them the light of the Gospel, by denying the Bible to the slave? (Hear, hear.) No education, no marriage, every thing done to keep the mind of the slave in darkness. There was a wish on the part of the people of the Northern States to shield themselves from the charge of slaveholding, but as they shared in the guilt, he was not satisfied with letting them off without their share in the odium.

And now, a word about the Fugitive Slave Bill. That measure was in every respect an unconstitutional measure. It set aside the right formerly enjoyed by the fugitive of trial by jury—it annulled his claim to the writ of habeas corpus—it afforded to him no protection, no opportunity of proving his right to be free, and it placed every free colored person at the mercy of every unprincipled person who might wish to lay claim to him. (Hear.) That law is opposed to the principles of Christianity—foreign alike to the laws of God and man; it had converted the whole population of the free States into a band of slavecatchers, and every rood of territory is but so much hunting-ground, over which they might chase the fugitive. But while they were speaking of slavery in the United States, they must not omit to mention that there was a strong feeling in that land, not only against the Fugitive Slave Law, but also against the existence of slavery in any form. There was a band of fearless men and women in the city of Boston, whose labor for the slave had resulted in good beyond calculation. This noble and heroic class had caused the whole country to be in agitation, until their principles have taken root in almost every association in the land, and which, with God's blessing, will in due time cause the Americans to put in practice what they have so long professed. (Hear, hear.) He wished it to be constantly held up before the country, [th]at the Northern States are as deeply implicated in the guilt of slavery as [the] South. The North had a population of 13,553,328; the South had a population of only 6,393,756 freemen; the North has 152 representatives in the House, the South only 81; and it would be seen by this that the balance of power was with the free States. Looking therefore, at the question in all its aspects, he was sure that there was no one in this country but who would find out that the slavery of the United States of America was a system the most abandoned and the most tyrannical. (Hear, hear.)

With reference to Mr. Thompson's visit to America, the Chairman proceeded:

I am glad that we have upon this platform one who has recently returned from America. (Cheers.) I am somewhat acquainted with the doings of the noble friend that I have alluded to. I had some acquaintance with his connection with the anti-slavery movement before I came to this country. I have had ample opportunity of judging of his zeal in the cause of the slave since I have been here. I have myself been a frequent guest at his table, where I have met many fugitives who have been entrusted to his care, and I know that they have received from him the most friendly advice, and more than that, substantial assistance, to help them on their way in this country. I was present at the farewell Soiree given to him before he embarked this second time for America. I was the last to shake hands with him as he left the railway station, and the first to welcome him on his return at the same place. I watched his movements in every direction. I gained information from every source, public and private, from slaveholders and abolitionists, respecting the course of Mr. Thompson through the country, and I am satisfied that he gave an impetus to the cause of freedom there which it had not received for years before. His tour through the States of Massachusetts and New York, the zeal with which the people came forth to welcome him at every meeting—the fact that when he left the city of Boston, the friends in Boston accompanied him a long distance to where the steamer was moored, is enough to satisfy my mind as to the value placed upon his labors and talents by the friends of my oppressed race. I was anxious, in common with many other fugitives—those who are present as well as numbers who cannot attend this meeting—to meet together here, not only to celebrate this, the anniversary of West India emancipation, but also to welcome our friend, and thank him for his labors in the United States within the past eight months. And now I will take my seat by welcoming Mr. Thompson, and expressing to him the thanks of the fugitives in this country for the labors, co-operation and noble zeal with which he has aided the cause of the slave in the U. States. I am sure that this audience will be better satisfied with hearing remarks from him than almost any one in the meeting. And now, Sir (turning to Mr. Thompson), I beg to thank you for your noble exertions in behalf of my oppressed people (shaking Mr. Thompson by the hand, amidst the loud applause of the meeting). I had the assurance of William and Ellen Craft, two of the noblest fugitives from the United States of America, that they would be present at this meeting; but at a late hour, I received a letter from them, informing me that unfortunate circumstances beyond their control prevented their attendance. We have, I am happy to say, the presence of a noble man upon this platform, who has been lynched within the last year in the State of Kentucky, simply because he was a sharer in abolition feelings.

Speech delivered at the Town Hall, Manchester, England, August 1, 1854

from C. Peter Ripley et al., editors, *The Black Abolitionist Papers*, vol. 1,
The British Isles, 1830–1865 (Chapel Hill: University of North Carolina Press,
1985; used by permission of the publisher); originally published
in the *Manchester Examiner and Times*, August 5, 1854

*Delivered much later in his tour of England, this speech allows Brown to
address his audience as an insider, "almost an Englishman," he explains,
having been in England five years at the time of this speech. Departing
from his ealier care at developing a rapport with his British audience, here
Brown assumes a more direct rhetorical stance, listing example after example of the horrors of slavery in the United States and continuing to appeal
to the British to bolster the work of American abolitionists. Of note in this
speech is Brown's defense of Harriet Beecher Stowe's* Uncle Tom's Cabin.

Mr. Chairman, and ladies and gentlemen, I would much have preferred
that my friend Mr. Pillsbury should have occupied the time that is
intended for myself. As has been said, he is not only thoroughly
acquainted with the working of slavery in the United States, but he is one
of its oldest and best pioneers. He has had the advantage of early education, he has the advantage of me at the present time, and I feel confident
could not only claim your attention, but could give you better information
in a better manner than I could possibly hope to do. I stand to-night without ever having had a day's schooling in my life. You have been called
together to hear men speak to-night—I am here as a piece of property. I
am a slave according to the laws of the United States at the present time.
Something has been said this afternoon about my having been purchased
by the liberality of the English people; I know not that such a purchase has
taken place; I know it is the contemplation, and many suppose it may have

33

been accomplished by this time, but I do not know that such is the case. I stand here, this evening, therefore, not only a slave, a piece of property according to the laws of the United States, but I am here without education or without having received a day's schooling in my life, and what education I have has been of my own seeking in my own way; and, therefore, I can hope to say but little that shall go to aid in making up the testimony that is intended by the holding of this conference. (Applause.) No one can read, Mr. Chairman, the declaration of the American independence, and compare that document with the history of the legislation of the federal government of the United States, without being struck with the marked inconsistency of the theory of the people and their acts; the one declaring that all men are created equally, endowed by their Creator with certain inalienable rights, among which are life, liberty, and the pursuit of happiness, and the other is the history of the encroachment of slavery upon liberty, or legislation in favour of slavery in that country against the cause of freedom. From the very hour that the convention that was held to form the constitution of the United States down to the present time, the acts of the government have been for the perpetuation and the spread of slavery in that land. As has been said, slavery was introduced into the constitution by allowing the African slave trade to be continued for twenty years, making it lawful and constitutional, which it had never been before; and then the slaveowner was allowed representation for this slave property, and every man that would go to the Coast of Africa, and steal five negroes and bring them to the United States, was allowed by the constitution, then, three votes for the five slaves. And it is carried down to the present time, as the American congress has more than twenty-five representatives based upon this slave representation. And that is one of the reasons why in the national congress the slaveowners have the power of carrying so many of their measures, and the twenty-five, I need not say, who are slaveowners themselves, do not represent, but misrepresent, their "property," and these slaveowners go for the purpose of spreading the system of slavery over the land. America is called a free and independent country, and yet there is not a single foot of soil over which the stars and the stripes wave upon which I could stand and be protected by law. (Sensation.) There is not a foot of soil in the United States upon which I could stand where the constitution would give me any protection; and let me return to the United States, I am liable to be seized at any moment and conveyed in chains to the southern states, and there handed over to a man who claims me as his property, and to be worked up as he may think fit. Such is true as regards even the early history of slavery. It is true that the congress of the United States, or the constitution, agreed to abolish slavery in 20 years, but the internal slave trade is carried on, and I aver that it is even worse—setting aside the middle passage—than anything connected with the foreign slave trade. In the old states, slaves are raised for the market; they have their family attachments, and they are probably, to some extent, more enlightened and not so much degraded by heathenism as the negroes upon the coast of Africa, and, as men become more enlightened, the separation of families, and the buying and selling of them to slavery, is so much the worse. They feel it the more, and therefore, I think that when we look and see that 100,000 slaves are annually taken from the slave-raising states, to supply the southern markets—the cotton, sugar, and rice plantations of the far south—we must be satisfied that the internal slave trade that is carried on by the people of the United States is as grievous in its effect as the African slave trade when carried on by the people of that country. I know that some suppose that the evils of slavery are exaggerated; I have been asked again and again if certain portions of *Uncle Tom's Cabin* were not exaggeration. Of the working of slavery, in my opinion, I don't think anything can exaggerate that infamous system. When we look and see that there are at the present time enslaved between three and four millions of God's children, who are put upon the auction stand and sold to the highest bidder, no language which we can use can exaggerate the workings or the evils of the system of slavery as it is carried on in that country. (Applause.) The fugitive slave law, that by many people here is considered a great evil, is at present the law in America, and it is the most atrocious law ever concocted by the human brain or human legislation—a law that sets every other statute in existence in the shade when we look at the barbarous enactments that it contains. By the fugitive slave law every coloured person in that country is liable to be arrested and carried off to the far south and made a slave of, no matter whether born in New York, Massachusetts, Vermont, or any free state. The gate of separation which has hitherto kept the inhabitants of the northern states from participating in slaveholding, is now thrown down; and every man who wishes to go into the slaveholding business, has now only to find some one who shall participate in the gain, and to swear that the coloured person whom he means to enslave, is the property of that man whom he has brought forward for that purpose, and so the poor coloured man is carried away to the south. In the state of Illinois, during the past few months, a coloured man was arrested under this fugitive slave law, who had lived in the same town some fifteen years, and had by his industry accumulated 1,500 or 2,000 dollars worth of property; and the man who came upon this man, and claimed and seized him as a slave, was not only a professing Christian, but was a minister of the gospel, and one who belonged to the same denomination as the man whom he claimed for his property. It was in vain this coloured man asserted that he was a free man, and had a right to be free; that no one had any right to take him away, that he was free born, and from the state of Ohio. The only respite he could obtain was, that he was allowed, as a favour, to go to prison, and to stay there for a while, until he could get his property and other affairs in the place disposed of; and in the meantime he was obliged to find security, and to pay an officer three dollars a day to watch him and see that he did not run away. He agreed to this, but after a while he had collected evidence by which he proved himself to be free, and was enabled to demand his release. But a debt had been accumulated during his detention, to the amount of some $3,000, so that, although he had thus escaped being sent into slavery, he was utterly ruined. This is the history of a free coloured man in the state of Illinois. There is a more atrocious case I can tell you. Within the last year, two villains from a southern state arrived in a certain town of Pennsylvania, and attempted to seize a coloured man, who was employed there as a waiter, in one of the inns. They approached him in a clandestine manner, and threw their chains upon his limbs; but the man, whom they would have made a slave, escaped from his pursuers; he ran out of the house, he ran to the nearest stream, and plunged into it, and there stood at bay, immersed up to his neck in the running water. The slave-hunters came up, and many people gathered around, sympathising with the hunted fugitive. He exclaimed to his persecutors, "If any of you come near me here, I will drown him in this water that flows about me." The slave-hunters answered him, "If you don't come out of the river, and surrender, we will shoot you where you are." And then, suddenly, to the horror and astonishment of all the bystanders, one of the slave-hunters raised his gun or pistol, aimed it at the fugitive, and fired at him. We are told how the water then ran red with the blood of the slave; and how a crowd of four or five hundred people, who stood by and saw this thing done, did nothing more than cry "Shame" upon those who had done it, because it was the law. Sir, I do feel confident, that if in this country such a law existed, and if any two persons came into a town of England, and dared openly to ill treat a human being in that way, there would not be three or four hundred Englishmen standing by so cold to the feelings of humanity as to let such a thing be done in their presence, and content themselves with crying "Shame!" I feel certain, that, in England, the villains who should do such an outrage would instantly be compelled to fly the spot. (Cheers.)

Well, now, you will recollect that all this was perpetrated in the state of Pennsylvania, in one of those which are called the free states. We hear people speak of free and slave states; but I hold that there is no such distinction; for now there are no free states in the United States of America. There are none of them free, because that cannot be a free state which cannot protect the freedom of its inhabitants; and there is no state in the union now which can give Liberty, or even secure his liberty, to the coloured man. His rights are nothing if the slaveholder pursues him. The courts of justice in some of those "free states" have been converted into prisons, in which the fugitive slaves of the southerners have been kept for them; and very recently, in Boston, a slave was arrested, and confined for six or seven days in the court house, which was guarded by muskets and cannon to prevent his rescue; thence he was put on board a vessel in the harbour and carried away to the far south, to a life of slavery. The boast of the "free states," that people there enjoy perfect freedom is most untrue; for under the fugitive slave law, the slaveowners of the south are empowered to enter those "free states," and employ not only the marshals of the union, in arresting any of the coloured people whom they choose to claim, but compel the inhabitants of the place, under severe penalties, to abet the seizure of the slave. I cannot exaggerate, sir, the effect of this fugitive slave law, and indeed, of everything else that is connected with slavery in the United States. If you had been, as I have been, for twenty years of your life in the southern states of America, and had seen there, as I have seen, the workings of slavery, the trading in human beings, the buying and selling of them, the whipping and abusing of them, as I have seen all that carried on there—and if you had seen the dear ones torn from you, and taken to be sold [on the] auction block, and handed over to the highest bidder, [as I] have seen my dear ones taken, never to see them again—if you had seen all this, you could not think anything, in the statements made at this conference, or in the publications you may have read, was at all exaggerated. (Cheers.) I know you read, with palpitating hearts, the history of the Bloody Assize in this country; you loathe the name of Judge Jeffreys, when you remember that Reign of Terror in England. Now, go to the United States, and you will see, that acts as cruel as ever were done in England, in that age, are done in America now—done every day in the southern states, and done almost every week in the northern states; you will see there judges who sit on the bench, giving their sentence in favour of slavery, and condemning freedom; judges who knew, too, that the persons whom their sentence orders thus to be seized and carried back into the southern states, will be cruelly tortured there. It was asserted not long since in Boston, by Theodore Parker, that one of those slaves, who had been seized in the north, and carried back to slavery, had been flogged to death, or nearly to death; and such will be the fate of many of them. Then, ought not facts like those to be known throughout this country? I am glad these meetings are held, and that this association has been formed. I hope it will do something to instruct the people here, and to maintain anti-slavery principles, so that Englishmen, when they visit the United States, may not do henceforth, as many of their countrymen have done, give their influence to the side of the oppressor, instead of the oppressed. (Cheers.) That is now most important to the cause; for thousands of persons, emigrants and others, are going to the United States every year, and they ought to understand this matter. If nothing else could be accomplished yet, meetings like these and lecturing would be worthy objects of the efforts of this association. It is true, there is already in England an anti-slavery society established. But I must say, and with great respect for the excellent persons who belong to it, that society is so inactive it scarcely does anything throughout the year but hold an anniversary meeting; and it is a fact, sir, that speeches like those which were made in the conference today, or to night upon this platform, would not be tolerated on the platform of the British and Foreign Anti-Slavery Society in London. (Cheers.) It may be said of us, that we have used very strong language. Why, sir, has not the time come for strong language? Those who want milk and water, let them go to London at anniversary time, and they will get it there, in homeopathic doses. (A laugh.) Probably, the fact of my having once been a slave, and of my feeling upon this subject so intensely, having relations of my own, still dragging out the life of slavery, has made me feel, that something strong should be uttered. (Cheers.) People want something strong—they are willing to hear it; then I say, why not give it them? There is need I think, of an association in this country, which shall expose to the British nation the working of slavery in America and the fact as it is; which shall give a true representation also, and not merely a partial account, of what the abolitionists in America are doing. (Cheers.) I am identified, as you may well believe, with the most ultra of the abolitionists, who are, I consider, speaking the truth more effectually than any other party or association in the United States; and I consider also, that the greatest of the champions of human liberty there is the present leader of the anti-slavery movement in the United States, William Lloyd Garrison. (Great cheering.) I know there are some who would be afraid to utter that sentiment, because they would be afraid of losing caste. I, sir, have nothing to lose, but everything to gain. (Cheers.) I have now been five years in this country. I have traveled through Great Britain, and am almost an Englishman. I think I know something of the public sentiment here; and I say, the people want to know the truth, and to know what they can do for us. I tell them, that those ultra abolitionists in America, to whom I have referred, are those who in America are considered to be the greatest foes of the fugitive slave law, and of all the acts of the pro-slavery party; those are the persons of whom slaveowners speak with most malignity, and who are more vilified by the American pro-slavery press than all other parties and associations put together. This may be, unless I can comply with an invitation to speak on Thursday (and I am afraid that I cannot do so), my last opportunity of speaking publicly in this country; but I shall return to the United States, after being five years in England, conscious that I may safely give to the free coloured people of the north, and to the abolitionists of the United States, the assurance that something is being done here for their cause, and that the English people only want to know what they can do, and they will set about it and do it. (Cheers.) We do not ask you to take up arms; we do not ask you to do any act, or utter any language, unbecoming Christians; but we ask you to learn the facts and the truth of this matter, and honestly and strongly to speak out upon it.

Autobiographical Writings

From *Narrative of William W. Brown, a Fugitive Slave, Written by Himself*

(Boston: Anti-Slavery Office, 1847)

Brown's narrative was a best seller: more than 10,000 copies were sold in two years. Written two years after Douglass's Narrative, *Brown largely follows the conventions of slave narrative, detailing his life under slavery and his escape at age twenty. Brown later dramatized some of these incidents in his 1858 play* The Escape; or, A Leap to Freedom *and in his now lost earlier play "Experience; or, How to Give a Northern Man a Backbone" (1856). In the excerpts of the Narrative offered in this collection, we see Brown employing familiar characters such as the tragic mulatto, the heartless master, and the easily manipulated mistress, as well as such conventional tropes as the thwarted escape, the kindness of northern strangers, and the attempts to rescue and reunite the slave family. We can read all this as a literary apprenticeship or as the theme around which Brown will organize his literary variations.*

> ———Is there not some chosen curse,
> Some hidden thunder in the stores of heaven,
> Red with uncommon wrath, to blast the man
> Who gains his fortune from the blood of souls?
>   —COWPER

CHAPTER I.

I was born in Lexington, Ky. The man who stole me as soon as I was born, recorded the births of all the infants which he claimed to be born his property, in a book which he kept for that purpose. My mother's name was Elizabeth. She had seven children, viz: Solomon,

Leander, Benjamin, Joseph, Millford, Elizabeth, and myself. No two of us were children of the same father. My father's name, as I learned from my mother, was George Higgins. He was a white man, a relative of my master, and connected with some of the first families in Kentucky.

My master owned about forty slaves, twenty-five of whom were field hands. He removed from Kentucky to Missouri, when I was quite young, and settled thirty or forty miles above St. Charles, on the Missouri, where, in addition to his practice as a physician, he carried on milling, merchandizing and farming. He had a large farm, the principal productions of which were tobacco and hemp. The slave cabins were situated on the back part of the farm, with the house of the overseer, whose name was Grove Cook, in their midst. He had the entire charge of the farm, and having no family, was allowed a woman to keep house for him, whose business it was to deal out the provisions for the hands.

A woman was also kept at the quarters to do the cooking for the field hands, who were summoned to their unrequited toil every morning at four o'clock, by the ringing of a bell, hung on a post near the house of the overseer. They were allowed half an hour to eat their breakfast, and get to the field. At half past four, a horn was blown by the overseer, which was the signal to commence work; and every one that was not on the spot at the time, had to receive ten lashes from the negro-whip, with which the overseer always went armed. The handle was about three feet long, with the butt-end filled with lead, and the lash six or seven feet in length, made of cowhide, with platted wire on the end of it. This whip was put in requisition very frequently and freely, and a small offence on the part of a slave furnished an occasion for its use. During the time that Mr. Cook was overseer, I was a house servant—a situation preferable to that of a field hand, as I was better fed, better clothed, and not obliged to rise at the ringing of the bell, but about half an hour after. I have often laid and heard the crack of the whip, and the screams of the slave. My mother was a field hand, and one morning was ten or fifteen minutes behind the others in getting into the field. As soon as she reached the spot where they were at work, the overseer commenced whipping her. She cried, "Oh! pray—Oh! pray—Oh! pray"—these are generally the words of slaves, when imploring mercy at the hands of their oppressors. I heard her voice, and knew it, and jumped out of my bunk, and went to the door. Though the field was some distance from the house, I could hear every crack of the whip, and every groan and cry of my poor mother. I remained at the door, not daring to venture any farther. The cold chills ran over me, and I wept aloud. After giving her ten lashes, the sound of the whip ceased, and I returned to my bed, and found no consolation but in my tears. It was not yet daylight.

CHAPTER II.

My master being a political demagogue, soon found those who were ready to put him into office, for the favors he could render them; and a few years after his arrival in Missouri, he was elected to a seat in the Legislature. In his absence from home, everything was left in charge of Mr. Cook, the overseer, and he soon became more tyrannical and cruel. Among the slaves on the plantation, was one by the name of Randall. He was a man about six feet high, and well-proportioned, and known as a man of great strength and power. He was considered the most valuable and able-bodied slave on the plantation; but no matter how good or useful a slave may be, he seldom escapes the lash. But it was not so with Randall. He had been on the plantation since my earliest recollection, and I had never known of his being flogged. No thanks were due to the master or overseer for this. I have often heard him declare, that no white man should ever whip him—that he would die first.

Cook, from the time that he came upon the plantation, had frequently declared, that he could and would flog any nigger that was put into the field to work under him. My master had repeatedly told him not to attempt to whip Randall, but he was determined to try it. As soon as he was left sole dictator, he thought the time had come to put his threats into execution. He soon began to find fault with Randall, and threatened to whip him, if he did not do better. One day he gave him a very hard task,—more than he could possibly do; and at night, the task not being performed, he told Randall that he should remember him the next morning. On the following morning, after the hands had taken breakfast, Cook called out to Randall, and told him that he intended to whip him, and ordered him to cross his hands and be tied. Randall asked why he wished to whip him. He answered, because he had not finished his task the day before. Randall said that the task was too great, or he should have done it. Cook said it made no difference,—he should whip him. Randall stood silent for a moment, and then said, "Mr. Cook, I have always tried to please you since you have been on the plantation, and I find you are determined not to be satisfied with my work, let me do as well as I may. No man has laid hands on me, to whip me, for the last ten years, and I have long since come to the conclusion not to be whipped by any man living."

45

Cook, finding by Randall's determined look and gestures, that he would resist, called three of the hands from their work, and commanded them to seize Randall, and tie him. The hands stood still;—they knew Randall—and they also knew him to be a powerful man, and were afraid to grapple with him. As soon as Cook had ordered the men to seize him, Randall turned to them, and said—"Boys, you all know me; you know that I can handle any three of you, and the man that lays hands on me shall die. This white man can't whip me himself, and therefore he has called you to help him." The overseer was unable to prevail upon them to seize and secure Randall, and finally ordered them all to go to their work together.

Nothing was said to Randall by the overseer, for more than a week. One morning, however, while the hands were at work in the field, he came into it, accompanied by three friends of his, Thompson, Woodbridge and Jones. They came up to where Randall was at work, and Cook ordered him to leave his work, and go with them to the barn. He refused to go; whereupon he was attacked by the overseer and his companions, when he turned upon them, and laid them, one after another, prostrate on the ground. Woodbridge drew out his pistol, and fired at him, and brought him to the ground by a pistol ball. The others rushed upon him with their clubs, and beat him over the head and face, until they succeeded in tying him. He was then taken to the barn, and tied to a beam. Cook gave him over one hundred lashes with a heavy cowhide, had him washed with salt and water, and left him tied during the day. The next day he was untied, and taken to a blacksmith's shop, and had a ball and chain attached to his leg. He was compelled to labor in the field, and perform the same amount of work that the other hands did. When his master returned home, he was much pleased to find that Randall had been subdued in his absence.

CHAPTER III.

Soon afterwards, my master removed to the city of St. Louis, and purchased a farm four miles from there, which he placed under the charge of an overseer by the name of Friend Haskell. He was a regular Yankee from New England. The Yankees are noted for making the most cruel overseers.

My mother was hired out in the city, and I was also hired out there to Major Freeland, who kept a public house. He was formerly from Virginia, and was a horse-racer, cock-fighter, gambler, and withal an inveterate drunkard. There were ten or twelve servants in the house, and when he was present, it was cut and slash—knock down and drag out. In his fits of anger, he would take up a chair, and throw it at a servant; and in his more rational moments, when he wished to chastise one, he would tie them up in the smoke-house, and whip them; after which, he would cause a fire to be made of tobacco stems, and smoke them. This he called "*Virginia play.*"

I complained to my master of the treatment which I received from Major Freeland; but it made no difference. He cared nothing about it, so long as he received the money for my labor. After living with Major Freeland five or six months, I ran away, and went into the woods back of the city; and when night came on, I made my way to my master's farm, but was afraid to be seen, knowing that if Mr. Haskell, the overseer, should discover me, I should be again carried back to Major Freeland; so I kept in the woods. One day, while in the woods, I heard the barking and howling of dogs, and in a short time they came so near, that I knew them to be the bloodhounds of Major Benjamin O'Fallon. He kept five or six, to hunt runaway slaves with.

As soon as I was convinced that it was them, I knew there was no chance of escape. I took refuge in the top of a tree, and the hounds were soon at its base, and there remained until the hunters came up in a half or three quarters of an hour afterwards. There were two men with the dogs, who, as soon as they came up, ordered me to descend. I came down, was tied, and taken to St. Louis jail. Major Freeland soon made his appearance, and took me out, and ordered me to follow him, which I did. After we returned home, I was tied up in the smoke-house, and was very severely whipped. After the Major had flogged me to his satisfaction, he sent out his son Robert, a young man eighteen or twenty years of age, to see that I was well smoked. He made a fire of tobacco stems, which soon set me to coughing and sneezing. This, Robert told me, was the way his father used to do to his slaves in Virginia. After giving me what they conceived to be a decent smoking, I was untied and again set to work.

Robert Freeland was a "chip of the old block." Though quite young, it was not unfrequently that he came home in a state of intoxication. He is now, I believe, a popular commander of a steamboat on the Mississippi river. Major Freeland soon after failed in business, and I was put on board the steamboat Missouri, which plied between St. Louis and Galena. The commander of the boat was William B. Culver. I remained on her during the sailing season, which was the most pleasant time for me that I had ever experienced. At the close of navigation, I was hired to Mr. John Colburn, keeper of the Missouri Hotel. He was from one of the Free States; but a more inveterate hater of the negro, I do not believe ever walked on God's green earth. This hotel was at that time one of the largest in the city, and there were employed in it twenty or thirty servants, mostly slaves.

Mr. Colburn was very abusive, not only to the servants, but to his wife also, who was an excellent woman, and one from whom I never knew a servant to receive a harsh word; but never did I know a kind one to a servant from her husband. Among the slaves employed in the hotel, was one by the name of Aaron, who belonged to Mr. John F. Darby, a lawyer. Aaron was the knife-cleaner. One day, one of the knives was put on the table, not as clean as it might have been. Mr. Colburn, for this offence, tied Aaron up in the wood-house, and gave him over fifty lashes on the bare back with a cowhide, after which, he made me wash him down with rum. This seemed to put him into more agony than the whipping. After being untied, he went home to his master, and complained of the treatment which he had received. Mr. Darby would give no heed to anything he had to say, but sent him directly back. Colburn, learning that he had been to his master with complaints, tied him up again, and gave him a more severe whipping than before. The poor fellow's back was literally cut to pieces; so much so, that he was not able to work for ten or twelve days.

There was also, among the servants, a girl whose master resided in the country. Her name was Patsey. Mr. Colburn tied her up one evening, and whipped her until several of the boarders came out and begged him to desist. The reason for whipping her was this. She was engaged to be married to a man belonging to Major William Christy, who resided four or five miles north of the city. Mr. Colburn had forbid her to see John Christy. The reason of this was said to be the regard which he himself had for Patsey. She went to meeting that evening, and John returned home with her. Mr. Colburn had intended to flog John, if he came within the inclosure; but John knew too well the temper of his rival, and kept at a safe distance;—so he took vengeance on the poor girl. If all the slave-drivers had been called together, I do not think a more cruel man than John Colburn,—and he too a northern man,—could have been found among them.

While living at the Missouri Hotel, a circumstance occurred which caused me great unhappiness. My master sold my mother, and all her children, except myself. They were sold to different persons in the city of St. Louis.

CHAPTER IV.

I was soon after taken from Mr. Colburn's, and hired to Elijah P. Lovejoy, who was at that time publisher and editor of the "St. Louis Times." My work, while with him, was mainly in the printing office, waiting on the hands, working the press, &c. Mr. Lovejoy was a very good man, and decidedly the best master that I had ever had. I am chiefly indebted to him, and to my employment in the printing office, for what little learning I obtained while in slavery.

Though slavery is thought, by some, to be mild in Missouri, when compared with the cotton, sugar and rice growing States, yet no part of our slave-holding country, is more noted for the barbarity of its inhabitants, than St. Louis. It was here that Col. Harney, a United States officer, whipped a slave woman to death. It was here that Francis McIntosh, a free colored man from Pittsburgh, was taken from the steamboat Flora, and burned at the stake. During a residence of eight years in this city, numerous cases of extreme cruelty came under my own observation;—to record them all, would occupy more space than could possibly be allowed in this little volume. I shall, therefore, give but a few more, in addition to what I have already related.

Capt. J. B. Brunt, who resided near my master, had a slave named John. He was his body servant, carriage driver, &c. On one occasion, while driving his master through the city,—the streets being very muddy, and the horses going at a rapid rate,—some mud spattered upon a gentleman by the name of Robert More. More was determined to be revenged. Some three or four months after this occurrence, he purchased John, for the express purpose, as he said, "to tame the d—d nigger." After the purchase, he took him to a blacksmith's shop, and had a ball and chain fastened to his leg, and then put him to driving a yoke of oxen, and kept him at hard labor, until the iron around his leg was so worn into the flesh, that it was thought mortification would ensue. In addition to this, John told me that his master whipped him regularly three times a week for the first two months:—and all this to "*tame him.*" A more noble looking man than he, was not to be found in all St. Louis, before he fell into the hands of More; and a more degraded and spirit-crushed looking being was never seen on a southern plantation, after he had been subjected to this "*taming*" process for three months. The last time that I saw him, he had nearly lost the entire use of his limbs.

While living with Mr. Lovejoy, I was often sent on errands to the office of the "Missouri Republican," published by Mr. Edward Charles. Once, while returning to the office with type, I was attacked by several large boys, sons of slave-holders, who pelted me with snow-balls. Having the heavy form of type in my hands, I could not make my escape by running; so I laid down the type and gave them battle. They gathered around me, pelting me with stones and sticks, until they overpowered me, and would have captured me, if I had not resorted to my heels. Upon my retreat, they took possession of the type; and what to do to regain it I could not devise. Knowing Mr. Lovejoy to be a very humane man, I went to the office, and laid the case before him. He told me to remain in the office. He took one of the apprentices with him, and went after the type, and soon returned with it; but on his return informed me that Samuel McKinney had told him that he would whip me, because I had hurt his boy. Soon after, McKinney was seen making his way to the office by one of the printers, who informed me of the fact, and I made my escape through the back door.

McKinney not being able to find me on his arrival, left the office in a great rage, swearing that he would whip me to death. A few days after, as I was walking along Main Street, he seized me by the collar, and struck me over the head five or six times with a large cane, which caused the blood to gush from my nose and ears in such a manner that my clothes were completely saturated with blood. After beating me to his satisfaction, he let me go, and I returned to the office so weak from the loss of blood, that Mr. Lovejoy sent me home to my master. It was five weeks before I was able to walk again. During this time, it was necessary to have some one to supply my place at the office, and I lost the situation.

After my recovery, I was hired to Capt. Otis Reynolds, as a waiter on board the steamboat Enterprize, owned by Messrs. John and Edward Walsh, commission merchants at St. Louis. This boat was then running on the upper Mississippi. My employment on board was to wait on gentlemen, and the captain being a good man, the situation was a pleasant one to me;—but in passing from place to place, and seeing new faces every day, and knowing that they could go where they pleased, I soon became unhappy, and several times thought of leaving the boat at some landing place, and trying to make my escape to Canada, which I had heard much about as a place where the slave might live, be free, and be protected.

But whenever such thoughts would come into my mind, my resolution would soon be shaken by the remembrance that my dear mother was a slave in St. Louis, and I could not bear the idea of leaving her in that condition. She had often taken me upon her knee, and told me how she had carried me upon her back to the field when I was an infant—how often she had been whipped for leaving her work to nurse me—and how happy I would appear when she would take me into her arms. When these thoughts came over me, I would resolve never to leave the land of slavery without my mother. I thought that to leave her in slavery, after she had undergone and suffered so much for me, would be proving recreant to the duty which I owed to her. Besides this, I had three brothers and a sister there,—two of my brothers having died.

My mother, my brothers Joseph and Millford, and my sister Elizabeth, belonged to Mr. Isaac Mansfield, formerly from one of the Free States, (Massachusetts, I believe.) He was a tinner by trade, and carried on a large manufacturing establishment. Of all my relatives, mother was first, and sister next. One evening, while visiting them, I made some allusion to a proposed journey to Canada, and sister took her seat by my side, and taking my hand in hers, said, with tears in her eyes,—"Brother, you are not going to leave mother and your dear sister here without a friend, are you?"

I looked into her face, as the tears coursed swiftly down her cheeks, and bursting into tears myself, said—

"No, I will never desert you and mother."

She clasped my hand in hers, and said—

"Brother, you have often declared that you would not end your days in slavery. I see no possible way in which you can escape with us; and now, brother, you are on a steamboat where there is some chance for you to escape to a land of liberty. I beseech you not to let us hinder you. If we cannot get our liberty, we do not wish to be the means of keeping you from a land of freedom."

I could restrain my feelings no longer, and an outburst of my own feelings, caused her to cease speaking upon that subject. In opposition to their wishes, I pledged myself not to leave them in the hand of the oppressor. I took leave of them, and returned to the boat, and laid down in my bunk; but "sleep departed from my eyes, and slumber from my eyelids."

A few weeks after, on our downward passage, the boat took on board, at Hannibal, a drove of slaves, bound for the New Orleans market. They numbered from fifty to sixty, consisting of men and women from eighteen to forty years of age. A drove of slaves on a southern steamboat, bound for the cotton or sugar regions, is an occurrence so common, that no one, not even the passengers, appear to notice it, though they clank their chains at every step. There was, however, one in this gang that attracted the attention of the passengers and crew. It was a beautiful girl, apparently about twenty years of age, perfectly white, with straight light hair and blue eyes. But it was not the whiteness of her skin that created such a sensation among those who gazed upon her—it was her almost unparalleled beauty. She had been on the boat but a short time, before the attention of all the passengers, including the ladies, had been called to her, and the common topic of conversation was about the beautiful slave-girl. She was not in chains. The man who claimed this article of human merchandize was a Mr. Walker,—a well known slave-trader, residing in St. Louis. There was a general anxiety among the passengers and crew to learn the history of the girl. Her master kept close by her side, and it would have been considered impudent for any of the passengers to have spoken to her, and the crew were not allowed to have any conversation with them. When we reached St. Louis, the slaves were removed to a boat bound for New Orleans, and the history of the beautiful slave-girl remained a mystery.

I remained on the boat during the season, and it was not an unfrequent occurrence to have on board gangs of slaves on their way to the cotton, sugar and rice plantations of the South.

Toward the latter part of the summer, Captain Reynolds left the boat, and I was sent home. I was then placed on the farm under Mr. Haskell, the overseer. As I had been some time out of the field, and not accustomed to work in the burning sun, it was very hard; but I was compelled to kee[p] up with the best of the hands.

I found a great difference between the work in a steamboat cabin and that in a corn-field.

My master, who was then living in the city, soon after removed to the farm, when I was taken out of the field to work in the house as a waiter. Though his wife was very peevish, and hard to please, I much preferred to be under her control than the overseer's. They brought with them Mr. Sloane, a Presbyterian minister; Miss Martha Tulley, a neice of theirs from Kentucky; and their nephew William. The latter had been in the family a number of years, but the others were all new-comers.

Mr. Sloane was a young minister, who had been at the South but a short time, and it seemed as if his whole aim was to please the slaveholders, especially my master and mistress. He was intending to make a visit during the winter, and he not only tried to please them, but I think he succeeded admirably. When they wanted singing, he sung; when they wanted praying, he prayed; when they wanted a story told, he told a story. Instead of his teaching my master theology, my master taught theology to him. While I was with Captain Reynolds, my master "got religion," and new laws were made on the plantation. Formerly, we had the privilege of hunting, fishing, making splint brooms, baskets, &c. on Sunday; but this was all stopped. Every Sunday, we were all compelled to attend meeting. Master was so religious, that he induced some others to join him in hiring a preacher to preach to the slaves.

CHAPTER V.

My master had family worship, night and morning. At night, the slaves were called in to attend; but in the mornings, they had to be at their work, and master did all the praying. My master and mistress were great lovers of mint julep, and every morning, a pitcher-full was made, of which they all partook freely, not excepting little master William. After drinking freely all round, they would have family worship, and then breakfast. I cannot say but I loved the julep as well as any of them, and during prayer was always careful to seat myself close to the table where it stood, so as to help myself when they were all busily engaged in their devotions. By the time prayer was over, I was about as happy as any of them. A sad accident happened one morning. In helping myself, and at the same time keeping an eye on my old mistress, I accidentally let the pitcher fall upon the floor, breaking it in pieces, and spilling the contents. This was a bad affair for me; for as soon as prayer was over, I was taken and severely chastised.

My master's family consisted of himself, his wife, and their nephew, William Moore. He was taken into the family, when only a few weeks of age. His name being that of my own, mine was changed, for the purpose of giving precedence to his, though I was his senior by ten or twelve years. The plantation being four miles from the city, I had to drive the family to church. I always dreaded the approach of the Sabbath; for, during service, I was obliged to stand by the horses in the hot broiling sun, or in the rain just as it happened.

One Sabbath, as we were driving past the house of D. D. Page, a gentleman who owned a large baking establishment, as I was sitting upon the box of the carriage, which was very much elevated, I saw Mr. Page pursuing a slave around the yard, with a long whip, cutting him at every jump. The man soon escaped from the yard, and was followed by Mr. Page. They came running past us, and the slave perceiving that he would be overtaken, stopped suddenly, and Page stumbled over him, and falling on the stone pavement, fractured one of his legs, which crippled him for life. The same gentleman, but a short time previous, tied up a woman of his, by the name of Delphia, and whipped her nearly to death; yet he was a deacon in the Baptist church, in good and regular standing. Poor Delphia! I was well acquainted with her, and called to see her while upon her sick bed; and I shall never forget her appearance. She was a member of the same church with her master.

Soon after this, I was hired out to Mr. Walker; the same man whom I have mentioned as having carried a gang of slaves down the river, on the steamboat Enterprize. Seeing me in the capacity of steward on the boat, and thinking that I would make a good hand to take care of slaves, he determined to have me for that purpose; and finding that my master would not sell me, he hired me for the term of one year.

When I learned the fact of my having been hired to a negro speculator, or a "soul-driver" as they are generally called among slaves, no one can tell my emotions. Mr. Walker had offered a high price for me, as I afterwards learned, but I suppose my master was restrained from selling me by the fact that I was a near relative of his. On entering the service of Mr. Walker, I found that my opportunity of getting to a land of liberty was gone, at least for the time being. He had a gang of slaves in readiness to start for New Orleans, and in a few days we were on our journey. I am at a loss for language to express my feelings on that occasion. Although my master had told me that he had not sold me, and Mr. Walker had told me that he had not purchased me, I did not believe them; and not until I had been to New Orleans, and was on my return, did I believe that I was not sold.

There was on the boat a large room on the lower deck, in which the slaves were kept, men and women, promiscuously—all chained two and two, and a strict watch kept that they did not get loose; for cases have occurred in which slaves have got off their chains, and made their escape at landing-places, while the boats were taking in wood;—and with all our care, we lost one woman who had been taken from her husband and children, and having no desire to live without them, in the agony of her soul jumped overboard, and drowned herself. She was not chained.

It was almost impossible to keep that part of the boat clean.

On landing at Natchez, the slaves were all carried to the slave-pen, and there kept one week, during which time, several of them were sold. Mr. Walker fed his slaves well. We took on board, at St. Louis, several hundred pounds of bacon (smoked meat) and corn-meal, and his slaves were better fed than slaves generally were in Natchez, so far as my observation extended.

At the end of a week, we left for New Orleans, the place of our final destination, which we reached in two days. Here the slaves were placed in a negro-pen, where those who wished to purchase could call and examine them. The negro-pen is a small yard, surrounded by buildings, from fifteen to twenty feet wide, with the exception of a large gate with iron bars. The slaves are kept in the buildings during the night, and turned out into the yard during the day. After the best of the stock was sold at private sale at the pen, the balance were taken to the Exchange Coffee House Auction Rooms, kept by Isaac L. McCoy, and sold at public auction. After the sale of this lot of slaves, we left New Orleans for St. Louis.

CHAPTER VI.

On our arrival at St. Louis, I went to Dr. Young, and told him that I did not wish to live with Mr. Walker any longer. I was heart-sick at seeing my fellow-creatures bought and sold. But the Dr. had hired me for the year, and stay I must. Mr. Walker again commenced purchasing another gang of slaves. He bought a man of Colonel John O'Fallon, who resided in the suburbs of the city. This man had a wife and three children. As soon as the purchase was made, he was put in jail for safe keeping, until we should be ready to start for New Orleans. His wife visited him while there, several times, and several times when she went for that purpose was refused admittance.

In the course of eight or nine weeks Mr. Walker had his cargo of human flesh made up. There was in this lot a number of old men and women, some of them with gray locks. We left St. Louis in the steamboat Carlton, Captain Swan, bound for New Orleans. On our way down, and before we reached Rodney, the place where we made our first stop, I had to prepare the old slaves for market. I was ordered to have the old men's whiskers shaved off, and the grey hairs plucked out, where they were not too numerous, in which case he had a preparation of blacking to color it, and with a blacking-brush we would put it on. This was new business to me, and was performed in a room where the passengers could not see us. These slaves were also taught how old they were by Mr. Walker, and after going through the blacking process, they looked ten or fifteen years younger; and I am sure that some of those who purchased slaves of Mr. Walker, were dreadfully cheated, especially in the ages of the slaves which they bought.

We landed at Rodney, and the slaves were driven to the pen in the back part of the village. Several were sold at this place, during our stay of four or five days, when we proceeded to Natchez. There we landed at night, and the gang were put in the warehouse until morning, when they were driven to the pen. As soon as the slaves are put in these pens, swarms of planters may be seen in and about them. They knew when Walker was expected, as he always had the time advertised beforehand when he would be in Rodney, Natchez, and New Orleans. These were the principal places where he offered his slaves for sale.

When at Natchez the second time, I saw a slave very cruelly whipped. He belonged to a Mr. Broadwell, a merchant who kept a store on the wharf. The slave's name was Lewis. I had known him several years, as he was formerly from St. Louis. We were expecting a steamboat down the river, in which we were to take passage for New Orleans. Mr. Walker sent me to the landing to watch for the boat, ordering me to inform him on its arrival. While there, I went into the store to see Lewis. I saw a slave in the store, and asked him where Lewis was. Said he, "They have got Lewis hanging between the heavens and the earth." I asked him what he meant by that. He told me to go into the warehouse and see. I went in, and found

Lewis there. He was tied up to a beam, with his toes just touching the floor. As there was no one in the warehouse but himself, I inquired the reason of his being in that situation. He said Mr. Broadwell had sold his wife to a planter six miles from the city, and that he had been to visit her,—that he went in the night, expecting to return before daylight, and went without his master's permission. The patrol had taken him up before he reached his wife. He was put in jail, and his master had to pay for his catching and keeping, and that was what he was tied up for.

Just as he finished his story, Mr. Broadwell came in, and inquired what I was doing there. I knew not what to say, and while I was thinking what reply to make, he struck me over the head with the cowhide, the end of which struck me over my right eye, sinking deep into the flesh, leaving a scar which I carry to this day. Before I visited Lewis, he had received fifty lashes. Mr. Broadwell gave him fifty lashes more after I came out, as I was afterwards informed by Lewis himself.

The next day we proceeded to New Orleans, and put the gang in the same negro-pen which we occupied before. In a short time, the planters came flocking to the pen to purchase slaves. Before the slaves were exhibited for sale, they were dressed and driven out into the yard. Some were set to dancing, some to jumping, some to singing, and some to playing cards. This was done to make them appear cheerful and happy. My business was to see that they were placed in those situations before the arrival of the purchasers, and I have often set them to dancing when their cheeks were wet with tears. As slaves were in good demand at that time, they were all soon disposed of, and we again set out for St. Louis.

On our arrival, Mr. Walker purchased a farm five or six miles from the city. He had no family, but made a housekeeper of one of his female slaves. Poor Cynthia! I knew her well. She was a quadroon, and one of the most beautiful women I ever saw. She was a native of St. Louis, and bore an irreproachable character for virtue and propriety of conduct. Mr. Walker bought her for the New Orleans market, and took her down with him on one of the trips that I made with him. Never shall I forget the circumstances of that voyage! On the first night that we were on board the steamboat, he directed me to put her into a state-room he had provided for her, apart from the other slaves. I had seen too much of the workings of slavery, not to know what this meant. I accordingly watched him into the state-room, and listened to hear what passed between them. I heard him make his base offers, and her reject them. He told her that if she would accept his vile proposals, he would take her back with him to St. Louis, and establish her as his housekeeper at his farm. But if she persisted in rejecting them, he would sell her as a field hand on the worst plantation on the river. Neither threats nor bribes prevailed, however, and he retired, disappointed of his prey.

The next morning, poor Cynthia told me what had past, and bewailed her sad fate with floods of tears. I comforted and encouraged her all I could; but I foresaw but too well what the result must be. Without entering into any farther particulars, suffice it to say that Walker performed his part of the contract, at that time. He took her back to St. Louis, established her as his mistress and housekeeper at his farm, and before I left, he had two children by her. But, mark the end! Since I have been at the North, I have been credibly informed that Walker has been married, and, as a previous measure, sold poor Cynthia and her four children (she having had two more since I came away) into hopeless bondage!

He soon commenced purchasing to make up the third gang. We took steamboat, and went to Jefferson City, a town on the Missouri river. Here we landed, and took stage for the interior of the State. He bought a number of slaves as he passed the different farms and villages. After getting twenty-two or twenty-three men and women, we arrived at St. Charles, a village on the banks of the Missouri. Here he purchased a woman who had a child in her arms, appearing to be four or five weeks old.

We had been travelling by land for some days, and were in hopes to have found a boat at this place for St. Louis, but were disappointed. As no boat was expected for some days, we started for St. Louis by land. Mr. Walker had purchased two horses. He rode one, and I the other. The slaves were chained together, and we took up our line of march, Mr. Walker taking the lead, and I bringing up the rear. Though the distance was not more than twenty miles, we did not reach it the first day. The road was worse than any that I have ever travelled.

Soon after we left St. Charles, the young child grew very cross, and kept up a noise during the greater part of the day. Mr. Walker complained of its crying several times, and told the mother to stop the child's d—d noise, or he would. The woman tried to keep the child from crying, but could not. We put up at night with an acquaintance of Mr. Walker, and in the morning, just as we were about to start, the child again commenced crying. Walker stepped up to her, and told her to give the child to him. The mother tremblingly obeyed. He took the child by one arm, as you would a cat by the leg, walked into the house, and said to the lady,

"Madam, I will make you a present of this little nigger; it keeps such a noise that I can't bear it."

"Thank you, sir," said the lady.

The mother, as soon as she saw that her child was to be left, ran up to Mr. Walker, and falling upon her knees begged him to let her have her child; she clung around his legs, and cried, "Oh, my child! my child! master, do let me have my child! oh, do, do, do. I will stop its crying, if you will only let me have it again." When I saw this woman crying for her child so piteously, a shudder,—a feeling akin to horror, shot through my frame. I have often since in imagination heard her crying for her child:—

"O, master, let me stay to catch
My baby's sobbing breath,
His little glassy eye to watch,
And smooth his limbs in death,

And cover him with grass and leaf,
Beneath the large oak tree:
It is not sullenness, but grief,—
O, master, pity me!

The morn was chill—I spoke no word,
But feared my babe might die,
And heard all day, or thought I heard,
My little baby cry.

At noon, oh, how I ran and took
My baby to my breast!
I lingered—and the long lash broke
My sleeping infant's rest.

I worked till night—till darkest night,
In torture and disgrace;
Went home and watched till morning light,
To see my baby's face.

Then give me but one little hour—
O! do not lash me so!
One little hour—one little hour—
And gratefully I'll go."

Mr. Walker commanded her to return into the ranks with the other slaves. Women who had children were not chained, but those that had none were. As soon as her child was disposed of, she was chained in the gang.

The following song I have often heard the slaves sing, when about to be carried to the far south. It is said to have been composed by a slave.

"See these poor souls from Africa
Transported to America;
We are stolen, and sold to Georgia,
Will you go along with me?
We are stolen, and sold to Georgia,
Come sound the jubilee!

See wives and husbands sold apart,
Their children's screams will break my heart;—
There 's a better day a coming,
Will you go along with me?
There 's a better day a coming,
Go sound the jubilee!

O, gracious Lord! when shall it be,
That we poor souls shall all be free;
Lord, break them slavery powers—
Will you go along with me?
Lord break them slavery powers,
Go sound the jubilee!

Dear Lord, dear Lord, when slavery 'll cease,
Then we poor souls will have our peace;—
There 's a better day a coming,
Will you go along with me?
There 's a better day a coming,
Go sound the jubilee!"

We finally arrived at Mr. Walker's farm. He had a house built during our absence to put slaves in. It was a kind of domestic jail. The slaves were put in the jail at night, and worked on the farm during the day. They were kept here until the gang was completed, when we again started for New Orleans, on board the steamboat North America, Capt. Alexander Scott. We had a large number of slaves in this gang. One, by the name of Joe, Mr. Walker was training up to take my place, as my time was nearly out, and glad was I. We made our first stop at Vicksburg, where we remained one week and sold several slaves.

Mr. Walker, though not a good master, had not flogged a slave since I had been with him, though he had threatened me. The slaves were kept in the pen, and he always put up at the best hotel, and kept his wines in his room, for the accommodation of those who called to negotiate with him for the purchase of slaves. One day while we were at Vicksburg, several gentlemen came to see him for this purpose, and as usual the wine was called for. I took the tray and started around with it, and having accidentally filled some of the glasses too full, the gentlemen spilled the wine on their clothes as they went to drink. Mr. Walker apologized to them for my carelessness, but looked at me as though he would see me again on this subject.

After the gentlemen had left the room, he asked me what I meant by my carelessness, and said that he would attend to me. The next morning, he gave me a note to carry to the jailer, and a dollar in money to give to him. I suspected that all was not right, so I went down near the landing where I met with a sailor, and walking up to him, asked him if he would be so kind as to read the note for me. He read it over, and then looked at me. I asked him to tell me what was in it. Said he,

"They are going to give you hell."

"Why?" said I.

He said, "This is a note to have you whipped, and says that you have a dollar to pay for it."

He handed me back the note, and off I started. I knew not what to do, but was determined not to be whipped. I went up to the jail—took a look at it, and walked off again. As Mr. Walker was acquainted with the jailer, I feared that I should be found out if I did not go, and be treated in consequence of it still worse.

While I was meditating on the subject, I saw a colored man about my size walk up, and the thought struck me in a moment to send him with my note. I walked up to him, and asked him who he belonged to. He said he was a free man, and had been in the city but a short time. I told him I had a note to go into the jail, and get a trunk to carry to one of the steamboats; but was so busily engaged that I could not do it, although I had a dollar to pay for it. He asked me if I would not give him the job. I handed him the note and the dollar, and off he started for the jail.

I watched to see that he went in, and as soon as I saw the door close behind him, I walked around the corner, and took my station, intending to see how my friend looked when he came out. I had been there but a short time, when a colored man came around the corner, and said to another colored man with whom he was acquainted—

"They are giving a nigger scissors in the jail."

"What for?" said the other. The man continued,

"A nigger came into the jail, and asked for the jailer. The jailer came out, and he handed him a note, and said he wanted to get a trunk. The jailer told him to go with him, and he would give him the trunk. So he took him into the room, and told the nigger to give up the dollar. He said a man had given him the dollar to pay for getting the trunk. But that lie would not answer. So they made him strip himself, and then they tied him down, and are now whipping him."

I stood by all the while listening to their talk, and soon found out that the person alluded to was my customer. I went into the street opposite the jail, and concealed myself in such a manner that I could not be seen by any one coming out. I had been there but a short time, when the young man made his appearance, and looked around for me.

I, unobserved, came forth from my hiding-place, behind a pile of brick, and he pretty soon saw me and came up to me complaining bitterly, saying that I had played a trick upon him. I denied any knowledge of what the note contained, and asked him what they had done to him. He told me in substance what I heard the man tell who had come out of the jail.

"Yes," said he, "they whipped me and took my dollar, and gave me this note."

He showed me the note which the jailer had given him, telling him to give it to his master. I told him I would give him fifty cents for it,—that being all the money I had. He gave it to me, and took his money. He had received twenty lashes on his bare back, with the negro-whip.

I took the note and started for the hotel where I had left Mr. Walker. Upon reaching the hotel, I handed it to a stranger whom I had not seen before, and requested him to read it to me. As near as I can recollect, it was as follows:—

"DEAR SIR:—By your direction, I have given your boy twenty lashes. He is a very saucy boy, and tried to make me believe that he did not belong to you, and I put it on to him well for lying to me.
I remain,
Your obedient servant."

It is true that in most of the slave-holding cities, when a gentleman wishes his servants whipped, he can send him to the jail and have it done. Before I went in where Mr. Walker was, I wet my cheeks a little, as though I had been crying. He looked at me, and inquired what was the matter. I told him that I had never had such a whipping in my life, and handed him the note. He looked at it and laughed;—"and so you told him that you did not belong to me." "Yes, sir," said I. "I did not know that there was any harm in that." He told me I must behave myself, if I did not want to be whipped again.

This incident shows how it is that slavery makes its victims lying and mean; for which vices it afterwards reproaches them, and uses them as arguments to prove that they deserve no better fate. I have often, since my escape, deeply regretted the deception I practised upon this poor fellow; and I heartily desire that it may be, at some time or other, in my power to make him amends for his vicarious sufferings in my behalf.

From *My Southern Home;*
or, The South and Its People

(Boston: A. G. Brown, 1880)

In the excerpts from My Southern Home *offered in this collection we see Brown at his wittiest, even his silliest. Written late in Brown's life,* My Southern Home *focuses on the wit and wisdom of slavery, rather than on its bitterness. Set "ten miles north of the city of St. Louis," this work humorously recounts life on Poplar Farm.* My Southern Home, *seldom considered in estimates of Brown's work, is an intriguing example of Brown's ability to turn situations on end and point out, with poignant humor, the inhumanity of southern slavery. In fact, Brown emulates many popular sentimental works of the time from the outset, seemingly establishing his ironic tone from the first page. Complete with thorough descriptions of the proud flora and fauna of the estate, Brown immediately establishes his comic frame.*

In addition to the numerous black characters who outwit their owner, Brown presents a comical version of Poplar Farm's proprietor, Dr. John Gaines. Gaines, who apparently chose as a profession medicine over religion when his father flipped a coin to make the decision, is immediately established as a mockery of Christian goodness. His wife Sarah, who repeatedly insists that she has married beneath herself, is shown as a cruel mistress, though notably less cruel than her peers. Central to this plot, however, is the existence of Billy, a slave who bears a marked resemblance to Dr. Gaines and is "mistaken" as his son. In addition, the plot is peopled by Cato, Dolly, and a host of other stock black characters.

In My Southern Home, *Brown takes up with a comic lens the role of religion in southern slavery—a role that he had outlined in* Clotel. *Brown repeatedly mocks the hypocrisy of southern white "Christians." Brown's use of humor deserves greater scholarly attention.*

63

"Go, little book, from this thy solitude!
I cast thee on the waters—go thy ways!
And if, as I believe, th[y] vein be good,
The world will find thee after many days."

—Southey.

CHAPTER I.

Ten miles north of the city of St. Louis, in the State of Missouri, forty years ago, on a pleasant plain, sloping off toward a murmuring stream, stood a large frame-house, two stories high; in front was a beautiful lake, and, in the rear, a[n] old orchard filled with apple, peach, pear, and plum trees, with boughs untrimmed, all bearing indifferent fruit. The mansion was surrounded with piazzas, covered with grape-vines, clematis, and passion flowers; the Pride of China mixed its oriental-looking foliage with the majestic magnolia, and the air was redolent with the fragrance of buds peeping out of every nook, and nodding upon you with a most unexpected welcome.

The tasteful hand of art, which shows itself in the grounds of European and New-England villas, was not seen there, but the lavish beauty and harmonious disorder of nature was permitted to take its own course, and exhibited a want of taste so commonly witnessed in the sunny South.

The killing effects of the tobacco plant upon the lands of "Poplar Farm," was to be seen in the rank growth of the brier, the thistle, the burdock, and the jimpson weed, showing themselves wherever the strong arm of the bondman had not kept them down.

Dr. Gaines, the proprietor of "Poplar Farm," was a good-humored, sunny-sided old gentleman, who, always feeling happy himself, wanted everybody to enjoy the same blessing. Unfortunately for him, the Doctor had been born and brought up in Virginia, raised in a family claiming to be of the "F. V.'s," but, in reality, was comparatively poor. Marrying Mrs. Sarah Scott Pepper, an accomplished widow lady of medium fortune, Dr. Gaines emigrated to Missouri, where he became a leading man in his locality.

Deeply imbued with religious feeling of the Calvinistic school, well-versed in the Scriptures, and having an abiding faith in the power of the Gospel to regenerate the world, the Doctor took great pleasure in presenting his views wherever his duties called him.

As a physician, he did not rank very high, for it was currently reported, and generally believed, that the father, finding his son unfit for mercantile business, or the law, determined to make him either a clergyman or a physician. Mr. Gaines, Senior, being somewhat superstitious, resolved not to settle the question too rashly in regard to the son's profession, therefore, it is said, flipped a cent, feeling that "heads or tails" would be a better omen than his own judgment in the matter. Fortunately for the cause of religion, the head turned up in favor of the medical profession. Nevertheless, the son often said that he believed God had destined him for the sacred calling, and devoted much of his time in exhorting his neighbors to seek repentance.

Most planters in our section cared but little about the religious training of their slaves, regarding them as they did their cattle,—an investment, the return of which was only to be considered in dollars and cents. Not so, however, with Dr. John Gaines, for he took special pride in looking after the spiritual welfare of his slaves, having them all in the "great house," at family worship, night and morning.

On Sabbath mornings, reading of the Scriptures, and explaining the same, generally occupied from one to two hours, and often till half of the negroes present were fast asleep. The white members of the family did not take as kindly to the religious teaching of the doctor, as did the blacks.

For his Christian zeal, I had the greatest respect, for I always regarded him as a truly pious and conscientious man, willing at all times to give of his means the needful in spreading the Gospel.

Mrs. Sarah Gaines was a lady of considerable merit, well-educated, and of undoubted piety. If she did not join heartily in her husband's religious enthusiasm, it was not for want of deep and genuine Christian feeling, but from the idea that he was of more humble origin than herself, and, therefore, was not a capable instructor.

This difference in birth, this difference in antecedents does much in the South to disturb family relations wherever it exists, and Mrs. Gaines, when wishing to show her contempt for the Doctor's opinions, would allude to her own parentage and birth in comparison to her husband's. Thus, once, when they were having a "family jar," she, with tears streaming down her cheeks, and wringing her hands, said,—

"My mother told me that I was a fool to marry a man so much beneath me,—one so much my inferior in society. And now you show it by hectoring and aggravating me all you can. But, never mind; I thank the Lord that He has given me religion and grace to stand it. Never mind, one of these days the Lord will make up His jewels,— take me home to glory, out of your sight,—and then I'll be devilish glad of it!"

These scenes of unpleasantness, however, were not of everyday occurrence, and, therefore, the great house at the "Poplar Farm," may be considered as having a happy family.

Slave children, with almost an alabaster complexion, straight hair, and blue eyes, whose mothers were jet black, or brown, were often a great source of annoyance in the Southern household, and especially to the mistress of the mansion.

Billy, a quadroon of eight or nine years, was amongst the young slaves, in the Doctor's house, then being trained up for a servant. Any one taking a hasty glance at the lad would never suspect that a drop of negro blood coursed through his blue veins. A gentleman, whose acquaintance Dr. Gaines had made, but who knew nothing of the latter's family relations, called at the house in the Doctor's absence. Mrs. Gaines received the stranger, and asked him to be seated, and remain till the host's return. While thus waiting, the boy, Billy, had occasion to pass through the room. The stranger, presuming the lad to be a son of the Doctor, exclaimed, "How do you do?" and turning to the lady, said, "how much he looks like his father; I should have known it was the Doctor's son, if I had met him in Mexico!"

With flushed countenance and excited voice, Mrs. Gaines informed the gentleman that the little fellow was "only a slave and nothing more." After the stranger's departure, Billy was seen pulling up grass in the garden, with bare head, neck and shoulders, while the rays of the burning sun appeared to melt the child.

This process was repeated every few days for the purpose of giving the slave the color that nature had refused it. And yet, Mrs. Gaines was not considered a cruel woman,—indeed she was regarded as a kind-feeling mistress. Billy, however, a few days later, experienced a roasting far more severe than the one he had got in the sun.

The morning was cool, and the breakfast table was spread near the fireplace, where a newly-built fire was blazing up. Mrs. Gaines, being seated near enough to feel very sensibly the increasing flames, ordered Billy to stand before her.

The lad at once complied. His thin clothing giving him but little protection from the fire, the boy soon began to make up faces and to twist and move about, showing evident signs of suffering.

"What are you riggling about for?" asked the mistress. "It burns me," replied the lad; "turn round, then," said the mistress; and the slave commenced turning around, keeping it up till the lady arose from the table.

Billy, however, was not entirely without his crumbs of comfort. It was his duty to bring the hot biscuit from the kitchen to the great house table while the whites were at meal. The boy would often watch his opportunity, take a "cake" from the plate, and conceal it in his pocket till breakfast was over, and then enjoy his stolen gain. One morning Mrs. Gaines, observing that the boy kept moving about the room, after bringing in the "cakes," and also seeing the little fellow's pocket sticking out rather largely, and presuming that there was something hot there, said, "Come here." The lad came up; she pressed her hand against the hot pocket, which caused the boy to jump back. Again the mistress repeated, "Come here," and with the same result.

This, of course, set the whole room, servants and all, in a roar. Again and again the boy was ordered to "come up," which he did, each time jumping back, until the heat of the biscuit was exhausted, and then he was made to take it out and throw it into the yard, where the geese seized it and held a carnival over it. Billy was heartily laughed at by his companions in the kitchen and the quarters, and the large blister, caused by the hot biscuit, created merriment among the slaves, rather than sympathy for the lad.

Mrs. Gaines, being absent from home one day, and the rest of the family out of the house, Billy commenced playing with the shot-gun, which stood in the corner of the room, and which the boy supposed was unloaded; upon a corner shelf, just above the gun, stood a band-box, in which was neatly laid away all of Mrs. Gaines' caps and cuffs, which, in, those days, were in great use.

The gun having the flint lock, the boy amused himself with bringing down the hammer and striking fire. By this action powder was jarred into the pan, and the gun, which was heavily charged with shot was discharged, the contents passing through band-box of caps, cutting them literally to pieces and scattering them over the floor.

Billy gathered up the fragments, put them in the box and placed it upon the shelf,—he alone aware of the accident.

A few days later, and Mrs. Gaines was expecting company; she called to Hannah to get her a clean cap. The servant, in attempting to take down box, exclaimed: "Lor, misses, ef de rats ain't bin at dees caps an' cut 'em all to pieces, jes look here." With a degree of amazement not easily described the mistress beheld the fragments as they were emptied out upon the floor.

Just then a new idea struck Hannah, and she said: "I lay anything dat gun has been shootin' off."

"Where is Billy? Where is Billy?" exclaimed the mistress; "Where is Billy?" echoed Hannah; fearing that the lady would go into convulsions, I hastened out to look for the boy, but he was nowhere to be found; I returned only to find her weeping and wringing her hands, exclaiming,

"O, I am ruined, I am ruined; the company's coming and not a clean cap about the house; O, what shall I do, what shall I do?"

I tried to comfort her by suggesting that the servants might get one ready in time; Billy soon made his appearance, and looked on with wonderment; and when asked how he came to shoot off the gun, declared that he knew nothing about it; and "ef de gun went off, it was of its own accord." However, the boy admitted the snapping of the lock or trigger. A light whipping was all that he got, and for which he was well repaid by having an opportunity of telling how the "caps flew about the room when de gun went off."

Relating the event some time after in the quarters he said: "I golly, you had aughty seen dem caps fly, and de dust and smok' in de room. I thought de judgment day had come, sure nuff." On the arrival of the company, Mrs. Gaines made a very presentable appearance, although the caps and laces had been destroyed. One of the visitors on this occasion was a young Mr. Sarpee, of St. Louis, who, although above twenty-one years of age, had never seen anything of country life, and, therefore, was very anxious to remain over night, and go on a coon hunt. Dr. Gaines, being lame, could not accompany the gentleman, but sent Ike, Cato, and Sam; three of the most expert coon-hunters on the farm. Night came, and off went the young man and the boys on the coon hunt. The dogs scented game, after being about half an hour in the woods, to the great delight of Mr. Sarpee, who was armed with a double barrel pistol, which, he said, he carried both to "protect himself, and to shoot the coon."

The halting of the boys and the quick, sharp bark of the dogs announced that the game was "treed," and the gentleman from the city pressed forward with fond expectation of seeing the coon, and using his pistol. However, the boys soon raised the cry of "polecat, polecat; get out de way"; and at the same time, retreating as if they were afraid of an attack from the animal. Not so with Mr. Sarpee; he stood his ground, with pistol in hand, waiting to get a sight of the game. He was not long in suspense, for the white and black spotted creature soon made its appearance, at which the city gentleman opened fire upon the skunk, which attack was immediately answered by the animal, and in a manner that caused the young man to wish that he, too, had retreated with the boys. Such an odor, he had never before inhaled; and, what was worse, his face, head, hands and clothing was covered with the cause of the smell, and the gentleman, at once, said: "Come, let's go home; I've got enough of coon-hunting." But, didn't the boys enjoy the fun.

The return of the party home was the signal for a hearty laugh, and all at the expense of the city gentleman. So great and disagreeable was the smell, that the young man had to go to the barn, where his clothing was removed, and he submitted to the process of washing by the servants. Soap, scrubbing brushes, towels, indeed, everything was brought into requisition, but all to no purpose. The skunk smell was there, and was likely to remain. Both family and visitors were at the breakfast table, the next morning, except Mr. Sarpee. He was still in the barn, where he had slept the previous night. Nor did there seem to be any hope that he would be able to visit the house, for the smell was intolerable The substitution of a suit of the Doctor's clothes for his own failed to remedy the odor.

Dinkie, the conjurer, was called in. He looked the young man over, shook his head in a knowing manner, and said it was a big job. Mr. Sarpee took out a Mexican silver dollar, handed it to the old negro, and told him to do his best. Dinkie smiled, and he thought that he could remove the smell.

His remedy was to dig a pit in the ground large enough to hold the man, put him in it, and cover him over with fresh earth; consequently, Mr. Sarpee was, after removing his entire clothing, buried, all except his head, while his clothing was served in the same manner. A servant held an umbrella over the unhappy man, and fanned him during the eight hours that he was there.

Taken out of the pit at six o'clock in the evening, all joined with Dinkie in the belief that Mr. Sarpee "smelt sweeter," than when interred in the morning; still the smell of the "polecat" was there. Five hours longer in the pit, the following day, with a rub down by Dinkie, with his "Goopher," fitted the young man for a return home to the city.

I never heard that Mr. Sarpee ever again joined in a "coon hunt."

No description of mine, however, can give anything like a correct idea of the great merriment of the entire slave population on "Poplar Farm," caused by the "coon hunt." Even Uncle Ned, the old superannuated slave, who seldom went beyond the confines of his own cabin, hobbled out, on this occasion, to take a look at "de gentleman fum de city," while buried in the pit.

At night, in the quarters, the slaves had a merry time over the "coon hunt."

"I golly, but didn't de polecat give him a big dose?" said Ike.

"But how Mr. Sarpee did talk French to hissef when de ole coon peppered him," remarked Cato.

"He won't go coon huntin' agin, soon, I bet you," said Sam.

"De coon hunt," and "de gemmen fum de city," was the talk for many days.

CHAPTER II.

I have already said that Dr. Gaines was a man of deep religious feeling, and this interest was not confined to the whites, for he felt that it was the Christian duty to help to save all mankind, white and black. He would often say, "I regard our negroes as given to us by an All Wise Providence, for their especial benefit, and we should impart to them Christian civilization." And to this, end, he labored most faithfully.

No matter how driving the work on the plantation, whether seed-time or harvest, whether threatened with rain or frost, nothing could prevent his having the slaves all in at family prayers, night and morning. Moreover, the older servants were often invited to take part in the exercises. They always led the singing, and, on Sabbath mornings, were permitted to ask questions eliciting Scriptural explanations. Of course, some of the questions and some of the prayers were rather crude, and the effect, to an educated person, was rather to call forth laughter than solemnity.

Leaving home one morning, for a visit to the city, the Doctor ordered Jim, an old servant, to do some mowing in the rye-field; on his return, finding the rye-field as he had left it in the morning, he called Jim up, and severely flogged him without giving the man an opportunity of telling why the work had been neglected. On relating the circumstance at the supper-table, the wife said,—

"I am very sorry that you whipped Jim, for I took him to do some work in the garden, amongst my flowerbeds."

To this the Doctor replied, "Never mind, I'll make it all right with Jim."

And sure enough he did, for that night, at prayers, he said, "I am sorry, Jim, that I corrected you, to-day, as your mistress tells me that she set you to work in the flower-garden. Now, Jim," continued he, in a most feeling manner, "I always want to do justice to my servants, and you know that I never abuse any of you intentionally, and now, tonight, I will let you lead in prayer."

Jim thankfully acknowledged the apology, and, with grateful tears, and an overflowing heart, accepted the situation; for Jim aspired to be a preacher, like most colored men, and highly appreciated an opportunity to show his persuasive powers; and that night the old man made splendid use of the liberty granted to him. After praying for everything generally, and telling the Lord what a great sinner he himself was, he said,—

"Now, Lord, I would specially ax you to, try to save marster. You knows dat marster thinks he's mighty good; you knows dat marster says he's gwine to heaven; but Lord, I have my doubts: an' yet, I want marster saved. Please to convert him over agin; take him, dear Lord, by de nap of de neck, and shake him over hell and show him his condition. But Lord, don't let him fall into hell, jes let him see whar he ought to go to, but don't let him go dar. An' now, Lord, ef you jes save marster, I will give you de glory."

The indignation expressed by the doctor, at the close of Jim's prayer, told the old negro that for once he had overstepped the mark. "What do you mean, Jim, by insulting me in that manner? Asking the Lord to convert me over again. And praying that I might be shaken over hell. I have a great mind to tie you up, and give you a good correcting. If you ever make another such a prayer, I'll whip you well, that I will."

Dr. Gaines felt so intensely the duty of masters to their slaves that he, with some of his neighbors, inaugurated a religious movement, whereby the blacks at the Corners could have preaching once a fortnight, and that, too, by an educated white man. Rev. John Mason, the man selected for this work, was a heavy-set, fleshy, lazy man who, when entering a house, sought the nearest chair, taking possession, of it, and holding it to the last.

He had been employed many years as a colporteur or missionary, sometimes preaching to the poor whites, and, at other times, to the slaves, for which service he was compensated either by planters, or by the dominant religious denomination in the section where he labored. Mr. Mason had carefully studied the character of the people, to whom he was called to preach, and took every opportunity to shirk his duties, and to throw them upon some of the slaves, a large number of whom were always ready and willing to exhort when called upon.

We shall never forget his first sermon, and the profound sensation that it created both amongst masters and slaves, and especially the latter. After taking for his text, "He that knoweth his master's will, and doeth it not, shall be beaten with many stripes," he spoke substantially as follows:—

"Now when *correction* is given you, you either deserve it, or you do not deserve it. But whether you really deserve it or not, it is your duty, and Almighty God requires that you bear it patiently. You may, perhaps, think that this is hard doctrine, but if you consider it right you must needs think otherwise of it. Suppose then, that you deserve correction, you cannot but say that it is just and right you should meet with it. Suppose you do not, or at least you do not deserve so much, or so severe a correction for the fault you have committed, you, perhaps, have escaped a great many more, and are at last paid for all. Or suppose you are quite innocent of what is laid to your charge, and suffer wrongfully in that particular thing, is it not possible you may have done some other bad thing which was never discovered, and that Almighty God, who saw you doing it, would not let you escape without punishment one time or another? And ought you not, in such a case, to give glory to Him, and be thankful that he would rather punish

71

you in this life for your wickedness, than destroy your souls for it in the next life? But suppose that even this was not the case (a case hardly to be imagined), and that you have by no means, known or unknown, deserved the correction you suffered, there is this great comfort in it, that if you bear it patiently, and leave your cause in the hands of God, he will reward you for it in heaven, and the punishment you suffer unjustly here, shall turn to your exceeding great glory, hereafter."

At this point, the preacher hesitated a moment, and then continued, "I am now going to give you a description of hell, that awful place, that you will surely go to, if you don't be good and faithful servants.

"Hell is a great pit, more than two hundred feet deep, and is walled up with stone, having a strong, iron grating at the top. The fire is built of pitch pine knots, tar barrels, lard kegs, and butter firkins. One of the devil's imps appears twice a day, and throws about half a bushel of brimstone on the fire, which is never allowed to cease burning. As sinners die they are pitched headlong into the pit, and are at once taken up upon the pitchforks by the devil's imps, who stand, with glaring eyes and smiling countenances, ready to do their master's work."

Here the speaker was disturbed by the "Amens," "Bless God, I'll keep out of hell," "Dat's my sentiments," which plainly told him that he had struck the right key.

"Now," continued the preacher, "I will tell you where heaven is, and how you are to obtain a place there. Heaven is above the skies; its streets are paved with gold; seraphs and angels will furnish you with music which never ceases. You will all be permitted to join in the singing and you will be fed on manna and honey, and you will drink from fountains, and will ride in golden chariots."

"I am bound for hebben," ejaculated one.

"Yes, blessed God, hebben will be my happy home," said another.

These outbursts of feeling were followed, while the man of God stood with folded arms, enjoying the sensation that his eloquence had created.

After pausing a moment or two, the reverend man continued, "Are there any of you here who would rather burn in hell than rest in heaven? Remember that once in hell you can never get out. If you attempt to escape little devils are stationed at the top of the pit, who will, with their pitchforks, toss you back into the pit, *curchunk*, where you must remain forever. But once in heaven, you will be free the balance of your days." Here the wildest enthusiasm showed itself, amidst which the preacher took his seat.

A rather humorous incident now occurred which created no little merriment amongst the blacks, and to the somewhat discomfiture of Dr. Gaines,—who occupied a seat with the whites who were present.

Looking about the room, being unacquainted with the negroes, and presuming that all or nearly so were experimentally interested in religion, Mr. Mason called on Ike to close with prayer. The very announcement of Ike's name in such a connection called forth a broad grin from the larger portion of the audience.

Now, it so happened that Ike not only made no profession of religion, but was in reality the farthest off from the church of any of the servants at "Poplar Farm"; yet Ike was equal to the occasion, and at once responded, to the great amazement of his fellow slaves.

Ike had been, from early boyhood, an attendant upon whites, and he had learned to speak correctly for an uneducated person. He was pretty well versed in Scripture and had learned the principal prayer that his master was accustomed to make, and would often get his follow-servants together at the barn on a rainy day and give them the prayer, with such additions and improvements as the occasion might suggest. Therefore, when called upon by Mr. Mason, Ike at once said, "Let us pray."

After floundering about for a while, as if feeling his way, the new beginner struck out on the well-committed prayer, and soon elicited a loud "amen," and "bless God for that," from Mr. Mason, and to the great amusement of the blacks. In his eagerness, however, to make a grand impression, Ike attempted to weave into his prayer some poetry on "Cock Robin," which he had learned, and which nearly spoiled his maiden prayer.

After the close of the meeting, the Doctor invited the preacher to remain over night, and accepting the invitation, we in the great house had an opportunity of learning more of the reverend man's religious views.

When comfortably seated in the parlor, the Doctor said, "I was well pleased with your discourse, I think the tendency will be good upon the servants."

"Yes," responded the minister, "The negro is eminently a religious being, more so, I think, than the white race. He is emotional, loves music, is wonderfully gifted with gab; the organ of alimentativeness largely developed, and is fond of approbation. I therefore try always to satisfy their vanity; call upon them to speak, sing, and pray, and sometimes to preach. That suits for this world. Then I give them a heaven with music in it, and with something to eat. Heaven without singing and food would be no place for the negro. In the cities, where many of them are free, and have control of their own time, they are always late to church meetings, lectures, or almost anything else. But let there be a festival or supper announced and they are all there on time."

"But did you know," said Dr. Gaines, "that the prayer that Ike made to-day he learned from me?"

"Indeed?" responded the minister.

"Yes, that boy has the imitative power of his race in a larger degree than most negroes that I have seen. He remembers nearly everything that he hears, is full of wit, and has most excellent judgment. However, his dove-tailing the Cock Robin poetry into my prayer was too much, and I had to laugh at his adroitness."

The Doctor was much pleased with the minister, but Mrs. Gaines was not. She had great contempt for professional men who sprung from the lower class, and she regarded Mr. Mason as one to be endured but not encouraged. The Rev. Henry Pinchen was her highest idea of a clergyman. This gentleman was then expected in the neighborhood, and she made special reference to the fact, to her husband, when speaking of the "negro missionary," as she was wont to call the new-comer.

The preparation made, a few days later, for the reception of Mrs. Gaines' favorite spiritual adviser, showed plainly that a religious feast was near at hand, and in which the lady was to play a conspicuous part; and whether her husband was prepared to enter into the enjoyment or not, he would have to tolerate considerable noise and bustle for a week.

"Go, Hannah," said Mrs. Gaines, "and tell Dolly to kill a couple of fat pullets, and to put the biscuit to rise. I expect Brother Pinchen here this afternoon, and I want everything in order. Hannah, Hannah, tell Melinda to come here. We mistresses do have a hard time in this world; I don't see why the Lord should have imposed such heavy duties on us poor mortals. Well, it can't last always. I long to leave this wicked world, and go home to glory."

At the hurried appearance of the waiting maid the mistress said: "I am to have company this afternoon, Melinda. I expect Brother Pinchen here, and I want everything in order. Go and get one of my new caps, with the lace border, and get out my scalloped-bottomed dimity petticoat, and when you go out, tell Hannah to clean the white-handled knives, and see that not a speck is on them; for I want everything as it should be while Brother Pinchen is here."

Mr. Pinchen was possessed with a large share of the superstition that prevails throughout the South, not only with the ignorant negro, who brought it with him from his native land, but also by a great number of well educated and influential whites.

On the first afternoon of the reverend gentleman's visit, I listened with great interest to the following conversation between Mrs. Gaines and her ministerial friend.

"Now, Brother Pinchen, do give me some of your experience since you were last here. It always does my soul good to hear religious experience. It draws me nearer and nearer to the Lord's side. I do love to hear good news from God's people."

"Well, Sister Gaines," said the preacher, "I've had great opportunities in my time to study the heart of man. I've attended a great many camp-meetings, revival meetings, protracted meetings, and death-bed scenes, and I am satisfied, Sister Gaines, that the heart of man is full of sin, and desperately wicked. This is a wicked world, Sister Gaines, a wicked world."

"Were you ever in Arkansas, Brother Pinchen?" inquired Mrs. Gaines; "I've been told that the people out there are very ungodly."

Mr. P. "Oh, yes, Sister Gaines. I once spent a year at Little Rock, and preached in all the towns round about there; and I found some hard cases out there, I can tell you. I was once spending a week in a district where there were a great many horse thieves, and, one night, somebody stole my pony. Well, I knowed it was no use to make a fuss, so I told Brother Tarbox to say nothing about it, and I'd get my horse by preaching God's everlasting gospel; for I had faith in the truth, and knowed that my Saviour would not let me lose my pony. So the next Sunday I preached on horse-stealing, and told the brethren to come up in the evenin' with their hearts filled with the grace of God. So that night the house was crammed brimfull with anxious souls, panting for the bread of life. Brother Bingham opened with prayer, and Brother Tarbox followed, and I saw right off that we were gwine to have a blessed time. After I got 'em pretty well warmed up, I jumped on to one of the seats, stretched out my hands' and said: 'I know who stole my pony; I've found out; and you are in here tryin' to make people believe that you've got religion; but you ain't got it. And if you don't take my horse back to Brother Tarbox's pasture this very night, I'll tell your name right out in meetin' to-morrow night. Take my pony back, you vile and wretched sinner, and come up here and give your heart to God.' So the next mornin', I went out to Brother Tarbox's pasture, and sure enough, there was my bob-tail pony. Yes, Sister Gaines, there he was, safe and sound. Ha, ha, ha!"

Mrs. G. "Oh, how interesting, and how fortunate for you to get your pony! And what power there is in the gospel! God's children are very lucky. Oh, it is so sweet to sit here and listen to such good news from God's people? [Aside.] 'You Hannah, what are you standing there listening for, and neglecting your work? Never mind, my lady, I'll whip you well when I am done here. Go at your work this moment, you lazy huzzy! Never mind, I'll whip you well.' Come, do go on, Brother Pinchen, with your godly conversation. It is so sweet! It draws me nearer and nearer to the Lord's side."

Mr. P. "Well, Sister Gaines, I've had some mighty queer dreams in my time, that I have. You see, one night I dreamed that I was dead and in heaven, and such a place I never saw before. As soon as I entered the gates of the celestial empire, I saw many old and familiar faces that I had seen before. The first person that I saw was good old Elder Pike, the preacher that first called my attention to religion. The next person I saw was Deacon Billings, my first wife's father, and then I saw a host of godly faces. Why, Sister Gaines, you knowed Elder Goosbee, didn't you?"

Mrs. G. "Why, yes; did you see him there? He married me to my first husband."

Mr. P. "Oh, yes, Sister Gaines, I saw the old Elder, and he looked for all the world as if he had just come out of a revival meetin'."

Mrs. G. "Did you see my first husband there, Brother Pinchen?"

Mr. P. "No, Sister Gaines, I didn't see Brother Pepper there; but I've no doubt but that Brother Pepper was there."

Mrs. G. "Well, I don't know; I have my doubts. He was not the happiest man in the world. He was always borrowing trouble about something or another. Still, I saw some happy moments with Mr. Pepper. I was happy when I made his acquaintance, happy during our courtship, happy a while after our marriage, and happy when he died." [Weeps.]

Hannah. "Massa Pinchen, did you see my ole man Ben up dar in hebben?"

Mr. P. "No, Hannah, I didn't go amongst the niggers."

Mrs. G. "No, of course Brother Pinchen didn't go among the blacks. What are you asking questions for? [Aside.] 'Never mind, my lady, I'll whip you well when I'm done here. I'll skin you from head to foot.' Do go on with your heavenly conversation, Brother Pinchen; it does my very soul good. This is indeed a precious moment for me. I do love to hear of Christ and Him crucified."

Mr. P. "Well, Sister Gaines, I promised Sister Daniels that I'd come over and see her a few moments this evening, and have a little season of prayer with her, and I suppose I must go."

Mrs. G. "If you must go, then I'll have to let you; but before you do, I wish to get your advice upon a little matter that concerns Hannah. Last week Hannah stole a goose, killed it, cooked it, and she and her man Sam had a fine time eating the goose; and her master and I would never have known anything about it if it had not been for Cato, a faithful servant, who told his master all about it. And then, you see, Hannah had to be severely whipped before she'd confess that she stole the goose. Next Sabbath is sacrament day, and I want to know if you think that Hannah is fit to go to the Lord's Supper, after stealing the goose."

"Well, Sister Gaines," responded the minister, "that depends on circumstances. If Hannah has confessed that she stole the goose, and has been sufficiently whipped, and has begged her master's pardon, and begged your pardon, and thinks she will not do the like again, why then I suppose she can go to the Lord's Supper; for—

> 'While the lamp holds out to burn,
> The vilest sinner may return.'

But she must be sure that she has repented, and won't steal any more."

"Do you hear that, Hannah?" said the mistress. "For my part," continued she, "I don't think she's fit to go to the Lord's Supper; for she had no cause to steal the goose. We give our servants plenty of good food. They have a full run to the meal-tub, meat once a fortnight, and all the sour milk on the place, and I am sure that's enough for any one. I do think that our negroes are the most ungrateful creatures in the world. They aggravate my life out of me."

During this talk on the part of the mistress, the servant stood listening with careful attention, and at its close Hannah said:—

"I know, missis, dat I stole de goose, an' massa whip me for it, an' I confess it, an' I is sorry for it. But, missis, I is gwine, to de Lord's Supper, next Sunday, kase I ain't agwine to turn my back on my bressed Lord an' Massa for no old tough goose, dat I ain't." And here the servant wept as if she would break her heart.

Mr. Pinchen, who seemed moved by Hannah's words, gave a sympathizing look at the negress, and said, "Well, Sister Gaines, I suppose I must go over and see Sister Daniels; she'll be waiting for me."

After seeing the divine out, Mrs. Gaines said, "Now, Hannah, Brother Pinchen is gone, do you get the cowhide and follow me to the cellar, and I'll whip you well for aggravating me as you have to-day. It seems as if I can never sit down to take a little comfort with the Lord, without you crossing me. The devil always puts it into your head to disturb me, just when I am trying to serve the Lord. I've no doubt but that I'll miss going to heaven on your account. But I'll whip you well before I leave this world, that I will. Get the cowhide and follow me to the cellar."

In a few minutes the lady returned to the parlor, followed by the servant whom she had been correcting, and she was in a high state of perspiration, and, on taking a seat, said, "Get the fan, Hannah, and fan me; you ought to be ashamed of yourself to put me into such a passion, and cause me to heat myself up in this way, whipping you. You know that it is a great deal harder for me than it is for you. I have to exert myself, and it puts me all in a fever; while you have only to stand and take it."

On the following Sabbath,—it being Communion,—Mr. Pinchen officiated. The church being at the Corners, a mile or so from "Poplar Farm," the Communion wine, which was kept at the Doctor's, was sent over by the boy, Billy. It happened to be in the month of April, when the maple trees had been tapped, and the sap freely running.

Billy, while passing through the "sugar camp," or sap bush, stopped to take a drink of the sap, which looked inviting in the newly-made troughs. All at once it occurred to the lad that he could take a drink of the wine, and fill it up with sap. So, acting upon this thought, the youngster put the decanter to his mouth, and drank freely, lowering the beverage considerably in the bottle.

But filling the bottle with the sap was much more easily contemplated than done. For, at every attempt, the water would fall over the sides, none going in. However, the boy, with the fertile imagination of his race, soon conceived the idea of sucking his mouth full of the sap, and then squirting it into the bottle. This plan succeeded admirably, and the slave boy sat in the church gallery that day, and wondered if the communicants would have partaken so freely of the wine, if they had known that his mouth had been the funnel through which a portion of it had passed.

Slavery has had the effect of brightening the mental powers of the negro to a certain extent, especially those brought into close contact with the whites. It is also a fact, that these blacks felt that when they could get the advantage of their owners, they had a perfect right to do so; and the boy, Billy, no doubt, entertained a consciousness that he had done a very cunning thing in thus drinking the wine entrusted to his care.

CHAPTER III.

Dr. Gaines' practice being confined to the planters and their negroes, in the neighborhood of "Poplar Farm," caused his income to be very limited from that source, and consequently he looked more to the products of his plantation for support. True, the new store at the Corners, together with McWilliams' Tannery and Simpson's Distillery, promised an increase of population, and, therefore, more work for the physician. This was demonstrated very clearly by the Doctor's coming in one morning somewhat elated, and exclaiming: "Well, my dear, my practice is steadily increasing. I forgot to tell you that neighbor Wyman engaged me yesterday as his family physician; and I hope that the fever and ague, which is now taking hold of the people, will give me more patients. I see by the New Orleans papers that the yellow fever is raging there to a fearful extent. Men of my profession are reaping a harvest in that section this year. I would that we could have a touch of the yellow fever here, for I think I could invent a medicine that would cure it. But the yellow fever is a luxury that we medical men in this climate can't expect to enjoy; yet we may hope for the cholera."

"Yes," replied Mrs. Gaines, "I would be glad to see it more sickly, so that your business might prosper. But we are always unfortunate. Everybody here seems to be in good health, and I am afraid they'll keep so. However, we must hope for the best. We must trust in the Lord. Providence may possibly send some disease amongst us for our benefit."

On going to the office the Doctor found the faithful servant hard at work, and saluting him in his usual kind and indulgent manner, asked, "Well, Cato, have you made the batch of ointment I that I ordered?"

Cato. "Yes, massa; I dun made de intment, an' now I is making the bread pills. De tater pills is up on the top shelf."

Dr. G. "I am going out to see some patients. If any gentlemen call, tell them I shall be in this afternoon. If any servants come, you attend to them. I expect two of Mr. Campbell's boys over. You see to them. Feel their pulse, look at their tongues, bleed them, and give them each a dose of calomel. Tell them to drink no cold water, and to take nothing but water gruel."

Cato. "Yes, massa; I'll tend to 'em."

The negro now said, "I allers knowed I was a doctor, an' now de ole boss has put me at it; I muss change my coat. Ef any niggers comes in, I wants to look suspectable. Dis jacket don't suit a doctor; I'll change it."

Cato's vanity seemed at this point to be at its height, and having changed his coat, he walked up and down before the mirror, and viewed himself to his heart's content, and saying to himself, "Ah! now I looks like a doctor. Now I can bleed, pull teef, or cut off a leg. Oh, well, well! ef I ain't put de pill stuff an' de intment stuff togedder. By golly, dat ole cuss will be mad when he finds it out, won't he? Nebber mind, I'll make it up in pills, and when de flour is on dem, he won't know what's in' em; an' I'll make some new intment. Ah! yonder comes Mr. Campbell's Pete an' Ned; dem's de ones massa sed was comin'. I'll see ef I looks right. [Goes to the looking-glass and views himself.] I 'em some punkins, ain't I? [Knock at the door.] Come in." *Enter* PETE *and* NED.

Pete. "Whar is de Doctor?"

Cato. "Here I is; don't you see me?"

Pete. "But whar is de ole boss?"

Cato. "Dat's none you business. I dun tole you dat I is de doctor, an' dat's enuff."

Ned. "Oh, do tell us whar de Doctor is. I is almos' dead. Oh, me! oh, dear me! I is so sick." [Horrible faces.]

Pete. "Yes, do tell us; we don't want to stan' here foolin.'"

Cato. "I tells you again dat I is de doctor. I larn de trade under massa."

Ned. "Oh! well den; give me somethin' to stop dis pain. Oh, dear me! I shall die."

Cato. "Let me feel your pulse. Now, put out your tongue. You is berry sick. Ef you don't mine, you'll die. Come out in de shed, an' I'll bleed you. [Taking them out and bleeding them.] [D]ar, now, take dese pills, two in de mornin', and two at night, and ef you don't feel better, double de dose. Now, Mr. Pete, what's de matter wid you?"

Pete. "I is got de cole chills, an' has a fever in de night."

"Come out in de shed, an' I'll bleed you," said Cato, at the same time viewing himself in the mirror, as he passed out. After taking a quart of blood, which caused the patient to faint, they returned, the black doctor saying, "Now, take dese pills, two in de mornin', and two at night, an' ef dey don't help you, double de dose. Ah! I like to forget to feel your pulse, and look at your tongue. Put out your tongue. [Feels his pulse.] Yes, I tells by de feel ob your pulse dat I is gib you de right pills?"

Just then, Mr. Parker's negro boy Bill, with his hand up to his mouth, and evidently in great pain, entered the office without giving the usual knock at the door, and which gave great offence to the new physician.

"What you come in dat door widout knockin' for?" exclaimed Cato.

Bill. "My toof ache so, I didn't tink to knock. Oh, my toof! my toof! Whar is de Doctor?"

Cato. "Here I is; don't you see me?"

Bill. "What! you de Doctor, you brack cuss! You looks like a doctor! Oh, my toof! my toof! Whar is de Doctor?"

Cato. "I tells you I is de doctor. Ef you don't believe me, ax dese men. I can pull your toof in a minnit."

Bill. "Well, den, pull it out. Oh, my toof! how it aches! Oh, my toof!" [Cato gets the rusty turnkeys.]

Cato. "Now lay down on your back."

Bill. "What for?"

Cato. "Dat's de way massa does."

Bill. "Oh, my toof! Well, den, come on." [Lies down. Cato gets astraddle of Bill's breast, puts the turnkeys on the wrong tooth, and pulls—Bill kicks and cries out]—["]Oh, do stop! Oh, oh, oh!["] [Cato pulls the wrong tooth—Bill jumps up.]

Cato. "Dar, now, I tole you I could pull your toof for you."

Bill. ["]Oh, dear me! Oh, it aches yet! Oh, me! Lor-e-massy! You dun pull de wrong toof. Drat your skin! ef I don't pay you for this, you brack cuss!["] [They fight, and turn over table, chairs, and bench—Pete and Ned look on.]

During the *melée*, Dr. Gaines entered the office, and unceremoniously went at them with his cane, giving both a sound drubbing before any explanation could be offered. As soon as he could get an opportunity, Cato said, "Oh, massa! He's to blame, sir, he's to blame. He struck me fuss."

Bill. "No, sir; he's to blame; he pull de wrong toof. Oh, my toof! oh, my toof!"

Dr. G. "Let me see your tooth. Open your mouth. As I live, you've taken out the wrong tooth. I am amazed. I'll whip you for this; I'll whip you well. You're a pretty doctor. Now, lie down, Bill, and let him take out the right tooth; and if he makes a mistake this time, I'll cowhide him well. Lie down, Bill." [Bill lies down, and Cato pulls the tooth.] "There, now, why didn't you do that in the first place?"

Cato. "He wouldn't hole still, sir."

Bill. "I did hole still."

Dr. G. "Now go home, boys; go home."

"You've made a pretty muss of it, in my absence," said the Doctor. "Look at the table! Never mind, Cato; I'll whip you well for this conduct of yours to-day. Go to work now, and clear up the office."

As the office door closed behind the master, the irritated negro, once more left to himself, exclaimed, "Confound dat nigger! I wish he was in Ginny. He bite my finger, and scratch my face. But didn't I give it to him? Well, den, I reckon I did. [He goes to the mirror, and discovers that his coat is torn—weeps.] Oh, dear me! Oh, my coat—my coat is tore! Dat nigger has tore my coat. [He gets angry, and rushes about the room frantic.] Cuss dat nigger! Ef I could lay my hands on him, I'd tare him all to pieces,—dat I would. An' de old boss hit me wid his cane after dat nigger tore my coat. By golly, I wants to fight somebody. Ef ole massa should come in now, I'd fight him. [Rolls up his sleeves.] Let 'em come now, ef dey dare—old massa, or anybody else; I'm ready for 'em."

Just then the Doctor returned and asked, "What's all this noise here?"

Cato. "Nuffin', sir; only jess I is puttin' things to rights, as you tole me. I didn't hear any noise, except de rats."

Dr. G. "Make haste, and come in; I want you to go to town."

Once more left alone, the witty black said, "By golly, de ole boss like to cotch me dat time, didn't he? But wasn't I mad? When I is mad, nobody can do nuffin' wid me. But here's my coat tore to pieces. Cuss dat nigger! [Weeps.] Oh, my coat! oh, my coat! I rudder he had broke my head, den to tore my coat. Drat dat nigger! Ef he ever comes here agin, I'll pull out every toof he's got in his head—dat I will."

CHAPTER IV.

During the palmy days of the South, forty years ago, if there was one class more thoroughly despised than another, by the high-born, well-educated Southerner, it was the slave-trader who made his money by dealing in human cattle. A large number of the slave-traders were men of the North or free States, generally from the lower order, who, getting a little money by their own hard toil, invested it in slaves purchased in Virginia, Maryland, or Kentucky, and sold them in the cotton, sugar, or rice-growing States. And yet the high-bred planter, through mismanagement, or other causes, was compelled to sell his slaves, or some of them, at auction, or to let the "soul-buyer" have them.

Dr. Gaines' financial affairs being in an unfavorable condition, he yielded to the offers of a noted St. Louis trader by the name of Walker. This man was the terror of the whole South-west amongst the black population, bond and free,—for it was not unfrequently that even free colored persons were kidnapped and carried to the far South and sold. Walker had no conscientious scruples, for money was his God, and he worshipped at no other altar.

An uncouth, ill-bred hard-hearted man, with no education, Walker had started at St. Louis as a dray-driver, and ended as a wealthy slave-trader. The day was set for this man to come and purchase his stock, on which occasion, Mrs. Gaines absented herself from the place; and even the Doctor, although alone, felt deeply the humiliation. For myself, I sat and bit my lips with anger, as the vulgar trader said to the faithful man,—

"Well, my boy, what's your name?"

Sam. "Sam, sir, is my name.["]

Walk. "How old are you, Sam?"

Sam. "Ef I live to see next corn plantin' time I'll be twenty-seven, or thirty, or thirty-five,—I don't know which, sir."

Walk. "Ha, ha, ha ! Well, Doctor, this is rather a green boy. Well, mer feller, are you sound?"

Sam. "Yes, sir, I spec I is."

Walk. "Open your mouth and let me see your teeth. I allers judge a nigger's age by his teeth, same as I dose a hoss. Ah! pretty good set of grinders. Have you got a good appetite?"

Sam. "Yes, sir."

Walk. "Can you eat your allowance?"

Sam. "Yes, sir, when I can get it."

Walk. "Get out on the floor and dance; I want to see if you are supple."

Sam. "I don't like to dance; I is got religion."

Walk. "Oh, ho! you've got religion, have you? That's so much the better. I likes to deal in the gospel. I think he'll suit me. Now, mer gal, what's your name?"

Sally. "I is Big Sally, sir."

Walk. "How old are you, Sally?"

Sally. "I don't know, sir; but I heard once dat I was born at sweet pertater diggin' time."

Walk. "Ha, ha, ha! Don't you know how old you are? Do you know who made you?"

Sally. "I hev heard who it was in de Bible dat made me, but I dun forget de gentman's name."

Walk. "Ha, ha, ha! Well, Doctor, this is the greenest lot of niggers I've seen for some time."

The last remark struck the Doctor deeply, for he had just taken Sally for debt, and, therefore, he was not responsible for her ignorance. And he frankly told him so.

"This is an unpleasant business for me, Mr. Walker," said the Doctor, "but you may have Sam for $1,000, and Sally for $900. They are worth all I ask for them. I never banter, Mr. Walker. There they are; you can take them at that price, or let them alone, just as you please."

Walk. "Well, Doctor, I reckon I'll take 'em; but it's all they are worth. I'll put the handcuffs on 'em, and then I'll pay you. I likes to go accordin' to Scripter. Scripter says ef eatin' meat will offend your brother, you must quit it; and I say ef leavin' your slaves without the handcuffs will make 'em run away, you must put the handcuffs on 'em. Now, Sam, don't you and Sally cry. I am of a tender heart, and it allers makes me feel bad to see people cryin'. Don't cry, and the first place I get to, I'll buy each of you a great big ginger cake,—that I will."

And with the last remark the trader took from a small satchel two pairs of handcuffs, putting them on, and with a laugh said: "Now, you look better with the ornaments on."

Just then, the Doctor remarked,—"There comes Mr. Pinchen." Walker, looking out and seeing the man of God, said: "It is Mr. Pinchen, as I live; jest the very man I wants to see." And as the reverend gentleman entered, the trader grasped his hand, saying: "Why, how do you do, Mr. Pinchen? What in the name of Jehu brings you down here to Muddy Creek? Any camp-meetins, revival meetins, death-bed scenes, or anything else in your line going on down here? How is religion prosperin' now, Mr. Pinchen? I always like to hear about religion.["]

Mr. Pin. "Well, Mr. Walker, the Lord's work is in good condition every-where now. I tell you, Mr. Walker, I've been in the gospel ministry these thirteen years, and I am satisfied that the heart of man is full of sin and desperately wicked. This is a wicked world, Mr. Walker, a wicked world, and we ought all of us to have religion. Religion is a good thing to live by, and we all want it when we die. Yes, sir, when the great trumpet blows, we ought to be ready. And a man in your business of buying and selling slaves needs religion more than anybody else, for it makes you treat your people as you should. Now, there is Mr. Haskins,—he is a slave-trader, like your-self. Well, I converted him. Before he got religion, he was one of the worst men to his niggers I ever saw; his heart was as hard as stone. But religion has made his heart as soft as a piece of cotton. Before I converted him he would sell husbands from their wives, and seem to take delight in it; but now he won't sell a man from his wife, if he can get any one to buy both of them together. I tell you, sir, religion has done a wonderful work for him."

Walk. "I know, Mr. Pinchen, that I ought to have religion, and I feel that I am a great sinner; and whenever I get with good pious people like you and the Doctor, it always makes me feel that I am a desperate sinner. I feel it the more, because I've got a religious turn of mind. I know that I would be happier with religion, and the first spare time I get, I am going to try to get it. I'll go to a protracted meeting, and I won't stop till I get religion."

The departure of the trader with his property left a sadness even amongst the white members of the family, and special sympathy was felt for Hannah for the loss of her husband by the sale. However, Mrs. Gaines took it coolly, for as Sam was a field hand, she had often said she wanted her to have one of the house servants, and as Cato was without a wife, this seemed to favor her plans. Therefore, a week later, as Hannah entered the sitting-room one evening, she said to her:—"You need not tell me, Hannah, that you don't want another husband, I know better. Your master has sold Sam, and he's gone down the river, and you'll never see him again. So go and put on your calico dress, and meet me in the kitchen. I intend for you to *jump the broom-stick* with Cato. You need not tell me you don't want another man. I know there's no woman living that can be happy and satisfied without a husband."

Hannah said: "Oh, missis, I don't want to jump de broomstick wid Cato. I don't love Cato; I can't love him."

Mrs. G. "Shut up, this moment! What do you know about love? I didn't love your master when I married him, and people don't marry for love now. So go and put on your calico dress, and meet me in the kitchen."

As the servant left for the kitchen, the mistress remarked: "I am glad that the Doctor has sold Sam, for now I'll have her marry Cato, and I'll have them both in the house under my eyes."

As Hannah entered the kitchen, she said: "Oh, Cato, do go and tell missis dat you don't want to jump de broomstick wid me,—dat's a good man. Do,

Cato; kase I nebber can love you. It was only las week dat massa sold my Sammy, and I don't want any udder man. Do go tell missis dat you don't want me." To which Cato replied: "No, Hannah, I ain't a-gwine to tell missis no such thing, kase I does want you, and I ain't a-gwine to tell a lie for you ner nobody else. Dar, now you's got it! I don't see why you need to make so much fuss. I is better lookin' den Sam; an' I is a house servant, an' Sam was only a fiel hand; so you ought to feel proud of a change. So go and do as missis tells you."

As the woman retired, the man continued: "Hannah needn't try to get me to tell a lie; I ain't a-gwine to do it, kase I dose want her, an' I is bin wantin' her dis long time, an' soon as massa sold Sam, I knowed I would get her. By golly, I is gwine to be a married man. Won't I be happy? Now, ef I could only jess run away from ole massa, an' get to Canada wid Hannah, den I'd show 'em who I was. Ah! dat reminds me of my song 'bout ole massa and Canada, an' I'll sing it. Dis is my moriginal hyme. It comed into my head one night when I was fass asleep under an apple tree, looking up at de moon."

While Hannah was getting ready for the nuptials, Cato amused himself by singing—

> De happiest day I ever did see,
> I'm bound fer my heavenly home,
> When missis give Hannah to me,
> Through heaven dis chile will roam.

> CHORUS.—Go away, Sam, you can't come a-nigh me,
> Gwine to meet my friens in hebben,
> Hannah is gwine along;
> Missis ses Hannah is mine,
> So Hannah is gwine along.

> Chorus, *repeated.*

> Father Gabriel, blow your horn,
> I'll take wings and fly away,
> Take Hannah up in the early morn,
> An' I'll be in hebben by de break of day.

> CHORUS.—Go away, Sam, you can't come a-nigh me,
> Gwine to meet my friens in hebben,
> Hannah is gwine along;
> Missis ses Hannah is mine,
> So Hannah is gwine along.

Mrs. Gaines, as she approached the kitchen, heard the servant's musical voice and knew that he was in high glee; entering, she said, "Ah! Cato, you're ready, are you? Where is Hannah?"

Cato. "Yes, missis; I is bin waitin' dis long time. Hannah has bin here tryin' to swade me to tell you dat I don't want her; but I telled her dat you sed I must jump de broomstick wid her, an' I is gwine to mind you."

Mrs. G. "That's right, Cato; servants should always mind their masters and mistresses, without asking a question."

Cato. "Yes, missis, I allers dose what you and massa tells me, an' axes nobody."

While the mistress went in search of Hannah, Dolly came in saying, "Oh, Cato, do go an' tell missis dat you don't want Hannah. Don't yer he hear how she's whippin' her in de cellar? Do go an' tell missis dat you don't want Hannah, and den she'll stop whippin' her."

Cato. "No, Dolly, I ain't a gwine to do no such a thing, kase ef I tell missis dat I don't want Hannah, den missis will whip me; an' I ain't a-gwine to be whipped fer you, ner Hannah, ner nobody else. No, I'll jump the broomstick wid every woman on de place, ef missis wants me to, before I'll be whipped."

Dolly. "Cato, ef I was in Hannah's place, I'd see you in de bottomless pit before I'd live wid you, you great, big, wall-eyed, empty-headed, knock-kneed fool. You're as mean as your devilish old missis."

Cato. "Ef you don't quit dat busin' me, Dolly, I'll tell missis as soon as she comes in, an' she'll whip you, you know she will."

As Mrs. Gaines entered she said, "You ought to be ashamed of yourself, Hannah, to make me fatigue myself in this way, to make you do your duty. It's very naughty in you, Hannah. Now, Dolly, you and Susan get the broom, and get out in the middle of the room. There, hold it a little lower—a little higher; there, that'll do. Now, remember that this is a solemn occasion; you are going to jump into matrimony. Now, Cato, take hold of Hannah's hand. There, now, why could n't you let Cato take hold of your hand before? Now, get ready, and when I count three, do you jump. Eyes on the *broomstick!* All ready. One, two, three, and over you go. There, now you're husband and wife, and if you don't live happy together, it's your own fault; for I am sure there's nothing to hinder it. Now, Hannah, come up to the house, and I'll give you some whiskey, and you can make some apple-toddy, and you and Cato can have a fine time. Now, I'll go back to the parlor."

Dolly. "I tell you what, Susan, when I get married, I is gwine to have a preacher to marry me. I ain't a-gwine to jump de broomstick. Dat will do for fiel' hands, but house servants ought to be 'bove dat."

86

Susan. "Well, chile, you can't spect any ting else from ole missis. She come from down in Carlina, from 'mong de poor white trash. She don't know any better. You can't speck nothin' more dan a jump from a frog. Missis says she is one ob de akastocacy; but she ain't no more of an akastocacy dan I is. Missis says she wits born wid a silver spoon in her mouf; ef she was I wish it had a-choked her, dat' what I wish."

The mode of jumping the broomstick was the general custom in the rural districts of the South, forty years ago; and, as there was no law whatever in regard to the marriage of slaves, this custom had as binding force with the negroes, as if they had been joined by a clergyman; the difference being the one was not so high-toned as the other. Yet, it must be admitted that the blacks always preferred being married by a clergyman.

CHAPTER V.

Dr. Gaines and wife having spent the heated season at the North, travelling for pleasure and seeking information upon the mode of agriculture practised in the free States, returned home filled with new ideas which they were anxious to put into immediate execution, and, therefore, a radical change was at once commenced.

Two of the most interesting changes proposed, were the introduction of a plow, which was to take the place of the heavy, unwieldy one then in use, and a washing-machine, instead of the hard hand-rubbing then practised. The first called forth much criticism amongst the men in the field, where it was christened the "Yankee Dodger," and during the first half a day of its use, it was followed by a large number of the negroes, men and women wondering at its superiority over the old plow, and wanting to know where it was from.

But the excitement in the kitchen, amongst the women, over the washing-machine, threw the novelty of the plow entirely in the shade.

"An' so dat tub wid its wheels an' fixin' is to do de washin', while we's to set down an' look at it," said Dolly, as ten or a dozen servants stood around the new comer, laughing and making fun at its ungainly appearance.

"I don't see why massa didn't buy a woman, out dar whar de ting was made, an' fotch 'em along, so she could learn us how to wash wid it," remarked Hannah, as her mistress came into the kitchen to give orders about the mode of using the "washer."

"Now, Dolly," said the mistress, "we are to have new rules, hereafter, about the work. While at the North, I found that the women got up at four o'clock, on Monday mornings, and commenced the washing, which was all finished, and out on the lines, by nine o'clock. Now, remember that, hereafter, there is to be no more washing on Fridays, and ironing on Saturdays, as you used to do. And instead of six of you great, big women to do the washing, two of you with the 'washer,' can do the work." And out she went, leaving the negroes to the contemplation of the future.

"I wish missis had stayed at home, 'stead of goin' round de world, bringin' home new rules. Who she tinks gwine to get out of bed at four o'clock in de mornin', kase she fotch home dis wash-box," said Dolly, as she gave a knowing look at the other servants.

"De Lord knows dat dis chile ain't a-gwine to git out of her sweet bed at four o'clock in de mornin', for no body; you hears dat, don't you?" remarked Winnie, as she gave a loud laugh, and danced out of the room.

Before the end of the week, Peter had run the new plow against a stump, and had broken it beyond the possibility of repair.

When the lady arose on Monday morning, at half-past nine, her usual time, instead of finding the washing out on the lines, she saw, to her great disappointment, the inside works of the "washer" taken out, and Dolly, the chief laundress, washing away with all her power, in the old way, rubbing with her hands, the perspiration pouring down her black face.

"What have you been doing, Dolly, with the 'washer?' " exclaimed the mistress, as she threw up her hands in astonishment.

"Well, you see, missis," said the servant, "dat merchine won't work no way. I tried it one way, den I tried it an udder way, an' still it would not work. So, you see, I got de screw-driver an' I took it to pieces. Dat's de reason I ain't got along faster wid de work."

Mrs. Gaines returned to the parlor, sat down, and had a good cry, declaring her belief that "negroes could not be made white folks, no matter what you should do with them."

Although the "patent plow" and the "washer" had failed, Dr. and Mrs. Gaines had the satisfaction of knowing that one of their new ideas was to be put into successful execution in a few days.

While at the North, they had eaten at a farmhouse, some new cheese, just from the press, and on speaking of it, she was told by old Aunt Nancy, the black *mamma* of the place, that she understood all about making cheese. This piece of information gave general satisfaction, and a cheese-press was at once ordered from St. Louis.

The arrival of the cheese-press, the following week, was the signal for the new sensation. Nancy was at once summoned to the great house for the purpose of superintending the making of the cheese. A prouder person than the old negress could scarcely have been found. Her early days had been spent on the eastern shores of Maryland, where the blacks have an idea that they are, by nature, superior to their race in any other part of the habitable globe. Nancy had always spoken of the Kentucky and Missouri negroes as "low brack trash," and now, that all were to be passed over, and the only Marylander on the place called in upon this "great occasion," her cup of happiness was filled to the brim.

"What do you need, besides the cheese-press, to make the cheese with, Nancy?" inquired Mrs. Gaines, as the old servant stood before her, with her hands resting upon her hips, and looking at the half-dozen slaves who loitered around, listening to what was being said.

"Well, missis," replied Nancy, "I mus' have a runnet."

"What's a runnet?" inquired Mrs. Gaines.

"Why, you see, missis, you's got to have a sheep killed, and get out of it de maw, an' dat's what's called de runnet. An' I puts dat in de milk, an' it curdles the milk so it makes cheese."

"Then I'll have a sheep killed at once," said the mistress, and orders were given to Jim to kill the sheep. Soon after the sheep's carcass was distributed amongst the negroes, and "de runnet," in the hands of old Nancy.

That night there was fun and plenty of cheap talk in the negro quarters and in the kitchen, for it had been discovered amongst them that a calf's runnet, and not a sheep's, was the article used to curdle the milk for making cheese.

The laugh was then turned upon Nancy, who, after listening to all sorts of remarks in regard to her knowledge of cheese-making, said, in a triumphant tone, suiting the action to the words,—

"You niggers tink you knows a heap, but you don't know as much as you tink. When de sheep is killed, I knows dat you niggers would git de meat to eat. I knows dat."

With this remark Nancy silenced the entire group. Then putting her hand akimbo, the old woman sarcastically exclaimed: "To-morrow you'll all have calf's meat for dinner, den what will you have to say 'bout old Nancy?" Hearing no reply, she said: "Whar is you smart niggers now? Whar is you, I ax you?"

"Well, den, ef Ant Nancy ain't some punkins, dis chile knows nuffin," remarked Ike, as he stood up at full length, viewing the situation on, as if he had caught a new idea. "I allers tole yer dat Ant Nancy had moo in her head dan what yer catch out wid a fine-toof comb," exclaimed Peter.

"But how is you going to tell missis 'bout killin' de sheep?" asked Jim.

Nancy turned to the head man and replied: "De same mudder wit dat tole me to get some sheep fer you niggers will tell me what to do. De Lord always guides me through my troubles an' trials. Befoe I open my mouf, He always fills it."

The following day Nancy presented herself at the great house door, and sent in for her mistress. On the lady's appearing, the servant, putting on a knowing look, said: "Missis, when de moon is cold an' de water runs high in it, den I have to put calf's runnet in de milk, instead of sheep's. So, lass night, I see dat de moon is cold an' de water is runnin' high."

"Well, Nancy," said the mistress, "I'll have a calf killed at once, for I can't wait for a warm' moon. Go and tell Jim to kill a calf immediately, for I must not be kept out of cheese much longer." On Nancy's return to the quarters, old Ned, who was past work, and who never did anything but eat, sleep, and talk, heard the woman's explanation, and clapping his wrinkled hands exclaimed: "Well den, Nancy, you is wof moo den all de niggers on dis place, fer you gives us fresh meat ebbry day."

After getting the right runnet, and two weeks' work on the new cheese, a little, soft, sour, hard-looking thing, appearing like anything but a cheese, was exhibited at "Poplar Farm," to the great amusement of the blacks, and the disappointment of the whites, and especially Mrs. Gaines, who had frequently remarked that her "mouth was watering for the new cheese."

No attempt was ever made afterwards to renew the cheesemaking, and the press was laid under the shed, by the side of the washing machine and the patent plow. While we had three or four trustworthy and faithful servants, it must be admitted that most of the negroes on "Poplar Farm" were always glad to shirk labor, and thought that to deceive the whites was a religious duty.

Wit and religion has ever been the negro's forte while in slavery. Wit with which to please his master, or to soften his anger when displeased, and religion to enable him to endure punishment when inflicted.

Both Dr. and Mrs. Gaines were easily deceived by their servants. Indeed, I often thought that Mrs. Gaines took peculiar pleasure in being misled by them; and even the Doctor, with his long experience and shrewdness, would allow himself to be carried off upon almost any pretext. For instance, when he retired at night, Ike, big body servant, would take his master's clothes out of the room, brush them off and return them in time for the Doctor to dress for breakfast. There was nothing in this out of the way; but the master would often remark that he thought Ike brushed his clothes too much, for they appeared to wear out a great deal faster than they had formerly. Ike, however, attributed the wear to the fact that the goods were wanting in soundness. Thus the master, at the advice of his servant, changed his tailor.

About the same time the Doctor's watch stopped at night, and when taken to be repaired, the watchmaker found it badly damaged, which he pronounced had been done by a fall. As the Doctor was always very careful with his time-piece, he could in no way account for the stoppage. Ike was questioned as to his handling of it, but he could throw no light upon the subject. At last, one night about twelve o'clock, a message came for the Doctor to visit a patient who had a sudden attack of cholera morbus. The faithful Ike was nowhere to be found, nor could any traces of the Doctor's clothes be discovered. Not even the watch, which was always laid upon the mantle-shelf, could be seen anywhere.

It seemed clear that Ike had run away with his master's daily wearing apparel, watch and all. Yes, and further search showed that the boots, with one heel four inches higher than the other, had also disappeared. But go, the Doctor must; and Mrs. Gaines and all of us went to work to get the Doctor ready.

While Cato was hunting up the old boots, and Hannah was in the attic getting the old hat, Jim returned from the barn and informed his master that the sorrel horse, which he had ordered to be saddled, was nowhere to be found; and that he had got out the bay mare, and as there was no saddle on the place, Ike having taken the only one, he, Jim, had put the buffalo robe on the mare.

It was a bright moonlight night, and to see the Doctor on horseback without a saddle, dressed in his castaway suit, was, indeed, ridiculous in the extreme. However, he made the visit, saved the patient's life, came home and went snugly to bed. The following morning, to the Doctor's great surprise, in walked Ike, at his usual time, with the clothes in one hand and the boots nicely blacked in the other. The faithful slave had not seen any of the other servants, and consequently did not know of the master's discomfiture on the previous night.

"Were any of the servants off the place last night?" inquired the Doctor, as Ike laid the clothes carefully on a chair, and was setting down the boots.

"No, I speck not," answered Ike.

"Were you off anywhere last night?" asked the master.

"No, sir," replied the servant.

"What! not off the place at all?" inquired the Doctor sharply. Ike looked confused and evidently began to "smell a mice."

"Well, massa, I was not away only to step over to de prayer-meetin' at de Corners, a little while, dat's all," said Ike.

"Where's my watch?" asked the Doctor.

"I speck it's on de mantleshelf dar, whar I put it lass night, sir," replied Ike, and at the same time reached to the timepiece, where he had laid it a moment before, and holding it up triumphantly, "Here it is, sir, right where I left it lass night."

Ike was told to go, which he was glad to do. "What shall I do with that fellow?" said the Doctor to his wife, as the servant quitted the room.

Ike had scarcely reached the back yard when he met Cato, who told him of his absence on the previous night being known to his master. When Ike had heard all, he exclaimed, "Well, den ef de ole boss knows it, dis nigger is kotched sure as you is born."

"I would not be in your shoes, Ike, fer a heap, dis mornin'," said Cato.

"Well," replied Ike, "I thank de Lord dat I is got religion to stand it."

Dr. Gaines, as he dressed himself, found nothing out of the way until he came to look at the boots. The Doctor was lame from birth. Here he saw unmistakable evidence that the high heel had been taken off, and had been replaced by a screw put through the inside, and the seam waxed over. Dr. Gaines had often thought, when putting his boots on in the morning, that they appeared a little loose, and on speaking of it to his servant, the negro would attribute it to the blacking, which he said "made de lether stretch."

That morning when breakfast was over, and the negroes called in for family prayers, all eyes were upon Ike.

It has always appeared strange that the negroes should seemingly take such delight in seeing their fellow-servants in a "bad fix." But it is never-theless true, and Ike's "bad luck" appeared to furnish sport for old and young of his own race. At the conclusion of prayers, the Doctor said, "Now, Ike, I want you to tell me the truth, and nothing but the truth, of your whereabouts last night, and why you wore away my clothes?"

"Well, massa," said, Ike, "I'm gwine to tell you God's truth."

"That's what I want, Ike," remarked the master.

"Now," continued the negro, "I ware de clothes to de dance, kase you see, massa, I knowed dat you didn't want your body servant to go to de ball look-ing poorer dressed den udder gentmen's boys. So you see I had no clothes myself, so I takes yours. I had to knock the heel off de lame leg boot, so dat I could ware it. An' den I took 'ole Sorrel,' kase he paces so fass an' so easy. No udder hoss could get me to de city in time for de ball, ceptin' 'Ole Sorrel.' You see, massa, ten miles is a good ways to go after you is gone to bed. Now, massa, I hope you'll forgive me dis time, an' I'll never do so any moo."

During Ike's telling his story, his master kept his eyes rivetted upon him, and at its conclusion said: "You first told me that you were at the prayer-meeting at the Corners; what did you do that for?"

"Well, massa," replied Ike, "I knowed dat I ought to had gone to de prar-meetin', an' dat's de reason I said I was dar."

"And you're a pretty Christian, going to a dance, instead of your prayer-meeting. This is the fifth time you've fallen from grace," said the master.

"Oh, no," quickly responded Ike; "dis is only de fourf time dat I is back slid."

"But this is not the first time that you have taken my clothes and worn them. And there's my watch, you could not tell the time, what did you want with that?" said the Doctor.

"Yes, massa," replied Ike, "I'll tell de truth; I wore de clothes afore dis time, an' I take de watch too, an' I let it fall, an' dat's de reason it stop dat time. An' I know I could not tell do time by de watch, but I guessed at it, an' dat made de niggers star at me, to see me have a watch."

The announcement that Col. Lemmy was at the door cut short the further investigation of Ike's case. The Colonel was the very opposite to Dr. Gaines, believing that there was no good in the negro, except to toil, and feeling that all religious efforts to better the condition of the race was time thrown away.

The Colonel laughed heartily as the Doctor told how Ike had worn his clothes. He quickly inquired if the servant had been punished, and when informed that he had not, he said: "The lash is worth more than all the religion in the world. Your boy, Ike, with the rest of the niggers around here, will go to a prayer meetin' and will tell how good they feel or how bad they feel, just as it may suit the case. They'll cry, groan, clap their hands, pat their feet, worry themselves into a lather of sweat, sing,

> I'm a-gwine to keep a-climbin' high,
> See de hebbenly land;
> Till I meet dem er angels in a de sky
> See de hebbenly lan'.

> Dem pooty angels I shall see,
> See de hebbenly lan';
> Why don't de debbil let a-me be,
> See de hebbenly lan'.

"Yes, Doctor; these niggers will pray till twelve o'clock at night; break up their meeting and go home shouting and singing, 'Glory hallelujah!' and every darned one of them will steal a chicken, turkey, or pig, and cry out 'Come down, sweet chariot, an' carry me home to hebben!' yes, and still continue to sing till they go to sleep. You may give your slaves religion, and I'll give mine the whip, an' I'll bet that I'll get the most tobacco and hemp out of the same number of hands."

"I hardly think," said the Doctor, after listening attentively to his neighbor, "that I can let Ike pass without some punishment. Yet I differ with you in regard to the good effects of religion upon all classes, more espe-cially our negroes, for the African is preeminently a religious being; with them, I admit, there is considerable superstition. They have a permanent belief in good and bad luck, ghosts, fortune-telling, and the like; but we whites are not entirely free from such notions."

At the last sentence or two, the Colonel's eyes sparkled, and he began to turn pale, for it was well known that he was a firm believer in ghosts, and fortune-telling.

"Now, Doctor," said Col. Lemmy, "every sensible man must admit the fact that ghosts exist, and that there is nothing in the world truer than that the future can be told. Look at Mrs. McWilliams' lawsuit with Major Todd. She went to old Frank, the nigger fortune-teller, and asked him which lawyer she should employ. The old man gazed at her for a moment or two, and said, 'missis, you's got your mind on two lawyers,—a big man and a little man. Ef you takes de big man, you loses de case; ef you takes do little man, you wins de case.' Sure enough, she had in contemplation the employment of either McGuyer or Darby. The first is a large man; the latter was, as you know, a small man. So, taking the old negro's advice, she obtained the services of John F. Darby, and gained the suit."

"Yes," responded the Doctor, "I have always heard that the Widow McWilliams gained her case by consulting old Frank."

"Why, Doctor," continued the Colonel, in an animated manner, "When the races were at St. Louis, three years ago, I went to old Betty, the blind fortune-teller, to see which horse was going to win; and she said, 'Massa, bet your money on de gray mare.' Well, you see, everybody thought that Johnson's black horse would win, and piles of money was bet on him. However, I bet one hundred dollars on the gray mare, and, to the utter sur-prise of all, she won. When the race was over, I was asked how I come to bet on the mare, when everybody was putting their funds on the horse. I then told them that I never risked my money on any horse, till I found out which was going to win.

"Now, with regard to ghosts, just let me say to you, Doctor, that I saw the ghost of the peddler that was murdered over on the old road, just as sure as you are born."

"Do you think so?" asked the Doctor.

"Think so! Why, I know it, just as well as I know that I see you now. He had his pack on his back; and it was in the daytime, no night-work about it. He looked at me, and I watched him till he got out of sight. But wasn't I frightened; it made the hair stand up on my head, I tell you."

"Did he speak to you?" asked the Doctor.

"Oh, no! he didn't speak, but he had a sorrowful look, and, as he was getting out of sight, he turned and looked over his shoulder at me."

Most of the superstition amongst the whites, in our section, was the result of their close connection with the blacks; for the servants told the most foolish stories to the children in the nurseries, and they learned more, as they grew older, from the slaves in the quarters, or out on the premises.

CHAPTER VI.

Profitable and interesting amusements were always needed at the Corners, the nearest place to the "Poplar Farm." At the tavern, post-office, and the store, all the neighborhood assembled to read the news, compare notes, and to talk politics.

Shows seldom ventured to stop there, for want of sufficient patronage. Once in three months, however, they had a "Gander Snatching," which never failed to draw together large numbers of ladies as well as gentlemen, the *elite*, as well as the common. The getter-up of this entertainment would procure a gander of the wild goose species. This bird had a long neck, which was large as it rose above the breast, but tapered gradually, for more than half the length, until it became small, and serpent-like in form, terminating in a long, slim head, and peaked bill. The head and neck of the gander was well-greased; the legs were tied together with a strong cord, and the bird was then fastened by its legs, to a swinging limb of a tree. The *Snatchers* were to be on horseback, and were to start fifteen or twenty rods from the gander, riding at full speed, and, as they passed along under the bird, they had the right to pull his head off if they could. To accelerate the speed of the horses, a man was stationed a few feet from the gander, with orders to give every horse a cut with his whip, as he went by.

Sometimes the bird's head would be caught by ten or a dozen before they would succeed in pulling it off, which was necessary; often by the sudden jump of the animal, or the rider having taken a little too much wine, he would fall from his horse, which event would give additional interest to the "Snatching."

The poor gander would frequently show far more sagacity than its torturers. After having its head caught once or twice, the gander would draw up its head, or dodge out of the way. Sometimes the snatcher would have in his hand a bit of sand-paper, which would enable him to make a tighter grasp. But this mode was generally considered unfair, and, on one occasion, caused a duel in which both parties were severely wounded.

But the most costly and injurious amusement that the people in our section entered into was that of card-playing, a species of gambling too much indulged in throughout the entire South. This amusement causes much sadness, for it often occurs that gentlemen lose large sums at the gambling-table, frequently seriously embarrassing themselves, sometimes bringing ruin upon whole families.

Mr. Oscar Smith, residing near "Poplar Farm," took a trip to St. Louis, thence to New Orleans and back. On the steamer he was beguiled into gaming.

"Go call my boy, steward," said Mr. Smith, as he took his cards one by one from the table.

In a few moments a fine-looking, bright-eyed mulatto boy, apparently about fifteen years of age, was standing by his master's side at the table.

"I will see you and five hundred dollars better," said Smith, as his servant Jerry approached the table.

"What price do you set on that boy?" asked Johnson, as he took a roll of bills from his pocket.

"He will bring a thousand dollars, any day, in the New Orleans market," replied Smith.

"Then you bet the whole of the boy, do you?"

"Yes."

"I call you, then," said Johnson, at the same time spreading his cards out upon the table.

"You have beat me," said Smith, as soon as he saw the cards.

Jerry, who was standing on top of the table, with the bank-notes and silver dollars round his feet, was now ordered to descend from the table.

"You will not forget that you belong to me," said Johnson, as the young slave was stepping from the table to a chair.

"No, sir," replied the chattel.

"Now go back to your bed, and be up in time to-morrow morning to brush my clothes and clean my boots, do you hear?"

"Yes, sir," responded Jerry, as he wiped the tears from his eyes.

As Mr. Smith left the gaming-table, he said: "I claim the right of redeeming that boy, Mr. Johnson. My father gave him to me when I came of age, and I promised not to part with him."

"Most certainly, sir, the boy shall be yours whenever you hand me over a cool thousand," replied Johnson.

The next morning, as the passengers were assembling in the breakfast saloons, and upon the guards of the vessel, and the servants were seen running about waiting upon or looking for their masters, poor Jerry was entering his new master's state-room with his boots.

The genuine wit of the negro is often a marvel to the whites, and this wit or humor, as it may be called, is brought out in various ways. Not unfrequently is it exhibited by the black, when he really means to be very solemn.

Thus our Sampey met Davidson's Joe, on the road to the Corners, and called out to him several times without getting an answer. At last, Joe, appearing much annoyed, stopped, looked at Sampey in an attitude of surprise, and exclaimed: "Ain't you got no manners? Whare's your eyes? Don't you see I is a funeral?"

It was not till then that Sampey saw that Joe had a box in his arms, resembling a coffin, in which was a deceased negro child. The negro would often show his wit to the disadvantage of his master or mistress.

When visitors were at "Poplar Farm," Dr. Gaines would frequently call in Cato to sing a song or crack a joke, for the amusement of the company. On one occasion, requesting the servant to give a toast, at the same time handing the negro a glass of wine, the latter took the glass, held it up, looked at it, began to show his ivory, and said:

> "De big bee flies high,
> De little bee makes de honey,
> De black man raise de cotton,
> An' de white man gets de money."

The same servant going to meeting one Sabbath, was met on the road by Major Ben. O'Fallon, who was riding on horseback, with a hoisted umbrella to keep the rain off. The Major, seeing the negro trudging along bareheaded and with something under his coat, supposing he had stolen some article which he was attempting to hide said, "What's that you've got under your coat, boy?"

"Nothin', sir, but my hat," replied the slave, and at the same time drawing forth a second-hand beaver.

"Is it yours?" inquired the Major.

"Yes, sir," was the quick response of the negro.

"Well," continued the Major, "if it is yours, why don't you wear it and save your head from the rain?"

"Oh!" replied the servant, with a smile of seeming satisfaction, "de head belongs to massa an' de hat belongs to me. Let massa take care of his property, an' I'll take care of mine."

Dr. Gaines, while taking a neighbor out to the pig sty, to show him some choice hogs that he intended for the next winter's bacon, said to Dolly who was feeding the pigs: "How much lard do you think you can get out of that big hog, Dolly?"

The old negress scratched her wooly head, put on thoughtful look, and replied, "I specks I can get a pail full, ef de pail aint too big."

"I reckon you can," responded the master.

The ladies are not without their recreation, the most common of which is snuff-dipping. A snuff-box or bottle is carried, and with it a very small stick or cane, which has been chewed at the end until it forms a small mop. The little dippers or sticks are sold in bundles for the use of the ladies, and can be bought simply cut in the requisite lengths or chewed ready for use. This the dipper moistens with saliva, and dips into the snuff-box, and then lifts the mop thus loaded inside the lips. In some parts they courteously hand round the snuff and dipper, or place a plentiful supply of snuff on the table, into which all the company may dip.

Amongst even the better classes of whites, the ladies would often assemble in considerable numbers, especially during revival meeting times, place a wash-dish in the middle of the room, all gather around it, commence, snuff-dipping, and all using the wash-dish as a common spittoon.

Every well bred lady carries her own snuff-box and dipper. Generally during church service, where the clergyman is a little prosy, snuff-dipping is indispensible.

CHAPTER VII.

Forty years ago, in the Southern States, superstition, held an exalted place wit[h] all classes, but more especially with the blacks and uneducated, or poor, whites. This was shown more clearly in their belief in witchcraft in general, and the devil in particular. To both of these classes, the devil was a real being, sporting a club-foot, horns, tail, and a hump on his back.

The influence of the devil was far greater than that of the Lord. If one of these votaries had stolen a pig, and the fear of the Lord came over him, he would most likely ask the Lord to forgive him, but still cling to the pig. But if the fear of the devil came upon him, in all probability he would drop the pig and take to his heels.

In those days the city of St. Louis had a large number who had implicit faith in Voudooism. I once attended one of their midnight meetings. In the pale rays of the moon the dark outlines of a large assemblage was visible, gathered about a small fire, conversing in different tongues. They were negroes of all ages,—women, children, and men. Finally, the noise was hushed, and the assembled group assumed an attitude of respect. They made way for their queen, and a short, black, old negress came upon the scene, followed by two assistants, one of whom bore a cauldron, and the other, a box.

The cauldron was placed over the dying embers, the queen drew forth, from the folds of her gown, a magic wand, and the crowd formed a ring around her. Her first act was to throw some substance on the fire, the flames shot up with a lurid glare—now it writhed in serpent coils, now it darted upward in forked tongues, and then it gradually transformed itself into a veil of dusky vapors. At this stage, after a certain amount of gibberish and wild gesticulation from the queen, the box was opened, and frogs, lizards, snakes, dog liver, and beef hearts drawn forth and thrown into the cauldron. Then followed more gibberish and gesticulation, when the congregation joined hands, and began the wildest dance imaginable, keeping it up until the men and women sank to the ground from mere exhaustion.

In the ignorant days of slavery, there was a general belief that a horseshoe hung over the door would insure good luck. I have seen negroes, otherwise comparatively intelligent, refuse to pick up a pin, needle, or other such object, dropped by a negro, because, as they alleged, if the person who dropped the articles had a spite against them, to touch anything they dropped would voudou them, and make them seriously ill.

Nearly every large plantation, with any considerable number of negroes, had at least one, who laid claim to be a fortune-teller, and who was regarded with more than common respect by his fellow-slaves. Dinkie, a full-blooded African, large in frame, coarse featured, and claiming to be a descendant of a king in his native land, was the oracle on the "Poplar Farm." At the time of which I write, Dinkie was about fifty years of age, and had lost an eye, and was, to say the least, a very ugly-looking man.

No one in that section was considered so deeply immersed in voudooism, goopherism, and fortune-telling, as he. Although he had been many years in the Gaines family, no one could remember the time when Dinkie was called upon to perform manual labor. He was not sick, yet he never worked. No one interfered with him. If he felt like feeding the chickens, pigs, or cattle, he did so. Dinkie hunted, slept, was at the table at meal time, roamed through the woods, went to the city, and returned when he pleased, with no one to object, or to ask a question. Everybody treated him with respect. The whites, throughout the neighborhood, tipped their hats to the old one-eyed negro, while the policemen, or patrollers, permitted him to pass without a challenge. The negroes, everywhere, stood in mortal fear of "Uncle Dinkie." The blacks who saw him every day, were always thrown upon their good behavior, when in his presence. I once asked a negro why they appeared to be afraid of Dinkie. He looked at me, shrugged his shoulders, smiled, shook his head and said,—

"I ain't afraid of de debble, but I ain't ready to go to him jess yet." He then took a look around and behind, as if he feared some one would hear what he was saying, and then continued: "Dinkie's got de power, ser; he knows things seen and unseen, an' dat's what makes him his own massa."

It was literally true, this man was his own master. He wore a snake's skin around his neck, carried a petrified frog in one pocket, and a dried lizard in the other.

A slave speculator once came along and offered to purchase Dinkie. Dr. Gaines, no doubt, thought it a good opportunity to get the elephant off his hands, and accepted the money. A day later, the trader returned the old negro, with a threat of a suit at law for damages.

A new overseer was employed, by Dr. Gaines, to take charge of "Poplar Farm." His name was Grove Cook, and he was widely known as a man of ability in managing plantations, and in raising a large quantity of produce from a given number of hands. Cook was called a "hard overseer." The negroes dreaded his coming, and, for weeks before his arrival, the overseer's name was on every slave's tongue.

Cook came, he called the negroes up, men and women; counted them, looked them over as a purchaser would a drove of cattle that he intended to buy. As he was about to dismiss them he saw Dinkie come out of his cabin. The sharp eye of the overseer was at once on him.

"Who is that nigger?" inquired Cook.

"That is Dinkie," replied Dr. Gaines.

"What is his place?" continued the overseer.

"Oh, Dinkie is a gentleman at large!" was the response.

"Have you any objection to his working?"

"None, whatever."

"Well, sir," said Cook, "I'll put him to work to-morrow morning."

Dinkie was called up and counted in.

At the roll call, the following morning, all answered except the conjurer; he was not there.

The overseer inquired for Dinkie, and was informed that he was still asleep.

"I will bring him out of his bed in a hurry," said Cook, as he started towards the negro's cabin. Dinkie appeared at his door, just as the overseer was approaching.

"Follow me to the barn," said the impatient driver to the negro. "I make it a point always to whip a nigger, the first day that I take charge of a farm, so as to let the hands know who I am. And, now, Mr. Dinkie, they tell me that you have not had your back tanned for many years; and, that being the case, I shall give you a flogging that you will never forget. Follow me to the barn." Cook started for the barn, but turned and went into his house to get his whip.

At this juncture, Dinkie gave a knowing look to the other slaves, who were standing by, and said, "Ef he lays the weight ob his finger on me, you'll see de top of dat barn come off."

The reappearance of the overseer, with the large negro whip in one hand, and a club in the other, with the significant demand of "follow me," caused a deep feeling in the breast of every negro present.

Dr. Gaines, expecting a difficulty between his new driver and the conjurer, had arisen early, and was standing at his bedroom window looking on.

The news that Dinkie was to be whipped, spread far and near over the place, and had called forth men, women, and children. Even Uncle Ned, the old negro of ninety years, had crawled out of his straw, and was at his cabin door. As the barn doors closed behind the overseer and Dinkie, a death-like silence pervaded the entire group, who, instead of going to their labor, as ordered by the driver, were standing as if paralyzed, gazing intently at the barn, expecting every moment to see the roof lifted.

Not a word was spoken by anyone, except Uncle Ned, who smiled, shook his head, put on a knowing countenance, and said, "My word fer it, de oberseer ain't agwine to whip Dinkie."

Five minutes, ten minutes, fifteen minutes passed, and the usual sound of "Oh, pray, massa! Oh, pray, massa!" heard on the occasion of a slave being punished, had not yet proceeded from the barn.

Many of the older negroes gathered around Uncle Ned, for he and Dinkie occupied the same cabin, and the old, superannuated slave knew more about the affairs of the conjurer, than anyone else. Ned told of how, on the previous night, Dinkie had slept but little, had closely inspected the snake's skin around his neck, the petrified frog and dried lizard, in his pockets, and had rubbed himself all over with goopher; and when he had finished, he knelt, and exclaimed,—

"Now, good and lovely devil, for more than twenty years, I have served you faithfully. Before I got into your service, de white folks bought an' sold me an' my old wife an' chillen, an' whip me, and half starve me. Dey did treat me mighty bad, dat you knows. Den I use to pray to de Lord, but dat did no good, kase de white folks don't fear de Lord. But dey fears you, an' ever since I got into your service, I is able to do as I please. No white dares to la his hand on me; and dis is all owing to de power dat you give me. Oh, good and lovely devil! please to continer dat power. A new oberseer is to come here to-morrow, an' he wants to get me in his hands. But, dear devil, I axe you to stand by me in dis my trial hour, an' I will neber desert you as long as I live. Continer dis power; make me strong in your cause, make me to be more faithful to you, an' let me still be able to conquer my enemies, an' I will give you all de glory, and will try to deserve a seat at your right hand."

With bated breath, everyone listened to Uncle Ned. All had the utmost confidence in Dinkie's "power." None believed that he would be punished, while a large number expected to see the roof of the barn burst off at any moment. At last the suspence was broken. The barn door flew open; the overseer and the conjurer came out together, walking side by side, and separated when half-way up the walk. As they parted, Cook went to the field, and Dinkie to his cabin.

The slaves all shook their heads significantly. The fact that the old negro had received no punishment, was evidence of his victory over the slave driver. But how the feat had been accomplished, was a mystery. No one dared to ask Dinkie, for he was always silent, except when he had something to communicate. Everyone was afraid to inquire of the overseer.

There was, however, one faint chance of getting an inkling of what had occurred in the barn, and that was through Uncle Ned. This fact made the old, superannuated slave the hero and centre of attraction, for several days. Many were the applications made to Ned for information, but the old man did not know, or wished to exaggerate the importance of what he had learned.

"I tell you,["] said Dolly, "Dinkie is a power."

"He's nobody's fool," responded Hannah.

"I would not make him mad wid me, fer dis whole world," ejaculated Jim.

Just then, Nancy, the cook, came in brim full of news. She had given Uncle Ned some "cracklin bread," which had pleased the old man so much that he had opened his bosom, and told her all that he got from Dinkie. This piece of information flew quickly from cabin to cabin, and brought the slaves hastily into the kitchen.

It was night. Nancy sat down, looked around, and told Billy to shut the door. This heightened the interest, so that the fall of a pin could have been heard. All eyes were upon Nancy, and she felt keenly the importance of her position. Her voice was generally loud, with a sharp ring, which could be heard for a long distance, especially in the stillness of the night. But now, Nancy spoke in a whisper, occasionally putting her finger to her mouth, indicating a desire for silence, even when the breathing of those present could be distinctly heard.

"When dey got in de barn, de oberseer said to Dinkie, 'Strip yourself; I don't want to tear your clothes with my whip. I'm going to tear your black skin.'

"Den, you see, Dinkie tole de oberseer to look in de east corner ob de barn. He looked, an' he saw hell, wid all de torments, an' de debble, 'wid his cloven foot, a-struttin' about dar, jes as ef he was cock ob de walk. An' Dinkie tole Cook, dat ef he lay finger on him, he'd call de debble up to take him away."

"An' what did Cook say to dat?" asked Jim.

"Let me 'lone; I didn't tell you all," said Nancy. "Den you see de oberseer turn pale in de face, an' he say to Dinkie, 'Let me go dis time, an' I'll nebber trouble you any more.' "

This concluded Nancy's story, as related to her by old Ned, and religiously believed by all present. Whatever caused the overseer to change his mind regard to the flogging of Dinkie, it was certain that he was most thoroughly satisfied to let the old negro off without the threatened punishment and, although he remained at "Poplar Farm," as overseer, for five years, he never interfered with the conjurer again.

It is not strange that ignorant people should believe in characters of Dinkie's stamp; but it is really marvellous that well-educated men and women should give any countenance whatever, to such delusions as were practised by the oracle of "Poplar Farm."

The following illustration may be taken as a fair sample of the easy manner in which Dinkie carried on his trade.

Miss Martha Lemmy, being on a visit to Mrs. Gaines, took occasion during the day to call upon Dinkie. The conjurer knew the antecedents of his visitor, and was ready to give complete satisfaction in his particular line. When the young lady entered the old man's cabin, he met her, bade her be welcome, and tell what she had come for. She took a seat on one stool, and he on another. Taking the lady's right hand in his, Dinkie spit into its palm, rubbed it, looked at it, shut his one eye, opened it, and said: "I sees a young gentman, an' he's rich, an' owns plenty of land an' a heap o' niggers; an', lo! Miss Marfa, he loves you."

The lady drew a long breath of seeming satisfaction, and asked, "Are you sure that he loves me, Uncle Dinkie?"

"Oh! Miss Marfa, I knows it like a book."

"Have you ever seen the gentleman?" the lady inquired.

The conjurer began rubbing the palm of the snow-white hand, talked to himself in an undertone, smiled, then laughed out, and saying: "Why, Miss Marfa, as I lives it's Mr. Scott, an' he's thinkin' 'bout you now; yes, he's got his mind on you dis bressed minute. But how he's changed sense I seed him de lass time. Now he's got side whiskers an' a mustacher on his chin. But, let me see. Here is somethin' strange. De web looks a little smoky, an' when I gets to dat spot, I can't get along till a little silver is given to me."

Here the lady drew forth her purse and gave the old man a half dollar piece that made his one eye fairly twinkle.

He resumed: "Ah! now de fog is cleared away, an' I see dat Mr. Scott is settin in a rockin-cheer, wid boff feet on de table, an' smokin' a segar."

"Do you think Mr. Scott loves me?" inquired the lady.

"O! yes," responded Dinkie; "he jess sets his whole heart on you. Indeed, Miss Marfa, he's almos' dyin' 'bout you."

"He never told me that he loved me," remarked the lady.

"But den, you see, he's backward, he ain't got his eye-teef cut yet in love matters. But he'll git a little bolder ebbry time he sees you," replied the negro.

"Do you think he'll ever ask me to marry him?"

"O! yes, Miss Marfa, he's sure to do dat. As he sets dar in his rockin-cheer, he looks mighty solem-colly—looks like he wanted to ax you to haf him now."

"Do you think that Mr. Scott likes any other lady, Uncle Dinkie?" asked Miss Lemmy.

"Well, Miss Marfa, I'll jess consult de web an' see." And here the conjurer shut his one eye, opened it, shut it again, talked to himself in an undertone, opened his eye, looked into the lady's hand, and exclaimed: "Ah! Miss Marfa, I see a lady in de way, an' she's got riches; but de web is smoky, an' it needs a little silver to clear it up."

With tears in her eyes, and almost breathless, Miss Lemm[y] hastily took from her pocket her purse, and handed the old man another piece of money, saying: "Please go on."

Dinkie smiled, shook his head, got up and shut his cabin door, sat down, and again took the lady's hand in his.

"Yes, I, see," said he, "I see it's a lady; but bless you soul, Miss Marfa, it's a likeness of you dat Mr. Scott is lookin' at; dat's all."

This morsel of news gave great relief, and Miss Lemmy dried her eyes with joy.

Dinkie then took down the old rusty horseshoe from over his cabin door, held it up, and said: "Dis horseshoe neffer lies." Here he took out of his pocket a bag made of the skin of the rattlesnake, and took from it some goopher, sprinkled it over the horseshoe, saying: "Dis is de stuff, Miss Marfa, dat's gwine to make you Mr. Scott's conqueror. Long as you keeps dis goopher 'bout you he can't get away from you; he'll ax you fer a kiss, de berry next time he meets you, an' he can't help hisself fum doin' it. No woman can get him fum you so long as you keep dis goopher 'bout you."

Here Dinkie lighted a tallow candle, looked at it, smiled, shook his head,—"You's gwine to marry Mr. Scott in 'bout one year, an' you's gwine to haf thirteen children—sebben boys an' six gals, an' you's gwine to haf a heap of riches."

Just then, Dinkie's interesting revelations were cut short by Ike and Cato bringing along Peter, who, it was said, had been killed by the old bell sheep.

It appears that Peter had a way of playing with the old ram, who was always ready to butt at any one who got in his way. When seeing the ram coming, Peter would get down on his hands and knees and pretend that he was going to have a butting match with the sheep. And when the latter would come full tilt at him, Peter would dodge his head so as to miss the ram, and the latter would jump over the boy, turn around angrily, shake his head and start for another butt at Peter.

This kind of play was repeated sometimes for an hour or more, to the great amusement of both whites and blacks. But, on this occasion, Peter was completely caught. As he was on his hands and knees, the ram started on his usual run for the boy; the latter, in dodging his head, run his face against a stout stub of dry rye stalk, which caused him to quickly jerk up his head, just in time for the sheep to give him a fair butt squarely in the forehead, which knocked Peter senseless. The ram, elated with his victory, began to back himself for another lick at Peter, when the men, seeing what had happened to the poor boy, took him up and brought him to Dinkie's cabin to be resuscitated, or "brought to," as they termed it.

Nearly an hour passed in rubbing the boy, before he began to show signs of consciousness. He "come to," but he never again accepted a butting match with the ram.

CHAPTER VIII.

Cruelty to negroes was not practised in our section. It is true there were some exceptional cases, and some individuals did not take the care of their servants at all times, that economy seemed to demand. Yet a certain degree of punishment was actually needed to insure respect to the master, and good government to the slave population. If a servant disobeyed orders, it was necessary that he should be flogged, to deter others from following the bad example. If a servant ran away, he must be caught and brought back, to let the others see that the same fate awaited them if they made similar attempts.

While the keeping of bloodhounds, for running down and catching negroes, was not common, yet a few were kept by Mr. Tabor, an inferior white man, near the Corners, who hired them out, or hunted the runaway, charging so much per day, or a round sum for the *catch*.

Jerome, a slave owned by the Rev. Mr. Wilson, when about to be punished by his master, ran away. Tabor and his dogs were sent for. The slave-catcher came, and at once set his dogs upon the trail. The parson and some of the neighbors went along for the fun that was in store.

These dogs will attack a negro, at their master's bidding, and cling to him as a bull-dog will cling to a beast. Many are the speculations as to whether the negro will be secured alive or dead, when these dogs get on his track. However, on this occasion, there was not much danger of ill-treatment, for Mr. Wilson was a clergyman, and was of a humane turn, and bargained with Tabor not to injure the slave if he could help it.

The hunters had been in the wood a short time, ere they got on the track of two slaves, one of whom was Jerome. The negroes immediately bent their steps toward the swamp, with the hope that the dogs would, when put upon the scent, be unable to follow them through the water. Nearer and nearer the whimpering pack pressed on; their delusion began to dispel.

All at once the truth flashed upon the minds of the fugitives like a glare of light,—that it was Tabor with his dogs! They at last reached the river, and in the negroes plunged, followed by the catch-dog. Jerome was finally caught, and once more in the hands of his master; while the other man found a watery grave. They returned, and the preacher sent his slave to the city jail for safekeeping.

While the planters would employ Tabor, without hesitation, to hunt down their negroes, they would not receive him into their houses as a visitor any sooner than they would one of their own slaves. Tabor was, however, considered one of the better class of poor whites, a number of whom had a religious society in that neighborhood. The pastor of the poor whites was the Rev. Martin Louder, somewhat of a genius in his own way. The following sermon, preached by him, about the time of which I write, will well illustrate the character of the people for whom he labored.

More than two long, weary hours had now elapsed since the audience had been convened, and the people began to exhibit slight signs of fatigue. Some few scrapings and rasping of cowhide boots on the floor, an audible yawn or two, a little twisting and turning on the narrow, uncomfortable seats, while, in one or two instances, a somnolent soul or two snored outright. These palpable signs were not lost upon our old friend Louder. He cast an eye (emphatically, an eye) over the assemblage, and then—he spoke:—

"My dear breethering, and beloved sistering! You've ben a long time a settin' on your seats. You're tired, I know, an' I don't expect you want to hear the ole daddy preach. Ef you don't want to hear the ole man, jist give him the least bit of a sign. Cough. Hold up your hand. Ennything, an' Louder'll sit rite down. He'll dry up in a minit."

At this juncture of affairs, Louder paused for a reply. He glanced furtively over the audience, in search of the individual who might be "tired of settin' on his seat," but no sign was made: no such malcontent came within the visual range.

"Go on, Brother Louder!" said a sonorous voice in the "amen corner" of the house. Thus encourage[d], the speaker proceeded in his remarks:—

"Well, then, breethering, sense you say so, Louder'll perceed; but he don't intend to preach a reg'lar sermon, for it's a gittin' late, and our sect which hit don't believe in eatin' cold vittles on the Lord's day. My breethering, ef the ole Louder gits outen the rite track, I want you to call him back. He don't want to teach you any error. He don't want' to preach nuthin' but what's found between the leds of this blessed Book."

"My dear breethering, the Lord raised up his servant, Moses, that he should fetch his people Isrel up outen that wicked land—ah. Then Moses, he went out from the face of the Lord, and departed hence unto the courts of the old tyranickle king—ah. An' what sez you, Moses? Ah, sez he, Moses sez, sez he to that wicked old Faro: Thus sez the Lord God of hosts, sez he: Let my Isrel go—ah. An' what sez the ole, hard-hearted king—ah? Ah! sez Faro, sez he, who is the Lord God of hosts, sez he, that I should obey his voice—ah? An' now what sez you, Moses—ah. Ah, Moses sez, sez he: Thus saith the Lord God of Isrel, let my people go, that they mought worship me, sez the Lord, in the wilderness—ah. But—ah! my beloved breethering an' my harden', impenitent frien's—ah, did the ole, hard-hearted king harken to the words of Moses, and let my people go—ah? Nary time."

This last remark, made in an ordinary, conversational tone of voice, was so sudden and unexpected that the change, the transition from the singing state was electrical.

"An' then, my beloved breethering an' sistering, what next—ah? What sez you, Moses, to Faro—that contrary ole king—ah? Ah, Moses sez to Faro, sez he, Moses sez, sez he: Thus seth the Lord God of Isrel: Let my people go, sez the Lord, leest I come, sez he, and smite you with a cuss—ah! An' what sez Faro, the ole tyranickle king—ah? Ah, sez he, sez ole Faro, Let their tasks be doubled, and leest they mought grumble, sez he, those bricks shall be made without straw—ah! [Vox naturale.] Made 'em pluck up grass an' stubble outen the fields, breethering, to mix with their mud. Mity hard on the pore critters; warn't it, Brother Flood Gate?" [The individual thus interrogated replied, "Jess so;" and "ole Louder" moved along.]

"An' what next—ah? Did the ole king let my people Isrel go—ah? No, my dear breethering, he retched out his pizen hand, and he hilt 'em fash—

ah. Then the Lord was wroth with that wicked ole king—ah. An' the Lord, he sed to Moses, sez he: Moses, stretch forth now thy rod over the rivers an' the ponds of this wicked land—ah; an' behold, sez he, when thou stretch out thy rod, sez the Lord, all the waters shall be turned into blood—ah! Then Moses, he tuck his rod, an' he done as the Lord God of Isrel had commanded his servant Moses to do—ah. An' what then, say you, my breethering—ah? Why, lo an' behold! the rivers of that wicked land was all turned into blood—ah; an' all the fish an' all the frogs in them streams an' waters died a—h!"

"Yes!" said the speaker, lowering his voice to a natural tone, and glancing out of the open window at the dry and dusty road, for we were at the time suffering from a protracted drouth: "An' I believe the frogs will all die now, unless we get some rain purty soon. What do you think about it, Brother Waters?" [This interrogatory was addressed to a fine, portly-looking old man in the congregation. Brother W. nodded assent, and old Louder resumed the thread of his discourse.] "Ah, my beloved breethering, that was a hard time on old Faro an' his wicked crowd—ah. For the waters was loathsome to the people, an' it smelt so bad none of 'em, cood drink it; an' what next—ah? Did the ole king obey the voice of the Lord, and let my people Isrel go—ah? Ah, no, my breethering, not by a long sight—ah. For he hilt out agin the Lord, and obeyed not his voice—ah. Then the Lord sent a gang of bull-frogs into that wicked land—ah. An' they went hoppin' an' lopin' about all over the country, into the vittles, an' everywhere else—ah. My breethering, the old Louder thinks that was a des'prit time—ah. But all woodent do—ah. Ole Faro was as stubborn as one of Louder's mules—ah, an' he woodent let the chosen seed go up outen the land of bondage—ah. Then the Lord sent a mighty hail, an', arter that, his devourin' locuses—ah! An' they et up blamed nigh everything on the face of the eth—ah."

"Let not yore harts be trubbled, for the truth is mitay and must prevale—ah. Brother Creek, you don't seem to be doin' much of ennything, suppose you raise a tune!"

This remark was addressed to a tall, lank, hollow-jawed old man, in the congregation, with a great shock of "grizzled gray" hair.

"Wait a minit, Brother Louder, till I git on my glasses!" was the reply of Brother Creek, who proceeded to draw from his pocket an oblong tin case, which opened and shut with a tremendous snap, from which he drew a pair of iron-rimmed spectacles. These he carefully "dusted" with his handkerchief, and then turned to the hymn which the preacher had selected and read out to the congregation. After considerable deliberation, and some clearing of the throat, hawking, spitting, etc., and other preliminaries, Brother Creek, in a quavering, split sort of voice, opened out on the tune.

Louder seemed uneasy. It was evident that he feared a failure on the part of the worthy brother. At the end of the first line, he exclaimed:—

"'Pears to me, Brother Creek, you hain't got the right miter."

Brother Creek suspended operations a moment, and replied, "I am purty kerrect, ginerally, Brother Louder, an' I'm confident she'll come out all right!"

"Well," said Louder, "we'll try her agin," and the choral strain, under the supervision of Brother Creek, was resumed in the following words:—

"When I was a mourner just like you,
Washed in the blood of the Lamb,
I fasted and prayed till I got through,
Washed in the blood of the Lamb.

CHORUS.—"Come along, sinner, and go with us;
If you don't you will be cussed.

"Religion's like a blooming rose,
Washed in the blood of the Lamb,
As none but those that feel it knows,
Washed in the blood of the Lamb."—*Cho.*

The singing, joined in by all present, brought the enthusiasm of the assembly up to white heat, and the shouting, with the loud "Amen," "God save the sinner," "Sing it, brother, sing it," made the welkin ring.

CHAPTER IX.

While the "peculiar institution" was a great injury to both master and slaves, yet there was considerable truth in the oft-repeated saying that the slave "was happy." It was indeed, a low kind of happiness, existing only where masters were disposed to treat their servants kindly, and where the proverbial light-heartedness of the latter prevailed. History shows that of all races, the African was best adapted to be the "hewers of wood, and drawers of water."

Sympathetic in his nature, thoughtless in his feelings, both alimentativeness and amativeness large, the negro is better adapted to follow than to lead. His wants easily supplied, generous to a fault, large fund of humor, brimful of music, he has ever been found the best and most accommodating of servants. The slave would often get rid of punishment by his wit; and even when being flogged, the master's heart has been moved to pity, by the humorous appeals of his victim. House servants in the cities and villages, and even on plantations, were considered privileged classes. Nevertheless, the field hands were not without their happy hours.

An old-fashioned corn-shucking took place once a year, on "Poplar Farm," which afforded pleasant amusement for the out-door negroes for miles around. On these occasions, the servants, on all plantations, were allowed to attend by mere invitation of the blacks where the corn was to be shucked.

As the grain was brought in from the field, it was left in a pile near the corn-cribs. The night appointed, and invitations sent out, slaves from plantations five or six miles away, would assemble and join on the road, and in large bodies march along, singing their melodious plantation songs.

To hear three or four of these gangs coming from different directions, their leaders giving out the words, and the whole company joining in the chorus, would indeed surpass anything ever produced by "Haverly's Ministrels," and many of their jokes and witticisms were never equalled by Sam Lucas or Billy Kersands.

A supper was always supplied by the planter on whose farm the shucking was to take place. Often when approaching the place, the singers would speculate on what they were going to have for supper. The following song was frequently sung:—

> "All dem puty gals will be dar,
> Shuck dat corn before you eat.
> Dey will fix it fer us rare,
> Shuck dat corn before you eat.
> I know dat supper will be big,
> Shuck dat corn before you eat.
> I think I smell a fine roast pig,
> Shuck dat corn before you eat.
> A supper is provided, so dey said,
> Shuck dat corn before you eat.
> I hope dey'll have some nice wheat bread,
> Shuck dat corn before you eat.
> I hope dey'll have some coffee dar,
> Shuck dat corn before you eat.
> I hope dey'll have some whisky dar,
> Shuck dat corn before you eat.

I think I'll fill my pockets full,
Shuck dat corn before you eat.
Stuff dat coon an' bake him down,
Shuck dat corn before you eat.
I speck some niggers dar from town,
Shuck dat corn before you eat.
Please cook dat turkey nice an' brown.
Shuck dat corn before you eat.
By de side of dat turkey I'll be foun,
Shuck dat corn before you eat.
I smell de supper, dat I do,
Shuck dat corn before you eat.
On de table will be a stew,
Shuck dat corn, etc."

Burning pine knots, held by some of the boys, usually furnished light for the occasion. Two hours is generally sufficient time to finish up a large shucking; where five hundred bushels of corn is thrown into the cribs as the shuck is taken off. The work is made comparatively light by the singing, which never ceases till they go to the supper table. Something like the following is sung during the evening:

"De possum meat am good to eat,
Carve him to de heart;
You'll always find him good and sweet,
Carve him to de heart;
My dog did bark, and I went to see,
Carve him to de heart.
And dar was a possum up dat tree,
Carve him to de heart.

CHORUS.—"Carve dat possum, carve dat possum children,
Carve dat possum, carve him to de heart;
Oh, carve dat possum, carve dat possum children,
Carve dat possum, carve him to de heart.

"I reached up for to pull him in,
Carve him to de heart;
De possum he began to grin,
Carve him to de heart;
I carried him home and dressed him off,

Carve him to de heart;
I hung him dat night in de frost,
Carve him to de heart.

CHORUS.—"Carve dat possum, etc.

"De way to cook de possum sound,
Carve him to de heart;
Fust par-bile him, den bake him brown,
Carve him to de heart;
Lay sweet potatoes in de pan,
Carve him to de heart;
De sweetest eatin' in de lan,'
Carve him to de heart.

CHORUS.—["]Carve dat possum, etc."

Should a poor supper be furnished, on such an occasion, you would hear remarks from all parts of the table,—
"Take dat rose pig 'way from dis table."
"What rose pig? you see any rose pig here?"
"Ha, ha, ha! Dis ain't de place to see rose pig."
"Pass up some dat turkey wid clam sauce."
"Don't talk about dat turkey; he was gone afore we come."
"Dis is de las' time I shucks corn at dis farm."
"Dis is a cheap farm, cheap owner, an' a cheap supper."
"He's talkin' it, ain't he?"
"Dis is de tuffest meat dat I is been called upon to eat fer many a day; you's got to have teeth sharp as a saw to eat dis meat."
"Spose you ain't got no teef, den what you gwine to do?"
"Why, ef you ain't got no teef you muss *gum it!*"
"Ha, ha, ha!" from the whole company, was heard.
On leaving the corn-shucking farm, each gang of men, headed by their leader, would sing during the entire journey home. Some few, however, having their dogs with them, would start on the trail of a coon, possum, or some other game, which might keep them out till nearly morning.
To the Christmas holidays, the slaves were greatly indebted for winter recreation; for long custom had given to them the whole week from Christmas day to the coming in of the New Year.
On "Poplar Farm," the hands drew their share of clothing on Christmas day for the year. The clothing for both men and women was made up by

women kept for general sewing and housework. One pair of pants, and two shirts, made the entire stock for a male field hand.

The women's garments were manufactured from the same goods that the men received. Many of the men worked at night for themselves, making splint and corn brooms, baskets, shuck mats, and axe-handles, which they would sell in the city during Christmas week. Each slave was furnished with a pass, something like the following:—

"Please let my boy, Jim, pass anywhere in this county, until Jan. 1, 1834, and oblige
"Respectfully,
"JOHN GAINES, M.D.
"'Poplar Farm,' St. Louis County, Mo."

With the above precious document in his pocket, a load of baskets, brooms, mats, and axe-handles on his back, a bag hanging across his shoulders, with a jug in each end,—one for the whiskey, and the other for the molasses,—the slaves trudged off to town at night, singing,—

"Hurra, for good ole massa,
He give me de pass to go to de city.
Hurra, for good ole missis,
She bile de pot, and giv me de licker.
Hurra, I'm goin to de city[.]

"When de sun rise in de mornin',
Jes' above de yaller corn,
You'll fin' dis nigger has take warnin',
An's gone when de driver blows his horn.

["]Hurra, for good ole massa,
He giv me de pass to go to de city.
Hurra for good ole missis,
She bile de pot, and give me de licker.
Hurra, I'm goin to de city."

Both the Methodists and Baptists,—the religious denominations to which the blacks generally belong,—never fail to be in the midst of a revival meeting during the holidays, and, most of the slaves from the country hasten to these gatherings. Some, however, spend their time at the dances, raffles, cock-fights, foot-races, and other amusements that present themselves.

CHAPTER X.

A young and beautiful lady, closely veiled and attired in black, arrived one morning at "Poplar Farm," and was shown immediately into a room in the eastern wing, where she remained, attended only by old Nancy. That the lady belonged to the better class was evident from her dress, refined manners, and the inviolable secrecy of her stay at the residence of Dr. Gaines. At last the lady gave birth to a child, which was placed under the care of Isabella, a quadroon servant, who had recently lost a baby of her own.

The lady left the premises as mysteriously as she had come, and nothing more was ever seen or heard of her, certainly not by the negroes. The child, which was evidently of pure Anglo-Saxon blood, was called Lola, and grew up amongst the negro children of the place, to be a bright, pretty girl, to whom her adopted mother seemed very much attached. At the time of which I write, Lola was eight years old, and her presence on the plantation began to annoy the white members of Dr. Gaines' family, especially when strangers visited the place.

The appearance of Mr. Walker, the noted slave speculator, on the plantation, and whom it was said, had been sent for, created no little excitement amongst the slaves; and great was the surprise to the blacks, when they saw the trader taking Isabella and Lola with him at his departure. Unable to sell the little white girl at any price, Mr. Walker gave her to Mr. George Savage, who having no children of his own adopted the child.

Isabella was sold to a gentleman, who took her to Washington. The grief of the quadroon at being separated from her adopted child was intense, and greatly annoyed her new master, who determined to sell her on his arrival home. Isabella was sold to the slave-trader, Jennings, who placed the woman in one of the private slave-pens, or prisons, a number of which then disgraced the national capital.

Jennings intended to send Isabella to the N[e]w Orleans market, as soon as he purchased a sufficient number. At the dusk of the evening, previous to the day she was to be sent off, as the old prison was being closed for the night, Isabella suddenly darted past the keeper, and ran for her life. It was not a great distance from the prison to the long bridge which passes from the lower part of the city, across the Potomac to the extensive forests and woodlands of the celebrated Arlington Heights, then occupied by that distinguished relative and descendant of the immortal Washington, Mr. Geo. W. Custis. Thither the poor fugitive directed her flight. So unexpected was her escape, that she had gained several rods the start before the keeper had secured the other prisoners, and rallied his assistants to aid in the pursuit. It was at an hour, and in a part of the city where horses could not easily be obtained for the chase; no bloodhounds were at hand to run down the fly-ing woman, and for once it seemed as if there was to be a fair trial of speed and endurance between the slave and the slave-catchers.

The keeper and his force raised the hue-and-cry on her path as they fol-lowed close behind; but so rapid was the flight along the wide avenue, that the astonished citizens, as they poured forth from their dwellings to learn the cause of alarm, were only able to comprehend the nature of the case in time to fall in with the motley throng in pursuit, or raise an anxious prayer to heaven, as they refused to join in the chase (as many a one did that night), that the panting fugitive might escape, and the merciless soul-dealer for once be disappointed of his prey. And now, with the speed of an arrow, having passed the avenue, with the distance between her and her pursuers constantly increasing, this poor, hunted female gained the "Long Bridge," as it is called, where interruption seemed improbable. Already her heart began to beat high with the hope of success. She had only to pass three-quarters of a mile across the bridge, when she could bury herself in a vast forest, just at the time when the curtain of night would close around her, and protect her from the pursuit of her enemies.

But God, by His providence, had otherwise determined. He had ordained that an appalling tragedy should be enacted that night within plain sight of the President's house, and the Capitol of the Union, which would be an evidence, wherever it should be known, of the unconquerable love of liberty which the human heart may inherit, as well as a fresh admo-nition to the slave-dealer of the cruelty and enormity of his crimes.

Just as the pursuers passed the high draw, soon after entering upon the bridge, they beheld three men slowly approaching from the Virginia side. They immediately called to them to arrest the fugitive, proclaiming her a runaway slave. True to their Virginia instincts, as she came near, they formed a line across the narrow bridge to intercept her. Seeing that escape was impossible in that quarter, she stopped suddenly, and turned upon her pursuers.

On came the profane and ribald gang, faster than ever, already exulting in her capture, and threatening punishment for her flight. For a moment, she looked wildly and anxiously around to see if there was no hope of escape, on either hand; far down below, rolled the deep, foaming waters of the Potomac, and before and behind were the rapidly approaching steps and noisy voices of her pursuers.

Seeing how vain would be any further effort to escape, her resolution was instantly taken. She clasped her hands convulsively together, raised her tearful and imploring eyes towards heaven, and begged for the mercy and compassion there, which was unjustly denied her on earth; then, with a single bound, vaulted over the railing of the bridge, and sank forever beneath the angry and foaming waters of the river.

In the meantime Mr. and Mrs. Savage were becoming more and more interested in the child, Lola, whom they had adopted, and who was fast developing into an intellectual and beautiful girl, whose bright, sparkling hazel eyes, snow-white teeth and alabaster complexion caused her to be admired by all. In time, Lola become highly educated, and was duly introduced into the best society.

The cholera of 1832, in its ravages, swept off many of St. Louis' most valued citizens, and among them, Mr. George Savage. Mrs. Savage, who was then in ill-health, regarded Lola with even greater solicitude, than during the lifetime of her late husband. Lola had been amply provided for by Mr. Savage, in his will. She was being courted by Mr. Martin Phelps, previous to the death of her adopted father, and the failing health of Mrs. Savage hastened the nuptials.

The marriage of Mr. Phelps and Miss Savage partook more of a private than of a public affair, owing to the recent death of Mr. Savage. Mr. Phelps' residence was at the outskirts of the city, in the vicinity of what was known as the "Mound," and was a lovely spot. The lady had brough[t] considerable property t[o] her husband.

One morning in the month of December, and only about three months after the marriage of the Phelps's, two men alighted from a carriage, at Mr. Phelps' door, rang the bell, and were admitted by the servant. Mr. Phelps hastened from the breakfast-table, as the servant informed him of the presence of the strangers.

On entering the sitting-room, the host recognized one of the men as Officer Mull, while the other announced himself as James Walker, and said,—

"I have come, Mr. Phelps, on rather an unpleasant errand. You've got a slave in your house that belongs to me."

"I think you are mistaken, sir," replied Mr. Phelps; "my servants are all hired from Major Ben. O'Fallon."

Walker put on a sinister smile, and blandly continued, "I see, sir, that you don't understand me. Ten years ago I bought a slave child from Dr. Gaines, and lent her to Mr. George Savage, and I understand she's in your employ, and I've come to get her," and, here the slave speculator took from his side pocket a large sheepskin pocket book, and drew forth the identical bill of sale of Lola, given to him by Dr. Gaines at the time of the selling of Isabella and the child.

"Good heavens!" exclaimed Mr. Phelps, "that paper, if it means anything, it means my wife."

"I can't help what it means," remarked Walker; "here's the bill of sale, and here's the officer to get me my nigger."

"There must be a mistake here. It is true that my wife was the adopted daughter of the late Mr. George Savage, but there is not a drop of negro blood in her veins; and I doubt, sir, if you have ever seen her."

"Well, sir," said Walker, "jest bring her in the room, and I guess she'll know me."

Feeling confident that the bill of sale had no reference to his wife, Mr. Phelps rang the bell, and told the boy that answered it to ask his mistress to come in. A moment or two later, and the lady entered the room.

"My dear," said Mr. Phelps, "are you acquainted with either of these gentlemen?"

The lady looked, hesitated, and replied, "I think not."

Then Walker arose, stepped towards the window, where he could be seen to better advantage, and said, "Why, Lola, have you forgotten me, its only about ten years since I brought you from 'Poplar Farm,' and lent you to Mr. Savage. Ha, ha, ha!"

This coarse laugh of the rough, uneducated negro-trader had not ceased, when Lola gave a heartrending shriek, and fell fainting upon the floor.

"I thought she'd know me when I jogged her memory," said Walker, as he re-seated himself.

Mr. Phelps sprang to his wife, and lifted her from the floor, and placed her upon the sofa.

"Throw a little of Adam's ale in her face, and that'll bring her to. I've seen 'em faint afore; but they aller[s] come to," said the trader.

"I thank you, sir, but I will attend to my own affairs," said Mr. Phelps, in a rather petulant tone.

"Yes," replied Walker; "but she's mine, and I want to see that she comes to."

As soon as she revived, Mr. Phelps led his wife from the room. A conference of an hour took place on the return of Mr. Phelps to the parlor, which closed with the understanding that a legal examination of the papers should settle the whole question the next day.

At the appointed time, on the following morning, one of the ablest lawyers in the city, Col. Strawther, pronounced the bill of sale genuine, for it had been drawn up by Justice McGuyer, and witnessed by George Kennelly and Wilson P. Hunt.

For this claim, Walker expressed a willingness to sell the woman for two thousand dollars. The payment of the money would have been a small matter, if it had not carried with it the proof that Lola was a slave, which was undeniable evidence that she had negro blood in her veins.

Yet such was the result, for Dr. Gaines had been dead these three years, and whoever Lola's mother was, even if living, she would not come forth to vindicate the free birth of her child.

Mr. Phelps was a man of fine sensibility and was affectionately attached to his wife. However, it was a grave question to be settled in his mind, whether his honor as a Southern gentleman, and his standing in society would allow him to acknowledge a woman as his wife, in whose veins coursed the accursed blood of the negro slave.

Long was the struggle between love and duty, but the shame of public gaze and the ostracism of society decided the matter in favor of duty, and the young and lovely wife was informed by the husband that they must separate, never to meet again. Indescribable were the feelings of Lola, as she begged him, upon her knees, not to leave her. The room was horrible in its darkness,—her mind lost its reasoning powers for a time. At last consciousness returned, but only to awaken in her the loneliness of her condition, and the unfriendliness of that law and society that dooms one to everlasting disgrace for a blood taint, which the victim did not have.

Ten days after the proving of the bill of sale, the innocent Lola died of a broken heart, and was interred in the negro burial ground, with not a white face to follow the corpse to its last resting-place. Such is American race prejudice.

CHAPTER XI.

The invention of the Whitney cotton gin, nearly fifty years ago, created a wonderful rise in the price of slaves in the cotton States. The value of able-bodied men, fit for field-hands, advanced from five hundred to twelve hundred dollars, in the short space of five years. In 1850, a prime field-hand was worth two thousand dollars. The price of women rose in proportion; they being valued at about three hundred dollars less each than the men. This change in the price of slaves caused a lucrative business to spring up, both in the breeding of slaves and the sending of them to the States needing their services. Virginia, Kentucky, Missouri, Tennessee, and North Carolina became the slave-raising sections; Virginia, however, was always considered the banner State. To the traffic in human beings, more than to any other of its evils, is the institution indebted for its over-throw.

From the picture on the heading of *The Liberator*, down to the smallest tract printed against slavery, the separation of families was the chief object of those exposing the great American sin. The tearing asunder of husbands and wives, of parents and children, and the gangs of men and women chained together, *en route* for the New Orleans' market, furnished newspaper correspondents with items that never wanted readers. These newspaper paragraphs were not unfrequently made stronger by the fact that many of the slaves were as white as those who offered them for sale, and the close resemblance of the victim to the trader, often reminded the purchaser that the same blood coursed through the veins of both.

The removal of Dr. Gaines from "Poplar Farm" to St. Louis, gave me an opportunity of seeing the worst features of the internal slave-trade. For many years Missouri drove a brisk business in the selling of her sons and daughters, the greater number of whom passed through the city of St. Louis. For a long time, James Walker was the principal speculator in this species of property. The early life of this man had been spent as a dray-man, first working for others, then for himself, and eventually purchasing men who worked with him. At last, disposing of his horses and drays, he took his faithful men to the Louisiana market and sold them. This was the commencement of a career of cruelty, that, in all probability, had no equal in the annals of the American slave trade.

A more repulsive-looking person could scarcely be found in any community of bad-looking men than Walker. Tall, lean, and lank, with high cheek-bones, face much pitted with the small-pox, gray eyes, with red eye-brows, and sandy whiskers, he indeed stood alone without mate or fellow in looks. He prided himself upon what he called his goodness of heart, and was always speaking of his humanity.

Walker often boasted that he never separated families if he could "persuade the purchaser to take the whole lot." He would always advertise in the New Orleans' papers that he would be there with a prime lot of able-bodied slaves, men and women, fit for field-service, with a few extra ones calculated for house servants,—all between the ages of fifteen and twenty-five years; but like most men who make a business of speculating in human beings, he often bought many who were far advanced in years, and would try to pass them off for five or six years younger than they were. Few persons can arrive at anything approaching the real age of the negro, by mere observation, unless they are well acquainted with the race. Therefore, the slave-trader frequently carried out the deception with perfect impunity.

As soon as the steamer would leave the wharf, and was fairly on the bosom of the broad Mississippi, the speculator would call his servant Pompey to him, and instruct him as to getting the slaves ready for the market. If any of the blacks looked as if they were older than they were advertised to be, it was Pompey's business to fit them for the day of sale.

119

Pomp, as he was usually called by the trader, was of real negro blood, and would often say, when alluding to himself, "Dis nigger am no counterfeit, he is de ginuine artikle. Dis chile is none of your haf-and-haf, dere is no bogus about him."

Pompey was of low stature, round face, and, like most of his race, had a set of teeth, which, for whiteness and beauty, could not be surpassed; his eyes were large, lips thick, and hair short and woolly. Pomp had been with Walker so long, and seen so much of buying and selling of his fellow-creatures, that he appeared perfectly indifferent to the heart-rendin[g] scenes which daily occurred in his presence. Such is the force of habit:—

> "Vice is a monster of such frightful mien,
> That to be hated, needs but to be seen;
> But seen too oft, familiar with its face,
> We first endure, then pity, then embrace."

Before reaching the place of destination, Pompey would pick out the older portion and say, "I is de chap dat is to get you ready for de Orleans market, so dat you will bring marser a good price. How old is you?" addressing himself to a man that showed some age.

"Ef I live to see next corn-plantin' time, I'll be forty."

"Dat may be," replied Pompey, "but now you is only thirty years old; dat's what marser says you is to be."

"I know I is mo' dan dat," responded the man.

"I can't help nuffin' 'bout dat," returned Pompey; "but when you get in de market, an' any one ax you how old you is, an' you tell um you is forty, massa will tie yo[u] up, an' when he is done whippin' you, you'll be glad to say you's only thirty."

"Well den, I reckon I is only thirty," said the slave.

"What is your name?" asked Pompey of another man in the group.

"Jeems," was the response.

"Oh! Uncle Jim, is it?"

"Yes."

"Den you muss' hab all dem gray whiskers shaved off, and dem gray hairs plucked out of your head. De fack is, you's got ole too quick." This was all said by Pompey in a manner which showed that he knew his business.

"How ole is you?" asked Pompey of a tall, strong-looking man.

"I am twenty-nine, nex' Christmas Eve," said the man.

"What's your name?"

"My name is Tobias," replied the slave.

"Tobias!" ejaculated Pompey, with a sneer, that told that he was ready to show his brief authority. "Now you's puttin' on airs. Your name is Toby, an' why can't you tell the truf? Remember, now, dat you is twenty-three years ole; an' afore' you goes in do market your face muss' be greased; fer I see you's one of dem kind o' ashy niggers, an' a little grease will make your face look black an' slick, an' make you look younger."

Pompey reported to his master the condition of affairs, when the latter said, "Be sure that the niggers don't forget what you have taught them, for our luck depends a great deal upon the appearance of our stock."

With this lot of slaves was a beautiful quadroon, a girl of twenty years, fair as most white women, with hair a little wavy, large black eyes, and a countenance that betokened intelligence beyond the common house servant. Her name was Marion, and the jealousy of the mistress, so common in those days, was the cause of her being sold.

Not far from Canal Street, in the city of New Orleans, in the old days of slavery, stood a two-story, flat building, surrounded by a stone wall, some twelve feet high, the top of which was covered with bits of glass, and so constructed as to prevent even the possibility of any one's passing over it without sustaining great injury. Many of the rooms in this building resembled the cells of a prison, and in a small apartment, near the "office," were to be seen any number of iron collars, hobbles, hand-cuffs, thumb-screws, cowhides, chains, gags, and yokes.

A back-yard, enclosed by a high wall, looked like the play-ground attached to one of our large New England schools, in which were rows of benches and swings. Attached to the back premises was a good-sized kitchen, where, at the time of which we write, two old negresses were at work, stewing, boiling, and baking, and occasionally wiping the perspiration from their furrowed and swarthy brows.

The slave-trader, Walker, on his arrival at New Orleans, took up his quarters here, with his gang of human cattle, and the morning after, at ten o'clock, they were exhibited for sale. First of all, came the beautiful Marion, whose pale countenance and dejected look, told how many sad hours she had passed since parting with her mother. There, too, was a poor woman, who had been separated from her husband, and another woman, whose looks and manners were expressive of deep anguish, sat by her side. There was "Uncle Jeems," with his whiskers off, his face shaven clean, and the gray hairs plucked out, ready to be sold for ten years younger than he was. Toby was also there, with his face shaven and greased, ready for inspection.

The examination commenced, and was carried on in such a manner as to shock the feelings of any one not entirely devoid of the milk of human kindness.

"What are you wiping your eyes for?" inquired a fat, red-faced man, with a white hat set on one side of his head and a cigar in his mouth, of a woman who sat on one of the benches.

"Because I left my man behind."

"Oh, if I buy you, I will furnish you with a better man than you left. I've got lots of young backs on my farm," responded the man.

"I don't want and never will have another man," replied the woman.

"What's your name?" asked a man, in a straw hat, of a tall negro, who stood with his arms folded across his breast, leaning against the wall.

"My name is Aaron, sar."

"How old are you?"

"Twenty-five."

"Where were you raised?"

"In ole Virginny, sar."

"How many men have owned you?"

"Four."

"Do you enjoy good health?"

"Yes, sar."

"How long did you live with your first owner?"

"Twenty years."

"Did you ever run away?"

"No, sar."

"Did you ever strike your master?"

"No sar."

"Were you ever whipped much?"

"No, sar; I spose I didn't desarve it, sar."

"How long did you live with your second master?"

"Ten years, sar."

"Have you a good appetite?"

"Yes, sar."

"Can you eat your allowance?"

"Yes, sar,—when I can get it."

"Where were you employed in Virginia?"

"I worked in de tobacker fiel'."

"In the tobacco field, eh?"

"Yes, sar."

"How old did you say you was?"

"Twenty-five, sar, nex' sweet-'tater-diggin' time."

"I am a cotton-planter, and if I buy you, you will have to work in the cotton field. My men pick one hundred and fifty pounds a day, and the women one hundred and forty pounds; and those who fail to perform their task receive five stripes for each pound that is wanting. Now do you think you could keep up with the rest of the hands?"

"I don't know, sar, but I reckon I'd have to."

"How long did you live with your third master?"

"Three years, sar," replied the slave.

"Why, that makes you thirty-three; I thought you told me you were only twenty-five."

Aaron now looked first at the planter, then at the trader, and seemed perfectly bewildered. He had forgotten the lesson given him by Pompey, relative to his age; and the planter's circuitous questions—doubtless to find out the slave's real age—had thrown the negro off his guard.

"I must see your back, so as to know how much you have been whipped, before I think of buying."

Pompey, who had been standing by during the examination, thought that his services were now required, and, stepping forth with a degree of officiousness, said to Aaron:—"Don't you hear de gemman tell you he wants to zamin you? Cum, unharness yo-seff, ole boy, an' don't be standin' dar."

Aaron was examined, and pronounced "sound"; yet the conflicting statement about his age was not satisfactory.

On the following trip down the river, Walker halted at Vicksburg, with a "prime lot of slaves," and a circumstance occurred which shows what the slaves in those days would resort to, to save themselves from flogging, while, at the same time, it exhibits the quick wit of the race.

While entertaining some of his purchasers at the hotel, Walker ordered Pompey to hand the wine around to his guests. In doing this, the servant upset a glass of wine upon a gentleman's lap. For this mishap, the trader determined to have his servant punished. He, therefore, gave Pompey a sealed note, and ordered him to take it to the slave prison. The servant, suspecting that all was not right, hastened to open the note before the wafer had dried; and passing the steamboat landing, he got a sailor to read the note, which proved to be, as Pompey had suspected, an order to have him receive "thirty-nine stripes upon the bare back."

Walker had given the man a silver dollar, with orders to deliver it, with the note, to the jailor, for it was common in those days for persons who wanted their servants punished and did not wish to do it themselves, to send them to the "slave pen," and have it done; the price for which was one dollar.

How to escape the flogging, and yet bring back to his master the evidence of having been punished, perplexed the fertile brain of Pompey. However, the servant was equal to the occasion. Standing in front of the "slave pen," the negro saw another well dressed colored man coming up the street, and he determined to inquire in regard to how they did the whipping there.

"How de do, sar," said Pompey, addressing the colored brother. "Do you live here?"

"Oh! no," replied the stranger, "I am a free man, and belong in Pittsburgh, Pa."

"Ah! ha, den you don't live here," said Pompey.

"No, I left my boat here last week, and I have been trying every day to get something to do. I'm pretty well out of money, and I'd do almost anything just now."

A thought flashed upon Pompey's mind—this was his occasion.

"Well," said the slave, "ef you want a job, whar you can make some money quick, I specks I can help you."

"If you will," replied the free man, ["]you'll do me a great favor."

"Here, then," said Pompey, "take dis note, an' go in to dat prison, dar, an' dey will give you a trunk, bring it out, an' I'll tell you where to carry it to, an' here's a dollar; dat will pay you, won't it?"

"Yes," replied the man, with many thanks; and taking the note and the shining coin, with smiles, he went to the "Bell Gate," and gave the bell aloud ring. The gate flew open, and in he went.

The man had scarcely disappeared, ere Pompey had crossed the street, and was standing at the gate, listening to the conversation then going on between the jailor and the free colored man.

"Where is the dollar that you got with this note?" asked the "whipper," as he finished reading the epistle.

"Here it is, sir; he gave it to me," said the man, with no little surprise.

"Hand it here," responded the jailor, in a rough voice. "There, now; take this nigger, Pete, and strap him down upon the stretcher, and get him ready for business."

"What are you going a to do to me!" cried the horrified man, at the jailor's announcement.

"You'll know, damn quick!" was the response.

The resistance of the innocent man caused the "whipper" to call in three other sturdy blacks, and, in a few minutes, the victim was fastened upon the stretcher, face downwards, his clothing removed, and the strong-armed white negro-whipper standing over him with uplifted whip.

The cries and groans of the poor man, as the heavy instrument of torture fell upon his bare back, aroused Pompey, who retreated across the street, stood awaiting the result, and wondering if he could obtain, from the injured man, the receipt which the jailor always gives the slave to take back to his master as evidence of his having been punished.

As the gate opened, and the colored brother made his appearance, looking wildly about for Pompey, the latter called out, "Here I is, sar!"

Maddened by the pain from the excoriation of his bleeding back, and the surprise and astonishment at the quickness with which the whole thing had been accomplished, the man ran across the street, upbraiding in the most furious manner his deceiver, who also appeared amazed at the epithets bestowed upon him.

"What have I done to you?" asked Pompey, with a seriousness that was indeed amusing.

"What hain't you done!" said the man, the tears streaming down his face. "You've got my back cut all to pieces," continued the victim.

"What did you let 'em whip you for?" said Pompey, with a concealed smile.

"You knew that note was to get somebody whipped, and you put it on me. And here is a piece of paper that he gave me, and told me to give it to my master. Just as if I had a master."

"Well,["] responded Pompey, "I have a half a dollar, an' I'll give that to you, ef you'll give me the paper."

Seeing that he could make no better bargain, the man gave up the receipt, taking in exchange the silver coin.

"Now," said Pompey, "I'm mighty sorry for ye, an' ef ye'll go down to de house, I'll pray for ye. I'm powerful in prayer, dat I is." However the free man declined Pompey's offer[.]

"I reckon you'll behave yourself and not spill the wine over gentlemen again," said Walker, as Pompey handed him the note from the jailor. "The next time you commit such a blunder, you'll not get off so easy," continued the speculator.

Pompey often spoke of the appearance of "my fren'," as he called the colored brother, and would enjoy a hearty laugh, saying "He was a free man, an' could afford to go to bed, an' lay dar till he got well."

Strangers to the institution of slavery and its effects upon its victims, would frequently speak with astonishment of the pride that slaves would show in regard to their own value in the market. This was especially so, at auction sales where town or city servants were sold.

"What did your marser pay for you?" would often be asked by one slave of another.

"Eight hundred dollars."

"Eight hundred dollars! Ha, ha! Well, ef I didn't sell for mo' dan eight hundred dollars, I'd neber show my head agin 'mong 'spectable people."

"You got so much to say 'bout me sellin' cheap, now I want to know how much your boss paid fer you?"

"My boss paid fifteen hundred dollars cash, for me; an' it was a rainy day, an' not many out to de auction, or he'd had to pay a heap mo', let me tell you. I'm none of your cheap niggers, I ain't."

"Hy, uncle! Did dey sell you, 'isterday? I see you down dar to de market."

"Yes, dey sole me."

"How much did you fetch?"

"Eighteen hundred dollars."

"Dat was putty smart for man like you, ain't it?"

"Well, I dunno; it's no mo' dan I is wuf; for you muss' 'member, I was raised by de Christy's. I'm none of yer common niggers, sellin' fer a picayune. I tink my new boss got me mighty cheap."

"An' so you sole, las' Sataday, for nine hundred dollars; so I herd."

"Well, what on it?"

"All I got to say is, of I was sole, to-morrow, an' did'nt bring more dan nine hundred dollars, I'd never look a decent man in de face agin."

These, and other sayings of the kind, were often heard in any company of colored men, in our Southern towns.

CHAPTER XII.

Throughout the Southern States, there are still to be found remnants of the old time Africans, who were stolen from their native land and sold in the Savannah, Mobile, and New Orleans markets, in defiance of all law. The last-named city, however, and its vicinity, had a larger portion of these people than any other section. New Orleans was their centre, and where their meetings were not uninteresting.

Congo Square takes its name, as is well known, from the Congo negroes who used to perform their dance on its sward every Sunday. They were a curious people, and brought over with them this remnant of their African jungles. In Louisiana there were six different tribes of negroes, named after the section of the country from which they came, and their representatives could be seen on the square, their teeth filed, and their cheeks still bearing tattoo marks. The majority of our city negroes came from the Kraels, a numerous tribe who dwell in stockades. We had here the Minahs, a proud, dignified, warlike race; the Congos, a treacherous, shrewd, relentless people; the Mandringas, a branch of the Congos; the Gangas, named after the river of that name, from which they had been taken; the Hiboas, called by the missionaries the "Owls," a sullen, intractable tribe, and the Foulas, the highest type of the African, with but few representatives here.

These were the people that one would meet on the square many years ago. It was a gala occasion, these Sundays in those years, and not less than two or three thousand people would congregate there to see the dusky dancers. A low fence enclosed the square, and on each street there was a little gate and turnstile. There were no trees then, and the ground was worn bare by the feet of the people. About three o'clock the negroes began to gather, each nation taking their places in different parts of the square. The Minahs would not dance near the Congos, nor the Mandringas near the Gangas. Presently the music would strike up, and the parties would prepare for the sport. Each set had its own orchestra. The instruments were a peculiar kind of banjo, made of a Louisiana gourd, several drums made of a gum stump dug out, with a sheepskin head, and beaten with the fingers, and two jaw-bones of a horse, which when shaken would rattle the loose teeth, keeping time with the drums. About eight negroes, four male and four female, would make a set, and generally they were but scantily clad.

It took some little time before the tapping of the drums would arouse the dull and sluggish dancers, but when the point of excitement came, nothing can faithfully portray the wild and frenzied motions they go through. Backward and forward, this way and that, now together and now apart every motion intended to convey the most sensual ideas. As the dance progressed, the drums were thrummed faster, the contortions became more grotesque, until sometimes, in frenzy, the women and men would fall fainting to the ground. All this was going on with a dense crowd looking on, and with a hot sun pouring its torrid rays on the infatuated actors of this curious ballet. After one set had become fatigued, they would drop out to be replaced by others, and then stroll off to the groups of some other tribe in a different portion of the square. Then it was that trouble would commence, and a regular set-to with short sticks followed, between the men, and broken heads ended the day's entertainment.

On the sidewalks, around the square, the old negresses, with their spruce-beer and peanuts, cocoa-nuts and pop-corn, did a thriving trade, and now and then, beneath petticoats, bottles of tafia, a kind of Louisiana rum, peeped out, of which the *gendarmes* were oblivious. When the sun went down, a stream of people poured out of the turn-stiles, and the *gendarmes*, walking through the square, would order the dispersion of the negroes, and by gun-fire, at nine o'clock, the place was well-nigh deserted. These dances were kept up until within the memory of men still living, and many who believe in them, and who would gladly revive them, may be found in every State in the Union.

The early traditions, brought down through the imported Africans, have done much to keep alive the belief that the devil is a personal being, with hoofs, horns, and having powers equal with God. These ideas give influence to the conjurer, goopher doctor, and fortune-teller.

While visiting one of the upper parishes, not long since, I was stopping with a gentleman who was accustomed to make weekly visits to a neighboring cemetery, sitting for hours amongst the graves at which occurrence the wife felt very sad.

I inquired of her the object of her husband's strange freak.

"Oh!" said she, "he's influenced out there by angels."

"Has he gone to the cemetery now?" I asked.

"Yes," was the reply.

"I think I can cure him of it, if you will promise to keep the whole thing a secret."

"I will," was the reply.

"Let me have a sheet, and unloose your dog, and I will put the cure in motion," I said. Rolla, the big Newfoundland dog, was unfastened, the sheet was well fitted around his neck, tightly sewed, and the pet told to go hunt his master.

Taking the trail, the dog at once made for the cemetery. Screams of "Help, help! God save me!" coming from the direction of the tombs, aroused the neighborhood. The cries of the man frightened the dog, and he returned home in haste; the sheet, half torn, was removed, and Rolla again fastened in his house.

Very soon Mr. Martin was led in by two friends, who picked him up from the sidewalk, with his face considerably bruised. His story was, that "The devil had chased him out of the cemetery, tripped him up on the sidewalk, and hence the flow of blood from the wound on his face."

The above is a fair index to most of the ghost stories.

CHAPTER XIII.

Forty years ago, the escapes of slaves from the South, although numerous, were nevertheless difficult, owing to the large rewards offered for their apprehension, and the easy mode of extradition from the Northern States. Little or no difficulty was experienced in capturing and returning a slave from Ohio, Indiana, Illinois, or Pennsylvania, the four States through which the fugitives had to pass in their flight to Canada. The Quaker element in all of the above States showed itself in the furnishing of food to the flying-bondman, concealing him for days, and even weeks, and at last conveying him to a place of safety, or carrying him to the Queen's dominions.

Instinct seemed to tell the negro that a drab coat and a broad-brimmed hat covered a benevolent heart, and we have no record of his ever having been deceived. It is possible that the few Friends scattered over the slave States, and the fact that they were never known to own a slave, gave the blacks a favorable impression of this sect, before the victim of oppression left his sunny birth-place.

A brave and manly slave resolved to escape from Natchez, Miss. This slave, whose name was Jerome, was of pure African origin, was perfectly black, very fine-looking, tall, slim, and erect as any one could possibly be. His features were not bad, lips thin, nose prominent, hands and feet small. His brilliant black eyes lighted up his whole countenance. His hair, which was nearly straight, hung in curls upon his lofty brow. George Combe or Fowler would have selected his head for a model. He was brave and daring, strong in person, fiery in spirit, yet kind and true in his affections, earnest in whatever he undertook.

To reach the free States or Canada, by travelling by night and lying by during the day, from a State so far south as Mississippi, no one would think for a moment of attempting to escape. To remain in the city would be a suicidal step. The deep sound of the escape of steam from a boat, which was at that moment ascending the river, broke upon the ears of the slave. "If that boat is going up the river," said he, "why not I conceal myself on board, and try to escape?" He went at once to the steamboat landing, where the boat was just coming in. "Bound for Louisville," said the captain, to one who was making inquiries. As the passengers were rushing on board, Jerome followed them, and proceeding to where some of the hands were stowing away bales of goods, he took hold and aided them.

"Jump down into the hold, there, and help the men," said the mate to the fugitive, supposing that, like many persons, he was working his way up the river. Once in the hull, among the boxes, the slave concealed himself. Weary hours, and at last days, passed without either water or food with the hidden slave. More than once did he resolve to let his case be known; but the knowledge that he would be sent back to Natchez, kept him from doing so. At last, with his lips parched and fevered to a crisp, the poor man crawled out into the freight-room, and began wandering about. The hatches were on, and the room dark. There happened to be on board, a wedding-party; and a box, containing some of the bridal cake, with several bottles of port wine, was near Jerome. He found the box, opened it, and helped himself. In eight days, the boat tied up at the wharf at the place of her destination. It was late at night; the boat's crew, with the single exception of the man on watch, were on shore. The hatches were off, and the fugitive quietly made his way on dock and jumped on shore. The man saw the fugitive, but too late to seize him.

Still in a slave State, Jerome was at a loss to know how he should proceed. He had with him a few dollars, enough to pay his way to Canada, if he could find a conveyance. The fugitive procured such food as he wanted from one of the many eating-houses, and then, following the direction of the North Star, he passed out of the city, and took the road leading to Covington. Keeping near the Ohio River, Jerome soon found an opportunity to pass over into the State of Indiana. But liberty was a mere name in the latter State, and the fugitive learned, from some colored persons that he met, that it was not safe to travel by daylight. While making his way one night, with nothing to cheer him but the prospect of freedom in the future, he was pounced upon by three men who were lying in wait for another fugitive, an advertisement of whom they had received through the mail. In vain did Jerome tell them that he was not a slave. True, they had not caught the man they expected; but, if they could make this slave tell from what place he had escaped, they knew that a good price would be paid them for the slave's arrest.

Tortured by the slave-catchers, to make him reveal the name of his owner and the place from whence he had escaped, Jerome gave them a fictitious name in Virginia, and said that his master would give a large reward, and manifested a willingness to return to his "old boss."

By this misrepresentation, the fugitive hoped to have another chance of getting away.

Allured with the prospect of a large sum of the needful the slave-catchers started back with their victim. Stopping on the second night at an inn, on the banks of the Ohio River, the kidnappers, in lieu of a suitable place in which to confine their prize during the night, chained him to the bed-post of their sleeping chamber.

The white men were late in retiring to rest, after an evening spent in drinking. At dead of night, when all was still, the slave arose from the floor, upon which he had been lying, looked around and saw that Morpheus had possession of his captors. "For once," thought he, "the brandy bottle has done a noble work." With palpitating heart and trembling limbs, he viewed his position. The door was fast, but the warm weather had compelled them to leave the window open. If he could but get the chains off, he might escape through the window to the piazza. The sleepers' clothes hung upon chairs by the bedside. The slave thought of the padlock key, examined the pockets, and found it. The chains were soon off, and the negro stealthily making his way to the window. He stopped, and said to himself, "These men are villains, they are enemies to all who, like me, are trying to be free. Then why not teach them a lesson?" He then dressed himself in the best suit, hung his own worn-out and tattered garments on the same chair, and silently passed through the window to the piazza, and let himself down by one of the pillars, and started once more for Canada.

Daylight came upon him before he had selected a hiding-place for the day, and he was walking at a rapid rate, in hopes of soon reaching some woodland or forest. The sun had just begun to show itself, when Jerome was astonished at seeing behind him, in the distance, two men upon horseback. Taking a road to the right he saw before him a farmhouse, and so near was he to it that he observed two men in front of him looking at him. It was too late to turn back. The kidnappers were behind—strange men before. Those in the rear he knew to be enemies, while he had no idea of what principles were the farmers. The latter also saw the white men coming, and called to the fugitive to come that way.

The broad-brimmed hats that the farmers wore told the slaves that they were Quakers.

Jerome had seen some of these people passing up and down the river, when employed on a steamer between Natchez and New Orleans, and had heard that they disliked slavery. He, therefore, hastened toward the drab-coated men, who, on his approach, opened the barn-door, and told him to "run in."

When Jerome entered the barn, the two farmers closed the door, remaining outside themselves, to confront the slave-catchers, who now came up and demanded admission, feeling that they had their prey secure.

"Thee can't enter my premises," said one of the Friends, in rather a musical voice.

The negro-catchers urged their claim to the slave, and intimated that, unless they were allowed to secure him, they would force their way in. By this time, several other Quakers had gathered around the barn-door. Unfortunately for the kidnappers, and most fortunately for the fugitive, the Friends had just been holding a quarterly meeting in the neighborhood, and a number of them had not yet returned to their homes.

After some talk, the men in drab promised to admit the hunters, provided they procured an officer and a search-warrant from a justice of the peace. One of the slave-catchers was left to see that the fugitive did not get away, while the other went in pursuit of an officer. In the mean time, the owner of the barn sent for a hammer and nails, and began nailing up the barn-door.

After an hour in search of the man of the law, they returned with an officer and a warrant. The Quaker demanded to see the paper, and, after looking at it for some time, called to his son to go into the house for his glasses. It was a long time before Aunt Ruth found the leather case, and when she did, the glasses wanted wiping before they could be used. After comfortably adjusting them on his nose, he read the warrant over leisurely.

"Come, Mr. Dugdale, we can't wait all day," said the officer.

"Well, will thee read it for me?" returned the Quaker.

The officer complied, and the man in drab said,—

"Yes, thee may go in, now. I am inclined to throw no obstacles in the way of the execution of the law of the land."

On approaching the door, the men found some forty or fifty nails in it, in the way of their progress.

"Lend me your hammer and a chisel, if you please, Mr. Dugdale," said the officer.

"Please read that paper over again, will thee?" asked the Quaker.

The officer once more read the warrant.

"I see nothing there which says I must furnish thee with tools to open my door. If thee wants a hammer, thee must go elsewhere for it; I tell thee plainly, thee can't have mine."

The implements for opening the door are at length obtained, and, after another half hour, the slave-catchers are in the barn. Three hours is a long time for a slave to be in the hands of Quakers. The hay is turned over, and the barn is visited in every part; but still the runaway is not found. Uncle Joseph has a glow upon his countenance; Ephraim shakes his head knowingly; little Elijah is a perfect know-nothing, and if you look toward the house you will see Aunt Ruth's smiling face ready to announce that breakfast is ready.

"The nigger is not in this barn," said the officer.

"I know he is not," quietly remarked the Quaker.

"What were you nailing up your door for, then, as if you were afraid we would enter?" inquired one of the kidnappers.

"I can do what I please with my own door, can't I?" said the Friend.

The secret was out; the fugitive had gone in at the front door, and out at the back; and the reading of the warrant, nailing up of the door, and other preliminaries of the Quaker, was to give the fugitive time and opportunity to escape.

It was now late in the morning, and the slave-catchers were a long way from home, and the horses were jaded by the rapid manner in which they had travelled. The Friends, in high glee, returned to the house for breakfast; the officer and the kidnappers made a thorough examination of the barn and premises, and satisfied that Jerome had gone into the barn, but had not come out, and equally satisfied that he was out of their reach, the owner said, "He's gone down into the earth, and has taken an underground railroad."

And thus was christened that famous highway over which so many of the oppressed sons and daughters of African descent were destined to travel, and an account of which has been published by one of its most faithful agents, Mr. William Still, of Philadelphia.

At a later period, Cato, servant of Dr. Gaines, was sold to Captain Enoch Price, of St. Louis. The Captain took his slave with him on board the steamer *Chester*, just about sailing for New Orleans. At the latter place, the boat obtained a cargo for Cincinnati, Ohio. The master, aware that the slave might give him the slip, while in a free State, determined to leave the chattel at Louisville, Ky., till his downward return. However, Mrs. Price, anxious to have the servant's services on the boat, questioned him with regard to the contemplated visit to Cincinnati.

"I don't want to go to a free State," said Cato; "fer I knowed a servant dat went up dar, once, an' dey kept beggin' him to run away; so I druther not go dar; kase I is satisfied wid my marser, an' don't want to go off, whar I'd have to take keer of mysef."

This was said in such an earnest and off-hand manner, that it removed all of the lady's suspicions in regard to his attempting to escape; and she urged her husband to take him to Ohio.

Cato wanted his freedom, but he well knew that if he expressed a wish to go to a free State, he would never be permitted to do so. In due season, the *Chester* arrived at Cincinnati, where she remained four days, discharging her cargo, and reloading for the return trip. During the time, Cato remained at his post, attending faithfully to his duties; no one dreaming that he had the slightest idea of leaving the boat. However, on the day previous to the *Chester's* leaving Cincinnati, Cato divulged the question to Charley, another slave, whom he wished to accompany him.

Charley heard the proposition with surprise; and although he wanted his freedom, his timid disposition would not allow him to make the trial.

"My master is a pretty good man, and treats me comparatively well; and should I be caught and taken back, he would no doubt sell me to a cotton or sugar-planter," said Charley to Cato's invitation. "But," continued he, "Captain Price is a mean man; I shall not blame you, Cato, for running away and leaving him. By the by, I am engaged to go to a surprise-party, to-night, and I reckon we'll have a good time. I've got a new pair of pumps to dance in, and I've got Jim, the cook, to bake me a pie, and I'll have some sandwiches, and I'm going with a pretty gal."

"So you won't go away with me, to-night?" said Cato to Charley.

"No," was the reply.

"It is true," remarked Cato, "your marser is better man, an' treats you a heap better den Captain Price does me, but, den, he may get to gambling, an' get broke, and den he'll have to sell you."

"I know that," replied Charley; "none of us are safe as long as we are slaves."

It was seven o'clock at night, Cato was in the pantry, washing the supper dishes, and contemplating his flight, the beginning of which was soon to take place. Charley had gone up to the steward's hall, to get ready for the surprise, and had been away some time, which caused uneasiness to Cato, and he determined to go up into the cabin, and see that everything was right. Entering the cabin from the Social Hall, Cato, in going down and passing the Captain's room, heard a conversation which attracted his attention, and caused him to halt at his master's room door.

He was not long, although the conversation was in a low tone, in learning that the parties were his master and his fellow-servant Charley.

"And so he is going to run away, to-night, is he?" said the Captain.

"Yes, sir," replied Charley; "he's been trying to get me to go with him, and I thought it my duty to tell you."

"Very well; I'll take him over to Covington, Ky., put him in jail, for the night, and when I get back to New Orleans, I will sell the ungrateful nigger. Where is he now?" asked the Captain.

"Cato is in the pantry, sir, washing up the tea things," was the reply.

The moving of the chairs in the room, and what he had last heard, satisfied Cato that the talk between his master and the treacherous Charley was at an end, and he at once returned to the pantry undetermined what course to pursue. He had not long been there, ere he heard the well-known squeak of the Captain's boots coming down the stairs. Just then Dick, the cook's boy, came out of the kitchen and threw a pan full of cold meat overboard. This incident seemed to furnish Cato with words, and he at once took advantage of the situation.

"What is dat you throw overboard dar?"

"None your business," replied Dick, as he slammed the door behind him and returned to the kitchen.

"You free niggers will waste everything dar is on dis boat," continued Cato. "It's my duty to watch dees niggers an' see dat dey don't destroy marser's property. Now, let me see, I'll go right off an' tell marser 'bout Charley, I won't keep his secrets any longer." And here Cato threw aside his dish towel and started for the cabin.

Captain Price, who, during Cato's soliloquy, was hid behind a large box of goods, returned in haste to his room, where he was soon joined by his dutiful servant.

In answer to the rap on the door, the Captain said "Come in."

Cato, with downcast look, and in an obsequious manner, entered the room, and said, "Marser, I is come to tell you somethin' dat hangs heavy on my mine, somethin' dat I had ought to tole you afore dis."

"Well," said the master, "what is it, Cato?"

"Now, marser, you hires Charley, don't you?"

"Yes."

"Well, den, ser, ef Charley runs away you'll have to pay fer him, won't you?"

"I think it very probable, as I brought him into a free State, and thereby giving him an opportunity to escape. Why, is he thinking of running away?"

"Yes, ser," answered Cato, "he's gwine to start to-night, an' he's bin pesterin' me all day to go wid him."

"Do you mean to say that Charley has been trying to persuade you to run away from me?" asked the Captain, rather sharply.

"Yes, ser, dats jess what he's bin a doin' all day. I axed him whar he's gwine to, an' he sed he's gwine to Canada, an' he call you some mighty mean names, an' dat made me mad."

"Why, Charley has just been here telling me that you were going to run away to-night."

[W]ith apparent surprise, and opening his large eyes, Cato exclaimed, "Well, well, well, ef dat nigger don't beat de debble!" And here the negro raised his hands, and looking upward said, "Afoe God, marser, I would'nt leave you for dis worl'. Now, ser, jess let me tell you how you can find out who tells de trufe. Charley has got ebry ting ready an' is a gwine right off. He's got two pies, some sweetcake, some sandwiches, bread an' butter, an' he's got a pair of pumps to dance in when he gets to Canada. An' ef you want to kotch him in de ack of runnin' away, you jess wait out on de dock an' you'll kotch him."

This was said in such an earnest manner, and with such protestations of innocence, that Captain Price determined to follow Cato's advice and watch for Charley.

"Go see if you can find where Charley is, and come back and let me know," said the Captain.

Away went Cato, on his tip-toes, in the direction of the steward's room, where, by looking through the key-hole, he saw the treacherous fellow-servant getting ready for the surprise party that he had engaged the night previous to attend.

Cato returned almost breathless, and in a whisper said, "I foun' him ser, he's gittin' ready to start. He's got a bundle of provisions tied up all ready, ser; you'll be shur to kotch him as he's gwine away, ef you go on de dock."

Throwing his camlet cloak over his shoulders, the Captain passed out upon the wharf, took a position behind a pile of wood, and awaited the coming of the negro; nor did he remain long in suspense.

With lighted cigar, dressed in his best apparel, and his eatables tied up in a towel, Charley was soon seen hastily leaving the boat.

Stepping out from his hiding-place, the Captain seized the negro by the collar and led him back to the steamer, exclaiming, "Where are you going, what's that you've got in that bundle?"

"Only some washin' I is takin' out to get done," replied the surprised and frightened negro.

As they reached the lighted deck, "Open that bundle," said the Captain.

Charley began to obey the command, and at [the] same time to give an explanation.

"Shut your mouth, you scoundrel," vociferously shouted the Captain.

As the man slowly undid the parcel, and the contents began to be seen, "There," said the Captain, "there's the pies, cake, sandwiches, bread and butter that Cato told me you had put up to eat while running away. Yes, there's the pumps, too, that you got to dance in when you reached Canada."

Here the frightened Charley attempted again to explain, "I was jess gwine to—"

"Shut your mouth, you villain; you were going to escape to Canada."

"No, Marser Price, afoe God I was only—"

"Shut your mouth, you black rascal; you told me you were taking some clothes to be washed, you lying scamp."

During this scene, Cato was inside the pantry, with the door ajar, looking out upon his master and Charley with unfeigned satisfaction.

Still holding the negro by the collar, and leading him to the opposite side of the boat, the Captain called to Mr. Roberts, the second mate, to bring up the small boat to take him and the "runaway" over the river.

A few moments more, and the Captain, with Charley seated by his side, was being rowed to Covington, where the negro was safely locked up for the night.

"A little longer," said the Captain to the second officer, as he returned to the boat, "a little longer and I'd a lost fifteen hundred dollars by that boy's running away."

"Indeed," responded the officer.

"Yes," continued the Commander, "my servant Cato told me, just in time to catch the rascal in the very act of running off."

One of the sailors who was rowing, and who had been attentively listening to the Captain, said, "I overheard Cato to-day, trying to persuade Charley to go somewhere with him to-night, and the latter said he was going to a 'surprise party.'"

"The devil you did," exclaimed the Captain. "Hasten up there," continued he, "for these niggers are a slippery set."

[A]s the yawl came alongside of the steamer, Captain Price leaped on deck and went directly in search of Cato, who could nowhere be found. And even Charley's bundle, which he left where he had been opening it, was gone. All search for the tricky man was in vain.

On the following morning, Charley was brought back to the boat, saying, as they were crossing the river, "I tole de boss dat Cato was gwine to run away, but he did'nt bleve me. Now he sees Cato's gone."

After the Captain had learned all that he could from Charley, the latter's account of his imprisonment in the lock-up caused great merriment amongst the boat's crew.

"But I tell you dar was de biggest rats in dat jail, eber I seed in my life. Dey run aroun' dar an' make so much fuss dat I was 'fraid to set down or lay down. I had to stan' up all night."

The *Chester* was detained until in the latter part of the day, during which time every effort was made to hunt up Cato, but without success.

When upbraided by the black servants on the boat for his treachery to Cato, Charley's only plea was, "I 'speck it was de debble dat made me do it."

Dressing himself in his warmest and best clothes, and getting some provisions that he had prepared during the day, and also taking with him Charley's pies, cakes, sandwiches, and pumps, Cato left the boat and made good his escape before his master returned from Covington.

It was during the cold winter of 1834, that the fugitive travelled by night and laid by in the woods in the day. After a week's journey, his food gave out, and then came the severest of his trials, cold coupled with hunger.

Often Cato would resolve to go to some of the farm-houses and apply for food and shelter, but the fear of being captured and again returned prevented him from following his inclinations. One night a pelting rain that froze as fast as it fell, drove the fugitive into a barn, where, creeping under the hay, he remained, sleeping sweetly while his garments were drying upon his person.

Sounds of the voices of the farmer and his men feeding the cattle and doing the chores, awakened the man from his slumbers, who, seeing that it was daylight, feared he would be arrested. However, the day passed, and the fugitive coming out at night-fall started once more on his weary journey, taking for his guide the North Star, and after travelling the entire night, he again lay by, but this time in the forest.

Three days of fasting had now forced hunger upon Cato, so that he once more determined to seek food. Waiting till night, he came upon the highway, and soon approached a farmhouse, of the olden style, built of logs. The sweet savor of the supper attracted the hungry man's attention as he neared the dwelling. For once there was no dog to herald his coming, and he had an opportunity of viewing the interior of the house, through the apertures that a log cabin generally presents.

As the fugitive stood with one eye gazing through the *crack*, looking at the table, already set, and snuffing in the delicious odor from a boiling pot, he heard the mother say,—"Take off the chicken, Sally Ann, I guess the dumplings are done. Your father will be home in half an hour; if he should catch that nigger and bring him along, we'll feed him on the cold meat and potatoes."

With palpitating heart, Cato listened to the last sentences that fell from the woman's lips. Who could the "nigger" be, thought he.

Finding only the woman and her daughter in the house, the black man had been debating in his own mind whether or not to go in and demand a part of the contents of the kettle. However, the talk about "catching a nigger," settled the question at once with him.

Seizing a sheet that hung upon the clothes-line, Cato covered himself with it; leaving open only enough to enable him to see, he rushed in, crying at the top of his voice,—"Come to judgment! Come to judgment."

Both women sprang from their seats, and, screaming, passed out of the room, upsetting the table as they went. Cato seized the pot of chicken with one hand, and a loaf of bread, that had fallen from the table, with the other; hastily leaving the house and taking to the road, he continued on his journey.

The fugitive, however, had gone but a short distance when he heard the tramp of horses and the voices of men; and, fearing to meet them, he took to the woods till they had passed by.

As he hid behind a large tree by the roadside, Cato heard distinctly:

"And what is your master's name?"

"Peter Johnson, ser," was the reply.

"How much do you think he will give to have you brought back?"

"Dunno, ser," responded a voice which Cato recognized by the language to be a negro.

It was evident that a fugitive slave had been captured, and was about to be returned for the reward. And it was equally evident to Cato that the slave had been caught by the owner of the pot of stewed chicken that he then held in his hand, and he felt a thrill of gladness as he returned to the road and pursued his journey.

Travel Writings

Brown published his travel letters, Three Years in Europe; or, Places I Have Seen and People I Have Met, *in London in 1852 and republished these letters under a separate title,* The American Fugitive in Europe: Sketches of Places and People Abroad, *in America in 1855 with a few additional notes. Both editions include versions of his Narrative, entitled "Memoirs of the Author." The British edition includes a final chapter on slavery in America that is excluded from the American edition. The American edition also includes a copy of an 1850 speech, "An Address Presented to Mr. William Wells Brown, the Fugitive Slave from America, by the Ladies of Bolton, March 22nd, 1850."*

This collection includes the preface and excerpts from the British edition, including the final chapter on American slavery, as well as the additional chapters, notes, and speech added to the American edition. Brown's preface to the British edition indicates that the letters were written to an American audience and alludes to their prior publication in Frederick Douglass's paper. Indeed, excerpts and summaries of many of Brown's letters from England were published in Douglass's paper. However, read together in full, these letters situate Brown in the larger body of travel writing that was so popular at the time. Brown seems careful, in fact, to mimic the patterns of white American travel writers, paying careful attention to the great halls he is visiting. However, Brown's letters are punctuated with reflections, even self-consciousness, on his experiences specifically as a black traveler.

From *Three Years in Europe; or, Places I Have Seen and People I Have Met*

(London: Charles Gilpin, 1852)

PREFACE.

While I feel conscious that most of the contents of these Letters will be interesting chiefly to American readers, yet I may indulge the hope, that the fact of their being the first production of a Fugitive Slave, as a history of travels, may carry with them novelty enough to secure for them, to some extent, the attention of the reading public of Great Britain. Most of the letters were written for the private perusal of a few personal friends in America; some were contributed to "Frederick Douglass's paper," a journal published in the United States. In a printed circular sent some weeks since to some of my friends, asking subscriptions to this volume, I stated the reasons for its publication: these need not be repeated here. To those who so promptly and kindly responded to that appeal, I tender my most sincere thanks. It is with no little diffidence that I lay these letters before the public; for I am not blind to the fact, that they must contain many errors; and to those who shall find fault with them on that account, it may not be too much for me to ask them kindly to remember, that the author was a slave in one of the Southern States of America, until he had attained the age of twenty years; and that the education he has acquired, was by his own exertions, he never having had a day's schooling in his life.

W. WELLS BROWN.

22, CECIL STREET, STRAND,
LONDON.

LETTER I.

Departure from Boston—the Passengers—Halifax—the Passage—
First Sight of Land—Liverpool.

LIVERPOOL, *July* 28.

On the 18th July, 1849, I took passage in the steam-ship *Canada*, Captain
Judkins, bound for Liverpool. The day was a warm one; so much so, that
many persons on board, as well as several on shore, stood with their
umbrellas up, so intense was the heat of the sun. The ringing of the ship's
bell was a signal for us to shake hands with our friends, which we did, and
then stepped on the deck of the noble craft. The *Canada* quitted her
moorings at half-past twelve, and we were soon in motion. As we were
passing out of Boston Bay, I took my stand on the quarter-deck, to take a
last farewell (at least for a time), of my native land. A visit to the old
world, up to that time had seemed but a dream. As I looked back upon the
receding land, recollections of the past rushed through my mind in quick
succession. From the treatment that I had received from the Americans as
a victim of slavery, and the knowledge that I was at that time liable to be
seized and again reduced to whips and chains, I had supposed that I would
leave the country without any regret; but in this I was mistaken, for when
I saw the last thread of communication cut off between me and the land,
and the dim shores dying away in the distance, I almost regretted that I
was not on shore.

An anticipated trip to a foreign country appears pleasant when talking
about it, especially when surrounded by friends whom we love; but when
we have left them all behind, it does not seem so pleasant. Whatever may
be the fault of the government under which we live, and no matter how
oppressive her laws may appear, yet we leave our native land (if such it be)
with feelings akin to sorrow. With the steamer's powerful engine at work,
and with a fair wind, we were speedily on the bosom of the Atlantic,
which was as calm and as smooth as our own Hudson in its calmest aspect.
We had on board above one hundred passengers, forty of whom were the
"Vienneise children"—a troop of dancers. The passengers represented several different nations, English, French, Spaniards, Africans, and
Americans. One man who had the longest pair of mustaches that mortal
man was ever doomed to wear, especially attracted my attention. He
appeared to belong to no country in particular, but was yet the busiest man
on board. After viewing for some time the many strange faces around me,
I descended to the cabin to look after my luggage, which had been put
hurriedly on board. I hope that all who take a trip of so great a distance

may be as fortunate as I was, in being supplied with books to read on the voyage. My friends had furnished me with literature, from "Macaulay's History of England" to "Jane Eyre," so that I did not want for books to occupy my time.

A pleasant passage of about thirty hours, brought us to Halifax, at six o'clock in the evening. In company with my friend the President of the Oberlin Institute, I took a stroll through the town; and from what little I saw of the people in the streets, I am sure that the taking of the Temperance pledge would do them no injury. Our stay at Halifax was short. Having taken in a few sacks of coals, the mails, and a limited number of passengers, we were again out, and soon at sea. After a pleasant run of seven days more, and as I was lying in my bed, I heard the cry of "Land a-head." Although oar passage had been unprecedentedly short, yet I need not inform you that this news was hailed with joy by all on board. For my own part, I was soon on deck. Away in the distance, and on our larboard quarter, were the grey hills of Ireland. Yes! we were in sight of the land of Emmitt and O'Connell. While I rejoiced with the other passengers at the sight of land, and the near approach to the end of the voyage, I felt low spirited, because it reminded me of the great distance I was from home. But the experience of above twenty years' travelling, had prepared me to undergo what most persons must lay their account with, in visiting a strange country. This was the last day but one that we were to be on board; and as if moved by the sight of land, all seemed to be gathering their different things together—brushing up their old clothes and putting on their new ones, as if this would bring them any sooner to the end of their journey.

The last night on board was the most pleasant, apparently, that we had experienced; probably, because it was the last. The moon was in her meridian splendour, pouring her broad light over the calm sea; while near to us, on our starboard side, was a ship with her snow-white sails spread aloft, and stealing through the water like a thing of life. What can present a more picturesque view, than two vessels at sea on a moonlight night, and within a few rods of each other? With a gentle breeze, and the powerful engine at work, we seemed to be flying to the embrace of our British neighbours.

The next morning I was up before the sun, and found that we were within a few miles of Liverpool. The taking of a pilot on board at eleven o'clock, warned us to prepare to quit our ocean palace and seek other quarters. At a little past three o'clock, the ship cast anchor, and we were all tumbled, bag and baggage, into a small steamer, and in a few moments were at the door of the Custom-House. The passage had only been nine days and twenty-two hours, the quickest on record at that time, yet it was long enough. I waited nearly three hours before my name was called, and when it was, I unlocked my trunks and handed them over to one of the officers, whose dirty hands made no improvement on the work of the laundress. First one article was taken out, and then another, till an *Iron Collar* that had been worn by a female slave on the banks of the Mississippi, was hauled out, and this democratic instrument of torture became the centre of attraction; so much so, that instead of going on with the examination, all hands stopped to look at the "Negro Collar."

Several of my countrymen who were standing by, were not a little displeased at answers which I gave to questions on the subject of Slavery; but they held their peace. The interest created by the appearance of the Iron Collar, closed the examination of my luggage. As if afraid that they would find something more hideous, they put the Custom-House mark on each piece, and passed them out, and I was soon comfortably installed at Brown's Temperance Hotel, Clayton Square.

No person of my complexion can visit this country without being struck with the marked difference between the English and the Americans. The prejudice which I have experienced on all and every occasion in the United States, and to some extent on board the *Canada*, vanished as soon as I set foot on the soil of Britain. In America I had been bought and sold as a slave, in the Southern States. In the so-called free States, I had been treated as one born to occupy an inferior position,—in steamers, compelled to take my fare on the deck; in hotels, to take my meals in the kitchen; in coaches, to ride on the outside; in railways, to ride in the "negro car;" and in churches, to sit in the "negro pew." But no sooner was I on British soil, than I was recognised as a man, and an equal. The very dogs in the streets appeared conscious of my manhood. Such is the difference, and such is the change that is brought about by a trip of nine days in an Atlantic steamer.

I was not more struck with the treatment of the people, than with the appearance of the great seaport of the world. The grey appearance of the stone piers and docks, the dark look of the magnificent warehouses, the substantial appearance of every thing around, causes one to think himself in a new world instead of the old. Every thing in Liverpool looks old, yet nothing is worn out. The beautiful villages on the opposite side of the river, in the vicinity of Birkenhead, together with the countless number of vessels in the river, and the great ships to be seen in the stream, give life and animation to the whole scene.

Every thing in and about Liverpool seems to be built for the future as well as the present. We had time to examine but few of the public buildings, the first of which was the Custom-House, an edifice that would be an ornament to any city in the world.

For the first time in my life, I can say "I am truly free." My old master may make his appearance here, with the Constitution of the United States in his pocket, the Fugitive Slave Law in one hand and the chains in the other, and claim me as his property, but all will avail him nothing. I can here stand and look the tyrant in the face, and tell him that I am his equal! England is, indeed, the "land of the free, and the home of the brave."

LETTER XII.

Kirkstall Abbey—Mary the Maid of the Inn—Newstead Abbey: Residence of Lord Byron—Parish Church of Hucknall—Burial Place of Lord Byron—Bristol: "Cook's Folly"—Chepstow Castle and Abbey—Tintern Abbey—Redcliffe Church.

January 29.

In passing through Yorkshire, we could not resist the temptation it offered, to pay a visit to the extensive and interesting ruin of Kirkstall Abbey, which lies embosomed in a beautiful recess of Airedale, about three miles from Leeds. A pleasant drive over a smooth road, brought us abruptly in sight of the Abbey. The tranquil and pensive beauty of the desolate Monastery, as it reposes in the lap of pastoral luxuriance, and amidst the touching associations of seven centuries, is almost beyond description when viewed from where we first beheld it. After arriving at its base, we stood for some moments under the mighty arches that lead into the great hall, gazing at its old grey walls frowning with age. At the distance of a small field, the Aire is seen gliding past the foot of the lawn on which the ruin stands, after it has left those precincts, sparkling over a weir with a pleasing murmur. We could fully enter into the feelings of the Poet when he says:—

> "Beautiful fabric! even in decay
> And desolation, beauty still is thine;
> As the rich sunset of an autumn day,
> When gorgeous clouds in glorious hues combine
> To render homage to its slow decline,
> Is more majestic in its parting hour:
> Even so thy mouldering, venerable shrine
> Possesses now a more subduing power,
> Than in thine earlier sway, with pomp and pride thy dower."

The tale of "Mary, the Maid of the Inn," is supposed, and not without foundation, to be connected with this Abbey. "Hark to Rover," the name of the house where the key is kept, was, a century ago, a retired inn or pot-house, and the haunt of many a desperate highwayman and poacher. The anecdote is so well known, that it is scarcely necessary to relate it. It, however, is briefly this:—

"One stormy night, as two travellers sat at the inn, each having exhausted his news, the conversation was directed to the Abbey, the boisterous night, and Mary's heroism; when a bet was at last made by one of them, that she would not go and bring back from the nave a slip of the alder-tree growing there. Mary, however, did go; but having nearly reached the tree, she heard a low, indistinct dialogue; at the same time, something black fell and rolled towards her, which afterwards proved to be a hat. Directing her attention to the place whence the conversation proceeded, she saw, from behind a pillar, two men carrying a murdered body: they passed near the place where she stood, a heavy cloud was swept from off the face of the moon, and Mary fell senseless—one of the murderers was her intended husband! She was awakened from her swoon, but—her reason had fled for ever." Mr. Southey wrote a beautiful poem founded on this story, which will be found in his published works. We spent nearly three hours in wandering through these splendid ruins. It is both curious and interesting to trace the early history of these old piles, which become the resort of thousands, nine-tenths of whom are unaware either of the classic ground on which they tread, or of the peculiar interest thrown around the spot by the deeds of remote ages.

During our stay in Leeds, we had the good fortune to become acquainted with Wilson Armistead, Esq. This gentleman is well known as an able writer against Slavery. His most elaborate work is "A Tribute for the Negro." This is a volume of 560 pages, and is replete with facts refuting the charges of inferiority brought against the Negro race. Few English gentlemen have done more to hasten the day of the American slave's liberation, than Wilson Armistead.

We have just paid a visit to Newstead Abbey, the far-famed residence of Lord Byron. I posted from Hucknall over to Newstead one pleasant morning, and, being provided with a letter of introduction to Colonel Wildman, I lost no time in presenting myself at the door of the Abbey. But, unfortunately for me, the Colonel was at Mansfield, in attendance at the Assizes—he being one of the County Magistrates. I did not however lose the object of my visit, as every attention was paid in showing me about the premises. I felt as every one must, who gazes for the first time upon these walls, and remembers that it was here, even amid the comparative ruins of a building once dedicated to the sacred cause of Religion and her twin sister, Charity, that the genius of Byron was first developed. Here

that he paced with youthful melancholy the halls of his illustrious ancestors, and trode the walks of the long-banished monks. The housekeeper—
a remarkably good looking and polite woman—showed us through the
different apartments, and explained in the most minute manner every
object of interest connected with the interior of the building. We first visited the Monks' Parlour, which seemed to contain nothing of note, except
a very fine stained window—one of the figures representing St. Paul, surmounted by a cross. We passed through Lord Byron's Bedroom, the
Haunted Chamber, the Library, and the Eastern Corridor, and halted in
the Tapestry Bedroom, which is truly a magnificent apartment, formed by
the Byrons for the use of King Charles II. The ceiling is richly decorated
with the Byron arms. We next visited the grand Drawing-room, probably
the finest in the building. This saloon contains a large number of splendid
portraits, among which is the celebrated portrait of Lord Byron, by
Phillips. In this room we took into our hand the Skull-cup, of which so
much has been written, and that has on it a short inscription, commencing
with—"Start not—nor deem my spirit fled." Leaving this noble room, we
descended by a few polished oak steps into the West Corridor, from which
we entered the grand Dining Hall, and through several other rooms, until
we reached the Chapel. Here we were shown a stone coffin which had
been found near the high altar, when the workmen were excavating the
vault, intended by Lord Byron for himself and his dog. The coffin contained the skeleton of an Abbot, and also the identical skull from which
the cup, of which I have made mention, was made. We then left the building, and took a stroll through the grounds. After passing a pond of cold
crystal water, we came to a dark wood in which are two leaden statues of
Pan, and a female satyr—very fine specimens as works of art. We here
inspected the tree whereon Byron carved his own name and that of his sister, with the date, all of which are still legible. However, the tree is now
dead, and we were informed that Colonel Wildman intended to have it
cut down so as to preserve the part containing the inscription. After crossing an interesting and picturesque part of the gardens, we arrived within
the precincts of the ancient Chapel, near which we observed a neat marble
monument, and which we supposed to have been erected to the memory
of some of the Byrons; but, on drawing near to it, we read the following
inscription:—

"Near this spot
are deposited the remains of one
who possessed beauty without vanity,
strength without insolence,

courage without ferocity,
and all the virtues of man without his vices.
This praise, which would be unmeaning flattery,
if inscribed over human ashes,
is but a just tribute to the memory of
BOATSWAIN, a dog,
Who was born at Newfoundland, May, 1803,
and died at Newstead Abbey, November 18, 1808.["]

By a will which his Lordship executed in 1811, he directed that his own body should be buried in a vault in the garden, near his faithful dog. This feeling of affection to his dumb and faithful follower, commendable in itself, seems here to have been carried beyond the bounds of reason and propriety.

In another part of the grounds we saw the oak tree planted by the poet himself. It has now attained a goodly size, considering the growth of the oak, and bids fair to become a lasting memento to the Noble Bard, and to be a shrine to which thousands of pilgrims will resort in future ages, to do homage to his mighty genius. This tree promises to share in after times the celebrity of Shakspere's mulberry, and Pope's willow. Near by, and in the tall trees, the rooks were keeping up a tremendous noise. After seeing everything of interest connected with the great poet, we entered our chaise, and left the premises. As we were leaving, I turned to take a farewell look at the Abbey, standing in solemn grandeur, the long ivy clinging fondly to the rich tracery of a former age. Proceeding to the little town of Hucknall, we entered the old grey Parish Church, which has for ages been the last resting-place of the Byrons, and where repose the ashes of the Poet, marked only by a neat marble slab, bearing the date of the poet's birth, death, and the fact that the tablet was placed there by his sister. This closed my visit to the interesting scenes associated with Byron's strange eventful history—scenes that ever acquire a growing charm as the lapse of years softens the errors of the man, and confirms the genius of the poet.

May 10.
It was on a lovely morning that I found myself on board the little steamer *Wye*, passing out of Bristol harbour. In going down the river, we saw on our right, the stupendous rocks of St. Vincent towering some four or five hundred feet above our heads. By the swiftness of our fairy steamer, we were soon abreast of Cook's Folly, a singular tower, built by a man from whom it takes its name, and of which the following romantic story is

told:—"Some years since a gentleman, of the name of Cook, erected this tower, which has since gone by the name of 'Cook's Folly.' A son having been born, he was desirous of ascertaining, by means of astrology, if he would live to enjoy his property. Being himself a firm believer, like the poet Dryden, that certain information might be obtained from the above science, he caused the child's horoscope to be drawn, and found, to his dismay, that in his third, sixteenth, or twenty-first year, he would be in danger of meeting with some fearful calamity or sudden death, to avert which he caused the turret to be constructed, and the child placed therein. Secure, as he vainly thought, there he lived, attended by a faithful servant, their food and fuel being conveyed to them by means of a pully-basket, until he was old enough to wait upon himself. On the eve of his twenty-first year, his parent's hopes rose high, and great were the rejoicings prepared to welcome the young heir to his home. But, alas! no human skill could avert the dark fate which clung to him. The last night he had to pass alone in the turret, a bundle of faggots was conveyed to him as usual, in which lay concealed a viper, which clung to his hand. The bite was fatal; and, instead of being borne in triumph, the dead body of his only son was the sad spectacle which met the sight of his father."

We crossed the channel and soon entered the mouth of that most picturesque of rivers, the Wye. As we neared the town of Chepstow the old Castle made its appearance, and a fine old ruin it is. Being previously provided with a letter of introduction to a gentleman in Chepstow, I lost no time in finding him out. This gentleman gave me a cordial reception, and did what Englishmen seldom ever do, lent me his saddle horse to ride to the Abbey. While lunch was in preparation I took a stroll through the Castle which stood near by. We entered the Castle through the great door-way and were soon treading the walls that had once sustained the cannon and the sentinel, but were now covered with weeds and wild flowers. The drum and fife had once been heard within these walls—the only music now is the cawing of the rook and daw. We paid a hasty visit to the various apartments, remaining longest in those of most interest. The room in which Martin the Regicide was imprisoned nearly twenty years, was pointed out to us. The Castle of Chepstow is still a magnificent pile, towering upon the brink of a stupendous cliff, on reaching the top of which, we had a splendid view of the surrounding country. Time, however, compelled us to retrace our steps, and after partaking of a lunch, we mounted a horse for the first time in ten years, and started for Tintern Abbey. The distance from Chepstow to the Abbey is about five miles, and the road lies along the banks of the river. The river is walled in on either side by hills of much beauty, clothed from base to summit with the richest verdure. I can conceive of nothing more striking than the first appearance of the Abbey. As we rounded a hill, all at once we saw the old ruin standing before us in all its splendour. This celebrated ecclesiastical relic of the olden time is doubtless the finest ruin of its kind in Europe. Embosomed amongst hills, and situated on the banks of the most fairy-like river in the world, its beauty can scarcely be surpassed. We halted at the "Beaufort Arms," left our horse, and sallied forth to view the Abbey. The sun was pouring a flood of light upon the old grey walls, lighting up its dark recesses, as if to give us a better opportunity of viewing it. I gazed with astonishment and admiration at its many beauties, and especially at the superb gothic windows over the entrance door. The beautiful gothic pillars, with here and there a representation of a praying priest, and mailed knights, with saints and Christian martyrs, and the hundreds of Scriptural representations, all indicate that this was a place of considerable importance in its palmy days. The once stone floor had disappeared, and we found ourselves standing on a floor of unbroken green grass, swelling back to the old walls, and looking so verdant and silken that it seemed the very floor of fancy. There are more romantic and wilder places than this in the world, but none more beautiful. The preservation of these old abbeys should claim the attention of those under whose charge they are, and we felt like joining with the poet and saying—

["]O ye who dwell
Around yon ruins, guard the precious charge
From hands profane! O save the sacred pile—
O'er which the wing of centuries has flown
Darkly and silently, deep-shadowing all
Its pristine honours—from the ruthless grasp
Of future violation."

In contemplating these ruins more closely, the mind insensibly reverts to the period of feudal and regal oppression, when structures like that of Tintern Abbey necessarily became the scenes of stirring and highly-important events. How altered is the scene! Where were formerly magnificence and splendour; the glittering array of priestly prowess; the crowded halls of haughty bigots, and the prison of religious offenders; there is now but a heap of mouldering ruins. The oppressed and the oppressor have long since lain down together in the peaceful grave. The ruin, generally speaking, is unusually perfect, and the sculpture still beautifully sharp. The outward walls are nearly entire, and are thickly clad with ivy. Many of the windows are also in a good state of preservation; but the roof has long since fallen in. The feathered songsters were fluttering about, and pouring forth their artless lays as a tribute of joy; while the lowing of the herds, the bleating of flocks, and the hum of bees upon the farm near by, all burst upon the ear, and gave the scene a picturesque sublimity that can be easier imagined than described. Most assuredly Shakspere had such ruins in view when he exclaimed—

> "The cloud-capp'd towers, the gorgeous palaces,
> The solemn temples, the great globe itself,
> Yea, all which it inherit, shall dissolve—
> And, like the baseless fabric of a vision,
> Leave not a wreck behind."

In the afternoon we returned to Bristol, and I spent the greater part of the next day in examining the interior of Redcliffe Church. Few places in the West of England have greater claims upon the topographer and historian than the church of St. Mary's, Redcliffe. Its antiquity, the beauty of its architecture, and above all the interesting circumstances connected with its history, entitle it to peculiar notice. It is also associated with the enterprise of genius; for its name has been blended with the reputation of Rowley, of Canynge, and of Chatterton; and no lover of poetry and admirer of art can visit it without a degree of enthusiasm. And when the old building shall have mouldered into ruins, even these will be trodden with veneration as sacred to the recollection of genius of the highest order. Ascending a winding stair, we were shown into the Treasury Room. The room forms an irregular octagon, admitting light through narrow unglazed apertures upon the broken and scattered fragments of the famous Rowleian chests, that with the rubble and dust of centuries cover the floor. It is here creative fancy pictures forth the sad image of the spirit of the spot—the ardent boy, flushed and fed by hope, musing on the brilliant deception he had conceived—whose daring attempt has left his name unto the intellectual world as a marvel and a mystery.

That a boy under twelve years of age should write a series of poems, imitating the style of the fifteenth century, and palm these poems off upon the world as the work of a monk, is indeed strange; and that these should become the object of interesting contemplation to the literary world, and should awaken inquiries, and exercise the talents of a Southey, a Bryant, a Miller, a Mathias, and others, savours more of romance than reality. I had visited the room in a garret in High Holborn, where this poor boy died. I had stood over a grave in the burial-ground of the Lane Workhouse, which was pointed out to me as the last resting-place of Chatterton; and now I was in the room where it was alleged he obtained the manuscripts that gave him such notoriety. We descended and viewed other portions of the church. The effect of the chancel, as seen behind the pictures, is very singular, and suggestive of many swelling thoughts. We look at the great east window, it is unadorned with its wonted painted glass; we look at the altar-screen beneath, on which the light of day again falls, and behold the injuries it has received at the hands of time. There is a dreary mournfulness in the scene which fastens on the mind, and is in unison with the time-worn mouldering fragments that are seen all around us. And this dreariness is not removed by our tracing the destiny of man on the storied pavements or on the graven brass, that still bears upon its surface the names of those who obtained the world's regard years back. This old pile is not only an ornament to the city, but it stands a living monument to the genius of its founder. Bristol has long sustained a high position as a place from which the American Abolitionists have received substantial encouragement in their arduous labours for the emancipation of the slaves of that land; and the writer of this received the best evidence that in this respect the character of the people had not been exaggerated, especially as regards the "Clifton Ladies' Anti-Slavery Society."

LETTER XXI.

The word Englishman is but another name for an American, and the word American is but another name for an Englishman—England is the father, America the son. They have a common origin and identity of language; they hold the same religions and political opinions; they study the same histories, and have the same literature. Steam and mechanical ingenuity have brought the two countries within nine days sailing of each other. The Englishman on landing at New-York finds his new neighbours speaking the same language which he last heard on leaving Liverpool, and he sees the American in the same dress that he had been accustomed to look upon at home, and soon forgets that he is three thousand miles from his native land, and in another country. The American on landing at Liverpool, and taking a walk through the great commercial city, finding no difficulty in understanding the people, supposes himself still in New-York; and if there seems any doubt in his own mind, growing out of the fact that the people have a more healthy look, seem more polite, and that the buildings have a more substantial appearance than those he had formerly looked upon, he has only to imagine, as did Rip Van Winkle, that he has been asleep these hundred years.

If the Englishman who has seen a Thompson silenced in Boston, or a Macready mobbed in New-York, upon the ground that they were foreigners, should sit in Exeter Hall and hear an American orator until he was hoarse, and wonder why the American is better treated in England than the Englishman in America, he has only to attribute it to John Bull's superior knowledge of good manners, and his being a more law-abiding man than brother Jonathan. England and America has each its reforms and its reformers, and they have more or less sympathy with each other. It has been said that one generation commences a reform in England, and that another generation finishes it. I would that so much could be said with regard to the great object of reform in America—the system of slavery!

No evil was ever more deeply rooted in a country than is slavery in the United States. Spread over the largest and most fertile States in the Union, with decidedly the best climate, and interwoven, as it is, with the religious, political, commercial, and social institutions of the country, it is scarcely possible to estimate its influence. This is the evil which claims the attention of American Reformers, over and above every other evil in the land, and thanks to a kind providence, the American slave is not without his advocates. The greatest enemy to the Anti-Slavery Society, and the most inveterate opposer of the men whose names stand at the head of the list as officers and agents of that association, will, we think, assign to William Lloyd Garrison, the first place in the ranks of the American Abolitionists. The first to proclaim the doctrine of immediate emancipation to the slaves of America, and on that account an object of hatred to the slave-holding interest of the country, and living for years with his life in danger, he is justly regarded by all, as the leader of the Anti-Slavery movement in the New World. Mr. Garrison is at the present time but little more than forty-five years of age, and of the middle size. He has a high and prominent forehead, well developed, with no hair on the top of the head, having lost it in early life; with a piercing eye, a pleasant, yet anxious countenance, and of a most loveable disposition; tender, and blameless in his family affections, devoted to his friends; simple and studious, upright, guileless, distinguished, and worthy, like the distinguished men of antiquity, to be immortalized by another Plutarch. How many services never to be forgotten, has he not rendered to the cause of the slave, and the welfare of mankind! As a speaker, he is forcible, clear, and logical, yet he will not rank with the many who are less known. As a writer, he is regarded as one of the finest in the United States, and certainly the most prominent in the Anti-Slavery cause. Had Mr. Garrison wished to serve himself, he might, with his great talents, long since, have been at the head of either of the great political parties. Few men can withstand the allurements of office, and the prize-money that accompanies them. Many of those who were with him fifteen years ago, have been swept down with the current of popular favour, either in Church or State. He has seen a Cox on the one hand, and a Stanton on the other, swept away like so much floating wood before the tide. When the sturdiest characters gave way, when the finest geniuses passed one after another under the yoke of slavery, Garrison stood firm to his convictions, like a rock that stands stirless amid the conflicting agitation of the waves. He is not only the friend and advocate of freedom with his pen and his tongue, but to the oppressed of every clime he opens his purse, his house, and his heart: yet he is not a man of money. The fugitive slave, fresh from the whips and chains, who is turned off by the politician, and experiences the cold shoulder of the divine, finds a bed and a breakfast under the hospitable roof of Mr. Lloyd Garrison.

The party of which he is the acknowledged head, is one of no inconsiderable influence in the United States. No man has more bitter enemies or stauncher friends than he. There are those among his friends who would stake their all upon his veracity and integrity; and we are sure that the coloured people throughout America, bond and free, in whose cause he has so long laboured, will, with one accord, assign the highest niche in their affection to the champion of universal emancipation. Every cause has its writers and its orators. We have drawn a hasty and imperfect sketch of the greatest writer in the Anti-Slavery field: we shall now call attention to the most distinguished public speaker. The name of Wendell Phillips is but another name for eloquence. Born in the highest possible position in America, Mr. Phillips has all the advantages that birth can give to one in that country. Educated at the first University, graduating with all the honours which the College could bestow on him, and studying the law and becoming a member of the bar, he has all the accomplishments that these advantages can give to a man of a great mind. Nature has treated him as a favourite. His stature is not tall, but handsome; his expressive countenance paints and reflects every emotion of his soul. His gestures are wonderfully graceful, like his delivery. There is a fascination in the soft gaze of his eyes, which none can but admire. Being a great reader, and endowed by nature with a good memory, he supplies himself with the most complicated dates and historical events. Nothing can equal the variety of his matter. I have heard him more than twenty different times on the same subject, but never heard the same speech. He is personal, but there is nothing offensive in his personalities. He extracts from a subject all that it contains, and does it as none but Wendell Phillips can. His voice is beautifully musical, and it is calculated to attract wherever it is heard. He is a man of calm intrepidity, of a patriotic and warm heart, with manners the most affable, temper the most gentle, a rectitude of principle entirely natural, a freedom from ambition, and a modesty quite singular. As Napoleon kept the Old Guard in reserve, to turn the tide in battle, so do the Abolitionists keep Mr. Phillips in reserve when opposition is expected in their great gatherings. We have soon the meetings turned into a bedlam, by the mobocratic slave-holding spirit, and when the speakers had one after another left the platform without a hearing, and the chairman had lost all control of the assembly, the appearance of this gentleman upon the platform would turn the tide of events. He would not beg for a hearing, but on the contrary, he would lash them as no preceding speaker had done. If, by their groans and yells, they stifled his voice, he would stand unmoved with his arms folded, and by the very eloquence of his looks put them to silence. His speeches against the Fugitive Slave Law, and his withering rebukes of Daniel Webster and other northern men who supported that measure, are of the most splendid character, and will compare in point of composition with anything ever uttered by Chatham or Sheridan in their palmiest days. As a public speaker, Mr. Phillips is, without doubt, the first in the United States. Considering his great talent, his high birth, and the prospects which lay before him, and the fact that he threw everything aside to plead the slave's cause, we must be convinced that no man has sacrificed more upon the altar of humanity than Wendell Phillips.

Within the past ten years, a great impetus has been given to the anti-slavery movement in America by coloured men who have escaped from slavery. Coming as they did from the very house of bondage, and being able to speak from sad experience, they could speak as none others could.

The gentleman to whom we shall now call attention is one of this class, and doubtless the first of his race in America. The name of Frederick Douglass is well known throughout this country as well as America. Born and brought up as a slave, he was deprived of a mother's care and of early education. Escaping when he was little more than twenty years of age, he was thrown upon his own resources in the free states, where prejudice against colour is but another name for slavery. But during all this time he was educating himself as well as circumstances would admit. Mr. Douglass commenced his career as a public speaker some ten years since, as an agent of the American or Massachusetts Anti-Slavery Societies. He is tall and well made. His vast and well-developed forehead announces the power of his intellect. His voice is full and sonorous. His attitude is dignified, and his gesticulation is full of noble simplicity. He is a man of lofty reason, natural, and without pretension, always master of himself, brilliant in the art of exposing and of abstracting. Few persons can handle a subject with which they are familiar better than Mr. Douglass. There is a kind of eloquence issuing from the depth of the soul, as from a spring, rolling along its copious floods, sweeping all before it, overwhelming by its very force, carrying, upsetting, engulphing its adversaries, and more dazzling and more thundering than the bolt which leaps from crag to crag. This is the eloquence of Frederick Douglass. He is one of the greatest mimics of the age. No man can put on a sweeter smile or a more sarcastic frown than he: you cannot put him off his guard. He is always in good humour. Mr. Douglass possesses great dramatic powers; and had he taken up the sock and buskin, instead of becoming a lecturer, he would have made as fine a Coriolanus as ever trod the stage.

However, Mr. Douglass was not the first coloured man that became a lecturer, and thereby did service to the cause of his countrymen. The earliest and most effective speaker from among the coloured race in America, was Charles Lennox Remond. In point of eloquence, this gentleman is not inferior to either Wendell Phillips or Frederick Douglass. Mr. Remond is of small stature, and neat figure, with a head well developed, but a remarkably thin face. As an elocutionist, he is, without doubt, the first on the anti-Slavery platform. He has a good voice, a pleasing countenance, a prompt intelligence, and when speaking, is calculated to captivate and carry away an audience by the very force of his eloquence. Born in the freest state of the Union, and of most respectable parents, he prides himself not a little on his birth and descent. One can scarcely find fault with this, for, in the United States, the coloured man is deprived of the advantages which parentage gives to the white man. Mr. Remond is a descendant of one of those coloured men who stood side by side with white men on the plains of Concord and Lexington, in the battles that achieved the independence of the colonies from the mother country, in the war of the Revolution. Mr. Remond has felt deeply, (probably more so than any other coloured man), the odious prejudice against colour. On this point he is sensitive to a fault. If any one will sit for an hour and hear a lecture from him on this subject, if he is not converted, he will at least become convinced, that the boiling cauldron of anti-slavery discussion has never thrown upon its surface a more fiery spirit than Charles Lennox Remond.

There are some men who neither speak nor write, but whose lives place them in the foremost ranks in the cause which they espouse. One of these is Francis Jackson. He was one of the earliest to give countenance and support to the anti-slavery movement. In the year 1835, when a mob of more than 5000 merchants and others, in Boston, broke up an anti-slavery meeting of females, at which William Lloyd Garrison and George

Thompson were to deliver addresses, and when the Society had no room in which to hold its meetings (having been driven from their own room by the mob), Francis Jackson, with a moral courage scarcely ever equalled, came forward and offered his private dwelling to the ladies, to hold their meeting in. The following interesting passage occurs in a letter from him to the Secretary of the Society a short time after, on receiving a vote of thanks from its members:—

"If a large majority of this community choose to turn a deaf ear to the wrongs which are inflicted upon their countrymen in other portions of the land—if they are content to turn away from the sight of oppression, and 'pass by on the other side'—so it must be.

"But when they undertake in any way to impair or annul my right to speak, write, and publish upon any subject, and more especially upon enormities, which are the common concern of every lover of his country and his kind—so it must not be—so it shall not be, if I for one can prevent it. Upon this great right let us hold on at all hazards. And should we, in its exercise, be driven from public halls to private dwellings, one house at least shall be consecrated to its preservation. And if, in defence of this sacred privilege, which man did not give me, and shall not (if I can help it) take from me, this roof and these walls shall be levelled to the earth, let them fall if they must; they cannot crumble in a better cause. They will appear of very little value to me after their owner shall have been whipt into silence."

There are among the contributors to the Anti-Slavery cause, a few who give with a liberality which has never been surpassed by the donors to any benevolent association in the world, according to their means—the chief of these is Francis Jackson.

In the month of May, 1834, while one evening strolling up Broadway, New York, I saw a crowd making its way into the Minerva Rooms, and, having no pressing engagement, I followed, and was soon in a splendid hall, where some twelve or fifteen hundred persons were seated, and listening to rather a strange-looking man. The speaker was tall and slim, with long arms, long legs, and a profusion of auburn or reddish hair hanging in ringlets down his shoulders; while a huge beard of the same colour fell upon his breast. His person was not at all improved by his dress. The legs of his trousers were shorter than those worn by smaller men: the sleeves of his coat were small and short, the shirt collar turned down in Byronic style, beard and hair hid his countenance, so that no redeeming feature could be found there; yet there was one redeeming quality about the man—that was the stream of fervid eloquence which escaped from his lips. I inquired his name, and was informed that it was Charles C. Burleigh. Nature has been profuse in showering her gifts upon Mr

159

Burleigh, but all has been bestowed upon his head and heart. There is a kind of eloquence which weaves its thread around the hearer, and gradually draws him into its web, fascinating him with its gaze, entangling him as the spider does the fly, until he is fast: such is the eloquence of C. C. Burleigh. As a debater he is unquestionably the first on the Anti-slavery platform. If he did not speak so fast, he would equal Wendell Phillips; if he did not reason his subject out of existence, he would surpass him. However, one would have to travel over many miles, and look in the faces of many men, before he would find one who has made more personal sacrifices, or done more to bring about the Emancipation of the American Slaves, than Mr Charles C. Burleigh.

Whoever the future historian of the Anti-Slavery movement may be, he will not be able to compile a correct history of this great struggle, without consulting the writings of Edmund Quincy, a member of one of the wealthiest, patriotic, and aristocratic families in New England: the prestige of his name is a passport to all that the heart could wish. Descended from a family, whose name is connected with all that was glorious in the great American Revolution, the son of one who has again and again represented his native State, in the National Congress, he too, like Wendell Phillips, throw away the pearl of political preferment, and devoted his distinguished talents to the cause of the Slave. Mr. Quincy is better known in this country as having filled the editorial chair of *The Liberator*, during the several visits of its Editor to Great Britain. As a speaker, he does not rank as high as some who are less known; as a writer, he has few equals. The "Annual Reports" of the American and Massachusetts Anti-Slavery Societies for the past fifteen or twenty years, have emanated from his pen. When posterity, in digging among the tombs of the friends of mankind, and of universal freedom, shall fail to find there the name of Edmund Quincy, it will be because the engraver failed to do his duty.

Were we sent out to find a man who should excel all others in collecting together new facts and anecdotes, and varnishing up old ones so that they would appear new, and bringing them into a meeting and emptying out, good or bad, the whole contents of his sack, to the delight and admiration of the audience, we would unhesitatingly select James N. Buffum as the man. If Mr. Buffum is not a great speaker, he has what many accomplished orators have not—*i.e.*, a noble and generous heart. If the fugitive slave, fresh from the cotton-field, should make his appearance in the town of Lynn, in Massachusetts, and should need a night's lodging or refreshments, he need go no farther than the hospitable door of James N. Buffum.

Most men who inherit large fortunes, do little or nothing to benefit mankind. A few, however, spend their means in the best possible manner:

one of the latter class is Gerrit Smith. The name of this gentleman should have been brought forward among those who are first mentioned in this chapter. Some eight or ten years ago, Mr. Smith was the owner of large tracts of land, lying in twenty-nine counties in the State of New York, and came to the strange conclusion to give the most of it away. Consequently, three thousand lots of land, containing from thirty to one hundred acres each, were given to coloured men residing in the State—the writer of this being one of the number.

Although universal suffrage is enjoyed by the whites in the State of Now York, a property-qualification is imposed on coloured men; and this act of Mr. Smith's not only made three thousand men the owners of land, but created also three thousand voters. The ability to give, and the willingness to do so, is not by any means the greatest quality of this gentleman. As a public speaker, Mr. Smith has few equals; and certainly no man in his State has done more to forward the cause of Negro Emancipation than he.

We have already swelled the pages of this chapter beyond what we intended when we commenced, but yet we have called attention to only one branch of American Reformers. The Temperance Reformers are next to be considered. This cause has many champions, and yet none who occupy a very prominent position before the world. The first temperance newspaper published in the United States, was edited by William Lloyd Garrison. Gerrit Smith has also done much in promulgating temperance views. But the most noted man in the movement at the present time, and the one best known to the British public, is John B. Gough. This gentleman was at one time an actor on the stage, and subsequently became an inebriate of the most degraded kind. He was, however, reclaimed through the great Washingtonian movement that swept over the United States a few years since. In stature, Mr. Gough is tall and slim, with black hair, which he usually wears too long. As an orator, he is considered among the first in the United States. Having once been an actor, he throws all his dramatic powers into his addresses. He has a facility of telling strange and marvellous stories which can scarcely be surpassed; and what makes them still more interesting, he always happens to be an eyewitness. While speaking, he acts the drunkard, and does it in a style which could not be equalled on the boards of the Lyceum or Adelphi. No man has obtained more signatures to the temperance pledge than he. After all, it is a question whether he has ever been of any permanent service to this reform or not. Mr. Gough has more than once fallen from his position as a teetotaler; more than once he has broken his pledge, and when found by his friends, was in houses of a questionable character. However, some are of opinion that these defects have been of use to him; for when he has made his appearance after one of these debaucheries, the people appear to sympathize more with him, and some thought he spoke better. If we believe that a person could enjoy good health with water upon the brain, we would be of opinion that Mr. Gough's cranium contained a greater quantity than that of any other living man. When speaking before an audience, he can weep when he pleases; and the tears shed on these occasions are none of your make-believe kind—none of your small drops trickling down the checks one at a time;—but they come in great showers, so as even to sprinkle upon the paper which he holds in his hand. Of course, he is not alone in shedding tears in his meetings, many of his hearers usually join him; especially the ladies, as these showers are intended for them. However, no one can sit for an hour and hear John. B. Gough, without coming to the conclusion that he is nothing more than a theatrical mountebank.

The ablest speaker on the subject of Peace, is Charles Sumner. Standing more than six feet in height, and well proportioned, Mr Sumner makes a most splendid and commanding appearance before an assembly. It is not his looks alone that attract attention—his very countenance indicates a superior mind. Born in the upper circle, educated in the first College in the country, and finally becoming a member of the Bar, he is well qualified to take the highest possible position as a public speaker. As an orator, Charles Sumner has but one superior in the United States, and that is Wendell Phillips. Mr Sumner is an able advocate for the liberation of the American Slaves as well as of the cause of Peace, and has rendered great aid to the abolition movement.

The name of Elihu Burritt, for many reasons, should be placed at the head of the Peace Movement. No man was ever more devoted to one idea than he is to that of peace. If he is an advocate of Temperance, it is because it will promote peace. If he opposes Slavery, it is upon the grounds of peace. Ask him why he wants an "Ocean Penny Postage," he will tell you to engender the principles of peace. Everything with him hinges upon the doctrine of peace. As a speaker, Mr Burritt does not rank amongst the first. However, his speeches are of a high order, some think them too high, and complain that he is too much of a cloud-traveller, and when he descends from these aerial flights and cloudy thrones, they are unwilling to admit that he can be practical. If Mr. Burritt should prove as good a statesman as a theorist, he would be an exception to most who belong to the aerial school. As a writer he stands deservedly high. In his "Sparks from the Anvil," and "Voice from the Forge," are to be found as fine pieces as have been produced by any writer of the day. His "Drunkard's Wife" is the most splendid thing of the kind in the language. His stature is of the middle size, head well developed, with eyes deeply set, and a prepossessing countenance, though not handsome; he wears an exterior of remarkable austerity, and everything about him is grave, even to his smile. Being well versed in the languages, ancient and modern, he does not lack vanity or imagination, either in his public addresses or private conversation; yet it would be difficult to find a man with a better heart, or sweeter spirit, than Elihu Burritt.

From *The American Fugitive in Europe:*
Sketches of Places and People Abroad

(Boston: John P. Jewett; Cleveland: Jewett, Proctor & Worthington; New York:
Sheldon, Lamport & Blakeman, 1855)

NOTE TO THE AMERICAN EDITION.

During my sojourn abroad I found it advantageous to my purse to publish a book of travels, which I did under the title of "Three Years in Europe, or Places I have seen and People I have met." The work was reviewed by the ablest journals in Great Britain, and from their favorable criticisms I have been induced to offer it to the American public, with a dozen or more additional chapters.

W. W. B.

BOSTON, *November*, 1854.

"AN ADDRESS PRESENTED TO MR. WILLIAM WELLS BROWN, THE FUGITIVE SLAVE FROM AMERICA, BY THE LADIES OF BOLTON, MARCH 22ND, 1850:

"DEAR FRIEND AND BROTHER: We cannot permit you to depart from among us without giving expression to the feelings which we entertain towards yourself personally, and to the sympathy which you have awakened in our breasts for the three millions of our sisters and brothers who still suffer and groan in the prison-house of American bondage. You came among us an entire stranger; we received you for the sake of your mission; and having heard the story of your personal wrongs, and gazed with horror on the atrocities of slavery as seen through the medium of your touching descriptions, we are resolved, henceforward, in reliance on divine assistance, to render what aid we can to the cause which you have so eloquently pleaded in our presence.

"We have no words to express our detestation of the crimes which, in the name of liberty, are committed in the country which gave you birth. Language fails to tell our deep abhorrence of the impiety of those who, in the still more sacred name of religion, rob immortal beings not only of an earthly citizenship, but do much to prevent them from obtaining a heavenly one; and, as mothers and daughters, we embrace this opportunity of giving utterance to our utmost indignation at the cruelties perpetrated upon our sex, by a people professedly acknowledging the equality of all mankind. Carry with you, on your return to the land of your nativity, this our solemn protest against the wicked institution which, like a dark and baleful cloud, hangs over it; and ask the unfeeling enslavers, as best you can, to open the prison-doors to them that are bound, and let the oppressed go free.

"Allow us to assure you that your brief sojourn in our town has been to ourselves, and to vast multitudes, of a character long to be remembered; and when you are far removed from us, and toiling, as we hope you may be long spared to do, in this righteous enterprise, it may be some solace to your mind to know that your name is cherished with affectionate regard, and that the blessing of the Most High is earnestly supplicated in behalf of yourself, your family, and the cause to which you have consecrated your distinguished talents."

A most respectable and enthusiastic public meeting was held at Sheffield to welcome Mr. Brown, and the next day he was invited to inspect several of the large establishments there. While going through the manufactory of Messrs. Broadhead and Atkin, silver and electro-platers, &c., in Love-street, and whilst he was being shown through the works, a subscription was hastily set on foot on his behalf, by the workmen and women of the establishment, which was presented to Mr. Brown, in the counting-house, by a deputation of the subscribers. The spokesman (the designer to Messrs. Broadhead & Atkin), addressing Mr. Brown on behalf of the work-people, begged his acceptance of the present as a token of esteem, as well as an expression of their sympathy in the cause be advocates, namely, that of the American slave. Mr. Brown briefly thanked the parties for their spontaneous free-will offering, accompanied, as it was, by a generous expression of sympathy for his afflicted brethren and sisters in bondage.

Mr. Brown was in England five years, and during his sojourn there travelled above twenty-five thousand miles through Great Britain, addressed more than one thousand public meetings, lectured in twenty-three mechanics' and literary institutions, and gave his services to many of the benevolent and religious societies on the occasion of their anniversary meetings. After a lecture which he delivered before the Whittington Club, he received from the managers of that institution the following testimonial:

"WHITTINGTON CLUB AND
METROPOLITAN ATHENÆUM,
189 STRAND, *June* 21, 1850.

"My DEAR SIR: I have much pleasure in conveying to you the best thanks of the Managing Committee of this institution for the excellent lecture you gave here last evening, and also in presenting you in their names with an honorary membership of the club. It is hoped that you will often avail yourself of its privileges by coming amongst us. You will then see, by the cordial welcome of the members, that they protest against the odious distinctions made between man and man, and the abominable traffic of which you have been the victim.

"For my own part, I shall be happy to be serviceable to you in any way, and at all times be glad to place the advantages of the institution at your disposal.

"I am, my dear sir, yours, truly,

"WILLIAM STRUDWICKE, *Secretary.*

"Mr. W. WELLS BROWN."

CHAPTER XXI.

"For 'tis the mind that makes the body rich;
And as the sun breaks through the darkest clouds,
So Honor peereth in the meanest habit."

SHAKSPEARE.

After strolling, for more than two hours, through the beautiful town of Lemington, in which I had that morning arrived, a gentleman, to whom I had a letter of introduction, asked me if I was not going to visit Shakspeare's House. It was only then that I called to mind the fact that I was within a few miles of the birthplace of the world's greatest literary genius. A horse and chaise was soon procured, and I on my way to

Stratford. A quick and pleasant ride brought me to the banks of the Avon, and, a short time after, to the little but picturesque town of Stratford. I gave the horse in charge of the man-of-all-work at the inn, and then started for the much-talked-of and celebrated cottage. I found it to be a small, mean-looking house of wood and plaster, the walls of which are covered with names, inscriptions and hieroglyphics, in every language, by people of all nations, ranks and conditions, from the highest to the lowest, who have made their pilgrimage there. The old shattered and worn-out stock of the gun with which Shakspeare shot Sir Thomas Lucy's deer was shown to us. The old-fashioned tobacco-box was also there. The identical sword with which he played Hamlet, the lantern with which Romeo and Juliet were discovered, lay on the table. A plentiful supply of Shakspeare's mulberry-tree was there, and we were asked if we did not want to purchase; but, fearing that it was not the genuine article, we declined. In one of the most gloomy and dilapidated rooms is the old chair in which the poet used to sit. After viewing everything of interest, and paying the elderly young woman (old maid) her accustomed fee, we left the poet's birthplace to visit his grave. We were soon standing in the chancel of the parish church, a large and venerable edifice, mouldering with age, but finely ornamented within, and the ivy clinging around without. It stands in a beautiful situation on the banks of the Avon. Garrick has most truthfully said:

> Thou soft-flowing Avon, by thy silver stream
> Of things more than mortal sweet Shakspeare would dream;
> The fairies by moonlight dance round his green bed,
> For hallowed the turf is which pillowed his head."

The picturesque little stream runs murmuring at the foot of the church-yard, disturbed only by the branches of the large elms that stand on the banks, and whose limbs droop down. A flat stone is the only thing that marks the place where the poet lies buried. I copied the following verse from the stone, and which is said to have been written by the bard himself:

> "Good friend, for Jesus' sake, forbeare
> To dig the dust enclosed here:
> Blessed be he that spares these stones,
> And cursed be he that moves my bones."

Above the grave, in a niche in the wall, is a bust of the poet, placed there not long after his death, and which is supposed to bear some resemblance.

Shakspeare's wife and daughter lie near him. After beholding everything of any possible interest, we stepped into our chaise and were soon again in Lemington; which, by the by, is the most beautiful town in all Great Britain, not excepting Cheltenham. In the evening I returned to Coventry, and was partaking of the hospitality of my excellent friend, Joseph Cash, Esq., of Sherburne House, and had stretched myself out on a sofa, with Carlyle's Life of Stirling in my hands, when I was informed that the younger members of the family were preparing to attend a lecture at the Mechanics' Institution. I did not feel inclined to stir from my easy position, after the fatigues of the day; but, learning that the lecturer was George Dawson, Esq., I resolved to join the company.

The hall was nearly filled when we reached it, which was only a few minutes before the commencement of the lecture. The stamping of feet and clapping of hands—which is the best evidence of an Englishman's impatience—brought before us a thin-faced, spare-made, wiry-looking man, with rather a dark complexion for an Englishman, but with prepossessing features. I must confess that I entered the room with some little prejudice against the speaker, caused by an unfavorable criticism from the pen of George Gilfillan, the essayist. However, I was happily disappointed. His style is witty, keen and gentle, with the language of the drawing-room. His smiling countenance, piercing glance and musical voice, captivated his audience. Mr. Dawson's subject was "The Rise and Spread of the Anglo-Saxon Race," and he showed that be understood his task. During his discourse he said:

"The Greeks and Romans sent out colonies; but no nation but England ever before gave a nation birth. The Americans are a nation, with no language, no creed, no grave-yards. Their names are a derivation; and it is laughable to see the pains an American takes to appear national. He will soon explain to you that he is not an Englishman, but a free-born citizen of the United States, with a pretty considerable contempt for them British-ers. These notions make an Englishman smile; the Americans are a nation without being a nation; they are impressed with an idea that they have characteristics,—they are odd, not national, and remind one of a long slender youth, somewhat sallow, who has just had a new watch, consequently blasphemes the old one; and as for the watch his father used, what is it?—a turnip; by this means he assumes the independent. The American *is* independent; he flaunts it in your face, and surprises you with his galvanic attempts at showing off his nationality. They have, in fact, no literature; we don't want them to have any, as long as they can draw from the old country; the feeling is kindly, and should be cherished; it is like the boy at Christmas coming home to spend the holidays. Long may they draw inspiration from

Shakspeare and Milton, and come again and again to the old well. Walking down Broadway is like looking at a page of the Polyglot Bible. America was founded in a great thought, peopled through liberty; and long may that country be the noblest thing that England has to boast of.

"Some people think that we, as a nation, are going down; that we have passed the millennium; but there is no reason yet. We have work to do,—gold mines to dig, railways to construct, &c. &c. When all the work is done, then, and not till then, will the Saxon folk have finished their destiny. We have continents to fill yet; our work is not done till Europe is free. When Emerson visited us, he said that England was not an old country, but had the two-fold character of youth and age; he saw now cities, new docks; a good day's work yet to be done, and many vast undertakings only just begun. The coal, the iron and the gold, are ours; we have noble days in store, but we must labor more than we have yet done. Talk of going down!—we have hardly arrived at our meridian. We have our faults; any Frenchman or German may point them out. We have our duties, and often waste our precious moments by indulging in one eternal grumble at what we do, compared to what we ought to do. A little praise is good sometimes,—we walk the taller for it, and work the better. Only as we know our work here, and do it as our fathers did, shall we promote good; working heartily, and not faltering until the object is gained. The more we add to the happiness of a people, the more we shall be worthy of the good gifts of God."

As an orator, Mr. Dawson stands deservedly high; and was on several occasions applauded to the echo. He was educated for the ministry in the Orthodox persuasion, but left it and became a Unitarian, and has since gone a step further. Mr. Dawson resides in Birmingham, where he has a fine chapel, and a most intellectual congregation, and is considered the Theodore Parker of England.

It is indeed strange, the impression which a mind well cultivated can make upon those about it; and in this we see more clearly the need of education. In whatever light we view education, it cannot fail to appear the most important subject that can engage the attention of mankind. When we contrast the ignorance, the rudeness and the helplessness of the savage, with the knowledge, the refinement and the resources of civilized man, the difference between them appears so wide, that they can scarcely be regarded as of the same species; yet compare the infant of the savage with that of the educated and enlightened philosopher, and you will find them in all respects the same. The same *high, capacious powers* of the mind lie folded up in both, and in both the organs of sensation adapted to these mental powers are exactly similar. All the difference which is afterwards to distinguish them depends entirely upon their education, energy and self-culture.

CHAPTER XXII.

> "Proud pile! that rearest thy hoary head,
> In ruin vast, in silence dread,
> O'er Teme's luxuriant vale,
> Thy moss-grown halls, thy precincts drear,
> To musing Fancy's pensive ear
> Unfold a varied tale."

It was in the latter part of December, and on one of the coldest nights that I have experienced, that I found myself seated before the fire, and alone, in the principal hotel in the town of Ludlow, and within a few minutes' walk of the famous old castle from which the town derives its name. A ride of one hundred and fifty miles by rail, in such uncomfortable carriages as no country except Great Britain furnishes for the weary traveller, and twenty miles on the top of a coach, in a drenching rain, caused me to remain by the fire's side to a later hour than I otherwise would have done. "Did you ring, sir?" asked the waiter, as the clock struck twelve. "No," I replied; but I felt that this was the servant's mode of informing me that it was time for me to retire to bed, and consequently I asked for a candle, and was shown to my chamber, and was soon in bed. From the weight of the covering on the bed, I felt sure that the extra blanket which I had requested to be put on was there; yet I was shivering with cold. As the sheets began to get warm, I discovered, to my astonishment, that they were damp; indeed, wet. My first thought was to ring the bell for the chambermaid, and have them changed; but, after a moment's consideration, I resolved to adopt a different course. I got out of bed, pulled the sheets off, rolled them up, raised the window, and threw them into the street. After disposing of the wet sheets, I returned to bed and got in between the blankets, and lay there trembling with cold till Morpheus came to my relief. The next morning I said nothing about the uncomfortable night I had experienced, and determined to leave it until they discovered the loss of the sheets. As soon as I had breakfasted, I went out to view the castle. For many years this was one of the strongest baronial fortifications in England. It was from Ludlow Castle that Edward, Prince of Wales, and his brother, were taken to London and put to death in the Tower, by order of their uncle, Richard III., before that villain seized upon the crown. The family of Mortimer for centuries held the castle, and, consequently, ruled Herefordshire. The castle rises from the point of a headland, and its foundations are ingrafted into a bare gray rock. The front consists of square towers, with high connecting walls. The castle is a complete ruin, and has been for centuries; large trees are still growing in the midst of the old pile, which give it a picturesque appearance. It was here that the exquisite effusion of the youthful genius of Milton—The Masque of Comus—was composed, and performed before His Majesty Charles I., in 1631. Little did the king think that the poet would one day be secretary to the man who should put him to death and rule his kingdom. Although a ruin, this fact is enough to excite interest, and to cause one to venerate the old building, and to do homage to the memory of the divine poet who hallowed it with his immortal strains. From a visitor's book that is kept at the gate-house, I copied the following verses:

"Here Milton sung; what needs a greater spell
To lure thee, stranger, to these far-famed walls?
Though chroniclers of other ages tell
That princes oft have graced fair Ludlow's halls,
Their honors glide along oblivion's stream,
And o'er the wreck a tide of ruin drives;
Faint and more faint the rays of glory beam
That gild their course—the bard alone survives.
And, when the rude, unceasing shocks of Time
In one vast heap shall whelm this lofty pile,
Still shall his genius, towering and sublime,
Triumphant o'er the spoils of grandeur smile;
Still in these haunts, true to a nation's tongue,
Echo shall love to dwell, and say, Here Milton sung."

I lingered long in the room pointed out to me as the one in which Milton wrote his "Comus." The castle was not only visited by the author of "Paradise Lost," but here, amidst the noise and bustle of civil dissensions, Samuel Butler, the satirical author of "Hudibras," found an asylum. The part of the tower in which it is said he composed his "Hudibras" was shown to us. In looking over the different apartments, we passed through a cell with only one small window through which the light found its way. On a stone, chiselled with great beauty, was a figure in a weeping position, and underneath it some one had written with pencil, in a legible hand:

"The Muse, too, weeps; in hallowed hour
Here sacred Milton owned her power,
And woke to nobler song."

The weather was exceedingly cold, and made more so by the stone walls partly covered with snow and frost around us; and I returned to the inn. It being near the time for me to leave by the coach for Hereford, I called for my bill. The servant went out of the room; but soon returned, and began stirring up the fire with the poker. I again told him that the coach would shortly be up, and that I wanted my bill. "Yes, sir, in a moment," he replied, and left in haste. Ten or fifteen minutes passed away, and the servant once more came in, walked to the window, pulled up the blinds, and then went out. I saw that something was in the wind; and it occurred to me that they had discovered the loss of the sheets. The waiter soon returned again, and, in rather an agitated manner, said, "I beg your pardon, sir, but the landlady is in the hall, and would like to speak to you." Out I went, and found the finest specimen of an English landlady that I had seen for many a day. There she stood, nearly as thick as she was high, with a red face, garnished around with curls, that seemed to say, "I have just been brushed and oiled." A neat apron covered a black alpacca dress that swept the ground with modesty, and a bunch of keys hung at her side. O, that smile! such a smile as none but a woman who had often been before a mirror could put on. However, I had studied human nature too successfully not to know that thunder and lightning were concealed tinder that smile; and I nerved myself up for the occasion. "I am sorry to have to name it, sir," said she, "but the sheets are missing off your bed." "O, yes," I replied; "I took them off last night." "Indeed!" exclaimed she; "and pray what have you done with them?" "I threw them out of the window," said I. "What! into the street?" "Yes, into the street," I said. "What did you do that for?" "They were wet; and I was afraid that if I left them in the room they would be put on at night, and give somebody else a cold." And here I coughed with all my might, to remind her that I had suffered from the negligence of her chambermaid. The heaving of the chest and panting for breath which the lady was experiencing at this juncture told me plainly that an explosion was at hand; and the piercing glance of those wicked-looking black eyes, and the rapid changes that came over that never-to-be-forgotten face, were enough to cause the most love-sick man in the world to give up all ideas of matrimony, and to be contented with being his own master.

"Then, sir," said the landlady, "you will have to pay for the sheets." "O, yes," replied I; "I will pay for them; put them in the bill, and I will send the bill to *The Times*, and have it published, and let the travelling public know how much you charge for wet sheets!" and I turned upon my heel and walked into the room.

A few minutes after, the servant came in and laid before me the bill. I looked, but in vain, to see how much I had been charged for my hasty indiscretion the previous night. No mention was made of the sheets; and I paid the bill as it stood. The blowing of the coachman's horn warned me that I must get ready; and I put on my top coat. As I was passing through the hall, there stood the landlady just where I had left her, looking as if she had not stirred a single peg. And that smile, that had often cheered or carried consternation to many a poor heart, was still to be seen. I would rather have gone without my dinner than to have looked her in the face, such is my timidity. But common courtesy demanded that I should at least nod as I passed by; and therefore I was thrown back upon my manners, and unconsciously found myself giving her one of my best bows. Whether this bow was the result of my early training while in slavery, the domestic discipline that I afterwards experienced in freedom, or the terror with which every nerve was shaken on first meeting the landlady, I am still unaware. However, the bow was made and the ice broken, and the landlady smilingly said, "You do not know, sir, how much I am grieved at your being put to so much trouble last night, with those wet sheets; it was all the fault of the chambermaid, and I have given her warning, and shall dismiss her a month from to-day. And I do hope, sir, that if you should ever mention this circumstance you will not name the house in which it occurred." How could I do otherwise than to acquiesce in her wishes? Yes, I promised that I would never name the inn at which I had caught the rheumatism; and, therefore, reader, you may ask me, but in vain,—I will not tell you. One more bow, and out I went, and mounted the coach. As the driver was pulling up his reins, and raising his whip in the air, I turned to take a farewell glance of the inn, when, to my surprise, I beheld the landlady at the door with a white handkerchief in her hand, and a countenance beaming with smiles that I still see in my mind's eye. I raised my hat, she nodded, and away went the coach. Although the ride was a cold and dreary one, I often caught myself smiling over the fright in which I had put the landlady by threatening to publish her house.

After a fatiguing stage twenty miles or more, over a bad road, we reached Hereford, a small city, situated in a fertile plain, bounded on all sides with orchards, and watered by the translucent Wye. I spent the greater part of the next day in seeing the lions of the little city. I first visited, what most strangers do, the cathedral; a building partly Gothic and partly Saxon in its architecture, the interior of which is handsome, and contains an excellent organ, a piece of furniture that often calls more hearers to a place of worship than the preacher. In passing through the cathedral I stood a moment or two over the grave of the poet Phillips, the author of the "Splendid Shilling," "Cider," etc. While in the library the verger showed me a manuscript Bible of Wickliffe's, the first in use, written on vellum in the old black letter, full of abbreviations. He also pointed out some Latin manuscripts, in various parts beautifully illuminated with most ingenious penmanship, the coloring of the figures very bright. After all, there is a degree of pleasure in bundling those old and laid-aside books. Hereford is noted for having been the birth-place of several distinguished persons. I was shown the house in which David Garrick was born. From Hereford he was removed to Litchfield and became the pupil of Dr. Johnson, and eventually both master and pupil went to London in search of bread; one became famous as an actor, the other noted as *surly Sam Johnson*. An obscure cottage in Pipe-lane was pointed out as the birthplace of the celebrated Nell Gwynne, who first appeared in London in the pit of Drury-lane Theatre as an apple-girl, and afterwards became an actress, in which position she was seen by King Charles II., who took her to his bed and board, and created her Duchess of St. Albans. However, she had many crooked paths to tread, after becoming an actress, before she captivated the heart of the *Merry Monarch*. The following story of her life, told by herself, is too good to be lost; so I insert it here.

"When I was a poor girl," said the Duchess of St. Albans, "working very hard for my thirty shillings a week, I went down to Liverpool during the holidays, where I was always well received. I was to perform in a new piece, something like those pretty little affecting dramas they get up now at our minor theatres; and in my character I represented a poor, friendless orphan-girl, reduced to the most wretched poverty. A heartless tradesman prosecutes the sad heroine for a heavy debt, and insists on putting her in prison, unless some one will be bail for her. The girl replies, 'Then I have no hope; I have not a friend in the world.' 'What! will no one be bail for you, to save you from going to prison?' asks the stern creditor. 'I have told you I have not a friend on earth,' was the reply. But just as I was uttering the words, I saw a sailor in the upper gallery springing over the railing, let-ting himself down from one tier to another, until he bounded clear over the orchestra and footlights, and placed himself beside me in a moment. 'Yes, you shall have *one* friend at least, my poor young woman,' said he, with the greatest expression in his honest, sunburnt countenance; 'I will go bail for you to any amount. And as for *you*,' turning to the frightened actor, 'if you don't bear a hand and shift your moorings, you lubber, it will be worse for you when I come athwart your bows!' Every creature in the house rose; the uproar was indescribable—peals of laughter, screams of terror, cheers from his tawny mess-mates in the gallery, preparatory scrapings of violins from the orchestra; and, amidst the universal din, there stood the unconscious cause of it, sheltering me, 'the poor, distressed young woman,' and breathing defiance and destruction against my mimic persecutor. He was only persuaded to relinquish his care of me, by the manager pretending to arrive and rescue me, with a profusion of theatrical bank-notes."

Hereford was also the birthplace of Mrs. Siddons, the unequalled tragic actress. The views around Hereford are very sylvan, and from some points, where the Welsh mountains are discernible, present something of the magnificent. All this part of the country still shows unmistakable evidence that war has had its day here. In those times the arts and education received no encouragement. The destructive exploits of conquerors may dazzle for a while, but the silent labors of the student and the artist, of the architect and the husbandman, which embellish the earth, and convert it into a terrestrial paradise, although they do not shine with so conspicuous a glare, diversify the picture with milder colors and more beautiful shades.

CHAPTER XXIII.

"To him no author was unknown,
Yet what he writ was all his own;
Horace's wit, and Virgil's state,
He did not steal, but emulate;
And when he would like them appear,
Their form, but not their clothes, did wear."

DENHAM.

If there be an individual living who has read the "Essay on Man," or "The Rape of the Lock," without a wish to become more acquainted with the writings of the gifted poet that penned those exquisite poems, I confess that such an one is made of different materials from myself.

It is possible that I am too great a devotee to authors, and especially poets; yet such is my reverence for departed writers, that I would rather walk five miles to see a poet's grave than to spend an evening at the finest entertainment that could be got up.

It was on a pleasant afternoon in September, that I had gone into Surrey to dine with Lord C——, that I found myself one of a party of nine, and seated at a table loaded with everything that the heart could wish. Four men-servants, in livery, with white gloves, waited upon the company.

After the different courses had been changed, the wine occupied the most conspicuous place on the table, and all seemed to drink with a relish unappreciated except by those who move in the higher walks of life. My glass was the only one on the table in which the juice of the grape had not been poured. It takes more nerve than most men possess to cause one to decline taking a glass of wine with a lady; and in English society they don't appear to understand how human beings can live and enjoy health without taking at least a little wine. By my continued refusal to drink with first one and then another of the company, I had become rather an object of pity than otherwise.

A lady of the party, and in company with whom I had dined on a previous occasion, and who knew me to be an abstainer, resolved to relieve me from the awkward position in which my principles had placed me, and therefore caused a decanter of raspberry vinegar to be adulterated and brought on the table. A note in pencil from the lady informed me of the contents of the new bottle. I am partial to this kind of beverage, and felt glad when it made its appearance. No one of the party, except the lady, knew of the fraud; and I was able, during the remainder of the time, to drink with any of the company. The waiters, as a matter of course, were in the secret; for they had to make the change while passing the wine from me to the person with whom I drank.

After a while, as is usual, the ladies all rose and left the room. The retiring of the fair sex left the gentlemen in a more free-and-easy position, and consequently the topics of conversation were materially changed, but not for the better. The presence of women is always a restraint in the right direction. An hour after the ladies had gone, the gentlemen were requested to retire to the drawing-room, where we found tea ready to be served up. I was glad when the time came to leave the dining-room, for I felt it a great bore to be compelled to remain at the table *three hours*. Tea over, the wine again brought on, and the company took a stroll through the grounds at the back of the villa. It was a bright moonlight night, and the stars were out, and the air came laden with the perfume of sweet flowers, and there were no sounds to be heard, except the musical splashing of the little cascade at the end of the garden, and the song of the nightingale, that seemed to be in one of the trees near by. How pleasant everything looked, with the flowers creeping about the summer-house, and the windows opening to the velvet lawn, with its modest front, neat trellis-work, and meandering vine! The small smooth fish-pond, and the lifelike statues standing or kneeling in different parts of the grounds, gave it the appearance of a very paradise.

"There," said his lordship, "is where Cowley used to sit, under that tree, and read."

This reminded me that I was near Chertsey, where the poet spent his last days; and, as I was invited to spend the night within a short ride of that place, I resolved to visit it the next day. We returned to the drawing-room, and a few moments after the party separated, at ten o'clock.

After breakfast the following morning, I drove over to Chertsey, a pretty little town, with but two streets of any note. In the principal street, and not far from the railway station, stands a low building of wood and plaster, known as the *Porch House*. It was in this cottage that Abraham Cowley, the poet, resided, and died in 1667, in the forty-ninth year of his age. It being the residence of a gentleman who was from home, I did not have an opportunity of seeing the interior of the building, which I much regretted. Having visited Cowley's house, I at once determined to do what I had long promised myself; that was, to see Pope's villa, at Twickenham; and I returned to London, took the Richmond boat, and was soon gliding up the Thames.

I have seldom had a pleasanter ride by water than from London Bridge to Richmond; the beautiful panoramic view which unfolds itself on either side of the river can scarcely be surpassed by the scenery in any country. In the centre of Twickenham stands the house made celebrated from its having been the residence of Alexander Pope. The house is not large, but occupies a beautiful site, and is to be seen to best advantage from the river. The garden and grounds have undergone some change since the death of the poet. The grotto leading from the villa to the Thames is in a sad condition.

The following lines, written by Pope soon after finishing this idol of his fancy, show in what estimate he held it, and should at least have preserved it from decay:

"Thou who shalt stop where *Thames'* translucent wave
Shines a broad mirror through the shadowy cave;
Where lingering drops from mineral roofs distill,
And pointed crystals break the sparkling rill;
Unpolished gems no ray on pride bestow,
And latent metals innocently glow—
Approach! Great nature studiously behold!
And eye the mine without a wish for gold.
Approach—but awful! Lo! the Ægerian grot,
Where, nobly pensive, St. John sate and thought;

Where *British* sighs from dying Wyndham stole,
And the bright flame was shot through Marchmont's soul.
Let such—such only—tread this sacred floor,
Who dare to love their country and be poor."

It is strange that there are some at the present day who deny that Pope was a poet; but it seems to me that such either show a want of appreciation of poetry, or themselves no judge of what constitutes poetry. Where can be found a finer effusion than the "Essay on Man"? Johnson, in his admirable Life of Pope, in drawing a comparison between him and Dryden, says, "If the flights of Dryden are higher, Pope continues longer on the wing; if of Dryden's fire the blaze is brighter, of Pope is the beat more regular and constant. Dryden often surpasses expectation, and Pope never falls below it; Dryden is read with frequent astonishment, and Pope with perpetual delight." In speaking of the "Rape of the Lock," the same great critic remarks that it "stands forward in the classes of literature, as the most exquisite example of ludicrous poetry." Another poet and critic of no mean authority calls him "The sweetest and most elegant of English poets, the severest chastiser of vice, and the most persuasive teacher of wisdom." Lord Byron terms him "the most perfect and harmonious of poets." How many have quoted the following lines without knowing that they were Pope's!

"To look through Nature up to Nature's God."
"An honest man's the noblest work of God."
"Just as the twig is bent, the tree's inclined."

"If to her share some female errors fall,
Look on her face, and you 'll forget them all."

"For modes of faith let graceless zealots fight,
His can't be wrong whose life is in the right."

Pope was certainly the most independent writer of his time; a poet who never sold himself, and never lent his pen to the upholding of wrong. And although a severe critic, the following verse will show that he did not wish to bestow his chastisement in a wrong direction:

"Curst be the verse, how well soe'er it flow,
That tends to make one honest man my foe,
Give Virtue scandal, Innocence a fear,
Or from the soft-eyed virgin steal a tear!"

No poet's pen was ever more thoroughly used to suppress vice than Pope's; and what he did was done conscientiously, as the following lines will show:

> "Ask you what provocation I have had?
> The strong antipathy of good to bad.
> When Truth or Virtue an affront endures,
> The affront is mine, my friend, and should be yours."

Pope is not only a poet of a high order, but as yet he is the unsurpassed translator of Homer.

My visit to Pope's villa was a short one, but it was attended with many pleasing incidents. I have derived much pleasure from reading his Iliad and other translations. The verse from the pen of Lord Denham, that heads this chapter, conveys but a faint idea of my estimate of Pope's genius and talents.

CHAPTER XXIV.

> "This modest stone, what few vain marbles can,
> May truly say, here lies an honest man:
> A poet, blest beyond the poet's fate,
> Whom heaven kept sacred from the proud and great."
>
> POPE.

While on a recent visit to Dumfries, I lodged in the same house with Robert Burns, the eldest son of the Scottish bard, who is now about sixty-five years old. I also visited the grave of the poet, which is in the church-yard at the lower end of the town. A few days afterwards I arrived at Ayr, and being within three miles of the birthplace of Burns, and having so lately stood over his grave, I felt no little interest in seeing the cottage in which he was born, and the monument erected to his memory; and there-fore, after inquiring the road, I started on my pilgrimage. In going up the High Street, we passed the Wallace Tower, a Gothic building, with a statue of the renowned chief, out by Thom, the famed sculptor of "Tam O'Shanter and Souter Johnny," occupying the highest niche. The Scottish hero is represented not in warlike attitude, but in a thoughtful mood, as if musing over the wrongs of his country. We were soon out of the town, and on the high road to the "Land of Burns." On the west side of the road, and about two miles from Ayr, stands the cottage in which the poet was born;

it is now used as an ale-house or inn. This cottage was no doubt the fancied scene of that splendid poem, "The Cottar's Saturday Night." A little further on, and we were near the old kirk, in the yard of which is the grave of Burns' father; marked by a plain tombstone, on which is engraved the following epitaph, from the pen of the poet:

"O ye whose cheek the tear of pity stains,
Draw near with pious reverence and attend;
Here lie the loving husband's dear remains,
The tender father, and the generous friend.
The pitying heart that felt for human woe,
The dauntless heart that feared no human pride,
The friend of man—to vice alone a foe;
'For e'en his failings leant to Virtue's side.'"

A short distance beyond the church, we caught a sight of the "Auld Brig" crossing the Doon's classic stream, along which Tam O'Shanter was pursued by the witches, his "Gray Mare Meg" losing her tail in the struggle on the keystone. On the banks of the Doon stands the beautiful monument, surrounded by a little plat of ground very tastefully laid out. The edifice is of the composite order, blending the finest models of Grecian and Roman architecture. It is about sixty feet high; on the ground floor there is a circular room lighted by a cupola of stained glass, in the centre of which stands a table with relics, and editions of Burns' writings. Amongst these relics is the Bible given by the poet to his Highland Mary. It is bound in two volumes, which are enclosed in a neat oaken box with a glass lid. In both volumes is written "Robert Burns, Mossgiel," in the bard's own hand-writing. In the same room are the original far-famed figures of "Tam O'Shanter and Souter Johnny," chiselled out of solid blocks of freestone, by the self-taught sculptor, Thom. No one can look at these statues without feeling that the poet has not more graphically described than the sculptor has delineated the jolly couple. Immediately on the banks of the river stands the Shell Palace. This most beautiful of little edifices is scarcely less to be admired than the monument itself.

Like its great prototype, the Shell Palace, to be judged of, must be seen. It is not easy to describe even this miniature. Lying in the heart of the Monument scenery, it forms a fitting spot for something dazzlingly beautiful; and it realizes the aspiration. It is a palace of which rare and beautiful shells, gathered in many climes, form the entire surface, internal and external. The erection is twenty feet long, by fourteen and a half feet broad, and fourteen feet high in the roof. It is in form an irregular or oblong octagon—the two sides long, and the three sections at each end, of course, narrow, thus giving, by the cross reflections of no fewer than nineteen mirrors, an infinite multiplicity of its internal treasures. Of these the shells are the leading feature, and many thousands of the rarest sorts go to make up this conchological wonder. The floor is covered with a very rich carpet, and rugs to match front two unique dwarf grates. The seats, set on imitation granite props, are covered with rich crimson velvet. Opposite the stained-glass entrance-door, in a recess, is a beautiful fountain, surrounded by large ornamental shells, playing from a delightful spring, the jet rising from a rich green vase, in tasteful contrast with the "winking gold-fish," now sporting and now lazily floating round its base. The side walls are inlaid in the most regular and artistic manner with shells, which vary in size, the roof being studded with large ornamental shells, the upward unseen points of which, being bored, act as ventilators, while in the centre of the roof some of the very choicest middle-sized shells are grouped together in the form of flowers, with a very rich and beautiful effect, seldom attained in the choicest bouquets. With so much of the beautiful so very attractively arranged, the mirrors work wonders. The large mirrors at either end show a line of table as far as the eye can carry, and multiply the visitors accordingly—green vases and golden fish presenting themselves anew at every turn. The Doon ran silently past as we entered; but here it meanders round us on every side, and our fairy palace seems the centre of some enchanted island. It is, indeed, a beautiful grotto, and all who have not seen it will, we dare say, on visiting it, not begrudge it the title of the "Shell Palace."

We next visited Newark Castle, about a mile from the monument. It is remarkable for its antiquity, and for the splendid view obtained from the balcony on its summit. While standing on this celebrated spot, we saw at one glance the Frith of Clyde and Bay of Ayr; in the immediate foreground the cradle-land of Burns, and the winding Doon; and in the distance the eye wonders over a vast tract of richly-wooded country, embracing a panoramic view of portions of at least seven counties, and the much-admired and celebrated rock, Ailsacraig. While in the neighborhood, we could not forego the temptation which presented itself of visiting the scene of Burns' tender parting with Mary Campbell. It is near the junction of the water of Fail with the river Ayr, where the poet met his Mary on a Sunday in the month of May, and, laying their hands in the stream, vowed, over Mary's Bible, love while the woods of Montgomery grew and its waters ran. The death of the girl before the appointed time of marriage caused the composition of the following poem, one of Burns' sweetest pieces.

HIGHLAND MARY.

"Ye banks, and braes, and streams around
The castle o' Montgomery,
Green be your woods, and fair your flowers,
Your waters never drumlie!
There Simmer first unfaulds her robes,
And there they langest tarry;
For there I took the last fareweel
O' my sweet Highland Mary.

"How sweetly bloomed the gay green birk,
How rich the hawthorn's blossom,
As underneath their fragrant shade
I clasped her to my bosom!
The golden hours, on angel wings,
Flew o'er me and my dearie:
For dear to me as light and life
Was my sweet Highland Mary.

"Wi' mony a vow, and locked embrace,
Our parting was fu' tender;
And, pledging aft to meet again,
We tore oursels asunder;
But, O! fell Death's untimely frost,
That nipt my flower sae early!
Now green's the sod, and cauld 's the clay,
That wraps my Highland Mary!

"O pale, pale now, those rosy lips,
I aft hae kissed sae fondly!
And closed for aye the sparkling glance
That dwalt on me sae kindly!
And mouldering now in silent dust
That heart that lo'ed me dearly!
But still within my bosom's core
Shall live my Highland Mary."

It was indeed pleasant to walk over the ground once pressed by the feet of the Scottish bard, and to look upon the scenes that inspired his youthful breast, and gave animation to that blaze of genius that burst upon the world. The classic Doon, the ruins of the old kirk Alloway, the cottage in which the poet first drew breath, and other places made celebrated by his pen, all filled us with a degree of enthusiasm we have seldom experienced. In every region where the English language is known the songs of Burns give rapture; and from every land, and from climes the most remote, comes the praise of Burns as a poet. In song-writing he surpassed Sir Walter Scott and Lord Byron; for in that department he was above "all Greek, above all Roman fame;" a more than Simonides in pathos, as in his "Highland Mary;" a more than Tyrtæus in fire, as in his "Scots wha ha'e wi' Wallace bled;" and a softer than Sappho in love, as in his—

"Had we never loved so kindly,
Had we never loved so blindly,
Never met or never parted,
We had ne'er been broken-hearted."

CHAPTER XXV.

"If thou art worn and hard beset
With sorrows, that thou wouldst forget;
If thou wouldst read a lesson, that would keep
Thy heart from fainting and thy soul from sleep,—
Go to the Colosseum."

LONGFELLOW.

It was in the middle of May, when London is usually inundated with strangers from the country, who come up to attend the anniversaries, that a party of friends called on me with a request that I would accompany them to some of the lions of the metropolis. We started for the Thames Tunnel, one of the wonders of London. The idea of making a thorough-fare under the largest river in England was a project that could scarcely have been carried out by any except a most enterprising people. We faintly heard the clock on St. Paul's striking eleven, as the Woolwich boat put us down at the Tunnel; which we entered, after paying the admission fee of one penny. After descending one hundred steps, we found ourselves under the river, and looking towards the faint glimmer of light that showed itself on the Surrey side. There are two arches, one of which is closed up, with here and there a stall, loaded with old maps, books, and views of the Tunnel. Lamps, some six or eight yards apart, light up the otherwise dark and dismal place. Signs of frequent repairs show that they must ever be on the watch to keep the water out. An hour spent in the Tunnel satisfied us all, and we left in the direction of the Tower, a description of which will be found in another chapter. Some of our party seemed bent on going next to the Colosseum, and to the Colosseum we went. On arriving at the doors, and entering a long, capacious passage, our eyes became quite dazzled by the gleams of colored light which shone upon them, both directly and reflectedly. The effect was heightened by the beautiful designs which figured on the walls, and by the graceful forms of the many statues which lined the path. In fact, the strength of the sense of sight became much greater, because the ear, which, all the day before, had listened to the busy hum of bustle and activity, now ceased to hear aught but a silent whisper or a wondering "O,"—no echo had even the foot-fall from the luxuriant softness of the carpeting.

Following up this fairy viaduct, we merged into a spacious circularly-formed apartment, on the downy conches of which reclined many an enraptured group; while nimble fingers and enticing lips caused sweet harmonious strains to chase each other from niche to niche, and among marbled figures within that charming temple.

Ascending a narrow flight of stairs, we landed on a balcony, from which we viewed the principal spectacle exhibited—and, O, it was a grand one! We found ourselves, as it were, upon the summit of some high building in the centre of the French metropolis, and there, all brilliant with gas-lights, and favored by the shining moon, Paris lay spread far out beneath us, though the canvas on which the scene was painted was but half a dozen feet from where we gazed in wonder. The moon herself seemed actually in the heavens. Nay, bets were laid that she had risen since we entered. Nothing can surpass the uniformity of appearance which every spire, and house, and wood, and river—yea, which every shop-window, ornamented, presented. All seemed natural, from the twinkling of the stars above us, to the monkey of the organ-man in the market-place below. Reader, if ever thou hast occasion to go to London, leave it not till thou hast seen the Colosseum.

Mustering our forces to return together, the cry was raised "A man a-wanting!" It seems there is an apparatus constructed in an apartment leading from the balcony, by which parties may, with a great degree of suddenness, be raised or lowered from or to the music-room. Our friend, at all times, anxious to make the most of a shilling, followed some parties into the "ascension-room," as it is called, and took his seat beside them, expecting that on the withdrawal of a curtain he should witness something which his companions would miss. A bell sounded, and suddenly our expectant found himself some twenty feet lower, and obliged to follow the example of his co-descendants still further, by furnishing the attendant with such a gratuity as became an imitator of the Queen Elizabeth.

To another, but extremely different, of nature's imitations, we now turned our steps. After traversing one or two passages, the lights of which became more dim as we advanced, we reached a cavern's mouth. Here our progress was arrested by an iron grating. Our inquisitive friend, however, soon discovered that this obstacle could be removed,—it being, in fact, similar to those revolving barriers (we forget the name given in the "trade") placed at the entrance to the Great Exhibition. Like them, too, they checked all egress, and, to the further astonishment of the man of prying propensity, we were soon called upon for so many extra sixpences, indicated by this tell-tale gateway as being the number of persons who had entered since the keeper left.

The damp and dripping stones, with their coat of foggy green,— the exclusion of every sound from without,—the stunted measure of our speech,—the sharp clank of our footsteps,—and the frowning gloom of every corner of this retreat, soon gave evidence of the excellence of the design and entire structure, in the impression which it raised that, in reality, we were in some secluded rendezvous of smugglers, or of outlaws. Yea, the question was put by one who had seldom crossed the Cree, Was Meg Merrilies' one like this? while a party who had explored Ben Lomond and its neighborhood was asked if from it there could not be formed some notion of that which bears the name of the chief, Rob Roy.

Relieved alike from depressing atmosphere and cloudy thoughts, we retired to a projecting window, from which to view the "Swiss cottage," as it is called. Upon the verge of a tremendous precipice is seen a lonely cot. All communication with it is cut off, save by the rugged trunk of a withered tree which spans an opposite projection. Under this unstable bridge gush torrents of foaming water, lashed down from the heights beyond. Yet morn and eve does an industrious peasant leave and return to his romantic home across this dangerous way. See now, as he returns from his toil, he paces cautiously along; and yonder, at the further end, stand wife and little ones waiting to greet him when he crosses. O! happy man, to live where thus thou'rt called to venture much and oft for those thou lovest, and be as oft rewarded by renewed tokens of their affection and most tender attachment!

Through openings in the walls we witnessed, also, the representation of mines and manufactures in full operation; and then, as we withdrew, we passed through artificial walks adorned with every kind of fantastical structure, and at some points of which, from the position of reflecting-glasses, we viewed in them hundreds of the very objects of which we could, with the unaided eye, see but one.

> "Passing we looked, and, looking, grieved to pass
> From the fair (?) figures smiling in the glass."

CHAPTER XXVI.

> "The treasures of the deep are not so precious
> As are the concealed comforts of a man
> Locked up in woman's love. I scent the air
> Of blessings, when I come but near the house.
> What a delicious breath marriage sends forth! . . .
> The violet bed 's not sweeter."
>
> MIDDLETON.

During a sojourn of five years in Europe, I have spent many pleasant hours in strolling through old church-yards, and reading the epitaphs upon the tombstones of the dead. Part of the pleasure was derived from a wish for solitude; and no place offers as quiet walks as a village burial-ground. And the curious epitaphs that are to be seen in a church-yard six or eight hundred years old are enough to cause a smile, even in so solemn a place as a grave-yard. While walking through Horsleydown church, in Cumberland, a short time since, I read an inscription over a tomb which I copied, and shall give in this chapter, although at the risk of bringing down upon my devoted head the indignation of the fair sex. Domestic enjoyment is often blasted by an intermixture of foibles with virtues of a superior kind; and if the following shall prove a warning to wives, I shall be fully compensated for my trouble.

> Here lie the bodies of
> THOMAS BOND, and MARY his wife.
> She was temperate, chaste and charitable;
> But
> She was proud, peevish and passionate.
> She was an affectionate wife and a tender mother;
> But
> Her husband and child, whom she loved, seldom saw her
> countenance without a disgusting frown,

Whilst she received visitors, whom she despised, with an
endearing smile.
Her behavior was discreet toward strangers;
But
imprudent in her family.
Abroad, her conduct was influenced by good-breeding;
But
at home, by ill-temper.
She was a professed enemy to flattery, and was
Seldom known to praise or commend;
But
the talents in which she principally excelled were
difference of opinion, and discovering
flaws and imperfections.
She was an admirable economist,
and, without prodigality,
dispensed plenty to every person in her family;
But
would sacrifice their eyes to a farthing candle.
She sometimes made her husband happy with her good qualities;
But
Much more frequently miserable with her many failings;
Insomuch, that, in thirty years' cohabitation, he often
lamented that, maugre her virtues,
He had not, in the whole, enjoyed two years
of matrimonial comfort.
At length,
finding that she had lost the affections of her
husband, as well as the regard of her neighbors, family
disputes having been divulged by servants,
She died of vexation, July 20, 1768,
Aged 48 years.
Her worn-out husband survived her four months
and two days, and departed this life November 28,1768,
in the 54th year of his age.
William Bond, brother to the deceased, erected
this stone,
a *weekly monitor* to the surviving wives of this
parish, that they may avoid the infamy
of having their memories handed down to posterity
with a *patch-work* character.

CHAPTER XXVII.

"To where the broken landscape, by degrees
Ascending, roughens into rigid hills;
O'er which the Cambrian mountains, like far clouds
That skirt the blue horizon, dusky rise."

THOMSON.

I have visited few places where I found warmer friends, or felt myself more at home, than in Aberdeen. The dwellings, being built mostly of granite, remind one of Boston, especially in a walk down Union-street, which is thought to be one of the finest promenades in Europe. The town is situated on a neck of land between the rivers Dee and Don, and is the most important commercial place in the north of Scotland.

During our stay in the city we visited, among other places, the old bridge of Don, which is not only resorted to owing to its antique celebrity and peculiar appearance, but also for the notoriety that it has gained by Lord Byron's poem for the "Bridge of Don." His lordship spent several years here during his minority, and this old bridge was a favorite resort of his. In one of his notes he alludes to how he used to hang over its one arch, and the deep black salmon stream below, with a mixture of childish terror and delight. While we stood upon the melancholy bridge, and although the scene around was severely grand and terrific,—the river swollen, the wind howling amongst the leafless trees, the sea in the distance,—and although the walk where Hall and Mackintosh were wont to melt down hours to moments in high converse was in sight, it was, somehow or other, the figure of the mild lame boy leaning over the parapet that filled our fancy; and the chief fascination of the spot seemed to breathe from the genius of the author of "Childe Harold."

To Anthony Cruikshank, Esq., whose hospitality we shared in Aberdeen, we are indebted for showing us the different places of interest in the town and vicinity. An engagement, however, to be in Edinburgh, cut short our stay in the north. The very mild state of the weather, and a wish to see something of the coast between Aberdeen and Edinburgh, induced us to make the journey by water. Consequently, after delivering a lecture before the Mechanics' Institute, with His Honor the Provost in the chair, on the evening of February 15th, we went on board the steamer bound for Edinburgh. On reaching the vessel we found the drawing-saloon almost entirely at our service, and, prejudice against color being unknown, we had no difficulty in obtaining the best accommodation that the steamer afforded. This was so unlike the pro-slavery, negro-hating spirit of America, that my colored friends who were with me were almost bewildered by the transition. The night was a glorious one. The sky was cloudless, and the clear, bracing air had a buoyancy I have seldom seen. The moon was in its zenith; the steamer and surrounding objects were beautiful in the extreme. The boat left her moorings at half-past twelve, and we were soon out at sea. The "Queen" is a splendid craft, and, without the aid of sails, was able to make fifteen miles within the hour. I was up the next morning extremely early,—indeed, before any of my fellow-passengers,—and found the sea, as on the previous night, as calm and as smooth as a mirror.

> "There was no sound upon the deep,
> The breeze lay cradled there;
> The motionless waters sank to sleep
> Beneath the sultry air;
> Out of the cooling brine to leap
> The dolphin scarce would dare."

It was a delightful morning, more like April than February; and the sun, as it rose, seemed to fire every peak of the surrounding hills. On our left lay the Island of May, while to the right was to be seen the small fishing-town of Anstruther, twenty miles distant from Edinburgh. Beyond these, on either side, was a range of undulating blue mountains, swelling, as they retired, into a bolder outline and a loftier altitude, until they terminated some twenty-five or thirty miles in the dim distance. A friend at my side pointed out a place on the right, where the remains of an old castle or look-out house, used in the time of the border wars, once stood, and which reminded us of the barbarism of the past.

But these signs are fast disappearing. The plough and roller have passed over many of those foundations, and the time will soon come when the antiquarian will look in vain for those places that history has pointed out to him as connected with the political and religious struggles of the past. The steward of the vessel came round to see who of the passengers wished for breakfast; and as the keen air of the morning had given me an appetite, and there being no prejudice on the score of color, I took my seat at the table, and gave ample evidence that I was not an invalid. On our return to the deck again, I found that we had entered the Frith of Forth, and that "Modern Athens" was in sight; and far above every other object, with its turrets almost lost in the clouds, could be seen Edinburgh Castle.

After landing, and a pleasant ride over one of the finest roads in Scotland, with a sprinkling of beautiful villas on either side, we were once more at Cannon's Hotel. While in the city, on this occasion, we went on the Calton Hill, from which we had a delightful view of the place and surrounding country.

I had an opportunity, during my stay in Edinburgh, of visiting the Infirmary; and was pleased to see among the two or three hundred students three colored young men, seated upon the same benches with those of a fairer complexion, and yet there appeared no feeling on the part of the whites towards their colored associates, except of companionship and respect. One of the cardinal truths, both of religion and freedom, is the equality and brotherhood of man. In the sight of God and all just institutions, the whites can claim no precedence or privilege on account of their being white; and if colored men are not treated as they should be in the educational institutions in America, it is a pleasure to know that all distinction ceases by crossing the broad Atlantic. I had scarcely left the lecture-room of the Institute and reached the street, when I met a large number of the students on their way to the college, and here again were seen colored men arm in arm with whites. The proud American who finds himself in the splendid streets of Edinburgh, and witnesses such scenes as these, can but behold in them the degradation of his own country, whose laws would make slaves of these same young men, should they appear in the streets of Charleston or New Orleans.

During my stay in Edinburgh I accepted an invitation to breakfast with George Combe, Esq., the distinguished philosophical phrenologist; and author of "The Constitution of Man." Although not far from seventy years of age, I found him apparently as active and as energetic as many men of half that number of years. Mr. Combe feels a deep interest in the cause of the American slave. I have since become more intimately acquainted with him, and am proud to reckon him amongst the warmest of my friends. In all of Mr. Combe's philanthropic exertions he is ably seconded by his wife, a lady of rare endowments, of an attractive person and engaging manners, and whose greatest delight is in doing good. She took much interest in Ellen Craft, who formed one of the breakfast party; and was often moved to tears on the recital of the thrilling narrative of her escape from slavery.

CHAPTER XXVIII.

"Look here, upon this picture, and on this."

HAMLET.

No one accustomed to pass through Cheapside could fail to have noticed a good-looking man, neither black nor white, engaged in distributing bills to the thousands who throng that part of the city of London. While strolling through Cheapside, one morning, I saw, for the fiftieth time, Joseph Jenkins, the subject of this chapter, handing out his bills to all who would take them as he thrust them into their hands. I confess that I was not a little amused, and stood for some moments watching and admiring his energy in distributing his papers. A few days after, I saw the same individual in Chelsea, sweeping a crossing; here, too, he was equally as energetic as when I met him in the city. Some days later, while going through Kensington, I heard rather a sweet, musical voice singing a familiar psalm, and on looking round was not a little surprised to find that it was the Cheapside bill-distributor and Chelsea crossing-sweeper. He was now singing hymns, and selling religious tracts. I am fond of patronizing genius, and therefore took one of his tracts and paid him for a dozen.

During the following week, I saw, while going up the city road, that Shakspeare's tragedy of Othello was to be performed at the Eagle Saloon that night, and that the character of the Moor was to be taken by "*Selim, an African prince.*" Having no engagement that evening, I resolved at once to attend, to witness the performance of the "African Roscius," as he was termed on the bills. It was the same interest that had induced me to go to the Italian opera to see Madames Sontag and Grisi in Norma, and to visit Drury Lane to see Macready take leave of the stage. My expectations were screwed up to the highest point. The excitement caused by the publication of "Uncle Tom's Cabin" had prepared the public for anything in the African line, and I felt that the *prince* would be sure of a good audience; and in this I was not disappointed, for, as I took my seat in one of the boxes near the stage, I saw that the house was crammed with an orderly company. The curtain was already up when I entered, and Iago and Roderigo were on the stage. After a while Othello came in, and was greeted with thunders of applause, which he very gracefully acknowledged. Just black enough to take his part with out coloring his face, and being tall, with a good figure and an easy carriage, a fine, full and musical voice, he was well adapted to the character of Othello. I immediately recognized in the countenance of the Moor a face that I had seen before, but could not at the moment tell where. Who could this "prince" be, thought I. He was too black for Douglass, not black enough for Ward, not tall enough for Garnet, too calm for Delany, figure, though fine, not genteel enough for Remond. However, I was soon satisfied as to who the *star* was. Reader, would you think it? it was no less a person than Mr. Jenkins, the bill-distributor from Cheapside, and crossing-sweeper from Chelsea! For my own part, I was overwhelmed with amazement, and it was some time before I could realize the fact. He soon showed that he possessed great dramatic power and skill; and his description to the senate of how he won the affections of the gentle Desdemona stamped him at once as an actor of merit. "What a pity," said a lady near me to a gentleman that was by her side, "that a prince of the royal blood of Africa should have to go upon the stage for a living! It it is indeed a shame!" When he came to the scene,

> "O, cursed, cursed slave!—whip me, ye devils,
> From the possession of this heavenly sight!
> Blow me about in winds, roast me in sulphur!
> Wash me in steep-down gulfs of liquid fire!
> O, Desdemona Desdemona! dead?
> Dead? O! O! O!"

the effect was indeed grand. When the curtain fell, the prince was called upon the stage, where he was received with deafening shouts of approbation, and a number of *bouquets* thrown at his feet, which he picked up, bowed, and retired. I went into Cheapside the next morning, at an early hour, to see if the prince had given up his old trade for what I supposed to be a more lucrative one; but I found the hero of the previous night at his post, and giving out his bills as energetically as when I had last soon him. Having to go to the provinces for some months, I lost sight of Mr. Jenkins, and on my return to town did not trouble myself to look him up. More than a year after I had witnessed the representation of Othello at the Eagle, I was walking, one pleasant Sabbath evening, through one of the small streets in the borough, when I found myself in front of a little chapel, where a number of persons were going in. As I was passing on slowly, an elderly man said to me, "I suppose you have come to hear your colored brother preach." "No," I answered; "I was not aware that one was to be here." "Yes," said he; "and a clever man he is, too." As the old man offered to find me a seat, I concluded to go in and hear this son of Africa. The room, which was not large, was already full. I had to wait but a short time before the reverend gentleman made his appearance. He was nearly black, and dressed in a black suit, with high shirt-collar, and an intellectual-looking cravat, that nearly hid his chin. A pair of spectacles covered his eyes. The preacher commenced by reading a portion of Scripture; and then announced that they would sing the twenty-eighth hymn in "the arrangement." O, that voice! I felt sure that I had heard that musical voice before; but where, I could not tell. I was not aware that any of my countrymen were in London; but felt that, whoever he was, he was no discredit to the race; for he was a most eloquent and accomplished orator. His sermon was against the sale and use of intoxicating drinks, and the bad habits of the working classes, of whom his audience was composed. Although the subject was intensely interesting, I was impatient for it to come to a close, for I wanted to speak to the preacher. But, the evening being warm, and the room heated, the reverend gentleman, on wiping the perspiration from his face (which, by the way, ran very freely), took off his spectacles on one occasion, so that I immediately recognized him, and saved me from going up to the pulpit at the end of the service. Yes; it was the bill-distributor of Cheapside, the crossing-sweeper of Chelsea, the tract-seller and psalm-singer of Kensington, and the Othello of the Eagle Saloon. I could scarcely keep from laughing right out when I discovered this to be the man that I had seen in so many characters. As I was about leaving my seat at the close of the services, the old man who showed me into the chapel asked me if I would not like to be introduced to the minister, and I immediately replied that I would. We proceeded up the aisle, and met the clergyman as he was descending. On seeing me, he did not wait for a formal introduction, but put out his hand and said, "I have seen you so often, sir, that I seem to know you." "Yes," I replied; "we have met several times, and under different circumstances." Without saying more, he invited me to walk with him towards his home, which was in the direction of my own residence. We proceeded; and, during the walk, Mr. Jenkins gave me some little account of his early history. "You think me rather an odd fish, I presume," said he. "Yes," I replied. "You are not the only one who thinks so," continued he. "Although I am not as black as some of my countrymen, I am a native of Africa. Surrounded by some beautiful mountain scenery, and situated between Darfour and Abyssinia, two thousand miles in the interior of Africa, is a small valley going by the name of Tegla. To that valley I stretch forth my affections, giving it the endearing appellation of my native home and fatherland. It was there that I was born, it was there that I received the fond looks of a loving mother, and it was there that I set my feet, for the first time, upon a world full of cares, trials, difficulties and dangers. My father being a farmer, I used to be sent out to take care of his goats. This service I did when I was between seven and eight years of age. As I was the eldest of the boys, my pride was raised in no small degree when I beheld my father preparing a farm for me. This event filled my mind with the grand anticipation of leaving the care of the goats to my brother, who was then beginning to work a little. While my father was making those preparations, I had the constant charge of the goats; and, being accompanied by two other boys, who resided near my father's house, we wandered many miles from home, by which means we acquired a knowledge of the different districts of our country.

"It was while in those rambles with my companions that I became the victim of the slave-trader. We were tied with cords, and taken to Tegla, and thence to Kordofan, which is under the jurisdiction of the Pacha of Egypt. From Kordofan I was brought down to Dongola and Korti, in Nubia, and from thence down the Nile to Cairo; and, after being sold nine times, I became the property of an English gentleman, who brought me to this country and put me into school. But he died before I finished my education, and his family feeling no interest in me, I had to seek a living as best I could. I have been employed for some years in distributing hand-bills for a barber in Cheapside in the morning, go to Chelsea and sweep a crossing in the afternoon, and sing psalms and sell religious tracts in the evening. Sometimes I have an engagement to perform at some of the small theatres, as I had when you saw me at the Eagle. I preach for this lit-tle congregation over here, and charge them nothing; for I want that the poor should have the Gospel without money and without price. I have now given up distributing bills; I have settled my son in that office. My eldest daughter was married about three months ago; and I have presented her husband with the Chelsea crossing, as my daughter's wedding por-tion." "Can he make a living at it?" I eagerly inquired. "O, yes! that cross-ing at Chelsea is worth thirty shillings a week, if it is well swept," said he. "But what do you do for a living for yourself?" I asked. "I am the leader of a band;" he continued; "and we play for balls and parties, and three times a week at the Holborn Casino."

By this time we had reached a point where we had to part; and I left Joseph Jenkins, impressed with the idea that he was the greatest genius that I had met in Europe.

CHAPTER XXIX.

> "Farewell! we did not know thy worth;
> But thou art gone, and now 't is prized.
> So angels walked unknown on earth,
> But when they flew were recognized."
>
> THOMAS HOOD.

It was on Tuesday, July 18, 1854, that I set out for Kensall Green Cemetery, to attend the inauguration of the monument erected to the memory of Thomas Hood, the poet. It was the first pleasant day we had had for some time, and the weather was exceedingly fine. The company was large, and many literary characters wore present. Near the monument sat Eliza Cook, author of the "Old Arm Chair," with her hair cut short and parted on one side like a man's. She is short in stature, and thick-set, with fair complexion, and bright eyes. Not far from Miss Cook was Mrs. Balfour, author of the "Working Women of the Last Half-century," "Morning Dew Drops," etc. etc. Mrs. Balfour is both taller and stouter than Miss Cook; and both are about the same age,—not far from forty. Murdo Young, Esq., of *The Sun*, and George Cruikshank, stood near the monument. Horace Mayhew, author of "London Labor and London Poor," was by the side of Cruikshank. The Hon. Mrs. Milnes sat near Eliza Cook. As the ceremony was about to commence, a short, stout man, with dark complexion, and black hair, took his stand on a tomb near by; this was R. Monckton Milnes, Esq., author of "Poetry for the People," and M.P. for Pontefract. He was the orator of the occasion.

The monument, which has been ably executed by Mr. Matthew Noble, consists of a bronze bust of the poet elevated on a pedestal of highly-polished red granite, the whole being twelve feet high. In front of the bust are placed wreaths in bronze, formed of the laurel, the myrtle, and the *immortelle*; and on a slab beneath the bast appears that well-known line of the poet, which he desired should be used as his epitaph:

"He sang the Song of the Shirt."

Upon the front of the pedestal is carved this inscription:

"In memory of Thomas Hood, born 23d May, 1798; died 3d May, 1845. Erected by public subscription, A. D. 1854."

At the base of the pedestal a lyre and comic mask in bronze are thrown together suggesting the mingled character of Hood's writings; whilst on the sides of the pedestal are bronze medallions illustrating the poem of "The Bridge of Sighs" and "The Dream of Eugene Aram." The whole design is worthy of the poet and the sculptor, and it is much to the honor of the latter that his sympathy with the object has entirely destroyed all hope of profit from the work.

Mr. Milnes was an intimate friend of the poet, and his selection as orator was in good taste. He spoke with great delicacy and kindness of Hood's personal characteristics, and with much taste upon the artistic value of the dead humorist's works. He touched with great felicity and subtlety upon the value of humor. He defined its province, and showed how closely it was connected with the highest forms in which genius manifests itself. Mr. Milnes spoke, however, more as a friend than as a critic, and his genial utterances excited emotions in the hearts of his hearers which told how deep was their sympathy both with the orator and the subject of his eulogium. There were not many dry eyes amongst his hearers when he quoted one or two exquisite portions of Hood's poems. It was evident that the greater part of the audience were well acquainted with the works of the poet, and were delighted to hear the quotations from poems which had afforded them exquisite gratification in the perusal.

Hood was not a merely ephemeral writer. He did not address himself to the feelings which more passing events generated in the minds of his readers. He smote deep down into the hearts of his admirers. Had he been nothing more than a literary man, the ceremony on this occasion would have been an impertinence. The nation cannot afford to have its time taken up by eulogiums on every citizen who does his work well in his own particular line. Nevertheless, when a man not only does his own work well, but acts powerfully on the national mind, then his fame is a national possession, and may be with all propriety made the subject of public commemoration. A great author is distinguished from the merely professional scribe by the fact of adding something to the stock of national ideas. Who can tell how much of the national character is due to the operation of the works of Shakspeare? The flood of ideas with which the great dramatist inundated the national mind has enriched it and fertilized it. We are most of us wiser and better by the fact of Shakspeare having lived and written. It would not be difficult to find in most modern works traces of the influence which Shakspeare has exercised over the writers. A great author, such as Shakspeare, is, then, a great public educator. The national mind is enlarged and enriched by the treasures which he pours into it. There is, therefore, a great propriety in making such a writer the subject of public eulogium.

Hood was one of those who not only enriched the national literature, but instructed the national mind. His conceptions, it is true, were not vast. His labors were not, like those of Shakspeare, colossal. But he has produced as permanent an effect on the nation as many of its legislators.

Englishmen are wiser and better because Hood has lived. In one of his own poems, "The Death-Bed," how sweetly he sang:

"We watched her breathing through the night,
Her breathing soft and low,
As in her breast the wave of life
Kept heaving to and fro.

"So silently we seemed to speak,
So slowly moved about,
As we had lent her half our powers
To eke her living out.

"Our very hopes belied our fears,
Our fears our hopes belied;
We thought her dying when she slept,
And sleeping when she died.

"For when the morn came dim and sad,
And chill with early showers,
Her quiet eyelids closed—she had
Another morn than ours."

Thomas Hood has another morn; may that morn have brightened into perfect day! It is well known that the poet died almost on the verge of starvation. Being seized, long before his death, with a malady that kept him confined to his bed the greater part of the time, he became much embarrassed. Still, in defiance of anguish and weakness, he toiled on, until nature could endure no more. Many of Hood's humorous pieces were written upon a sick bed, and taken out and sold to the publishers, that his family might have bread. Little did those who laughed over these comical sayings think of the pain that it cost the poet to write them. And, now that he is gone, we often hear some one say, "*Poor Hood!*" But peace to his ashes! He now lies in the finest cemetery in the world, and in one of its greenest spots. At the close of the inauguration, a rush was made to get a view of Eliza Cook, as being the next great novelty after the monument, if not its equal.

CHAPTER XXX.

"Dull rogues affect the politician's part,
And learn to nod, and smile, and shrug, with art;
Who nothing has to lose, the war bewails;
And he who nothing pays, at taxes rails."

CONGREVE.

The Abbey clock was striking nine, as we entered the House of Commons, and, giving up our ticket, were conducted to the strangers' gallery. We immediately recognized many of the members, whom we had met in private circles or public meetings. Just imagine, reader, that we are now seated in the strangers' gallery, looking down upon the representatives of the people of the British empire.

There, in the centre of the room, shines the fine, open, glossy brow and speaking face of Alexander Hastie, a Glasgow merchant, a mild and amiable man, of modest deportment, liberal principles, and religious profession. He has been twice elected for the city of Glasgow, in which he resides. He once presided at a meeting for us in his own city.

On the right of the hall, from where we sit, you see that small man, with fair complexion, brown hair, gray eyes, and a most intellectual countenance. It is Layard, with whom we spent a pleasant day at Hartwell Park, the princely residence of John Lee, Esq., LL.D. He was employed as consul at Bagdad, in Turkey. While there he explored the ruins of ancient Nineveh, and sent to England the Assyrian relics now in the British Museum. He is member for Aylesbury. He takes a deep interest in the Eastern question, and censures the government for their want of energy in the present war.

Not far from Layard you see the large frame and dusky visage of Joseph Hume. He was the son of a poor woman who sold apples in the streets of London. Mr. Hume spent his younger days in India, where he made a fortune; and then returned to England, and was elected a member of the House of Commons, where he has been ever since, with the exception of five or six years. He began political life as a tory, but soon went over to radicalism. He is a great financial reformer, and has originated many of the best measures of a practical character that have been passed in Parliament during the last thirty years. He is seventy-five years old, but still full of life and activity—capable of great endurance and incessant labor. No man enjoys to an equal extent the respect and confidence of the legislature. Though his opinions are called extreme, he contents himself with realizing, for the present, the good that is attainable. He is emphatically a progressive reformer; and the father of the House of Commons.

To the left of Mr. Hume you see a slim, thin-faced man, with spectacles, an anxious countenance, his hat on another seat before him, and in it a large paper rolled up. That is Edward Miall. He was educated for the Baptist ministry, and was called when very young to be a pastor. He relinquished his charge to become the conductor of a paper devoted to the abolition of the state church, and the complete political enfranchisement of the people. He made several unsuccessful attempts to go into Parliament, and at last succeeded Thomas Crawford in the representation of Rochdale, where in 1852 he was elected free of expense. He is one of the most democratic members of the legislature. Miall is an able writer and speaker—a very close and correct reasoner. He stands at the very head of the Nonconformist party in Great Britain; and *The Nonconformist*, of which he is editor, is the most radical journal in the United Kingdom.

Look at that short, thick-set man, with his hair parted on the crown of his head, a high and expansive forehead, and an uncommon bright eye.

That is William Johnson Fox. He was a working weaver at Norwich; then went to Holton College, London, to be educated for the Orthodox Congregational ministry; afterwards embraced Unitarian views. He was invited to Finsbury Chapel, where for many years he lectured weekly upon a wide range of subjects, embracing literature, political science, theology, government and social economy. He is the writer of the articles signed "Publicola," in the *Weekly Dispatch*, a democratic newspaper. He has retired from his pulpit occupations, and supports himself exclusively by his pen, in connection with the liberal journals of the metropolis. Mr. Fox is a witty and vigorous writer, an animated and brilliant orator.

Yonder, on the right of us, sits Richard Cobden. Look at his thin, pale face, and spare-made frame. He started as a commercial traveller; was afterwards a calico-printer and merchant in Manchester. He was the expounder, in the Manchester Chamber of Commerce and in the town council, of the principles of free trade. In the council of the Anti-Corn-Law League, he was the leader, and principal agitator of the question in public meetings throughout the kingdom. He was first elected for Stockport. When Sir Robert Peel's administration abolished the corn-laws, the prime minister avowed in the House of Commons that the great measure was in most part achieved by the unadorned eloquence of Richard Cobden. He is the representative of the non-intervention or political peace party; holding the right and duty of national defence, but opposing all alliances which are calculated to embroil the country in the affairs of other nations. His age is about fifty. He represents the largest constituency in the kingdom—the western division of Yorkshire, which contains thirty-seven thousand voters. Mr. Cobden has a reflective cast of mind; and is severely logical in his style, and very lucid in the treatment of his subjects. He may be termed the leader of the radical party in the House.

Three seats from Cobden you see that short, stout person, with his high head, large, round face, good-sized eyes. It is Macaulay, the poet, critic, historian and statesman. If you have not read his Essay on Milton, you should do so immediately; it is the finest thing of the kind in the language. Then there is his criticism on the Rev. R. Montgomery. Macaulay will never be forgiven by the divine for that onslaught upon his poetical reputation. That review did more to keep the reverend poet's works on the publisher's shelves than all other criticisms combined. Macaulay represents the city of Edinburgh.

Look at that tall man, apparently near seventy, with front teeth gone. That is Joseph Brotherton, the member for Salford. He has represented that constituency ever since 1832. He has always been a consistent liberal, and is a man of business. He is no orator, and seldom speaks, unless in favor of the adjournment of the House when the hour of midnight has arrived. At the commencement of every new session of Parliament he prepares a resolution that no business shall be entered upon after the hour of twelve at night, but has never been able to carry it. He is a teetotaller and a vegetarian, a member of the Peace Society, and a preacher in the small religious society to which he belongs.

In a seat behind Brotherton you see a young-looking man, with neat figure, white vest, frilled shirt, with gold studs, gold breast-pin, a gold chain round the neck, white kid glove on the right hand, the left bare with the exception of two gold rings. It is Samuel Morton Peto. He is of humble origin—has made a vast fortune as a builder and contractor for docks and railways. He is a Baptist, and contributes very largely to his own and other dissenting denominations. He has built several Baptist chapels in London and elsewhere. His appearance is that of a gentleman; and his style of speaking, though not elegant, yet pleasing.

Over on the same side with the liberals sits John Bright, the Quaker statesman, and leader of the Manchester school. He is the son of a Rochdale manufacturer, and first distinguished himself as an agitator in favor of the repeal of the corn-laws. He represents the city of Manchester, and has risen very rapidly. Mr. Cobden and he invariably act together, and will, doubtless, sooner or later, come into power together. Look at his robust and powerful frame, round and pleasing face. He is but little more than forty; an earnest and eloquent speaker, and commands the fixed attention of his audience.

See that exceedingly good-looking man just taking his seat. It is William Ewart Gladstone. He is the son of a Liverpool merchant, and represents the University of Oxford. He came into Parliament in 1832, under the auspices of the tory Duke of Newcastle. He was a disciple of the first Sir R. Peel, and was by that statesman introduced into official life. He has been Vice-president and President of the Board of Trade, and is now Chancellor of the Exchequer. Mr. Gladstone is only forty-four. When not engaged in speaking he is of rather unprepossessing appearance. His forehead appears low, but his eye is bright and penetrating. He is one of the ablest debaters in the House, and is master of a style of eloquence in which he is quite unapproached. As a reasoner he is subtle, and occasionally jesuitical; but, with a good cause and a conviction of the right, he rises to a lofty pitch of oratory, and may be termed the Wendell Phillips of the House of Commons.

There sits Disraeli, amongst the tories. Look at that Jewish face, those dark ringlets hanging round that marble brow. When on his feet he has a cat-like, stealthy step; always looks on the ground when walking. He is the son of the well-known author of the "Curiosities of Literature." His ancestors were Venetian Jews. He was himself born a Jew, and was initiated into the Hebrew faith. Subsequently he embraced Christianity. His literary works are numerous, consisting entirely of novels, with the exception of a biography of the late Lord George Bentinck, the leader of the protectionist party, to whose post Mr. Disraeli succeeded on the death of his friend and political chief. Mr. Disraeli has been all round the compass in politics. He is now professedly a conservative, but is believed to be willing to support any measures, however sweeping and democratical, if by so doing he could gratify his ambition—which is for office and power. He was the great thorn in the side of the late Sir R. Peel, and was never so much at home as when he could find a flaw in that distinguished statesman's political acts. He is an able debater and a finished orator, and in his speeches wrings applause even from his political opponents.

Cast your eyes to the opposite side of the House, and take a good view of that venerable man, full of years, just rising from his seat. See how erect he stands; he is above seventy years of age, and yet he does not seem to be forty. That is Lord Palmerston. Next to Joseph Hume, he is the oldest member in the House. He has been longer in office than any other living man. All parties have, by turns, claimed him, and he has belonged to all kinds of administrations; tory, conservative, whig, and coalition. He is a ready debater, and is a general favorite, as a speaker, for his wit and adroitness, but little trusted by any party as a statesman. His talents have secured him office, as he is useful as a minister, and dangerous as an opponent.

That is Lord Dudley Cutts Stuart speaking to Mr. Ewart. His lordship represents the populous and wealthy division of the district of Marylebone. He is a radical, the warm friend of the cause of Poland, Hungary and Turkey. He speaks often, but always with a degree of hesitation which makes it painful to listen to him. His solid frame, strongly-marked features, and unmercifully long eye-brows are in strange contrast to the delicate face of Mr. Ewart.

The latter is the representative for Dumfries, a Scotch borough. He belongs to a wealthy family, that has made its fortune by commerce. Mr. Ewart is a radical, a stanch advocate of the abolition of capital punishment, and a strenuous supporter of all measures for the intellectual improvement of the people.

Ah! we shall now have a speech. See that little man rising from his seat; look at his thin black hair, how it seems to stand up; hear that weak, but distinct voice. O, how he repeats the ends of his sentences! It is Lord John Russell, the leader of the present administration. He is now asking for three million pounds sterling to carry on the war. He is a terse and perspicuous speaker, but avoids prolixity. He is much respected on both sides of the House. Though favorable to reform measures generally, he is nevertheless an upholder of aristocracy, and stands at the head and firmly by his order. He is brother to the present Duke of Bedford, and has twice been Premier; and, though on the sunny side of sixty, he has been in office, at different times, more than thirty years. He is a constitutional whig and conservative reformer. See how earnestly he speaks, and keeps his eyes on Disraeli! He is afraid of the Jew. Now he scratches the bald place on his head, and then opens that huge roll of paper, and looks over towards Lord Palmerston.

That full-faced, well-built man, with handsome countenance, just behind him, is Sir Joshua Walmesley. He is about the same age of Lord John; and is the representative for Leicester. He is a native of Liverpool, where for some years he was a poor teacher, but afterwards became wealthy in the corn trade. When mayor of his native town, he was knighted. He is a radical reformer, and always votes on the right side.

Lord John Russell has finished and taken his seat. Joseph Hume is up. He goes into figures; he is the arithmetician of the House of Commons. Mr. Hume is in the Commons what James N. Buffum is in our Anti-Slavery meetings, the *man of facts*. Watch the old man's eye as he looks over his papers. He is of no religious faith, and said, a short time since, that the world would be better off if all creeds were swept into the Thames. His motto is that of Pope:

"For modes of faith let graceless zealots fight:
His can't be wrong whose life is in the right."

Mr. Hume has not been tedious; he is done. Now for Disraeli. He is going to pick Lord John's speech to pieces, and he can do it better than any other man in the House. See how his ringlets shake as he gesticulates! and that sarcastic smile! He thinks the government has not been vigorous enough in its prosecution of the war. He finds fault with the inactivity of the Baltic fleet; the allied army has made no movement to suit him. The Jew looks over towards Lord John, and then makes a good hit. Lord John shakes his head; Disraeli has touched a tender point, and he smiles as the minister turns on his seat. The Jew is delighted beyond measure. "The Noble Lord shakes his head; am I to understand that he did not say what I have just repeated?" Lord John: "The Right Hon. Gentleman is mistaken; I did not say what he has attributed to me." Disraeli: "I am glad that the Noble Lord has denied what I thought he had said." An attack is made on another part of the minister's speech. Lord John shakes his head again. "Does the Noble Lord deny that, too?" Lord John: "No, I don't, but your criticism is unjust." Disraeli smiles again: he has the minister in his hands, and he shakes him well before he lots him go. What cares he for justice? Criticism is his forte; it was that that made him what he is in the House. The Jew concludes his speech amid considerable applause.

All eyes are turned towards the seat of the Chancellor of the Exchequer: a pause of a moment's duration, and the orator of the House rises to his feet. Those who have been reading *The Times* lay it down; all whispering stops, and the attention of the members is directed to Gladstone, as he begins. Disraeli rests his chin upon his hat, which lies upon his knee: he too is chained to his seat by the fascinating eloquence of the man of letters. Thunders of applause follow, in which all join but the Jew. Disraeli changes his position on his seat, first one leg crossed, and then the other, but he never smiles while his opponent is speaking. He sits like one of those marble figures in the British Museum. Disraeli has furnished more fun for *Punch* than any other man in the empire. When it was resolved to have a portrait of the late Sir R. Peel painted for the government, Mr. Gladstone ordered it to be taken from one that appeared in *Punch* during the lifetime of that great statesman. This was indeed a compliment to the sheet of fun. But now look at the Chancellor of the Exchequer. He is in the midst of his masterly speech, and silence reigns throughout the House.

> "His words of learned length and thundering sound
> Amazed the gazing rustics ranged around;
> And still they gazed, and still the wonder grew
> That one small head could carry all he knew."

Let us turn for a moment to the gallery in which we are seated. It is now near the hour of twelve at night. The question before the House is an interesting one, and has called together many distinguished persons as visitors. There sits the Hon. and Rev. Baptist W. Noel. He is one of the first of the Nonconformist ministers in the kingdom. He is about fifty years of age; very tall, and stands erect; has a fine figure, complexion fair, face long and rather pale, eyes blue and deeply set. He looks every inch the gentleman. Near by Mr. Noel you see the Rev. John Cumming, D.D. We stood more than an hour last Sunday in his chapel in Crown-court to hear him preach; and such a sermon we have seldom ever heard. Dr. Cumming does not look old. He has rather a bronzed complexion, with dark hair, eyes covered with spectacles. He is an eloquent man, and seems to be on good terms with himself. He is the most ultra Protestant we have ever heard, and hates Rome with a perfect vengeance. Few men are more popular in an Exeter Hall meeting than Dr. Cumming. He is a most prolific writer; scarce a month passes by without something from his pen. But they are mostly works of a sectarian character, and cannot be of long or of lasting reputation.

Further along sits a man still more eloquent than Dr. Cumming. He is of dark complexion, black hair, light blue eyes, an intellectual countenance, and when standing looks tall. It is the Rev. Henry Melville. He is considered the finest preacher in the Church of England. There, too, is Washington Wilks, Esq., author of "The Half-century." His face is so covered with beard that I will not attempt a description; it may, however, be said that he has literally entered into the *Beard Movement.*

Come, it is time for us to leave the House of Commons. Stop a moment! Ah! there is one that I have not pointed out to you. Yonder he sits amongst the tories. It is Sir Edward Bulwer Lytton, the renowned novelist. Look at his trim, neat figure; his hair done up in the most approved manner; his clothes cut in the latest fashion. He has been in Parliament twenty-five years. Until the abolition of the corn-laws, he was a liberal; but as a land-owner he was opposed to free trade, and joined the protectionists. He has two country-seats, and lives in a style of oriental magnificence that is not equalled by any other man in the kingdom; and often gathers around him the brightest spirits of the age, and presses them into the service of his private theatre, of which he is very fond. In the House of Commons he is seldom heard, but is always listened to with profound attention when he rises to speak. He labors under the disadvantage of partial deafness. He is undoubtedly a man of refined taste, and pays a greater attention to the art of dress than any other public character I have ever seen. He has a splendid fortune, and his income from the labors of his pen is very great. His title was given to him by the queen, and his rank as a baronet he owes to his high literary attainments. Now take a farewell view of this assembly of senators. You may go to other climes, and look upon the representatives of other nations, but you will never see the like again.

CHAPTER XXXI.

"Take the spade of Perseverance,
Dig the field of Progress wide;
Every bar to true instruction
Carry out and cast aside."

The anniversary of West India emancipation was celebrated here on Monday last. But little notice of the intended meeting had been given, yet the capacious lecture-room of St. Martin's Hall was filled at an early hour with a most respectable audience, who appeared to have assembled for the sake of the cause.

Our old and well-tried friend, Geo. Thompson, Esq., was unanimously called to preside, and he opened the proceedings with one of his characteristic speeches. The meeting was then addressed by the Rev. Wm. Douglass, a colored clergyman of Philadelphia, in a most eloquent and feeling manner. Mr. Douglass is a man of fine native talent.

Francis W. Kellogg, of the United States, was the next speaker. Mr. Kellogg is an advocate of temperance, of some note, I believe, in his own country, and has been lecturing with considerable success in Great Britain. He is one of the most peculiar speakers I have ever heard. Born in Massachusetts, and brought up in the West, he has the intelligence of the one and the roughness of the other. He has the retentive memory of Wendell Phillips, the overpowering voice of Frederick Douglass, and the too rapid gestures of Dr. Delany. He speaks faster than any man I ever heard, except C. C. Burleigh. His speech, which lasted more than an hour, was one stream of fervid eloquence. He gave the audience a better idea of a real American stump orator than they ever had before. Altogether, he is the best specimen of the rough material out of which great public speakers are manufactured that I have yet seen. Mr. Kellogg's denunciations of Clay and Webster (the dead lion and the living dog) reminded us of Wendell Phillips; his pictures of slavery called to memory Frederick Douglass in his palmiest days; and his rebuke of his own countrymen for their unchristian prejudice against color brought before us the favorite topic and best speeches of C. L. Remond. It was his maiden speech on the subject of slavery, yet it was the speech of the evening.

Hatred to oppression is so instilled into the minds of the people in Great Britain, that it needs but little to arouse their enthusiasm to its highest point; yet they can scarcely comprehend the real condition of the slaves of the United States. They have heard of the buying and selling of men, women and children, without any regard to the tenderest ties of nature; of the passage and execution of the infamous Fugitive Slave Law; and, as we walk through the streets of London, they occasionally meet an American slave, who reminds them of the fact that while their countrymen are boasting of their liberty, and offering an asylum to the exiled of other countries, they refuse it to their own citizens.

Much regret has been expressed on this side of the Atlantic that Kossuth should have kept so silent on the slavery question while in

America; and this act alone has, to a great extent, neutralized his further operations in this country. He certainly is not the man now that he was before his visit to the New World.

I seldom pass through the Strand, or other great thoroughfares of the metropolis, without meeting countrymen of mine. I encountered one, a short time since, under peculiar circumstances. It was one of those days commonly experienced in London, of half cloud and half sunshine, with just fog enough to give everything a gray appearance, that I was loitering through Drury Lane, and came upon a crowd of poor people and street beggars, who were being edified by an exhibition of Punch and Judy, on the one hand, and an organ-grinder, with a well-dressed and intelligent-looking monkey, on the other. Punch looked happy, and was performing with great alacrity, while the organ-grinder, with his loud-toned instrument, was furnishing music for the million. Pushing my way through the crowd, and taking the middle of the street for convenience' sake, I was leaving the infected district in greater haste than I entered it. I had scarcely taken my eyes off the motley group, when I observed a figure approaching me from the opposite direction, and walking with a somewhat hasty step. I have seen so much oddity in dress, and the general appearance of members of the human family, that my attention is seldom ever attracted by the uncivilized look of any one. But this being whom I was meeting, and whose appearance was such as I had not seen before, threw the monkey and his companions entirely in the shade. In fact, all that I had beheld in the Great Exhibition, of a ludicrous nature, dwindled away into utter insignificance when compared to this Robinson Crusoe looking man; for, after all, it turned out to be a man. He was of small stature, and, although not a cold day, his person was enveloped in a heavy over-coat, which looked as if it had seen some service, and had passed through the hands of some of the second-hand gentlemen of Brattle-street, Boston. The trousers I did not see, as they were benevolently covered by the long skirts of the above garment. A pair of patent-leather boots covered a small foot. The face was entirely hidden by a huge beard, apparently from ten to fifteen inches in length, and of a reddish color. Long, dark hair joined the beard, and upon the head was thrown, in a careless manner, one of those hats known in America as the wide-awake, but here as the billy-cock. A pair of bright eyes were entirely hid by the hair around the face. I was not more attracted by his appearance than astonished at the man's stopping before me, as if he knew me. I now observed something like smoke emanating from the long beard round the mouth. I was immediately seized by the individual by his right hand, while the left hand took from his mouth a pipe about three inches in length, stem included, and, in a sharp, shrill voice, sounding as if it came from the interior of a hogshead or from a sepulchre, he called me by my name. I stood for a moment and eyed the figure from head to foot, "from top to toe," to see if I could discover the resemblance of any one I had ever seen before. After satisfying myself that the object was now, I said, "Sir, you have the advantage of me." "Don't you know me?" he exclaimed, in a still louder voice. I looked again, and shook my head. "Why," said he, it is C——." I stepped back a few feet, and viewed him once more from top to bottom, and replied, "You don't mean to say that this is H. C——?" "Yes, it is he, and nobody else." After taking another look, I said, "An't you mistaken, sir, about this being H. C——?" "No," said he, "I am sure I know myself." So I very reluctantly had to admit that I was standing in presence of the ex-editor of the "L. P. and H. of F." Indeed, one meets with strange faces in a walk through the streets of London. But I must turn again to the question of slavery.

Some months since a lady, apparently not more than fifty years of age, entered a small dwelling on the estate of the Earl of Lovelace, situated in the county of Surrey. After ascending a flight of stairs, and passing through a narrow passage, she found herself in a small but neat room, with plain furniture. On the table lay copies of the *Liberator* and *Frederick Douglass' Paper*. Near the window sat a young woman, busily engaged in sewing, with a spelling-book laying open on her lap. The light step of the stranger had not broken the silence enough to announce the approach of any one, and the young woman still sat at her task, unconscious that any one was near. A moment or two, and the lady was observed, when the diligent student hastily rose, and apologized for her apparent inattention. The stranger was soon seated, and in conversation with the young woman. The lady had often heard the word "slave," and knew something of its application, but had never before seen one of her own sex who had actually been born and brought up in a state of chattel slavery; and the one in whose company she now [was] so white, and had so much the appearance of an educated and well-bred lady, that she could scarcely realize that she was in the presence of an American slave. For more than an hour the illustrious lady and the poor exile sat and carried on a most familiar conversation. The thrilling story of the fugitive often brought tears to the eyes of the stranger. O, how I would that every half-bred, aristocratic, slave-holding, woman-whipping, negro-hating woman of America could have been present and heard what passed between these two distinguished persons! They would, for once, have seen one who, though moving in the most elevated and aristocratic society in Europe, felt it an honor to enter the small cottage and take a seat by the side of a poor, hunted and exiled American fugitive slave. Let it be rung in the ears of the thin-skinned aristocracy of the United States, who would rather receive a flogging from the cat-o'-nine-tails than to sit at the table of a negro, that Lady Noel Byron, widow of the great poet, felt it a peculiar pleasure to sit at the table and take tea with Ellen Craft. It must, indeed, be an interesting fact to the reader, and especially to those who are acquainted with the facts connected with the life and escape of William and Ellen Craft, to know that they are industrious students in a school, and attracting the attention of persons occupying the most influential positions in society. The wonderful escape of William and Ellen Craft is still fresh in the minds of all who take an interest in the cause of humanity; and their eluding the pursuit of the slave-hunters at Boston, and final escape from the Athens of the New World, will not be soon forgotten.

Every American should feel a degree of humiliation when the thought occurs to him that there is not a foot of soil over which the *Stars and Stripes* wave upon which Ellen Craft can stand and be protected by the constitution or laws of the country. Yet Ellen Craft is as white as most white women. Had she escaped from Austrian tyranny, and landed on the shores of America, her reception would have been scarcely less enthusiastic than that which greeted the arrival of Jenny Lind. But Ellen Craft had the misfortune to be born in one of the Slave States of the American Union, and that was enough to cause her to be driven into *exile* for daring to escape from American despotism.

CHAPTER XXXII.

"——when I left the shore,
The distant shore, which gave me birth,
I hardly thought to grieve once more,
To quit another spot on earth."

BYRON.

What a change five years make in one's history! The summer of 1849 found me a stranger in a foreign land, unknown to its inhabitants; its laws, customs and history, were a blank to me. But how different the summer of 1854! During my sojourn I had travelled over nearly every railroad in England and Scotland, and had visited Ireland and Wales, besides spending some weeks on the continent. I had become so well acquainted with the British people and their history, that I had begun to fancy myself an Englishman by habit, if not by birth. The treatment which I had experienced at their hands had endeared them to me, and caused me to feel myself at home wherever I went. Under such circumstances, it was not strange that I commenced with palpitating heart the preparation to return to my *native land*. Native land! How harshly that word sounds to my ears! True, America was the land of my birth; my grandfather had taken part in her Revolution, had enriched the soil with his blood, yet upon this, soil I had been worked as a slave. I seem still to hear the sound of the auctioneer's rough voice, as I stood on the block in the slave-market at St. Louis. I shall never forget the savage grin with which he welcomed a higher bid, when he thought that he had received the last offer. I had seen a mother sold and taken to the cotton-fields of the far South; three brothers had been bartered to the soul-driver in my presence; a dear sister had been sold to the negro-dealer, and driven away by him; I had seen the rusty chains fastened upon her delicate wrists; the whip had been applied to my own person, and the marks of the brutal driver's lash were still on my body. Yet this was my native land, and to this land was I about to embark.

In Edinburgh, I had become acquainted with the Wighams; in Glasgow, the Patens and Smeals; in Manchester, the Langdons; in Newcastle, the Mawsons and Richardsons. To Miss Ellen Richardson, of this place, I was mainly indebted for the redemption of my body from slaver and the privilege of again returning to my native country. I had also met, and become acquainted with, John Bishop Estlin, Esq., of Bristol, and his kindhearted and accomplished daughter. Of the hundreds of British Abolitionists with whom I had the pleasure of shaking hands while abroad, I know of none whose hearts beat more fervently for the emancipation of the American slave than Mr. Estlin's. He is indeed a model Christian. His house, his heart and his purse, were always open to the needy, without any regard to sect, color or country. When those distinguished fugitive slaves, William and Ellen Craft, arrived in England, unknown and without friends, Mr. Estlin wrote to me and said, "If the Crafts are in want, send to me. If you cannot find a home for them, let them come to Bristol, and I will keep them, at my expense, until something better turns up." And nobly did he keep his word. He put the two fugitives in school, and saw that they did not want for the means of support. I have known him to keep concealed what he had given to benevolent objects. To Mr. Estlin I am indebted for many acts of kindness; and now that the broad Atlantic lies between us, and in all probability we shall never again meet on earth, it is with heartfelt gratitude and pleasure that I make this mention of him.

And last, though not the least, I had become intimate with that most generous-hearted philanthropist, George Thompson, who never feels so well as when giving a welcome to an American fugitive slave. I had spent hours at the hospitable firesides of Harriet Martineau, R. D. Webb, and other distinguished authors. You will not, reader, think it strange that my heart became sad at the thought of leaving all these dear friends, to return to a country in which I had spent some of the best days of my life as a slave, and where I knew that prejudice would greet me on my arrival.

Most of the time I had resided in London. Its streets, parks, public buildings and its fog, had become "as familiar as household words." I had heard the deep, bass voice of the Bishop of London, in St. Paul's Cathedral. I had sat in Westminster Abbey, until I had lost all interest in the services, and then wandered about amongst the monuments, reading the epitaphs placed over the dead. Like others, I had been locked in the Temple Church, and compelled to wait till service was over, whether I liked it or not. I had spent days in the British Museum and National Gallery, and in all these I had been treated as a man. The "negro pew," which I had seen in the churches of America, was not to be found in the churches of London. There, too, were my daughters. They who had been denied education upon equal terms with children of a fairer complexion, in the United States, had been received in the London schools upon terms of perfect equality. They had accompanied me to most of the noted places in the metropolis. We had strolled through Regent-street, the Strand, Piccadilly and Oxford-street, so often, that sorrow came over me as the thought occurred to me that I should never behold them again.

Then the English manner of calling on friends before one's departure. I can meet an enemy with pleasure, but it is with regret that I part with a friend. As the time for me to leave drew near, I felt more clearly my iden-tity with the English people. By and by the last hour arrived that I was to spend in London. The cab stood at the door, with my trunks on its top; and, bidding the household "good-by," I entered the vehicle, the driver raised his whip, and I looked for the last time on my old home in Cecil-street. As we turned into the Strand, Nelson's monument, in Trafalgar-square, greeted me on the left, and Somerset House on the right. I took a farewell look at Covent Garden Market, through whose walks I had often passed, and where I had spent many pleasant hours. My youngest daugh-ter was in France, but the eldest met me at the dépôt, and after a few moments the bell rang, and away we went.

As the train was leaving the great metropolis of the world behind, I caught a last view of the dome of St. Paul's, and the old pile of Westminster Abbey.

In every town through which we passed on our way to Liverpool I could call to mind the name of some one whose acquaintance I had made, and whose hospitality I had shared. The steamer City of Manchester had her fires kindled when we arrived, and we went immediately on board. We found one hundred and seventy-five passengers in the cabin, and above five hundred in the steerage. After some delay, the ship weighed anchor, the machinery was put in motion, and, bidding Liverpool a long farewell, the vessel moved down the Mersey, and was in a short time out at sea. The steam tender accompanied the ship about thirty miles, during which time search was made throughout the Manchester to see that no "stow-aways" were on board. No vessel ever leaves an English port without some one trying to get his passage out without pay. When the crew are at work, or not on the watch, these persons come on board, hide themselves under the berths in the steerage cabin, or amongst the freight, until the vessel is out to sea, and then they come out. As they are always poor persons, without either baggage or money, they succeed in getting their passage without giving anything in return. As the tender was about quitting us to return to Liverpool, it came along-side to take on board those who had come with the vessel to see their friends off. Any number of white napkins were called into requisition, as friends were shaking hands with each other, and renewing their promises to write by the first post. One young man had come out to spend a few more hours with a handsome Scotch lass, with whom he, no doubt, had a matrimonial engagement. Another, an English lady, seemed much affected when the last bell of the tender rung, and the captain cried "All on board." Having no one to look after, I found time to survey others. The tender let go her cables amid three hearty cheers, and a deafening salute from the two-pounder on board the City of Manchester. A moment more, and the two steamers were leaving each other with rapid speed. The two young ladies of whom I have already made mention, together with many others, had their faces buried in their handkerchiefs, and appeared to be dying with grief. However, all of them seemed to get over it very soon. On the second day out at sea I saw the young English lady walking the quarter-deck with a fine-looking gentleman, and holding as tightly to his arm as if she had left no one behind; and as for the Scotch lass, she was seated on a settee with a countryman of hers, who had made her acquaintance on board, and, from all appearance, had entirely forgotten her first love. Such is the waywardness of man and woman, and the unfaithfulness of the human heart.

In the latter part of the second day a storm overtook us, and for the ten succeeding days we scarcely knew whether we were on our heads or our heels. The severest part of the gale was on the eighth and ninth nights out. On one of those evenings a fellow-roommate came in and said, "If you wish to see a little fun, go into the forward steerage." It was about eight o'clock, and most of the passengers were either in bed, or preparing for the night's rest, such as is to be had on board a ship in a gale of wind. This cabin contained about two hundred and fifty persons; some Germans, some Irish, and twenty-five or thirty Gypsies. Forty or fifty of these were on their knees in their berths, engaged in prayer. No camp-meeting ever presented a more noisy spectacle than did this cabin. The ship was rolling, and the sea running mountains high, and many of these passengers had given up all hope of ever seeing land again. The Gypsies were foremost amongst those who were praying; indeed, they seemed to fancy themselves in a camp-meeting, for many of them shouted at the top of their voices. One of them, known as the "Queen of the Gypsies," came to me and said, "O, Master! do get down and help us to ask God to stop the wind! You are a black man; may be he 'll pay more attention to what you say. Now do, master, do! and when the storm is over I will tell your fortune for nothing." At this juncture one of the chests which had been fastened to the floor broke away from its moorings, and came sliding across the cabin at the rate of about twenty miles per hour; soon another got loose, and these two locomotives broke up the prayer-meeting. Trunk after trunk became unfastened, until some eight or ten were crossing the cabin every time the vessel went over. At last the loose boxes upset the tables, on which were some of the passengers' eatables, and in a short time the whole cabin was in splendid confusion. The lamps, one after another, were knocked down and extinguished, so that the cabin was in total darkness. As I turned to retrace my steps, I heard the company joining in the prayer, and I was informed the next day that it was kept up during most of the night.

With all the watchfulness on the day of sailing, several persons succeeded in stowing themselves away. First one came out, and then another, until not less than five made their appearance on deck. As fast as these men were discovered they were put to work; so that labor, if not money, might be obtained for their passage. On the sixth day out I missed a small leather trunk, and search was immediately made in every direction, but no tidings of it could be found. However, after its being lost two days, I offered a reward for its recovery, and it was soon found, hid away in the forecastle. It had been broken open, and a few things, together with a little money, had been taken. The ships Chieftain and Harmony were the only vessels we met during the first ten days. An iceberg made its appearance while we were on the banks, but it was some distance to the larboard.

After a long passage of twenty days we arrived at the mouth of the Delaware, and took a pilot on board. The passengers were now all life; the Irish were basking in the sun, the Germans were singing, and the Gypsies were dancing. Some fifteen miles below Philadelphia, the officers came on board, to see that no sickness was on the vessel; and, after being passed by the doctors, each person began to get his luggage on deck, and prepare to go on shore. About four o'clock, on the twenty-sixth day of September, 1854, the City of Manchester hauled alongside the Philadelphia wharf, and the passengers all on the move; the Scotch lass clinging to the arm of her new Highland laddie, and the young English lady in company with her "fresh" lover. It is a dangerous thing to allow the Atlantic Ocean to separate one from his or her "affectionate friend." The City of Manchester, though not a fast steamer, is, nevertheless, a safe one. Her officers are men of experience and activity. Captain Wyly was always at his post; the first officer was an able seaman, and Mr. John Mirehouse, the second officer, was a most gentlemanly and obliging, as well as experienced officer. To this gentleman I am much indebted for kind attention shown me on the voyage. I had met him on a former occasion at Whitehaven. He is a stanch friend of humanity.

At Philadelphia I met with a most cordial reception at the hands of the Motts, J. M. M'Kim, the Stills, the Fortens, and that distinguished gentleman and friend of the slave, Robert Purvis, Esq. There is no colored man in this country to whom the Anti-slavery cause is more indebted than to Mr. Purvis. Endowed with a capacious and reflective mind, he is ever in search after truth; and, consequently, all reforms find in him an able and devoted advocate. Inheriting a large fortune, he has had the means, as well as the will, to do good. Few men in this country, either colored or white, possess the rare accomplishments of Robert Purvis. In no city in the Free States does the Anti-slavery movement have more bitter opponents than in Philadelphia. Close to two of our Southern States, and connected as it is in a commercial point of view, it could scarcely be otherwise. Colorphobia is more rampant there than in the pro-slavery, negro-hating city of New York. I was not destined to escape this unnatural and anti-christian prejudice. While walking through Chestnut-street, in company with two of my fellow-passengers, we hailed an omnibus going in the direction which we wished to go. It immediately stopped, and the white men were furnished with seats, but I was told that "We don't allow niggers to ride in here." It so happened that these two persons had rode in the same car with me from London to Liverpool. We had put up at the same hotel at the latter place, and had crossed the Atlantic in the same steamer. But as soon as we touch the soil of America we can no longer ride in the same conveyance, no longer eat at the same table, or be regarded with equal justice, by our thin-skinned democracy. During five years' residence in monarchical Europe I had enjoyed the rights allowed to all foreigners in the countries through which I passed; but on returning to my NATIVE LAND the influence of slavery meets me the first day that I am in the

country. Had I been an escaped felon, like John Mitchell, no one would
have questioned my right to a seat in a Philadelphia omnibus. Neither of
the foreigners who were allowed to ride in this carriage had ever visited
our country before. The constitution of these United States was as a blank
to them: the Declaration of Independence, in all probability, they had
never seen,—much less, read. But what mattered it? They were white, and
that was enough. The fact of my being an American by birth could not be
denied; that I had read and understood the constitution and laws, the most
pro-slavery, negro-hating professor of Christianity would admit; but I was
colored, and that was enough. I had partaken of the hospitality of noble-
men in England, had sat at the table of the French Minister of Foreign
Affairs; I had looked from the strangers' gallery down upon the great legislators of England, as they sat in the House of Commons; I had stood in
the House of Lords, when Her Britannic Majesty prorogued her
Parliament; I had eaten at the same table with Sir Edward Bulwer Lytton,
Charles Dickens, Eliza Cook, Alfred Tennyson, and the son-in-law of Sir
Walter Scott; the omnibuses of Paris, Edinburgh, Glasgow and Liverpool,
had stopped to take me up; I had often entered the "Caledonia,"
"Bayswater," "Hammersmith," "Chelsea," "Bluebell," and other omnibuses
that rattle over the pavements, of Regent-street, Cheapside, and the west
end of London,—but what mattered that? My face was not white, my hair
was not straight; and, therefore, I must be excluded from a seat in a third-
rate American omnibus. Slavery demanded that it should be so. I charge
this prejudice to the pro-slavery pulpits of our land, which first set the
example of proscription by erecting in their churches the "negro pew." I
charge it to that hypocritical profession of democracy which will welcome
fugitives from other countries, and drive its own into exile. I charge it to
the recreant sons of the men who carried on the American revolutionary
war, and who come together every fourth of July to boast of what their
fathers did, while they, their sons, have become associated with bloodhounds, to be put at any moment on the track of the fugitive slave.

But I had returned to the country for the express purpose of joining in
the glorious battle against slavery, of which this Negrophobia is a legitimate offspring. And why not meet it in its stronghold? I might have
remained in a country where my manhood was never denied; I might have
remained in ease in other climes; but what was ease and comfort abroad,
while more than three millions of my countrymen were groaning in the
prison-house of slavery in the Southern States? Yes, I came to the land of
my nativity, not to be a spectator, but a soldier—a soldier in this moral
warfare against the most cruel system of oppression that ever blackened
the character or hardened the heart of man. And the smiles of my old

associates, and the approval of my course while abroad by my colored fel-low-citizens, has amply compensated me for the twenty days rough pas-sage on my return.

OPINIONS OF THE BRITISH PRESS.

"While all the world is reading 'Uncle Tom's Cabin,' it is quite possible that what a real fugitive slave has to say for himself may meet with less attention than it deserves. Mr. Brown's book is pleasingly written."—*The Critic*, Dec. 10, 1852.

"When he writes on the wrongs of his race, or the events of his own career, he is always interesting or amusing."—*The Athenæum*, Nov. 15, 1852.

"The appearance of this book is too remarkable a literary event to pass without a notice. At the moment when attention in this country is directed to the state of the colored people in America, the book appears with additional advantage; if nothing else were attained by its publication, it is well to have another proof of the capability of the negro intellect. Altogether, Mr. Brown has written a pleasing and amusing volume. Contrasted with the caricature and bombast of his white countryman Mr. Willis' description of 'People he has Met,' a comparison suggested by the similarity of the title, it is both in intellect and in style a superior perform-ance, and we are glad to bear this testimony to the literary merit of a work by a negro author."—*The Literary Gazette*, Oct. 2, 1852.

"That a man who was a slave for the first twenty years of his life, and who has never had a day's schooling, should produce such a book as this, can-not but astonish those who speak disparagingly of the African race."—*The Weekly News and Chronicle*, Sept. 6, 1852.

"It is something new for a self-educated slave to publish such a work. It is really wonderful how one who has had to surmount so many difficulties in his literary career should have been able to produce a volume of so sparkling a character. The author is personally known to many of our read-ers, and, therefore, we need not enlarge respecting his abilities or his mer-its. We recommend them to procure his book, and are induced to do so by the consideration that his main object in bringing out the work is to enable him to educate his family; an object at all times honorable and praiseworthy, but in one occupying the position of William Wells Brown eminently commendable, and in which every friend of humanity must wish him success."—*British Friend*, Aug. 1852.

"This remarkable book of a remarkable man cannot fail to add to the practical protests already entered in Britain against the absolute bondage of three millions of our fellow-creatures. The impressions of a self-educated son of slavery, here set forth, must hasten the period when the senseless and impious denial of common claims to a common humanity, on the score of color, shall be scouted with scorn in every civilized and Christian country. And when this shall be attained, among the means of destruction of the hideous abomination his compatriots will remember with respect and gratitude the doings and sayings of William Wells Brown. The volume consists of a sufficient variety of scenes, persons, arguments, inferences, speculations and opinions, to satisfy and amuse the most *exigeant* of those who read *pour se desennuyer*, while those who look deeper into things, and view with anxious hope the progress of nations and of mankind, will feel that the good cause of humanity and freedom, of Christianity, enlightenment and brotherhood, cannot fail to be served by such a book as this."—*Morning Advertiser*, Sept. 10, 1852.

"He writes with ease and ability, and his intelligent observations upon the great question to which he has devoted and is devoting his life will be read with interest, and will command influence and respect."—*Daily News*, Sept. 24, 1852.

"The extraordinary excitement produced by 'Uncle Tom's Cabin' will, we hope, prepare the public of Great Britain and America for this lively book of travels by a real fugitive slave. Though he never had a day's schooling in his life, he has produced a literary work not unworthy of a highly-educated gentleman. Our readers will find in these letters much instruction, not a little entertainment, and the beatings of a manly heart, on behalf of a down-trodden race, with which they will not fail to sympathize."—*The Eclectic Review*, Nov. 1852.

"We have read this book with an unusual measure of interest. Seldom, indeed, have we met with anything more captivating. It somehow happens that all these fugitive slaves are persons of superior talents. The pith of the volume consists in narratives of voyages and journeys made by the author in England, Scotland, Ireland and France; and we can assure our readers that Mr. Brown has travelled to some purpose. The number of white men is not great who could have made more of the many things that came before them. There is in the work a vast amount of quotable matter, which, but for want of space, we should be glad to extract. As the volume, however, is published with a view to promote the benefit of the interesting fugitive, we deem it better to give a general opinion, by which curiosity may be whetted, than to gratify it by large citation. A book more worth the money has not, for a considerable time, come into our hands."—*British Banner*, Dec. 15, 1852.

"THREE YEARS IN EUROPE—The remarkable man who is the author of this work is not unknown to many of our readers. He was received with kindness in this city, and honored with various marks of respect by many eminent characters in the sister country. Since his arrival Mr. Brown has contributed much to the press; and the work before us, though small and unpretending, is of a high character, and evinces a superior and cultivated mind."—*Dublin General Advertiser*, October 30, 1852.

"This is a thrilling book, independent of adventitious circumstances, which will enhance its popularity. The author of it is not a man in America, but a chattel, a thing to be bought, and sold, and whipped: but in Europe he is an author, and a successful one, too. He gives in this book an interesting and graphic description of a three years' residence in Europe. The book will no doubt obtain, as it well deserves, a rapid and wide popularity."—*Glasgow Examiner.*

"The above is the title of an intelligent and otherwise well-written book, in which the author details, in a pleasing and highly-interesting manner, an account of places he has seen and people he has met; and we take much pleasure in recommending it to our readers."—*Weekly Dispatch.*

"This is an interesting volume, ably written, hearing on every page the impress of honest purpose and noble aspiration. One is amused by the well-told anecdotes, and charmed with the painter-like descriptions of towns, cities and natural scenery. Indeed, our author gives many very recognizable sketches of the places he has seen and people he has met. His three years in Europe have been well spent. The work will be appreciated by all the friends of the negro."—*The Leader.*

W. Wells Brown is no ordinary man, or he could not have so remarkably surmounted the many difficulties and impediments of his training as a slave. By dint of resolution, self-culture and force of character, he has rendered himself a popular lecturer to a British audience, and vigorous expositor of the evils and atrocities of that system whose chains he has shaken off so triumphantly and forever. We may safely pronounce William Wells Brown a remarkable man, and a full refutation of the doctrine of the inferiority of the negro."—*Glasgow Citizen.*

"We can assure those who are inclined to take up this volume that they will find it written with commendable care, as well as fluency, and will derive much pleasure from a perusal of it."—*Bristol Mercury.*

"The profound Anti-slavery feeling produced by 'Uncle Tom's Cabin' needed only such a book as this, which shows so forcibly the powers and capacity of the negro intellect, to deepen the impression. The work certainly exhibits a most favorable contrast to the more ambitious productions of many of his white countrymen, N. P. Willis among others."
—*Caledonian Mercury.*

Fiction

From *Clotel; or, The President's Daughter:*
A Narrative of Slave Life in the United States

(London: Partridge and Oakey, 1853)

Still considered the first novel published by an African American, Clotel *tells the story of Thomas Jefferson's slave mistress and her children, and depicts the horrors of slavery and racism. Initially published in England, the American edition removed references to Jefferson. Brown published three revisions and expansions of his novel as* Miralda; or, The Beautiful Quadroon *(1860–1861),* Clotelle: A Tale of the Southern States *(1864),* and Clotelle; or, The Colored Heroine *(1867). Most of the scholarship on William Wells Brown focuses on this, his pastiche novel.* Clotel *draws upon many of the same scenes, characters, and tropes that Brown's* Narrative *does, but what truly makes the story noteworthy and daring, of course, is the novel's bold representation of an enslaved black heroine who is descended from an American Founding Father. Yet despite the current popularity of the text in African American literature courses, Robert Fanuzzi, in his review of the Bedford Cultural Edition, acknowledges, "With its fair-skinned heroine and improbable sentimental romance,* Clotel *has always had the distinction and the curse of being incredibly derivative."[1]*

"We hold these truths to be self-evident: that all men are created equal; that they are endowed by their Creator with certain inalienable rights, and that among these are LIFE, LIBERTY, and the PURSUIT OF HAPPINESS."

—*Declaration of American Independence.*

PREFACE.

More than two hundred years have elapsed since the first cargo of slaves was landed on the banks of the James River, in the colony of Virginia, from the West coast of Africa. From the introduction of slaves in 1620, down to the period of the separation of the Colonies from the British Crown, the number had increased to five hundred thousand; now there are nearly four million. In fifteen of the thirty-one States, Slavery is made lawful by the Constitution, which binds the several States into one confederacy.

On every foot of soil, over which *Stars* and *Stripes* wave, the negro is considered common property, on which any white man may lay his hand with perfect impunity. The entire white population of the United States, North and South, are bound by their oath to the constitution, and their adhesion to the Fugitive Slave Law, to hunt down the runaway slave and return him to his claimant, and to suppress any effort that may be made by the slaves to gain their freedom by physical force. Twenty-five millions of whites have banded themselves in solemn conclave to keep four millions of blacks in their chains. In all grades of society are to be found men who either hold, buy, or sell slaves, from the statesmen and doctors of divinity, who can own their hundreds, down to the person who can purchase but one.

Were it not for persons in high places owning slaves, and thereby giving the system a reputation, and especially professed Christians, Slavery would long since have been abolished. The influence of the great "honours the corruption, and chastisement doth therefore hide his head." The great aim of the true friends of the slave should be to lay bare the institution, so that the gaze of the world may be upon it, and cause the wise, the prudent, and the pious to withdraw their support from it, and leave it to its own fate. It does the cause of emancipation but little good to cry out in tones of execration against the traders, the kidnappers, the hireling overseers, and brutal drivers, so long as nothing is said to fasten the guilt on those who move in a higher circle.

The fact that slavery was introduced into the American colonies, while they were under the control of the British Crown, is a sufficient reason why Englishmen should feel a lively interest in its abolition; and now that the genius of mechanical invention has brought the two countries so near together, and both having one language and one literature, the influence of British public opinion is very great on the people of the New World.

If the incidents set forth in the following pages should add anything new to the information already given to the Public through similar publications, and should thereby aid in bringing British influence to bear upon

American slavery, the main object for which this work was written will have been accomplished.

W. WELLS BROWN

22, Cecil Street, Strand, London.

CHAPTER I.
THE NEGRO SALE.

> "Why stands she near the auction stand,
> That girl so young and fair?
> What brings her to this dismal place,
> Why stands she weeping there?"

With the growing population of slaves in the Southern States of America, there is a fearful increase of half whites, most of whose fathers are slave-owners, and their mothers slaves. Society does not frown upon the man who sits with his mulatto child upon his knee, whilst its mother stands a slave behind his chair. The late Henry Clay, some years since, predicted that the abolition of negro slavery would be brought about by the amalgamation of the races. John Randolph, a distinguished slaveholder of Virginia, and a prominent statesman, said in a speech in the legislature of his native state, that "the blood of the first American statesmen coursed through the veins of the slave of the South." In all the cities and towns of the slave states, the real negro, or clear black, does not amount to more than one in every four of the slave population. This fact is, of itself, the best evidence of the degraded and immoral condition of the relation of master and slave in the United States of America.

In all the slave states, the law says:—"Slaves shall be deemed, sold, taken, reputed, and adjudged in law to be chattels personal in the hands of their owners and possessors, and their executors, administrators and assigns, to all intents, constructions, and purposes whatsoever." A slave is one who is in the power of a master to whom he belongs. The master may sell him, dispose of his person, his industry, and his labour. He can do nothing, possess nothing, nor acquire anything, but what must belong to his master. The slave is entirely subject to the will of his master, who may correct and chastise him, though not with unusual rigour, or so as to maim and mutilate him, or expose him to the danger of loss of life, or to cause his death. The slave, to remain a slave, must be sensible that there is no appeal from his master[.] Where the slave is placed by law entirely under the control of the man who claims him, body and soul, as property, what else could be expected than the most depraved social condition? The marriage relation, the oldest and most sacred institution given to man by his Creator, is unknown and unrecognised in the slave laws of the United States. Would that we could say, that the moral and religious teaching in the slave states were better than the laws; but, alas! we cannot. A few years since, some slaveholders became a little uneasy in their minds about the rightfulness of permitting slaves to take to themselves husbands and wives, while they still had others living, and applied to their religious teachers for advice; and the following will show how this grave and important subject was treated:—

"Is a servant, whose husband or wife has been sold by his or her master into a distant country, to be permitted to marry again?"

The query was referred to a committee, who made the following report; which, after discussion, was adopted:—

"That, in view of the circumstances in which servants in this country are placed, the committee are unanimous in the opinion, that it is better to permit servants thus circumstanced to take another husband or wife."

Such was the answer from a committee of the "Shiloh Baptist Association;" and instead of receiving light, those who asked the question were plunged into deeper darkness!

A similar question was put to the "Savannah River Association," and the answer, as the following will show, did not materially differ from the one we have already given:—

"Whether, in a case of involuntary separation, of such a character as to preclude all prospect of future intercourse, the parties ought to be allowed to marry again."

Answer—

"That such separation among persons situated as our slaves are, is civilly a separation by death; and they believe that, in the sight of God, it would be so viewed. To forbid second marriages in such cases would be to expose the parties, not only to stronger hardships and strong temptation, but to church-censure for acting in obedience to their masters, who cannot be expected to acquiesce in a regulation at variance with justice to the slaves, and to the spirit of that command which regulates marriage among Christians. The slaves are not free agents; and a dissolution by death is not more entirely without their consent, and beyond their control, than by such separation."

Although marriage, as the above indicates, is a matter which the slaveholders do not think is of any importance, or of any binding force with their slaves; yet it would be doing that degraded class an injustice, not to acknowledge that many of them do regard it as a sacred obligation, and show a willingness to obey the commands of God on this subject. Marriage is, indeed, the first and most important institution of human existence—the foundation of all civilisation and culture—the root of church and state. It is the most intimate covenant of heart formed among mankind; and for many persons the only relation in which they feel the true sentiments of humanity. It gives scope for every human virtue, since each of these is developed from the love and confidence which here predominate. It unites all which ennobles and beautifies, life,—sympathy, kindness of will and deed, gratitude, devotion, and every delicate, intimate feeling. As the only asylum for true education, it is the first and last sanctuary of human culture. As husband and wife through each other become conscious of complete humanity, and every human feeling, and every human virtue; so children, at their first awakening in the fond covenant of love between parents, both of whom are tenderly concerned for the same object, find an image of complete humanity leagued in free love. The spirit of love which prevails between them acts with creative power upon the young mind, and awakens every germ of goodness within it. This invisible and incalculable influence of parental life acts more upon the child than all the efforts of education, whether by means of instruction, percept, or exhortation. If this be a true picture of the vast influence for good of the institution of marriage, what must be the moral degradation of that people to whom marriage is denied? Not content with depriving them of all the higher and holier enjoyments of this relation, by degrading and darkening their souls, the slaveholder denies to his victim even that slight alleviation of his misery, which would result from the marriage relation being protected by law and public opinion. Such is the influence of slavery in the United States, that the ministers of religion, even in the so-called free states, are the mere echoes, instead of the correctors, of public sentiment.

We have thought it advisable to show that the present system of chattel slavery in America undermines the entire social condition of man, so as to prepare the reader for the following narrative of slave life, in that otherwise happy and prosperous country.

In all the large towns in the Southern States, there is a class of slaves who are permitted to hire their time of their owners, and for which they pay a high price. These are mulatto women, or quadroons, as they are familiarly known, and are distinguished for their fascinating beauty. The handsomest usually pays the highest price for her time. Many of these women are the favourites of persons who furnish them with the means of paying their owners, and not a few are dressed in the most extravagant manner. Reader, when you take into consideration the fact, that amongst the slave population no safeguard is thrown around virtue, and no inducement held out to slave women to be chaste, you will not be surprised when we tell you that immorality and vice pervade the cities of the Southern States in a manner unknown in the cities and towns of the Northern States. Indeed most of the slave women have no higher aspiration than that of becoming the finely-dressed mistress of some white man. And at negro balls and parties, this class of women usually cut the greatest figure.

At the close of the year—the following advertisement appeared in a newspaper published in Richmond, the capital of the state of Virginia:— "Notice: Thirty-eight negroes will be offered for sale on Monday, November 10th, at twelve o'clock, being the entire stock of the late John Graves, Esq. The negroes are in good condition, some of them very prime; among them are several mechanics, able-bodied field hands, plough-boys, and women with children at the breast, and some of them very prolific in their generating qualities, affording a rare opportunity to any one who wishes to raise a strong and healthy lot of servants for their own use. Also several mulatto girls of rare personal qualities: two of them very superior. Any gentleman or lady wishing to purchase, can take any of the above slaves on trial for a week, for which no charge will be made." Amongst the above slaves to be sold were Currer and her two daughters, Clotel and Althesa; the latter were the girls spoken of in the advertisement as "very superior." Currer was a bright mulatto, and of prepossessing appearance, though then nearly forty years of ago. She had hired her time for more than twenty years, during which time she had lived in Richmond. In her younger days Currer had been the housekeeper of a young slaveholder; but of later years had been a laundress or washerwoman, and was considered to be a woman of great taste in getting up linen. The gentleman for whom she had kept house was Thomas Jefferson, by whom she had two daughters. Jefferson being called to Washington to fill a government appointment, Currer was left behind, and thus she took herself to the business of washing, by which means she paid her master, Mr. Graves, and supported herself and two children. At the time of the decease of her master, Currer's daughters, Clotel and Althesa, were aged respectively sixteen and fourteen years, and both, like most of their own sex in America, were well grown. Currer early resolved to bring her daughters up as ladies, as she termed it, and therefore imposed little or no work upon them. As her daughters grew older, Currer had to pay a stipulated price for them; yet her notoriety as a laundress of the first class enabled her to put an extra price upon her charges, and thus she and her daughters lived in comparative luxury. To bring up Clotel and Althesa to attract attention, and especially at balls and parties, was the great aim of Currer. Although the term "negro ball" is applied to most of these gatherings, yet a majority of the attendants are often whites. Nearly all the negro parties in the cities and towns of the Southern States are made up of quadroon and mulatto girls, and white men. These are democratic gatherings, where gentlemen, shopkeepers, and their clerks, all appear upon terms of perfect equality. And there is a degree of gentility and decorum in these companies that is not surpassed by similar gatherings of white people in the Slave States. It was at one of these parties that Horatio Green, the son of a wealthy gentleman of Richmond, was first introduced to Clotel. The young man had just returned from college, and was in his twenty-second year. Clotel was sixteen, and was admitted by all to be the most beautiful girl, coloured or white, in the city. So attentive was the young man to the quadroon during the evening that it was noticed by all, and became a matter of general conversation; while Currer appeared delighted beyond measure at her daughter's conquest. From that evening, young Green became the favourite visitor at Currer's house. He soon promised to purchase Clotel, as speedily as it could be effected, and make her mistress of her own dwelling; and Currer looked forward with pride to the time when she should see her daughter emancipated and free. It was a beautiful moonlight night in August, when all who reside in tropical climes are eagerly gasping for a breath of fresh air, that Horatio Green was seated in the small garden behind Currer's cottage, with the object of his affections by his side. And it was here that Horatio drew from his pocket the newspaper, wet from the press, and read the advertisement for the sale of the slaves to which we have alluded; Currer and her two daughters being of the number. At the close of the evening's visit, and as the young man was leaving, he said to the girl, "You shall soon be free and your own mistress."

As might have been expected, the day of sale brought an unusual large number together to compete for the property to be sold. Farmers who make a business of raising slaves for the market were there; slave-traders and speculators were also numerously represented; and in the midst of this throng was one who felt a deeper interest in the result of the sale than any other of the bystanders; this was young Green. True to his promise, he was there with a blank bank check in his pocket, awaiting with impatience to enter the list as a bidder for the beautiful slave. The less valuable slaves were first placed upon the auction block, one after another, and sold to the highest bidder. Husbands and wives were separated with a degree of indifference that is unknown in any other relation of life, except that of slavery. Brothers and sisters were torn from each other; and mothers saw their children leave them for the last time on this earth.

It was late in the day, when the greatest number of persons were thought to be present, that Currer and her daughters were brought forward to the place of sale. Currer was first ordered to ascend the auction stand, which she did with a trembling step. The slave mother was sold to a trader. Althesa, the youngest, and who was scarcely less beautiful than her sister, was sold to the same trader for one thousand dollars. Clotel was the last, and, as was expected, commanded a higher price than any that had been offered for sale that day. The appearance of Clotel on the auction block created a deep sensation amongst the crowd. There she stood, with a complexion as white as most of those who were waiting with a wish to become her purchasers; her features as finely defined as any of her sex of pure Anglo-Saxon; her long black wavy hair done up in the neatest manner; her form tall and graceful, and her whole appearance indicating one superior to her position. The auctioneer commenced by saying, that "Miss Clotel had been reserved for the last, because she was the most valuable. How much gentlemen? Real Albino, fit for a fancy girl for any one. She enjoys good health, and has a sweet temper. How much do you say?" "Five hundred dollars." "Only five hundred for such a girl as this? Gentlemen, she is worth a deal more than that sum; you certainly don't know the value of the article you are bidding upon. Here, gentlemen, I hold in my hand a paper certifying that she has a good moral character." "Seven hundred." "Ah, gentlemen, that is something like. This paper also states that she is very intelligent." "Eight hundred." "She is a devoted Christian, and perfectly trustworthy." "Nine hundred." "Nine fifty." "Ten." "Eleven." "Twelve hundred." Here the sale came to a dead stand. The auctioneer stopped, looked around, and began in a rough manner to relate some anecdotes relative to the sale of slaves, which, he said, had come under his own observation. At this juncture the scene was indeed strange. Laughing, joking, swearing, smoking, spitting, and talking kept up a continual hum and noise amongst the crowd; while the slave-girl stood with tears in her eyes, at one time looking towards her mother and sister, and at another towards the young man whom she hoped would become her purchaser. "The chastity of this girl is pure; she has never been from under her mother's care, she is a virtuous creature." "Thirteen." "Fourteen." "Fifteen." "Fifteen hundred dollars," cried the auctioneer, and the maiden was struck for that sum. This was a Southern auction, at which the bones, muscles, sinews, blood, and nerves of a young lady of sixteen were sold for five hundred dollars; her moral character for two hundred; her improved intellect for one hundred; her Christianity for three hundred; and her chastity and virtue for four hundred dollars more. And this, too, in a city thronged with churches, whose tall spires look like so many signals pointing to heaven, and whose ministers preach that slavery is a God-ordained institution!

What words can tell the inhumanity, the atrocity, and the immorality of that doctrine which, from exalted office, commends such a crime to the favour of enlightened and Christian people? What indignation from all the world is not due to the government and people who put forth all their strength and power to keep in existence such an institution? Nature abhors it; the age repels it; and Christianity needs all her meekness to forgive it.

Clotel was sold for fifteen hundred dollars, but her purchaser was Horatio Green. Thus closed a negro sale, at which two daughters of Thomas Jefferson, the writer of the Declaration of American Independence, and one of the presidents of the great republic, were disposed of to the highest bidder!

"O God! my every heart-string cries,
Dost thou these scenes behold
In this our boasted Christian land,
And must the truth be told?

"Blush, Christian, blush! for e'en the dark,
Untutored heathen see
Thy inconsistency; and, lo!
They scorn thy God, and thee!"

CHAPTER IV.
THE QUADROON'S HOME.

"How sweetly on the bill side sleeps
The sunlight with its quickening rays!
The verdant trees that crown the steeps,
Crow greener in its quivering blaze.["]

About three miles from Richmond is a pleasant plain, with here and there a beautiful cottage surrounded by trees so as scarcely to be seen. Among them was one far retired from the public roads, and almost hidden among the trees. It was a perfect model of rural beauty. The piazzas that surrounded it were covered with clematis and passion flower. The pride of China mixed its oriental looking foliage with the majestic magnolia, and the air was redolent with the fragrance of flowers, peeping out of every nook and nodding upon you with a most unexpected welcome. The tasteful hand of art had not learned to imitate the lavish beauty and harmonious disorder of nature, but they lived together in loving amity, and spoke in accordant tones. The gateway rose in a gothic arch, with graceful tracery in iron work, surmounted by a cross, round which fluttered and played the mountain fringe, that lightest and most fragile of vines. This cottage was hired by Horatio Green for Clotel, and the quadroon girl soon found herself in her new home.

The tenderness of Clotel's conscience, together with the care her mother had with her and the high value she placed upon virtue, required an outward marriage; though she well knew that a union with her prescribed race was unrecognised by law, and therefore the ceremony would give her no legal hold on Horatio's constancy. But her high poetic nature regarded reality rather than the semblance of things; and when he playfully asked how she could keep him if he wished to run away, she replied, "If the mutual love we have for each other, and the dictates of your own conscience do not cause you to remain my husband, and your affections fall from me, I would not, if I could, hold you by a single fetter." It was indeed a marriage sanctioned by heaven, although unrecognised on earth. There the young couple lived secluded from the world, and passed their time as happily as circumstances would permit. It was Clotel's wish that Horatio should purchase her mother and sister, but the young man pleaded that he was unable, owing to the fact that he had not come into possession of his share of property, yet he promised that when he did, he would seek them out and purchase them. Their first-born was named Mary, and her complexion was still lighter than her mother. Indeed she was not darker than other white children. As the child grew older, it more and more resembled its mother. The iris of her large dark eye had the melting mezzotinto, which remains the last vestige of African ancestry, and gives that plaintive expression, so often observed, and so appropriate to that docile and injured race. Clotel was still happier after the birth of her dear child; for Horatio, as might have been expected, was often absent day and night with his friends in the city, and the edicts of society had built up a wall of separation between the quadroon and them. Happy as Clotel was in Horatio's love, and surrounded by an outward environment of beauty, so well adapted to her poetic spirit, she felt these incidents with inexpressible pain. For herself she cared but little; for she had found a sheltered home in Horatio's heart, which the world might ridicule, but had no power to profane. But when she looked at her beloved Mary, and reflected upon the unavoidable and dangerous position which the tyranny of society had awarded her, her soul was filled with anguish. The rare loveliness of the child increased daily, and was evidently ripening into most marvellous beauty. The father seemed to rejoice in it with unmingled pride; but in the deep tenderness of the mother's eye, there was an indwelling sadness that spoke of anxious thoughts and fearful foreboding. Clotel now urged Horatio to remove to France or England, where both her and her child would be free, and where colour was not a crime. This request excited but little opposition, and was so attractive to his imagination, that he might have overcome all intervening obstacles, had not "a change come over the spirit of his dreams." He still loved Clotel; but he was now becoming engaged in political and other affairs which kept him oftener and longer from the young mother; and ambition to become a statesman was slowly gaining the ascendancy over him.

Among those on whom Horatio's political success most depended was a very popular and wealthy man, who had an only daughter. His visits to the house were at first purely of a political nature; but the young lady was pleasing, and he fancied he discovered in her a sort of timid preference for himself. This excited his vanity, and awakened thoughts of the great worldly advantages connected with a union. Reminiscences of his first love kept these vague ideas in check for several months; for with it was associated the idea of restraint. Moreover, Gertrude, though inferior in beauty, was yet a pretty contrast to her rival. Her light hair fell in silken ringlets down her shoulders, her blue eyes were gentle though inexpressive, and her healthy cheeks were like opening rosebuds. He had already become accustomed to the dangerous experiment of resisting his own inward convictions; and this new impulse to ambition, combined with the strong temptation of variety in love, met the ardent young man weakened in moral principle, and unfettered by laws of the land. The change wrought upon him was soon noticed by Clotel.

CHAPTER V.
THE SLAVE MARKET.

"What! mothers from their children riven!
What! God's own image bought and sold!
Americans to market driven,
And barter'd as the brute for gold."

—*Whittier.*

Not far from Canal-street, in the city of New Orleans, stands a large two story flat building surrounded by a stone wall twelve feet high, the top of which is covered with bits of glass, and so constructed as to prevent even the possibility of any one's passing over it without sustaining great injury. Many of the rooms resemble cells in a prison. In a small room near the "office" are to be seen any number of iron collars, hobbles, handcuffs, thumbscrews, cowhides, whips, chains, gags, and yokes. A back yard inclosed by a high wall looks something like the playground attached to one of our large New England schools, and in which are rows of benches and swings. Attached to the back premises is a good-sized kitchen, where two old negresses are at work, stewing, boiling, and baking, and occasionally wiping the sweat from their furrowed and swarthy brows.

The slave-trader Walker, on his arrival in New Orleans, took up his quarters at this slave pen with his gang of human cattle; and the morning after, at ten o'clock, they were exhibited for sale. There, first of all, was the beautiful Althesa, whose pale countenance and dejected look told how many sad hours she had passed since parting with her mother at Natchez. There was a poor woman who had been separated from her husband and five children. Another woman, whose looks and manner were expressive of deep anguish, sat by her side. There, too, was "Uncle Geemes," with his whiskers off, his face shaved clean, and the grey hair plucked out, and ready to be sold for ten years younger than he was. Toby was also there, with his face shaved and greased, ready for inspection. The examination commenced, and was carried on in a manner calculated to shock the feelings of any one not devoid of the milk of human kindness. "What are you wiping your eyes for?" inquired a fat, red-faced man, with a white hat set on one side of his head, and a cigar in his mouth, of a woman who sat on one of the stools. "I s'pose I have been crying." "Why do you cry?" "Because I have left my man behind." "Oh, if I buy you I will furnish you with a better man than you left. I have lots of young bucks on my farm." "I don't want, and will never have, any other man," replied the woman. "What's your name?" asked a man in a straw hat of a tall negro man, who stood with his arms folded across his breast, and leaning against the wall. "My name is Aaron, sir." "How old are you?" "Twenty-five." "Where were you raised?" "In old Virginny, sir." "How many men have owned you?" "Four." "Do you enjoy good health?" "Yes, sir." "How long did you live with your first owner?" "Twenty years." "Did you ever run away?" "No, sir." "Did you ever strike your master[?]" "No, sir." "Were you ever whipped much?" "No, sir, I s'pose I did not deserve it." "How long did you live with your second master?" "Ten years, sir." "Have you a good appetite?" "Yes, sir." "Can you eat your allowance?" "Yes, sir, when I can get it." "What were you employed at in Virginia?" "I worked in de terbacar feel." "In the tobacco field?" "Yes, sir." "How old did you say you were?" "I will be twenty-five if I live to see next sweet potater-digging time." "I am a cotton planter, and if I buy you, you will have to work in the cotton field. My men pick one hundred and fifty pounds a day, and the women one hundred and forty, and those who fail to pick their task receive five stripes from the cat for each pound that is wanting. Now, do you think you could keep up with the rest of the hands?" "I don't know, sir, I 'spec I'd have to." "How long did you live with your third master?" "Three years, sir." "Why, this makes you thirty-three, I thought you told me you was only twenty-five?" Aaron now looked first at the planter, then at the trader, and seemed perfectly bewildered. He had forgotten the lesson given him by Pompey as to his age, and the planter's circuitous talk (doubtless to find out the slave's real age) had the negro off his guard. "I must see your back, so as to know how much you have been whipped, before I think of buying," said the planter. Pompey, who had been standing by during the examination, thought that his services were now required, and stepping forward with a degree of officiousness, said to Aaron, "Don't you hear de gentman tell you he want to zamon your limbs. Come, unharness yeself, old boy, an don't be standing dar." Aaron was soon examined and pronounced "sound;" yet the conflicting statement about the age was not satisfactory.

Fortunate for Althesa she was spared the pain of undergoing such an examination[.] Mr. Crawford, a teller in one of the banks, had just been married, and wanted a maid-servant for his wife; and passing through the market in the early part of the day, was pleased with the young slave's appearance and purchased her, and in his dwelling the quadroon found a much better home than often falls to the lot of a slave sold in the New Orleans market. The heart-rending and cruel traffic in slaves which has been so often described, is not confined to any particular class of persons. No one forfeits his or her character or standing in society, by buying or selling slaves; or even raising slaves for the market. The precise number of slaves carried from the slave-raising to the slave-consuming states, we have no means of knowing. But it must be very great, as more than forty thousand were sold and taken out of the state of Virginia in one year. Known to God only is the amount of human agony and suffering which sends its cry from the slave markets and negro pens, unheard and unheeded by man, up to his ear; mothers weeping for their children, breaking the night-silence with the shrieks of their breaking hearts. From some you will hear the burst of bitter lamentation, while from others the loud hysteric laugh, denoting still deeper agony. Most of them leave the market for cotton or rice plantations,

> "Where the slave-whip ceaseless swings,
> Where the noisome insect stings,
> Where the fever demon strews
> Poison with the falling dews,
> Where the sickly sunbeams glare
> Through the hot and misty air."

CHAPTER VIII.
THE SEPARATION.

"In many ways does the full heart reveal
The presence of the love it would conceal;
But in far more the estranged heart lets know
The absence of the love, which yet it fain would show."

At length the news of the approaching marriage of Horatio met the ear of Clotel. Her head grew dizzy, and her heart fainted within her; but, with a strong effort at composure, she inquired all the particulars, and her pure mind at once took its resolution. Horatio came that evening, and though she would fain have met him as usual, her heart was too full not to throw a deep sadness over her looks and tones. She had never complained of his decreasing tenderness, or of her own lonely hours; but he felt that the mute appeal of her heart-broken looks was more terrible than words. He kissed the hand she offered, and with a countenance almost as sad as her own, led her to a window in the recess shadowed by a luxuriant passion flower. It was the same seat where they had spent the first evening in this beautiful cottage, consecrated to their first loves. The same calm, clear moonlight looked in through the trellis. The vine then planted had now a luxuriant growth; and many a time had Horatio fondly twined its sacred blossoms with the glossy ringlets of her raven hair. The rush of memory almost overpowered poor Clotel; and Horatio felt too much oppressed and ashamed to break the long deep silence. At length, in words scarcely audible, Clotel said: "Tell me, dear Horatio, are you to be married next week?" He dropped her hand as if a rifle ball had struck him; and it was not until after long hesitation, that he began to make some reply about the necessity of circumstances. Mildly but earnestly the poor girl begged him to spare apologies. It was enough that he no longer loved her, and that they must bid farewell. Trusting to the yielding tenderness of her character, he ventured, in the most soothing accents, to suggest that as he still loved her better than all the world, she would ever be his real wife, and they might see each other frequently. He was not prepared for the storm of indignant emotion his words excited. True, she was his slave; her bones, and sinews had been purchased by his gold, yet she had the heart of a true woman, and hers was a passion too deep and absorbing to admit of partnership, and her spirit was too pure to form a selfish league with crime.

At length this painful interview came to an end. They stood together by the Gothic gate, where they had so often met and parted in the moonlight. Old remembrances melted their souls. "Farewell, dearest Horatio," said

Clotel. "Give me a parting kiss." Her voice was choked for utterance, and the tears flowed freely, as she bent her lips toward him. He folded her convulsively in his arms, and imprinted a long impassioned kiss on that mouth, which had never spoken to him but in love and blessing. With efforts like a death-pang she at length raised her head from his heaving bosom, and turning from him with bitter sobs, "It is our last. To meet thus is henceforth crime. God bless you. I would not have you so miserable as I am. Farewell. A last farewell." "The last?" exclaimed he, with a wild shriek. "Oh God, Clotel, do not say that;" and covering his face with his hands, he wept like a child. Recovering from his emotion, he found himself alone. The moon looked down upon him mild, but very sorrowfully; as the Madonna seems to gaze upon her worshipping children, bowed down with consciousness of sin. At that moment he would have given worlds to have disengaged himself from Gertrude, but he had gone so far, that blame, disgrace, and duels with angry relatives would now attend any effort to obtain his freedom. Oh, how the moonlight oppressed him with its friendly sadness! It was like the plaintive eye of his forsaken one, like the music of sorrow echoed from an unseen world. Long and earnestly he gazed at that cottage, where he had so long known earth's purest foretaste of heavenly bliss. Slowly he walked away; then turned again to look on that charmed spot, the nestling-place of his early affections. He caught a glimpse of Clotel, weeping beside a magnolia, which commanded a long view of the path leading to the public road. He would have sprung toward her but she darted from him, and entered the cottage. That graceful figure, weeping in the moonlight, haunted him for years. It stood before his closing eyes, and greeted him with the morning dawn. Poor Gertrude, had she known all, what a dreary lot would hers have been; but fortunately she could not miss the impassioned tenderness she never experienced; and Horatio was the more careful in his kindness, because he was deficient in love. After Clotel had been separated from her mother and sister, she turned her attention to the subject of Christianity, and received that consolation from her Bible that is never denied to the children of God. Although it was against the laws of Virginia, for a slave to be taught to read, Currer had employed an old free negro, who lived near her, to teach her two daughters to read and write. She felt that the step she had taken in resolving never to meet Horatio again would no doubt expose her to his wrath, and probably cause her to be sold, yet her heart was too guileless for her to commit a crime, and therefore she had ten times rather have been sold as a slave than do wrong. Some months after the marriage of Horatio and Gertrude their barouche rolled along a winding road that skirted the forest near Clotel's cottage, when the attention of Gertrude was suddenly attracted by two figures among the trees by the wayside; and touching Horatio's arm, she exclaimed, "Do look at that beautiful child." He turned and saw Clotel and Mary. His lips quivered, and his face became deadly pale. His young wife looked at him intently, but said nothing. In returning home, he took another road; but his wife seeing this, expressed a wish to go back the way they had come. He objected, and suspicion was awakened in her heart, and she soon after learned that the mother of that lovely child bore the name of Clotel, a name which she had often heard Horatio murmur in uneasy slumbers. From gossiping tongues she soon learned more than she wished to know. She wept, but not as poor Clotel had done; for she never had loved, and been beloved like her, and her nature was more proud: henceforth a change came over her feelings and her manners, and Horatio had no further occasion to assume a tenderness in return for hers. Changed as he was by ambition, he felt the wintry chill of her polite propriety, and sometimes, in agony of heart, compared it with the gushing love of her who was indeed his wife. But these and all his emotions were a sealed book to Clotel, of which she could only guess the contents. With remittances for her and her child's support, there sometimes came earnest pleadings that she would consent to see him again; but these she never answered, though her heart yearned to do so.

She pitied his young bride, and would not be tempted to bring sorrow into her household by any fault of hers. Her earnest prayer was, that she might not know of her existence. She had not looked on Horatio since she watched him under the shadow of the magnolia, until his barouche passed her in her rambles some months after. She saw the deadly paleness of his countenance, and had he dared to look back, he would have seen her tottering with faintness. Mary brought water from a rivulet, and sprinkled her face. When she revived, she clasped the beloved child to her heart with a vehemence that made her scream. Soothingly she kissed away her fears, and gazed into her beautiful eyes with a deep, deep sadness of expression, which poor Mary never forgot. Wild were the thoughts that passed round her aching heart, and almost maddened her poor brain; thoughts which had almost driven her to suicide the night of that last farewell. For her child's sake she had conquered the fierce temptation then; and for her sake, she struggled with it now. But the gloomy atmosphere of their once happy home overclouded the morning of Mary's life. Clotel perceived this, and it gave her unutterable pain.

> "'Tis ever thus with woman's love,
> True till life's storms have passed;
> And, like the vine around the tree,
> It braves them to the last."

CHAPTER X.
THE YOUNG CHRISTIAN.

"Here we see *God dealing in slaves*; giving them to his own favourite child [Abraham], a man of superlative worth, and as a reward for his eminent goodness."

—*Rev. Theodore Clapp, of New Orleans.*

On Carlton's return the next day from the farm, he was overwhelmed with questions from Mr. Peck, as to what he thought of the plantation, the condition of the negroes, Huckelby and Snyder; and especially how he liked the sermon of the latter. Mr. Peck was a kind of a patriarch in his own way. To begin with, he was a man of some talent. He not only had a good education, but was a man of great eloquence, and had a wonderful command of language. He too either had, or thought he had, poetical genius; and was often sending contributions to the *Natchez Free Trader*, and other periodicals. In the way of raising contributions for foreign missions, he took the lead of all others in his neighbourhood. Everything he did, he did for the "glory of God," as he said: he quoted Scripture for almost everything he did. Being in good circumstances, he was able to give to almost all benevolent causes to which he took a fancy. He was a most loving father, and his daughter exercised considerable influence over him, and, owing to her piety and judgment, that influence had a beneficial effect. Carlton, though a schoolfellow of the parson's, was nevertheless nearly ten years his junior; and though not an avowed infidel, was, however, a freethinker, and one who took no note of to-morrow. And for this reason Georgiana took peculiar interest in the young man, for Carlton was but little above thirty and unmarried. The young Christian felt that she would not be living up to that faith that she professed and believed in, if she did not exert herself to the utmost to save the thoughtless man from his downward career; and in this she succeeded to her most sanguine expectations. She not only converted him, but in placing the Scriptures before him in their true light, she redeemed those sacred writings from the charge of supporting the system of slavery, which her father had cast upon them in the discussion some days before.

Georgiana's first object, however, was to awaken in Carlton's breast a love for the Lord Jesus Christ. The young man had often sat under the sound of the gospel with perfect indifference. He had heard men talk who had grown grey bending over the Scriptures, and their conversation had passed by him unheeded; but when a young girl, much younger than himself, reasoned with him in that innocent and persuasive manner that woman is wont to use when she has entered with her whole soul upon an object, it was too much for his stout heart, and he yielded. Her next aim was to vindicate the Bible from sustaining the monstrous institution of slavery. She said, "God has created of one blood all the nations of men, to dwell on all the face of the earth[.] To claim, hold, and treat a human being as property is felony against God and man. The Christian religion is opposed to slaveholding in its spirit and its principles; it classes men-stealers among murderers; and it is the duty of all who wish to meet God in peace, to discharge that duty in spreading these principles. Let us not deceive ourselves into the idea that slavery is right, because it is profitable to us. Slaveholding is the highest possible violation of the eighth commandment. To take from a man his earnings, is theft; but to take the earner is a compound, life-long theft; and we who profess to follow in the footsteps of our Redeemer, should do our utmost to extirpate slavery from the land. For my own part, I shall do all I can. When the Redeemer was about to ascend to the bosom of the Father, and resume the glory which he had with him before the world was, he promised his disciples that the power of the Holy Ghost should come upon them, and that they should be witnesses for him to the uttermost parts of the earth. What was the effect upon their minds? 'They all continued with one accord in prayer and supplication with the women.' Stimulated by the confident expectation that Jesus would fulfil his gracious promise, they poured out their hearts in fervent supplications, probably for strength to do the work which he had appointed them unto, for they felt that without him they could do nothing, and they consecrated themselves on the altar of God, to the great and glorious enterprise of preaching the unsearchable riches of Christ to a lost and perishing world. Have we less precious promises in the Scriptures of truth? May we not claim of our God the blessing promised unto those who consider the poor: the Lord will preserve them and keep them alive, and they shall be blessed upon the earth? Does not the language, 'Inasmuch as ye did it unto one of the least of these my brethren, ye did it unto me,' belong to all who are rightly engaged in endeavouring to unloose the bondman's fetters? Shall we not then do as the apostles did? Shall we not, in view of the two millions of heathen in our very midst, in view of the souls that are going down in an almost unbroken phalanx to utter perdition, continue in prayer and supplication, that God will grant us the supplies of his Spirit to prepare us for that work which he has given us to do? Shall not the wail of the mother as she surrenders her only child to the grasp of the ruthless kidnapper, or the trader in human blood, animate our devotions? Shall not the manifold crimes and horrors of slavery excite more ardent outpourings at the throne of grace to grant repentance to our guilty country, and permit us to aid in preparing the way for the glorious second advent of the Messiah, by preaching deliverance to the captives, and the opening of the prison doors to those who are bound."

Georgiana had succeeded in rivetting the attention of Carlton during her conversation, and as she was finishing her last sentence, she observed the silent tear stealing down the cheek of the newly born child of God. At this juncture her father entered, and Carlton left the room. "Dear papa," said Georgiana, "will you grant me one favour; or, rather, make me a promise?" "I can't tell, my dear, till I know what it is," replied Mr. Peck. "If it is a reasonable request, I will comply with your wish," continued he. "I hope, my dear," answered she, "that papa would not think me capable of making an unreasonable request." "Well, well," returned he; "tell me what it is." "I hope," said she, "that in your future conversation with Mr. Carlton, on the subject of slavery, you will not speak of the Bible as sustaining it." "Why, Georgiana, my dear, you are mad, aint you?" exclaimed he, in an excited tone. The poor girl remained silent; the father saw in a moment that he had spoken too sharply; and taking her hand in his he said, "Now, my child, why do you make that request?" "Because," returned she, "I think he is on the stool of repentance, if he has not already been received among the elect. He, you know, was bordering upon infidelity, and if the Bible sanctions slavery, then he will naturally enough say that it is not from God; for the argument from internal evidence is not only refuted, but actually turned against the Bible. If the Bible sanctions slavery, then it misrepresents the character of God. Nothing would be more dangerous to the soul of a young convert than to satisfy him that the Scriptures favoured such a system of sin." "Don't you suppose that I understand the Scriptures better than you? I have been in the world longer." "Yes," said she, "you have been in the world longer, and amongst slaveholders so long that you do not regard it in the same light that those do who have not become so familiar with its every-day scenes as you. I once heard you say, that you were opposed to the institution, when you first came to the South." "Yes," answered he, "I did not know so much about it then." "With great deference to you, papa," replied Georgiana, "I don't think that the Bible sanctions slavery. The Old Testament contains this explicit condemnation of it, 'He that stealeth a man, and selleth him, or if he be found in his hand, he shall surely be put to death;' and 'Woe unto him that buildeth his house by unrighteousness, and his chambers by wrong; that useth his neighbour's service without wages, and giveth him not for his work;' when also the New Testament exhibits such words of rebuke as these, 'Behold the hire of the labourers who have reaped down your fields, which is of you kept back by fraud, crieth; and the cries of them who have reaped are entered into the ears of the Lord of Sabaoth.' 'The law is not made for a righteous man, but for the lawless and disobedient, for the ungodly and for sinners, for unholy and profane, for murderers of fathers and murderers of mothers, for manslayers, for whoremongers, for them that defile themselves with mankind, for *menstealers*, for liars, for perjured persons.' A more scathing denunciation of the sin in question is surely to be found on record in no other book. I am afraid," continued the daughter, "that the acts of the professed friends of Christianity in the South do more to spread infidelity than the writings of all the atheists which have ever been published. The infidel watches the religious world. He surveys the church, and, lo! thousands and tens of thousands of her accredited members actually hold slaves. Members 'in good and regular standing,' fellowshipped throughout Christendom except by a few anti-slavery churches generally despised as ultra and radical, reduce their fellow men to the condition of chattels, and by force keep them in that state of degradation. Bishops, ministers, elders, and deacons are engaged in this awful business, and do not consider their conduct as at all inconsistent with the precepts of either the Old or New Testaments. Moreover, those ministers and churches who do not themselves hold slaves, very generally defend the conduct of those who do, and accord to them a fair Christian character, and in the way of business frequently take mortgages and levy executions on the bodies of their fellow men, and in some cases of their fellow Christians.

"Now is it a wonder that infidels, beholding the practice and listening to the theory of professing Christians, should conclude that the Bible inculcates a morality not inconsistent with chattelising human beings? And must not this conclusion be strengthened, when they hear ministers of talent and learning declare that the Bible does sanction slaveholding, and that it ought not to be made a disciplinable offence in churches? And must not all doubt be dissipated, when one of the most learned professors in our theological seminaries asserts that the Bible 'recognises that the relation may still exist, *salva fide et salva ecclesia*' (without injury to the Christian faith or church) and that only 'the *abuse* of it is the essential and fundamental wrong?' Are not infidels bound to believe that these professors, ministers, and churches understand their own Bible, and that, consequently, notwithstanding solitary passages which appear to condemn slaveholding, the Bible sanctions it? When nothing can be further from the truth. And as for Christ, his whole life was a living testimony against slavery and all that it inculcates. When he designed to do us good, he took upon himself the form of a servant. He took his station at the bottom of society. He voluntarily identified himself with the poor and the despised. The warning voices of Jeremiah and Ezekiel were raised in olden time, against sin. Let us not forget what followed. 'Therefore, thus saith the

Lord—ye have not hearkened unto me in proclaiming liberty every one to his brother, and every one to his neighbour—behold I proclaim a liberty for you saith the Lord, to the sword, to the pestilence, and to the famine.' Are we not virtually as a nation adopting the same impious language, and are we not exposed to the same tremendous judgments? Shall we not, in view of those things, use every laudable means to awaken our beloved country from the slumbers of death, and baptize all our efforts with tears and with prayers, that God may bless them. Then, should our labour fail to accomplish the end for which we pray, we shall stand acquitted at the bar of Jehovah, and although we may share in the national calamities which await unrepented sins, yet that blessed approval will be ours.—'Well done good and faithful servants, enter ye into the joy of your Lord.'"

"My dear Georgiana," said Mr. Peck, "I must be permitted to entertain my own views on this subject, and to exercise my own judgment."

"Believe me, dear papa," she replied, "I would not be understood as wishing to teach you, or to dictate to you in the least; but only grant my request, not to allude to the Bible as sanctioning slavery, when speaking with Mr. Carlton."

"Well," returned he, "I will comply with your wish."

The young Christian had indeed accomplished a noble work; and whether it was admitted by the father, or not, she was his superior and his teacher. Georgiana had viewed the right to enjoy perfect liberty as one of those inherent and inalienable rights which pertain to the whole human race, and of which they can never be divested, except by an act of gross injustice. And no one was more able than herself to impress those views upon the hearts of all with whom she came in contact. Modest and self-possessed, with a voice of great sweetness, and a most winning manner, she could, with the greatest ease to herself, engage their attention.

CHAPTER XI.
THE PARSON POET.

"Unbind, unbind my galling chain,
And set, oh! set me free:
No longer say that I'll disdain
The gift of liberty."

Through the persuasion of Mr. Peck, and fascinated with the charms of Georgiana, Carlton had prolonged his stay two months with his old school-fellow. During the latter part of the time he had been almost as one of the family. If Miss Peck was invited out, Mr. Carlton was, as a matter of course. She seldom rode out, unless with him. If Mr. Peck was absent, he took the head of the table; and, to the delight of the young lady, he had on several occasions taken part in the family worship. "I am glad," said Mr. Peck, one evening while at the tea table, "I am glad, Mr. Carlton, that my neighbour Jones has invited you to visit him at his farm. He is a good neighbour, but a very ungodly man; I want that you should see his people, and then, when you return to the North, you can tell how much better a Christian's slaves are situated than one who does nothing for the cause of Christ." "I hope, Mr. Carlton," said Georgiana, "that you will spend the Sabbath with him, and have a religious interview with the negroes." "Yes," replied the parson, "that's well thought of, Georgy." "Well, I think I will go up on Thursday next, and stay till Monday," said Carlton; "and I shall act upon your suggestion, Miss Peck," continued he; "and try to get a religious interview with the blacks. By-the-by," remarked Carlton, "I saw an advertisement in the *Free Trader* to-day that rather puzzled me. Ah, here it is now; and," drawing the paper from his pocket, "I will read it, and then you can tell me what it means:

'TO PLANTERS AND OTHERS.—*Wanted fifty negroes.* Any person having *sick negroes*, considered *incurable* by their respective physicians, (their owners of course,) and wishing to dispose of them, Dr. Stillman will pay cash for negroes affected with scrofula or king's evil, confirmed hypochondriacism, apoplexy, or diseases of the brain, kidneys, spleen, stomach and intestines, bladder and its appendages, diarrhoea, dysentery, &c. *The highest cash price will be paid as above.*'

["]When I read this to-day I thought that the advertiser must be a man of eminent skill as a physician, and that he intended to cure the sick negroes; but on second thought I find that some of the diseases enumerated are certainly incurable. What can he do with these sick negroes?" "You see," replied Mr. Peck, laughing, "that he is a doctor, and has use for them in his lectures. The doctor is connected with a small college. Look at his prospectus, where he invites students to attend, and that will explain the matter to you." Carlton turned to another column, and read the following:

"Some advantages of a peculiar character are connected with this institution, which it may be proper to point out. No place in the United States offers as great opportunities for the acquisition of anatomical knowledge. Subjects being obtained from among the coloured population in sufficient numbers *for every purpose*, and proper dissections carried on *without offending any individuals in the community!*"

"These are for dissection, then?" inquired Carlton with a trembling voice. "Yes," answered the parson. "Of course they wait till they die before they can use them." "They keep them on hand, and when they need one they bleed him to death," returned Mr. Peck. "Yes, but that's murder." "Oh, the doctors are licensed to commit murder, you know; and what's the difference, whether one dies owing to the loss of blood, or taking too many pills? For my own part, if I had to choose, I would rather submit to the former." "I have often heard what I considered hard stories in abolition meetings in New York about slavery; but now I shall begin to think that many of them are true." "The longer you remain here the more you will be convinced of the iniquity of the institution," remarked Georgiana. "Now, Georgy, my dear, don't give us another abolition lecture, if you please," said Mr. Peck. "Here, Carlton," continued the parson, "I have written a short poem for your sister's album, as you requested me; it is a domestic piece, as you will see." "She will prize it the more for that," remarked Carlton; and taking the sheet of paper, he laughed as his eyes glanced over it. "Read it out, Mr. Carlton," said Georgiana, "and let me hear what it is; I know papa gets off some very droll things at times." Carlton complied with the young lady's request, and read aloud the following rare specimen of poetical genius . . .

CHAPTER XIV.
A FREE WOMAN REDUCED TO SLAVERY.

Althesa found in Henry Morton a kind and affectionate husband; and his efforts to purchase her mother, although unsuccessful, had doubly endeared him to her. Having from the commencement resolved not to hold slaves, or rather not to own any, they were compelled to hire servants for their own use. Five years had passed away, and their happiness was increased by two lovely daughters. Mrs. Morton was seated, one bright afternoon, busily engaged with her needle, and near her sat Salome, a servant that she had just taken into her employ. The woman was perfectly white; so much so, that Mrs. Morton had expressed her apprehensions to her husband, when the woman first came, that she was not born a slave. The mistress watched the servant, as the latter sat sewing upon some coarse work, and saw the large silent tear in her eye. This caused an uneasiness to the mistress, and she said, "Salome, don't you like your situation here?" "Oh yes, madam," answered the woman in a quick tone, and then tried to force a smile. "Why is it that you often look sad, and with tears in your eyes?" The mistress saw that she had touched a tender chord, and continued, "I am your friend; tell me your sorrow, and, if I can, I will help you." As the last sentence was escaping the lips of the mistress, the slave woman put her check apron to her face and wept. Mrs. Morton saw plainly that there was cause for this expression of grief, and pressed the woman more closely. "Hear me, then," said the woman calming herself: "I will tell you why I sometimes weep. I was born in Germany, on the banks of the Rhine. Ten years ago my father came to this country, bringing with him my mother and myself. He was poor, and I, wishing to assist all I could, obtained a situation as nurse to a lady in this city. My father got employment as a labourer on the wharf, among the steamboats; but he was soon taken ill with the yellow fever, and died. My mother then got a situation for herself, while I remained with my first employer. When the hot season came on, my master, with his wife, left New Orleans until the hot season was over, and took me with them. They stopped at a town on the banks of the Mississippi river, and said they should remain there some weeks. One day they went out for a ride, and they had not been gone more than half an hour, when two men came into the room and told me that they had bought me, and that I was their slave. I was bound and taken to prison, and that night put on a steamboat and taken up the Yazoo river, and set to work on a farm. I was forced to take up with a negro, and by him had three children. A year since my master's daughter was married, and I was given to her. She came with her husband to this city, and I have ever since been hired out."

"Unhappy woman," whispered Althesa, "why did you not tell me this before?" "I was afraid," replied Salome, "for I was once severely flogged for telling a stranger that I was not born a slave." On Mr. Morton's return home, his wife communicated to him the story which the slave woman had told her an hour before, and begged that something might be done to rescue her from the situation she was then in. In Louisiana as well as many others of the slave states, great obstacles are thrown in the way of persons who have been wrongfully reduced to slavery regaining their freedom. A person claiming to be free must prove his right to his liberty. This, it will be seen, throws the burden of proof upon the slave, who, in all probability, finds it out of his power to procure such evidence. And if any free person shall attempt to aid a freeman in regaining his freedom, he is compelled to enter into security in the sum of one thousand dollars, and if the person claiming to be free shall fail to establish such fact, the thousand dollars are forfeited to the state. This cruel and oppressive law has kept many a freeman from espousing the cause of persons unjustly held as slaves. Mr. Morton inquired and found that the woman's story was true, as regarded the time she had lived with her present owner; but the latter not only denied that she was free, but immediately removed her from Morton's. Three months after Salome had been removed from Morton's and let out to another family, she was one morning cleaning the door steps, when a lady passing by, looked at the slave and thought she recognised some one that she had seen before. The lady stopped and asked the woman if she was a slave, "I am," said she[.] "Were you born a slave?" "No, I was born in Germany." "What's the name of the ship in which you came to this country?" inquired the lady. "I don't know," was the answer. "Was it the *Amazon*?" At the sound of this name, the slave woman was silent for a moment, and then the tears began to flow freely down her care-worn cheeks. "Would you know Mrs. Marshall, who was a passenger in the *Amazon*, if you should see her?" inquired the lady. At this the woman gazed at the lady with a degree of intensity that can be imagined better than described, and then fell at the lady's feet. The lady was Mrs. Marshall. She had crossed the Atlantic in the same ship with this poor woman. Salome, like many of her countrymen, was a beautiful singer, and had often entertained Mrs. Marshall and the other lady passengers on board the *Amazon*. The poor woman was raised from the ground by Mrs. Marshall, and placed upon the door step that she had a moment before been cleaning. "I will do my utmost to rescue you from the horrid life of a slave," exclaimed the lady, as she took from her pocket her pencil, and wrote down the number of the house, and the street in which the German woman was working as a slave.

After a long and tedious trial of many days, it was decided that Salome Miller was by birth a free woman, and she was set at liberty. The good and generous Althesa had contributed some of the money toward bringing about the trial, and had done much to cheer on Mrs. Marshall in her benevolent object. Salome Miller is free, but where are her three children? They are still slaves, and in all human probability will die as such.

This, reader, is no fiction; if you think so, look over the files of the New Orleans newspapers of the years 1845–6, and you will there see reports of the trial.

TO-DAY A MISTRESS, TO MORROW A SLAVE.

> "I promised thee a sister tale
> Of man's perfidious cruelty;
> Come, then, and hear what cruel wrong
> Befel the dark ladie."
>
> —*Coleridge.*

Let us return for a moment to the home of Clotel. While she was passing lonely and dreary hours with none but her darling child, Horatio Green was trying to find relief in that insidious enemy of man, the intoxicating cup. Defeated in politics, forsaken in love by his wife, he seemed to have lost all principle of honour, and was ready to nerve himself up to any deed, no matter how unprincipled. Clotel's existence was now well known to Horatio's wife, and both her and her father demanded that the beautiful quadroon and her child should be sold and sent out of the state. To this proposition he at first turned a deaf ear; but when he saw that his wife was about to return to her father's roof, he consented to leave the matter in the hands of his father-in-law. The result was, that Clotel was immediately sold to the slave-trader, Walker, who, a few years previous, had taken her mother and sister to the far South. But, as if to make her husband drink of the cup of humiliation to its very dregs, Mrs. Green resolved to take his child under her own roof for a servant. Mary was, therefore, put to the meanest work that could be found, and although only ten years of age, she was often compelled to perform labour, which, under ordinary circumstances, would have been thought too hard for one much older. One condition of the sale of Clotel to Walker was, that she should be taken out of the state, which was accordingly done. Most quadroon women who are taken to the lower countries to be sold are either purchased by gentlemen for their own use, or sold for waiting-maids; and Clotel, like her sister, was fortunate enough to be bought for the latter purpose. The town of Vicksburgh stands on the left bank of the Mississippi, and is noted for the severity with which slaves are treated. It was here that Clotel was sold to Mr. James French, a merchant.

Mrs. French was severe in the extreme to her servants. Well dressed, but scantily fed, and overworked were all who found a home with her. The quadroon had been in her new home but a short time ere she found that her situation was far different from what it was in Virginia. What social virtues are possible in a society of which injustice is the primary characteristic? in a society which is divided into two classes, masters and slaves? Every married woman in the far South looks upon her husband as unfaithful, and regards every quadroon servant as a rival. Clotel had been with her new mistress but a few days, when she was ordered to cut off her long hair. The negro, constitutionally, is fond of dress and outward appearance. He that has short, woolly hair, combs it and oils it to death. He that has long hair, would sooner have his teeth drawn than lose it. However painful it was to the quadroon, she was soon seen with her hair cut as short as any of the full-blooded negroes in the dwelling.

Even with her short hair, Clotel was handsome. Her life had been a secluded one, and though now nearly thirty years of age, she was still beautiful. At her short hair, the other servants laughed, "Miss Clo needn't strut round so big, she got short nappy har well as I," said Nell, with a broad grin that showed her teeth. "She tinks she white, when she come here wid dat long har of hers," replied Mill. "Yes," continued Nell; "missus make her take down her wool so she no put it up to-day."

The fairness of Clotel's complexion was regarded with envy as well by the other servants as by the mistress herself. This is one of the hard features of slavery. To-day the woman is mistress of her own cottage; to-morrow she is sold to one who aims to make her life as intolerable as possible. And be it remembered, that the house servant has the best situation which a slave can occupy. Some American writers have tried to make the world believe that the condition of the labouring classes of England is as bad as the slaves of the United States.

The English labourer may be oppressed, he may be cheated, defrauded, swindled, and even starved; but it is not slavery under which he groans. H[e] cannot be sold; in point of law he is equal to the prime minister. "It is easy to captivate the unthink[i]ng and the prejudiced, by eloquent declamation about the oppression of English operatives being worse than that of American slaves, and by exaggerating the wrongs on one side and hiding them on the other. But all informed and reflecting minds, knowing that bad as are the social evils of England, those of Slavery are immeasurably worse." But the degradation and harsh treatment that Clotel experienced in her new home was nothing compared with the grief she underwent at being separated from her dear child. Taken from her without scarcely a moment's warning, she knew not what had become of her. The deep and heartfelt grief of Clotel was soon perceived by her owners, and fearing that her refusal to take food would cause her death, they resolved to sell her. Mr. French found no difficulty in getting a purchaser for the quadroon woman, for such are usually the most marketable kind of property. Clotel was sold at private sale to a young man for a housekeeper; but even he had missed his aim.

CHAPTER XVI.
DEATH OF THE PARSON.

Carlton was above thirty years of age, standing on the last legs of a young man, and entering on the first of a bachelor. He had never dabbled in matters of love, and looked upon all women alike. Although he respected woman for her virtues, and often spoke of the goodness of heart of the sex, he had never dreamed of marriage. At first he looked upon Miss Peck as a pretty young woman, but after she became his religious teacher, he regarded her in that light, that every one will those whom they know to be their superiors. It was soon seen, however, that the young man not only respected and reverenced Georgiana for the incalculable service she had done him, in awakening him to a sense of duty to his soul, but he had learned to bow to the shrine of Cupid. He found, weeks after he had been in her company, that when he met her at table, or alone in the drawing-room, or on the piazza, he felt a shortness of breath, a palpitating of the heart, a kind of dizziness of the head; but he knew not its cause.

This was love in its first stage. Mr. Peck saw, or thought he saw, what would be the result of Carlton's visit, and held out every inducement in his power to prolong his stay. The hot season was just commencing, and the young Northerner was talking of his return home, when the parson was very suddenly taken ill. The disease was the cholera, and the physicians pronounced the case incurable. In less than five hours John Peck was a corpse. His love for Georgiana, and respect for her father, had induced Carlton to remain by the bedside of the dying man, although against the express orders of the physician. This act of kindness caused the young orphan henceforth to regard Carlton as her best friend. He now felt it his duty to remain with the young woman until some of her relations should be summoned from Connecticut. After the funeral, the family physician advised that Miss Peck should go to the farm, and spend the time at the country seat; and also advised Carlton to remain with her, which he did.

At the parson's death his negroes showed little or no signs of grief. This was noticed by both Carlton and Miss Peck, and caused no little pain to the latter. "They are ungrateful," said Carlton, as he and Georgiana were seated on the piazza. "What," asked she, "have they to be grateful for?" "Your father was kind, was he not?" "Yes, as kind as most men who own slaves; but the kindness meted out to blacks would be unkindness if given to whites. We would think so, should we not?" "Yes," replied he. "If we would not consider the best treatment which a slave receives good enough for us, we should not think he ought to be grateful for it. Everybody knows that slavery in its best and mildest form is wrong. Whoever denies this, his lips libel his heart. Try him! Clank the chains in his ears, and tell him they are for him; give him an hour to prepare his wife and children for a life of slavery; bid him make haste, and get ready their necks for the yoke, and their wrists for the coffle chains; then look at his pale lips and trembling knees, and you have nature's testimony against slavery."

"Let's take a walk," said Carlton, as if to turn the conversation. The moon was just appearing through the tops of the trees, and the animals and insects in an adjoining wood kept up a continued din of music. The croaking of bull-frogs, buzzing of insects, cooing of turtle-doves, and the sound from a thousand musical instruments, pitched on as many different keys, made the welkin ring. But even all this noise did not drown the singing of a party of the slaves, who were seated near a spring that was sending up its cooling waters. "How prettily the negroes sing," remarked Carlton, as they were wending their way towards the place from whence the sound of the voices came. "Yes," replied Georgiana; "master Sam is there, I'll warrant you: he's always on hand when there's any singing or dancing. We must not let them see us, or they will stop singing." "Who makes their songs for them?" inquired the young man. "Oh, they make them up as they sing them; they are all impromptu songs." By this time they were near enough to hear distinctly every word; and, true enough, Sam's voice was heard above all others. At the conclusion of each song they all joined in a hearty laugh, with an expression of "Dats de song for me;" "Dems dems."

"Stop," said Carlton, as Georgiana was rising from the log upon which she was seated; "stop, and let's hear this one." The piece was sung by Sam, the others joining in the chorus, and was as follows:

Sam.

"Come, all my brethren, let us take a rest,
While the moon shines so brightly and clear;
Old master is dead, and left us at last,
And has gone at the Bar to appear.
Old master has died, and lying in his grave,
And our blood will awhile cease to flow;
He will no more trample on the neck of the slave;
For he's gone where the slaveholders go.

Chorus.

"Hang up the shovel and the hoe—
Take down the fiddle and the bow—
Old master has gone to the slaveholder's rest;
He has gone where they all ought to go.

Sam.

"I heard the old doctor say the other night,
As he passed by the dining-room door—

249

'Perhaps the old man may live through the night,
But I think he will die about four.'
Young mistress sent me, at the peril of my life,
For the parson to come down and pray,
For says she, 'Your old master is now about to die,'
And says I, 'God speed him on his way.'

"Hang up the shovel, &c.

"At four o'clock at morn the family was called
Around the old man's dying bed;
And oh! but I laughed to myself when I heard
That the old man's spirit had fled.
Mr. Carlton cried, and so did I pretend;
Young mistress very nearly went mad;
And the old old person's groans did the heavens fairly rend;
But I tell you I felt mighty glad.

"Hang up the shovel, &c.

"We'll no more be roused by the blowing of his horn,
Our backs no longer he will score;
He no more will feed us on cotton-seeds and corn;
For his reign of oppression now is o'er.
He no more will hang our children on the tree,
To be ate by the carrion crow;
He no more will send our wires to Tennessee;
For he's gone where the slaveholders go.

"Hang up the shovel and the hoe,
Take down the fiddle and the bow,
We'll dance and sing,
And make the forest ring,
With the fiddle and the old banjo."

The song was not half finished before Carlton regretted that he had caused the young lady to remain and hear what to her must be anything but pleasant reflections upon her deceased parent. "I think we will walk," said he, at the same time extending his arm to Georgiana. "No," said she "let's hear them out. It is from these unguarded expressions of the feelings of the negroes, that we should learn a lesson." At its conclusion they walked towards the house in silence: as they were ascending the steps, the young man said, "They are happy, after all. The negro, situated as yours are, is not aware that he is deprived of any just rights." "Yes, yes," answered Georgiana: "you may place the slave where you please; you may dry up to your utmost the fountains of his feelings, the springs of his thought; you may yoke him to your labour, as an ox which liveth only to work, and worketh only to live; you may put him under any process which, without destroying his value as a slave, will debase and crush him as a rational being; you may do this, and *the idea that he was born to be free will survive it all*. It is allied to his hope of immortality; it is the ethereal part of his nature, which oppression cannot reach; it is a torch lit up in his soul by the hand of Deity, and never meant to be extinguished by the hand of man."

On reaching the drawing-room, they found Sam snuffing the candles, and looking as solemn and as dignified as if he had never sung a song or laughed in his life. "Will Miss Georgy have de supper got up now?" asked the negro. "Yes," she replied. "Well," remarked Carlton, "that beats anything I ever met with. Do you think that was Sam we heard singing?" "I am sure of it," was the answer. "I could not have believed that that fellow was capable of so much deception," continued he. "Our system of slavery is one of deception; and Sam, you see, has only been a good scholar. However, he is as honest a fellow as you will find among the slave population here. If we would have them more honest, we should give them their liberty, and then the inducement to be dishonest would be gone. I have resolved that these creatures shall all be free." "Indeed!" exclaimed Carlton. "Yes, I shall let them all go free, and set an example to those about me." "I honour your judgment," said he. "But will the state permit them to remain?" "If not, they can go where they can live in freedom. I will not be unjust because the state is."

CHAPTER XVII.
RETALIATION.

> "I HAD a dream, a happy dream;
> I thought that I was free:
> That in my own bright land again
> A home there was for me."

With the deepest humiliation Horatio Green saw the daughter of Clotel, his own child, brought into his dwelling as a servant. His wife felt that she had been deceived, and determined to punish her deceiver. At first Mary was put to work in the kitchen, where she met with little or no sympathy from the other slaves, owing to the fairness of her complexion. The child was white, what should be done to make her look like other negroes, was the question Mrs. Green asked herself. At last she hit upon a plan: there was a garden at the back of the house over which Mrs. Green could look from her parlour window. Here the white slave-girl was put to work, without either bonnet or handkerchief upon her head. A hot sun poured its broiling rays on the naked face and neck of the girl, until she sank down in the corner of the garden, and was actually broiled to sleep. "Dat little nigger ain't working a bit, missus," said Dinah to Mrs. Green, as she entered the kitchen.

"She's lying in the sun, seasoning; she will work better by and by," replied the mistress. "Dees white niggers always tink dey sef good as white folks," continued the cook. "Yes, but we will teach them better; won't we, Dinah?" "Yes, missus, I don't like dees mularter niggers, no how; dey always want to set dey sef up for something big." The cook was black, and was not without that prejudice which is to be found among the negroes, as well as among the whites of the Southern States. The sun had the desired effect, for in less than a fortnight Mary's fair complexion had disappeared, and she was but little whiter than any other mulatto children running about the yard. But the close resemblance between the father and child annoyed the mistress more than the mere whiteness of the child's complexion. Horatio made proposition after proposition to have the girl sent away, for every time he beheld her countenance it reminded him of the happy days he had spent with Clotel. But his wife had commenced, and determined to carry out her unfeeling and fiendish designs. This child was not only white, but she was the granddaughter of Thomas Jefferson, the man who, when speaking against slavery in the legislature of Virginia, said,

"The whole commerce between master and slave is a perpetual exercise of the most boisterous passions; *the most unremitting despotism on the one part, and degrading submission on the other.* With what execration should the statesman be loaded who, permitting one half the citizens thus to trample on the rights of the other, transforms those into despots and these into enemies, destroys the morals of the one part, and the *amor patriæ* of the other! For if the slave can have a country in this world, it must be any other in preference to that in which he is born to live and labour for another; in which be must lock up the faculties of his nature, contribute as far as depends on his individual endeavours to the evanishment of the human race, or entail his own miserable condition on the endless generations proceeding from him. And can the liberties of a nation be thought secure when we have removed their only firm basis, a conviction in the minds of the people that these liberties are the gift of God? that they are not to be violated but with his wrath? Indeed, I tremble for my country when I reflect that God is just; that his justice cannot sleep for ever; that, considering numbers, nature, and natural means only, a revolution of the wheel of fortune, an exchange of situation, is among possible events; that it may become probable by supernatural interference! The Almighty has no attribute which can take side with us in such a contest. . . .

"What an incomprehensible machine is man! Who can endure toil, famine, stripes, imprisonment, and death itself, in vindication of his own liberty, and the next moment be deaf to all those motives, whose power supported him through his trial, and inflict on his fellow men a bondage, *one hour of which is fraught with more misery than ages of that which he rose in rebellion to oppose!* But we must wait with patience the workings of an overruling Providence, and hope that that is preparing the deliverance of these our suffering brethren. When the measure of their tears shall be full—when their tears shall have involved heaven itself in darkness—doubtless a God of justice will awaken to their distress, and by diffusing light and liberality among their oppressors, or at length by his exterminating thunder, manifest his attention to things of this world, and that they are not left to the guidance of blind fatality."

The same man, speaking of the probability that the slaves might some day attempt to gain their liberties by a revolution, said,

"I tremble for my country, when I recollect that God is just, and that His justice cannot sleep for ever. The Almighty has no attribute that can take sides with us in such a struggle."

But, sad to say, Jefferson is not the only American statesman who has spoken high-sounding words in favour of freedom, and then left his own children to die slaves.

CHAPTER XVIII.
THE LIBERATOR.

"We hold these truths to be self-evident, that all men are created free and equal; that they are endowed by their Creator with certain inalienable rights; among these are *life*, *liberty*, and the pursuit of happiness."

—*Declaration of American Independence.*

The death of the parson was the commencement of a new era in the history of his slaves. Only a little more than eighteen years of age, Georgiana could not expect to carry out her own wishes in regard to the slaves, although she was sole heir to her father's estate. There were distant relations whose opinions she had at least to respect. And both law and public opinion in the state were against any measure of emancipation that she might think of adopting; unless, perhaps, she might be permitted to send them to Liberia. Her uncle in Connecticut had already been written to, to come down and aid in settling up the estate. He was a Northern man, but she knew him to be a tight-fisted yankee, whose whole counsel would go against liberating the negroes. Yet there was one way in which the thing could be done. She loved Carlton, and she well knew that he loved her; she read it in his countenance every time they met, yet the young man did not mention his wishes to her. There were many reasons why he should not. In the first place, her father was just deceased, and it seemed only right that he should wait a reasonable time. Again, Carlton was poor, and Georgiana was possessed of a large fortune; and his high spirit would not, for a moment, allow him to place himself in a position to be regarded as a fortune-hunter. The young girl hinted, as best she could, at the probable future; but all to no purpose. He took nothing to himself. True, she had read much of "woman's rights;" and had even attended a meeting, while at the North, which had been called to discuss the wrongs of woman; but she could not nerve herself up to the point of putting the question to Carlton, although she felt sure that she should not be rejected. She waited, but in vain. At last, one evening, she came out of her room rather late, and was walking on the piazza for fresh air. She passed near Carlton's room, and heard the voice of Sam. The negro had just come in to get the young man's boots, and had stopped, as he usually did, to have some talk. "I wish," said Sam, "dat Marser Carlton an Miss Georgy would get married; den, I 'spec, we'd have good times." "I don't think your mistress would have me," replied the young man. "What make tink dat, Marser Carlton?" "Your mistress would marry no one, Sam, unless she loved them." "Den I wish she would lub you, cause I tink we have good times den. All our folks is de same 'pinion like me," returned the negro, and then left the room with the boots in his hands. During the conversation between the Anglo-Saxon and the African, one word had been dropped by the former that haunted the young lady the remainder of the night—"Your mistress would marry no one unless she loved them." That word awoke her in the morning, and caused her to decide upon this important subject. Love and duty triumphed over the woman's timid nature, and that day Georgiana informed Carlton that she was ready to become his wife. The young man, with grateful tears, accepted and kissed the hand that was offered to him. The marriage of Carlton and Miss Peck was hailed with delight by both the servants in the house and the negroes on the farm. New rules were immediately announced for the working and general treatment of the slaves on the plantation. With this, Huckelby, the overseer, saw his reign coming to an end; and Snyder, the Dutch preacher, felt that his services would soon be dispensed with, for nothing was more repugnant to the feelings of Mrs. Carlton than the sermons preached by Snyder to the slaves. She regarded them as something intended to make them better satisfied with their condition, and more valuable as pieces of property, without preparing them for the world to come. Mrs. Carlton found in her husband a congenial spirit, who entered into all her wishes and plans for bettering the condition of their slaves. Mrs. Carlton's views and sympathies were all in favour of immediate emancipation; but then she saw, or thought she saw, a difficulty in that. If the slaves were liberated they must be sent out of the state. This, of course, would incur additional expense; and if they left the state, where had they better go? "Let's send them to Liberia," said Carlton. "Why should they go to Africa, any more than to the Free States or to Canada?" asked the wife. "They would be in their native land," he answered. "Is not this their native land? What right have we, more than the negro to the soil here, or to style ourselves native Americans? Indeed it is as much their homes as ours, and I have sometimes thought it was more theirs. The negro has cleared up the lands, built towns, and enriched the soil with his blood and tears; and in return, he is to be sent to a country of which he knows nothing. Who fought more bravely for American independence than the blacks? A negro, by the name of Attucks, was the first that fell in Boston at the commencement of the revolutionary war; and, throughout the whole of the struggles for liberty in this country, the negroes have contributed their share. In the last war with Great Britain, the country was mainly indebted to the blacks in New Orleans for the achievement of the victory at that place; and even General Jackson, the commander in chief, called the negroes together at the close of the war, and addressed them in the following terms:—

"[']Soldiers!—When on the banks of the Mobile I called you to take up arms, inviting you to partake the perils and glory of your *white fellow citizens, I expected much from you*; for I was not ignorant that you possessed qualities most formidable to an invading enemy. I knew with what fortitude you could endure hunger and thirst, and all the fatigues of a campaign. *I knew well how you loved your native country*, and that you, as well as ourselves, had to defend what *man* holds most dear—his parents, wife, children, and property. *You have done more than I expected*. In addition to the previous qualities I before knew you to possess, I found among you a noble enthusiasm, which leads to the performance of great things.

"'Soldiers! The President of the United States shall hear how praiseworthy was your conduct in the hour of danger, and the representatives of the American people will give you the praise your exploits entitle you to. Your general anticipates them in applauding your noble ardour.'

"And what did these noble men receive in return for their courage, their heroism? Chains and slavery. Their good deeds have been consecrated only in their own memories. Who rallied with more alacrity in response to the summons of danger? If in that hazardous hour, when our homes were menaced with the horrors of war, we did not disdain to call upon the negro to assist in repelling invasion, why should we, now that the danger is past, deny him a home in his native land?" "I see," said Carlton, "you are right, but I fear you will have difficulty in persuading others to adopt your views." "We will set the example," replied she, "and then hope for the best; for I feel that the people of the Southern States will one day see their error. Liberty has always been our watchword, as far as profession is concerned. Nothing has been held so cheap as our common humanity, on a national average. If every man had his aliquot proportion of the injustice done in this land, by law and violence, the present freemen of the northern section would many of them commit suicide in self-defence, and would court the liberties awarded by Ali Pasha of Egypt to his subjects. Long ere this we should have tested, in behalf of our bleeding and crushed American brothers of every hue and complexion, every new constitution, custom, or practice, by which inhumanity was supposed to be upheld, the injustice and cruelty they contained, emblazoned before the great tribunal of mankind for condemnation; and the good and available power they possessed, for the relief, deliverance and elevation of oppressed men, permitted to shine forth from under the cloud, for the refreshment of the human race."

Although Mr. and Mrs. Carlton felt that immediate emancipation was the right of the slave and the duty of the master, they resolved on a system of gradual emancipation, so as to give them time to accomplish their wish, and to prepare the negro for freedom. Huckelby was one morning told that his services would no longer be required. The negroes, ninety-eight in number, were called together and told that the whip would no longer be used, and that they would be allowed a certain sum for every bale of cotton produced. Sam, whose long experience in the cotton-field before he had been taken into the house, and whose general intelligence justly gave him the first place amongst the negroes on the Poplar Farm, was placed at their head. They were also given to understand that the money earned by them would be placed to their credit; and when it amounted to a certain sum, they should all be free[.]

The joy with which this news was received by the slaves, showed their grateful appreciation of the boon their benefactors were bestowing upon them. The house servants were called and told that wages would be allowed them, and what they earned set to their credit, and they too should be free. The next were the bricklayers. There were eight of these, who had paid their master two dollars per day, and boarded and clothed themselves. An arrangement was entered into with them, by which the money they earned should be placed to their credit; and they too should be free, when a certain amount should be accumulated; and great was the change amongst all these people. The bricklayers had been to work but a short time, before their increased industry was noticed by many. They were no longer apparently the same people. A sedateness, a care, an econ-omy, an industry, took possession of them, to which there seemed to be no bounds but in their physical strength. They were never tired of labouring, and seemed as though they could never effect enough. They became tem-perate, moral, religious, setting an example of innocent, unoffending lives to the world around them, which was seen and admired by all. Mr. Parker, a man who worked nearly forty slaves at the same business, was attracted by the manner in which these negroes laboured. He called on Mr. Carlton, some weeks after they had been acting on the new system, and offered 2.000 dollars for the head workman, Jim. The offer was, of course, refused. A few days after the same gentleman called again, and made an offer of double the sum that he had on the former occasion.

Mr. Parker, finding that no money would purchase either of the negroes, said, "Now, Mr. Carlton, pray tell me what it is that makes your negroes work so? What kind of people are they?" "I suppose," observed Carlton, "that they are like other people, flesh and blood." "Why, sir," con-tinued Parker, "I have never seen such people; building as they are next door to my residence, I see and have my eye on them from morning till night. You are never there, for I have never met you, or seen you once at the building. Why, sir, I am an early riser, getting up before day; and do you think that I am not awoke every morning in my life by the noise of their trowels at work, and their singing and noise before day; and do you suppose, sir, that they stop or leave off work at sundown? No, sir, but they work as long as they can see to lay a brick, and then they carry up brick and mortar for an hour or two afterward, to be ahead of their work the next morning. And again, sir, do you think that they walk at their work? No, sir, they run all day. You see, sir, those immensely long ladders, five stories in height; do you suppose they walk up them? No, sir, they run up and down them like so many monkeys all day long. I never saw such people as these in my life. I don't know what to make of them. Were a white man with them and over them with a whip, then I should see and understand the cause of the running and incessant labour; but I cannot comprehend it; there is something in it, sir. Great man, sir, that Jim; great man; I should like to own him." Carlton here informed Parker that their liberties depended upon their work; when the latter replied, "If niggers can work so for the promise of freedom, they ought to be made to work without it." This last remark was in the true spirit of the slaveholder, and reminds us of the fact that, some years since, the overseer of General Wade Hampton offered the niggers under him a suit of clothes to the one that picked the most cotton in one day; and after that time that day's work was given as a task to the slaves on that plantation; and, after a while, was adopted by other planters.

The negroes on the farm, under "Marser Sam," were also working in a manner that attracted the attention of the planters round about. They no longer feared Huckelby's whip, and no longer slept under the preaching of Snyder. On the Sabbath, Mr. and Mrs. Carlton read and explained the Scriptures to them; and the very great attention paid by the slaves showed plainly that they appreciated the gospel when given to them in its purity. The death of Currer, from yellow fever, was a great trial to Mrs. Carlton; for she had not only become much attached to her, but had heard with painful interest the story of her wrongs, and would, in all probability, have restored her to her daughter in New Orleans.

CHAPTER XXI.
THE CHRISTIAN'S DEATH.

"O weep, ye friends of freedom weep!
Your harps to mournful measures sweep."

On the last day of November, 1620, on the confines of the Grand Bank of Newfoundland, lo! we behold one little solitary tempest-tost and weather-beaten ship; it is all that can be seen on the length and breadth of the vast intervening solitudes, from the melancholy wilds of Labrador and New England's iron-bound shores, to the western coasts of Ireland and the rock-defended Hebrides, but one lonely ship greets the eye of angels or of men, on this great thoroughfare of nations in our age. Next in moral grandeur, was this ship, to the great discoverer's: Columbus found a continent; the May-flower brought the seed-wheat of states and empire. That is the May-flower, with its servants of the living God, their wives and little ones, hastening to lay the foundations of nations in the occidental lands of the setting-sun. Hear the voice of prayer to God for his protection, and the glorious music of praise, as it breaks into the wild tempest of the mighty deep, upon the ear of God. Here in this ship are great and good men. Justice, mercy, humanity, respect for the rights of all; each man honoured, as he was useful to himself and others; labour respected, law-abiding men, constitution-making and respecting men; men, whom no tyrant could conquer, or hardship overcome, with the high commission sealed by a Spirit divine, to establish religious and political liberty for all. This ship had the embryo elements of all that is useful, great, and grand in Northern institutions; it was the great type of goodness and wisdom, illustrated in two and a quarter centuries gone by; it was the good genius of America.

But look far in the South-east, and you behold on the same day, in 1620, a low rakish ship hastening from the tropics, solitary and alone, to the New World. What is she? She is freighted with the elements of unmixed evil. Hark! hear those rattling chains, hear that cry of despair and wail of anguish, as they die away in the unpitying distance. Listen to those shocking oaths, the crack of that fleshcutting whip. Ah! it is the first cargo of slaves on their way to Jamestown, Virginia. Behold the Mayflower anchored at Plymouth Rock, the slave-ship in James River. Each a parent, one of the prosperous, labour-honouring, law-sustaining institutions of the North; the other the mother of slavery, idleness, lynch-law, ignorance, unpaid labour, poverty, and duelling, despotism, the ceaseless swing of the whip, and the peculiar institutions of the South. These ships are the representation of good and evil in the New World, even to our day. When shall one of those parallel lines come to an end?

The origin of American slavery is not lost in the obscurity of by-gone ages. It is a plain historical fact, that it owes its birth to the African slave trade, now pronounced by every civilised community the greatest crime ever perpetrated against humanity. Of all causes intended to benefit mankind, the abolition of chattel slavery must necessarily be placed amongst the first, and the negro hails with joy every new advocate that appears in his cause. Commiseration for human suffering and human sacrifices awakened the capacious mind, and brought into action the enlarged benevolence, of Georgiana Carlton. With respect to her philosophy—it was of a noble cast. It was, that all men are by nature equal; that they are wisely and justly endowed by the Creator with certain rights, which are irrefragable; and that, however human pride and human avarice may depress and debase, still God is the author of good to man—and of evil, man is the artificer to himself and to his species. Unlike Plato and Socrates, her mind was free from the gloom that surrounded theirs; her philosophy was founded in the school of Christianity; though a devoted member of her father's church, she was not a sectarian.

We learn from Scripture, and it is a little remarkable that it is the only exact definition of religion found in the sacred volume, that "pure religion and undefiled before God, even the Father, is this, to visit the fatherless and widows in their affliction, and to keep oneself unspotted from the world." "Look not every man on his own things, but every man also on the things of others." "Remember them that are in bonds as bound with them." "Whatsoever ye would that others should do to you, do ye even so to them."

This was her view of Christianity, and to this end she laboured with all her energies to convince her slaveholding neighbours that the negro could not only take care of himself, but that he also appreciated liberty, and was willing to work and redeem himself. Her most sanguine wishes were being realized when she suddenly fell into a decline. Her mother had died of consumption, and her physician pronounced this to be her disease. She was prepared for this sad intelligence, and received it with the utmost composure. Although she had confidence in her husband that he would carry out her wishes in freeing the negroes after her death, Mrs. Carlton resolved upon their immediate liberation. Consequently the slaves were all summoned before the noble woman, and informed that they were no longer bondsmen. "From this hour," said she, "you are free, and all eyes will be fixed upon you. I dare not predict how far your example may affect the welfare of your brethren yet in bondage. If you are temperate, industrious, peaceable, and pious, you will show to the world that slaves can be eman-cipated without danger. Remember what a singular relation you sustain to society. The necessities of the case require not only that you should behave as well as the whites, but better than the whites; and for this reason: if you behave no better than they, your example will lose a great portion of its influence. Make the Lord Jesus Christ your refuge and exemplar. His is the only standard around which you can successfully rally. If ever there was a people who needed the consolations of religion to sustain them in their grievous afflictions, you are that people. You had better trust in the Lord than to put confidence in man. Happy is that people whose God is the Lord. Get as much education as possible for yourselves and your children. An ignorant people can never occupy any other than a degraded station in society; they can never be truly free until they are intelligent. In a few days you will start for the state of Ohio, where land will be purchased for some of you who have families, and where I hope you will all prosper. We have been urged to send you to Liberia, but we think it wrong to send you from your native land. We did not wish to encourage the Colonization Society, for it originated in hatred of the free coloured people. Its pretences are false, its doctrines odious, its means contemptible. Now, whatever may be your situation in life, 'Remember those in bonds as bound with them.' You must get ready as soon as you can for your journey to the North."

Seldom was there ever witnessed a more touching scene than this. There sat the liberator,—pale, feeble, emaciated, with death stamped upon her countenance, surrounded by the sons and daughters of Africa; some of whom had in former years been separated from all that they had held near and dear, and the most of whose backs had been torn and gashed by the negro whip. Some were upon their knees at the feet of their benefactress; others were standing round her weeping. Many begged that they might be permitted to remain on the farm and work for wages, for some had wives and some husbands on other plantations in the neighbourhood, and would rather remain with them.

But the laws of the state forbade any emancipated negroes remaining, under penalty of again being sold into slavery. Hence the necessity of sending them out of the state. Mrs. Carlton was urged by her friends to send the emancipated negroes to Africa. Extracts from the speeches of Henry Clay, and other distinguished Colonization Society men, were read to her to induce her to adopt this course. Some thought they should be sent away because the blacks are vicious; others because they would be missionaries to their brethren in Africa. "But," said she, "if we send away the negroes because they are profligate and vicious, what sort of missionaries will they make? Why not send away the vicious among the whites for the same reason, and the same purpose?"

Death is a leveller, and neither age, sex, wealth, nor usefulness can avert when he is permitted to strike. The most beautiful flowers soon fade, and droop, and die; this is also the case with man; his days are uncertain as the passing breeze. This hour he glows in the blush of health and vigour, but the next he may be counted with the number no more known on earth.

Although in a low state of health, Mrs. Carlton had the pleasure of seeing all her slaves, except Sam and three others, start for a land of freedom. The morning they were to go on board the steamer, bound for Louisville, they all assembled on the large grass plot, in front of the drawing-room window, and wept while they bid their mistress farewell. When they were on the boat, about leaving the wharf, they were heard giving the charge to those on shore—"Sam, take care of Misus, take care of Marser, as you love us, and hope to meet us in de Hio (Ohio), and in heben; be sure and take good care of Misus and Marser."

In less than a week after her emancipated people had started for Ohio, Mrs. Carlton was cold in death. Mr. Carlton felt deeply, as all husbands must who love their wives, the loss of her who had been a lamp to his feet, and a light to his path. She had converted him from infidelity to Christianity; from the mere theory of liberty to practical freedom. He had looked upon the negro as an ill-treated distant link of the human family; he now regarded them as a part of God's children. Oh, what a silence pervaded the house when the Christian had been removed. His indeed was a lonesome position.

> "'Twas midnight, and he sat alone—
> The husband of the dead,
> That day the dark dust had been thrown
> Upon the buried head."

In the midst of the buoyancy of youth, this cherished one had drooped and died. Deep were the sounds of grief and mourning heard in that stately dwelling, when the stricken friends, whose office it had been to nurse and soothe the weary sufferer, beheld her pale and motionless in the sleep of death.

Oh what a chill creeps through the breaking heart when we look upon the insensible form, and feel that it no longer contains the spirit we so dearly loved! How difficult to realise that the eye which always glowed with affection and intelligence—that the ear which had so often listened to the sounds of sorrow and gladness—that the voice whose accents had been to us like sweet music, and the heart, the habitation of benevolence and truth, are now powerless and insensate as the bier upon which the form rests. Though faith be strong enough to penetrate the cloud of gloom which hovers near, and to behold the freed spirit safe, *for ever*, safe in its home in heaven, yet the thoughts *will* linger sadly and cheerlessly upon the grave.

Peace to her ashes! she fought the fight, obtained the Christian's victory, and wears the crown. But if it were that departed spirits are permitted to note the occurrences of this world, with what a frown of disapprobation would hers view the effort being made in the United States to retard the work of emancipation for which she laboured and so wished to see brought about.

In what light would she consider that hypocritical priesthood who gave their aid and sanction to the infamous "Fugitive Slave Law." If true greatness consists in doing good to mankind, then was Georgiana Carlton an ornament to human nature. Who can think of the broken hearts made whole, of sad and dejected countenances now beaming with contentment and joy, of the mother offering her free-born babe to heaven, and of the father whose cup of joy seems overflowing in the presence of his family, where none can molest or make him afraid. Oh, that God may give more such persons to take the whip-scarred negro by the hand, and raise him to a level with our common human-ity! May the professed lovers of freedom in the new world see that true liberty is freedom for all! and may every American continually hear it sounding in his ear:—

> "Shall every flap of England's flag
> Proclaim that all around are free,
> From 'farthest Ind' to each blue crag
> That beetles o'er the Western Sea?
> And shall we scoff at Europe's kings,
> When Freedom's fire is dim with us,
> And round our country's altar clings
> The damning shade of Slavery's curse?["]

Note

1 *Resources for American Literary Study*

The Escape: or, A Leap of Freedom: A Drama in Five Acts

(Boston: R. F. Walcutt, 1858)

The Escape *is considered the first play published by an African American, though it was never staged. Brown frequently read from the play during his lectures, which delighted his audiences.* The Escape *is a five-act drama focusing on the negative repercussions of slavery on the enslavers; it portrays a cruel master and mistress who endlessly seek to thwart the marriage of two slaves who eventually marry and escape to Canada.* The Escape *was actually predated by another, unpublished, play that Brown read aloud on several occasions: "Experience; or, How to Give a Northern Man a Backbone," which was a thinly veiled attack on a northern clergyman with whose views Brown disagreed vehemently. The minstrel-like Cato from* The Escape, *for example, can be read in such a way as to cast Brown as a real-life Uncle Tom, but then again, the irony of Brown's soft rendition of the South in* My Southern Home *no doubt also escaped many readers.*

AUTHOR'S PREFACE

This play is solely written for my own amusement, and not with the remotest thought that it would ever be seen by the public eye. I read it privately however, to a circle of my friends, and through them was invited to read it before a Literary Society. Since then, the Drama has been given in various parts of the country. By the earnest solicitation of some in whose judgment I have the greatest confidence, I now present it in printed form to the public. As I never aspired to be a dramatist, I ask no favor for it, and have little or no solicitude for its fate. If it is not readable, no word of mine can make it so: if it is, to ask favor for it would be needless.

The main features in the Drama are true. GLEN and MELINDA are actual characters, and still reside in Canada. Many of the incidents were drawn from my own experience of eighteen years at the South. The marriage ceremony, as performed in the second act, is still adhered to in many of the Southern States, especially in the farming districts.

The ignorance of the slave, as seen in the case of "BIG SALLY," is common wherever chattel slavery exists. The difficulties created in the domestic circle by the presence of beautiful slave women, as found in DR. GAINES'S family, is well understood by all who have ever visited the valley of the Mississippi.

The play, no doubt, abounds in defects, but as I was born in slavery and never had a day's schooling in my life, I owe the public no apology for my errors.

W. W. B.

CHARACTERS REPRESENTED

DR. GAINES, *proprietor of the farm at Muddy Creek.*
REV. JOHN PINCHEN, *a clergyman.*
DICK WALKER, *a slave speculator.*
MR. WILDMARSH, *neighbor to Dr. Gaines.*
MAJOR MOORE, *a friend of Dr. Gaines.*
MR. WHITE, *a citizen of Massachusetts.*
BILL JENNINGS, *a slave speculator.*
JACOB SCRAGG, *overseer to Dr. Gaines.*
MRS. GAINES, *wife of Dr. Gaines.*
MR. and MRS. NEAL, and DAUGHTER, *Quakers, in Ohio.*
THOMAS, *Mr. Neal's hired man.*
GLEN, *slave of Mr. Hamilton, brother-in-law of Dr. Gaines.*
CATO, SAM, SAMPEY, MELINDA, DOLLY, SUSAN, and BIG SALLY, *slaves of Dr. Gaines.*
PETE, NED, and BILL,
OFFICERS, LOUNGERS, BARKEEPER, *&c.*

ACT I.

Scene 1.—A SITTING-ROOM.

MRS. GAINES, *looking at some drawings—SAMPEY, a white slave, stands behind the lady's chair.*

Enter DR. GAINES, R.

Dr. Gaines. Well, my dear, my practice is steadily increasing. I forgot to tell you that neighbor Wyman engaged me yesterday as his family physician; and I hope that the fever and ague, which is now taking hold of the people, will give me more patients. I see by the New Orleans papers that the yellow fever is raging there to a fearful extent. Men of my profession are reaping a harvest in that section of this year. I would that we could have a touch of the yellow fever here, for I think I could invent a medicine that would cure it. But the yellow fever is a luxury that we medical men in this climate can't expect to enjoy; yet we may hope for the cholera.

Mrs. Gaines. Yes, I would be glad to see it more sickly here, so that your business might prosper. But we are always unfortunate. Every body here seems to be in good health, and I'm afraid that they'll keep so. However, we must hope for the best. We must trust in the Lord. Providence may possibly send some disease amongst us for our benefit.

Enter CATO, R.

Cato. Mr. Campbell is at de door, massa.
Dr. G. Ask him in, Cato.

Enter MR. CAMPBELL, R.

Dr. G. Good morning, Mr. Campbell. Be seated.
Mr. Campbell. Good morning, doctor. The same to you, Mrs. Gaines. Fine morning, this.
Mrs. G. Yes, sir; beautiful day.
Mr. C. Well, doctor, I've come to engage you for my family physician. I am tired of Dr. Jones. I've lost another very valuable nigger under his treatment; and, as my old mother used to say, "change of pastures makes fat calves."
Dr. G. I shall be most happy to become your doctor. Of course, you want me to attend to your niggers, as well as to your family?
Mr. C. Certainly, sir. I have twenty-three servants. What will you charge me by the year?
Dr. G. Of course, you'll do as my other patients do, send your servants to me when they are sick, if able to walk?
Mr. C. Oh, yes; I always do that.
Dr. G. Then I suppose I'll have to lump it, and say $500 per annum.
Mr. C. Well, then, we'll consider that matter settled; and as two of the boys are sick, I'll send them over. So I'll bid you good day, doctor. I would be glad if you came over some time, and bring Mrs. Gaines with you.
Dr. G. Yes, I will; and shall be glad if you pay us a visit, and bring with you Mrs. Campbell. Come over and spend the day.
Mr. C. I will. Good morning, doctor.

[*Exit* MR. CAMPBELL, R.

Dr. G. There, my dear, what do you think of that? Five hundred dollars more added to our income. That's patronage worth having! And I am glad to get all the negroes I can to doctor, for Cato is becoming very useful to me in the shop. He can bleed, pull teeth, and do almost any thing that the blacks require. He can put up medicine as well as any one. A valuable boy, Cato!

Mrs. G. But why did you ask Mr. Campbell to visit you, and to bring his wife? I am sure I could never consent to associate with her, for I understand that she was the daughter of a tanner. You must remember, my dear, that I was born with a silver spoon in my mouth. The blood of the Wyleys runs in my veins. I am surprised that you should ask him to visit you at all; you should have known better.

Dr. G. Oh, I did not mean for him to visit me. I only invited him for the sake of compliments, and I think he so understood it; for I should be far from wishing you to associate with Mrs. Campbell. I don't forget, my dear, the family you were raised in, nor do I overlook my own family. My father, you know, fought by the side of Washington, and I hope some day to have a handle to my own name. I am certain Providence intended me for something higher than a medical man. Ah! by-the-by, I had forgotten that I have a couple of patients to visit this morning, I must go at once.

[*Exit* DR. GAINES, R.

Enter HANNAH, L.

Mrs. G. Go, Hannah, and tell Dolly to kill a couple of fat pullets, and to put the biscuit to rise. I expect brother Pinchen here this afternoon, and I want everything in order. Hannah, Hannah, tell Melinda to come here.

[*Exit* HANNAH, L.

We mistresses do have a hard time in this world; I don't see why the Lord should have imposed such heavy duties on us poor mortals. Well, it can't last always. I long to leave this wicked world, and go home to glory.

Enter MELINDA.

I am to have company this afternoon, Melinda. I expect brother Pinchen here, and I want every thing in order. Go and get one of my new caps, with the lace border, and get out my scalloped-bottomed dimity petticoat, and when you go out, tell Hannah to clean the white-handled knives, and see that not a speck is on them; for I want every thing as it should be while brother Pinchen is here.

[*Exit* MRS. GAINES, L, HANNAH, R.

Scene 2.—DOCTOR'S SHOP—CATO MAKING PILLS.

Enter DR. GAINES, L.

Dr. G. Well, Cato, have you made the batch of ointment that I ordered?

Cato. Yes, massa; I dun made de intment, an' now I is making the bread pills. De tater pills is up on the top shelf.

Dr. G. I am going out to see some patients. If any gentlemen call, tell them that I shall be in this afternoon. If any servants come, you attend to them. I expect two of Mr. Campbell's boys over. You see to them. Feel their pulse, look at their tongues, bleed them, and give each a dose of calomel. Tell them to drink no cold water, and to take nothing but water gruel.

Cato. Yes, massa; I'll tend to 'em.

[*Exit* DR. GAINES, L.

Cato. I allers knowed I was a doctor, an' now de ole boss has put me at it, I muss change my coat. Ef any niggers comes in, I wants to look suspectable. Dis jacket don't suit a doctor, I'll change it. [*Exit* CATO—*immediately returning in a long coat.*] Ah! now I looks like a doctor. Now I can bleed, pull teef, or cut off a leg. Oh! well, well, ef I aint put de pill stuff an' de intment stuff togedder. By golly, dat ole cuss will be mad when he finds it out, won't he? Nebber mind, I'll make it up in pills, and when de flour is on dem, he won't know what's in 'em; an' I'll make some new intment. Ah! yonder comes Campbell's Pete an' Ned; dems de ones massa sed was comin'. I'll see ef I looks right. [*Goes to the looking-glass and views himself.*] I em some punkins, ain't I? [*Knock at the door.*] Come in.

Enter PETE *and* NED, R.

Pete. Whar is de doctor?

Cato. Here I is; don't you see me?

Pete. But whar is de ole boss?

Cato. Dat's none you business. I dun tole you dat I is de doctor, an dat's enuff.

Ned. Oh! do tell us whar de doctor is. I is almos dead. Oh me! oh dear me! I is so sick. [*Horrible faces.*]

Pete. Yes, do tell us; we don't want to stan here foolin'.

Cato. I tells you again dat I is de doctor. I larn de trade under massa.

Ned. Oh! well, den, give me somethin' to stop dis pain. Oh dear me! I shall die. [*He tries to vomit, but can't—ugly faces.*]

Cato. Let me feel your pulse. Now put out your tongue. You is berry sick. Ef you don't mine, you'll die. Come out in de shed, an' I'll bleed you. [*Exit all—re-enter.*

Cato. Dar, now take dese pills, two in de mornin' and two at night, and ef you don't feel better, double de dose. Now, Mr. Pete, what's de matter wid you?

Pete. I is got de cole chills, an' has a fever in de night.

Cato. Come out, an' I'll bleed you.

[*Exit all—re-enter.*

Now take dese pills, two in de mornin' and two at night, an' ef dey don't help you, double de dose. Ah! I like to forget to feel your pulse and look at your tongue. Put out your tongue. [*Feels his pulse.*] Yes, I tells by de feel ob your pulse dat I is gib you de right pills.

Enter MR. Parker's BILL, L.

Cato. What you come in dat door widout knockin' for?

Bill. My toof ache so, I didn't tink to knock. Oh, my toof! my toof! Whar is de doctor?

Cato. Here I is; don't you see me?

Bill. What! you de doctor, you brack cuss! You looks like a doctor! Oh, my toof! my toof! Whar is de doctor?

Cato. I tells you I is de doctor. Ef you don't believe me, ax dese men. I can pull your toof in a minnit.

Bill. Well, den, pull it out. Oh, my toof! how it aches! Oh, my toof! [*Cato gets the rusty turnkeys.*]

Cato. Now lay down on your back.

Bill. What for?

Cato. Dat's de way massa does.

Bill. Oh, my toof! Well, den, come on. [*Lies down, Cato goes astraddle of Bill's breast, puts the turnkeys on the wrong tooth, and pulls—Bill kicks, and cries out*]—Oh, do stop! Oh! oh! oh! [*Cato pulls the wrong tooth—Bill jumps up.*

Cato. Dar, now, I tole you I could pull your toof for you.

Bill. Oh, dear me! Oh, it aches yet! Oh me! Oh, Lor-e-massy! You dun pull de wrong toof. Drat your skin! ef I don't pay you for this, you brack cuss! [*They fight, and turn over table, chairs, and bench—Pete and Ned look on.*

Enter DR. GAINES, R.

Dr. G. Why, dear me, what's the matter? What's this all about? I'll teach you a lesson, that I will. [*The doctor goes at them with his cane.*

Cato. Oh massa! he's to blame, sir. He's to blame. He struck me fuss.

Bill. No, sir; he's to blame; he pull de wrong toof. Oh, my toof! oh, my toof!

Dr. G. Let me see your tooth. Open your mouth. As I live, you've taken out the wrong tooth. I am amazed. I'll whip you for this; I'll whip you well. You're a pretty doctor. Now lie down, Bill, and let him take out the right tooth; and if he makes a mistake this time, I'll cowhide him well. Lie down, Bill. [*Bill lies down, and Cato pulls the tooth.*] There now, why didn't you do that in the first place?

Cato. He wouldn't hole still, sir.

Bill. He lies, sir. I did hole still.

Dr. G. Now go home, boys; go home.

[*Exit* PETE, NED *and* Bill, L.

Dr. G. You've made a pretty muss of it, in my absence. Look at the table! Never mind, Cato; I'll whip you well for this conduct of yours today. Go to work now, and clear up the office.

[*Exit* DR. GAINES, R.

Cato. Confound dat nigger! I wish he was in Ginny. He bite my finger and scratch my face. But didn't I give it to him? Well, den, I reckon I did. [*He goes to the mirror, and discovers that his coat is torn—weeps.*] Oh, dear me! Oh, my coat—my coat is tore! Dat nigger has tore my coat. [*He gets angry, and rushes about the room frantic.*] Cuss dat nigger! Ef I could lay my hands on him, I'd tare him all to pieces,—dat I would. An' de ole boss hit me wid his cane after dat nigger tore my coat. By golly, I wants to fight somebody. Ef ole massa should come in now, I'd fight him. [*Rolls up sleeves.*] Let 'em come now, ef dey dare—ole massa, or any body else; I'm ready for 'em.

Enter DR. GAINES, R.

Dr. G. What's all this noise here?

Cato. Nuffin', sir; only juss I is puttin' things to rights, as you tole me. I didn't hear any noise except de rats.

Dr. G. Make haste, and come in; I want you to go to town.

[*Exit* DR. GAINES, R.

Cato. By golly, de ole boss like to cotch me dat time, didn't he? But wasn't I mad? When I was mad, nobody can do nuffin' wid me. But here's my coat, tore to pieces. Cuss dat nigger! [*Weeps.*] Oh, my coat! oh, my coat! I rudder he had broke my head den to tore my coat. Drat dat nigger! Ef he ever comes here agin, I'll pull out every toof he's got in his head—dat I will.

270

[*Exit*, R.

Scene 3.—A ROOM IN THE QUARTERS.

Enter GLEN, L.

Glen. How slowly the time passes away. I've been waiting here two hours, and Melinda has not yet come. What keeps her, I cannot tell. I waited long and late for her last night, and when she approached, I sprang to my feet, caught her in my arms, pressed her to my heart, and kissed away the tears from her moistened cheeks. She placed her trembling hand in mine, and said, "Glen, I am yours; I will never be the wife of another." I clasped her to my bosom, and called God to witness that I would ever regard her as my wife. Old Uncle Joseph joined us in holy wedlock by moonlight; that was the only marriage ceremony. I look upon the vow as ever binding on me, for I am sure that a just God will sanction our union in heaven. Still, this man, who claims Melinda as his property, is unwilling for me to marry the woman of my choice, because he wants her himself. But he shall not have her. What will he say when he finds out that we are married, I cannot tell; but I am determined to protect my wife or die. Ah! here comes Melinda.

Enter MELINDA, R.

I am glad to see you, Melinda. I've been waiting long, and feared you would not come. Ah! in tears again?

Melinda. Glen, you are always thinking I am in tears. But what did master say to-day?

Glen. He again forbade our union.

Melinda. Indeed! Can he be so cruel?

Glen. Yes, he can be just so cruel.

Melinda. Alas! alas! how unfeeling and heartless! But did you appeal to his generosity?

Glen. Yes, I did; I used all the persuasive powers that I was master of but to no purpose; he was inflexible. He even offered me a new suit of clothes, if I would give you up; and when I told him that I could not, he said he would flog me to death if I ever spoke to you again.

Melinda. And what did you say to him?

Glen. I answered, that, while I loved life better than death, even life itself could not tempt me to consent to a separation that would make life an unchanging curse. Oh, I would kill myself, Melinda, if I thought that, for the sake of life, I could consent to your degradation. No, Melinda, I can die, but shall never live to see you the mistress of another man. But, my dear girl, I have a secret to tell you, and no one must know it but you. I will go out and see that no person is within hearing. I will be back soon.

[*Exit* GLEN, L.

Melinda. It is often said that the darkest hour of the night precedes the dawn. It is ever thus with the vicissitudes of human suffering. After the soul has reached the lowest depths of despair, and can no deeper plunge amid its rolling, fœtid shades, than the reactionary force of man's nature begin to operate, resolution takes the place of despondency, energy succeeds instead of apathy, and an upward tendency is felt and exhibited. Men then hope against power, and smile in defiance of despair. I shall never forget when first I saw Glen. It is now more than a year since he came here with his master, Mr. Hamilton. It was a glorious moonlight night in autumn. The wide and fruitful face of nature was silent and buried in repose. The tall trees on the borders of Muddy Creek waved their leafy branches in the breeze, which was wafted from afar, refreshing over hill and vale, over the rippling water, and the waving corn and wheat fields. The starry sky was studded over with a few light, flitting clouds, while the moon, as if rejoicing to witness the meeting of two hearts that should be cemented by the purest love, sailed triumphantly along among the shifting vapors.

Oh, how happy I have been in my acquaintance with Glen! That he loves me, I do well believe it; that I love him, it is most true. Oh, how I would that those who think the slave incapable of the finer feelings, could only see our hearts, and learn our thoughts,—thoughts that we dare not utter in the presence of our masters! But I fear that Glen will be separated from me, for there is nothing too base and mean for masters to do, for the purpose of getting me entirely in his power. But, thanks to Heaven, he does not own Glen, and therefore cannot sell him. Yet he might purchase him from his brother-in-law, so as to send him out of the way. But here comes my husband.

Enter GLEN, L.

Glen. I've been as far as the overseer's house, and all is quiet. Now, Melinda, as you are my wife, I will confide to you a secret. I've long been thinking of making my escape to Canada, and taking you with me. It is true that I don't belong to your master, but he might buy me from Hamilton, and then sell me out of the neighborhood.

Melinda. But we could never succeed in the attempt to escape.

Glen. We will make the trial, and show that we at least deserve success. There is a slave trader expected here next week, and Dr. Gaines would sell you at once if he knew that we were married. We must get ready and start, and if we can pass the Ohio river, we'll be safe on the road to Canada.

[*Exit*, R.

Scene 4.—DINING-ROOM.

REV. MR. PINCHEN *giving* MRS. GAINES *an account of his*
experience as a minister—HANNAH *clearing away the breakfast table—*
SAMPEY *standing behind* MRS. GAINES' *chair*.

Mrs. Gaines. Now, do give me more of your experience, brother
Pinchen. It always does my soul good to hear religious experience. It
draws me nearer and nearer to the Lord's side. I do love to hear good news
from God's people.

Mr. Pinchen. Well, sister Gaines, I've had great opportunities in my time
to study the heart of man. I've attended a great many camp-meetings,
revival meetings, protracted meetings, and death-bed scenes, and I am satisfied, sister Gaines, that the heart of man is full of sin, and desperately
wicked. This is a wicked world, sister Gaines, a wicked world.

Mrs. G. Were you ever in Arkansas, brother Pinchen? I've been told that
the people out there are very ungodly.

Mr. P. Oh yes, sister Gaines. I once spent a year at Little Rock, and
preached in all the towns round about there; and I found some hard cases
out there, I can tell you. I was once spending a week in a district where there
were a great many horse thieves, and one night, somebody stole my pony.
Well, I knowed it was no use to make a fuss, so I told brother Tarbox to say
nothing about it, and I'd get my horse by preaching God's everlasting
gospel; for I had faith in the truth, and knowed that my savior would not let
me lose my pony. So the next Sunday I preached on horse-stealing, and told
the brethren to come up in the evenin' with their hearts filled with the grace
of God. So that night the house was crammed brim full of anxious souls,
panting for the bread of life. Brother Bingham opened with prayer, and
brother Tarbox followed, and I saw right off that we were gwine to have a
blessed time. After I got 'em all pretty warmed up, I jumped on to one of the
seats, stretched out my hands, and said, "I know who stole my pony; I've
found out; and you are in here tryin' to make people believe that you've got
religion; but you ain't got it. And if you don't take my horse back to brother
Tarbox's pasture this very night, I'll tell your name right out in meetin' to-
morrow night. Take my pony back, you vile and wretched sinner, and come
up here and give your heart to God." So the next mornin', I went out to
brother Tarbox's pasture, and sure enough, there was my bobtail pony. Yes,
sister Gaines, there he was, safe and sound. Ha, ha, ha.

Mrs. G. Oh, how interesting, and how fortunate for you to get your
pony! And what power there is in the gospel! God's children are very

lucky. Oh, it is so sweet to sit here and listen to such good news from God's people! You Hannah, what are you doing standing there listening for, and neglecting your work? Never mind, my lady, I'll whip you well when I'm done here. Go at your work this moment, you lazy huzzy! Never mind, I'll whip you well. [*Aside*] Come, do go on, brother Pinchen, with your godly conversation. It is so sweet! It draws me nearer and nearer to the Lord's side.

Mr. P. Well, sister Gaines, I've had some mighty queer dreams in my time, that I have. You see, one night I dreamed that I was dead and in heaven, and such a place I never saw before. As soon as I entered the gates of the celestial empire, I saw many old and familiar faces that I had seen before. The first person that I saw was good old Elder Pike, the preacher that first called my attention to religion. The next person I saw was Deacon Billings, my first wife's father, and then I saw a host of godly faces. Why, sister Gaines, you knowed Elder Goosbee, didn't you?

Mrs. G. Why, yes; did you see him there? He married me to my first husband.

Mr. P. Oh, yes, sister Gaines, I saw the old Elder, and he looked for all the world as if he had just come out of a revival meetin'.

Mrs. G. Did you see my first husband there, brother Pinchen?

Mr. P. No, sister Gaines, I didn't see brother Pepper there; but I've no doubt but that brother Pepper was there.

Mrs. G. Well, I don't know; I have my doubts. He was not the happiest man in the world. He was always borrowing trouble about something or another. Still, I saw some happy moments with Mr. Pepper. I was happy when I made his acquaintance, happy during our courtship, happy a while after our marriage, and happy when he died. [*Weeps.*]

Hannah. Massa Pinchen, did you see my ole man Ben up dar in hebben?

Mr. P. No, Hannah; I didn't go amongst the niggers.

Mrs. G. No, of course Pinchen didn't go amongst the blacks. What are you asking questions for? Never mind, my lady, I'll whip you well when I'm done here. I'll skin you from head to foot. [*Aside.*] Do go on with your heavenly conversation, brother Pinchen; it does my very soul good. This is indeed a precious moment for me. I do love to hear of God and Him crucified.

Mr. P. Well, sister Gaines, I promised sister Daniels that I'd come over and see her this morning, and have a little season of prayer with her, and I suppose I must go. I'll tell you more of my religious experience when I return.

274

Mrs. G. If you must go, then I'll have to let you; but before you do, I wish to get your advice upon a little matter that concerns Hannah. Last week, Hannah stole a goose, killed it, cooked it, and she and her man Sam had a fine time eating the goose; and her master and I would never have known a word about it, if it had not been for Cato, a faithful servant, who told his master. And then, you see, Hannah had to be severely whipped before she'd confess that she stole the goose. Next Sabbath is sacrament day, and I want to know if you think Hannah is fit to go to the Lord's supper after stealing the goose.

Mr. P. Well, sister Gaines, that depends on circumstances. If Hannah has confessed that she stole the goose, and has been sufficiently whipped, and has begged her master's pardon, and thinks she'll never do the like again, why then I suppose she can go to the Lord's supper; for

"While the lamp holds out to burn,
    The vilest sinner may return."

But she must be sure that she has repented, and won't steal any more.

Mrs. G. Now, Hannah, do you hear that? For my own part, I don't think she's fit to go to the Lord's supper, for she had no occasion to steal the goose. We give our niggers plenty of good wholesome food. They have a full run to the meal tub, meat once a fortnight, and all the sour milk about the place, and I'm sure there's enough for any one. I do think that our niggers are the most ungrateful creatures in the world, that I do. They aggravate my life out of me.

Hannah. I know, missis, dat I steal de goose, and massa whip me for it, and I confess it, and I is sorry for it. But, missis, I is gwine to de Lord's supper, next Sunday, kase I ain't agwine to turn my back on my bressed Lord an' Massa for no old tough goose, dat I ain't. [*Weeps.*]

Mr. P. Well, sister Gaines, I suppose I must go over and see sister Daniels; she'll be waiting for me.

[*Exit* MR. PINCHEN, M.D.

Mrs. G. Now, Hannah, brother Pinchen is gone, do you get the cowhide and follow me to the cellar, and I'll whip you well for aggravating me as you have to-day. It seems as if I can never sit down to take a little comfort with the Lord, without you crossing me. The devil always puts it into your head to disturb me, just when I'm trying to serve the Lord. I've no doubt but that I'll miss going to heaven on your account. But I'll whip you well before I leave this world, that I will. Get the cowhide and follow me to the cellar.

[*Exit* MRS. GAINES *and* HANNAH, R.

275

ACT II.

Scene 1.—PARLOR.

DR. GAINES *at a table, letters and papers before him.*

Enter SAMPEY, L.

Sampey. Dar's a gemman at de doe, massa, dat wants to see you, seer.
Dr. Gaines. Ask him to walk in, Sampey.

[*Exit* SAMPEY, L.

Enter WALKER.

Walker. Why, how do you do Dr. Gaines? I em glad to see you, I'll swear.
Dr. G. How do you do, Mr. Walker? I did not expect to see you up here
so soon. What has hurried you?
Walk. Well, you see, doctor, I comes when I em not expected. The price of
niggers is up, and I em gwine to take advantage of the times. Now, doctor, ef
you've got any niggers that you wants to sell, I em your man. I am paying the
highest price of any body in the market. I pay cash down, and no grumblin'.
Dr. G. I don't know that I want to sell any of my people now. Still, I've got
to make up a little money next month, to pay in bank; and another thing, the
doctors say we are likely to have a touch of cholera this summer, and if that's
the case, I suppose I had better turn as many of my slaves into cash as I can.
Walk. Yes, doctor, that is very true. The cholera is death on slaves, and a
thousand dollars in your pocket is a great deal better than a nigger in the
field, with cholera at his heels. Why, who is that coming up the lane? It's
Mr. Wildmarsh, as I live! Jest the very man I wants to see.

Enter MR. WILDMARSH.

Why, how do you do squire? I was jest thinkin' about you.
Wildmarsh. How are you Mr. Walker? and how are you, doctor? I am
glad to see you both looking so well. You seem in remarkably good health,
doctor?
Dr. G. Yes, Squire, I was never in the enjoyment of better health. I hope
you left all well at Licking?
Wild. Yes, I thank you. And now, Mr. Walker, how goes times with you?
Walk. Well, you see, Squire, I em in good spirits. The price of niggers is
up in the market, and I'm looking out for bargains; and I was just intendin'
to come over to Lickin' to see you, to see if you had any niggers to sell. But
it seems as ef the Lord knowed that I wanted to see you, and directed your
steps over here. Now, Squire, ef you've got any niggers you wants to sell, I

em your man. I am payin' the highest cash price of any body in the market. Now's your time, Squire.

Wild. No, I don't think I want to sell any of my slaves now. I sold a very valuable gal to Mr. Haskins last week. I tell you, she was a smart one. I got eighteen hundred dollars for her.

Walk. Why, Squire, how you do talk! Eighteen hundred dollars for one gal? She must have been a screamer to bring that price. What sort of a lookin' critter was she? I should like to have bought her.

Wild. She was a little of the smartest gal I've ever raised; that she was.

Walk. Then she was of your own raising, was she?

Wild. Oh, yes; she was raised on my place, and if I could have kept her three or four years longer, and taken her to the market myself, I am sure I could have sold her for three thousand dollars. But you see, Mr. Walker, my wife got a little jealous, and you know jealousy sets the women's heads a tee-tering, and so I had to sell the gal. She's got straight hair, blue eyes, promi-nent features, and is almost white. Haskins will make a spec, and no mistake.

Walk. Why, Squire, was she that pretty little gal that I saw on your knee the day that your wife was gone, when I was at your place three years ago?

Wild. Yes, the same.

Walk. Well, now, Squire, I thought that was your daughter; she looked mightily like you. She was your daughter, wasn't she? You need not be ashamed to own it to me, for I am mum upon such matters.

Wild. You know, Mr. Walker, that people will talk, and when they talk, they say a great deal; and people did talk, and many said the gal was my daughter; and you know we can't help people's talking. But here comes the Rev. Mr. Pinchen; I didn't know that he was in the neighborhood.

Walk. It is Mr. Pinchen, as I live; jest the very man I wants to see.

Enter MR. PINCHEN, R.

Why, how do you do, Mr. Pinchen? What in the name of Jehu brings you down here to Muddy Creek? Any camp-meetins, revival meetins, death-bed scenes, or any thing else in your line going on down there? How is religion prosperin' now, Mr. Pinchen? I always like to hear about religion.

Mr. Pin. Well, Mr. Walker, the Lord's work is in good condition every where now. I tell you, Mr. Walker, I've been in the gospel ministry these thirteen years, and I am satisfied that the heart of man is full of sin and desperately wicked. This is a wicked world, Mr. Walker, a wicked world, and we ought all of us to have religion. Religion is a good thing to live by, and we all want it when we die. Yes, sir, when the great trumpet blows, we ought to be ready. And a man in your business of buying and selling slaves needs religion more than any body else, for it makes you treat your people as you should. Now, there is Mr. Haskins,—he is a slave-trader, like your-self. Well, I converted him. Before he got religion, he was one of the worst men to his niggers I ever saw; his heart was as hard as stone. But religion has made his heart as soft as a piece of cotton. Before I converted him, he would sell husbands from their wives, and seem to take delight in it; but now he won't sell a man from his wife, if he can get any one to buy both of them together. I tell you, sir, religion has done wonderful work for him.

Walk. I know, Mr. Pinchen, that I ought to have religion, and I feel that I am a great sinner; and whenever I get with pious people like you and the doctor, and Mr. Wildmarsh, it always makes me feel that I am a desperate sinner. I feel it the more, because I've got a religious turn of mind. I know that I would be happier with religion, and the first spare time I get, I am going to try to get it. I'll go to a protracted meeting, and I won't stop till I get religion. Yes, I'll scuffle with the Lord till I gets forgiven. But it always makes me feel bad to talk about religion, so I'll change the subject. Now, doctor, what about them thar niggers you thought you could sell me?

Dr. Gaines. I'll see my wife, Mr. Walker, and if she is willing to part with Hannah, I'll sell you Sam and his wife, Hannah. Ah! here comes my wife; I'll mention it.

Enter MRS. GAINES, L.

Ah! my dear, I'm glad you've come. I was just telling Mr. Walker, that if you were willing to part with Hannah, I'd sell him Sam and Hannah.

Mrs. G. Now, Dr. Gaines, I am astonished and surprised that you should think of such a thing. You know what trouble I've had in training up Hannah for a house servant, and now that I've got her so that she knows my ways, you want to sell her. Hav n't you niggers enough on the planta-tion to sell, without selling the servants from under my very nose?

Dr. G. Oh, yes, my dear; but I can spare Sam, and don't like to separate him from his wife; and I thought if you could let Hannah go, I'd sell them both. I don't like to separate husbands from their wives.

Mrs. G. Now, gentlemen, that's just the way with my husband. He thinks more about the welfare and comfort of his slaves, than he does of himself or his family. I am sure you need not feel so bad at the thought of separating Sam from Hannah. They've only been married eight months. And their attachment can't be very strong in that short time. Indeed, I shall be glad if you do sell Sam, for then I'll make Hannah *jump the broom-stick* with Cato, and I'll have them both here under my eye. I never will again let one of my house servants marry a field hand—never! For when night comes on, the servants are off to the quarters, and I have to holler and holler enough to split my throat before I can make them hear. And another thing: I want you to sell Melinda. I don't intend to keep that mulatto wench about the house any longer.

Dr. Gaines. My dear, I'll sell any servant from the place to suit you, except Melinda. I can't think of selling her—I can't think of it.

Mrs. G. I tell you that Melinda shall leave this house, or I'll go. There, now you have it. I've had my life tormented out of me by the presence of that yellow wench, and I'll stand it no longer. I know you love her more than you do me, and I'll—I'll—I'll write—write to my father. [*Weeps.*]

[*Exit* MRS. GAINES, L.

Walk. Why, doctor, your wife's a screamer, ain't she? Ha, ha, ha. Why, doctor, she's got a tongue of her own, ain't she? Why, doctor, it was only last week that I thought of getting a wife myself; but your wife has skeered the idea out my head. Now, doctor, if you wants to sell the gal, I'll buy her. Husband and wife should be on good terms, and your wife won't feel well till the gal is gone. Now, I'll pay you all she's worth, if you wants to sell.

Dr. G. No, Mr. Walker; the girl my wife spoke of is not for sale. My wife does not mean what she says, she's only a little jealous. I'll get brother Pinchen to talk to her, and get her mind upon religious matters and then she'll forget it. She's only a little jealous.

Walk. I tell you what, doctor, ef you call that a little jealous, I'd like to know what's a heap. I tell you, it will take something more than religion to set your wife right. You had better sell me the gal; I'll pay you cash down, and no grumblin'.

Dr. G. The girl is not for sale, Mr. Walker; but if you want two good, able-bodied servants, I'll sell you Sam and Big Sally. Sam is trustworthy, and Sally is worth more than her weight in gold for rough usage.

Walk. Well, doctor, I'll go out and take a look at 'em, for I never buys slaves without examining them well, because they are sometimes injured by over-work or under-feedin'. I don't say that is the case with yours, for I don't believe it is; but as I sell on honor, I must buy on honor.

Dr. G. Walk out, sir, and you can examine them to your heart's content. Walk right out, sir.

Scene 2.—VIEW IN FRONT OF THE GREAT HOUSE.

Examination of SAM *and* BIG SALLY.—DR. GAINES, WILDMARSH, MR. PINCHEN *and* WALKER *present.*

Walk. Well, my boy, what's your name?
Sam. Sam, sir, is my name.
Walk. How old are you, Sam?

Sam. Ef I live to see next corn plantin' time, I'll be 27, or 30, or 35, or 40—I don't know which, sir.

Walk. Ha, ha, ha. Well, doctor, this is a rather green boy. Well, mer feller, are you sound?

Sam. Yes, sir, I spec I is.

Walk. Open your mouth and let me see your teeth. I allers judge a nigger's age by his teeth, same as I does a hoss. Ah! pretty good set of grinders. Have you got a good appetite?

Sam. Yes, sir.

Walk. Can you eat your allowance?

Sam. Yes, sir, when I can get it.

Walk. Get out on the floor and dance; I want to see if you are supple.

Sam. I don't like to dance; I is got religion.

Walk. Oh, ho! you've got religion, have you? That's so much the better. I likes to deal in the gospel. I think he'll suit me. Now, mer gal, what's your name?

Sally. I is Big Sally, sir.

Walk. How old are you, Sally?

Sally. I don't know, sir; but I heard once dat I was born at pertater diggin' time.

Walk. Ha, ha, ha. Don't know how old you are! Do you know who made you?

Sally. I hev heard who it is in de Bible dat made me, but I dun forget de gentman's name.

Walk. Ha, ha, ha. Well, doctor, this is the greenest lot of niggers I've seen for some time. Well, what do you ask for them?

Dr. Gaines. You may have Sam for $1000, and Sally for $900. They are worth all I ask for them. You know I never banter, Mr. Walker. There they are; you can take them at that price, or let them alone, just as you please.

Walk. Well, doctor, I reckon I'll take 'em; but it's all they are worth. I'll put handcuffs on 'em and then I'll pay you. I likes to go according to Scripter. Scripter says ef eating' meat will offend your brother, you must quit it; and I says, ef leavin' your slaves without the handcuffs will make 'em run away, you mus put the handcuffs on 'em. Now, Sam, don't you and Sally cry. I am of a tender heart, an it allers makes me feel bad to see people cryin'. Don't cry, and the first place I get to, I'll buy each of you a great big *ginger cake*,—that I will. Now, Mr. Pinchen, I wish you were going down the river. I'd like to have your company, for I allers likes the company of preachers.

Mr. Pinchen. Well, Mr. Walker, I would be much pleased to go down the river with you, but it's too early for me. I expect to go to Natchez in four or five weeks, to attend a camp-meetin', and if you were going down then, I'd like it. What kind of niggers sells best in the Orleans market, Mr. Walker?

Walk. Why, field hands. Did you think of goin' in the trade?

Mr. P. Oh, no; only it's a long ways down to Natchez, and I thought I'd just buy five or six niggers, and take 'em down and sell 'em to pay for my travellin' expenses. I only want to clear my way.

Scene 3.—SITTING-ROOM—TABLE AND ROCKING-CHAIR.

Enter MRS. GAINES, R, *followed by* SAMPEY

Mrs. Gaines. I do wish your master would come; I want supper. Run to the gate, Sampey, and see if he is coming.

[*Exit* SAMPEY, L.

That man is enough to break my heart. The patience of an angel could not stand it.

Enter SAMPEY, L.

Samp. Yes, missis, master is coming.

Enter DR. GAINES, L.

[*The Doctor walks about with his hands under his coat, seeming very much elated.*]

Mrs. Gaines. Why, doctor, what is the matter?

Dr. Gaines. My dear, don't call me *doctor.*

Mrs. G. What should I call you?

Dr. G. Call me Colonel, my dear—Colonel. I have been elected Colonel of Militia, and I want you to call me by my right name. I always felt that Providence had designed me for something great, and He has just begun to shower His Blessings upon me.

Mrs. G. Dear me, I could never get to calling you Colonel; I've called you Doctor for the last twenty years.

Dr. G. Now, Sarah, if you will call me Colonel, other people will, and I want you to set the example. Come, my darling, call me Colonel, and I'll give you any thing you wish for.

Mrs. G. Well, as I want a new gold watch and bracelets, I'll commence now. Come, Colonel, we'll go to supper. Ah! now for my new shawl. [*Aside.*] Mrs. Lemme was here to-day, Colonel, and she had on, Colonel, one of the prettiest shawls, Colonel, I think, Colonel, that I ever saw, Colonel, in my life, Colonel. An there is only one, Colonel, in Mr.

Watson's store, Colonel; and that, Colonel, will do, Colonel, for a Colonel's wife.

Dr. G. Ah! my dear, you never looked so much the lady since I've known you. Go, my darling, get the watch, bracelets, and shawl, and tell them to charge them to Colonel Gaines; and when you say "Colonel," always emphasize the word.

Mrs. G. Come, Colonel, let's go to supper.

Dr. G. My dear, you're a jewel,—you are!

[*Exit*, R.

Enter CATO, L.

Cato. Why, whar is massa and missis? I tought dey was here. Ah! by golly, yonder comes a mulatter gal: Yes, it's Mrs. Jones's Tapioca. I'll set up to dat gal, dat I will.

Enter TAPIOCA, R.

Good ebenin', Miss Tappy. How is your folks?

Tapioca. Pretty well, I tank you.

Cato. Miss Tappy, dis wanderin' heart of mine is yours. Come, take a seat! Please to squze my manners; love discommodes me. Take a seat. Now, Miss Tappy, I loves you; an ef you will jess marry me, I'll make you a happy husbands, dat I will. Come, take me as I is.

Tap. But what will Big Jim say?

Cato. Big Jim! Why, let dat nigger go to Ginny. I want to know, now, if you is tinkin' about dat common nigger? Why, Miss Tappy, I is surstonished dat you should tink 'bout frowin' yousef away wid a common, ugly lookin' cuss like Big Jim, when you can get a fine lookin', suspectable man like me. Come, Miss Tappy, choose dis day who you have. Afore I go any furder, give me one kiss. Come, give me one kiss. Come, let me kiss you.

Tap. No you shan't—dare now! You shan't kiss me widout you is stronger den I is and I know you is dat. [*He kisses her.*]

Enter DR. GAINES, R, *and hides.*

Cato. Did you know, Miss Tappy, dat I is de head doctor 'bout dis house? I beats de ole boss all to pieces.

Tap. I hev heard dat you bleeds and pulls teef.

Cato. Yes, Miss Tappy; massa could not get along widout me, for massa was made a doctor by books; but I is a natral doctor. I was born a doctor, jess as Lorenzo Dow was born a preacher. So you see I can't be nuffin' but a doctor, while massa is a bunglin' ole cuss at de bissness.

Dr. Gaines, (in a low voice.) Never mind; I'll teach you a lesson, that I will.

Cato. You see, Miss Tappy, I was gwine to say—Ah! but afore I forget, jess give me anudder kiss, jess to keep company wid de one dat you gave me jess now,—dat's all. [*Kisses her.*] Now, Miss Tappy, duse you know de fuss time dat I seed you?

Tap. No, Mr. Cato, I don't.

Cato. Well, it was at de camp-meetin'. Oh, Miss Tappy, dat pretty red cal-liker dress you had on dat time did de work for me. It made my heart flutter—

Dr. G. (low voice.) Yes, and I'll make your black hide flutter.

Cato. Didn't I hear some noise? By golly, dar is teves in dis house, and I'll drive 'em out. [*Takes a chair and runs at the Doctor, and knocks him down. The Doctor chases Cato around the table.*

Cato. Oh, massa, I didn't know 'twas you!

Dr. G. You scoundrel! I'll whip you well. Stop! I tell you.

[*Curtain falls.*

ACT III.

Scene 1. —SITTING-ROOM.

MRS. GAINES, *seated in an arm chair, reading a letter.*

Enter HANNAH, L.

Mrs. Gaines. You need not tell me, Hannah, that you don't want another husband, I know better. Your master has sold Sam, and he's gone down the river, and you'll never see him again. So, go and put on your calico dress, and meet me in the kitchen. I intend for you to *jump the broomstick* with Cato. You need not tell me that you don't want another man. I know that there's no woman living that can be happy and satisfied without a husband.

Hannah. Oh, missis, I don't want to jump de broomstick wid Cato. I don't love Cato; I can't love him.

Mrs. G. Shut up, this moment! What do you know about love? I didn't love your master when I married him, and people don't marry for love now. So go and put on your calico dress, and meet me in the kitchen.

[*Exit* HANNAH, L.

I am glad that the Colonel has sold Sam; now I'll make Hannah marry Cato, and I have them both here under my eye. And I am also glad that the Colonel has parted with Melinda. Still, I'm afraid that he is trying to deceive me. He took the hussy away yesterday, and says he sold her to a

283

trader; but I don't believe it. At any rate, if she's in the neighborhood, I'll find her, that I will. No man ever fools me.

[*Exit* MRS. GAINES, L.

Scene 2.—THE KITCHEN—SLAVES AT WORK.

Enter HANNAH, R.

Hannah. Oh, Cato, do go and tell missis dat you don't want to jump de broomstick with me,—dat's a good man! Do, Cato; kase I nebber can love you. It was only last week dat massa sold my Sammy, and I don't want any udder man. Do go tell missis dat you don't want me.

Cato. No, Hannah, I ain't a gwine to tell missis no such thing, kase I does want you, and I ain't a-gwine to tell a lie for you ner nobody else. Dar, now you's got it! I don't see why you need to make so much fuss. I is better lookin' den Sam; an' I is a house servant, an' Sam was only a fiel' hand; so you ought to feel proud of a change. So go and do as missis tells you.

[*Exit* HANNAH, L.

Hannah needn't try to get me to tell a lie; I ain't a-gwine to do it, kase I dose want her, an' I is bin wantin' her dis long time, an' soon as massa sold Sam, I knowed I would get her. By golly, I is gwine to be a married man. Won't I be happy! Now, ef I could only jess run away from ole massa, an' get to Canada wid Hannah, den I'd show 'em who I was. Ah! dat reminds me of my song 'bout ole massa and Canada, an' I'll sing it fer yer. Dis is my moriginal hyme. It comed into my head one night when I was fass asleep under an apple tree, looking up at de moon. Now for my song:—

AIR—"*Dandy Jim.*"

Come all ye bondmen far and near,
Let's put a song in massa's ear,
It is a song for our poor race,
Who're whipped and trampled with disgrace.
CHORUS.
My old massa tells me, Oh,
This is a land of freedom, Oh;
Let's take a look about and see if it's so,
Just as massa tells me, Oh.

He tells us of that glorious one,
I think his name was Washington,
How he did fight for liberty,
To save a threepence tax on tea. [*Chorus.*]

But now we look about and see
That we poor blacks are not so free;
We're whipped and thrashed about like fools,
And have no chance at common schools. [*Chorus.*]

They take our wives, insult and mock,
And sell our children on the block,
They choke us if we say a word,
And say that "niggers" shan't be heard. [*Chorus.*]

Our preachers, too, with whip and cord,
Command obedience in the Lord:
They say they learn it from the big book,
But for ourselves, we dare not look. [*Chorus.*]

There is a country far away,
I think they call it Canada,
And if we reach Victoria's shore,
They say that we are slaves no more.

    Now hasten, all bondmen, let us go,
    And leave this *Christian* country, Oh;
    Haste to the land of the British Queen,
    Where whips for negroes are not seen.
Now, if we go, we must take the night,
And never let them come in sight;
The bloodhounds will be on our track,
And wo to us if they fetch us back.

    Now hasten all bondmen, let us go,
    And leave this *Christian* country, Oh;
    God help us to Victoria's shore,
    Where we are free and slaves no more!

Enter MRS. GAINES, L.

Mrs. Gaines. Ah! Cato, you're ready, are you? Where is Hannah?

Cato. Yes, missis; I is bin waitin' dis long time. Hannah has been here tryin' to swade me to tell you dat I don't want her; but I telled her dat you sed I must jump de broomstick wid her, an' I is gwine to mind you.

Mrs. G. That's right, Cato; servants should always mind their masters and mistresses, without asking a question.

Cato. Yes, missis, I allers dose what you and massa tells me, an' axes nobody.

Enter HANNAH, R.

Mrs. Gaines. Ah! Hannah; come we are waiting for you. Nothing can be done till you come.

Hannah. Oh, missis, I do n't want to jump de broomstick wid Cato; I can't love him.

Mrs. G. Shut up, this moment. Dolly, get the broom. Susan, you take hold of the other end. There, now hold it a little lower—there, a little higher. There, now, that'll do. Now Hannah, take hold of Cato's hand. Let Cato take hold of your hand.

Hannah. Oh, missis, do spare me. I do n't want to jump de broom stick wid Cato.

Mrs. G. Get the cowhide, and follow me to the cellar, and I'll whip you well. I'll let you know how to disobey my orders. Get the cowhide, and follow me to the cellar.

[*Exit* MRS. GAINES *and* HANNAH, R.

Dolly. Oh, Cato, do go an' tell missis dat you don't want Hannah. Don't you here how she's whippin' her in de cellar. Do go an' tell missis dat you don't want Hannah, and den she'll stop whippin' her.

Cato. No, Dolly, I ain't a-gwine to do no such thing, kase ef I tell missis dat I don't want Hannah, den missis will whip me; an' I ain't a-gwine to be whipped fer you, ner Hannah, ner nobody else. No, I'll jump de broomstick wid every woman on de place, ef missis wants me to, before I'll be whipped.

Dolly. Cato, ef I was in Hannah's place, I'd see you in de bottomless pit before I'd live wid you, you great big wall-eyed, empty-headed, knock-kneed fool. You're as mean as your devilish old missis.

Cato. Ef you do n't quit dat busin' me, Dolly, I'll tell missis as soon as she comes in, an' she'll whip you, you know she will.

Enter MRS. GAINES *and* HANNAH, R.

[*Mrs. G. fans herself with her handkerchief, and appears fatigued.*]

Mrs. G. You ought to be ashamed of yourself, Hannah, to make me fatigue myself in this way, to make you do your duty. It's very naughty in you, Hannah. Now, Dolly, you and Susan get the broom, and get out in the middle of the room. There, hold it a little lower—a little higher; there that'll do. Now, remember that this is a solemn occasion; you are going to jump into matrimony. Now, Cato, take hold of Hannah's hand. There, now, why could n't you let Cato take hold of your hand before? Now get ready, and when I count to three, do you jump. Eyes on the *broomstick!* All ready. One, two, three, and over you go. There, now you're husband and wife, and if you do n't live happily together, it's your own fault; for I am sure there's nothing to hinder it. Now, Hannah, come up to the house, and I'll give you some whiskey, and you can make some apple toddy, and you and Cato can have a fine time.

[*Exit* MRS. GAINES *and* HANNAH, L.

Dolly. I tell you what, Susan, when I get married, I is gwine to have a preacher to marry me. I aint' a-gwine to jump de broomstick. Dat will do for fiel' hands, but house servants ought to be 'bove dat.

Susan. Well, chile, you can't speck any ting else from ole missis. She come down from Carlina, from 'mong de poor white trash. She don't know any better. You can't speck nothin' more dan a jump from a frog. Missis says she is one of de akastocacy; but she ain't no more of an akastocacy dan I is. Missis says she was born with a silver spoon in her mouf; ef she was, I wish it had a-choked her, dat's what I wish. Missis wanted to make Linda jump de broomstick wid Glen, but massa ain't a-gwine to let Linda jump de broomstick wid anyone. He's gwine to keep Linda fer heself.

Dolly. You know massa took Linda 'way las' night, an' tell missis dat he has sold her and sent her down the river; but I do n't believe he has sold her at all. He went ober towards poplar farm, an' I tink Linda is ober dar right now. Ef she is dar, missis'll find it out, fer she tell'd massa las' night, dat ef Linda was in de neighborhood, she'd find her.

[*Exit* DOLLY *and* SUSAN.

Scene 3.—SITTING ROOM—CHAIRS AND TABLE.

Enter HANNAH, R.

Hannah. I don't keer what missis says; I don't like Cato, an' I won't live wid him. I always love my Sammy, an' I loves him now. [*Knock at the door—goes to the door.*

287

Enter MAJ. MOORE, M.D.

Walk in, sir; take a seat. I'll call missis, sir; massa is gone away.

[*Exit* HANNAH, R.

Maj. Moore. So I am here at last, and the Colonel is not at home. I hope his wife is a good-looking woman. I rather like fine-looking women, especially when their husbands are from home. Well, I've studied human nature to some purpose. If you wish to get the good will of a man, do n't praise his wife, and if you wish to gain the favor of a woman, praise her children, and swear that they are the picture of their father, whether they are or not. Ah! here comes the lady.

Enter MRS. GAINES, R.

Mrs. G. Good morning, sir!

Maj. M. Good morning, madam! I am Maj. Moore, of Jefferson. The Colonel and I had seats near each other in the last Legislature.

Mrs. G. Be seated, sir. I think I've heard the Colonel speak of you. He's away now; but I expect him every moment. You're a stranger here, I presume?

Maj. K. Yes, madam, I am. I rather like the Colonel's situation here.

Mrs. G. It is thought to be a fine location.

Enter SAMPEY, R.

Hand me my fan, will you, Sampey? [*Sampey gets the fan and passes near the Major, who mistakes the boy for the Colonel's son. He reaches out his hand.*

Maj. M. How do you do, bub? Madam, I should have known that this was the Colonel's son, if I had met him in California; for he looks so much like his papa.

Mrs. G. [*To the boy.*] Get out of here this minute. Got to the kitchen.

[*Exit* SAMPEY, R.

That is one of the niggers, sir.

Maj. M. I beg your pardon, madam; I beg your pardon.

Mrs. G. No offence, sir; mistakes will be made. Ah! here comes the colonel.

Enter DR. GAINES, M.D.

Dr. Gaines. Bless my soul, how are you, Major? I'm exceedingly pleased to see you. Be seated, be seated, Major.

Mrs. G. Please excuse me, gentlemen; I must go and look after dinner, for I've no doubt that the Major will have an appetite for dinner, by the time it is ready.

[*Exit* MRS. GAINES, R.

Maj. M. Colonel, I'm afraid I've played the devil here to-day.

Dr. G. Why, what have you done?

Maj. M. You see, Colonel, I always make it a point, wherever I go, to praise the children, if there are any, and so to-day, seeing one of your little children come in, and taking him to be your son, I spoke to your wife of the marked resemblance between you and the boy. I'm afraid I've insulted madam.

Dr. G. Oh! do n't let it trouble you. Ha, ha, ha. If you did call him my son, you did n't miss much. Ha, ha, ha. Come, we'll take a walk, and talk over matters about old times.

[*Exit*, L.

Scene 4.—FOREST SCENERY.

Enter GLEN, L.

Glen. Oh, how I want to see Melinda! My heart pants and my soul is moved whenever I hear her voice. Human tongue cannot tell how my heart yearns toward her. God! Thou who gavest me life, and implanted in my bosom the love of liberty, and gave me a heart to love, Oh, pity the poor out-raged slave! Thou, who canst rend the veil of centuries, speak, Oh, speak, and put a stop to this persecution! What is death, compared to slavery? Oh, heavy curse, to have thoughts, reason, taste, judgment, conscience and pas-sions like another man, and not have equal liberty to use them! Why was I born with a wish to be free, and still be a slave? Why should I call another man master? And my poor Melinda, she is taken away from me, and I dare not ask the tyrant where she is. It is childish to stand here weeping. Why should my eyes be filled with tears, when my brain is on fire? I will find my wife—I will; and wo to him who shall try to keep me from her!

Scene 5.—ROOM IN A SMALL COTTAGE
ON THE POPLAR FARM,
(Ten miles from Muddy Creek, and owned by Dr. Gaines)

Enter MELINDA, R.

Melinda. Here I am, watched, and kept a prisoner in this place. Oh, I would that I could escape, and once more get with Glen. Poor Glen! He does not know where I am. Master took the opportunity, when Glen was in the city with his master, to bring me here to this lonely place, and fearing that mistress would know where I was, he brought me here at night. Oh, how I wish I could rush into the arms of sleep!—that sweet sleep, which visits all alike, descending, like the dews of heaven upon the bond as well as the free. It would drive from my troubled brain the agonies of this terrible night.

Enter DR. GAINES, L.

Dr. Gaines. Good evening, Melinda! Are you not glad to see me?

Melinda. Sir, how can I be glad to see the one who has made life a burden, and turned my sweetest moments into bitterness?

Dr. G. Come, Melinda, no more reproaches! You know that I love you, and I have told you, and I tell you again, that if you will give up all idea of having Glen for a husband, I will set you free, let you live in this cottage, and be your own mistress, and I'll dress you like a lady. Come, now, be reasonable.

Melinda. Sir, I am your slave; you can do as you please with the avails of my labor, but you shall never tempt me to swerve from the path of virtue.

Dr. G. Now, Melinda, that black scoundrel Glen has been putting these notions into your head. I'll let you know that you are my property and I'll do as I please with you. I'll teach you that there is no limit to my power.

Melinda. Sir, let me warn you that if you compass my ruin, a woman's bitterest curse will be laid upon your head, with all the crushing, withering weight that my soul can impart to it; a curse that shall cling to you throughout the remainder of your wretched life; a curse that shall haunt you like a spectre in your dreams by night, and attend upon you by day; a curse, too, that shall embody itself in the ghastly form of a woman whose chastity you will have outraged. Command me to bury myself in yonder stream, and I will obey you. Bid me to do anything else, but I beseech you not to commit a double crime,—outrage a woman, and make her false to her husband.

Dr. G. You got a husband! Who is your husband, and when were you married?

Melinda. Glen is my husband, and I've been married four weeks. Old Uncle Joseph married us one night by moonlight. I see you are angry; I pray you not to injure my husband.

Dr. G. Melinda, you shall never see Glen again. I have bought him from Hamilton, and I will return to Muddy Creek, and roast him at the stake. A black villain, to get into my way in that manner! Here I've come ten miles tonight to see you, and this is the way you receive me!

Melinda. Oh, master, I beg you not to injure my husband! Kill me, but spare him! Do! do! he is my husband!

Dr. G. You shall never see that black imp again, so good night, my lady! When I come again, you'll give me a more cordial reception. Good night!

[*Exit* DR. GAINES, L.

Melinda. I shall go distracted. I cannot remain here and know that Glen is being tortured on my account. I must escape from this place,—I must,—I must.

Enter CATO, R.

Cato. No, you ain't a-gwine to 'scape, nudder. Massa tells me to keep dese eyes on you, an' I is gwine to do it.

Melinda. Oh, Cato, do let me get away! I beg you, do!

Cato. No; I tells you massa told me to keep you safe; an' ef I let you go, massa will whip me.

[*Exit* CATO, L.

Enter MRS. GAINES, R.

Mrs. Gaines. Ah, you trollop! here you are! Your master had told me that he had sold you and sent you down the river, but I knew better; I knew it was a lie. And when he left home this evening, he said he was going to the city on business, and I knew that was a lie too, and determined to follow him, and see what he was up to. I rode all the way over here to-night. My side-saddle was lent out, and I had to ride ten miles bare-back, and I can scarcely walk; and your master has just left here. Now deny that, if you dare.

Melinda. Madam, I will deny nothing which is true. Your husband has just gone from here, but God knows I am innocent of any thing wrong with him.

Mrs. G. It's a lie! I know better. If you are innocent, what are you doing here, cooped up in this cottage by yourself? Tell me that!

Melinda. God knows that I was brought here against my will, and I will beg that you will take me away.

Mrs. G. Yes, Melinda, I will see that you are taken away, but it shall be after a fashion that you won't like. I know that your master loves you, and I intend to put a stop to it. Here, drink the contents of this vial,—drink it!

Melinda. Oh, you will not take my life,—you will not!

Mrs. G. Drink the poison this moment!

Melinda. I cannot drink it.

Mrs. G. I tell you to drink this poison at once. Drink it, or I will thrust this knife to your heart! The poison at once. Drink it, or I will thrust this knife to your heart! The poison or the dagger, this instant! [*She draws a dagger; Melinda retreats, to the back of the room, and seizes a broom.*

Melinda. I will not drink this poison! [*They fight;* MELINDA *sweeps off* MRS. GAINES,—*cap, combs and curls.*

Curtain falls.

ACT IV.

Scene 1.—INTERIOR OF A DUNGEON—GLEN IN CHAINS.

Glen. When I think of my unmerited sufferings, it almost drives me mad. I struck the doctor, and for that, I must remain here loaded with chains. But why did he strike me? He takes my wife from me, sends her off, and then comes back and beats me over the head with his cane. I did right to strike him back. I would have killed him. Oh! there is a volcano pent up in the hearts of the slaves of these Southern States that will burst forth ere long. When that day comes, wo to those whom its unpitying fury may devour! I would be willing to die, if I could smite down with these chains every man who attempts to enslave his fellow-man.

Enter SAMPEY, R.

Sampey. Glen, I jess bin hear the massa call de oberseer, and I spec somebody is gwine to be whipped. Anudder thing: I know where massa took Linda to. He took her to de poplar farm, an' he went away las' night, an' missis she follow after massa, an' she ain't come back yet. I tell you, Glen, de debil will be to pay on dis place, but don't tell any body dat I tole you.

[*Exit* SAMPEY, R.

Scene 2.—Parlor.

DR. GAINES, *alone.*

Dr. Gaines. Yes, I will have the black rascal well whipped, and then I'll sell him. It was most fortunate for me that Hamilton was willing to sell him to me.

Enter MR. SCRAGG, L.

I have sent for you, Mr. Scragg. I want you to take Glen out of the dungeon, take him into the tobacco house, fasten him down upon the stretcher, and give him five hundred lashes upon his bare back; and when you have whipped him, feel his pulse, and report to me how it stands, an if he can bear any more, I'll have you give him an additional hundred or two as the case may be.

Scragg. I tell you, doctor, that suits me to a charm. I've long wanted to whip that nigger. When your brother-in-law came here to board, and brought that boy with him, I felt bad to see a nigger dressed up in such fine clothes, and I wanted to whip him right off. I tell you, doctor, I had rather whip that nigger than go to heaven, any day,—that I had!

Dr. G. Go, Mr. Scragg, and do your duty. Don't spare the whip!

Scragg. I will, sir; I'll do it in order.

[*Exit* SCRAGG, L.

Dr. G. Every thing works well now, and when I get Glen out of the way, I'll pay Melinda another visit, and she'll give me a different reception. But I wonder where my wife is? She left word that she was going to see her brother, but I am afraid that she has got on my track. That woman is the pest of my life. If there's any place in heaven for her, I'd be glad if the Lord would take her home, for I've had her too long already. But what noise is that? What can it be? What is the matter?

Enter SCRAGG, L., *with face bloody.*

Scragg. Oh, dear me! oh, my head! That nigger broke away from me, and struck me over the head with a stick. Oh, dear me! Oh!

Dr. G. Where is he, Mr. Scragg?

Scragg. Oh! sir, he jumped out of the window; he's gone. Oh! my head; he's cracked my skull. Oh, dear me, I'm kilt! Oh! oh! oh!

Enter SLAVES, R.

Dr. G. Go, Dolly, and wash Mr. Scragg's head with some whiskey, and bind it up. Go at once. And Bob, you run over to Mr. Hall, and tell him to come with his hounds; we must go after the rascal.

[*Exit all except the* DOCTOR, R.

This will never do. When I catch the scoundrel, I'll make an example of him; I'll whip him to death. Ah! here comes my wife. I wonder what she comes for now? I must put on a sober face, for she looks angry.

Enter MRS. GAINES, L.

Ah! my dear, I am glad you've come, I've been so lonesome without you. Oh! Sarah, I do n't know what I should do if the Lord should take you home to heaven. I do n't think that I should be able to live without you.

Mrs. G. Dr. Gaines, you ought to be ashamed to sit there and talk in that way. You know very well that if the Lord should call me home to glory to-night, you'd jump for joy. But you need not think that I am going to leave this world before you. No; with the help of the Lord, I'll stay here to foil you in your meanness. I've been on your track, and a dirty track it is, too. You ought to be ashamed of yourself. See what promises you made me before we

293

were married; and this is the way you keep your word. When I married you, every body said that it was a pity that a woman of my sweet temper should be linked to such a man as you. [*She weeps and wrings her hands.*

Dr. G. Come, my dear, do n't make a fool of yourself. Come, let's go to supper, an a strong cup of tea will help your head.

Mrs. G. Tea help my head! tea won't help my head! You're a brute of a man; I always knew I was a fool marrying you. There was Mr. Comstock, he wanted me, he loved me, and he said I was an angel, so he did; and he loved me, and he was rich; and mother always said that he loved me more than you, for when he used to kiss me, he always squeezed my hand. You never did such a thing in your life. [*She weeps and wrings her hands.*

Dr. G. Come, my dear, do n't act so foolish.

Mrs. G. Yes; every thing I do is foolish. You're a brute of a man; I won't live with you any longer. I'll leave you—that I will. I'll go and see a lawyer, and get a divorce from you—so I will.

Dr. G. Well, Sarah, if you want a divorce, you had better engage Mr. Barker. He's the best lawyer in town; and if you want some money to facilitate the business, I'll draw a check for you.

Mrs. G. So you want me to get a divorce, do you? Well, I won't have a divorce; no, I'll never leave you, as long as the Lord spares me.

[*Exit* MRS. GAINES, R.

Scene 3.—FOREST AT NIGHT—LARGE TREE.

Enter MELINDA, L.

Melinda. This is indeed a dark night to be out and alone on this road. But I must find my husband, I must. Poor Glen! if he only knew that I was here, and could get to me, he would. What a curse slavery is! It separates husbands from their wives, and tears mothers from their helpless offspring, and blights all our hopes for this world. I must try to reach Muddy Creek before daylight, and seek out my husband. What's that I hear?—footsteps? I'll get behind this tree.

Glen. It is so dark, I'm afraid I've missed the road. Still, this must be the right way to the poplar farm. I will soon be with her; and if I once get her in my arms, it will be a strong man that shall take her from me. Aye, a dozen strong men shall not be able to wrest her from my arms. [*Melinda rushes from behind the tree.*

Melinda. Oh, Glen! It is my husband;—it is!

Glen. Melinda! Melinda! it is, it is. Oh God! I thank Thee for this manifestation of Thy kindness. Come, come, Melinda, we must go at once to

Canada. I escaped from the overseer, whom Dr. Gaines sent to flog me. Yes, I struck him over the head with his own club, and I made the wine flow freely; yes, I pounded his old skillet well for him, and then jumped out of the window. It was a leap for freedom. Yes, Melinda, it was a leap for freedom. I've said "master" for the last time. I am free; I'm bound for Canada. Come, let's be off, at once, for the negro dogs will be put out upon our track. Let us once get beyond the Ohio river, and all will be right.

[*Exit* R.

ACT V.

Scene 1.—BAR-ROOM IN THE AMERICAN HOTEL— TRAVELERS LOUNGING IN CHAIRS, AND AT THE BAR.

Enter BILL JENNINGS, R.

Barkeeper. Why, Jennings, how do you do?

Jennings. Say Mr. Jennings, if you please.

Barkeeper. Well, Mr. Jennings, if that suits you better. How are times? We've been expecting you, for some days.

Jennings. Well, before I talk about the times, I want my horses put up, and want you to tell me where my niggers are to stay to-night. Sheds, stables, barns, and every thing else here, seems pretty full, if I am a judge.

Barkeeper. Oh! I'll see to your plunder.

1st Lounger. I say, Barkeeper, make me a brandy cocktail, strong. Why, how o you do, Mr. Jennings?

Jennings. Pretty well, Mr. Peters. Cold evening, this.

1st Loun. Yes, this is cold. I heard you speak of your niggers. Have you got a pretty large gang?

Jennings. No, only thirty-three. But they are the best that the country can afford. I shall clear a few dimes, this trip. I hear that the price is up.

Enter MR. WHITE, R.

White. Can I be accommodated here to-night, landlord?

Barkeeper. Yes, sir; we've bed for man and beast. Go, Dick, and take the gentleman's coat and hat. [*To the waiter.*] You're a stranger in these parts I rec'on.

White. Yes, I am a stranger here.

2d Loun. Where mout you come from, ef it's a far question?

White. I am from Massachusetts.

3rd Loun. I say, cuss Massachusetts!

White. I say, landlord, if this is the language that I am to hear, I would like to go into a private room.

Barkeeper. We ain't got no private room empty.

1st Loun. Maybe you're mad 'bout what I said 'bout your State. Ef you is, I've only to say that this is a free country, and people talks what they please; an' ef you do n't like it, you can better yourself.

White. Sir, if this is a free country, why do you have slaves here? I saw a gang at the door, as I came in.

2d Loun. He did n't mean that this was a free country for niggers. He meant that it's free for white people. And another thing, ef you get to taking 'bout freedom for niggers, you'll catch what you won't like, mister. It's right for niggers to be slaves.

White. But I saw some white slaves.

1st Loun. Well, they're white niggers.

White. Well, sir, I am from a free State, and I thank God for it; for the worst act that a man can commit upon his fellow-man, is to make him a slave. Conceive of a mind, a living soul, with the germs of faculties which infinity cannot exhaust, as it first beams upon you in its glad morning of existence, quivering with life and joy, exulting in the glorious sense of its developing energies, beautiful, and brave, and generous, and joyous, and free,—the clear spirit bathed in the auroral lights of its unconscious immortality,—and then follow it in its dark and dreary passage through slavery, until oppression stifles and kills, one by one, every inspiration and aspiration of its being, until it becomes a dead soul entombed in a living frame!

3d Loun. Stop that; stop that, I say. That's treason to the country; that's downright rebellion.

Barkeeper. Yes, it is. And another thing,—this is not a meeting-house.

1st Loun. Yes, if you talk such stuff as that, you'll get a chunk of cold lead in you, that you will.

Enter DR. GAINES *and* SCRAGG, *followed by* CATO, R..

Dr. G. Gentlemen, I am in pursuit of two valuable slaves, and I will pay five hundred dollars for their arrest.

[*Exit* MR. WHITE, L.

1st Loun. I'll bet a picayune that your niggers have been stolen by that cussed feller from Massachusetts. Don't you see he's gone?

Dr. G. Where is the man? If I can lay my hands on him, he'll never steal another nigger. Where is the scoundrel?

1st Loun. Let's go after the feller. I'll go with you. Come, foller me.

[*Exit all*, L., *except* CATO *and the waiter.*

Cato. Why don't you bring in massa's saddle-bags? What de debil you standin' dar for? You common country niggers don't know nuffin', no how. Go an' get massa's nsaddle-bags, and bring 'em in.

[*Exit* SERVANT, R.

By golly! ebry body's gone, an' de bar-keeper too. I'll tend de bar myself now; an' de fuss gemman I waits on will be dis gemman of color. [*Goes behind the counter, and drinks.*] Ah, dis is de stuff for me; it makes my head swim; it makes me happy right off. I'll take a little more.

Enter BARKEEPER, L.

Barkeeper. What are you doing behind that bar, you black cuss?
Cato. I is lookin' for massa's saddle-bags, sir. is dey here?
Barkeeper. But what were you drinking there?
Cato. Me drinkin'! Why, massa, you muss be mistaken. I ain't drink nuffin'.
Barkeeper. You infernal whelp, to stand there and lie in that way!
Cato. Oh, yes, seer, I did tase dat coffee in dat bottle; dat's all I did.

Enter MR. WHITE, L., *excited.*

Mr. White. I say, sir, is there no place of concealment in your house? They are after me, and my life is in danger. Say sir, can't you hide me away?
Barkeeper. Well, you ought to hold your tongue when you come into our State.
Mr. White. But, sir, the Constitution gives me the right to speak my sentiments, at all times and in all places.
Barkeeper. We don't care for Constitution nor nothin' else. We made the Constitution, and we'll break it. But you had better hide away; they are coming, and they'll lynch you, that they will. Come with me; I'll hide you in the cellar. Foller me.

[*Exit* BARKEEPER *and* WHITE, L.

Enter the MOB, R.

Dr. Gaines. If I can once lay my hands on that scoundrel, I'll blow a hole through his head.
Jennings. Yes, I say so too; for no one knows whose niggers are safe now-a-days. I must look after my niggers. Who is that I see in the distance? I believe it's that cussed Massachusetts feller. Come, let's go after him.

[*Exit the* MOB, R.

Scene 2.—FOREST AT NIGHT.

Enter GLEN *and* MELINDA, R.

Melinda. I am so tired and hungry, that I cannot go further. It is so cloudy that we cannot see the North Star, and therefore cannot tell whether we're going to Canada, or further South. Let's sit down here.

Glen. I know we cannot see the North Star, Melinda, and I fear we've lost our way. But, see! the clouds are passing away, and it'll soon be clear. See! yonder is a star; yonder is another and another. Ah! yonder is the North Star, and we are safe!

"Star of the North! though night winds drift
        The fleecy drapery of the sky
Between thy lamp and me, I lift,
        Yea, lift with hope my sleepless eye,
To the blue heights wherin thou dwellest,
And of a land of freedom tellest.

"Star of the North! while blazing day
        Pours round me its full tide of light,
And hides thy pale but faithful ray,
        I, too, lie hid, and long for night:
For night: I dare not walk at noon,
Nor dare I trust the faithless moon—

"Nor faithless man, whose burning lust
        For gold hath riveted my chain,—
Nor other leader can I trust
        But thee, of even the starry train;
For all the host around thee burning,
Like faithless man, keep turning, turning.

"I may not follow where thee go:—
        Star of the North! I look to thee
While on I press; for well I know,
        Thy light and truth shall set me free:—

Thy light, that no poor slave deceiveth;
Thy truth, that all my soul believeth.

"Thy beam is on the glassy breast
    Of the still spring, upon whose brink
I lay me weary limbs to rest,
    And bow my parching lips to drink.
Guide of the friendless negro's way,
I bless thee for this quiet ray!

"In the dark top of the southern pines
    I nestled, when the Driver's horn
Called to the field, in lengthening lines,
    My fellows, at the break of morn.
And there I lay till thy sweet face
Looked in upon "my hiding place."

The tangled cane-break, where I crept
    For shelter from the heat of noon,
And where, while others toiled, I slept,
    Till wakening by the rising moon,
As its stalks felt the night wind free,
Gave me to catch a glimpse of thee.

"Star of the North! in bright array
    The constellations round thee sweep,
Each holding on its nightly way,
    Rising, or sinking in the deep,
And, as it hangs in mid heaven flaming,
The homage of some nation claiming.

"*This* nation to the eagle cowers;
    Fit ensign! she's a bird of spoil:—
Like worships like! for each devours
    The earnings of another's toil.

I've felt her talons and her beak,
And now the gentler Lion seek.

"The Lion, at the Monarch's feet
    Crouches, an lays his mighty paw
Into her lap!—an emblem meet
    Of England's Queen, and English law:
Queen, that hath made her islands free!
Law, that holds out its shield to me!

Star of the North! upon that shield
    Thou shinest,—Oh, for ever shine!
The negro, from the cotton field
    Shall, then, beneath its orb recline,
And feed the Lion, couched before it,
Nor heed the Eagle, screaming o'er it!"

With the thoughts of servitude behind us, and the North Star before us, we will go forward with cheerful hearts. Come, Melinda, let's go on.

                                              [Exit, L.

Scene 3.—A STREET.

Enter MR. WHITE, R.

Mr. White. I am glad to be once more in a free State. If I am caught once again south of Mason and Dixon's line, I'll give them leave to lynch me. I came near losing my life. This is the way out constitutional rights are trampled upon. But what care these men about Constitutions, or any thing else that does not suit them? But I must hasten on.

                                              [Exit, L.

Enter CATO, *in disguise,* R.

Cato. I wonder ef dis is me? By golly, I is free as a frog. But maybe I is mistaken; maybe dis ain't me. Cato, is that you? Yes, seer. Well, now it is me, an' I em a free man. But, stop! I muss change my name, kase ole massa might foller me, and somebody might tell him dat dey seed Cato; so I'll change my name, and den he won't know me ef he sees me. Now, what shall I call myself? I'm

300

now in a suspectable part of de country, an' I muss have a suspectable name. Ah! I'll call myself Alexander Washington Napoleon Pompey Cæsar. Dar, now, dat's a good long, suspectable name, and every body will suspect me. Let me see; I wonder ef I can't make up a song on my escape? I'll try.

AIR—"*Dearest Mae.*"

Now, freemen, listen to my song, a story I'll relate,
It happened in de valley of de ole Kentucky State:
Dey marched me out into de fiel', at every break of day,
And work me dar till late sunset, widout a cent of pay.

  Chorus.—Dey work me all de day,
    Widout a bit of pay,
    And thought, because dey fed me well,
    I would not run away.

Massa gave me his ole coat, an' thought I'd happy be,
But I had my eye on de North Star, an' thought of liberty;
Ole massa lock de door, an' den he went to sleep,
I dress myself in his bess clothes, an' jump into de street.

  Chorus.—Dey work me all de day,
    Widout a bit of pay,
    So I took my flight, in the middle of de night,
    When de sun was gone away.

Sed I, dis chile's a freeman now, he'll be a slave no more;
I travell'd faster all dat night, dan I ever did before.
I came up to a farmer's house, jest at de break of day,
And saw a white man standin' dar, sed he, "You are a runaway."

  Chorus.—Dey work me all day, &c.

I tole him I had left de whip, an' bayin' of de hound,
To a place where man is man, ef sich dar can be found;
Dat I had heard, in Canada, dat all mankind is free,
An' dat I was going dar in search of liberty.

Chorus.—Dey work me all day, &c.

I've not committed any crime, why should I run away?
Oh! shame upon your laws, dat drive me off to Canada.
You loudly boast of liberty, an' say your State is free,
But ef I tarry in your midst, will you protect me?

Chorus.—Dey work me all de day, &c.

[*Exit*, L.

Scene 4.—DINING-ROOM.—TABLE SPREAD.
MRS. NEAL *and* CHARLOTTE.

Mrs. Neal. Thee may put the tea to draw, Charlotte. Thy father will be in soon, and we must have breakfast.

Enter MR. NEAL, L.

I think, Simeon, it is time that those people were called. Thee knows that they may be pursued, and we ought not to detain them long here.

Mrs. Neal. Yes, Ruth, thou art right. Go, Charlotte, and knock on their chamber door, and tell them that breakfast is ready.

[*Exit* CHARLOTTE, R.

Mrs. N. Poor creatures! I hope they'll reach Canada in safety. They seem to be worthy persons.

Enter CHARLOTTE, R.

Charlotte. I've called them, mother, and they'll be soon down. I"ll put the breakfast on the table.

Enter NEIGHBOR JONES, L.

Mr. N. Good morning, James. Thee has heard, I presume, that we have two very interesting persons in the house?

Jones. Yes, I heard that you had two fugitives by the Underground road, last night; and I've come over to fight for them, if any persons come to take them back.

Enter THOMAS, R.

Mr. N. Go, Thomas, and harness up the horses and put them to the covered wagon, and be ready to take these people on, as soon as they get their breakfast. Go, Thomas, and hurry thyself.

[*Exit* THOMAS, R.

And so thee wants to fight, this morning, James?

Jones. Yes; as you belongs to a society that don't believe in fighting, and I does believe in that sort of thing, I thought I'd come by and relieve you of that work, if there is any to be done.

Enter GLEN *and* MELINDA, R.

Mr. N. Good morning, friends. I hope thee rested well, last night.

Mrs. N. Yes, I hope thee had a good night's rest.

Glen. I thank you, madam, we did.

Mr. N. I'll introduce thee to our neighbor, James Jones. He's a staunch friend of thy people.

Jones. I am glad to see you. I've come over to render assistance, if any is needed.

Mrs. N. Come, friends, take seats at the table. Thee'll take seats there. [*To* GLEN *and* MELINDA.] [*All take seats at the table.*] Does thee take sugar and milk in thy tea?

Melinda. I thank you, we do.

Jones. I'll look at your *Tribune,* Uncle Simeon, while you're eating.

Mr. N. Thee'll find it on the table.

Mrs. N. I presume thee's anxious to get to thy journey's end?

Glen. Yes, madam, we are. I am told that we are not safe in any of the free States.

Mr. N. I am sorry to tell them that that is too true. Thee will not be safe until thee gets on British soil. I wonder what keeps Thomas; he should have been here with the team.

Enter THOMAS, L.

Thomas. All's ready; and I've written the prettiest song that was ever sung. I call it "The Underground Railroad."

Mr. N. Thomas, thee can eat thy breakfast far better than thee can write a song, as thee calls it. Thee must hurry thyself, when I send thee for the horses, Thomas. Here lately, thee takes thy time.

Thomas. Well, you see I've been writing poetry; that's the reason I've been so long. If you wish it, I'll sing it to you.

Jones. Do let us hear the song.

Mrs. Neal. Yes, if Thomas has written a ditty, do let us hear it.

Mr. Neal. Well, Thomas, if thee has a ditty, thee may recite it to us.

Thomas. Well, I'll give it to you. Remember that I call it "The Underground Railroad."

AIT—"*Waiting for the Wagon.*"

Oh, where is the invention
    Of this growing age,
Claiming the attention
    Of statesman, priest, or sage,
In the many railways
    Through the nation found,
Equal to the Yankees'
    Railway under-ground?

    Chorus.—No one hears the whistle,
        Or rolling of the cars,
        While negroes ride to freedom
        Beyond the stripes and stars.

On the Southern borders
    Are the Railway stations,
Negroes get free orders
    While on the plantations;
For all, of ev'ry color,
    First-class cars are found,
While they ride to freedom
    By Railway under-ground.

    Chorus.—No one hears the whistle, &c.

Masters in the morning
    Furiously rage,
Cursing the inventions
    Of this knowing age;
Order out the bloodhounds,
    Swear they'll bring them back,
Dogs return exhausted,
    Cannot find the track.

Chorus.—No one hears the whistle, &c.

Travel is increasing,
> Build a double track,

Cars and engines wanted,
> They'll come, we hve no lack.

Clear the track of loafers,
> See that crowded car!

Thousands passing yearly,
> Stock is more than par.

Chorus.—No one hears the whistle, &c.

Jones. Well done! That's a good song. I'd like to have a copy of them verses. [*Knock at the door. Charlotte goes to the door, and returns.*

Enter CATO, L., *still in disguise.*

Mr. Neal. Who is this we have? Another of the outcasts, I presume?

Cato. Yes, seer; I is gwine to Canada, an' I met a man, an' he tole me dat you would give me some wittals an' help me on de way. By golly! ef dar ain't Glen an' Melinda. Dey do n't know me in dese fine clothes. [*Goes up to them.*] Ah, chillen! I is one wid you. I golly, I is here too! [*They shake hands.*]

Glen. Why, it is Cato, as I live!

Melinda. Oh, Cato, I am so glad to see you! But how did you get here?

Cato. Ah, chile, I came wid ole massa to hunt you; an' you see I get tired huntin' you, an' I am now huntin' for Canada. I left de ole boss in de bed at de hotel; an' you see I thought, afore I left massa, I'd jess change clothes with him; so you see, I is fixed up,—ha, ha, ha. Ah, chillen! I is gwine wid you.

Mrs. Neal. Come, sit thee down, and have some breakfast.

Cato. Tank you, madam, I'll do dat. [*Sits down and eats.*

Mr. Neal. This is pleasant for thee to meet one of thy friends.

Glen. Yes, sir, it is; I would be glad if we could meet more of them. I have a mother and sister still in slavery, and I would give worlds, if I possessed them, if by doing so I could release them from their bondage.

Thomas. We are all ready, sir, an the wagon is waiting.

Mrs. Neal. Yes, thee had better start.

Cato. Ef any body tries to take me back to ole massa, I'll pull ebry toof out of dar heads, dat I will! As soon as I get to Canada, I'll set up a doctor shop, an won't I be poplar? Den I rec'on I will. I'll pull teef fer all de people in

Canada. Oh, how I wish I had Hannah wid me! It makes me feel bad when I tink I ain't a-gwine to see my wife no more. But, come, chillen, let's be makin' tracks. Dey say we is most to de British side.

Mr. Neal. Yes, a few miles further, and you'll be safe beyond the reach of the Fugitive-Slave Law.

Cato. Ah, dat's de talk fer dis chile.

[*Exit*, M.D.

Scene 5.—THE NIAGARA RIVER—A FERRY.

FERRYMAN, *fastening his small boat.*

Ferryman, [*advancing, takes out his watch.*] I swan, if it ain't one o'clock. I thought it was dinner time. Now there's no one here, I'll go to dinner, and if any body comes, they can wait until I return. I'll go at once.

[*Exit*, L.

Enter MR. WHITE, R., *with an umbrella.*

Mr. White. I wonder where that ferryman is? I want to cross to Canada. It seems a little showery, or else the mist from the Falls is growing thicker. [*Takes out his sketch-book and pencils,—sketches.*

Enter CANE PEDLAR, R.

Pedlar. Want a good cane to-day, sir? Here's one from Goat island,— very good, sir,—straight and neat,—only one dollar. I've a wife and nine small children,—youngest is nursing, and the oldest only three years old. Here's a cane from Table Rock, sir. Please buy one! I've had no breakfast to-day: My wife's got the rheumatics, and the children's got the measles. Come, sir, do buy a cane! I've a lame shoulder, and can't work.

Mr. White. Will you stop your confounded talk, and let me alone? Don't you see that I am sketching? You've spoiled a beautiful scene for me, with your nonsense.

Enter 2d PEDLAR, R.

2d Pedlar. Want any bead bags, or money purses? These are real Ingen bags, made by the Black Hawk Ingens. Here's a pretty bag, sir, only 75 cents. Here's a money purse, 50 cents. Please, sir, buy something! My wife's got the fever and ague, and the house is full of children, and they're all sick. Come, sir, do help a worthy man!

Mr. White. Will you hold your tongue? You've spoiled some of the finest pictures in the world. Don't you see that I'm sketching?

[*Exit* PEDLARS, R., *grumbling.*

I am glad those fellows have gone; now I'll go a little further up the shore, and see if I can find another boat. I want to get over.

[*Exit*, L.

Enter DR. GAINES, SCRAGG, *and an* OFFICER.

Officer. I do n't think that your slaves have crossed yet, and my officers will watch the shore below here, while we stroll up the river. If once I get my hands on them, all the Abolitionists in the State shall not take them from me.

Dr. G. I hope they have not gone over, for I would not lose them for two hundred dollars, especially the gal.

Enter 1st PEDLAR.

Pedlar. Wish to get a good cane, sir? This stick was cut on the very spot where Sam Patch jumped over the falls. Only fifty cents. I have a sick wife and thirteen children. Please buy a cane; I ain't had no dinner.

Officer. Get out of the way! Gentlemen, we'll go up the shore.

[*Exit*, L.

Enter CATO, R.

Cato. I is loss fum de cumpny, but dis is de ferry, and I spec dey'll soon come. But did n't we have a good time las' night in Buffalo? Dem dar Buffalo gals make my heart flutter, dat dey did. But, tanks be to de Lord, I is got religion. I git it las' night in de meetin'. Before I got religion, I was a great sinner; I got drunk, an' took de name of de Lord in vain. But now I is a conwerted man; I is bound for hebben; I toats de witness in my bosom; I feel dat my name is rote in the book of life. But dem niggers in de Vince Street Church las' night shout an' make sich a fuss, dey gave me de headache. But, tank de lord, I is got religion, an' now I'll be a preacher, and den dey'll call me Rev. Alexander Washington Napoleon Pompey Cæsar. Now I'll preach and pull teef, bofe at de same time. Oh, how I wish I had Hannah wid me! Cuss ole massa, fer ef it warn't for him, I could have my wife wid me. Ef I had n't religion, I'd say "Damn ole massa!" but as I is a religious man, an' belongs to de church, I won't say no such thing. But who is dat I see comin'? Oh, it's a whole heap of people. Good Lord! what is de matter?

Enter GLEN *and* MELINDA, L., *followed by* OFFICERS.

Glen. Let them come; I am ready for the,. He that lays hands on me or my wife shall feel the weight of this club.

Melinda. Oh, Glen, let's die right here, rather than again go into slavery.

Officer. I am the United States Marshal. I have a warrant from the Commissioner to take you, and bring you before him. I command assistance.

Enter DR. GAINES, SCRAGG, *and* OFFICER, R.

Dr. Gaines. Here they are. Down with the villain! Down with him! But do n't hurt the gal!

Enter MR. WHITE, R.

Mr. White. Why, bless me! These are the slaveholding fellows. I'll fight for freedom! [*Takes hold of his umbrella with both hands.—The fight commence, in which* GLEN, CATO, DR. GAINES, SCRAGG, WHITE, *and the* OFFICERS, *take part.—*FERRYMAN *enters, and runs to his boat.—* DR. GAINES, SCRAGG, *and the* OFFICERS *are knocked down,* GLEN, MELINDA *and* CATO *jump into the boat, and as it leaves the shore and floats away,* GLEN *and* CATO *wave their hats, and shout loudly for freedom.—Curtain falls.*

THE END.

Writing Race and Gender

Just as he republished his Narrative *and his travel letters, William Wells Brown published and republished his notes on the role of black people in American history. In his first chronicle of black contributions,* The Black Man: His Antecedents, His Genius, and His Achievements, *Brown prefaced his "vindicat[ion of] the Negro character" with his personal narrative; this version emphasizes his treatment as a privileged house servant but also notes the floggings he received, usually unfairly. In addition to this version of his personal narrative, Brown displays his education and erudition by quoting well-known authors and historical figures liberally and casually. His later version,* The Rising Son; or, The Antecedents and Advancement of the Colored Race, *includes identical entries on many black authors and figures with a few additions. Excerpted in this collection are Brown's entire preface, followed by short entries on Phillis Wheatley, Frances Ellen Watkins, Frederick Douglass, and Charlotte Forten.*

Also included is a brief excerpt from The Negro in the American Rebellion: His Heroism and his Fidelity. *Boston: Lee & Shepard, 1867.* [The Negro in the American Rebellion, *Johnson Reprint Corporation, 1968, pp. 1–8.*] *Brown's prose is erudite but not particularly engaging in these historical works, which have not remained in the public imagination.*[1] *Yet they deserve to be read by Brown scholars if only to compare with the more appealing personal style of his speeches and travel writings.*

From *The Black Man: His Antecedents, His Genius, and His Achievements*

(New York: Thomas Hamilton; Boston, R. F. Wallcut, 1863)

EX PEDE HERCULEM

TO
The Advocates and Friends
OF
NEGRO FREEDOM AND EQUALITY,
WHEREVER FOUND,
This Volume is Respectfully Dedicated,
BY THE AUTHOR.

PREFACE.

The calumniators and traducers of the Negro are to be found, mainly, among two classes. The first and most relentless are those who have done them the greatest injury, by being instrumental in their enslavement and consequent degradation. They delight to descant upon the "natural inferiority" of the blacks, and claim that we were destined only for a servile condition, entitled neither to liberty nor the legitimate pursuit of happiness. The second class are those who are ignorant of the characteristics of the race, and are the mere echoes of the first. To meet and refute these misrepresentations, and to supply a deficiency, long felt in the community, of a work containing sketches of individuals who, by their own genius, capacity, and intellectual development, have surmounted the many obstacles which slavery and prejudice have thrown in their way, and raised themselves to positions of honor and influence, this volume was written. The characters represented in most of these biographies are for the first time put in print. The author's long sojourn in Europe, his opportunity of research amid the archives of England and France, and his visit to the West Indies, have given him the advantage of information respecting the blacks seldom acquired.

If this work shall aid in vindicating the Negro's character, and show that he is endowed with those intellectual and amiable qualities which adorn and dignify human nature, it will meet the most sanguine hopes of the writer.

CAMBRIDGEPORT, MASS., 1863.

MEMOIR OF THE AUTHOR.

I was born at Lexington, Kentucky. My father, as I was informed, was a member of the Wickliffe family; my mother was of mixed blood; her father, it was said, was the noted Daniel Boone, and her mother a negress. My early life on the plantation was such as generally falls to the lot of the young slave, till I arrived at the age of nine years, when my position was changed. My master's brother lost his wife, she leaving an infant son a few months old, whom my mistress took to bring up. When this boy became old enough to need a playmate to watch over him, mistress called the young slaves together, to select one for the purpose. We were all ordered to run, jump, wrestle, turn somersets, walk on our hands, and go through the various gymnastic exercises that the imagination of our brain could invent, or the strength and activity of our limbs could endure. The selection was to be an important one, both to the mistress and the slave. Whoever should gain the place was in the future to become a house servant; the ask-cake thrown aside, that unmentionable garment that buttons around the neck, which we all wore, and nothing else, was to give way to the whole suit of tow linen. Every one of us joined heartily in the contest, while old mistress sat on the piazza, watching our every movement—some fifteen of us, each dressed in his one garment, sometimes standing on our heads with feet in the air—still the lady looked on. With me it seemed a matter of life and death; for, being blood kin to master, I felt that I had more at stake than my companions. At last the choice was made, and I was told to step aside as the "lucky boy," which order I obeyed with an alacrity seldom surpassed. That night I was put to soak, after which I was scraped, scrubbed, washed, and dried. The next day, the new suit came down to the quarters; I slipped into it; the young slaves gathered about me, and I was the star of the plantation. My mother, one of the best of mothers, placed her hands on my head, and, with tears in her eyes, said, "I knowed you was born for good luck, for a fortune-teller told me so when you was a baby layin' in your little sugar trough. Go up to de great house where you belong." With this blessing I bade farewell to the log hut and the dirt floor, and started towards the "big house." Mistress received me, and laid down the law which was to govern my future actions. "I give your young master over to you," said she; "and if you let him hurt himself, I'll pull your ears; if you let him cry, I'll pull your ears; if he wants any thing, and you don't give it to him, I'll pull your ears; when he goes to sleep, if you let him wake before it is time, I'll pull your ears." And right well did she keep her promise, for my ears felt the impress of her tender fingers and gold rings almost every day, and at times nearly every hour.

Yet I would not have you suppose, gentle reader, that my old mistress was of low or common origin; but on the contrary, she boasted that the best blood of the south coursed through her blue veins. My master, Dr. John Young, was a man of considerable standing in his section of the state. A member of the church, his se[a]t was not often empty during religious service. He was very strict as to the observance of the Sabbath, held prayer night and morning, and entertained more travelling preachers than almost any one in his neighborhood.

The doctor did not surpass his wife in devotedness to religious observances. Of these travelling ministers, each had a favorite, who in turn used to spend several days on the plantation, hunting, shooting, fishing, visiting, and at times preaching. The Rev. Mr. Pinchen was my mistress's favorite, and he was indeed an interesting character. Short and stout, somewhat inclined to corpulency, deeply pock-marked, quick in his motions, and with a strong voice, he was one of the funniest of men when telling his long stories about his religious and other experiences in the south.

I had been in the great house nearly three years, when Mr. Pinchen was expected to make his annual visit. The stir about the dwellings, the cleaning of paint, the scalding out of the bedbugs, an[d] the orders and counter-orders from Mrs. Young, showed plainly that something uncommon was to take place. High and angry words had passed between master and mistress, one morning, when the latter weepingly and snuffingly exclaimed, "Never mind; you'll not have me here always to hector and to worry: I'll die one of these days, and then you'll be glad of it. Never mind, keep on, and you'll send me to my grave before the time. Never mind; one of these days the Lord will make up his *jewels, call me home to glory*, and I'll be out of your way, and I'll be devilish glad of it too." Her weeping increased, and she continued, "Never mind, brother Pinchen will be here soon, and then I'll have somebody to talk to me about religion." At this moment, Hannah, the waiting maid, entered the room, and Mrs. Young gave orders with regard to Mr. Pinchen's visit. "Go, Hannah," said she, "and get the chamber ready for brother Pinchen: put on the new linen sheets, and see that they are dry, and well aired; if they are not, I'll air *you*, my lady." The arrival of the clergyman, the next day, was the signal for new and interesting scenes. After the first morning's breakfast was over, family prayer finished, the Bible put away, the brandy replaced in the sideboard, and Dr. Young gone to his office, Mr. Pinchen commenced the delivery of one of those religious experiences for which be was so celebrated wherever he was known. Mrs. Young and the minister were seated at the round table, I standing behind her chair, and Hannah clearing off the breakfast table, when the servant of God began by saying, "Well, sister Young, I've seen a heap since I was here last."

"I am so glad to hear it," responded she, "for I want to bear something good. Now do give me your experience, brother Pinchen; it always draws me nearer and nearer to the Lord's side."

"Well, sister Young, I've had great opportunity in my time to study the human heart. I've attended a great many camp meetings, revival meetings, protracted meetings, and death-bed scenes, and I am satisfied, sister Young, that the heart of man is full of sin and desperately wicked. This is a wicked world, sister, a wicked world."

Mrs. Young asked, "Were you ever in Arkansas, brother Pinchen? I've been told that the people out there are very ungodly."

Mr. Pinchen said, "O, yes, sister Young; I once spent a year at Little Rock, and preached in all the towns round about there; and I found some hard cases out there, I can tell you. I was once spending a week in a district where there were a great many horse thieves, and one night somebody stole my pony. Well, I knowed it was no use to make a fuss; so I told brother Tarbox to say nothing about it, and I'd get my horse by preaching God's everlasting gospel; for I had faith in the truth, and knowed that my Saviour would not let me lose my pony. So the next Sunday I preached on horse-stealing, and told the brethren to come up in the evenin' with their hearts filled with the grace of God. So that night the house was crammed brim full with anxious souls, panting for the bread of life. Brother Bingham opened with prayer, and brother Tarbox followed, and I saw right off that we were gwine to have a blessed time. After I got 'em pretty well warmed up, I jumped on to one of the seats, stretched out my hands, and said: 'I know who stole my pony; I've found out; and you are here tryin' to make people believe that you've got religion; but you ain't got it. And if you don't take my horse back to brother Tarbox's pasture this very night, I'll tell your name right out in meetin' to-mor-row night. Take my pony back, you vile and wretched sinner, and come up here and give your heart to God.' So the next mornin', I went out to brother Tarbox's pasture, and sure enough, there was my bob-tail pony. Yes, sister, there he was, safe and sound. Ha, ha, ha!"

With uplifted hands, old mistress exclaimed, "O, how interesting, and how fortunate for you to get your pony! And what power there is in the gospel! God's children are very lucky. O, it is so sweet to sit here and listen to such good news from God's people!"

Hannah was so entranced with the conversation that she had left her work, and, with eyes and mouth open, was listening to the preacher. Turning aside, and in a low voice, Mrs. Young harshly said, "Hannah, what are you standing there listening for, and neglecting your work? Never mind, my lady, I'll whip you well when I am done here. Go at your work this moment, you lazy hussy. Never mind, I'll whip you well." Then, turning again to the preacher, she said, "Come, do go on, brother Pinchen, with your godly conversation. It is so sweet! It draws me nearer and nearer to the Lord's side."

"Well, sister Young," continued he, "I've had some mighty queer dreams in my time—that I have. You see, one night I dreamed that I was dead and in heaven; and such a place I never saw before. As soon as I entered the gates of the celestial empire, I saw many old and familiar faces that I had seen before. The first person that I saw was good old Elder Pike, the preacher that first called my attention to religion. The next person I saw was Deacon Billings, my first wife's father; and then I saw a host of godly faces. Why, sister Young, you knew Elder Goosbee—didn't you?"

"Yes," replied she; "did you see him there?"

"O yes, sister Young, I saw the elder, and he looked for all the world as if he had just come out of a revival meeting."

"Did you see my first husband there, brother Pinchen?"

"No, sister Young, I didn't see brother Pepper, but I've no doubt but that he was there."

"Well, I don't know," said she; "I have my doubts. He was not the happiest man in the world. He was always borrowing trouble about something or another. Still, I saw some happy moments with Mr. Pepper. I was happy when I made his acquaintance, happy during our courtship, happy a while after our marriage, and happy when he died."

Here she put her handkerchief to her eyes, and wept bitterly for a moment. At this juncture Hannah asked, "Did you see my husband, Ben, up in hebben, Massa Pinchen?"

"No, no, Hannah, I didn't go amongst the blacks," answered he.

"Of course not," said mistress; "brother Pinchen didn't go among the niggers." Turning aside to Hannah, and in a whisper, she exclaimed, "What are you asking questions for? Never mind, my lady, I'll whip you well when I'm done here. I'll skin you from head to foot. Do go on with your heavenly conversation, brother Pinchen; it does my very soul good. This is indeed a precious moment for me. I do love to hear of Christ and him crucified."

After the conversation had ceased, and the preacher gone out to call on Mrs. Daniels, Mrs. Young said to the maid, "Now, Hannah, brother Pinchen is gone; you get the cowhide, and I'll whip you well, for aggravating me as you did to-day. It seems as if I can never sit down to take a little comfort with the Lord, without the devil putting it into your head to cross me. I've no doubt, Hannah, that I'll miss going to heaven on your account; but I'll whip you well before I leave this world—that I will." The servant received a flogging, Mrs. Young felt easier, and I was in the kitchen amusing my fellow-slaves[,] with telling over Mr. Pinchen's last experience. Here let me say, that we regarded the religious profession of the whites around us as a farce, and our master and mistress, together with their guest, as mere hypocrites. During the entire visit of the preacher, the servants had a joyful time over my representations of what was going on in the great house.

The removal of my master's family and slaves to the centre of the State of Missouri about this time, caused some change in our condition. My young master, William, had now grown to be a stout boy of five years of age. No restraint thrown around him by the doctor or his wife, aunt Dolly, his nurse, not permitted to control any of his actions, William had become impudent, petulant, peevish and cruel. Sitting at the tea table, he would often desire to make his entire meal out of the sweetmeats, the sugar-bowl, or the cake; and when mistress would not allow him to have them, he, in a fit of anger, would throw any thing within his reach at me; spoons, knives, forks, and dishes would be hurled at my head, accompanied with language such as would astonish any one not well versed in the injurious effects of slavery upon the rising generation. Thomas Jefferson, in 1788, in a letter to M. Warville, Paris, writing upon slavery, alludes to its influence upon the young as follows:—

"The parent storms, the child looks on, catches the lineaments of wrath, puts on the same airs in the circle of smaller slaves, GIVES LOOSE TO HIS WORST PASSIONS; and, thus *nursed, educated, and daily exercised in tyranny*, cannot but be stamped by it with odious peculiarities."

In the Virginia legislature, in the year 1832, Hon. Lewis Summers said,—

"A slave population exercises the *most pernicious influence* upon the manners, habits and character of those whom it exists. *Lisping infancy* learns the vocabulary of abusive epithets, and struts, the *embryo tyrant* of its little domain. The consciousness of *superior destiny* takes possession of his mind at its earliest dawning, and *love of power and rule* 'grows with his growth and strengthens with his strength.' Unless enabled to rise above the operation of those powerful causes, *he enters the world with miserable notions of self-importance, and under the government of an unbridled temper.*"

Having, by speculation and mismanagement, lost the most of his property, Dr. Young resumed the practice of medicine in Missouri, and soon obtained a lucrative run of custom. Here, as in Kentucky, the doctor took great interest in matters of religion, and was considered one of the pillars in the church.

Being sent one Sabbath morning to carry the sacramental wine to the church, about a mile distant, I could not withstand the temptation it presented of tasting it. Having had one swallow, I was tempted further on, till the beverage disappeared out of the neck of the bottle, so that I felt afraid that if noticed by master, I should be flogged. It occurred to me that I might fill up the bottle from one of the sap tubs, as I passed through the sugar camp; for it was the spring of the year, and we were making maple sugar. I tried to pour the sap into the bottle, but it flared over the top, leaving the wine still some inches down the neck. After ransacking my inventive faculties, I fortunately bit upon a plan and filled it up. Placing the bottle on the ground, and sucking my mouth full of the juice, I stood directly over the bottle and let it stream in until it was full. Putting the stopple in, I started off towards the church, feeling that I had got the advantage of master once more.

My fair complexion was a great obstacle to my happiness, both with whites and blacks, in and about the great house. Often mistaken by strangers for a white boy, it annoyed my mistress very much. On one occasion, a visitor came to the place in the absence of the doctor. While Mrs. Young was entertaining the major (for he was a military man), I passed through the room, and going near the stranger, he put out his hand and said to me, "How do you do, bub?" and turning to the lady, he exclaimed, "Madam, I would have known that he was the doctor's son, if I had met him in California, for he is so much like his papa." Mistress ordered me out of the room, and remarked that I was one of the servants, when the major begged pardon for the mistake. After the stranger was gone, I was flogged for his blunder.

Dr. Young sold his large farm, which was situated in the central part of the state, and removed to St. Louis, where a number of the servants were let out. I was put to work tending upon the hands in the office of the "St. Louis Times," a newspaper owned and published by Lovejoy & Miller, and edited by Elijah P. Lovejoy. Here my young heart began to feel more longings for liberty. The love of freedom is a sentiment natural to the human heart, and the want of it is felt by him who does not possess it. He feels it a reproach; and with this sting, this wounded pride, hating degradation, and looking forward to the cravings of the heart, the enslaved is always on the alert for an opportunity to escape from his oppressors and to avenge his wrongs. What greater injury and indignity can be offered to man, than to make him the bond-slave of his fellow-man?

My sojourn in the printing office was of short duration, and I was afterwards let out to a slave-trader named Walker. This heartless, cruel, ungodly man, who neither loved his Maker nor feared Satan, was a fair representative of thousands of demons in human form that are engaged in buying and selling God's children.

One year with Walker, beholding scenes of cruelty that can be better imagined than described, I was once more taken home, and soon after hired out as an under steward on the steamer Patriot, running to New Orleans. This opened to me a new life, and gave me an opportunity to see different phases of slave life, and to learn something more of the world. Life on the Mississippi River is an exciting one. I had not been on the boat but a few weeks when one of those races for which the southern steamers are so famous took place.

At eight o'clock on the evening of the third day of the passage, the lights of another steamer were seen in the distance, and apparently coming up very fast. This was the signal for a general commotion on board the Patriot, and every thing indicated that a steamboat race was at hand. Nothing can exceed the excitement attendant upon the racing of steamers on the Mississippi.

By the time the boats had reached Memphis they were side by side, and each exerting itself to get in advance of the other. The night was clear, the moon shining brightly, and the boats so near to each other that the passengers were within speaking distance. On board the Patriot the firemen were using oil, lard, butter, and even bacon, with wood, for the purpose of raising the steam to its highest pitch. The blaze mingled with the black smoke that issued from the pipes of the other boat, which showed that she also was burning something more combustible than wood.

The firemen of both boats, who were slaves, were singing songs such as can only be heard on board a southern steamer. The boats now came abreast of each other, and nearer and nearer, until they were locked so that men could pass from one to the other. The wildest excitement prevailed among the men employed on the steamers, in which the passengers freely participated.

At this moment the engineer of the Patriot was seen to fasten down the safety-valve, so that no steam should escape. This was indeed a dangerous resort, and a few who saw what had taken place, fearing that an explosion would be the consequence, left that part of the boat for more secure quarters.

The Patriot now stopped to take in passengers; but still no steam was permitted to escape. On the starting of the boat again, cold water was forced into the boilers by the feed-pumps, and, as might have been expected, one of the boilers exploded with terrific force, carrying away the boiler deck and tearing to pieces much of the machinery. One dense fog of steam filled every part of the vessel, while shrieks, groans, and cries were heard on every side. Men were running hither and thither looking for their wives, and women were flying about, in the wildest confusion, seeking for their husbands. Dismay appeared on every countenance.

The saloons and cabins soon looked more like hospitals than any thing else; but by this time the Patriot had drifted to the shore, and the other steamer had come alongside to render assistance to the disabled boat. The killed and wounded (nineteen in number) were put on shore, and the Patriot, taken in tow by the Washington, was once more on her journey.

It was half past twelve, and the passengers, instead of retiring to their berths, once more assembled at the gaming tables. The practice of gambling on the western waters has long been a source of annoyance to the more moral persons who travel on our great rivers. Thousands of dollars often change owners during a passage from St. Louis or Louisville to New Orleans on a Mississippi steamer. Many men are completely ruined on such occasions, and duels are often the consequence.

"Go call my boy, steward," said Mr. Jones, as he took his cards one by one from the table.

In a few minutes a fine-looking, bright-eyed mulatto boy, apparently about sixteen years of age, was standing by his master's side at the table.

"I am broke, all but my boy," said Jones, as he ran his fingers through his cards; "but he is worth a thousand dollars, and I will bet the half of him."

"I will call you," said Thompson, as he laid five hundred dollars at the feet of the boy, who was standing on the table, and at the same time throwing down his cards before his adversary.

"You have beaten me," said Jones; and a roar of laughter followed from the other gentleman as poor Joe stepped down from the table.

"Well, I suppose I owe you half the nigger," said Thompson, as he took hold of Joe and began examining his limbs.

"Yes," replied Jones, "he is half yours. Let me have five hundred dollars, and I will give you a bill of sale of the boy."

"Go back to your bed," said Thompson to his chattel, "and remember that you now belong to me."

The poor slave wiped the tears from his eyes, as, in obedience, he turned to leave the table.

"My father gave me that boy," said Jones, as he took the money, "and I hope, Mr. Thompson, that you will allow me to redeem him."

"Most certainly, sir," replied Thompson; "whenever you hand over the cool thousand the negro is yours."

Next morning, as the passengers were assembling in the cabin and on deck, and while the slaves were running about waiting on or looking for their masters, poor Joe was seen entering his new master's state-room, boots in hand.

Such is the uncertainty of a slave's life. He goes to bed at night the pampered servant of his young master, with whom he has played in childhood, and who would not see his slave abused under any consideration, and gets up in the morning the property of a man whom he has never before seen.

To behold five or six tables in the saloon of a steamer, with half a dozen men playing cards at each, with money, pistols, and bowie-knives spread in splendid confusion before them, is an ordinary thing on the Mississippi River.

Continued intercourse with educated persons, and meeting on the steamer so many travellers from the free states, caused me to feel more keenly my degraded and unnatural situation. I gained much information respecting the north and Canada that was valuable to me, and I resolved to escape with my mother, who had been sold to a gentleman in St. Louis. The attempt was made, but we were unsuccessful. I was then sold to Mr. Samuel Willi, a merchant tailor. I was again let out to be employed on a Mississippi steamboat, but was soon after sold to Captain E. Price, of the Chester. To escape from slavery and become my own master, was now the ruling passion of my life. I would dream at night that I was free, and, on awaking, weep to find myself still a slave.

"I would think of Victoria's domain;
In a moment I seemed to be there;
But the fear of being taken again
Soon hurried me back to despair."

Thoughts of the future, and my heart yearning for liberty, kept me always planning to escape.

The long-looked-for opportunity came, and I embraced it. Leaving the steamer upon which my now master had me at work, I started for the north, travelling at night and lying by during the day. It was in the winter season, and I suffered much from cold and hunger. Supposing every person to be my enemy, I was afraid to appeal to any one, even for a little food, to keep body and soul together. As I pressed forward, my escape to Canada seemed certain, and this feeling gave me a light heart; for

"Behind I left the whips and chains,
Before me were sweet Freedom's plains."

While on my journey at night, and passing farms, I would seek a corn-crib, and supply myself with some of its contents. The next day, while buried in the forest, I would make a fire and roast my corn, and drink from the nearest stream. One night, while in search of corn, I came upon what I supposed to be a hill of potatoes, buried in the ground for want of a cellar. I obtained a sharp-pointed piece of wood, with which I dug away for more than an hour, and on gaining the hidden treasure, found it to be turnips. However, I did not dig for nothing. After supplying myself with about half a dozen of the turnips, I again resumed my journey. This uncooked food was indeed a great luxury, and gave strength to my fatigued limbs. The weather was very cold,—so cold, that it drove me one night into a barn, where I lay in the hay until morning. A storm overtook me when about a week out. The rain fell in torrents, and froze as it came down. My clothes became stiff with ice. Here again I took shelter in a barn, and walked about to keep from freezing. Nothing but the fear of being arrested and returned to slavery prevented me, at this time, seeking shelter in some dwelling.

After many days of weary travelling, and sick from e[x]posure, I determined to seek shelter and aid; and for this purpose, I placed myself behind some fallen trees near the main road, hoping to see some colored person, thinking I should be more safe under the care of one of my own color. Several farmers with their teams passed, but the appearance of each one frightened me out of the idea of asking for assistance. After lying on the ground for some time, with my sore, frost-bitten feet benumbed with cold, I saw an old, white-haired man, dressed in a suit of drab, with a broad-brimmed bat, walking along, leading a horse. The man was evidently walking for exercise. I came out from my hiding-place and told the stranger I must die unless I obtained some assistance. A moment's conversation satisfied the old man that I was one of the oppressed, fleeing from the house of bondage. From the difficulty with which I walked, the shivering of my limbs, and the trembling of my voice, he became convinced that I had been among *thieves*, and be acted the part of the Good Samaritan. This was the first person I had ever seen of the religious sect called "Quakers," and his name was Wells Brown. I remained here about a fortnight, and being fitted out with clothes, shoes, and a little money, by these good people, I was again ready to resume my journey. I entered their house with the single name that I was known by at the south, "William;" I left it with the one I now bear.

A few days more, and I arrived at Cleveland, Ohio, where I found employment during the remainder of the winter. Having no education, my first thoughts went in that direction. Obtaining a situation the following spring on a Lake Erie Steamer, I found that I could be very serviceable to slaves who were escaping from the south to Canada. In one year alone I assisted *sixty* fugitives in crossing to the British queen's dominions. Many of these escapes were attended with much interest. On one occasion, a fugitive had been hid away in the house of a noted abolitionist in Cleveland for ten days, while his master was in town, and watching every steamboat and vessel that left the port. Several officers were also on the watch, guarding the house of the abolitionist every night. The slave was a young and valuable man, of twenty-two years of age, and very black. The friends of the slave had almost despaired of getting him away from his hiding-place, when I was called in, and consulted as to the best course to be taken. I at once inquired if a painter could be found who would paint the fugitive white. In an hour, by my directions, the black man was as white, and with as rosy cheeks, as any of the Anglo-Saxon race, and disguised in the dress of a woman, with a thick veil over her face. As the steamer's bell was tolling for the passengers to come on board, a tall lady, dressed in deep mourning, and leaning on the arm of a gentleman of more than ordinary height, was seen entering the ladies' cabin of the steamer North America, who took her place with the other *ladies*. Soon the steamer left the wharf, and the slave-catcher and his officers, who had been watching the boat since her arrival, went away, satisfied that their slave had not escaped by the North America, and returned to guard the house of the abolitionist. After the boat had got out of port, and fairly on her way to Buffalo, I showed the tall lady to her state-room. The next morning, the fugitive, dressed in his plantation suit, bade farewell to his native land, crossed the Niagara River, and took up his abode in Canada.

I remained on Lake Erie during the sailing season, and resided in Buffalo in the winter. In the autumn of 1843 I was invited by the officers of the Western New York Anti-Slavery Society to take an agency as a lecturer in behalf of my enslaved countrymen, which offer I accepted, and soon commenced my labors. Mobs were very frequent in those days. Being advertised to address the citizens of Aurora, Erie County, New York, on one occasion, I went to fulfil the appointment, and found the church surrounded by a howling set of men and boys, waiting to give me a warm reception. I went in, opened the meeting, and began my address. But they were resolved on having a good time, and the disturbance was so great that I had to stop. In the mean time, a bag of flour had been brought to the church, taken up into the belfry, directly over the entrance door, and a plan laid to throw the whole of it over me as I should pass out of the house, of all which my friends and I were unaware. After I [h]ad been driven from the pulpit by the unsalable eggs, which were thrown about very freely, I stopped in the body of the church to discuss a single point with one of the respectable rowdies, when the audience became silent, and I went on and spoke above an hour, all the while receiving the strictest attention from every one present. At the conclusion the lights were put out, and preparation made to flour me over, although I had evidently changed the opinions of many of their company. As we were jamming along towards the door, one of the mob whispered to me, "They are going to throw a bag of flour on you; so when you hear any one say, 'Let it slide,' you look out." Thus on my guard, and in possession of their signal, I determined to have a little fun at their expense. Therefore, when some of the best dressed and most respectable looking of their own company, or those who had no sympathy with my mission, filled up the doorway, I cried out in a disguised voice, "Let it slide;" and down came the contents of the bag, to the delight of my friends and the consternation of the *enemy*. A quarrel arose among the men at the door, and while they were settling their difficulty, my few friends and I quietly walked away unharmed.

Invited by influential English abolitionists, and elected a delegate to the Peace Congress at Paris, I sailed for Liverpool in the Royal Mail Steamship Canada, in the month of July, 1849. The passage was pleasant, and we arrived out in less than ten days.

I visited Dublin, where I partook of the hospitality of Richard D. Webb, Esq., and went from there to London; thence to Paris, to discharge the duties of my mission on peace.

In the French capital I met some of the most noted of the English philanthropists, who were also there in attendance on the Congress—Joseph Sturge, Richard Cobden, and men of that class.

Returning to London after the adjournment of the peace gathering, I was invited to various parts of the United Kingdom, and remained abroad a little more than five years, during which time I wrote and published three books, lectured in every town of any note in England, Ireland, Scotland, and Wales, besides visiting the Continent four times.

Anxious to be again in my native land, battling the monster *Slavery*, I returned home to America in the autumn of 1854; since which time I have travelled the length and breadth of the free states.

THE BLACK MAN AND HIS ANTECEDENTS.

Of the great family of man, the negro has, during the last half century, been more prominently before the world than any other race. He did not seek this notoriety. Isolated away in his own land, he would have remained there, had it not been for the avarice of other races, who sought him out as a victim of slavery. Two and a half centuries of the negro's enslavement have created, in many minds, the opinion that he is intellectually inferior to the rest of mankind; and now that the blacks seem in a fair way to get their freedom in this country, it has been asserted, and from high authority in the government, that the natural inferiority of the negro makes it impossible for him to live on this continent with the white man, unless in a state of bondage.

In his interview with a committee of the colored citizens of the District of Columbia, on the 14th of August last, the President of the United States intimated that the whites and the blacks could not live together in peace, on account of one race being superior intellectually to the other. Mr. Postmaster General Blair, in his letter to the Union mass meeting held at the Cooper Institute, in New York, in March last, takes this ground. The Boston "Post" and "Courier" both take the same position.

I admit that the condition of my race, whether considered in a mental, moral, or intellectual point of view, at the present time cannot compare favorably with the Anglo-Saxon. But it does not become the whites to point the finger of scorn at the blacks, when they have so long been degrading them. The negro has not always been considered the inferior race. The time was when he stood at the head of science and literature. Let us see.

It is the generally received opinion of the most eminent historians and ethnologists, that the Ethiopians were really negroes, although in them the physical characteristics of the race were exhibited in a less marked manner than in those dwelling on the coast of Guinea, from whence the stock o[f] American slaves has been chiefly derived. That, in the earliest periods of history, the Ethiopians had attained a high degree of civilization, there is every reason to believe; and that to the learning and science derived from them we must ascribe those wonderful monuments which still exist to attest the power and skill of the ancient Egyptians.

Among those who favor this opinion is our own distinguished country-man, Alexander H. Everett, and upon this evidence I base my argument. Volney assumes it as a settled point that the Egyptians were black. Herodotus, who travelled extensively through that interesting land, set them down as black, with curled hair, and having the negro features. The sacred writers were aware of their complexion: hence the question, "Can the Ethiopian change his skin?" The image of the negro is engraved upon the monuments of Egypt, not as a bondman, but as the master of art. The Sphinx, one of the wonders of the world, surviving the wreck of centuries, exhibits these same features at the present day. Minerva, the goddess of wisdom, was supposed to have been an African princess. Atlas, whose shoulders sustained the globe, and even the great Jupiter Ammon himself, were located by the mythologists in Africa. Though there may not be much in these fables, they teach us, nevertheless, who were then considered the nobles of the human race. Euclid, Homer, and Plato were Ethiopians. Terence, the most refined and accomplished scholar of his time, was of the same race. Hanno, the father of Hamilcar, and grandfather of Hannibal, was a negro. These are the antecedents of the enslaved blacks on this continent.

From whence sprang the Anglo-Saxon? For, mark you, it is he that denies the equality of the negro. "When the Britons first became known to the Tyrian mariners," says Macaulay, "they were little superior to the Sandwich Islanders."

Hume says they were a rude and barbarous people, divided into numerous tribes, dressed in the skins of wild beasts. Druidism was their religion, and they were very superstitious. Such is the first account we have of the Britons. When the Romans invaded that country, they reduced the people to a state of vassalage as degrading as that of slavery in the Southern States. Their king, Caractacus, was captured and sent a slave to Rome. Still later, Hengist and Horsa, the Saxon generals, presented another yoke, which the Britons wore compelled to wear. But the last dregs of the bitter cup of humiliation were drunk when William of Normandy met Harold at Hastings, and, with a single blow, completely annihilated the nationality of the Britons. Thousands of the conquered people were then sent to the slave markets of Rome, where they were sold very cheap on account of their inaptitude to learn.

This is not very flattering to the President's ancestors, but it is just. Cæsar, in writing home, said of the Britons, "They are the most ignorant people I ever conquered. They cannot be taught music." Cicero, writing to his friend Atticus, advised him not to buy slaves from England, "because," said he, "they cannot be taught to read, and are the ugliest and most stupid race I ever saw." I am sorry that Mr. Lincoln came from such a low origin; but he is not to blame. I only find fault with him for making mouths at me.

> "You should not the ignorant negro despise;
> Just such your sires appeared in Cæsar's eyes."

The Britons lost their nationality, became amalgamated with the Romans, Saxons, and Normans, and out of this conglomeration sprang the proud Anglo-Saxon of to-day. I once stood upon the walls of an English city, built by enslaved Britons when Julius Cæsar was their master. The image of the ancestors of President Lincoln and Montgomery Blair, as represented in Britain, was carved upon the monuments of Rome, where they may still be seen in their chains. Ancestry is something which the white American should not speak of, unless with his lips to the dust.

"Nothing," says Macaulay, "in the early existence of Britain, indicated the greatness which she was destined to attain." Britain has risen, while proud Rome, [o]nce the mistress of the world, has fallen; but the image of the early Englishman in his chains, as carved twenty centuries ago, is still to be seen upon her broken monuments. So has Egypt fallen; and her sable sons and daughters have been scattered into nearly every land where the white man has introduced slavery and disgraced the soil with his footprint. As I gazed upon the beautiful and classic obelisk of Luxor, removed from Thebes, where it had stood four thousand years, and transplanted to the Place de la Concorde, at Paris, and contemplated its hieroglyphic inscription of the noble daring of Sesostris, the African general, who drew kings at his chariot wheels, and left monumental inscriptions from Ethiopia to India, I felt proud of my antecedents, proud of the glorious past, which no amount of hate and prejudice could wipe from history's page, while I had to mourn over the fall and the degradation of my race. But I do not despair; for the negro has that intellectual genius which God has planted in the mind of man, that distinguishes him from the rest of creation, and which needs only cultivation to make it bring forth fruit. No nation has ever been found, which, by its own unaided efforts, by some powerful inward impulse, has arisen from barbarism and degradation to civilization and respectability. There is nothing in race or blood, in color or features, that imparts susceptibility of improvement to one race over another. The mind left to itself from infancy, without culture, remains a blank. Knowledge is not innate. Development makes the man. As the Greeks, and Romans, and Jews drew knowledge from the Egyptians three thousand years ago, and the Europeans received it from the Romans, so must the blacks of this land rise in the same way. As one man learns from another, so nation learns from nation. Civilization is handed from one people to another, its great fountain and source being God our Father. No one, in the days of Cicero and Tacitus, could have predicted that the barbarism and savage wildness of the Germans would give place to the learning, refinement, and culture which that people now exhibit. Already the blacks on this continent, though kept down under the heel of the white man, are fast rising in the scale of intellectual development, and proving their equality with the brotherhood of man.

In his address before the Colonization Society, at Washington, on the 18th of January, 1853, Hon. Edward Everett said, "When I lived in Cambridge, a few years ago, I used to attend, as one of the board of visitors, the examinations of a classical school, in which was a colored boy, the son of a slave in Mississippi, I think. He appeared to me to be of pure African blood. There were at the same time two youths from Georgia, and one of my own sons, attending the same school. I must say that this poor negro boy, Beverly Williams, was one of the best scholars at the school, and in the Latin language he was the best scholar in his class. There are others, I am told, which show still more conclusively the aptitude of the colored race for *every kind of intellectual culture.*"

Mr. Everett cited several other instances which had fallen under his notice, and utterly scouted the idea that there was any general inferiority of the African race. He said, "They have done as well as persons of European or Anglo-American origin would have done, after three thousand years of similar depression and hardship. The question has been asked, 'Does not the negro labor under some incurable, natural inferiority?' *In this, for myself, I have no belief.*"

I think that this is ample refutation of the charge of the natural inferiority of the negro. President Lincoln, in the interview to which I have already referred, said, "But for your race among us there would not be a war." This reminds me of an incident that occurred while travelling in the State of Ohio, in 1844. Taking the stage coach at a small village, one of the passengers (a white man) objected to my being allowed a seat inside, on account of my color. I persisted, however, in claiming the right which my ticket gave me, and got in. The objector at once took a seat on a trunk on the top of the coach. The wire netting round the top of the stage not being strong, the white passenger, trunks and all, slid off as we were going down a steep hill. The top passenger's shoulder was dislocated, and in his pain he cried out, "If you had not been black, I should not have left my seat inside."

The "New York Herald," the "Boston Post," the "Boston Courier," and the "New York Journal of Commerce," take the lead in misrepresenting the effect which emancipation in the West Indies had upon the welfare of those islands. It is asserted that general ruin followed the black man's liberation. As to the British colonies, the fact is well established that slavery had impoverished the soil, demoralized the people, bond and free, brought the planters to a state of bankruptcy, and all the islands to ruin, long before Parliament had passed the act of emancipation. All the colonies, including Jamaica, had petitioned the home government for assistance, ten years prior to the liberation of their slaves. It is a noticeable fact, that the free blacks were the least embarrassed, in a pecuniary point of view, and that they appeared in more comfortable circumstances than the whites. There was a large proportion of free blacks in each of the colonies, Jamaica alone having fifty-five thousand before the day of emancipation. A large majority of the West India estates were owned by persons residing in Europe, and who had never seen the colonies. These plantations were carried on by agents, overseers, and clerks, whose mismanagement, together with the blighting influence which chattel slavery takes with it wherever it goes, brought the islands under impending ruin, and many of the estates were mortgaged in Europe for more than their value. One man alone, Neil Malcomb, of London, had forty plantations to fall upon his hands for money advanced on them before the abolition of slavery. These European proprietors, despairing of getting any returns from the West Indies, gladly pocketed their share of the twenty million pounds sterling, which the home government gave them, and abandoned their estates to their ruin. Other proprietors residing in the colonies formed combinations to make the emancipated people labor for scarcely enough to purchase food for them. If found idle, the tread-wheel, the chain-gang, the dungeon, with black bread, and water from the moat, and other modes of legalized torture, were inflicted upon the negroes. Through the determined and combined efforts of the land owners, the condition of the freed people was as bad, if not worse, for the first three years after their liberation, than it was before. Never was all experiment more severely tested than that of emancipation in the West Indies.

Nevertheless, the principles of freedom triumphed; not a drop of blood was shed by the enfranchised blacks; the colonies have arisen from the blight which they labored under in the time of slavery; the land has increased in value; and, above all, that which is more valuable than cotton, sugar, or rice—the moral and intellectual condition of both blacks and whites is in a better state now than ever before. Sir William Colebrook, governor of Antigua, said, six years after the islands were freed, "At the lowest computation, the land, without a single slave upon it, is fully as valuable now as it was, including all the slaves, before emancipation." In a report made to the British Parliament, in 1859, it was stated that three fifths of the cultivated land of Jamaica was the *bona fide* property of the blacks. The land is in a better state of cultivation now than it was while slavery existed, and both imports and exports show a great increase. Every thing, demonstrates that emancipation in the West India islands has resulted in the most satisfactory manner, and fulfilled the expectation of the friends of freedom throughout the world.

Rev. Mr. Underhill, secretary of the English Baptist Missionary Society, who has visited Jamaica, and carefully studied its condition, said, in a recent speech in London, that the late slaves in that island had built some two hundred and twenty chapels. The churches that worship in them number fifty-three thousand communicants, amounting to one eighth of the total population. The average attendance, in other than the state churches, is ninety-one thousand—a fourth of the population. One third of the children—twenty-two thousand—are in the schools. The blacks voluntarily contribute twenty-two thousand pounds (one hundred and ten thousand dollars) annually for religious purposes. Their landed property exceeds five million dollars. Valuing their cottages at only fifty dollars each, these amount to three million dollars. They have nearly three hundred thousand dollars deposited in the savings banks. The sum total of their property is much above eleven million dollars. All this has been accumulated since their emancipation.

Thus it is seen that all parties have been benefited by the abolition of negro slavery in the British possessions. Now we turn to our own land. Among the many obstacles which have been brought to bear against emancipation, one of the most formidable has been the series of objections urged against it upon what has been supposed to be the slave's want of appreciation of liberty, and his ability to provide for himself in a state of freedom; and now that slavery seems to be near its end, these objections are multiplying, and the cry is heard all over the land, "What shall be done with the slave if freed?"

It has been clearly demonstrated, I think, that the enslaved of the south are as capable of self-support as any other class of people in the country. It is well known that, throughout the entire south, a large class of slaves have been for years accustomed to hire their time from their owners. Many of these have paid very high prices for the privilege. Some able mechanics have been known to pay as high as six hundred dollar per annum, besides providing themselves with food and clothing; and this class of slaves, by their industry, have taken care of themselves so well, and their appearance has been so respectable, that many of the states have passed laws prohibiting masters from letting their slaves out to themselves, because, as it was said, it made the other slaves dissatisfied to see so many of their fellows well provided, and accumulating something for themselves in the way of pocket money.

The Rev. Dr. Nehemiah Adams, whose antecedents have not been such as to lead to the suspicion that he favors the free colored men, or the idea of giving to the slaves their liberty, in his "South-Side View," unconsciously and unintentionally gives a very valuable statement upon this particular point. Dr. Adams says, "A slave woman having had three hundred dollars stolen from her by a white man, her master was questioned in court as to the probability of her having had so much money. The master said that he not unfrequently had borrowed fifty and a hundred dollars from her himself, and added that she was always very strict as to his promised time of payment." There was a slave woman who had not only kept every agreement with her master—paying him every cent she had promised—but had accumulated three hundred dollars towards purchasing her liberty; and it was stolen from her, not by a black man, but, as Dr. Adams says, by a white man.

But one of the clearest demonstrations of the ability of the slave to provide for himself in a state of freedom is to be found in the prosperous condition of the large free colored population of the Southern States. Maryland has eighty thousand, Virginia seventy thousand, and the other slave states have a large number. These free people have all been slaves, or they are the descendants of those who were once slaves; what they have gained has been acquired in spite of the public opinion and laws of the south, in spite of prejudice, and every thing. They have acquired a large amount of property; and it is this industry, this sobriety, this intelligence, and this wealth of the free colored people the south, that has created so much prejudice on the part of slaveholders against them. They have felt that the very presence of a colored man, looking so genteelly and in such a prosperous condition, made the slaves unhappy and discontented. In the Southern Rights Convention which assembled at Baltimore, June 8, 1860, a resolution was adopted, calling on the legislature to pass a law driving the free colored people out of the state. Nearly every speaker took the ground that the free colored people must be driven out to make the slave's obedience more secure. Judge Mason, in his speech, said, "It is the thrifty and well-to-do free negroes, that are seen by our slaves, that make them dissatisfied." A similar appeal was made to the legislature of Tennessee. Judge Catron, of the Supreme Court of the United States, in a long and able letter to the Nashville "Union," opposed the driving out of the colored people. He said they were among the best mechanics, the best artisans, and the most industrious laborers in the state, and that to drive them, out would be an injury to the state itself. This is certainly good evidence in their behalf.

The New Orleans "True Delta" opposed the passage of a similar law by the State of Louisiana. Among other things it said, "There are a large free colored population here, correct in their general deportment, honorable in their intercourse with society, and free from reproach so far as the laws are concerned, not surpassed in the inoffensiveness of their lives by any equal number of persons in any place, north or south."

A movement was made in the legislature of South Carolina to expel the free blacks from that state, and a committee was appointed to investigate the matter. In their report the committee said, "We find that the free blacks of this state are among our most industrious people; in this city (Charleston) we find that they own over two and a half millions of dollars worth of property; that they pay two thousand seven hundred dollars tax to the city."

Dr. Nehemiah Adams, whom I have already quoted, also testifies to the good character of the free colored people; but he does it unintentionally; it was not a part of the programme; how it slipped in I cannot tell. Here it is, however, from page 41 of his "South-Side View:"—

"A prosecuting officer, who had six or eight counties in his district, told me that, during eight years service, he had made out about two thousand bills of indictment, of which not more than twelve were against colored persons."

Hatred of the free colored people, and abuse of them, have always been popular with the pro-slavery people of this country; yet, an American senator from one of the Western States—a man who never lost an opportunity to vilify and traduce the colored man, and who, in his last canvass for a seat in the United States Senate, argued that the slaves were better off in slavery than they would be if set free, and declared that the blacks were unable to take care of themselves while enjoying liberty—died, a short time since, twelve thousand dollars in debt to a black man, who was the descendant of a slave.

There is a Latin phrase—*De mortuis nil nisi bonum*. It is not saying any thing against the reputation of Hon. Stephen A. Douglas to tell the fact that he had borrowed money from a negro. I only find fault with him that he should traduce the class that befriended him in the time of need. James Gordon Bennett, of the New York Herald, in a time of great pecuniary distress, soon after establishing his paper, borrowed three hundred dollars of a black man; and now he is one of our most relentless enemies. Thus it is that those who fattened upon us often turn round and traduce us: Reputation is, indeed, dear to every nation and race; but to us, the colored people of this country, who have so many obstacles to surmount, it is doubly dear:—

> "Who steals my purse steals trash;
> 'Twas mine, 'tis his, and has been slave to thousands;
> But he who filches from me my good name,
> Robs me of that which not enriches him,
> And makes me poor indeed."

You know we were told by the slaveholders, before the breaking out of the rebellion, that if we got into any difficulty with the south, their slaves would take up arms and fight to a man for them. Mr. Toombs, I believe, threatened that he would arm his slaves, and other men in Congress from the slave states made the same threat. They were going to arm the slaves and turn them against the north. They said they could be trusted; and many people here at the north really believed that the slave did not want his liberty, would not have it if he could, and that the slave population was a very dangerous element against the north; but at once, on the approach of our soldiers, the slaves are seen, with their bundles and baskets, and hats and coats, and without bundles or baskets, and without hats or coats, rushing to our lines; demonstrating what we have so often said, that all the slave was waiting for was the opportunity to get his liberty. Why should you not have believed this? Why should you have supposed for a moment, that, because a man's color differs a little from yours, he is better contented to remain a slave than you would be, or that he has no inclination, no wish, to escape from the thraldom that holds him so tight? What is it that does not wish to be free?

> "Go, let a cage with grates of gold,
> And pearly roof, the eagle hold;
> Let dainty viands be its fare,
> And give the captive tenderest care;

But say, in luxury's limits pent,
Find you the king of birds content?
No; oft he'll sound the startling shriek,
And dash the cage with angry beak:
Precarious freedom's far more dear
Than all the prison's pampering cheer."

As with the eagle, so with man. He loves to look upon the bright day and the stormy night; to gaze upon the broad, free ocean, its eternal surging tides, its mountain billows, and its foam-crested waves; to tread the steep mountain side; to sail upon the placid river; to wander along the gurgling stream; to trace the sunny slope, the beautiful landscape, the majestic forest, the flowery meadow; to listen to the howling of the winds and the music of the birds. These are the aspirations of man, without regard to country, clime, or color.

"What shall we do with the slave of the south? Expatriate him," say the haters of the negro. Expatriate him for what? He has cleared up the swamps of the south, and has put the soil under cultivation; he has built up her towns, and cities, and villages; he has enriched the north and Europe with his cotton, and sugar, and rice; and for this you would drive him out of the country! "What shall be done with the slaves if they are freed?" You had better ask "What shall we do with the slaveholders if the slaves are freed?" The slave has shown himself better fitted to take care of himself than the slaveholder. He is the bone and sinew of the south; he is the producer, while the master is nothing but a consumer, and a very poor consumer at that. The slave is the producer, and he alone can be relied upon. He has the sinew, the determination, and the will; and if you will take the free colored people of the south as the criterion, take their past history as a sample of what the colored people are capable of doing, every one must be satisfied that the slaves can take care of themselves. Some say, "Let them alone; they are well cared for, and that is enough."

"O, tell us not they're clothed and fed—
'Tis insult, stuff, and a' that;
With freedom gone, all joy is fled,
For Heaven's best gift is a' that."

But it is said, "The two races cannot live together in a state of freedom." Why, that is the cry that rung all over England thirty years ago: "If you liberate the slaves of the West Indies, they can't live with the whites in a state of freedom." Thirty years have shown the contrary. The blacks and the whites live together in Jamaica; they are all prosperous, and the island in a better condition than it ever was before the act of emancipation was passed.

But they tell us, "If the slaves are emancipated, we won't receive them upon an equality." Why, every man must make equality for himself. No society, no government, can make this equality. I do not expect the slave of the south to jump into equality; all I claim for him is, that he may be allowed to jump into liberty, and let him make equality for himself. I have some white neighbors around me in Cambridge; they are not very intellectual; they don't associate with my family; but whenever they shall improve themselves, and bring themselves up by their own intellectual and moral worth, I shall not object to their coming into my society—all things being equal.

Now, this talk about not letting a man come to this place or that, and that we won't do this for him, or won't do that for him, is all idle. The anti-slavery agitators have never demanded that you shall take the colored man, any more than that you shall take the uncultivated and uncouth white man, and place him in a certain position in society. All I demand for the black man is, that the white people shall take their heels off his neck, and let him have a chance to rise by his own efforts.

The idea of colonizing the slaves in some other country, outside of the United States, seems the height of folly. Whatever may be the mineral wealth of a country, or the producing capabilities of the soil, neither can be made available without the laborer. Four millions of strong hands cannot be spared from the Southern States. All time has shown that the negro is the best laborer in the tropics.

The slaves once emancipated and left on the lands, four millions of new consumers will spring into existence. Heretofore, the bondmen have consumed nothing scarcely from the north. The cost of keeping a slave was only about nineteen dollars per annum, including food, clothing, and doctors' bills. Negro cloth, negro shoes, and negro whips were all that were sent south by northern manufacturers. Let slavery be abolished, and stores will be opened and a new trade take place with the blacks south. Northern manufacturers will have to run on extra time till this new demand will have been supplied. The slave owner, having no longer an inducement to be idle, will go to work, and will not have time to concoct treason against the *stars and stripes*. I cannot close this appeal without a word about the free blacks in the non-slaveholding states.

The majority of the colored people in the Northern States descended from slaves: many of the[m] were slaves themselves. In education, in morals, and in the development of mechanical genius, the free blacks of the Northern States will compare favorably with any laboring class in the world. And considering the fact that we have been shut out, by a cruel prejudice, from nearly all the mechanical branches, and all the professions, it is marvellous that we have attained the position we now occupy. Notwithstanding those bars, our young men have learned trades, become artists, gone into the professions, although bitter prejudice may prevent their having a great deal of practice. When it is considered that they have mostly come out of bondage, and that their calling has been the lowest kind in every community, it is still more strange that the colored people have amassed so much wealth in every state in the Union. If this is not an exhibition of capacity, I don't understand the meaning of the term. And if true patriotism and devotion to the cause of freedom be tests of loyalty, and should establish one's claim to all the privileges that the government can confer, then surely the black man can demand his rights with a good grace. From the fall of Attucks, the first martyr of the American revolution in 1770, down to the present day, the colored people have shown themselves worthy of any confidence that the nation can place in its citizens in the time that tries men's souls. At the battle of Bunker Hill, on the heights of Groton, at the ever-memorable battle of Red Bank, the sable sons of our country stood side by side with their white brethren. On Lakes Erie and Champlain, on the Hudson, and down in the valley of the Mississippi, they established their valor and their invincibility. Whenever the rights of the nation have been assailed, the negro has always responded to his country's call, at once, and with every pulsation of his heart beating for freedom. And no class of Americans have manifested more solicitude for the success of the federal arms in the present struggle with rebellion, than the colored people. At the north, they were among the earliest to respond to the president's first proclamation, calling for troops. At the south, they have ever shown a preference for the *stars and stripes.* In his official despatch to Minister Adams, Mr. Secretary Seward said,—

"Every where the American general receives his most useful and reliable information from the negro, *who hails his coming as the harbinger of freedom.*"

PHILLIS WHEATLEY.

In the year 1761, when Boston had her slave market, and the descendants of the Pilgrims appeared to be the most pious and God-fearing people in the world, Mrs. John Wheatley went into the market one day, for the purpose of selecting and purchasing a girl for her own use. Among the group of children just imported from the African coast was a delicately built, rather good-looking child of seven or eight years, apparently suffering from the recent sea voyage and change of climate. Mrs. Wheatley's heart was touched at the interesting countenance and humble modesty of this little stranger. The lady bought the child, and she was named Phillis. Struck with the slave's uncommon brightness, the mistress determined to teach her to read, which she did with no difficulty. The child soon mastered the English language, with which she was totally unacquainted when she landed upon the American shores. Her school lessons were all perfect, and she drank in the scriptural teachings as if by intuition. At the age of twelve, she could write letters and keep up a correspondence that would have done honor to one double her years. Mrs. Wheatley, seeing her superior genius, no longer regarded Phillis as a servant, but took her as a companion. It was not surprising that the slave girl should be an object of attraction, astonishment, and attention with the refined and highly cultivated society that weekly assembled in the drawing room of the Wheatleys. As Phillis grew up to womanhood, her progress and attainments kept pace with the promise of her earlier years. She drew around her the best educated of the white ladies, and attracted the attention and notice of the literary characters of Boston, who supplied her with books and encouraged the ripening of her intellectual powers. She studied the Latin tongue, and translated one of Ovid's tales, which was no sooner put in print in America, than it was republished in London, with eloquent commendations from the reviews. In 1773, a small volume of her poems, containing thirty-nine pieces, was published in London, and dedicated to the Countess of Huntingdon. The genuineness of this work was established in the first page of the volume, by a document signed by the governor of Massachusetts, the lieutenant-governor, her master, and fifteen of the most respectable and influential citizens of Boston, who were acquainted with her talents and the circumstances of her life. Her constitution being naturally fragile, she was advised by her physician to take a sea voyage as the means of restoring her declining health.

Phillis was emancipated by her master at the age of twenty-one years, and sailed for England. On her arrival, she was received and admired in the first circles of London society; and it was at that time that her poems were collected and published in a volume, with a portrait and memoir of the authoress. Phillis returned to America, and married Dr. Peters, a man of her own color, and of considerable talents. Her health began rapidly to decline, and she died at the age of twenty-six years, in 1780. Fortunately rescued from the fate that awaits the victims of the slave trade, this injured daughter of Africa had an opportunity of developing the genius that God had given her, and of showing to the world the great wrong done to her race. The limited place allowed for this sketch will not permit of our giving more than one short poem from the pen of the gifted Phillis Wheatley.

ON THE DEATH OF A YOUNG GIRL.

From dark abodes to fair ethereal light,
The enraptured innocent has winged her flight;
On the kind bosom of eternal love
She finds unknown beatitudes above.
This know, ye parents, nor her loss deplore—
She feels the iron hand of pain no more;
The dispensations of unerring grace
Should turn your sorrows into grateful praise;
Let, then, no tears for her henceforward flow
Nor stiffer grief in this dark vale below.

Her morning sun, which rose divinely bright,
Was quickly mantled with the gloom of night;
But hear, in heaven's best bowers, your child so fair,
And learn to imitate her language there.
Thou, Lord, whom I behold with glory crowned,
By what sweet name, and in what tuneful sound,
Wilt thou be praised? Seraphic powers are faint
Infinite love and majesty to paint.
To thee let all their grateful voices raise,
And saints and angels join their songs of praise[.]

Perfect in bliss, now from her heavenly home
She looks, and, smiling, beckons you to come;
Why then, fond parents, why these fruitless groans?
Restrain your tears, and cease your plaintive moans.
Freed from a world of sin, and snares, and pain,
Why would ye wish your fair one back again?
Nay, bow resigned; let hope your grief control,
And check the rising tumult of the soul.
Calm in the prosperous and the adverse day,
Adore the God who gives and takes away;

See him in all, his holy name revere,
Upright your actions, and your hearts sincere,
Till, having sailed through life's tempestuous sea,
And from its rocks and boisterous billows free,
Yourselves, safe landed on the blissful shore,
Shall join your happy child to part no more.

FRANCES ELLEN WATKINS.

Miss Watkins is a native of Baltimore, where she received her education. She has been before the public some years as an author and public lecturer. Her "Poems on Miscellaneous Subjects," published in a small volume, show a reflective mind and no ordinary culture. Her "Essay on Christianity" is a beautiful composition. Many of her poems are soul-stirring, and all are characterized by chaste language and much thought. The following is entitled

THE SLAVE MOTHER.

Heard you that shriek? It rose
So wildly on the air,
It seemed as if a burdened heart
Was breaking in despair.

Saw you those hands so sadly clasped,
The bowed and feeble head,
The shuddering of that fragile form,
That look of grief and dread?

Saw you the sad, imploring eye?
Its every glance was pain,
As if a storm of agony
Were sweeping through the brain.

She is a mother pale with fear;
Her boy clings to her side,
And in her kirtle vainly tries
His trembling form to hide.

He is not hers, although she bore
For him a mother's pains;

He is not hers, although her blood
Is coursing through his veins.

He is not hers, for cruel hands
May rudely tear apart
The only wreath of household love
That binds her breaking heart.

His love has been a joyous light
That o'er her pathway smiled,
A fountain, gushing ever new,
Amid life's desert wild.

His lightest word has been a tone
Of music round her heart;
Their lives a streamlet blent in one—
O Father, must they part?

They tear him from her circling arms,
Her last and fond embrace;
O, never more may her sad eyes
Gaze on his mournful face.

No marvel, then, these bitter shrieks
Disturb the listening air;
She is a mother, and her heart
Is breaking in despair.

Miss Watkins's advice to her own sex on the selection of a husband should be appreciated by all.

Nay, do not blush! I only heard
You had a mind to marry;
I thought I'd speak a friendly word
So just one moment tarry.

Wed not a man whose merit lies
In things of outward show,
In raven hair or flashing eyes,
That please your fancy so.

341

But marry one who's good and kind,
And free from all pretence;
Who, if without a gifted mind,
At least has common sense.

Miss Watkins is about thirty years of age, of a fragile form, rather nervous, keen and witty in conversation, outspoken in her opinions, and yet appears in all the simplicity of a child.

FREDERICK DOUGLASS.

The career of the distinguished individual whose name heads this page is more widely known than that of any other living colored man, except, perhaps, Alexandre Dumas. The narrative of his life, published in 1845, gave a new impetus to the black man's literature. All other stories of fugitive slaves faded away before the beautifully written, highly descriptive, and thrilling memoir of Frederick Douglass. Other narratives had only brought before the public a few heart-rending scenes connected with the person described. But Mr. Douglass, in his book, brought not only his old master's farm and its occupants before the reader, but the entire country around him, including Baltimore and its ship yard. The manner in which he obtained his education, and especially his learning to write, has been read and re-read by thousands in both hemispheres. His escape from slavery is too well understood to need a recapitulation here. He took up his residence in New Bedford, where he still continued the assiduous student—mastering the different branches of education which the accursed institution had deprived him of in early life.

His advent as a lecturer was a remarkable one. White men and black men had talked against slavery, but none had ever spoken like Frederick Douglass. Throughout the north the newspapers were filled with the sayings of the "eloquent fugitive." He often travelled with others, but they were all lost sight of in the eagerness to hear Douglass. His travelling companions would sometimes get angry, and would speak first at the meetings; then they would take the last turn; but it was all the same—the fugitive's impression was the one left upon the mind. He made more persons angry, and pleased more, than any other man. He was praised, and he was censured. He made them laugh, he made them weep, and he made them swear. His "Slaveholder's Sermon" was always a trump card. He awakened an interest in the hearts of thousands who before were dead to the slave and his condition. Many kept away from his lectures, fearing lest they should be converted against their will. Young men and women, in those days of pro-slavery hatred, would return to their fathers' roofs filled with admiration for the "runaway slave," and would be rebuked by hearing the old ones grumble out, "You'd better stay at home and study your lessons, and not be running after the nigger meetings."

In 1841, he was induced to accept an agency as a lecturer for the Antislavery Society, and at once became one of the most valuable of its advocates. He visited England in 1845. There he was kindly received, and heartily welcomed; and after going through the length and breadth of the land, and addressing public meetings out of number on behalf of his countrymen in chains, with a power of eloquence which captivated his auditors, and brought the cause which he pleaded home to their hearts, he returned home and commenced the publication of the *North Star*, a weekly newspaper devoted to the advocacy of the cause of freedom.

Mr. Douglass is tall and well made. His vast and fully-developed forehead shows at once that he is a superior man intellectually. He is polished in his language, and gentlemanly in his manners. His voice is full and sonorous. His attitude is dignified, and his gesticulation is full of noble simplicity. He is a man of lofty reason; natural, and without pretension; always master of himself; brilliant in the art of exposing and abstracting. Few persons can handle a subject, with which they are familiar, better than he. There is a kind of eloquence issuing from the depth of the soul as from a spring, rolling along its copious floods, sweeping all before it, overwhelming by its very force, carrying, upsetting, ingulfing its adversaries, and more dazzling and more thundering than the bolt which leaps from crag to crag. This is the eloquence of Frederick Douglass. One of the best mimics of the age, and possessing great dramatic powers, had he taken up the sock and buskin, instead of becoming a lecturer, he would have made as fine a Coriolanus as ever trod the stage.

In his splendidly conceived comparison of Mr. Douglass to S. R. Ward, written for the "Autographs for Freedom," Professor William J. Wilson says of the former, "In his very look, his gesture, his whole manner, there is so much of genuine, earnest eloquence, that they leave no time for reflection. Now you are reminded of one rushing down some fearful steep, bidding you follow; now on some delightful stream, still beckoning you onward. In either case, no matter what your prepossessions or oppositions, you, for the moment at least, forget the justness or unjustness of his cause, and obey the summons, and loath, if at all, you return to your former post. Not always, however, is he successful in retaining you. Giddy as you may be with the descent you have made, delighted as you are with the pleasure afforded, with the Elysium to which he has wafted you, you return too often dissatisfied with his and your own impetuosity and want of firmness. You feel that you had only a dream, a pastime,—not a reality.

"This great power of momentary captivation consists in his eloquence of manners, his just appreciation of words. In listening to him, your whole soul is fired, every nerve strung, every passion inflated, and every faculty you possess ready to perform at a moment's bidding. You stop not to ask why or wherefore. 'Tis a unison of mighty yet harmonious sounds that play upon your imagination; and you give yourself up, for a time, to their irresistible charm. At last, the cataract which roared around you is hushed, the tornado is passed, and you find yourself sitting upon a bank, (at whose base roll but tranquil waters,) quietly asking yourself why, amid such a display of power, no greater effect had really been produced. After all, it must be admitted there is a power in Mr. Douglass rarely to be found in any other man."

As a speaker, Frederick Douglass has had more imitators than almost any other American, save, perhaps, Wendell Phillips. Unlike most great speakers, he is a superior writer also. Some of his articles, in point of ability, will rank with any thing ever written for the American press. He has taken lessons from the best of teachers, amid the homeliest realities of life; hence the perpetual freshness of his delineations, which are never over-colored, never strained, never aiming at difficult or impossible effects, but which always read like living transcripts of experience. The following, from his pen, on "What shall be done with the slaves, if emancipated?" is characteristic of his style.

"What shall be done with the four million slaves, if they are emancipated? This question has been answered, and can be answered in many ways. Primarily, it is a question less for man than for God—less for human intellect than for the laws of nature to solve. It assumes that nature has erred; that the law of liberty is a mistake; that freedom, though a natural want of the human soul, can only be enjoyed at the expense of human welfare, and that men are better off in slavery than they would or could be in freedom; that slavery is the natural order of human relations, and that liberty is an experiment. What shall be done with them?

"Our answer is, Do nothing with them; mind your business, and let them mind theirs. Your *doing* with them is their greatest misfortune. They have been undone by your doings, and all they now ask, and really have need of at your hands, is just to let them alone. They suffer by every interference, and succeed best by being let alone. The negro should have been let alone in Africa—let alone when the

pirates and robbers offered him for sale in our Christian slave markets (more cruel and inhuman than the Mohammedan slave markets)—let alone by courts, judges, politicians, legislators, and
slave-drivers—let alone altogether, and assured that they were thus to
be let alone forever, and that they must now make their own way in
the world, just the same as any and every other variety of the human
family. As colored men, we only ask to be allowed to do with ourselves, subject only to the same great laws for the welfare of human
society which apply to other men—Jews, Gentiles, Barbarian,
Scythian. Let us stand upon our own legs, work with our own hands,
and eat bread in the sweat of our own brows. When you, our white
fellow-countrymen, have attempted to do any thing for us, it has
generally been to deprive us of some right, power, or privilege, which
you yourselves would die before you would submit to have taken
from you. When the planters of the West Indies used to attempt to
puzzle the pure-minded Wilberforce with the question, 'How shall
we get rid of slavery?' his simple answer was, 'Quit stealing.' In like
manner we answer those who are perpetually puzzling their brains
with questions as to what shall be done with the negro, 'Let him
alone, and mind your own business.' If you see him ploughing in the
open field, levelling the forest, at work with a spade, a rake, a hoe, a
pickaxe, or a bill—let him alone; he has a right to work. If you see
him on his way to school, with spelling-book, geography, and arith-
metic in his hands—let him alone. Don't shut the door in his face,
nor bolt your gates against him; he has a right to learn—let him
alone. Don't pass laws to degrade him. If he has a ballot in his hand,
and is on his way to the ballot-box to deposit his vote for the man
who, he thinks, will most justly and wisely administer the government which has the power of life and death over him, as well as others
—let him ALONE; his right of choice as much deserves respect and
protection as your own. If you see him on his way to church, exercis-
ing religious liberty in accordance with this or that religious persuasion—let him alone. Don't meddle with him, nor trouble yourselves
with any questions as to what shall be done with him.

"What shall be done with the negro, if emancipated? Deal justly
with him. He is a human being, capable of judging between good and
evil, right and wrong, liberty and slavery, and is as much a subject of
law as any other man; therefore, deal justly with him. He is, like other
men, sensible of the motives of reward and punishment. Give him
wages for his work, and let hunger pinch him if he don't work. He
knows the difference between fulness and famine, plenty and scarcity.

"But will he work?" Why should he not? He is used to it, and is not afraid of it. His hands are already hardened by toil, and he has no dreams of ever getting a living by any other means than by hard work. "But would you turn them all loose?" Certainly! We are no better than our Creator. He has turned them loose, and why should not we? "But would you let them all stay here?" Why not? What better is *here* than *there*? Will they occupy more room as freemen than as slaves? Is the presence of a black freeman less agreeable than that of a black slave? Is an object of your injustice and cruelty a more ungrateful sight than one of your justice and benevolence? You have borne the one more than two hundred years—can't you bear the other long enough to try the experiment?["]

CHARLOTTE L. FORTEN.

In the autumn of 1854, a young colored lady of seventeen summers, unable to obtain admission into the schools of her native city (Philadelphia) on account of her complexion, removed to Salem, Massachusetts, where she at once entered the Higginson Grammar School. Here she soon secured the respect and esteem of the teachers and her fellow-pupils. Near the end of the last term, the principal of the establishment invited the scholars to write a poem each, to be sung at the last day's examination, and at the same time expressing the desire that the authors should conceal their names. As might have been expected, this drew out all the poetical genius of the young aspirants. Fifty or more manuscripts were sent in, and one selected, printed on a neat sheet, and circulated through the vast audience who were present. The following is the piece:—

A PARTING HYMN.

When Winter's royal robes of white
From hill and vale are gone,
And the glad voices of the spring
Upon the air are borne,
Friends, who have met with us before,
[W]ithin these walls shall meet no more.

Forth to a noble work they go:
O, may their hearts keep pure,

And hopeful zeal and strength be theirs
To labor and endure,
That they an earnest faith may prove
By words of truth and deeds of love.

May those, whose holy task it is
To guide impulsive youth,
Fail not to cherish in their souls
A reverence for truth;
For teachings which the lips impart
Must have their source within the heart.

May all who suffer share their love—
The poor and the oppressed;
So shall the blessing of our God
Upon their labors rest.
And may we meet again where all
Are blest and freed from every thrall.

The announcement that the successful competitor would be called out at the close of the singing, created no little sensation amongst the visitors, to say nothing of the pupils.

The principal of the school, after all parties had taken their seats, mounted the platform, and said, "Ladies and gentlemen, the beautiful hymn just sung is the composition of one of the students of this school, but who the talented person is I am unaware. Will the author step forward?" A moment's silence, and every eye was turned in the direction of the principal, who, seeing no one stir, looked around with a degree of amazement. Again he repeated, "Will the author of the hymn step forward?" A movement now among the female pupils showed that the last call had been successful. The buzzing and whispering throughout the large hall indicated the intense interest felt by all. "Sit down; keep your seats," exclaimed the principal, as the crowd rose to their feet, or bent forward to catch a glimpse of the young lady, who had now reached the front of the platform. Thunders of applause greeted the announcement that the distinguished authoress then before them was Miss Charlotte L. Forten. Her finely-chiselled features, well-developed forehead, countenance beaming with intelligence, and her dark complexion, showing her identity with an oppressed and injured race, all conspired to make the scene an exciting one. The audience was made up in part of some of the most aristocratic people in one of the most aristocratic towns in America. The impression left upon their minds was great in behalf of the race thus so nobly represented by the granddaughter of the noble-hearted, brave, generous, and venerable James Forten, whose whole life was a vindication of the character of his race.

> "'Tis the mind that makes the body rich;
> And as the sun breaks through the darkest clouds,
> So honor peereth in the meanest habit."

For several days after the close of the school, the name of Charlotte L. Forten was mentioned in all the private circles of Salem; and to imitate her was the highest aspiration of the fairest daughters of that wealthy and influential city. Miss Forten afterwards entered the State Normal School, where, in the language of the *Salem Register*, "she graduated with decided eclat." She was then appointed by the school committee to be a teacher in the Epes Grammar School, where she "was graciously received," says the same journal, "by parents of the district, and soon endeared herself to the pupils under her charge." These pupils were all white. Aside from having a finished education, Miss Forten possesses genius of a high order. An excellent student and a lover of books, she has a finely-cultivated mind, well stored with incidents drawn from the classics. She evinces talent, as a writer, for both prose and poetry. The following extracts from her "Glimpses of New England," published in the *National Anti-Slavery Standard*, are characteristic of her prose. "The Old Witch House," at Salem, is thus described:—

"This street has also some interesting associations. It contains a very great attraction for all lovers of the olden time. This is an ancient, dingy, yellow frame house, known as "The Old Witch House." Our readers must know that Salem was, two hundred years ago, the headquarters of the witches. And this is the veritable old Court House where the so-called witches were tried and condemned. It is wonderful with what force this singular delusion possessed the minds, not only of the poor and ignorant, but of the wisest and gravest of the magistrates appointed by his majesty's government.

"Those were dark days for Salem. Woe to the housewife or the household over whose door latch the protecting horseshoe was not carefully placed; and far greater woe to the unlucky dame who chanced to be suspected of such fanciful freaks as riding through the air on a broomstick, or muttering mystic incantations wherewith to undo her innocent neighbors. Hers was a summary and terrible punishment.

Well, it is very pleasant to think how times have changed, and to say with Whittier,—

> 'Our witches are no longer old
> And wrinkled beldams, Satan-sold,
> But young, and gay, and laughing creatures,
> With the heart's sunshine on their features.'

["]Troops of *such* witches now pass the old house every day. I grieve to say that the 'Old Witch House' has recently been defaced and desecrated by the erection of an apothecary's shop in front of one of its wings. People say that the new shop is very handsome; but to a few of us, lovers of antiquity, it seems a profanation, and we can see no beauty in it."

The hills in the vicinity of Salem are beautifully pictured. "The pure, bracing air, the open sky," and the sheet of water in the distance, are all brought in with their lights and shades. Along with the brilliancy of style and warmth of imagination which characterize her writings, we find here and there gravity of thought and earnestness of purpose, befitting her literary taste. Of Marblehead Beach she writes,—

"The beach, which is at some distance from the town, is delightful. It was here that I first saw the sea, and stood 'entranced in silent awe,' gazing upon the waves as they marched, in one mass of the richest green, to the shore, then suddenly broke into foam, white and beautiful as the winter snow. I remember one pleasant afternoon which I spent with a friend, gathering shells and seaweed on the beach, or sitting on the rocks, listening, to the wild music of the waves, and watching the clouds of spray as they sprang high up in the air, then fell again in snowy wreaths at our feet. We lingered there until the sun had sunk into his ocean bed. On our homeward walk we passed Forest River, a winding, picturesque little stream, dotted with rocky islands. Over the river, and along our quiet way, the moon shed her soft and silvery light. And as we approached Salem, the lights, gleaming from every window of the large factory, gave us a cheerful welcome."

She "looks on nature with a poet's eye." The visit to Lynn is thus given:—

"Its chief attraction to me was 'High Rock,' on whose summit the pretty little dwelling of the Hutchinsons is perched like an eagle's eyrie. In the distance this rock looks so high and steep that one marvels how a house could ever have been built upon it. At its foot there once lived a famous fortune-teller of the olden time—'Moll Pitcher.' She at first resided in Salem, but afterwards removed to Lynn, where her fame spread over the adjoining country far and near. Whittier has made her the subject of a poem, which every one should read, not only for its account of the fortune-teller, but for its beautiful descriptions of the scenery around Lynn, especially of the bold Promontory of Nahant, whose fine beach, invigorating sea air, and, more than all, its grand, rugged old rocks,—the grandest I have ever seen,—washed by the waves of old Ocean, make it the most delightful of summer resorts."

The gifts of nature are of no rank or color; they come unbidden and unsought: as the wind awakes the chords of the Æolian harp, so the spirit breathes upon the soul, and brings to life all the melody of its being. The following poem recalls to recollection some of the beautiful yet solemn strains of Miss Landon, the gifted "L. E. L.," whose untimely death at Cape Coast Castle, some years since, carried sorrow to so many English hearts:—

THE ANGEL'S VISIT.

'Twas on a glorious summer eve,—
A lovely eve in June,—
Serenely from her home above
Looked down the gentle moon;
And lovingly she smiled on me,
And softly soothed the pain—
The aching, heavy pain that lay
Upon my heart and brain.

And gently 'mid the murmuring leaves,
Scarce by its light wings stirred,
Like spirit voices soft and clear,
The night wind's song was heard;
In strains of music sweet and low
It sang to me of peace;
It bade my weary, troubled soul
Her sad complainings cease.

For bitter thoughts had filled my breast,
And sad, and sick at heart,
I longed to lay me down and rest,

From all the world apart.
"Outcast, oppressed on earth," I cried,
"O Father, take me home;
O take me to that peaceful land
Beyond the moon-lit dome.

"On such a night as this," methought,
"Angelic forms are near;
In beauty unrevealed to us
They hover in the air.
O mother, loved and lost," I cried,
"Methinks thou'rt near me now;
Methinks I feel thy cooling touch
Upon my burning brow.

"O, guide and soothe thy sorrowing child;
And if 'tis not His will
That thou shouldst take me home with thee,
Protect and bless me still;
For dark and drear had been my life
Without thy tender smile,
Without a mother's loving care,
Each sorrow to beguile."

I ceased: then o'er my senses stole
A soothing, dreamy spell,
And gently to my ear were borne
The tones I loved so well;
A sudden flood of rosy light
Filled all the dusky wood,
And, clad in shining robes of white,
My angel mother stood.

She gently drew me to her side,
She pressed her lips to mine,
And softly said, "Grieve not, my child;
A mother's love is thine.
I know the cruel wrongs that crush
The young and ardent heart;
But falter not; keep bravely on,
And nobly bear thy part.

351

"For thee a brighter day's in store;
And every earnest soul
That presses on, with purpose high,
Shall gain the wished-for goal.
And thou, beloved, faint not beneath
The weary weight of care;
Daily before our Father's throne
I breathe for thee a prayer.

"I pray that pure and holy thoughts
May bless and guard thy way;
A noble and unselfish life
For thee, my child, I pray."
She paused, and fondly bent on me
One lingering look of love,
Then softly said,—and passed away,—
"Farewell! we'll meet above."

I woke, and still the silver moon
In quiet beauty shone;
And still I heard amid the leaves
The night wind's murmuring tone;
But from my heart the weary pain
Forevermore had flown;
I knew a mother's prayer for me
Was breathed before the throne.

Nothing can be more touching than Miss Forten's [a]llusion to her sainted mother. In some of her other poems she is more light and airy, and her muse delights occasionally to catch the sunshine on its aspiring wings. Miss Forten is still young, yet on the sunny side of twenty-five, and has a splendid future before her. Those who know her best consider her on the road to fame. Were she white, America would recognize her as one of its brightest gems.

From *The Rising Son; or, The Antecedents and Advancement of the Colored Race*

Boston: A. G. Brown, 1874

PREFACE.

After availing himself of all the reliable information obtainable, the author is compelled to acknowledge the scantiness of materials for a history of the African race. He has throughout endeavored to give a faithful account of the people and their customs, without concealing their faults.

Several of the biographical sketches are necessarily brief, owing to the difficulty in getting correct information in regard to the subjects treated upon. Some have been omitted on account of the same cause.

WM. WELLS BROWN.

Cambridgeport, Mass.

CHAPTER I.
THE ETHIOPIANS AND EGYPTIANS.

The origin of the African race has provoked more criticism than any other of the various races of man on the globe. Speculation has exhausted itself in trying to account for the Negro's color, features, and hair, that distinguish him in such a marked manner from the rest of the human family.

All reliable history, and all the facts which I have been able to gather upon this subject, show that the African race descended from the country of the Nile, and principally from Ethiopia.

353

The early history of Ethiopia is involved in great obscurity. When invaded by the Egyptians, it was found to contain a large population, consisting of savages, hunting and fishing tribes wandering herdsmen, shepherds, and lastly, a civilized class, dwelling in houses and in large cities, possessing a government and laws, acquainted with the use of hieroglyphics, the fame of whose progress in knowledge and the social arts had, in the remotest ages, spread over a considerable portion of the earth. Even at that early period, when all the nations were in their rude and savage state, Ethiopia was full of historical monuments, erected chiefly on the banks of the Nile.

The earliest reliable information we have of Ethiopia, is (B. C. 971) when the rulers of that country assisted Shishank in his war against Judea, "with very many chariots and horsemen." Sixteen years later, we have an account of Judea being again invaded by an army of a million Ethiopians, unaccompanied by any Egyptian force.[2] The Ethiopian power gradually increased until its monarchs were enabled to conquer Egypt, where three of them reigned in succession, Sabbackon, Sevechus, and Tarakus, the Tirhakah of Scripture.[3]

Sevechus, called so in Scripture, was so powerful a monarch that Hoshed, king of Israel, revolted against the Assyrians, relying on his assistance,[4] but was not supported by his ally. This indeed, was the immediate cause of the captivity of the Ten Tribes; for "in the ninth year of Hoshed the king, the king of Assyria took Samaria, and carried Israel away into Assyria," as a punishment for unsuccessful rebellion.

Tirhakah was a more war-like prince; he led an army against Sennacherib,[5] king of Assyria, then besieging Jerusalem; and the Egyptian traditions, preserved in the age of Herodotus, give an accurate account of the providential interposition by which the pride of the Assyrians was humbled.

It is said that the kings of Ethiopia were always elected from the priestly caste; and there was a strange custom for the electors, when weary of their sovereign, to send him a courier with orders to die. Ergamenes was the first monarch who ventured to resist this absurd custom; he lived in the reign of the second Ptolemy, and was instructed in Grecian philosophy. So far from yielding, he marched against the fortress of the priests, massacred most of them, and instituted a new religion.

Queens frequently ruled in Ethiopia; one named Candace made war on Augustus Cæsar, about twenty years before the birth of Christ, and though not successful, obtained peace on very favorable conditions.

The pyramids of Ethiopia, though inferior in size to those in Egypt, are said to surpass them in architectural beauty, and the sepulchers evince the greatest purity of taste.

But the most important and striking proof of the progress of the Ethiopians in the art of building, is their knowledge and employment of the arch. Hoskins has stated that their pyramids are of superior antiquity to those of Egypt. The Ethiopian vases depicted on the monuments, though not richly ornamented, display a taste and elegance of form that has never been surpassed. In sculpture and coloring, the edifices of Ethiopia, though not so profusely adorned, rival the choicest specimens of Egyptian art.

Meroe was the *entrepot* of trade between the North and the South, between the East and the West, while its fertile soil enabled the Ethiopians to purchase foreign luxuries with native productions. It does not appear that fabrics were woven in Ethiopia so extensively as in Egypt; but the manufacture of metal must have been at least as flourishing.

But Ethiopia owed its greatness less to the produce of its soil or its factories than to its position on the intersection of the leading caravan routes of ancient commerce.

The Ethiopians were among the first nations that organized a regular army, and thus laid the foundation for the whole system of ancient warfare. A brief account of their military affairs will therefore illustrate not only their history, but that of the great Asiatic monarchies, and of the Greeks during the heroic ages. The most important division of an Ethiopian army was the body of war-chariots, used instead of cavalry. These chariots were mounted on two wheels and made low; open behind, so that the warrior could easily step in and out; and without a seat.

They were drawn by two horses and generally contained two warriors, one of whom managed the steeds while the other fought. Nations were distinguished from each other by the shape and color of their chariots.

Great care was taken in the manufacturing of the chariots and also of the breeding of horses to draw them. Nothing in our time can equal the attention paid by the ancients in the training of horses for the battle-field.

The harness which these animals wore was richly decorated; and a quiver and bow-case, decorated with extraordinary taste and skill, were securely fixed to the side of each chariot. The bow was the national weapon, employed by both cavalry and infantry. No nation of antiquity paid more attention to archery than the Ethiopians; their arrows better aimed than those of any other nation, the Egyptians perhaps excepted. The children of the warrior caste were trained from early infancy to the practice of archery.

The arms of the Ethiopians were a spear, a dagger, a short sword, a helmet, and a shield. Pole-axes and battle-axes were occasionally used. Coats of mail were used only by the principal officers, and some remarkable warriors, like Goliath, the champion of the Philistines. The light troops were armed with swords, battle-axes, maces, and clubs. Some idea of the manly forms, great strength, and military training of the Ethiopians, may be gathered from Herodotus, the father of ancient history.

After describing Arabia as "a land exhaling the most delicious fragrance," he says,—"Ethiopia, which is the extremity of the habitable world, is contiguous to this country on the south-west. Its inhabitants are very remarkable for their size, beauty, and their length of life."[6]

In his third book he has a detailed description of a single tribe of this interesting people, called the Macrobian, or long-lived Ethiopians. Cambyses, the Persian king, has made war upon Egypt, and subdued it. He is then seized with an ambition of extending his conquests still farther, and resolves to make war upon the Ethiopians. But before undertaking his expedition, he sends spies into the country disguised as friendly ambassadors, who carry costly presents from Cambyses. They arrive at the court of the Ethiopian prince, "a man superior to all others in the perfection of size and beauty," who sees through their disguise, and takes down a bow of such enormous size that no Persian could bend it. "Give your king this bow, and in my name speak him thus:—

"'The king of Ethiopia sends this counsel to the king of Persia. When his subjects shall be able to bend this bow with the same ease that I do, then let him venture to attack the long-lived Ethiopians. Meanwhile, let him be thankful to the gods, that the Ethiopians have not been inspired with the same love of conquests as himself.'"[7]

Homer wrote at least eight hundred years before Christ, and his poems are well ascertained to be a most faithful mirror of the manners and customs of his times, and the knowledge of his age.

In the first book of the Iliad, Achilles is represented as imploring his goddess-mother to intercede with Jove in behalf of her aggrieved son. She grants his request, but tells him the intercession must be delayed for twelve days. The gods are absent. They have gone to the distant climes of Ethiopia to join in its festal rites. "Yesterday Jupiter went to the feast with the *blameless* Ethiopians, away upon the limits of the ocean, and all the gods followed together."[8] Homer never wastes an epithet. He often alludes to the Ethiopians elsewhere, and always in terms of admiration and praise, as being the most just of men; the favorite of the gods.[9]

The same allusion glimmers through the Greek mythology, and appears in the verses of almost all the Greek poets ere the countries of Italy and Sicily were even discovered. The Jewish Scripture and Jewish literature abound in allusion to this distinct and mysterious people; the annals of the

Egyptian priests are full of them, uniformly the Ethiopians are there lauded as among the best, most religious, and most civilized of men.[10]

Let us pause here one moment, and follow the march of civilization into Europe. Wherever its light has once burned clearly, it has been diffused, but not extinguished. Every one knows that Rome got her civilization from Greece; that Greece again borrowed hers from Egypt, that thence she derived her earliest science and the forms of her beautiful mythology.

The mythology of Homer is evidently hieroglyphical in its origin, and has strong marks of family resemblance to the symbolical worship of Egypt.

It descended the Nile; it spread over the delta of that river, as it came down from Thebes, the wonderful city of a hundred gates. Thebes, as every scholar knows, is more ancient than the cities of the delta. The ruins of the colossal architecture are covered over with hieroglyphics, and strewn with the monuments of Egyptian mythology. But whence came Thebes? It was built and settled by colonies from Ethiopia, or from cities which were themselves the settlements of that nation. The higher we ascend the Nile, the more ancient are the ruins on which we tread, till we come to the "hoary Meroe," which Egypt acknowledged to be the cradle of her institutions.

But Meroe was the queenly city of Ethiopia, into which all Africa poured its caravans laden with ivory, frankincense, and gold. So it is that we trace the light of Ethiopian civilizations first into Egypt, thence into Greece, and Rome, whence, gathering new splendor on its way, it hath been diffusing itself all the world over.[11]

We now come to a consideration of the color of the Ethiopians, that distinguish their descendants of the present time in such a marked manner from the rest of the human race.

Adam, the father of the human family, took his name from the color of the earth from which he was made.[12]

The Bible says but little with regard to the color of the various races of man, and absolutely nothing as to the time when or the reasons why these varieties were introduced. There are a few passages in which color is descriptive of the person or the dress. Job said, "My skin is black upon me." Job had been sick for a long time, and no doubt this brought about a change in his complexion. In Lamentations, it is said, "Their visage is blacker than a coal;" also, "Our skin was blacker than an oven." Both of these writers, in all probability, had reference to the change of color produced by the famine. Another writer says, "I am black, but comely." This may have been a shepherd, and lying much in the sun might have caused the change.

However, we now have the testimony of one whom we clearly understand, and which is of the utmost importance in settling this question. Jeremiah asks, "Can the Ethiopian change his skin, or the leopard his spots?" This refers to a people whose color is peculiar, fixed, and unalterable. Indeed, Jeremiah seems to have been as well satisfied that the Ethiopian was colored, as he was that the leopard had spots; and that the one was as indelible as the other. The German translation of Luther has "Negro-land," for Ethiopia, *i. e.*, the country of the blacks.

All reliable history favors the belief that the Ethiopians descended from Cush, the eldest son of Ham, who settled first in Shina in Asia. Eusebius informs us that a colony of Asiatic Cushites settled in that part of Africa which has since been known as Ethiopia proper. Josephus asserts that these Ethiopians were descended from Cush, and that in his time they were still called Cushites by themselves and by the inhabitants of Asia. Homer divides the Ethiopians into two parts, and Strabo, the geographer, asserts that the dividing line to which he alluded was the Red Sea. The Cushites emigrated in part to the west of the Red Sea; these, remaining unmixed with other races, engrossed the general name of Cushite, or Ethiopian, while Asiatic Cushites became largely mingled with other nations, and are nearly or quite absorbed, or, as a distinct people well-nigh extinct. Hence, from the allusion of Jeremiah to the skin of the Ethiopian, confirmed and explained by such authorities as Homer, Strabo, Herodotus, Josephus, and Eusebius, we conclude that the Ethiopians were an African branch of the Cushites who settled first in Asia. Ethiop, in the Greek, means "sunburn," and there is not the slightest doubt but that these people, in and around Meroe, took their color from the climate. This theory does not at all conflict with that of the common origin of man. Although the descendants of Cush were black, it does not follow that all the offspring of Ham were dark-skinned; but only those who settled in a climate that altered their color.

The word of God by his servant Paul has settled forever the question of the equal origin of the human races, and it will stand good against all scientific research. "God hath made of one blood all the nations of men for to dwell on all the face of the earth."

The Ethiopians are not constitutionally different from the rest of the human family, and therefore, we must insist upon *unity*, although we see and admit the variety.

Some writers have endeavored to account for this difference of color, by connecting it with the curse pronounced upon Cain. This theory, however, has no foundation; for if Cain was the progenitor of Noah, and if Cain's new peculiarities were perpetuated, then, as Noah was the father of the world's new population, the question would be, not how to account for any of the human family being black, but how can we account for any being white? All this speculation as to the change of Cain's color, as a theory for accounting for the variety peculiar to Cush and the Ethiopians, falls to the ground when we trace back the genealogy of Noah, and find that he descended not from Cain, but from Seth.

Of course Cain's descendants, no matter what their color, became extinct at the flood. No miracle was needed in Ethiopia to bring about a change in the color of its inhabitants. The very fact that the nation derived its name from the climate should be enough to satisfy the most skeptical. What was true of the Ethiopians was also true of the Egyptians, with regard to color; for Herodotus tells us that the latter were colored and had curled hair.

The vast increase of the population of Ethiopia, and a wish of its rulers to possess more territory, induced them to send expeditions down the Nile, and towards the shores of the Mediterranean Sea. Some of these adventurers, as early as B. C. 885, took up their abode on the Mediterranean coast, and founded the place which in later years became the great city of Carthage. Necho, king of Egypt, a man distinguished for his spirit of enterprise, sent an expedition (B. C. 616) around the African coast. He employed Phoenecian navigators. This fleet sailed down the Red Sea, passed the straits of Balel-Mandeb, and, coasting the African continent, discovered the passage around the Cape of Good Hope, two thousand years before its re-discovery by Dias and Vasco de Gama. This expedition was three years in its researches, and while gone, got out of food, landed, planted corn, and waited for the crop. After harvesting the grain, they proceeded on their voyage. The fleet returned to Egypt through the Atlantic Ocean, the straits of Gibralter, and the Mediterranean.

The glowing accounts brought back by the returned navigators of the abundance of fruits, vegetables, and the splendor of the climate of the new country, kindled the fire of adventurous enthusiasm in the Ethiopians, and they soon followed the example set them by the Egyptians. Henceforward, streams of emigrants were passing over the Isthmus of Suez, that high road to Africa, who became permanent residents of the promised land.

CHAPTER IV.
CAUSES OF COLOR.

The various colors seen in the natives in Africa, where amalgamation with other races is impossible, has drawn forth much criticism, and puzzled the ethnologist not a little. Yet nothing is more easily accounted for than this difference of color amongst the same people, and even under the same circumstances. Climate, and climate alone, is the sole cause.

And now to the proof. Instances are adduced, in which individuals, transplanted into another climate than that of their birth, are said to have retained their peculiarities of form and color unaltered, and to have transmitted the same to their posterity for generations. But cases of this kind, though often substantiated to a certain extent, appear to have been much exaggerated, both as to the duration of time ascribed, and the absence of any change. It is highly probable, that the original characteristics will be found undergoing gradual modifications, which tend to assimilate them to those of the new country and situation.

The Jews, however slightly their features may have assimilated to those of other nations amongst whom they are scattered, from the causes already stated, certainly form a very striking example as regards the uncertainty of perpetuity in color.

Descended from one stock, and prohibited by the most sacred institutions from intermarrying with the people of other nations, and yet dispersed, according to the divine prediction, into every country on the globe, this one people is marked with the colors of all; fair in Briton and Germany; brown in France and in Turkey; swarthy in Portugal and Spain; olive in Syria and Chaldea; tawny or copper-colored in Arabia and in Egypt;[13] whilst they are "black at Congo, in Africa."[14]

Let us survey the gradations of color on the continent of Africa itself. The inhabitants of the north are whitest; and as we advance southwards towards the line, and those countries in which the sun's rays fall more perpendicularly, the complexion gradually assumes a darker shade. And the same men, whose color has been rendered black by the powerful influence of the sun, if they remove to the north, gradually become whiter (I mean their posterity), and eventually lose their dark color.[15]

The Portuguese who planted themselves on the coast of Africa a few centuries ago, have been succeeded by descendants blacker than many Africans.[16] On the coast of Malabar there are two colonies of Jews, the old colony and the new, separated by color, and known as the "black Jews," and the "white Jews." The old colony are the black Jews, and have been longer subjected to the influence of the climate. The hair of the black Jews are curly, showing a resemblance to the Negro. The white Jews are as dark as the Gipsies, and each generation growing darker.

Dr. Livingstone says,— "I was struck with the appearance of the people in Londa, and the neighborhood; they seemed more slender in form, and their color a lighter olive, than any we had hitherto met."[17]

Lower down the Zambesi, the same writer says: "Most of the men are muscular, and have large, ploughman hands. Their color is the same admixture from very dark to light olive, that we saw at Londa."[18]

In the year 1840, the writer was at Havana, and saw on board a vessel just arrived from Africa some five hundred slaves, captured in different parts of the country. Among these captives were colors varying from light brown to black, and their features represented the finest Anglo-Saxon and the most degraded African.

There is a nation called Tuaricks, who inhabit the oases and southern borders of the great desert, whose occupation is commerce, and whose caravans ply between the Negro countries and Fezzan. They are described by the travellers Hornemann and Lyon.

The western tribes of this nation are white, so far as the climate and their habits will allow. Others are of the yellow cast; others again, are swarthy; and in the neighborhood of Soudan, there is said to be a tribe completely black. All speak the same dialect, and it is a dialect of the original African tongue. There is no reasonable doubt of their being aboriginal.

Lyon says they are the finest race of men he ever saw, "tall, straight, and handsome, with a certain air of independence and pride, which is very imposing."[19] If we observe the gradations of color in different localities in the meridian numbers under which we live, we shall perceive a very close relation to the heat of the sun in each respectively. Under the equator we have the deep black of the Negro, then the copper or olive of the Moors of Northern Africa; then the Spaniard and Italian, swarthy, compared with other Europeans, the French, still darker than the English, while the fair and florid complexion of England and Germany passes more northerly into the bleached Scandinavian white.[20]

It is well-known, that in whatever region travellers ascend mountains, they find the vegetation at every successive level altering its character, and gradually assuming the appearances presented in more Northern countries; thus indicating that the atmosphere, temperature, and physical agencies in general, assimilate, as we approach Alpine regions, to the peculiarities locally connected with high latitudes.

If, therefore, complexion and other bodily qualities belonging to races of men, depend upon climate and external conditions, we should expect to find them varying in reference to elevation of surface; and if they should be found actually to undergo such variations, this will be a strong argument that these external characteristics do, in fact, depend upon local conditions.

Now, if we inquire respecting the physical characters of the tribes inhabiting high tracts in warm countries, we shall find that they coincide with those which prevail in the level or low parts of more northern tracts.

The Swiss, in the high mountains above the plains of Lombardy, have sandy or brown hair. What a contrast presents itself to the traveller who descends into the Milanese territory, where the peasants have black hair and eyes, with strongly marked Italian, and almost Oriental features.

In the higher part of Biscayan country, instead of the swarthy complexion and black hair of the Castilians, the natives have a fair complexion, with light blue eyes, and flaxen, or auburn hair.[21]

In the intertropical region, high elevations of surface, as they produce a cooler climate, occasion the appearance of light complexions. In the higher parts of Senegambia, which front the Atlantic, and are cooled by winds from the Western Ocean, where, in fact, the temperature is known to be moderate, and even cool at times, the light copper-colored Fulahs are found surrounded on every side by black Negro nations inhabiting lower districts; and nearly in the same parallel, but on the opposite coast of Africa, are the high plains of Enared and Kaffa, where the inhabitants are said to be fairer than the inhabitants of Southern Europe.[22]

Do we need any better evidence of the influence of climate on man, than to witness its effect on beasts and birds? Aeolian informs us that the Eubaea was famous for producing white oxen.[23] Blumenbach remarks, that "all the swine of Piedmont are black, those of Normandy white, and those of Bavaria are of a reddish brown. The turkeys of Normandy," he states, "are all black; those of Hanover almost all white. In Guinea, the dogs and the gallinaceous fowls are as black as the human inhabitants of the same country."[24]

The lack of color, in the northern regions, of many animals which possess color in more temperate latitudes,—as the bear, the fox, the hare, beasts of burden, the falcon, crow, jackdaw, and chaffinch,—seems to arise entirely from climate. The common bear is differently colored in different regions. The dog loses its coat entirely in Africa, and has a smooth skin.

We all see and admit the change which a few years produces in the complexion of a Caucasian going from our northern latitude into the tropics.

CHAPTER V.
CAUSES OF THE DIFFERENCE IN FEATURES.

We now come to a consideration of the difference in the features of the human family, and especially the great variety to be seen in the African race. From the grim worshippers of Odin in the woods of Germany, down to the present day, all uncivilized nations or tribes have more or less been addicted to the barbarous custom of disfiguring their persons.

Thus, among the North American Indians, the tribe known as the "flat heads," usually put their children's heads to press when but a few days old; and consequently, their name fitly represents their personal appearance. While exploring the valley of the Zambesi, Dr. Livingstone met with several tribes whose mode of life will well illustrate this point. He says:—

"The women here are in the habit of piercing the upper lip and gradually enlarging the orifice until they can insert a shell. The lip then appears drawn out beyond the perpendicular of the nose, and gives them a most ungainly aspect. Sekwebu remarked,—'These women want to make their mouths like those of ducks.' And indeed, it does appear as if they had the idea that female beauty of lip had been attained by the *Ornithorhynchus paradoxus* alone. This custom prevails throughout the country of the Maravi, and no one could see it without confessing that fashion had never led women to a freak more mad." [25]

There is a tribe near the coast of Guinea, who consider a flat nose the paragon of beauty; and at early infancy, the child's nose is put in press, that it may not appear ugly when it arrives to years of maturity.

Many of the tribes in the interior of Africa mark the face, arms, and breasts; these in some instances, are considered national identifications. Knocking out the teeth is a common practice, as will be seen by reference to Dr. Livingstone's travels. Living upon roots, as many of the more degraded tribes do, has its influence in moulding the features.

There is a decided coincidence between the physical characteristics of the varieties of man, and their moral and social condition; and it also appears that their condition in civilized society produces marked modification in the intellectual qualities of the race. Religious superstition and the worship of idols have done much towards changing the features of the Negro from the original Ethiopian of Meroe, to the present inhabitants of the shores of the Zambesi.

The farther the human mind strays from the ever-living God as a spirit, the nearer it approximates to the beasts; and as the mental controls the physical, so ignorance and brutality are depicted upon the countenance.

As the African by his fall has lost these qualities that adorn the visage of man, so the Anglo-Saxon, by his rise in the scale of humanity, has improved his features, enlarged his brain, and brightened in intellect.

Let us see how far history will bear us out in this assertion. We all acknowledge the Anglo-Saxon to be the highest type of civilization. But from whence sprang this refined, proud, haughty, and intellectual race? Go back a few centuries, and we find their ancestors described in the graphic touches of Cæsar and Tacitus. See them in the gloomy forests of Germany, sacrificing to their grim and gory idols; drinking the warm blood of their prisoners, quaffing libations from human skulls; infesting the shores of the Baltic for plunder and robbery; bringing home the reeking scalps of enemies as an offering to their king.

Macaulay says:—"When the Britons first became known to the Tyrian mariners, they were little superior to the Sandwich Islanders.

Hume says:—"The Britons were a rude and barbarous people, divided into numerous clans, dressed in the skins of wild beasts: druidism was their religion, and they were very superstitious." Cæsar writing home, said of the Britons,—"They are the most degraded people I ever conquered." Cicero advised his friend Atticus not to purchase slaves from Briton, "because," said he, "they cannot be taught music, and are the ugliest people I ever saw."

An illustration of the influence of circumstances upon the physical appearance of man may be found still nearer our own time. In the Irish rebellion in 1641, and 1689, great multitudes of the native Irish were driven from Armagh and the South down into the mountainous tract extending from the Barony of Flews eastward to the sea; on the other side of the kingdom the same race were expelled into Litrin, Sligo, and Mayo. Here they have been almost ever since, exposed to the worst effects of hunger and ignorance, the two great brutalizers of the human race.

The descendants of these exiles are now distinguished physically, from their kindred in Meath, and other districts, where they are not in a state of personal debasement. These people are remarkable for open, projecting mouths, prominent teeth, and exposed gums; their advancing cheek-bones and depressed noses carry barbarism on their very front.

In Sligo and northern Mayo, the consequences of two centuries of degradation and hardship exhibit themselves in the whole physical condition of the people, affecting not only the features, but the frame and giving such an example of human degradation as to make it revolting.

They are only five feet two inches, upon an average, bow-legged, bandy-shanked, abortively-featured; the apparitions of Irish ugliness and Irish want.[26]

Slavery is, after all, the great demoralizer of the human race. In addition to the marks of barbarism left upon the features of the African, he has the indelible imprint of the task-master. Want of food, clothing, medical attention when sick, over-work, under the control of drunken and heartless drivers, the hand-cuffs and Negro whip, together with the other paraphernalia of the slave-code, has done much to distinguish the blacks from the rest of the human family. It must also be remembered that in Africa, the people, whether living in houses or in the open air, are oppressed with a hot climate, which causes them to sleep, more or less, with their mouths open. This fact alone is enough to account for the large, wide mouth and flat nose; common sense teaching us that with the open mouth, the features must fall.

As to the hair, which has also puzzled some scientific men, it is easily accounted for. It is well-known that heat is the great crisper of the hair, whether it be on men's heads or on the backs of animals. I remember well, when a boy, to have witnessed with considerable interest the preparations made on great occasions by the women, with regard to their hair.

The curls which had been carefully laid away for months, were taken out of the drawer, combed, oiled, rolled over the prepared paper, and put in the gently-heated stove, there to remain until the wonted curl should be gained. When removed from the stove, taken off the paper rolls, and shaken out, the hair was fit to adorn the head of any lady in the land.

Now, the African's hair has been under the influence for many centuries, of the intense heat of his native clime, and in each generation is still more curly, till we find as many grades of hair as we do of color, from the straight silken strands of the Malay, to the wool of the Guinea Negro. Custom, air, food, and the general habits of the people, spread over the great area of the African continent, aid much in producing the varieties of hair often met in the descendants of the country of the Nile.

In the recent reports of Dr. Livingstone, he describes the physical appearance of a tribe which he met, and which goes to substantiate what has already been said with regard to the descent of the Africans from the region of the Nile. He says:—

"I happened to be present when all the head men of the great chief Msama who lives west of the south end of Tanganayika, had come together to make peace with certain Arabs who had burned their chief town, and I am certain one would not see more finely-formed, intellectual heads in any assembly in London or Paris, and the faces and forms corresponded with the finely-shaped heads. Msama himself had been a sort of Napoleon for fighting and conquering in his younger days.

"Many of the women are very pretty, and, like all ladies, would be much prettier if they would only let themselves alone. Fortunately, the dears cannot change their darling black eyes, beautiful foreheads, nicely-rounded limbs, well-shaped forms, and small hands and feet; but they must adorn themselves, and this they will do by filing their splendid teeth to points like cats' teeth. These specimens of the fair sex make shift by adorning their fine, warm brown skins, and tattooing various pretty devices without colors. They are not black, but of a light warm brown color.

"The Cazembe's queen would be esteemed a real beauty, either in London, Paris, or New York; and yet she had a small hole through the cartilage, near the tip of her fine aquiline nose. But she had only filed one side of two of the front swan-white teeth, and then what a laugh she had! Large sections of the country northwest of Cazembe, but still in the same inland region, are peopled with men very much like those of Msama and Cazembe."

CHAPTER VI.
CIVIL AND RELIGIOUS CEREMONIES.

While paganism is embraced by the larger portion of the African races, it is by no means the religion of the land. Missionaries representing nearly every phase of religious belief have made their appearance in the country, and gained more or less converts. Mohammedanism, however, has taken by far the greatest hold upon the people.

Whatever may be said of the followers of Mohammed in other countries, it may truly be averred that the African has been greatly benefited by this religion.

Recent discussions and investigations have brought the subject of Mohammedanism prominently before the reading public, and the writings of Weil, and Nodeke, and Muir, and Sprenger, and Emanuel Deutsch, have taught the world that "Mohammedanism is a thing of vitality, fraught with a thousand fruitful germs;" and have amply illustrated the principal enunciated by St. Augustine, showing that there are elements both of truth and goodness in a system which has had so wide-spread an influence upon mankind, embracing within the scope of its operations more than one hundred millions of the human race; that the exhibition of the germs of truth, even though "suspended in a gallery of counterfeits," has vast power over the human heart.

Whatever may be the intellectual inferiority of the Negro tribes (if, indeed, such inferiority exist), it is certain that many of these tribes have received the religion of Islam without its being forced upon them by the overpowering arms of victorious invaders. The quiet development and organization of a religious community in the heart of Africa has shown that Negroes, equally with other races, are susceptible of moral and spiritual impressions, and of all the sublime possibilities of religion.

The history of the progress of Islam in the country would present the same instances of real and eager mental conflict of minds in honest transition, of careful comparison and reflection, that have been found in other communities where new aspects of truth and fresh considerations have been brought before them. And we hold that it shows a stronger and more healthy intellectual tendency to be induced by the persuasion and reason of a man of moral nobleness and deep personal convictions to join with him in the introduction of beneficial changes, than to be compelled to follow the lead of an irresponsible character, who forces us into measures by his superior physical might.

Mungo Park, in his travels seventy years ago, everywhere remarked the contrast between the pagan and Mohammedan tribes of interior Africa. One very important improvement noticed by him was abstinence from intoxicating drinks.

"The beverage of the pagan Negroes," he says, "is beer and mead, of which they often drink to excess; the Mohammedan converts drink nothing but water."

Thus, throughout Central Africa there has been established a vast total abstinence society; and such is the influence of this society that where there are Moslem inhabitants, even in pagan towns, it is a very rare thing to see a person intoxicated. They thus present an almost impenetrable barrier to the desolating flood of ardent spirits with which the traders from Europe and America inundate the coast at Caboon.

Wherever the Moslem is found on the coast, whether Jalof, Fulah, or Mandingo, he looks upon himself as a separate and distinct being from his pagan neighbor, and immeasurably his superior in intellectual and moral respects. He regards himself as one to whom a revelation has been "sent down" from Heaven. He holds constant intercourse with the "Lord of worlds," whose servant he is. In his behalf Omnipotence will ever interpose in times of danger. Hence he feels that he cannot indulge in the frivolities and vices which he considers as by no means incompatible with the character and professions of the Kafir, or unbeliever.

There are no caste distinctions among them. They do not look upon the privileges of Islam as confined by tribal barriers or limitations. On the contrary, the life of their religion is aggressiveness. They are constantly making proselytes. As early as the commencement of the present century, the elastic and expansive character of their system was sufficiently marked to attract the notice of Mr. Park.

"In the Negro country," observes that celebrated traveller, "the Mohammedan religion has made, and continues to make, considerable progress." "The yearning of the native African," says Professor Crummell, "for a higher religion, is illustrated by the singular fact that Mohammedanism is rapidly and peaceably spreading all through the tribes of Western Africa, even to the Christian settlements of Liberia."

From Senegal to Lagos, over two thousand miles, there is scarcely an important town on the seaboard where there is not at least one mosque, and active representatives of Islam often side by side with the Christian teachers. And as soon as a pagan, however obscure or degraded, embraces the Moslem faith, he is at once admitted as an equal to their society. Slavery and slave-trade are laudable institutions, provided the slaves are Kafirs. The slave who embraces Islamism is free, and no office is closed against him on account of servile blood.[27]

Passing over into the southern part, we find the people in a state of civilization, and yet superstitious, as indeed are the natives everywhere.

The town of Noble is a settlement of modern times, sheltering forty thousand souls, close to an ancient city of the same name, the Rome of aboriginal South Africa. The religious ceremonies performed there are of the most puerile character, and would be thought of by most equally idolatrous with those formerly held in the same spot by the descendants of Mumbo Jumbo.

On Easter Monday is celebrated the *Festa del Señor de los Temblores*, or Festival of the Lord of Earthquakes. On this day the public plaza in front of the cathedral is hung with garlands and festoons, and the belfry utters its loudest notes. The images of the saints are borne out from their shrines, covered with fresh and gaudy decorations. The Madonna of Bethlehem, San Cristoval, San Blas, and San José, are borne on in elevated state, receiving as they go the prayers of all the Maries, and Christophers, and Josephs, who respectively regard them as patrons. But the crowning honors are reserved for the miraculous Crucifix, called the Lord of Earthquakes, which is supposed to protect the city from the dreaded terrestrial shocks, the *Temblores*.

The procession winds around a prescribed route, giving opportunity for public prayers and the devotions of the multitude; the miraculous image, in a new spangled skirt, that gives it the most incongruous resemblance to an opera-dancer, is finally shut up in the church; and then the glad throng, feeling secure from earthquakes another year, dance and sing in the plaza all night long.

The Borers, a hardy, fighting, and superstitious race, have a showy time at weddings and funerals. When the appointed day for marriage has arrived, the friends of the contracting parties assemble and form a circle; into this ring the bridegroom leads his lady-love.

The woman is divested of her clothing, and stands somewhat as mother Eve did in the garden before she thought of the fig-leaf. The man then takes oil from a shell and anoints the bride from the crown of her head to the soles of her feet; at the close of this ceremony, the bridegroom breaks forth into joyful peals of laughter, in which all the company join, the musicians strike up a lively air, and the dance commences. At the close of this, the oldest woman in the party comes forward, and taking the bride by the right hand, gives her to her future husband.

Two maids standing ready with clothes, jump to the bride, and begin rubbing her off. After this, she is again dressed, and the feast commences, consisting mainly of fruits and wines.

The funeral services of the same people are not less interesting. At the death of one of their number, the body is stripped, laid out upon the ground, and the friends of the deceased assemble, forming a circle around it, and commence howling like so many demons. They then march and counter-march around, with a subdued chant. After this, they hop around first on one foot, then on the other; stopping still, they cry at the top of their voices—"She's in heaven, she's in Heaven!" Here they all fall flat upon the ground, and roll about for a few minutes, after which they simultaneously rise, throw up their hands, and run away yelling and laughing.

Among the Bechuanas, when a chief dies, his burial takes place in his cattle-yard, and all the cattle are driven for an hour over the grave, so that it may be entirely obliterated. [28] In all the Backwain's pretended dreams and visions of their God, he has always a crooked leg like the Egyptian. [29]

Musical and dancing festivities form a great part of the people's time. With some of the tribes, instrumental music had been carried to a high point of culture. Bruce gives an account of a concert, the music of which he heard at the distance of a mile or more, on a still night in October. He says: "It was the most enchanting strain I ever listened to."

It is not my purpose to attempt a detailed account of the ceremonies of the various tribes that inhabit the continent of Africa; indeed, such a thing would be impossible, even if I were inclined to do so.

CHAPTER XII.
HAYTI.

In sketching an account of the people of Hayti, and the struggles through which they were called to pass, we confess it to be a difficult task. Although the writer visited the Island thirty years ago, and has read everything of importance given by the historians, it is still no easy matter to give a true statement of the revolution which placed the colored people in possession of the Island, so conflicting are the accounts.

The beautiful island of St. Domingo, of which Hayti is a part, was pronounced by the great discoverer to be the "Paradise of God."

The splendor of its valleys, the picturesqueness of its mountains, the tropical luxuriance of its plains, and the unsurpassed salubrity of its climate, confirms the high opinion of the great Spaniard. Columbus found on the Island more than a million of people of the Caribbean race. The warlike appearance of the Spaniards caused the natives to withdraw into the interior. However, the seductive genius of Columbus soon induced the Caribbeans to return to their towns, and they extended their hospitality to the illustrious stranger.

After the great discoverer had been recalled home and left the Island, Dovadillo, his successor, began a system of unmitigated oppression towards the Caribbeans, and eventually reduced the whole of the inhabitants to slavery; and thus commenced that hateful sin in the New World. As fresh adventurers arrived in the Island, the Spanish power became more consolidated and more oppressive. The natives were made to toil in the gold-mines without compensation, and in many instances without any regard whatever to the preservation of human life; so much so, that in 1507, the number of natives had, by hunger, toil, and the sword, been reduced from a million to sixty thousand. Thus, in the short space of fifteen years, more than nine hundred thousand perished under the iron hand of slavery in the island of St. Domingo.

The Island suffered much from the loss of its original inhabitants; and the want of laborers to till the soil and to work in the mines, first suggested the idea of importing slaves from the coast of Africa. The slave-trade was soon commenced and carried on with great rapidity. Before the Africans were shipped, the name of the owner and the plantation on which they were to toil was stamped on their shoulders with a burning iron. For a number of years St. Domingo opened its markets annually to more than twenty thousand newly-imported slaves. With the advance of commerce and agriculture, opulence spread in every direction. The great tide of immigration from France and Spain, and the vast number of Africans imported every year, so increased the population that at the commencement of the French Revolution, in 1789, there were nine hundred thousand souls on the Island. Of these, seven hundred thousand were Africans, sixty thousand mixed blood, and the remainder were whites and Caribbeans. Like the involuntary servitude in our own Southern States, slavery in St. Domingo kept morality at a low stand. Owing to the amalgamation between masters and slaves, there arose the mulatto population, which eventually proved to be the worst enemies of their fathers.

Many of the planters sent their malatto sons to France to be educated. When these young men returned to the Island, they were greatly dissatisfied at the proscription which met them whenever they appeared. White enough to make them hopeful and aspiring, many of the mulattoes possessed wealth enough to make them influential. Aware, by their education, of the principles of freedom that were being advocated in Europe and the United States, they were ever on the watch to seize opportunities to better their social and political conditions. In the French part of the island alone, twenty thousand whites lived in the midst of thirty thousand free mulattoes and five hundred thousand slaves. In the Spanish portion, the odds were still greater in favor of the slaves. Thus the advantage of numbers and physical strength was on the side of the oppressed. Right is the most dangerous of weapons—woe to him who leaves it to his enemies!

The efforts of Wilberforce, Sharp, Buxton, and Clarkson, to abolish the African slave-trade, and their advocacy of the equality of the races, were well understood by the men of color. They had also learned their own strength in the Island, and that they had the sympathy of all Europe with them. The news of the oath of the Tennis Court, and the taking of the Bastile at Paris, was received with the wildest enthusiasm by the people of St. Domingo.

The announcement of these events was hailed with delight by both the white planters and the mulattoes; the former, because they hoped the revolution in the Mother Country would secure to them the independence of the colony; the latter, because they viewed it as a movement that would give them equal rights with the whites; and even the slaves regarded it as a precursor to their own emancipation. But the excitement which the outbreak at Paris had created amongst the free men of color and the slaves, at once convinced the planters that a separation from France would be the death-knell of slavery in St. Domingo.

Although emancipated by law from the dominion of individuals, the mulattoes had no rights; shut out from society by their color, deprived of religious and political privileges, they felt their degradation even more keenly than the bond slaves. The mulatto son was not allowed to dine at his father's table, kneel with him in his devotions, bear his name, inherit his property, nor even to lie in his father's graveyard. Laboring as they were under the sense of their personal social wrongs, the mulattoes tolerated, if they did not encourage, low and vindictive passions. They were haughty and disdainful to the blacks, whom they scorned, and jealous and turbulent to the whites, whom they hated and feared.

The mulattoes at once despatched one of their number to Paris, to lay before the Constitutional Assembly their claim to equal rights with the whites. Vincent Oge, their deputy, was well received at Paris by Lafayette, Brisot, Barnave, and Gregoire, and was admitted to a seat in the assembly, where he eloquently portrayed the wrongs of his race. In urging his claims, he said if equality was withheld from the mulattoes, they would appeal to force. This was seconded by Lafayette and Barnave, who said: "Perish the colonies, rather than a principle."

371

The Assembly passed a decree, granting the demands of the men of color, and Oge was made bearer of the news to his brethren. The planters armed themselves, met the young deputy on his return to the Island, and a battle ensued. The free colored men rallied around Oge, but they were defeated and taken, with their brave leader; were first tortured, and then broken alive on the wheel.

The prospect of freedom was put down for the time, but the blood of Oge and his companions bubbled silently in the hearts of the African race; they swore to avenge them.

The announcement of the death of Oge in the halls of the Assembly at Paris, created considerable excitement, and became the topic of conversation in the clubs and on the boulevards. Gregoire defended the course of the colored men and said: "If liberty was right in France, it was right in St. Domingo." He well knew that the crime for which Oge had suffered in the West Indies, had constituted the glory of Mirabeau and Lafayette at Paris, and Washington and Hancock in the United States. The planters in the Island trembled at their own oppressive acts, and terror urged them on to greater violence. The blood of Oge and his accomplices had sown everywhere despair and conspiracy. The French sent an army to St. Domingo to enforce the law.

The planters repelled with force the troops sent out by France, denying its prerogatives, and refusing the civic oath. In the midst of these thickening troubles, the planters who resided in France were invited to return, and to assist in vindicating the civil independence of the Island. Then was it that the mulattoes earnestly appealed to the slaves, and the result was appalling. The slaves awoke as from an ominous dream, and demanded their rights with sword in hand. Gaining immediate success, and finding that their liberty would not be granted by the planters, they rapidly increased in numbers; and in less than a week from its commencement, the storm had swept over the whole plain of the north, from east to west, and from the mountains to the sea. The splendid villas and rich factories yielded to the furies of the devouring flames; so that the mountains, covered with smoke and burning cinder, borne upward by the wind looked like volcanoes; and the atmosphere as if on fire, resembled a furnace.

Such were the outraged feelings of a people whose ancestors had been ruthlessly torn from their native land and sold in the shambles of St. Domingo. To terrify the blacks and convince them that they could never be free, the planters were murdering them on every hand by thousands.

The struggle in St. Domingo was watched with intense interest by the friends of the blacks, both in Paris, and London, and all appeared to look with hope to the rising up of a black chief, who should prove himself adequate to the emergency. Nor did they look in vain. In the midst of the disorder that threatened on all sides, the Negro chief made his appearance in the person of a slave named Toussaint. This man was the grandson of the King of Ardra, one of the most powerful and wealthy monarchs on the west coast of Africa. By his own energy and perseverance, Toussaint had learned to read and write, and was held in high consideration by the surrounding planters, as well as their slaves.

In personal appearance he was of middle stature, strongly-marked African features, well-developed forehead, rather straight and neat figure, sharp and bright eye, with an earnestness in conversation that seemed to charm the listener. His dignified, calm, and unaffected demeanor would cause him to be selected in any company of men as one who was born for a leader.

His private virtues were many, and he had a deep and pervading sense of religion; and in the camp carried it even as far as Oliver Cromwell. Touissant was born on the Island, and was fifty years of age when called into the field. One of his chief characteristics was his humanity.

Before taking any part in the revolution, he aided his master's family to escape from the impending danger. After seeing them beyond the reach of the revolutionary movement, he entered the army as an inferior officer, but was soon made aid-de-camp to General Bissou. Disorder and bloodshed reigned through the Island, and every day brought fresh intelligence of depredations committed by whites, mulattoes, and blacks.

Hitherto, the blacks had been guided by Jean-François, Bissou, and Jeannot. The first of these was a slave, a young Creole of good exterior; he had long before the revolution obtained his liberty. At the commencement of the difficulties, he fled to the mountains and joined the Maroons, a large clan of fugitive slaves then wandering about in the woods and mountains, that furnished this class a secure retreat. This man was mild, vain, good-tempered, and fond of luxury.

Bissou belonged to the religious body designated "The Fathers of Charity." He was fiery, wrathful, rash, and vindictive; always in action, always on horseback, with a white sash, and feathers in his hat, or basking in the sunshine of the women, of whom he was very fond. Jeannot, a slave of the plantation of M. Bullet, was small and slender in person, and of boundless activity. Perfidious of soul, his aspect was frightful and revolting. Capable of the greatest crimes, he was inaccessible to regret or remorse.

Having sworn implacable hatred against the whites, he thrilled with rage when he saw them; and his greatest pleasure was to bathe his hands in their blood. These three were the leaders of the blacks till the appearance of Toussaint; and under their rule, the cry was "Blood, blood, blood!" Such was the condition of affairs when a decree was passed by the Colonial Assembly, giving equal rights to the mulattoes, and asking their aid in restoring order and reducing the slaves again to their chains. Overcome by this decree, and having gained all they wished, the free colored men joined the planters in a murderous crusade against the slaves. This union of the whites and mulattoes to prevent the bondman getting his freedom, created an ill-feeling between the two proscribed classes, which seventy years have not been able to efface. The French government sent a second army to St. Domingo to enforce the laws, giving freedom to the slaves, and Toussaint joined it on its arrival in the Island, and fought bravely against the planters.

While the people of St. Domingo were thus fighting amongst themselves, the revolutionary movement in France had fallen into the hands of Robespierre and Danton and the guillotine was beheading its thousands daily. When the news of the death of Louis XVI. reached St. Domingo, Toussaint and his companions left the French and joined the Spanish army, in the eastern part of the Island, and fought for the King of Spain. Here Toussaint was made brigadier-general, and appeared in the field as the most determined foe of the French planters.

The two armies met; a battle was fought in the streets, and many thousands were slain on both sides; the planters, however, were defeated. During the conflict the city was set on fire, and on every side presented shocking evidence of slaughter, conflagration, and pillage. The strifes of political and religious partisanship, which had raged in the clubs and streets of Paris, were transplanted to St. Domingo, where they raged with all the heat of a tropical clime, and the animosities of a civil war. Truly did the flames of the French revolution at Paris, and the ignorance and self-will of the planters, set the island of St. Domingo on fire. The commissioners with their retinue retired from the burning city into the neighboring highlands, where a camp was formed to protect the ruined town from the opposing party. Having no confidence in the planters, and fearing a reaction, the commissioners proclaimed a general emancipation to the slave population, and invited the blacks who had joined the Spaniards to return. Toussaint and his followers accepted the invitation, returned, and were enrolled in the army under the commissioners. Fresh troops arrived from France, who were no sooner in the Island then they separated—some siding with the planters, and others with the commissioners. The white republicans of the Mother country were arrayed against the white republicans of St. Domingo, whom they were sent out to assist.

The blacks and the mulattoes were at war with each other; old and young of both sexes, and of all colors, were put to the sword, while the fury of the flames swept from plantation to plantation, and from town to town.

CHAPTER XIII.
SUCCESS OF TOUSSAINT.

During these sad commotions, Toussaint, by his superior knowledge of the character of his race, his humanity, generosity, and courage, had gained the confidence of all whom he had under his command. The rapidity with which he traveled from post to post astonished every one. By his genius and surpassing activity, Toussaint levied fresh forces, raised the reputation of the army, and drove the English and Spanish from the Island.

The boiling caldron of the revolution during its progress, had thrown upon its surface several new military men, whose names became household words in St. Domingo. First of these, after Toussaint, was Christophe, a man of pure African origin, though a native of New Grenada. On being set free at the age of fifteen, he came to St. Domingo, where he resided until the commencement of the revolution. He had an eye full of fire, and a braver man never lived. Toussaint early discovered his good qualities, and made him his lieutenant, from which he soon rose to be a general of division.

As a military man, Christophe was considered far superior to Toussaint; and his tall, slim figure, dressed in the uniform of a general, was hailed with enthusiasm wherever he appeared.

Next to Christophe was Dessalines. No one who took part in the St. Domingo revolution has been so severely censured as this chief. At the commencement of the difficulties, Dessalines was the slave of a house carpenter, with whom he had learned the trade. He was a small man, of muscular frame, and of a dingy black. He had a haughty and ferocious look. Hunger, thirst, fatigue, and loss of sleep he seemed made to endure, as if by peculiarity of constitution. Dessalines was not a native of either of the West India Islands, for the marks upon his arms and breast, and the deep furrows and incisions on his face, pointed out the coast of Africa as his birth-place. Inured by exposure and toil to a hard life, his frame possessed a wonderful power of endurance. By his activity and singular fierceness on the field of battle he first attracted the attention of Toussaint, who placed him amongst his guides and attendants, and subsequently advanced him rapidly through several grades, to the dignity of third in command. A more courageous man never appeared upon the battle-field. What is most strange in the history of Dessalines is, that he was a savage, a slave, a soldier, a general, and died when an emperor.

Among the mulattoes were several valiant chiefs. The ablest of these was Rigaud, the son of a wealthy planter. Having been educated at Paris, his manner was polished, and his language elegant. Had he been born in Asia, Rigaud would have governed an empire, for he had all the elements of a great man.

In religion he was very opposite of Toussaint. An admirer of Voltaire and Rousseau, he had made their works his study. A long residence in Paris had enabled him to become acquainted with many of the followers of these two distinguished philosophers.

He had seen two hundred thousand persons following the bones of Voltaire, when removed to the Pantheon; and, in his admiration for the great writer, had confounded liberty with infidelity.

Rigaud was the first amongst the mulattoes, and had sided with the planters in their warfare against the blacks. But the growing influence of this chief early spread fear in the ranks of the whites, which was seen and felt by the mulattoes everywhere.

In military science, horsemanship, and activity, Rigaud was the first man on the Island, of any color, Toussaint bears the following testimony to the great skill of the mulatto general: "I know Rigaud well. He leaps from his horse when at full gallop, and he puts all his force in his arm when he strikes a blow." He was boundless in resources as he was brave and daring. High-tempered and irritable, he at times appeared haughty. The charmed power that he held over the men of his color can scarcely be described. At the breaking out of the revolution, he headed the mulattoes in his native town, and soon drew around him a formidable body of men. Rigaud's legion was considered to be by far the best drilled and most reliable in battle of all the troops raised on the Island.

The mulattoes were now urging their claims to citizenship and political enfranchisement, by arming themselves in defence of their rights; the activity and talent of their great leader, Rigaud, had been the guidance and support of their enterprise. He was hated by the whites in the same degree as they feared his influence with his race.

The unyielding nature of his character, which gave firmness and consistency to his policy while controlling the interest of his brethren, made him dear to them.

Intrigue and craftiness could avail nothing against the designs of one who was ever upon the watch, and who had the means of counteracting all secret attempts against him; and open force in the field could not be successful in destroying a chieftain whose power was often felt, but whose person was seldom seen.

Thus to accomplish a design which had long been in contemplation, the whites of Aux Cayes were now secretly preparing a mine for Rigaud,—which, though it was covered with flowers, and to be sprung by the hand of professed friendship,—it was thought would prove a sure and efficacious method of ridding them of such an opponent, and destroying the pretensions of the mulattoes forever.

It was proposed that the anniversary of the destruction of the Bastile should be celebrated in the town by both whites and mulattoes, in union and gratitude. A civic procession marched to the church, where the Te Deum was chanted and an oration pronounced by citizen Delpech. The Place d'Armes was crowded with tables of refreshments, at which both whites and mulattoes seated themselves. But beneath this seeming patriotism and friendship a dark and fatal conspiracy lurked, plotting treachery and death.

It had been resolved that at a preconcerted signal every white at the table should plunge his knife into the bosom of the mulatto who was seated nearest to him. Cannon had been planted around the place of festivity, that no fugitive from the massacre should have the means of escaping; and that Rigaud should not fail to be secured as the first victim to a conspiracy prepared especially against his life, the commander-in-chief of the national guard had been planted at his side, and his murder of the mulatto chieftain was to be the signal for a general onset upon all his followers.

But between the conception and the accomplishment of the guilty deed, man's abhorrence of crime often interposes many obstacles to success. The officer to whom had been entrusted the assassination of Rigaud, found it no small matter to screw his courage up to the sticking-place, and the expected signal which he was to display in blood to his associates, was so long delayed that secret messengers began to come to him from all parts of the table, demanding why execution was not done on Rigaud. Urged on by these successive appeals, the white general at last applied himself to the fatal task which had been allotted him. But instead of silently plunging his dagger into the bosom of the mulatto chief, he sprang upon him with a pistol in his hand, and with a loud execration, fired it at his intended victim. But Rigaud remained unharmed, and in the scuffle which ensued the white assassin was disarmed and put to flight.

The astonishment of the mulattoes soon gave way to tumult and indignation, and this produced a drawn battle, in which both whites and mulattoes, exasperated as they were to the utmost, fought man to man.

The struggle continued fiercely, until the whites were driven from the town, having lost one hundred and fifty of their number, and slain many of their opponents. Tidings of this conspiracy flew rapidly in all directions; and such was the indignation of the mulattoes at this attack on their chief, whose death had been announced in several places as certain, that they seized upon all the whites within their reach, and their immediate massacre was only prevented by the arrival of intelligence that Rigaud was still alive.[30]

The hostile claims of Toussaint and Rigaud, who shared between them the whole power of the Island, soon brought on a bloody struggle between the blacks and the mulattoes.

The contest was an unequal one, for the blacks numbered five hundred thousand, while the mulattoes were only thirty thousand. The mulattoes, alarmed by the prospect that the future government of the Island was likely to be engrossed altogether by the blacks, thronged from all parts of the Island to join the ranks of Rigaud. As a people, the mulattoes were endowed with greater intelligence; they were more enterprising, and in all respects their physical superiority was more decided than their rivals, the blacks. They were equally ferocious, and confident as they were in their superior powers, they saw without a thought of discouragement or fear the enormous disparity of ten to one in the respective numbers of their adversaries and themselves. Rigaud began the war by surprising Leogane, where a multitude of persons of every rank and color were put to death without mercy.

Toussaint, on learning this, hastened together all the troops which he then had in the neighborhood of Port au Prince, and ordered all the mulattoes to assemble at the church of that town, where he mounted the pulpit, and announced to them his intended departure to war against their brethren. He said, "I see into the recesses of your bosoms; you are ready to rise against me; but though my troops are about to leave this province, you cannot succeed, for I shall leave behind me both my eyes and my arms; the one to watch, ant the other to reach you." At the close of this admonition, threatening as it was, the mulattoes were permitted to leave the church and they retired, awe-struck and trembling with solicitude, to their homes.

The forces of Rigaud, fighting under the eyes of the chief whom they adored, defended with vigor the passes leading to their territory; and though they were but a handful, in comparison with the hordes who marched under the banners of Toussaint, their brave exertions were generally crowned with success.

The mulattoes under Rigaud, more skilled in the combinations of military movements, made up for their deficiency in numbers by greater rapidity and effectiveness in their operations. A series of masterly manoeuvres and diversions were followed up in quick succession, which kept the black army in full employment. But Toussaint was too strong, and he completely broke up the hopes of the mulattoes in a succession of victories, which gave him entire control of the Island, except, perhaps, a small portion of the South, which still held out. Rigaud, reduced in his means of defence, had the misfortune to see his towns fall one after another into the power of Toussaint, until he was driven to the last citadel of his strength—the town of Aux Cayes. As he thus yielded foot by foot, everything was given to desolation before it was abandoned, and the genius of Toussaint was completely at fault in his efforts to force the mulatto general from his last entrenchments.

He was foiled at every attempt, and his enemy stood immovably at bay, notwithstanding the active assaults and overwhelming number of his forces.

The government of France was too much engaged at home with her own revolution, to pay any attention to St. Domingo. The republicans in Paris, after getting rid of their enemies, turned upon each other. The revolution, like Saturn, devoured its own children; priest and people were murdered upon the thresholds of justice. Marat died at the hands of Charlotte Corday; Louis XVI. and Marie Antoinette was guillotined, Robespierre had gone to the scaffold, and Bonaparte was master of France.

The conqueror of Egypt now turned his attention to St. Domingo. It was too important an island to be lost to France, or to be destroyed by civil war; and through the mediation of Bonaparte, the war between Toussaint and Rigaud was brought to a close.

With the termination of this struggle, every vestige of slavery, and all obstacles to freedom, disappeared. Toussaint exerted every nerve to make Hayti what it had formerly been. He did everything in his power to promote agriculture; and in this he succeeded beyond the most sanguine expectations of the friends of freedom, both in England and France. Even the planters who had remained on the Island acknowledged the prosperity of Hayti under the governship of the man whose best days had been spent in slavery.

The peace of Amiens left Bonaparte without a rival on the continent, and with a large and experienced army which he feared to keep idle; and he determined to send a part of it to St. Domingo.

The army for the expedition to St. Domingo was fitted out, and no pains or expense spared to make it an imposing one. Fifty-six ships of war, with twenty-five thousand men, left France for Hayti. It was indeed, the most valiant fleet that had ever sailed from the French dominions. The Alps, the Nile, the Rhine, and all Italy had resounded with the exploits of the men who were now leaving their country for the purpose of placing chains again on the limbs of the heroic people of St. Domingo. There were men in that army that had followed Bonaparte from the siege of Toulon to the battle under the shades of the pyramids of Egypt,—men who had grown gray in the camp. Among them were several colored men, who had distinguished themselves on the field of battle.

There was Rigaud, the bravest of the mulatto chiefs, whose valor had disputed the laurels with Touissant. There, too, was Pétion, the most accomplished scholar of whom St. Domingo could boast; and lastly, there was Boyer, who was destined at a future day to be President of the Republic of Hayti. These last three brave men had become dupes and tools of Bonaparte, and were now on their way to assist in reducing the land of their birth to slavery.

CHAPTER XIV.
CAPTURE OF TOUISSANT.

Le Clerc, the brother-in-law of Bonaparte, the man who had married the voluptuous Pauline, was commander-in-chief of the army. Le Clerc was not himself a man of much distinction in military affairs; his close relationship with the ruler of France was all that he had to recommend him to the army of invasion. But he had with him Rochambeau, and other generals, who had few superiors in arms. Before arriving at Hayti the fleet separated, so as to attack the island on different sides.

News of the intended invasion reached St. Domingo some days before the squadron had sailed from Brest; and therefore the blacks had time to prepare to meet their enemies. Touissant had concentrated his forces at such points as he expected would be first attacked. Christophe was sent to defend Cape City, and Port au Prince was left in the hands of Dessalines.

Le Clerc, with the largest part of the squadron, came to anchor off Cape City, and summoned the place to surrender. The reply which he received from Christophe was such as to teach the captain-general what he had to expect in the subjugation of St. Domingo. "Go tell your general that the French shall march here only over ashes; and that the ground shall burn beneath their feet," was the answer that Le Clerc obtained in return to his command. The French general sent another messenger to Christophe, urging him to surrender, and promising the black chief a commission of higher rank in the French army. But he found he had a man, and not a slave, to deal with. The exasperated Christophe sent back the heroic reply, "The decision of arms can admit you only into a city in ashes; and even on these ashes will I fight still." The black chief then distributed torches to his principal officers, and awaited the approach of the French.

With no navy, and but little means of defence, the Haytians determined to destroy the towns rather than they should fall into the hands of the enemy. Late in the evening the French ships were seen to change their position, and Christophe, satisfied that they were about to effect a landing, set fire to his own house, which was the signal for the burning of the town. The French general wept as he beheld the ocean of flames rising from the tops of the houses in the finest city in St. Domingo.

Another part of the fleet landed in Samana, where Touissant, with an experienced wing of the army, was ready to meet them. On seeing the ships enter the harbor, the heroic chief said: "Here come the enslavers of our race. All France is coming to St. Domingo, to try again to put fetters upon our limbs; but not France with all her troops of the Rhine, the Alps, the Nile, the Tiber, nor all of Europe to help her, can extinguish the soul of Africa. That soul, when once the soul of a man, and no longer that of a slave, can overthrow the pyramids, and the Alps themselves, sooner than again be crushed down into slavery." The French, however, effected a landing, but they found nothing but smoldering ruins where once stood splendid cities. Touissant and his generals at once abandoned the cities, and betook themselves to the mountains, those citadels of freedom in St. Domingo, where the blacks have always proved too much for the whites.

Touissant put forth a proclamation to the colored people, in which he said: "You are now to meet and fight enemies who have neither faith, law, nor religion. Let us resolve that these French shall never leave our shores alive." The war commenced, and the blacks were victorious in nearly all the battles. Where the French gained a victory, they put their prisoners to the most excruciating tortures; in many instances burning them in pits and throwing them into boiling caldrons. This example of cruelty set by the whites, was followed by the blacks. Then it was that Dessalines, the ferocious chief, satisfied his long pent-up revenge against the white planters and French soldiers that he made prisoners. The French general saw that he could gain nothing from the blacks on the field of battle, and he determined upon a stratagem, in which he succeeded too well.

A correspondence was opened with Touissant, in which the captain-general promised to acknowledge the liberty of the blacks, and the equality of all, if he would yield. Overcome by the persuasions of his generals, and the blacks who surrounded him, and who were sick and tired of the shedding of blood, Touissant gave in his adhesion to the French authorities. This was the great error of his life.

The loss that the French army had sustained during the war, was great. Fifteen thousand of their best troops, and some of their bravest generals, had fallen before the arms of these Negroes, whom they despised.

Soon after Touissant gave in his adhesion, the yellow fever broke out in the French army, and carried off nearly all of the remaining great men,— more than seven hundred medical men, besides twenty-two thousand sailors and soldiers. Among these were fifteen hundred officers. It was at this time that Touissant might have renewed the war with great success. But he was a man of his word, and would not take the advantage of the sad condition of the French army.

Although peace reigned, Le Clerc was still afraid of Touissant; and by the advice of Napoleon, the black general was arrested, together with his family, and sent to France.

The great chief of St. Domingo had scarcely been conveyed on board the ship Creole, and she out of the harbor, ere Rigaud, the mulatto general who had accompanied Le Clerc to St. Domingo, was arrested, put in chains, and sent to France.

The seizure of Touissant and Rigaud caused suspicion and alarm among both blacks and mulattoes, and that induced them to raise again the flag of insurrection, in which the two proscribed classes were united.

Twenty thousand fresh troops arrived from France, but they were not destined to see Le Clerc, for the yellow fever had taken him off. In the mountains were many barbarous and wild blacks, who had escaped from slavery soon after being brought from the coast of Africa. One of these bands of savages were commanded by Lamour de Rance, an adroit, stern, savage man, half naked, with epaulettes tied to his bare shoulders for his only token of authority. This man had been brought from the coast of Africa, and sold as a slave in Port au Prince. On being ordered one day to saddle his master's horse, he did so; then mounted the animal, fled to the mountains and ever after made these fearful regions his home. Lamour passed from mountain to mountain with something of the ease of the birds of his own native land. Touissant, Christophe, and Dessalines, had each in their turn pursued him, but in vain. His mode of fighting was in keeping with his dress. This savage, united with others like himself, became complete master of the wilds of St. Domingo. They came forth from their mountain homes, and made war on the whites wherever they found them. Le Clerc was now dead, and Rochambeau, who succeeded him in the government of St. Domingo, sent Cuba to get bloodhounds, with which to hunt down the blacks in the mountains.

In personal appearance, Rochambeau was short and stout, with a deformed body, but of robust constitution; his manner was hard and severe, though he had a propensity to voluptuousness. He lacked neither ability nor experience in war. In his youth, he had, under the eyes of his illustrious father, served the cause of freedom in the United States; and while on duty in the slave portion of our government, formed a low idea of the blacks, which followed him even to St. Domingo.

The planters therefore hailed with joy Rochambeau as a successor to Le Clerc; and when the bloodhounds which he had sent to Cuba for arrived, cannon were fired, and demonstrations of joy were shown in various ways.

Even the women, wives of the planters, went to the sea-side, met the animals, and put garlands about their necks, and some kissed and caressed the dogs.[31]

Such was the degradation of human nature. While the white women were cheering on the French, who had imported bloodhounds as their auxiliaries, the black women were using all their powers of persuasion to rouse the blacks to the combat. Many of these women walked from camp to camp, and from battalion to battalion, exhibiting their naked bodies, showing their lacerated and scourged persons;—these were the marks of slavery, made many years before, but now used for the cause of human freedom.

Christophe, who had taken command of the insurgents, now gave unmistakable proofs that he was a great general; and scarcely second to Touissant. Twenty thousand fresh troops arrived from France to the aid of Rochambeau; yet the blacks were victorious wherever they fought. The French blindly thought that cruelty to the blacks would induce their submission, and to this end they bent all their energies. An amphitheatre was erected, and two hundred dogs, sharpened by hunger, put there, and black prisoners thrown in. The raging animals disputed with each other for the limbs of their victims until the ground was dyed with human blood.

Three hundred brave blacks were put to death in this horrible manner. The blacks, having spread their forces in every quarter of the island, were fast retaking the forts and towns. Christophe commanded in the north, Dessalines in the west, and Clervaux in the south.

Despotism and sensuality have often been companions. In Rochambeau, the one sharpened the appetite for the other, as though greediness of bodily pleasure welcomed the zest arising from the sight of bodily pain.

No small part of his time Rochambeau passed at table, or on sofas, with the Creole females, worshippers of pleasure, as well as most cruel towards their slaves. To satisfy these fascinating courtesans, scaffolds were raised in the cities, which were bathed in the blood of blacks. They even executed women and children, whose only crime was, that they had brothers, fathers, or husbands among the revolters. These brutal murders by the

French filled the blacks with terror. Dessalines started for the Cape, for the purpose of meeting Rochambeau, and avenging the death of the blacks. In his impetuous and terrible march, he surrounded and made prisoners of a body of Frenchmen; and with branches of trees, that ferocious chief raised, under the eyes of Rochambeau, five hundred gibbets, on which he hanged as many prisoners.

The numerous executions which began at the Cape soon extended to other places. Port au Prince had its salt waster made bloody, and scaffolds were erected and loaded, within and without the walls. The hand of tyranny spread terror and death over the shores of the north and the west. As the insurrection became more daring, it was thought that the punishments had not been either numerous enough, violent enough, or various enough. The colonists counseled and encouraged more vengeance. Children, women, and old men were confined in sacks, and thrown into the sea; this was the punishment of parricides among the Romans, ten centuries before; and now resorted to by these haters of liberty.

Rochambeau put five hundred blacks, prisoners whom he had taken in battle, to death in one day. Twenty of Touissant's old officers were chained to the rocks and starved to death.

But the blacks were gradually getting possession of the strongholds in the islands.

"To arms! To arms!" was the cry all over the Island, until everyone who could use even the lightest instrument of death, was under arms.

Dessalines, Belair, and Lamartiniere, defeated the French general at Verettes; in no place was the slaughter so terrible as there. At a mere nod of Dessalines, men who had been slaves, and who dreaded the new servitude with which they were threatened, massacred seven hundred of the whites that Dessalines had amongst his prisoners.

The child died in the arms of its sick and terrified mother; the father was unable to save the daughter, the daughter unable to save the father. Mulattoes took the lives of white fathers, to whom they had been slaves, or whom, allowing them to go free, had disowned them; thus revenging themselves for the mixture of their blood. So frightful was this slaughter, that the banks of the Artibonite were strewn with dead bodies, and the waters dyed with the blood of the slain. Not a grave was dug, for Dessalines had prohibited internment, in order that the eyes of the French might see his vengeance even in the repulsive remains of carnage.

The united enthusiasm and bravery of the blacks and mulattoes was too much for the French. Surrounded on all sides, Rochambeau saw his troops dying for want of food. For many weeks they lived on horse flesh, and were even driven to subsist on the dogs that they had imported from Cuba.

Reduced to the last extremity by starvation, the French general sued for peace, and promised that he would immediately leave the Island; it was accepted by the blacks, and Rochambeau prepared to return to France. The French embarked in their vessels of war, and the standard of the blacks once more waved over Cape City, the capital of St. Domingo. As the French sailed from the Island, they saw the tops of the mountains lighted up;—it was not a blaze kindled for war, but for freedom. Every heart beat for liberty, and every voice shouted for joy. From the ocean to the mountains, and from town to town, the cry was "Freedom! Freedom!" Thus ended Napoleon's expedition to St. Domingo. In less than two years the French lost more than fifty thousand persons. After the retirement of the whites, the men of color put forth a Declaration of Independence, in which they said: "We have sworn to show no mercy to those who may dare to speak to us of slavery."

CHAPTER XV.
TOUISSANT A PRISONER IN FRANCE.

While the cause of independence, forced at length on the aspirations of the natives of Hayti, was advancing with rapid strides, amid all the tumult of armies, and all the confusion of despotic cruelties, Touissant L'Ouverture pined away in the dark, damp, cold prison of Joux.

This castle stands on the brink of the river Daubs; on the land side, the road of Besancon, leading into Switzerland, gives the stronghold the command of the communications between that country and France. This dungeon built by the Romans, has in it a room fifteen feet square, with a stone floor, the same of which the entire castle is constructed. One small window, high up on the side, looking out on the snows of Switzerland, is the only aperture that gives light to the dismal spot. In winter, ice covers the floor; in summer, it is deep with water. In this living tomb, Touissant was placed, and left to die.

All communication was forbidden him with the outer world. He received no news of his wife and family. He wrote to Bonaparte, demanding a trial, but received no reply. His fare was limited to a sum not sufficient to give him the comforts of life. His servant was taken away, and food reduced to a still smaller quantity; and thus the once ruler of St. Domingo, the man to whom in the darkest day of the insurrection the white planters looked to for safety, knowing well his humanity, was little by little brought to the verge of starvation.

Touissant's wife and children had been arrested, sent to France, separated from him, and he knew nothing of their whereabouts. He wrote to Napoleon in behalf of them. The document contained these words:

"General Le Clerc employed towards me means which have never been employed towards the greatest enemies. Doubtless I owe that contempt to my color; but has that color prevented me from serving my country with zeal and fidelity? Does the color of my body injure my honor or courage. Suppose I was a criminal, and the general-in-chief had orders to arrest me; was it needful to employ carabineers to arrest my wife and children; to tear them from their residence without respect, and without charity? Was it necessary to fire on my plantations, and on my family, or to ransack and pillage my property? No! My wife, my children, my household, were under no responsibility; have no account to render to government. General Le Clerc had not even the right to arrest them. Was that officer afraid of a rival?

"I compare him to the Roman Senate, that pursued Hannibal even into his retirement. I request that he and I may appear before a tribunal, and that the government bring forward the whole of my correspondence with him. By that means, my innocence, and all I have done for the republic, will be seen."

Touissant was not even aware of Le Clerc's death. Finding that the humanity of Colomier, the governor of the castle, would not allow the prisoner to starve fast enough, Napoleon ordered the keeper to a distance; and on his return, Touissant was dead.

Thus in the beginning of April, in the year 1803, died Touissant L'Ouverture, a grandson of an African king. He passed the greater number of his days in slavery, and rose to be a soldier, a general, a governor, and today lives in the hearts of the people of his native isle. Endowed by nature with high qualities of mind, he owed his elevation to his own energies and his devotion to the welfare and freedom of his race. His habits were thoughtful, and, like most men of energetic temperaments, he crowded much into what he said.

So profound and original were his opinions, that they have been successively drawn upon by all the chiefs of St. Domingo since this era, and still without loss of adaptation to the circumstances of the country. His thoughts were copious and full of vigor; and what he could express well in his native patois, he found tame and unsatisfactory in the French language, which he was obliged to employ in the details of his official business.

He would never sign what he did not fully understand, obliging two or three secretaries to re-word the document, until they had succeeded in furnishing the particular phrase expressive of his meaning. While at the height of his power, and when all around him were furnished with every comfort, and his officers living in splendor, Touissant himself lived with an austere sobriety, which bordered on abstemiousness.

Clad in a common dress, with a red Madras handkerchief tied around his head, he would move amongst the people as though he were a laborer. On such occasions he would often take a musket, throw it up into the air, and catching it, kiss it; again hold it up, and exclaim to the gazing multitude, "Behold your deliverer; in this lies your liberty!" Touissant was entirely master of his own appetites and passions.

It was his custom to set off in his carriage with the professed object of going to some particular point of the Island, and when he had passed over several miles of the journey, quit the carriage, which continued its route under the same escort of guards, while Touissant, mounted on horseback, and followed by his officers, made rapid excursions across the country to places where he was least expected. It was upon one of these occasions that he owed his life to his singular mode of traveling. He had just left his carriage when an ambuscade of mulattoes, concealed in the thickets of Boucassin, fired upon the guard; several balls pierced the carriage, and one of them killed an old servant, who occupied the seat of his master.

No person knew better than he the art of governing the people under his jurisdiction. The greater part of the blacks loved him to idolatry. Veneration for Touissant was not confined to the boundaries of St. Domingo; it ran through Europe; and in France his name was frequently pronounced in the senate with the eulogy of polished eloquence. No one can look back upon his career without feeling that Touissant was a remarkable man. Without being bred to the science of arms, he became a valiant soldier, and baffled the skill of the most experienced generals that had followed Napoleon. Without military knowledge, he fought like one born in camp.

Without means, he carried on a war successfully. He beat his enemies in battle, and turned their weapons against them. He possessed splendid traits of genius, which were developed in the private circle, in the council chamber, and upon the field of battle. His very name became a tower of strength to his friends and a terror to his foes.

CHAPTER XXVII
SOUTH AMERICA.

The Portuguese introduced slavery into Brazil about the year 1558, and the increase of that class of the population was as rapid as in any part of the newly discovered country. The treatment of the slaves did not differ from Jamaica, St. Domingo, and Cuba.

Brazil has given the death-blow to the wicked system which has been so long both her grievous burden and her foul disgrace. Henceforth, every child born in the empire is free, and in twenty years the chains will fall from the limbs of her last surviving slave. By this decree, nearly three million blacks are raised up from the dust; and though but few of this generation can hope to see the day of general emancipation, it is much for them to know that the curse which rested on the parents will no longer be transmitted to the children; it is something that the younger of them have a bright although distant future to look toward and wait to for. Very likely, too, the dying institution will not be suffered to linger out the whole of the existence which the new law accords to it; as the benefits of free labor to the whole country become appreciated, fresh legislation may hasten the advent of national liberty and justice.

The first colonists enslaved the Indians; and, despite the futile measure of emancipation adopted by the Portuguese crown in 1570, in 1647, and in 1684, these unfortunate natives remained in servitude until 1755, and would perhaps have been held to this day, had they not proved very unprofitable. Negroes were accordingly imported from other Portuguese dominions, and a slave-trade with the African coast naturally sprang up, and it only just ended. Portugal bound herself by treaty with England, in 1815, to abolish the trade. Brazil renewed the obligation in her own name in 1826. Yet in 1839 it was estimated that eighty thousand blacks were imported every year; and, ten years later, the Minister of Foreign Affairs reported that the brutal traffic had only been reduced one-fourth. The energetic action of England, declaring in 1845 that Brazilian slave-ships should be amenable to English authorities, led to a long diplomatic contest, and threats of war; but it bore fruit in 1850 in a statute wherein Brazil assimilated the trade to piracy, and in 1852 the emperor declared it virtually extinct.

In the mean time, an opposition, not to the slave-trade alone, but to slavery, too, gradually strengthened itself within the empire. Manumission became frequent, and the laws made it very easy. A society was organized under the protection of the emperor, which, every year, in open church, solemnly liberated a number of slaves; and in 1856 the English Embassador wrote home that the government had communicated to him their resolution gradually to abolish slavery in every part of the empire. The grand step which they have now taken has no doubt been impelled by the example of our own country. It is one of the many precious fruits which have sprung, and are destined yet to spring from the soil which we watered so freely with patriot blood.

Information generally, with regard to Brazil, is scanty, especially in connection with the blacks; but in all the walks of life, men of color are found in that country.

In the Brazilian army, many of the officers are mulattoes, and some of a very dark hue. The prejudice of color is not so prominent here, as in some other slaveholding countries.

CHAPTER XXVIII.
CUBA AND PORTO RICO.

Cuba, the stronghold of Spain, in the Western world, has labored under the disadvantages of slavery for more than three hundred years. The Lisbon merchants cared more for the great profits made form the slave-trade, than for the development of the rich resources of this, one the most beautiful of the West India Islands, and therefore, they invested largely in that nefarious traffic. The increase of slaves, the demand for sugar and the products of the tropics, and the inducement which a race for wealth creates in the mind of man, rapidly built up the city of Havana, the capital of the Island. The colored population of Cuba, like the whites, have made but little impression on the world outside of their own southern home. There is, however, one exception in favor of the blacks. In the year 1830, there appeared in Havana a young colored man, whose mother had recently been brought from Africa. His name was Placido, and his blood was unmixed. Being with a comparatively kind master, he found the time to learn to read, and began developing the genius which at a later period showed itself.

The young slave took an interest in poetry, and often wrote poems which were set to music and sung in the drawing-rooms of the most refined assemblies in the city. His young master, paying his addresses to a rich heiress, the slave was ordered to write a poem embodying the master's passion for the young lady. Placido acquitted himself to the entire satisfaction of the lover, who copied the epistle in his own hand, and sent it on its mission. The slave's compositions were so much admired that they found their way into the newspapers; but no one knew the Negro as their author.

In 1838, these poems, together with a number which had never appeared in print, were entrusted to a white man, who sent them to England, where they were published and much praised for the talent and scholarly attainment which they evinced. A number of young whites, who were well acquainted with Placido, and appreciated his genius, resolved to purchase him, and present him his freedom, which was done in 1842.

But a new field had opened itself to the freed black, and he began to tread in its paths. Freedom for himself was only the beginning; he sighed to make others free.

The imaginative brain of the poet produced verses which the slaves sung in their own rude way, and which kindled in their hearts a more intense desire for liberty. Placido planned an insurrection of the slaves, in which he was to be their leader and deliverer; but the scheme failed.

After a hasty trial, he was convicted and sentenced to death. The fatal day came, he walked to the place of execution with as much calmness as if it had been to an ordinary resort of pleasure. His manly and heroic bearing excited the sympathy and admiration of all who saw him. As he arrived at the fatal spot, he began reciting the hymn, which he had written in his cell the previous night.

> "Almighty God; whose goodness knows no bound,
>   To Thee I flee in my severe distress;
>   O, let Thy potent arm my wrongs redress,
> And rend the odious veil by slander wound
> About my brow. The base world's arm confound,
>   Who on my front would now the seal of shame impress."

The free blacks in Cuba form an important element in her population, and these people are found in all the professions and trades. The first dentists are Blake and Coopat, mulattoes; the first musician, Joseito White, a mulatto; one of the best young ladies' academies at present existing at Havana is personally conducted by an accomplished Negro woman, Maria de Serra, to whom many a lady of high rank owes her social and intellectual accomplishments. The only Cuban who has distinguished herself as an actress on foreign states is Dacoste, a mulatto; Covarrubias, the great comedian and lively writer, for many years the star of the Cuban stage, was also a mulatto; Francisco Manzano, the poet, was a negro slave.

The prompter of the theatre of St. John, of Porto Rico, is Bartolo Antique, a Negro, so intelligent that the dramatic companies that come from Spain prefer him to their own prompters. The engineer of the only steamboat in Porto Rico is a colored man. The only artist worthy to be mentioned, in the same Island, is the religious painter, José Campeche, a mulatto. These are only a few known and acknowledged as colored, but should we search the sources of every family in Cuba and Porto Rico, we are sure that more or less, we could trace the African blood in the greatest number of our most illustrious citizens.

In Porto Rico, Dubois, a mulatto, paid the penalty of his head for his boldness and patriotism. There were in Cuba, in 1862, two hundred and twenty-one thousand four hundred and seventeen free colored people, and three hundred and sixty-eight thousand five hundred and fifty slaves. In Porto Rico, in the same year, there were two hundred and forty-one thousand and fifteen free colored people, and forty-one thousand seven hundred and thirty-six slaves.

When the English troops invaded the Island of Cuba, in 1762, the Negroes behaved so well during the siege at Havana, that a large number of them received from Governor Prado's hands, and in the name of the King, their letters of emancipation, in acknowledgement of their gallantry and good services.

CHAPTER XXX.
INTRODUCTION OF BLACKS INTO
THE AMERICAN COLONIES.

Simultaneously with the landing of the Pilgrims from the Mayflower, on Plymouth Rock, December 22d, 1620, a clumsy-looking brig, old and dirty, with paint nearly obliterated from every part, slowly sailed up the James River, and landed at Jamestown. The short, stout, fleshy appearance of the men in charge of the vessel, and the five empty sour-crout barrels which lay on deck, told plainly in what country the navigators belonged.

Even at that early day they had with them their "native beverage," which, though not like the lager of the present time, was a drink over which they smoked and talked of "Farderland," and traded for the Negroes they brought. The settlers of Jamestown, and indeed, all Virginia at that time, were mainly cavaliers, gentlemen-adventurers, aspiring to live by their wits and other men's labor. Few of the pioneers cherished any earnest liking for downright persistent muscular exertion, yet some exertion was urgently required to clear away the heavy forest which all but covered the soil of the infant colony, and to grow the tobacco which easily became the staple export by means of which nearly everything required by its people but food was to be paid for in England.

The landing of twenty slaves from the Dutch brig was the signal for all sorts of adventurers to embark in the same nefarious traffic. Worn-out and unseaworthy European ships, brigs, barks, schooners, and indeed, everything else that could float, no matter how unsafe, were brought into requisition to supply the demand for means of transportation in the new commerce.

391

Thousands of persons incarcerated in the prisons of the old world were liberated upon condition that they would man these slave-trading vessels. The discharged convicts were used in the slave factories on the African coast, and even in the marauding expeditions sent out from the slave ships in search of victims were mainly made up of this vile off-cast and scum of the prison population of England, France, Germany, Spain, and Portugal. So great was the increase of this traffic, that in a short time the importation in a single year amounted to forty thousand slaves.

The immense growth of the slave population in the Southern States, soon caused politicians to take sides for or against the institution. This, however, did not manifest itself to any very great extent, until the struggle for National Independence was over, and the people, North and South, began to look at their interests connected with each section of the country.

At the time that the Declaration of Independence was put forth, no authentic enumeration had been made; but when the first census was taken in 1791, the total number of slaves in what are now known as the Northern States, was forty thousand three hundred and seventy; in the Southern, six hundred and fifty-three thousand nine hundred and ten.

It is very common at this day to speak of our revolutionary struggle as commenced and hurried forward by a union of free and slave colonies; but such is not the fact. However slender and dubious its legal basis, slavery existed in each and all of the colonies that united to declare and maintain their Independence. Slaves were proportionately more numerous in certain portions of the South; but they were held with impunity throughout the North, advertised like dogs or horses, and sold at auction, or otherwise, as chattels. Vermont, then a territory in dispute between New Hampshire and New York, and with very few civilized inhabitants, mainly on its southern and eastern borders, is probably the only portion of the revolutionary confederation never polluted by the tread of a slave.

The spirit of liberty, aroused or intensified by the protracted struggle of the colonists against usurped and abused power in the mother-country, soon found itself engaged in natural antagonism against the current form of domestic despotism.

"How shall we complain of arbitrary or unlimited power exerted over us, while we exert a still more despotic and inexcusable power over a dependent and benighted race?" was very fairly asked. Several suits were brought in Massachusetts—where the fires of liberty burned earliest and brightest—to test the legal right of slaveholding; and the leading Whigs gave their money and their legal services to support these actions, which were generally, on one ground or another, successful. Efforts for an express law of emancipation, however, failed, even in Massachusetts; the

Legislature doubtless apprehended that such a measure, by alienating the slaveholders, would increase the number and power of the Tories; but in 1777, a privateer having brought a lot of captured slaves into Jamaica, and advertised them for sale, the General Court, as the legislative assembly was called, interfered, and had them set at liberty. The first Continental Congress which resolved to resist the usurpations and oppressions of Great Britain by force, had already declared that our struggle would be "for the cause of human nature," which the Congress of 1776, under the lead of Thomas Jefferson, expanded into the noble affirmation of the right of "all men to life, liberty, and the pursuit of happiness" contained in the immortal preamble to the Declaration of Independence. A like averment that "all men are born free and equal," was in 1780 inserted in the Massachusetts Bill of Rights; and the Supreme Court of that State, in 1783, on an indictment of a master for assault and battery, held this declaration a bar to slave-holding henceforth in the State.

A similar clause in the second Constitution of New Hampshire, was held by the courts of the State to secure freedom to every child born therein after its adoption. Pennsylvania, in 1780, passed an act prohibiting the further introduction of slaves, and securing freedom to all persons born in that state thereafter. Connecticut and Rhode Island passed similar acts in 1784. Virginia, in 1778, on motion of Mr. Jefferson, prohibited the further importation of slaves; and in 1782, removed all legal restrictions on emancipation. Maryland adopted both of these in 1783. North Carolina, in 1786, declared the introduction of slaves into the State "of evil consequences and highly impolitic," and imposed a duty of £5 per head thereon. New York and New Jersey followed the example of Virginia and Maryland, including the domestic in the same interdict with the foreign slave-trade. Neither of these states, however, declared a general emancipation until many years thereafter, and slavery did not wholly cease in New York until about 1830, nor in New Jersey till a much later date. The distinction of free and slave states, with the kindred assumption of a natural antagonism between the North and South, was utterly unknown to the men of the Revolution.

CHAPTER XXXI.
SLAVES IN THE NORTHERN COLONIES.

The earliest account we have of slavery in Massachusetts is recorded in Josselyn's description of his first visit to New England, in 1638. Even at that time, slave-raising on a small scale had an existence at the North.

Josselyn says: "Mr. Maverick had a Negro woman from whom he was desirous of having a breed of slaves; he therefore ordered his young Negro man to sleep with her. The man obeyed his master so far as to go to bed, when the young woman kicked him out."[32] This seems to have been the first case of an insurrection in the colonies, and commenced, too, by a woman. Probably this fact has escaped the notice of the modern advocates of "Woman's Rights." The public sentiment of the early Christians upon the question of slavery can be seen by the following form of ceremony, which was used at the marriage of slaves.

This was prepared and used by the Rev. Samuel Phillips, of Andover, whose ministry there, beginning in 1710, and ending with his death, in 1771, was a prolonged and eminently distinguished service of more than half the eighteenth century:—

"You, Bob, do now, in ye Presence of God and these Witnesses, Take Sally to be your wife;

"Promising, that so far as shall be consistent with ye Relation which you now Sustain as a servant, you will Perform ye Part of an Husband towards her: And in particular, as you shall have ye Opportunity & Ability, you will take proper Care of her in Sickness and Health, in Prosperity & Adversity;

"And that you will be True & Faithful to her, and will Cleave to her only, so long as God, in his Providence, shall continue your and her abode in Such Place (or Places) as that you can conveniently come together. — — Do You thus Promise?

"You, Sally, do now, in ye Presence of God, and these Witnesses, Take Bob to be your Husband;

"Promising, that so far as your present Relation as a Servant shall admit, you will Perform the Part of a Wife towards him; and in particular,

"You Promise that you will Love him; And that as you shall have the Opportunity & Ability, you will take a proper Care of him in Sickness and Health; in Prosperity and Adversity:

"And you will cleave to him only, so long as God, in his Providence, shall continue his & your Abode in such Place (or Places) as that you can come together. — — Do you thus Promise? I then, agreeable to your Request, and with ye Consent of your Masters & Mistresses, do Declare that you have License given you to be conversant and familiar together as Husband and Wife, so long as God shall continue your Places of Abode as foresaid; And so long as you Shall behave yourselves as it becometh servants to doe:

"For you must both of you bear in mind that you remain still, as really and truly as ever, your Master's Property, and therefore it will be justly expected, both by God and Man, that you behave and conduct yourselves as Obedient and faithfull Servants towards your respective Masters & Mistresses for the time being:

"And finally, I exhort and Charge you to beware lest you give place to the Devel, so as to take occasion from the license now given you, to be lifted up with Pride, and thereby fall under Displeasure, not of Man only, but of God also; for it is written, that God resisteth the Proud but giveth Grace to the humble.

"I shall now conclude with Prayer for you, that you may become good Christians, and that you may be enabled to conduct as such; and in particular, that you may have Grace to behave suitably towards each Other, as also dutifully towards your Masters & Mistresses, Not with Eye Service as Men pleasers, ye Servants of Christ doing ye Will of God from ye heart, &c.

"[ENDORSED]
"NEGRO MARRIAGE."

We have given the above form of marriage, *verbatim et literatim.*

In 1641, the Massachusetts Colony passed the following law:—

"There shall never be any bond slaverie, villinage, or captivitie amongst us unless it be lawfull captives taken in just warres, and such strangers as willingly sell themselves. And these shall have all the liberties and Christian usages, which the law of God established in Israel concerning such persons doth morally require. This exempts none from servitude, who shall be judged thereto by authority."

In 1646, one James Smith, a member of a Boston church, brought home two Negroes from the coast of Guinea, and had been the means of killing near a hundred more. In consequence of this conduct, the General Court passed the following order:—

"The General Court conceiving themselves bound by the first opportunity to bear witness against the heinous and crying sin of man-stealing, as also to prescribe such timely redress for what is passed, and such a law for the future as may sufficiently deter all others belonging to us to have to do in such vile and odious courses, justly abhorred of all good and just men, do order that the Negro interpreter with others unlawfully taken, be by the first opportunity at the charge of the country for the present, sent to his native country (Guinea) and a letter with him of the indignation of the Court thereabouts, and justice thereof desiring our honored Governor would please put this order in execution."

From this time till about 1700, the number of slaves imported into Massachusetts was not large. In 1680, Governor Simon Bradstreet, in answer to inquiries from "the lords of his Majesty's privy council," thus writes:—

"There hath been no company of blacks or slaves brought into the country since the beginning of this plantation, for the space of fifty years, only one small vessel about two years since after twenty months' voyage to Madagascar brought hither betwixt forty and fifty Negroes, most women and children, sold for £10, £15, and £20 apiece, which stood the merchants in near £40 apiece one with another: now and then two or three Negroes are brought hither from Barbadoes and other of His Majesty's plantations, and sold here for about £20 apiece, so that there may be within our government about one hundred, or one hundred and twenty, and it may be as many Scots brought hither and sold for servants in the time of the war with Scotland, and most now married and living here, and about halfe so many Irish brought hither at several times as servants."

The number of slaves at this period in the middle and southern colonies is not easily ascertained, as few books, and no newspapers were published in North America prior to 1704. In that year, the "Weekly News Letter" was commenced, and in the same year the "Society for the propagation of the Gospels in foreign parts opened a catechizing school for the slaves at New York, in which city there were then computed to be about fifteen hundred Negro and Indian slaves," a sufficient number to furnish materials for the "irrepressible conflict," which had long before begun. The catechist, whom the Society employed, was "Mr. Elias Neau, by nation a Frenchman, who having made a confession of the Protestant religion in France, for which he had been confined several years in prison, and seven years in the galleys." Mr. Neau entered upon his office "with great diligence, and his labors were very successful; but the Negroes were much discouraged from embracing the Christian religion upon the account of the very little regard showed them in any religious respect. Their marriages were performed by mutual consent only, without the blessing of the church; they were buried by those of their own country and complexion, in the common field, without any Christian office; perhaps some ridiculous heathen rites were performed at the grave by some of their own people. No notice was given of their being sick, that they might be visited; on the contrary, frequent discourses were made in conversation that they had no souls, and perished as the beasts, and that they grew by being taught and made Christians."[33]

From this time forward, the increase of slaves was very rapid in Virginia and South Carolina, and with this increase, discontent began to show itself amongst the blacks.

CHAPTER XXXII.
COLORED INSURRECTIONS IN THE COLONIES.

The first serious effort at rebellion by the slaves in the colonies, occurred in New York, in 1712; where, if it had not been for the timely aid from the garrison, the city would have been reduced to ashes. The next insurrection took place in South Carolina, in 1720, where the blacks in considerable numbers attacked the whites in their houses and in the streets.

Forces were immediately raised and sent after them, twenty-three of whom were taken, six convicted, three executed, and three escaped.

In October, 1722, about two hundred Negroes near the mouth of the Rappahannock River, Virginia, got together in a body, armed with the intent to kill the people in church, but were discovered, and fled.

On the 13th of April, 1723, Governor Dummer issued a proclamation with the following preamble, viz:—

"Whereas, within some short time past, many fires have broke out within the town of Boston, and divers buildings have thereby been consumed: which fires have been designedly and industriously kindled by some villainous and desperate Negroes, or other dissolute people, as appears by the confession of some of them (who have been examined by the authority), and many concurring circumstances; and it being vehemently suspected that they have entered into a combination to burn and destroy the town, I have therefore thought fit, with the advice of his Majesty's council, to issue forth this proclamation," etc.

On the 18th of April, 1723, Rev. Joseph Sewall preached a discourse, particularly occasioned "by the late fires yt have broken out in Boston, supposed to be purposely set by ye Negroes."

On the next day, April 19th, the Selectmen of Boston made a report to the town on the subject, consisting of nineteen articles, of which the following is No. 9:—

"That if more than two Indians, Negro or Mulatto Servants or Slaves be found in the Streets or Highways in or about Town, idling or lurking together unless in the service of their Master or Employer, every one so found shall be punished at the House of Correction."

So great at the time were the alarm and danger in Boston, occasioned by the slaves, that in addition to the common watch, a military force was not only kept up, but at the breaking out of every fire, a part of the militia were ordered out under arms to keep the slaves in order! !

In 1728, an insurrection of slaves occurred in Savannah, Georgia, who were fired on twice before they fled. They had formed a plot to destroy all the white, and nothing prevented them but a disagreement about the mode. At that time, the population consisted of three thousand whites and two thousands seven hundred blacks.

In August, 1730, an insurrection of blacks occurred in Williamsburgh, Virginia, occasioned by a report, on Colonel Spotswood's arrival, that he had directions from His Majesty to free all baptized persons. The negroes improved this to a great height. Five counties were in arms pursuing them, with orders to kill them if they did not submit.

In August, 1730, the slaves in South Carolina conspired to destroy all the whites. This was the first open rebellion in that State where the negroes were actually armed and embodied, and took place on the Sabbath.

In the same month, a negro man plundered and burned a house in Malden (Mass.,) and gave this reason for his conduct, that his master had sold him to a man in Salem, whom he did not like.

In 1731, Captain George Scott, of Rhode Island, was returning from Guinea with a cargo of slaves, who rose upon the ship, murdered three of the crew, all of whom soon after died, except the captain and boy.

In 1732, captain John Major, of Portsmouth, New Hampshire, was murdered, with all his crew, and the schooner and cargo seized by the slaves.

In 1741, there was a formidable insurrection among the slaves in New York. At that time the population consisted of twelve thousand whites, and two thousand blacks. Of the conspirators, thirteen were burned alive, eighteen hung, and eighty transported.

Those who were transported were sent to the West India islands. As a specimen of the persons who were suitable for transportation, I give the following from the "Boston Gazette," Aug. 17, 1761:—

"To be sold, a parcel of likely young Negroes, imported from Africa, cheap for cash. Inquire of John Avery. Also, if any person have any Negro men, strong and hearty, though not of the best moral character, which are proper subjects of transportation, they may have an exchange for small negroes"

In 1747, the slaves on board of a Rhode Island ship commanded by Captain Beers, rose, when off Cape Coast Castle, and murdered the captain and all the crew, except two mates, who swam ashore.

In 1754, C. Croft, Esq., of Charleston, South Carolina, had his buildings burned by his female negroes, two of whom were burned alive! !

In September, 1755, Mark and Phillis, slaves, were put to death at Cambridge (Mass.,) for poisoning their master, Mr. John Codman of Charlestown. Mark was hanged; and Phillis burned alive. Having ascertained that their master had, by his will, made them free at his death, they poisoned him in order to obtain their liberty so much the sooner.

In the year 1800, the city of Richmond, Virginia, and indeed the whole slave-holding country were thrown into a state of intense excitement, consternation and alarm, by the discovery of an intended insurrection among the slaves. The plot was laid by a slave named Gabriel, who was claimed as the property of Mr. Thomas Prosser. A full and true account of this General Gabriel, and of the proceedings consequent on the discovery of the plot, has never yet been published. In 1831, a short account which is false in almost every particular, appeared in the Albany "Evening Journal," under the head of "Gabriel's Defeat."

The following is the copy of a letter dated September 21, 1800, written by a gentleman of Richmond, Virginia, published in the "Boston Gazette," October 6th:—

"By this time, you have no doubt heard of the conspiracy formed in this country by the negroes, which, but for the interposition of Providence, would have put the metropolis of the State, and even the State itself, into their possession. A dreadful storm, with a deluge of rain, which carried away the bridges, and rendered the water-courses everywhere impassable, prevented the execution of their plot. It was extensive and vast in its design. Nothing could have been better contrived. The conspirators were to have seized on the magazine, the treasury, the mills, and the bridges across James River. They were to have entered the city of Richmond in three places with fire and sword, to commence an indiscriminate slaughter, the French only excepted. They were then to have called on their fellow-negroes and the friends of humanity throughout the continent, by proclamation, to rally round their standard. The magazine, which was defenceless, would have supplied them with arms for many thousand men.

"The treasury would have given them money, the mills bread, and the bridges would have enabled them to let in their friends and keep out their enemies. Never was there a more propitious season for the accomplishment of their purpose.

"The country is covered with rich harvests of Indian corn; flocks and herds are everywhere fat in the fields, and the liberty and equality doctrine, nonsensical and wicked as it is (in this land of tyrants and slaves), is for electioneering purposes sounding and resounding through our valleys and mountains in every direction. The city of Richmond and the circumjacent country are in arms, and have been so for ten or twelve days past. The patrollers are doubled through the State, and the Governor, impressed with the magnitude of the danger, has appointed for himself three aids-de-camp. A number of conspirators have been hung, and a great many more are yet to be hung. The trials and executions are going on day by day. Poor, deluded wretches! Their democratic deluders, conscious of their own guilt, and fearful of the public vengeance, are most active in bringing them to punishment."

CHAPTER XXXIII.
BLACK MEN IN THE REVOLUTIONARY WAR.

The Boston Massacre, March 5, 1770, may be regarded as the first act in the great drama of the American Revolution. "From that moment," said Daniel Webster, "we may date the severance of the British Empire." The presence of the British soldiers in King Street excited the patriotic indignation of the people, The whole community was stirred, and sage counselors were deliberating and writing and talking about the public grievances. But it was not for "the wise and prudent" to be the first to act against the encroachments of arbitrary power.

A motley rabble of men and boys, led by Crispus Attucks, a negro, and shouting, "The way to get rid of these soldiers is to attack the main guard; strike at the root; this is the nest!" with more valor than discretion, they rushed to King Street, and were fired upon by Captain Preston's company. Crispus Attucks was the first to fall; he and Samuel Gray and Jonas Caldwell were killed on the spot. Samuel Maverick and Patrick Carr were mortally wounded.

The excitement which followed was intense. The bells of the town were rung; an impromptu meeting was held, and a immense assembly was gathered. Three days after, on the 8th, a public funeral of the martyrs took place. The shops in Boston were closed; all the bells of Boston and neighboring towns were rung. It was said that a greater number of persons assembled on this occasion than were ever before gathered on the continent for a similar purpose.

The body of Attucks, the negro slave, had been placed in Faneuil Hall, with that of Caldwell, both being strangers in the city. Maverick was buried from his mother's house in Union Street, and Gray from his brother's, in Royal Exchange Lane. The four hearses formed a junction in King Street, and there the procession marched on in columns six deep, with a long file of coaches belonging to the most distinguished citizens, to the middle burying-ground, where the four victims were deposited in one grave, over which a stone was places with the following inscription:

> "Long as in Freedom's cause the wise contend,
> Dear to your country shall your fame extend;
> While to the world the lettered stone shall tell,
> Where Caldwell, Attucks, Gray and Maverick fell."

The anniversary of this event was publicly commemorated in Boston, by an oration and other exercises, every year until after our national independence was achieved, when the Fourth of July was substituted for the fifth of March, as the more proper day for general celebration. Not only was the occasion commemorated, but the martyrs who then gave up their lives were remembered and honored. For half a century after the close of the war, the name Crispus Attucks was honorably mentioned by the most noted men of the country, who were not blinded by foolish prejudice, which, to say the most, was only skin-deep.

A single passage from Bancroft's history will give a succinct and clear account of the condition of the army in respect to colored soldiers, at the time of the battle of Bunker Hill:—

"Nor should history forget to record, that, as in the army at Cambridge, so also in this gallant band, the free negroes of the colony had their representatives. For the right of free negroes to bear arms in the public defence was, at the day, as little disputed in New England as their other rights. They took their place not in separate corps, but in the ranks with the white man; and their names may be read on the pension-rolls of the country, side by side with those of other soldiers of the revolution."[34]

The capture of Major-General Prescott, of the British army, on the 9th of July, 1777, was an occasion of great rejoicing throughout the country. Prince, the valiant negro who seized that officer, ought always to be remembered with honor for his important service.

The battle of Red Bank, and the battle of Rhode Island, on the 29th of August, 1778, entitle the blacks to perpetual honor.[35]

When Colonel Green was surprised and murdered, near Points Bridge, New York, on 14th of May, 1781, his colored soldiers heroically defended him till they were cut to pieces; and the enemy reached him over the dead bodies of his faithful negroes. Of this last engagement, Arnold, in his "History of Rhode Island," says:—

"A third time the enemy, with desperate courage and increased strength, attempted to assail the redoubt and would have carried it, but form the timely aid of two continental battalions dispatched by Sullivan to support his almost exhausted troops. It was in repelling these furious onsets, that the newly raised black regiment, under Colonel Greene, distinguished itself by deeds of desperate valor. Posted behind a thicket in the valley, they three times drove back the Hessians, who charged repeatedly down the hill to dislodge them; and so determined were the enemy in these successive charges, that the day after the battle, the Hessian colonel, upon whom this duty had developed, applied to exchange his command, and go to New York, because he dared not lead his regiment again to battle, lest his men should shoot him for having caused them so much loss."

CHAPTER XXXIV.
BLACKS IN THE WAR OF 1812.

In the war of 1812, colored men again did themselves honor by volunteering their services in aid of American freedom, both at the North and at the South. In the latter section, even the slaves were invited, and entered the army, where their bravery was highly appreciated. The following document speaks for itself.

"HEAD QUARTERS, SEVENTH MILITARY DISTRICT,
MOBILE, September 21, 1814.

"To The Free Colored Inhabitants of Louisiana:
"Through a mistaken policy, you have heretofore been deprived of a participation in the glorious struggle for national rights, in which our country is engaged. This no longer shall exist.

"As sons of freedom, you are now called upon to defend our most inestimable blessing. As Americans, your country looks with confidence to her adopted children for a valorous support, as a faithful return for the advantages enjoyed under her mild and equitable government. As fathers, husbands, and brothers, you are summoned to rally around the standard of the Eagle, to defend all which is dear in existence,

"Your country, although calling for your exertions, does not wish you to engage in her cause without remunerating you for the services rendered. Your intelligent minds are not to be led away by false representations— your love of honor would cause you to despise the man who should attempt to deceive you,. With the sincerity of a soldier, and in the language of truth, I address you.

"To every noble-hearted free man of color, volunteering to serve during the present contest with Great Britain, and no longer, there will be paid the same bounty, in money and lands, now received by the white soldiers of the United States, namely—one hundred and twenty-four dollars in money, and one hundred and sixty acres of land. The non-commissioned officers and privates will also be entitled to the same monthly pay, daily rations, and clothes, furnished to any American soldier.

"On enrolling yourselves in companies, the Major-General commanding will select officers for your government, from your white fellow-citizens. Your non-commissioned officers will be appointed among yourselves.

"Due regard will be paid to the feelings of freemen and soldiers. You will not, by being associated with white men, in the same corps, be exposed to improper comparisons, or unjust sarcasm. As a distinct independent battalion or regiment, pursuing the path of glory, you will, undivided, receive the applause and gratitude of your countrymen.

"To assure you of the sincerity of my intentions, and my anxiety to engage your invaluable services to our country, I have communicated my wishes to the Governor of Louisiana, who is fully informed as to the manner of enrollments, and will give you every necessary information on the subject of this address.

"ANDREW JACKSON,
"Major-General Commanding."[36]

December 18th, 1814, General Jackson issued the following address to the colored members of his army:—

"SOLDIERS!—When, on the banks of the Mobile, I called you to take up arms, inviting you to partake of the perils and glory of your white fellow-citizens, I expected much from you; for I was not ignorant that you possessed qualities most formidable to an invading enemy. I knew with what fortitude you could endure hunger and thirst, and all the fatigues of a campaign. I know how well you loved your native country, and that you, as well as ourselves, had to defend what man holds most dear—his parents, wife, children, and property. You have done more than I expected. In addition to the previous qualities I before knew you to possess, I found among you a noble enthusiasm, which leads to the performance of great things.

"Soldiers! The President of the United States shall hear how praiseworthy was your conduct in the hour of danger, and the representatives of the American people will give you the praise your exploits entitle you to. Your general anticipates them in applauding your noble ardor.

"The enemy approaches; his vessels cover our lakes; our brave citizens are united, and all contention has ceased among them. Their only dispute is, who shall win the prize of valor, or who the most glory, its noblest prize.

"By order.
"THOMAS BUTLER, Aid-de-camp."

The "New Orleans Picayune," in an account of the celebration of the Battle of New Orleans, in that city, in 1851, says:—

"Not the least interesting, although the most novel feature of the procession yesterday, was the presence of ninety of the colored veterans who bore a conspicuous part in the dangers of the day they were now for the first time called to assist in celebrating, and who, by their good conduct in presence of enemy, deserved and received the approbation of their illustrious commander-in-chief. During the thirty-six years that have passed away since they assisted to repel the invaders from our shores, these faithful men have never before participated in the annual rejoicings for the victory which their valor contributed to gain.

"Their good deeds have been consecrated only in their memories, or lived but to claim a passing notice on the page of the historian. Yet who more than they deserve the thanks of the country, and the gratitude of succeeding generations? Who rallied with more alacrity in response to the summons of danger? Who endured more cheerfully the hardships of the camp, or faced with greater courage the perils of the fight? If, in that hazardous hour, when our homes were menaced with the horrors of war, we did not disdain to call upon the colored population to assist in repelling the invading horde, we should not, when the danger is past, refuse to permit them to unite with us in celebrating the glorious event which they helped to make so memorable an epoch in our history. We were not too exalted to mingle with them in the affray; they were not too humble to join in our rejoicings.

"Such, we think, is the universal opinion of our citizens, We conversed with many yesterday, and without exception, they expressed approval of the invitation which had been extended to the colored veterans to take part in the ceremonies of the day, and gratification at seeing them in a conspicuous place in the procession.

"The respectability of their appearance, and the modesty of their demeanor, made an impression on every observer and elicited unqualified approbation. Indeed, though in saying so we do not mean disrespect to any one else, we think that they constituted decidedly the most interesting portion of the pageant, as they certainly attracted the most attention."

On Lakes Erie and Champlain, colored men were also engaged in these battles which have become historical, exhibiting the same heroism that characterized them in all their previous efforts in defence of their country's rights.

CHAPTER XXXV.
THE CURSE OF SLAVERY.

The demoralization which the institution entailed upon all classes in the community in which it existed, was indeed fearful to contemplate; and we may well say that slavery is the curse of curses. While it made the victim a mere chattel, taking from him every characteristic of manhood, it degraded the mind of the master, brutalized his feelings, seared his conscience, and destroyed his moral sense.

Immorality to a great extent, pervaded every slave-holding city, town, village, and dwelling in the South. Morality and virtue were always the exceptions. The Southern clergy, backed by the churches, defended their right to hold slaves till the last. Houses of religious worship and the negro pen were often in sight of each other.

The Southern newspapers teemed with advertisements, which were in a fair index to this monstrous social evil. Now that slavery is wept away, it may be interesting to see some of these newspaper notices, in the light of the new dispensation of freedom.

The New Orleans "True Delta" in 1853, graced its columns with the following: "Mr. Joseph Jennings respectfully informs his friends and the public, that, at the request of many of his acquaintances, he has been induced to purchase from Mr. Osborn, of Missouri, the celebrated dark bay horse "Star," age five years, square trotter, and warranted sound, with a new light-trotting buggy and harness; also the stout mulatto girl "Sarah," aged about twenty years, general house servant, valued at nine hundred dollars, and guaranteed, will be raffled for at four o'clock, P. M., February 1st, at any hotel selected by the subscribers.

"The above is as represented, and those persons who may wish to engage in the usual practice of raffling will, I assure them, be perfectly satisfied with their destiny in this affair.

"Fifteen hundred chances, at one dollar each.

"The whole is valued at its just worth, fifteen hundred dollars.

"The raffle will be conducted by gentlemen selected by the interested subscribers present. Five nights allowed to complete the raffle. Both of above can be seen at my store, No. 78 Common Street, second door from Camp, at from 9 o'clock A. M., till, half-past two, P. M.

"Highest throw takes the first choice; the lowest throw the remaining prize, and the fortunate winners to pay twenty dollars each, for the refreshments furnished for the occasion."

The "Picayune," of the same city, gives the following:

"$100 REWARD.—Run away from the plantation of the undersigned, the negro man Shedrick, a preacher, five feet nine inches high, about forty years old, but not looking over twenty-three, stamped N. E. on the breast, and having both small toes cut off. He is of a very dark complexion, with eyes small, but bright, and a look quite insolent. He dresses good, and was arrested as a runaway at Donaldsonville, some three years ago. The above reward will be paid for his arrest, by addressing Messrs. Armant Brothers, St. James Parish, or A. Miltenberger & Co., 30 Carondelet Street."

A Savannah (Georgia) paper has the annexed notice.

"Committed to prison, three weeks ago, under suspicious circumstances, a negro woman, who calls herself Phebe, or Phillis. Says she is free, and lately from Beaufort District, South Carolina. Said woman is about fifty year of age, stout in stature, mild-spoken, five feet four inches high, and weighs about a hundred and forty pounds. Having made diligent inquiry by letter, and from what I can learn, said woman is a runaway. Any person owning said slave can get her by making application to me, properly authenticated."

The practice of capturing runaway slaves, with blood-hounds trained for the purpose, during the days of slave rule in the South, is well known. We give below one of the advertisements as it appeared in print at the time.

"The undersigned, having an excellent pack of hounds for trailing and catching runaway slaves, informs the public that his prices in future will be as follows for such services:

For each day employed in hunting or trailing	$2.50
For catching each slave	10.00
For going over ten miles, and catching slaves	20.00

"If sent for, the above prices will be exacted in cash. The subscriber resides one mile and a half south of Dadeville, Ala.

"B. BLACK."

Slavery so completely seared the conscience of the whites of the South, that they had no feeling of compassion for the blacks, as the following illustration will show. At St. Louis, in the year 1835, Francis McIntosh, a free colored man; while defending himself from an attack of white ruffians, one of the latter was killed. At once the colored man was taken, chained to a tree, and burned to death. One of the newspapers at the time gave the following account of the inhuman affair:—

"All was silent as death while the executioners were piling wood around their victim. He said not a word, until feeling that the flames had seized upon him. He then uttered an awful howl, attempting to sing and pray, then hung his head, and suffered in silence, except in the following instance. After the flames had surrounded their prey, his eyes burnt out of his head, and his mouth seemingly parched to a cinder, some one in the crowd, more compassionate then the rest, proposed to put an end to his misery by shooting him, when it was replied, 'That would be of no use, since he is already out of pain.' 'No, no,' said the wretch, 'I am not, I am suffering as much as ever; shoot me, shoot me.' "No, no,' said one of the fiends who was standing about the sacrifice they were roasting, 'he shall not be shot. I would sooner slacken the fire, if it would increase his misery;' and the man who said this was, as we understand, an officer of justice!"

Lest this demonstration of "public opinion" should be regarded as a sudden impulse merely, not an index of the settled tone of feeling in that community, it is important to add, that the Hon. Luke E. Lawless, Judge of the Circuit Court of Missouri, at a session of that court in the city of St. Louis, some months after the burning of this man, decided officially that since the burning of McIntosh was the act, either directly or by countenance of a majority of the citizens, it is "a case which transcends the jurisdiction" of the Grand Jury! Thus the State of Missouri proclaimed to the world that the wretches who perpetrated that unspeakably diabolical murder, and the thousands that stood by consenting to it, were her representatives, and the Bench sanctified it with the solemnity of a judicial decision.

CHAPTER XXXVI.
DISCONTENT AND INSURRECTION.

An undeveloped discontent always pervaded the black population of the South, bond and free. Human bondage is ever fruitful of insurrection, wherever it exists, and under whatever circumstances it may be found. The laws forbidding either free people of color or slaves to assemble in any considerable numbers for religious, or any other purpose, without two or more whites being present, and the rigorous enforcement of such laws, show how fearful the slave-masters were of their injured victims.

Everything was done to make the Negro feel that he was not a man, but a thing; his inferiority was impressed upon him in all possible ways. In the great cities of the South, free colored ladies were not allowed to wear a veil in the streets, or in any public places. A violation of this law was visited with thirty-nine lashes upon the bare back. The same was inflicted upon the free colored man who should be seen upon the streets with a cigar in his mouth, or a walking-stick in his hand. Both, when walking the streets, were forbidden to take inside of the pavement. Punishment of fine and imprisonment was laid upon any found out of their houses after nine o'clock at night.

An extra tax was placed upon every member of a free colored family. While all these odious edicts were silently borne by the free colored people of Charleston, South Carolina, in 1822, there was a suppressed feeling of indignation, mortification, and discontent, that was only appreciated by a few. Among the most dissatisfied of the free blacks was Denmark Vesey, a man who had purchased his freedom in the year 1800, and since that time had earned his living by his trade, being a carpenter and a joiner.

In person, Vesey was tall and of spare make; in color, a dark mulatto; high forehead; eyes, dark brown; nose, long and with a Roman cast. His education was superior to those of his associates, and he had read much, especially of the condition of his own race, and felt deeply for them in their degraded condition.

Vesey was a native of the West Indies. Having been employed on shipboard by his master, Captain Vesey, Denmark had seen a great deal of the world, and had acquired a large fund of information, and was regarded as a leading man among the blacks. He had studied the Scriptures, and never lost an opportunity of showing that they were opposed to chattel-slavery. He spoke freely with the slaves upon the subject, and often with the whites, where he found he could do so without risk to his own liberty.

After resolving to incite the slaves to rebellion, he began taking into his confidence such persons as he could trust, and instructing them to gain adherents from among the more reliable of both bond and free. Peter Poyas, a slave of more than ordinary foresight and ability, was selected by Vesey as his lieutenant; and to him was committed the arduous duty of arranging the mode of attack, and of acting as the military leader.

His plans showed some natural generalship; he arranged the night attack; he planned the enrollment of a mounted troop to scour the streets; and he had a list of all the shops where arms and ammunition were kept for sale. He voluntarily undertook the management of the most difficult parts of the enterprise,—the capture of the main guard-house,—and had pledged himself to advance alone, and surprise the sentinel. He was said to have a magnetism in his eye, of which his confederates stood in great awe; if he once got his eye upon a man, there was no resisting it.

Gullah Jack, Tom Russell, and Ned Bennett. The last two were not less valuable than Peter Poyas; for Tom was an ingenious mechanic, and made battle-axes, pikes, and other instruments of death, with which to carry on the war. All the above were to be generals of brigades, and were let into all the secrets all the intended rising. It has long been the custom in Charleston for the country slaves to visit the city in great numbers on Sunday, and return to their homes in time to commence work on the fol-lowing morning. It was therefore determined by Denmark to have the ris-ing take place on Sunday. The slaves of nearly every plantation in the vicinity were enlisted, and were to take part.

The details of the plan, however, were not rashly committed to the mass of the confederates; they were known only to a few, and were finally to have been announced after the evening prayer-meeting on the appointed Sunday. But each leader had his own company enlisted, and his own work marked out. When the clock struck twelve, all were to move. Peter Poyas was to lead a party ordered to assemble at South Bay, and to be joined by a force from James' Island; he was then to march up and seize the arsenal and guard-house opposite St. Michael's Church, and detach a sufficient number to cut off all white citizens who should appear at the alarm posts. A second body of negroes, from the country and the Neck, headed by Ned Bennett, was to assemble on the Neck and seize the arsenal there. A third was to meet at Governor Bennett's Mills, under command of Rolla, another leader, and, after putting the governor and intendant to death, to march through the city, or be posted at Cannon's Bridge, thus preventing the inhabitants of Cannonsborough from entering the city. A fourth, partly from the country and partly from the neighboring localities in the city, was to rendezvous on Gadsen's Wharf, and attack the upper guard-house.

A fifth, composed of country and Neck negroes, was to assemble at Bulkley's farm, two miles and a half from the city, seize the upper powder magazine, and then march down; and a sixth was to assemble at Denmark Vesey's, and obey his orders. A seventh detachment, under Gullah Jack, was to assemble in Boundary Street, at the head of King Street, to capture the arms of the Neck company of militia, and to take an additional supply from Mr. Duquercron's shop. The naval stores on Mey's Wharf were also to be attacked. Meanwhile a horse company, consisting of many draymen, hostlers, and butcher boys, was to meet at Lightwood's Alley, and then scour the streets to prevent the whites from assembling. Every white man coming out of his door was to be killed, and, if necessary, the city was to be fired in several places—slow match for this purpose having been purloined from the public arsenal and placed in an accessible position.

The secret and plan of attack, however, were incautiously divulged to a slave named Devany, belonging to Colonel Prioleau, and he at once informed his master's family. The mayor, on getting possession of the facts, called the city council together for consultation. The investigation elicited nothing new, for the slaves persisted in their ignorance of the matter, and the authorities began to feel that they had been imposed upon by Devany and his informant, when another of the conspirators, being bribed, revealed what he knew. Arrests after arrests were made, and the Mayor's Court held daily examinations for weeks. After several weeks of incarceration, the accused, one hundred and twenty in number, were brought to trial: thirty-four were sentenced to transportation, twenty-seven acquitted by the court, twenty-five discharged without trial, and thirty-five condemned to death. With but two or three exceptions, all of the conspirators went to the gallows feeling that they had acted right, and died like men giving their lives for the cause of freedom. A report of the trial, written soon after, says of Denmark Vesey:—

"For several years before he disclosed his intentions to any one, he appears to have been constantly and assiduously engaged in endeavoring to embitter the minds of the colored population against the white. He rendered himself perfectly familiar with all those parts of the Scriptures which he thought he could pervert to his purpose, and would readily quote them to prove that slavery was contrary to the laws of God,—that slaves were bound to attempt their emancipation, however shocking and bloody might be the consequences,—and that such efforts would not only be pleasing to the Almighty, but were absolutely enjoined, and their success predicted, in the Scriptures. His favorite texts, when he addressed those of his own color, were Zachariah xiv: 1–3, and Joshua vi: 21; and in all his conversation he identified their situation with that of the Israelites.

The number of inflammatory pamphlets on slavery brought into Charleston from some of our sister states within the last four years (and once from Sierra Leone), and distributed amongst the colored population of the city, for which there was a great facility, in consequence of the unrestricted intercourse allowed to the persons of color between the different states in the Union, and the speeches in Congress of those opposed to the admission of Missouri into the Union, perhaps garbled and misrepresented, furnished him with ample means for inflaming the minds of the colored population of this State; and by distorting certain parts of these speeches, or selecting from them particular passages, he persuaded but too many that Congress had actually declared them free, and that they were held in bondage contrary to the laws of the land.

Even whilst walking through the streets in company with another, he was not idle; for if his companion bowed to a white person, he would rebuke him, and observe that all men are born equal, and that he was surprised that any one would degrade himself by such conduct,—that he would never cringe to the whites, nor ought any one who had the feelings of a man. When answered, 'We are slaves,' he would sarcastically and indignantly reply, 'What can we do?' he would remark,' Go and buy a spelling-book and read the fable of Hercules and the Wagoner,' which he would then repeat, and apply it to their situation. He also sought every opportunity of entering it into conversation with white persons, when they could be overheard by negroes near by, especially in grog shops; during which conversation, he would artfully introduce some bold remark on slavery; ands sometimes, when, from the character he was conversing with, he found he might still be bolder, he would go so far, that, had not his declarations in such situations been clearly proved, they would scarcely have been credited. He continued this course until some time after the commencement of the last winter; by which time he had not only obtained incredible influence amongst persons of color, but many feared him more than their own owners, and, one of them declared, even more than his God."

The excitement which the revelations of the trial occasioned, and the continual fanning of the flame by the newspapers, were beyond description. Double guard in the city, the country patrol on horseback and on foot, the watchfulness that was observed on all plantations, showed the deep feelings of fear pervading the hearts of the slaveholders, not only in South Carolina, but the fever extended to the other Southern states, and all seemed to feel that a great crisis had been passed. And indeed, their fears seemed not to have been without ground, for a more complicated plan for an insurrection could scarcely have been conceived. And many were of the opinion that the rising once begun, they would have taken the city and held it, and might have sealed the fate of slavery in the South.[37] But a more successful effort in rebellion was made in Southampton,. Virginia, in the year 1831, at the head of which was Nat Turner.

On one of the oldest and largest plantations in Southampton County, Virginia, owned by Benjamin Turner, Esq., Nat was born a slave, on the 2d of October, 1800. His parents were of unmixed African descent. Surrounded as he was by the superstition of the slave quarters, and being taught by his mother that he was born for a prophet, a preacher, and a deliverer of his race, it is not strange that the child should have imbibed the principles which were afterwards developed in his career. Early impressed with the belief that he had seen visions, and received communications direct from God, he, like Napoleon, regarded himself as a being of destiny. In his childhood Nat was of an amiable disposition; but circumstances in which he was placed as a slave, brought out incidents that created a change in this disposition, and turned his kind and docile feeling into the most intense hatred to the white race.

Being absent one night from his master's plantation without a pass, he was caught by Whitlock and Mull, the two district patrolers, and severely flogged. This act of cruelty inflamed the young slave, and he resolved upon having revenge. Getting two of the boys of a neighboring plantation to join him, Nat obtained a long rope, went out at night on the road through which the officers had their beat, and stationing his companions, one on each side of the road, he stretched the rope across, fastening each end to a tree, and drawing it tight. His rope thus fixed, and his accomplices instructed how to act their part, Nat started off up the road. The night being dark, and the rope only six or eight inches from the ground, the slave felt sure that he would give his enemies a "high fall."

Nat hearing them, he called out in a disguised voice, "Is dat you Jim?" To this Whitlock replied, "Yes, dis is me." Waiting until the white men were near him, Nat started off upon a run, followed by the officers. The boy had placed a sheet of white paper in the road, so that he knew at what point to jump the rope, so as not to be caught by his own trap. Arriving at the signal he sprung over the rope, and went down the road like an antelope. But not so with the white men, for both caught by the legs and thrown so hard upon the ground that Mull had his shoulder put out of joint, and his face terribly lacerated by the fall; while Whitlock's left wrist was broken, and his head bruised in a shocking manner. Nat hastened home, while his companions did the same, not forgetting to take with them the clothes-line which had been so serviceable in the conflict. The patrollers were left on the field of battle, crying, swearing, and calling for help.

Snow seldom falls as far south as the southern part of Virginia; but when it does, the boys usually have a good time snow-balling, and on such occasions the slaves, old and young, women and men, are generally pelted without mercy, and with no right to retaliate. It was only a few months after his affair with the patrolers, that Nat was attacked by a gang of boys, who chased him some distance, snow-balling with all their power. The slave boy knew the lads, and determined upon revenge. Waiting till night, he filled his pockets with rocks, and went into the street. Very soon the same gang of boys were at his heels, and pelting him. Concealing his face so as not to be known, Nat discharged his rocks in every direction, until all his enemies had all taken to their heels.

The ill treatment he experienced at the hands of the whites and the visions he claimed to have seen, caused Nat to avoid, as far as he could, all intercourse with his fellow-slaves, and threw around him a gloom and melancholy that disappeared only with his life.

Both the young slave and his friends averred that a full knowledge of the alphabet came to him in a single night. Impressed with the belief that his mission was a religious one, and this impression strengthened by the advice of his grandmother, a pious but ignorant woman, Nat commenced preaching when about twenty-five years of age, but never went beyond his own master's locality. In stature he was under the middle size, long-armed, round-shouldered, and strongly marked with the African features. A gloomy fire burned in his looks, and he had a melancholy expression of countenance. He never tasted a drop of ardent spirits in his life, and was never known to smile. In the year 1828 new visions appeared to Nat, and he claimed to have a direct communication with God. Unlike most of those born under the influence of slavery, he had no faith in conjuring, fortune-telling, or dreams, and always spoke with contempt of such things.

Being hired out to cruel masters, he ran away and remained in the woods thirty days, and could have easily escaped to the free states, as did his father some years before; but he received, as he says in his confession a communication from the spirit, which said, "Return to your earthly master, for he who knoweth his Master's will, and doeth it not, shall be beaten with many stripes." It was not the will of his earthly, but his heavenly Master that he felt bound to do, and therefore Nat returned. His fellow-slaves were greatly incensed at him for coming back, for they knew well his ability to reach Canada, or some other land of freedom, if he was so inclined.

He says further: "About this time I had a vision, and saw white spirits and black spirits engaged in battle, and the sun was darkened, the thunder rolled in the heavens, and blood flowed in streams; and I heard a voice saying, 'Such is your luck; such as you are called on to see; and let it come, rough or smooth, you must surely bear it.'"

Some time after this, Nat had, as he says, another vision, in which the spirit appeared and said, "The serpent is loosened, and Christ has laid down the yoke he has borne for the sins of men, and you must take it up, and fight against the serpent, for the time is fast approaching when the first shall be last, and the last shall be first." There is no doubt but that this last sentence filled Nat with enthusiastic feeling in favor of the liberty of his race, that he had so long dreamed of. "The last shall be first, and the first shall be last," seemed to him to mean something. He saw in it the overthrow of the whites, and the establishing of the blacks in their stead, and to this end he bent the energies of his mind. In February, 1831, Nat received his last communication, and beheld his last vision. He said, "I was told I should arise and prepare myself, and slay my enemies with their own weapons."

The plan of an insurrection was now formed in his own mind, and the time had arrived for him to take others into the secret; and he at once communicated his ideas to four of his friends, in whom he had implicit confidence. Hark Travis, Nelson Williams, Sam Edwards, and Henry Porter were slaves like himself, and like him had taken their names from their masters. A meeting must be held with these, and it must take place in

413

some secluded place, where the whites would not disturb them; and a meeting was appointed. The spot where they assembled was as wild an romantic as were the visions that had been impressed upon the mind of their leader.

Three miles from where Nat lived was a dark swamp filled with reptiles, in the middle of which was a dry spot, reached by a narrow, winding path, and upon which human feet seldom trod, on account of its having been the place where a slave had been tortured to death by a low fire, for the crime of having flogged his cruel and inhuman master. The night for the meeting arrived, and they came together. Hark brought a pig; Sam, bread; Nelson, sweet potatoes, and Henry, brandy; and the gathering was turned into a feast. Others were taken in, and joined the conspiracy. All partook heartily of the food, except Nat. He fasted an prayed. It was agreed that the revolt should commence that night, and in their own master's households, and that each slave should give his oppressor the death-blow. Before they left the swamp Nat made a speech, in which he said, "Friends and brothers: We are to commence a great work to-night. Our race is to be delivered from slavery, and God has appointed us as the men to do his bidding, and let us be worthy of our calling. I am told to slay all the whites we encounter, without regard to age or sex. We have no arms or ammunition, but we will find these in the houses of our oppressor, and as we go on, others can join us. Remember that we do not go forth for the sake of blood and carnage, but it is necessary that in the commencement of this revolution all the whites we meet should die, until we shall have an army strong enough to carry on the war upon a Christian basis. Remember that ours is not a war for robbery and to satisfy our passions; it is a struggle for freedom. Ours must be deeds, and not words. Then let's away to the scene of action."

Among those who joined the conspirators was Will, a slave who scorned the idea of taking his master's name. Though his soul longed to be free, he evidently became one of the party, as much to satisfy revenge, as for the liberty that he saw in the dim distance. Will had seen a dear and beloved wife sold to the negro-trader and taken away, never to be beheld, by him again in this life. His own back was covered with scars from his shoulders to his feet. A large scar, running from his right eye down to his chin showed that he had lived with a cruel master.. Nearly six feet in height, and one of the strongest and most athletic of his race, he proved to be the most unfeeling of all the insurrectionists. His only weapon was a broad-axe, sharp and heavy.

Nat and his accomplices at once started for the plantation of Joseph Travis, with whom the four lived, and there the first blow was truck. In his confession, just before his execution, Nat said:—

"On returning to the house, Hark went to the door with an axe, for the purpose of breaking it open, as we knew we were strong enough to murder the family should they be awakened by the noise; but reflecting that it may create an alarm in the neighborhood, we determined to enter the house secretly, and murder them whilst sleeping. Hark got a ladder and set it against the chimney, on which I ascended, and hoisting a window, entered, and came down-stairs, unbarred the doors, and removed the guns from their places. It was then that I observed that I must spill first blood. On which, armed with a hatchet, and accompanied by Will, I entered my master's chamber. It being dark, I could not give a death-blow. The hatchet glanced from his head; he sprang from the bed and called his wife. It was his last word; Will laid him dead with a blow of his axe, and Mrs. Travis shared the same fate as she lay in bed. The murder of this family, five in number, was the work of a moment; not one of them awoke. There was a little infant sleeping in a cradle, that was forgotten until we had left the house and gone some distance, when Henry and Will returned and killed it. We got here four guns that would shoot, and several old muskets, with a pound or two of powder. We remained for some time at the barn, where we paraded; I formed them in line as soldiers, and after carrying them through all the manoeuvres I was master of, marched them off to Mr. Salathiel Francis's, about six hundred yards distant.

"Sam and Will went to the door and knocked. Mr. Francis asked who was there; Sam replied it was he and he had a letter for him; on this he got up and came to the door; they immediately seized him, and dragging him out a little from the door, he was dispatched by repeated blows on the head. There was no other white person in the family. We started from there to Mrs. Reese's, maintaining the most perfect silence on our march, where, finding the door unlocked, we entered and murdered Mrs. Reese in her bed while sleeping; her son awoke, but only to sleep the sleep of death; he only had time to say, 'Who is that?' and he was no more.

From Mrs. Reese's we went to Mrs. Turner's, a mile distant, when we reached about sunrise, on Monday morning. Henry, Austin, and Sam, went to the still, where, finding Mr. Peebles, Austin shot him; the rest of us went to the house. As we approached, the family discovered us and shut the door. Vain hope! Will, with one stroke of his axe, opened it, and we entered, and found Mrs. Turner and Mrs. Newsome in the middle of the room, almost frightened to death. Will immediately killed Mrs. Turner with one blow of his axe. I took Mrs. Newsome by the hand, and with the sword I had when apprehended, I struck her several blows over the head, but was not able to kill her, as the sword was dull. Will, turning round and discovering it, dispatched her also. A general destruction of property, and search for money and ammunition, always succeeded the murders.

"By this time, my company amounted to fifteen, nine men mounted, who started for Mrs. Whitehead's (the other six were to go through a by-way to Mr. Bryant's, and rejoin us at Mrs. Whitehead's).

"As we approached the house, we discovered Mr. Richard Whitehead standing in the cotton patch, near the lane fence; we called him over to the lane, and Will, the executioner, was near at hand, with his fatal axe, to send him to an untimely grave. As we pushed on to the house, I discovered some one running around the garden, and thinking it was some of the white family, I pursued; but finding it was a servant girl belonging to the house, I returned to commence the work of death; but they whom I left had not been idle; all the family were already murdered but Mrs. Whitehead and her daughter Margaret. As I came around the door, I saw Will pulling Mrs. Whitehead out of the house, and at the step he nearly severed her head from her body with his broadaxe. Miss Margaret, when I discovered her, had concealed herself in the corner formed by the projection of the cellar cap from the house; on my approach she fled, but was soon overtaken, and after repeated blows with a sword, I killed her with a blow over the head with a fence rail. By this time the six who had gone by Mr. Bryant's rejoined us, and informed me they had done the work of death assigned them.

"We again divided, part going to Mr. Richard Porter's, and from thence to Nathaniel Francis's, the others to Mr. Howell Harris's and Mr. T. Doyles's. On my reaching Mr. Porter's, he had escaped with his family. I understood there that the alarm had already spread, and I immediately returned to bring up those sent to Mr. Doyles's and Mr. Howell Harris's; the party I left going on to Mr. Francis's, having told them I would join them in that neighborhood. I met those sent to Mr. Doyle's and Mr. Howell Harris's returning, and having met Mr. Doyles on the road and killed him.

"Learning from some who joined then that Mr. Harris was from home, I immediately pursued the course taken by the party gone on before; but knowing that they would complete the work of death and pillage at Mr. Francis's before I could get there, I went to Mr. Peter Edwards's, expecting to find them there; but they had been there already. I then went to Mr. John T. Barrows's; they had been there and murdered him. I pursued on their track to Captain Newitt Harris's. I found the greater part mounted and ready to start; the men, now amounting to about forty, shouted and hurrahed as I rode up; some were in the yard loading their guns, others drinking. They said Captain Harris and his family had escaped; the property in the house they destroyed, robbing him of money and other valuables.

"I ordered them to mount and march instantly; this was about nine or ten o'clock, Monday morning. I proceeded to Mr. Levi Waller's, two or three miles distant. I took my station in the rear, and as it was my object to carry terror and devastation wherever we went, I placed fifteen or twenty of the best mounted and most to be relied on in the front, who generally approached the houses as fast as their horses could run. This was for two purposes; to prevent their escape, and strike terror to the inhabitants. On this account I never got to the houses, after leaving Mrs. Whitehead's, until the murders were committed, except in one case. I sometimes got in sight in time to see the work of death completed, view the mangled bodies as they lay, in silent satisfaction, and immediately start in quest of other victims. Having murdered Mrs. Waller and ten children, we started for Mr. William Williams's. We killed him and two little boys that were there: while engaged in this, Mrs. Williams fled, and got some distance from the house; but she was pursued, overtaken, and compelled to get up behind one of the company, who brought her back, and after showing her the mangled body of her lifeless husband, she was told to get down and lie by his side, where she was shot dead.

"I then started for Mr. Jacob Williams's, where the family was murdered. Here we found a young man named Drury, who had come on business with Mr. Williams; he was pursued, overtaken, and shot. Mrs. Vaughan's was the next place we visited; and after murdering the family here, I determined on starting for Jerusalem. Our number amounted now to fifty or sixty, all mounted and armed with guns, axes, swords, and clubs. On reaching Mr. James W. Parker's gate, immediately on the road leading to Jerusalem, and about three miles distant, it was proposed to me to call there; but I objected, as I knew he had gone to Jerusalem, and my object was to reach there as soon as possible; but some of the men having relations at Mr. Parker's, it was agreed that they might call and get his people.

"I remained at the gate on the road, with seven or eight, the others going across the field to the house, about half a mile off. After waiting some time for them, I became impatient, and started to the house for them, and on out return we were met by a party of white men, who had pursued our blood-stained track, and who had fired on those at the gate, and dispersed them, which I knew nothing of, not having been at that time rejoined by any of them. Immediately on discovering the whites, I ordered my men to halt and form, as they appeared to be alarmed. The white men, eighteen in number, approached us within one hundred yards, when one of them fired, and I discovered about half of them retreating. I then ordered my men to fire and rush on them; the few remaining stood their ground until we approached within fifty yards, when they fired and retreated.

We pursued and overtook some of them, whom we thought we left dead; after pursuing them about two hundred yards, and rising a little hill, I discovered they were met by another party, and had halted, and were reloading their guns, thinking that those who retreated first, and the party who fired on us at fifty or sixty yards distant, had only fallen back to meet others with ammunition. As I saw them reloading their guns, and more coming up than I saw at first, and several of my bravest men being wounded, the others became panic-stricken, and scattered over the field; the white men pursued and fired on us several times. Hark had his horse shot under him, and I caught another for him that was running by me; five or six of my men were wounded, but none left on the field. Finding myself defeated here, I instantly determined to go through a private way, and cross the Nottoway River at the Cypress Bridge, three miles below Jerusalem, and attack that place in the rear, as I expected they would look for me on the other road, and I had a great desire to get there to procure arms and ammunition."

Reënforcements came to the whites, and the blacks were overpowered and defeated by the superior numbers of their enemy. In this battle many were slain on both sides. Will, the bloodthirsty and revengeful slave, fell with his broad-axe uplifted, after having laid three of the whites dead at his feet with his own strong arm and his terrible weapon. His last words were, "Bury my axe with me," for he religiously believed that in the next world the blacks would have a contest with the whites, and that he would need his axe. Nat Turner, after fighting to the last with his short-sword, escaped with some orders to the woods near by, and was not captured for nearly two months. He had aroused the entire country by his deeds, and for sixty days had eluded a thousand armed men on his track. When taken, although half starved, and exhausted by fatigue, like a fox after a weary chase, he stood erect and dignified, proud and haughty, compact form, marked features, and flashing eye, declaring him to be every inch a man.

When brought to trial, he pleaded "not guilty;" feeling, as he said, that it was always right for one to strike for his own liberty. After going through a mere form of trial, he was convicted and executed at Jerusalem, the county seat for Southampton County, Virginia. Not a limb trembled nor a muscle was observed to move. Thus died Nat Turner, at the early age of thirty-one years—a martyr to the freedom of his race, and a victim to his own fanaticism. He meditated upon the wrongs of his oppressed and injured people, till the idea of their deliverance excluded all other ideas from his mind, and he devoted his life to its realization. Everything appeared to him a vision, and all favorable omens were signs of God. That he was sincere in all that he professed, there is not the slightest doubt. After being defeated, he might have escaped to the free states, but the hope of raising a new band kept him from doing so.

He impressed his image upon the minds of those who once beheld him. His looks, his sermons, his acts, and his heroism live in the hearts of his race, on every cotton, sugar, and rice plantation at the South. The present generation of slaves have a superstitious veneration for his name. He foretold that at his death the sun would refuse to shine, and that there would be signs of disapprobation given from Heaven. And it is true that the sun was darkened, a storm gathered, and more boisterous weather had never appeared in Southampton County than on the day of Nat's execution. The sheriff, warned by the prisoner, refused to cut the cord that held the trap. No black man would touch the rope. A poor old white man, long besotted by drink, was brought forty miles to be the executioner. And even the planters, with all their prejudice and hatred, believed him honest and sincere; for Mr. Gray, who had known Nat from boyhood, and to whom he made his confession, says of him:—

"It has been said that he was ignorant and cowardly, and that his object was to murder and rob, for the purpose of obtaining money to make his escape. It is notorious that he was never known to have a dollar in his life, to swear an oath, or drink a drop of spirits. As to his ignorance, he certainly never had the advantages of education; but he can read and write, and for natural intelligence and quickness of apprehension, is surpassed by few men I have ever seen. As to his being a coward, his reason, as given, for not resisting Mr. Phipps, shows the decision of his character. When he saw Mr. Phipps present his gun, he said he knew it was impossible for him to escape, as the woods were full of men; he therefore thought it was better for him to surrender, and trust to fortune for his escape.

He is a complete fanatic, or plays his part most admirably. In other subjects he possesses an uncommon share of intelligence, with a mind capable of attaining anything, but warped and perverted by the influence of early impressions. He is below the ordinary stature, though strong and active, having the true negro face, every feature of which is strongly marked. I shall not attempt to describe the effect of his narrative as told and commented on by himself, in the condemned hole of the prison; the calm, deliberate composure with which he spoke of his late deeds and intentions; the expression of his fiend-like face, when excited by enthusiasm—still bearing the stains of the blood of helpless innocence about him, clothed with rags, and covered with chains, yet daring to raise his manacled hands to Heaven, with sprit soaring above the attributes of man; I looked on him, and the blood curdled in my veins."

Fifty-five whites and seventy-three blacks lost their lives in the Southampton rebellion. On the fatal night when Nat and his companions were dealing death to all they found, Captain Harris, a wealthy planter, had his life saved by the devotion and timely warning of his slave Jim, said to have been half-brother to his master. After the revolt had been put down, and parties of whites were out hunting the suspected blacks, Captain Harris, with his faithful slave, went into the woods in search of the negroes. In saving his master's life, Jim felt that he had done his duty, and could not consent to become a betrayer of his race; and on reaching the woods, he handed his pistol to his master, and said, "I cannot help you hunt down these men; they, like myself, want to be free. Sir, I am tired of the life of a slave; please give me my freedom, or shoot me on the spot." Captain Harris took the weapon and pointed it at the slave. Jim, putting his right hand upon his heart, said, "This is the spot; aim here." The captain fired, and the slave fell dead at his feet.

CHAPTER XXXVII.
GROWING OPPOSITION TO SLAVERY.

The vast increase of the slave population in the Southern States, and their frequent insurrectionary efforts, together with the fact that the whole system was in direct contradiction to the sentiments expressed in the declaration of American independence, was fast creating a hatred to slavery.

The society of Friends, the first to raise a warning voice against the sin of human bondage had nobly done its duty; and as early as 1789 had petitioned Congress in favor of the abolition of slavery.

Previous to this, however, William Beorling, a Quaker, of Long Island, Ralph Sandiford of Philadelphia, Benjamin Lay, and several others of the society of Friends, had written brave words in behalf of negro freedom.

Benjamin Lundy, also a member of the Society of Friends, commence, in 1821, at Baltimore, the publication of a monthly paper, called "The Genius of Universal Emancipation." This journal advocated gradual, not immediate emancipation. It had, however, one good effect, and that was, to attract the attention of William Lloyd Garrison to the condition of the enslaved negro.

Out of this interest grew "The Liberator," which was commenced January 1, 1831, at Boston. Two years later, the American Anti-slavery Society was organized at Philadelphia.

After setting forth the causes which the patriots of the American Revolution had to induce then to throw off the British yoke, they nobly put forth the claim of the slave to his liberty.

The document was signed by sixty-four persons, among whom was William Lloyd Garrison, and John G. Whittier.

The formation of the American Anti-slavery Society created considerable excitement at the time, and exposed its authors to the condemnation of the servile pulpit and press of that period. Few, however, saw the great importance of such a work, and none of the movers in it imagined that they would live to witness the accomplishing of an object for which the society was brought into being.

One of the most malignant opposers that the abolitionists had to meet, in their commencement, was the American Colonization Society, an organization which began in 1817, in the interest of the slaveholders, and whose purpose was to carry off to Africa the free colored people. Garrison's "Thoughts on African Colonization," published in 1832, had already drawn the teeth of this enemy of the Negro, and for which the society turned all its batteries against him.

The people of the Southern States were not alone in the agitation, for the question had found its way into all of the ramifications of society in the North.

Miss Prudence Crandall, about this time, started a school for colored females, in Canterbury, Connecticut, which was soon broken up, and Miss Crandall thrown into prison.

David Walker, a colored man, residing at Boston, had published an appeal in behalf of his race, filled with enthusiasm, and well calculated to arouse the ire of the pro-slavery feeling of the country.

The liberation of his slaves, by James G. Binney of Kentucky, and his letters to the churches, furnished fuel to the agitating flames.

The free colored people of the North, especially in Boston, New York, and Philadelphia, were alive to their own interest, and were yearly holding conventions, at which they would recount their grievances, and press their claims to equal rights with their white fellow-citizens.

At these meeting, the talent exhibited, the able speeches made, and the strong appeals for justice which were sent forth, did very much to raise the blacks in the estimation of the whites generally, and gained for the Negroes' cause additional friends.

CHAPTER XXXVIII.
MOB LAW TRIUMPHANT.

In the year 1834, mob law was inaugurated in the free states, which extended into the years 1835–6 and 7.

The mobbing of the friends of freedom commenced in Boston, in October, 1835, with an attack upon William Lloyd Garrison, and the ladies' Anti-slavery Society. This mob, made up as it was by "Gentlemen of property and standing," and from whom Mr. Garrison had to be taken to prison to save his life, has become disgracefully historical.

The Boston mob was followed by one at Utica, New York, headed by Judge Beardsley, who broke up a meeting of the New York State Anti-slavery Society. Arthur Tappan's store was attacked by a mob in New York City, and his property destroyed, to the value of thirty thousand dollars. The Rev. Elijah P. Lovejoy, a brave man of the State of Maine, had located at St. Louis, where he took the editorial charge of "The St. Louis Times," and in its columns nobly pleaded for justice to the enslaved negro. The writer of this was for a period of six months employed in the office of "The Times," and knew Mr. Lovejoy well. Driven from St. Louis by mob law, he removed to Alton, Illinois. Here the spirit of slavery followed him, broke up his printing-press, threw it into the river, and murdered the heroic advocate of free speech.

Thus this good man died; but his death raised up new and strong friends for the oppressed. Wendell Phillips visited the grave of the martyr recently, and gave the following description of his burial-place:—

"Lovejoy lies buried now in the city cemetery, on a beautiful knoll. Near by rolls the great river. His resting-place is marked by an oblong stone, perhaps thirty inches by twenty, and rising a foot above the ground; on this rests a marble scroll bearing this inscription:

Hic
Jacet
LOVEJOY
Jam parce sepulto

[Here lies Lovejoy. Spare him, now, in his grave.]

A more marked testimonial would not, probably, have been safe from insult and disfigurement, previous to 1864. He fought his fight so far in the van, so much in the hottest of the battle, that not till after nigh thirty years and the final victory could even his dust be sure of quiet.

In the cities of New York, Philadelphia, Albany, Utica, and many other places in the free states, the colored people were hunted down like wild beasts and their property taken from them or destroyed.

In the two first-named places, the churches and dwellings of these unoffending citizens were set on fire in open day, and burnt to ashes without any effort of the authorities to prevent it.

Even the wives and children of the colored men were stoned in the streets, and the school-houses sought out, their inmates driven away, and many of the children with their parents had to flee to the country for safety.

Such was the feeling of hate brought out in the North by the influence of slavery at the South.

During this reign of terror among the colored people in the free states, their brethren in slavery were also suffering martyrdom. Free blacks were arrested, thrown into jail, scourged in their own houses, and if they made the slightest resistance, were shot down, hung at a lamp-post, or even burned at the stake.

CHAPTER XXXIX.
HEROISM AT SEA.

In the month of August, 1839, there appeared in the newspapers a shocking story:—that a schooner, going coastwise from Havana to Neuvitas, in the Island of Cuba, early in July, with about twenty white passengers, and a large number of slaves, had been seized by the slaves in the night time, and the passengers and crew all murdered except two, who made their escape to land in an open boat. About the 20th of the same month, a strange craft was seen repeatedly on our coast, which was believed to be the captured Spanish coaster, in the possession of the negroes. She was spoken by several pilot-boats and other vessels, and partially supplied with water, of which she was very much in want. It was also said that the blacks appeared to have a great deal of money. The custom-house department and the officers of the navy were instantly aroused to go in pursuit of the "pirates," as the unknown possessors of the schooner were spontaneously called. The United States steamer Fulton, and several revenue cutters were dispatched, and notice given to the collectors at the various seaports.

On the 10th of August, the "mysterious schooner" was near the shore at Culloden Point, on the east end of Long Island, where a part of the crew came on shore for water and fresh provisions, for which they paid with undiscriminating profuseness. Here they were met by Captain Green and another gentleman, who stated that they had in their possession a large box filled with gold. Shortly after, on the 26th, the vessel was espied by Captain Gedney, U. S. N., in command of the brig Washington, employed on the coast survey, who despatched an officer to board her. The officer found a large number of negroes, and two Spaniards, Pedro Montez and José Ruiz, one of whom immediately announced himself as the owner of the negroes, and claimed his protection. The schooner was thereupon taken possession of by Captain Gedney.

The leader of the blacks was pointed out by the Spaniards, and his name given as Joseph Cinque. He was a native of Africa, and one of the finest specimens of his race ever seen in this country. As soon as he saw that the vessel was in the hands of others, and all hope of his taking himself and countrymen back to their home land at an end, he leaped overboard with the agility of an antelope. The small boat was immediately sent after him, and for two hours did the sailors strive to capture him before they succeeded. Cinque swam and dived like the otter, first upon his back, then upon his breast, sometimes his head out of water, and sometimes his heel out. His countrymen on board the captured schooner seemed much amused at the chase, for they knew Cinque well, and felt proud of the untamableness of his nature. After baffling them for a time, he swam towards the vessel, was taken on board, and secured with the rest of the blacks, and they were taken into New London, Connecticut.

The schooner proved to be the Amistad, Captain Ramon Ferrer, from Havana, bound to Principe, about one hundred leagues distant, with fifty-four negroes held as slaves, and two passengers. The Spaniards said, that after being out four days, the negroes rose in the night and killed the captain and a mulatto cook; that the helmsman and another sailor took to the boat and went on shore; that the only two whites remaining were said passengers, Montez and Ruiz, who were confined below until morning; that Montez the elder, who had been a sea-captain, was required to steer the ship for Africa; that he steered easterly in the day-time, because the negroes could tell his course by the sun, but put the vessel about in the night. They boxed about some days in the Bahama Channel, and were several times near the Islands, but the negroes would not allow her to enter any port. Once they were near Long Island, but then put out to sea again, the Spaniards all the while hoping they might fall in with some ship of war that would rescue them from their awkward situation. One of the Spaniards testified that when the rising took place, he was awakened by the noise, and that he heard the captain order the cabin boy to get some bread and throw it to the negroes, in hope to pacify them. Cinque, however, the leader of the revolt, leaped on deck, seized a capstan bar, and attacked the captain, whom he killed at a single blow, and took charge of the vessel; his authority being acknowledged by his companions, who knew him as a prince in his native land.

After a long litigation in the courts, the slaves were liberated and sent back to their native land.

In the following year, 1840, the brig Creole, laden with slaves, sailed from Richmond, bound for New Orleans; the slaves mutinied, took the vessel, and carried her into the British West Indies, and thereby became free. The hero on this occasion was Madison Washington.

CHAPTER L.
REPRESENTATIVE MEN AND WOMEN.

In our Sketches of Representative Men and Women, some will be found to have scarcely more than a local reputation; but they are persons who have contributed, of their ability, towards the Freedom of the Race, and should not be forgotten. Others bid fair to become distinguished in the future. We commence with our first hero:—

CRISPUS ATTUCKS

The principle that taxation and representation were inseparable was in accordance with the theory, the genius, and the precedents of British legislation; and this principle was now, for the first time, intentionally invaded. The American colonies were not represented in Parliament; yet an act was passed by that body, the tendency of which was to invalidate all right and title to their property. This was the "Stamp Act," of March 23, 1765, which ordained that no sale, bond, note of hand, nor other instrument of writing, should be valid, unless executed on paper bearing the stamp prescribed by the home government. The intelligence of the passage of the stamp act at once roused the indignation of the liberty-loving portion of the people of the colonies, and meetings were held at various points to protest against this high-handed measure.

Massachusetts was the first to take a stand in opposition to the mother country. The merchants and traders in Boston, New York, and Philadelphia entered into non-importation agreements, with a view of obtaining a repeal of the obnoxious law. Under the pressure of public sentiment, the stamp act officers gave in their resignations. The eloquence of William Pitt and the sagacity of Lord Camden brought about a repeal of the stamp act in the British Parliament. A new ministry, in 1767, succeeded in getting through the House of Commons a bill to tax the tea imported into the American colonies, and it received the royal assent. Massachusetts again took the lead in opposing the execution of this last act, and Boston began planning to take the most conspicuous part in the great drama. The agitation in the colonies provoked the home government, and power was given to the governor of Massachusetts to take notice of all persons who might offer any treasonable objections to these oppressive enactments, that the same might be sent home to England to be tried there. Lord North was now at the head of affairs, and no leniency was to be shown to the colonies. The concentration of British troops in large numbers at Boston convinced the people that their liberties were at stake, and they began to rally.

A crowded and enthusiastic meeting, held in Boston, in the latter part of the year 1769, was addressed by the ablest talent that the progressive element could produce. Standing in the back part of the hall, eagerly listening to the speakers, was a dark mulatto man, very tall, rather good-looking, and apparently, about fifty years of age. This was Crispus Attucks. Though taking no part in the meeting, he was nevertheless destined to be conspicuous in the first struggle in throwing off the British yoke. Twenty years previous to this, Attucks was the slave of William Bruno, Esq., of Framingham, Massachusetts; but his was a heart beating for freedom, and not to be kept in the chains of mental or bodily servitude.

From the "Boston Gazette" of Tuesday, November 20, 1750, I copy the following advertisement:—

"Ran away from his master William Brouno Framingham, on the 30th of Sept., last, a Molatto Fellow, about 27 years of Age named Crispus, well set, six feet 2 inches high, short curl'd Hair, knees nearer together than common; had on a light colored Bearskin Coat, brown Fustian jacket, new Buckskin Breeches, blew yarn Stockins and Checkered Shirt. Whoever shall take up said Runaway, and convey him to his above said Master at Framingham, shall have Ten Pounds, old Tenor Reward and all necessary charges paid."

The above line is a *verbatim et literatim* advertisement for a runaway slave one hundred and twenty-two years ago. Whether Mr. Brouno succeeded in recapturing Crispus or not, we are left in the dark.

Ill-feeling between the mother country and her colonial subjects had begun gaining ground, while British troops were concentrating at Boston. On the 5th of March, 1770, the people were seen early congregating at the corners of the principle streets, at Dock Square, and near the Custom House. Captain Preston, with a body of redcoats, started out for the purpose of keeping order in the disaffected town, and was hissed at by the crowds in nearly every place where he appeared. The day passed off without any outward manifestation of disturbance, but all seemed to feel that something would take place after nightfall. The doubling of the guard in and about the Custom House showed the authorities felt an insecurity that they did not care to express. The lamps in Dock Square threw their light in the angry faces of a large crowd who appeared to be waiting for the crisis, in whatever form it should come. A part of Captain Preston's company was making its way from the Custom House, when they were met by the crowd from Dock Square, headed by the black man Attucks, who was urging them to meet the redcoats, and drive them from the streets. "These rebels have no business here," said he; "let's drive them away. Come on! Don't be afraid!" cried Attucks. "They dare not shoot; and, if they dare, let them do it."

Stones and sticks, with which the populace were armed, were freely used, to the great discomfiture of the English soldiers. "Don't hesitate! Come on! We'll drive these rebels out of Boston!" were the last words heard from the lips of the colored man, for the sharp crack of muskets silenced his voice, and he felt weltering in his blood. Two balls had pierced his sable breast. Thus died Crispus Attucks, the first martyr to American liberty, and the inaugurator of the revolution that was destined to take from the crown of George the Third its brightest star. An immense concourse of citizens followed the remains of the hero to its last resting-place, and his name was honorably mentioned in the best circles. The last words, the daring, and the death of Attucks gave spirit and enthusiasm to the revolution, and his heroism was imitated by both whites and blacks. His name was a rallying cry for the brave colored men who fought at the battle of Bunker's Hill. In the gallant defence of Redbank, where four hundred blacks met and defeated fifteen hundred Hessians, headed by Count Donop, the thought of Attucks filled them with ardor. When Colonel Green fell at Groton, surrounded by his black troops who perished with him, they went into the battle feeling proud of the opportunity of imitating the first martyr of the American revolution.

No monument has yet been erected to him. An effort was made in the legislature of Massachusetts a few years since, but without success. Five generations of accumulated prejudice against the negro had excluded from the American mind all inclination to do justice to one of her bravest sons. Now that slavery is abolished, we may hope, in future years, to see a monument raised to commemorate the heroism of Crispus Attucks.

PHILLIS WHEATLEY.

In the year 1761, when Boston had her slave market, and the descendants of the Pilgrims appeared to be the most pious and God-fearing people in the world, Mrs. John Wheatley went into the market one day, for the purpose of selecting and purchasing a girl for her own use. Among the group of children just imported from the African coast was a delicately-built, rather good-looking child of seven or eight years, apparently suffering from the recent sea-voyage and change of climate. Mrs. Wheatley's heart was touched at the interesting countenance and humble modesty of this little stranger. The lady bought the child, and she was named Phillis. Struck with the slave's uncommon brightness, the mistress determined to teach her to read, which she did with no difficulty, The child soon mastered the English language, with which she was totally unacquainted when she landed upon the American shores.

Her school lessons were all perfect, and she drank in the Scriptural teachings as if by intuition. At the age of twelve, she could write letters and keep up a correspondence that would have done honor to one double her years. Mrs. Wheatley, seeing her superior genius, no longer regarded Phillis as a servant, but took her as a companion. It was not surprising that the slave-girl should be an object of attraction with the refined and highly-cultivated society that weekly assembled in the drawing-room of the Wheatleys.

As Phillis grew up to womanhood, her progress and attainments kept pace with the promise of her earlier years. She drew around her the best educated of the white ladies, and attracted the notice and attention of the literary characters of Boston, who supplied her with books, and encouraged the ripening of her intellectual powers. She studied the Latin tongue, and translated one of Ovid's tales, which was no sooner put in print in America, than it was republished in London, with elegant commendations from the reviews.

In 1773, a small volume of her poems, containing thirty-nine pieces, was published in London, and dedicated to the Countess of Huntingdon. The genuineness of this work was established in the first page of the volume, by a document signed by the governor of Massachusetts, the lieutenant-governor, her master, and fifteen of the most respectable and influential citizens of Boston, who were acquainted with her talents and the circumstances of her life. Her constitution being naturally fragile, she was advised by her physician to take a sea voyage, as the means of restoring her declining health.

Phillis was emancipated by her master at the age of twenty-one years, and sailed for England. On her arrival, she was received and admired in the first circles of London society; and it was at that time that her poems were collected and published in a volume, with a portrait and a memoir of the authoress. Phillis returned to America, and married Dr. Peters, a man of her own color, and of considerable talents. Her health began rapidly to decline, and she died at the age of twenty-six years, in 1780. Fortunately rescued from the fate that awaits the victims of the slave-trade, this injured daughter of Africa had an opportunity of developing the genius that God had given her, and of showing to the world the great wrong done to her race.

Although her writings are not free from imperfections of style and sentiment, her verses are full of philosophy, beauty, and sublimity. It cost her no effort to round a period handsomely, or polish a sentence until it became transparent with splendor. She was easy, forcible, and eloquent in language, and needed but health and a few more years of experience to have made her a poet of greater note.

BENJAMIN BANNEKER.

The services rendered to science, to liberty, and to the intellectual character of the negro by Banneker, are too great for us to allow his name to sleep, and his genius and merits to remain hidden from the world.

Benjamin Banneker was born in the State of Maryland, in the year 1732, of pure African parentage; their blood never having been corrupted by the introduction of a drop of Anglo-Saxon. His father was a slave, and of course could do nothing towards the education of the child. The mother, however, being free, succeeded in purchasing the freedom of her husband, and they, with their son, settled on a few acres of land, where Benjamin remained during the lifetime of his parents.

His entire schooling was gained from an obscure country school, established for the education of the children of free negroes; and these advantages were poor, for the boy appears to have finished studying before he arrived at his fifteenth year. Although out of school, Banneker was still a student, and read with great care and attention such books as he could get. Mr. George Ellicott, a gentleman of fortune and considerable literary taste, and who resided near to Benjamin, became interested in him, and lent him books from his large library. Among these books were Mayor's Tables, Fergusson's Astronomy, and Leadbeater's Lunar Tables. A few old and imperfect astronomical instruments also found their way into the boy's hands, all of which he used with great benefit to his own mind.

Banneker took delight in the study of the languages, and soon mastered the Latin, Greek, and German. He was also proficient in the French. The classics were not neglected by him, and the general literary knowledge which he possessed caused Mr. Ellicott to regard him as the most learned

429

man in town, and he never failed to introduce Banneker to his most distinguished guests.

About this time, Benjamin turned his attention particularly to Astronomy, and determined on making calculations for an almanac, and completed a set for the whole year. Encouraged by this attempt, he entered upon calculations for subsequent years, which, as well as the former, he began and finished without the least assistance from any person or books than those already mentioned; so that whatever merits attached to his performance is exclusively his own.

He published an almanac in Philadelphia for the years 1792–3–4–5, and which contained his calculations, exhibiting the different aspects of the planets, a table of the motions of the sun and moon, their risings and settings, and of course of the bodies of the planetary system.

By this time, Banneker's acquirements had become generally known, and the best scholars in the country opened correspondence with him. Goddard & Angell, the well-known Baltimore publishers, engaged his pen for their establishment, and became the publishers of his almanacs. A copy of his first production was sent to Thomas Jefferson, together with a letter intended to interest the great statesman in the cause of negro emancipation and the elevation of the negro race, in which he says:—

"It is a truth too well attested to need a proof here, that we are a race of beings who have long labored under the abuse and censure of the world; that we have long been looked upon with an eye of contempt, and considered rather as brutish than human, and scarcely capable of mental endowments. I hope I may safely admit, in consequence of the report which has reached me, that you are a man far less inflexible in sentiments of this nature than many others; that you are measurably friendly and well disposed towards us and that you are willing to lend your aid and assistance for our relief from those many distresses and numerous calamities to which we are reduced.

"If this is founded in truth, I apprehend you will embrace every opportunity to eradicate the train of absurd and false ideas and opinions which so generally prevail with respect to us, and that your sentiments are concurrent with mine,—which are, that one universal Father hath given being to us all; that he hath not only made us all of one flesh, but that he hath also, without partiality, afforded us all the same sensations, and endowed us with all the same faculties; and that, however variable we may be in society or religion, however diversified in situation or in color, we are all of the same family, and stand in the same relation to him. If these are sentiments of which you are fully persuaded, you cannot but acknowledge that it is the indispensable duty of those who maintain rights of human nature, and who profess the obligations of Christianity, to extend their power and influence to the relief of every part of the human race from whatever burden or oppression they may unjustly labor under; and this, I apprehend a full conviction of the truth and obligation of these principles should lead all to.

"I have long been convinced that if your love for yourselves, and for those inestimable laws which preserved to you the rights of human nature, it is founded on sincerity, you cannot help being solicitous that every individual, of whatever rank or distinction, might with you equally enjoy the blessings thereof; neither can you rest satisfied short of the most active effusion of your exertions, in order to effect their promotion from any state of degradation to which the unjustifiable cruelty and barbarism of men have reduced them.

"I freely and cheerfully acknowledge that I am one of the African race, and in the color which is natural to them, of the deepest dye; and it is under a sense of the most profound gratitude to the Supreme Ruler of the universe, that I now confess to you that I am not under that state of tyrannical thralldom and inhuman captivity to which too many of my brethren are doomed; but that I have abundantly tasted of the fruition of those blessings which proceed from that free and unequalled liberty with which you are favored, and which I hope you will willingly allow you have mercifully received from the immediate hand of that Being from whom proceedeth every good and perfect gift.

"Your knowledge of the situation of my brethren is too extensive to need a recital here; neither shall I presume to prescribe methods by which they may be relieved, otherwise than by recommending to you and to others to wean yourselves from those narrow prejudices which you have imbibed with respect to them, and, as Job proposed to his friends, 'put your soul in their soul's stead.' Thus shall your hearts be enlarged with kindness and benevolence towards them; and thus shall you need neither the direction of myself or others in what manner to proceed herein. . . . The calculation for this almanac is the production of my arduous study in my advanced stage of life; for having long had unbounded desires to become acquainted with the secrets of nature, I have had to gratify my curiosity herein through my own assiduous application to astronomical study, in which I need not recount to you the many difficulties and disadvantages which I have had to encounter."

Mr. Jefferson at once replied, and said:—

"I thank you sincerely for your letter and the almanac it contained. Nobody wishes more than I do to see such proofs as you exhibit, that Nature has given to our black brethren talents equal to those of the other colors of men, and that the appearance of the want of them is owing merely to the degraded condition of their existence, both in Africa and America.

I can add with truth, that nobody wishes more ardently to see a good system commenced for raising their condition, both of their body and their mind, to what it ought to be, as far as the imbecility of their present existence, and other circumstances, which cannot be neglected, will admit. I have taken the liberty of sending your almanac to Monsieur de Condorcet, secretary of the Academy of Sciences at Paris, and a member of the Philanthropic Society, because I consider it as a document to which your whole color have a right, for their justification against the doubts which have been entertained of them."

The letter from Banneker, together with the almanac, created in the heart of Mr. Jefferson a fresh feeling of enthusiasm in behalf of freedom, and especially for the negro, which ceased only with his life. The American statesman wrote to Brissot, the celebrated French writer, I which he made enthusiastic mention of the "negro Philosopher." At the formation of the "Society of the Friends of the Blacks," at Paris, by Lafayette, Brissot, Barnave, Condorcet, and Gregoire, the name of Banneker was again and again referred to prove the equality of the races. Indeed, the genius of the "Negro Philosopher" did much towards giving liberty to the people of St . Domingo. In the British house of Commons, Pitt, Wilberforce, and Buxton often alluded to Banneker by name, a man fit to fill any position in society. At the setting off of the District of Columbia for the capital of the federal government, Banneker was invited by the Maryland commissioners, and took an honorable part in the settlement of the territory. But throughout all his intercourse with men of influence, he never lost sight of the condition of his race, and ever urged the emancipation and elevation of the slave. He well knew that everything that was founded upon the admitted inferiority of natural right in the African was calculated to degrade him and bring him nearer to the foot of the oppressor, and he therefore never failed to allude to the equality of the races when with those whites whom he could influence. He always urged self-elevation upon the colored people whom he met. He felt that to deprive the black man of the inspiration of ambition, of hope, of wealth, of standing, among his brethren of the earth, was to take from him all incentives to mental improvement.

What husbandman incurs the toil of seed-time and culture, except with a view to the subsequent enjoyment of a golden harvest? Banneker was endowed by Nature with all those excellent qualifications which are necessary previous to the accomplishment of a great man. His memory was large and tenacious, yet, by a curious felicity, chiefly susceptible of the finest impressions it received from the best authors he read, which he always preserved in their primitive strength and amiable order. He had a quickness of apprehension and a vivacity of understanding which easily took in and surmounted the most subtle and knotty parts of mathematics and metaphysics. He possessed in a large degree that genius which constitutes a man of letters; that equality, without which, judgment is cold, and knowledge is inert; that energy which collects, combines, amplifies, and animates.

He knew every branch of history, both natural and civil; he had read all the original historians of England, France, and Germany, and was a great antiquarian. Criticism, metaphysics, morals, politics, voyages, and travels, were all studied and well digested by him. With such a fund of knowledge, his conversation was equally interesting, instructive, and entertaining. Banneker was so favorably appreciated by the first families in Virginia, that in 1803 he was invited by Mr. Jefferson, then President of the United States, to visit him at Monticello, where the statesman had gone for recreation. But he was too infirm to undertake the journey. He died the following year, aged seventy-two. Like the golden sun that has sunk beneath the western horizon, but still throws upon the world, which he sustained and enlightened in his career, the reflected beams of his departed genius, his name can only perish with his language.

Banneker believed in the divinity of reason, and in the omnipotence of the human understanding, with Liberty for its handmaid. The intellect, impregnated by science, and multiplied by time, it appeared to him, must triumph necessarily over all the resistance of matter. He had faith in liberty, truth, and virtue. His remains still rest in the slave state where he lived and died, with no stone to mark the spot, or tell that it is the grave of Benjamin Banneker. He labored incessantly, lived irreproachably, and died in the literary harness, universally esteemed and regretted.

FREDERICK DOUGLASS

The carrier of this distinguished individual whose name heads this sketch, is more widely known than that of any other living colored man. Born and brought up under the institution of slavery, which denied its victims the right of developing those natural powers that adorn the children of men, and distinguish them from the beasts of the forest,—an institution that gave a premium to ignorance, and made intelligence a crime, when the possessor was a negro,—Frederick Douglass is, indeed, the most wonderful man that America has ever produced, white or black.

His days of servitude were like those of his race who were born at the South, differing but little from the old routines of plantation life. Douglass, however, possessed superior natural gifts, which began to show themselves even when a boy, but his history has become too well known for us to dwell on it here. The narrative of his life, published in 1845, gave a new impetus to the black man's literature. All other stories of fugitive slaves faded away before the beautifully-written, highly-descriptive, and thrilling memoir of Frederick Douglass. Other narratives had only brought before the public a few heart-rending scenes connected with the person described. But Mr. Douglass, in his book, brought not only his old master's farm and its occupants before the reader, but the entire country around him, including Baltimore and its ship-yard. The manner in which he obtained his education, and especially his learning to write, has been read and re-read by thousands in both hemispheres. His escape from slavery is too well understood to need a recapitulation here.

He took up his residence in New Bedford, where he still continued the assiduous student, mastering the different branches of education which the accursed institution had deprived him of in early life.

His advent as a lecturer was a remarkable one. White men and black men had talked against slavery, but none had ever spoken like Frederick Douglass. Throughout the North the newspapers were filled with the sayings of the "eloquent fugitive." He often traveled with others, but they were all lost sight of in the eagerness to hear Douglass. His traveling companions would sometimes get angry, and would speak first at meetings; then they would take the last turn; but it was all the same—the fugitive's impression was the one left upon the mind. He made more persons angry, and pleased more, than any other man. He was praised, and he was censured. He made them laugh, he made them weep, and then made them swear.

His "Slaveholders' Sermon" was always a trump card. He awakened an interest in the hearts of thousands who before were dead to the slave and his condition. Many kept away from his lectures, fearing lest they should be converted against their will. Young men and women, in those days of pro-slavery hatred, would return to their father's roofs filled with admiration for the "runaway slave," and would be rebuked by hearing the old ones grumble out, "You'd better stay at home and study your lessons, and not be running after the nigger meetings."

In 1841, he was induced to accept an agency as a lecturer for the Anti-slavery Society, and at once became one of the most valuable of its advocates. He visited England in 1845. There he was kindly received and heartily welcomed; and after going through the length and breadth of the land, and addressing public meetings out of number on behalf of his countrymen in chains, with a power of eloquence which captivated his auditors, and brought the cause which he pleaded home to their hearts, he returned home, and commenced the publication of the "North Star," a weekly newspaper devoted to the advocacy of the cause of freedom.

Mr. Douglass is tall and well made. His vast and fully-developed forehead shows at once that he is a superior man intellectually. He is polished in his language, and gentlemanly in his manners. His voice is full and sonorous. His attitude is dignified, and his gesticulation is full of noble simplicity. He is a man of lofty reason; natural, and without pretension; always master of himself; brilliant in the art of exposing and abstracting. Few persons can handle a subject, with which they were familiar better than he. There is a kind of eloquence issuing from the depth of the soul as from a spring, rolling along its copious floods, sweeping all before it, overwhelming by its very force, carrying, upsetting, ingulfing its adversaries, and more dazzling and more thundering than the bolt which leaps from crag to crag. This is the eloquence of Frederick Douglass. One of the best mimics of the age, and possessing great dramatic powers; he had taken up the sock and buskin, instead of becoming a lecturer, he would have made as fine a Coriolanus as ever trod the stage.

As a speaker, Frederick Douglass has had more imitators than almost any other American, save, perhaps, Wendell Phillips. Unlike most speakers, he is a superior writer also. Some of his articles, in point of ability, will rank with anything ever written for the American press. He has taken lessons from the best of teachers, amid the homeliest realities of life; hence the perpetual freshness of his delineations, which are never over-colored, never strained, never aiming at difficult or impossible effects, but which always read like living transcripts of experience.

Mr. Douglass has obtained a position in the front rank as a lyceum lecturer. His later addresses from manuscripts, however, do not, in our opinion, come up to his extemporaneous efforts.

But Frederick Douglass's abilities as an editor and publisher have done more for the freedom and elevation of his race than all his platform appeals. Previous to the year 1848, the colored people of the United States had no literature. True, the "National Reformer," the "Mirror of Liberty," the "Colored American," "The Mystery," the "Disfranchised American," the "Ram's Horn," and several others of smaller magnitude, had been in existence, had their run, and ceased to live. All of the above journals had done something towards raising the black man's standard, but they were merely the plows for breaking up the ground and getting the soil ready for seed-time. Newspapers, magazines, and books published in those days by colored men, were received with great allowance by the whites, who had always regarded the negro as an uneducated, inferior race, and who were considered out of their proper sphere when meddling with literature.

The commencement of the publication of the "North Star" was the beginning of a new era in the black man's literature. Mr. Douglass's well-earned fame gave his paper at once a place with the first journals in the country; and he drew around him a corps of contributors and correspondents from Europe, as well as all parts of America and the West Indies, that made its columns rich with the current news of the world.

While the "North Star" became a welcome visitor to the homes of whites who had never before read a newspaper edited by a colored man, its proprietor became still more popular as a speaker in every State in the Union where abolitionism was tolerated.

"My Bondage and My Freedom," a work published by Mr. Douglass a few years ago, besides giving a fresh impulse to anti-slavery literature, showed upon its pages the untiring industry of the ripe scholar.

Some time during the year 1850, we believe, his journal assumed the name of "Frederick Douglass's Paper." Its purpose and aim, was the same, and it remained the representative of the negro till it closed its career, which was not until the abolition of slavery.

Of all his labors, however, we regard Mr. Douglass's efforts as publisher and editor as most useful to his race. For sixteen years, against much opposition, single-handed and alone, he demonstrated the fact that the American colored man was equal to the white in conducting a useful and popular journal.

JAMES M'CUNE SMITH, M. D.

Unable to get justice done him in the educational institutions of his native country, James M'Cune Smith turned his face towards a foreign land. He graduated with distinguished honors at the University of Glasgow, Scotland, where he received his diploma of M. D. For the last twenty-five years he has been a practitioner in the city of New York, where he stands at the head of his profession. On his return from Europe, the doctor was warmly welcomed by his fellow-citizens, who were anxious to pay due deferences to his talents; since which time he has justly been esteemed among the leading men of his race on the American continent. When the natural ability of the negro was assailed, some years ago, in New York, Dr. Smith came forward as the representative of the black man, and his essays on the comparative anatomy and physiology of the races, read in the discussion, completely vindicated the character of the negro, and places the author among the most logical and scientific writers in the country.

The doctor has contributed many valuable papers to the different journals published by colored men during the last quarter of a century. The New York dailies have also received aid from him during the same period. History, antiquity, bibliography, translation, criticism, political economy, statistics,—almost every department of knowledge,—receive emblazon from his able, ready, versatile, and unwearied pen. The emancipation of the slave, and the elevation of the free colored people, has claimed the greatest share of his time as a writer.

The law of labor is equally binding on genius and mediocrity. The mind and body rarely visit this earth of ours so exactly fitted to each other, and so perfectly harmonizing together, as to rise without effort, and command in the affairs of men. It is not in the power of every one to become great. No great approximation, even towards that which is easiest attained, can be accomplished without exercise of much thought and vigor of action; and thus is demonstrated the supremacy of that law which gives excellence only when earned, and assigns labor its unfailing reward.

It is this energy of character, industry, and labor, combined with superior intellectual powers, which gave Dr. Smith so much influence in New York.

As a speaker, he was eloquent, and at times brilliant, but always clear, and to the point. In stature, the doctor was not tall, but thick, and somewhat inclined to corpulency. He had a fine and well-developed head; broad and lofty brow; round, full face; firm mouth; and an eye that dazzled. In blood he stood, apparently, equal between the Anglo-Saxon and the African.

ALEXANDER CRUMMELL, D. D.

Among the many bright examples of the black man which we present, one of the foremost is Alexander Crummell. Blood unadulterated, a tall and manly figure, commanding in appearance, a full and musical voice, fluent in speech, a graduate of Cambridge University, England, a mind stored with the richness of English literature, competently acquainted with the classical authors of Greece and Rome, from the grave Thucydides to the rhapsodical Lycophron, gentlemanly in all his movements, language chaste and refined, Dr. Crummell may well be put forward as one of the best and most favorable representatives of his race. He is a clergyman of the Episcopal denomination, and deeply versed in theology. His sermons are always written, but he reads them as few persons can.

In 1848, Dr. Crummell visited England, and delivered a well-conceived address before the Anti-slavery Society in London, where his eloquence and splendid abilities were at once acknowledged and appreciated. The year before his departure for the Old World, he delivered an "Eulogy on the Life and Character of Thomas Clarkson," which was a splendid, yet just tribute to the life-long labors of that great man.

Dr. Crummell is one of our ablest speakers. His style is polished, graceful, and even elegant, though never merely ornate or rhetorical. He has the happy faculty of using the expressions best suited to the occasion, and bringing in allusions which give a popular sympathy to the best cultivated style. He is, we think, rather too sensitive, and somewhat punctilious.

Dr. Crummell is a gentleman by nature, and could not be anything else, if he should try. Some ten years since, he wrote a very interesting work on Africa, to which country he emigrated in1852.

We have had a number of our public men to represent us in Europe within the past twenty-five years; and non have done it more honorably or with better success to the character and cause of the black man, than Alexander Crummell. We met him there again and again, and followed in his track whenever he preached or spoke before public assemblies, and we know whereof we affirm. Devotedly attached to the interest of the colored man, and having the moral, social, and intellectual elevation of the natives of Africa at heart, we do not regret that he considers it his fatherland. Warmly interested in the Republic, and so capable of filling the highest position that he can be called to, we shall not be surprised some day, to hear that Alexander Crummell is president of Liberia.

Avery College has just done itself the honor of conferring the degree of Doctor of Divinity upon this able man; and sure we are that a title was never better bestowed than in the present instance.

Since writing the above sketch, we learned that Dr. Crummell has returned, and taken up his residence in the City of New York, where he is now pastor of a church.

The Negro in the American Rebellion: His Heroism and His Fidelity

(Boston: Lee & Shepard, 1867)

Chapter I
Blacks in the Revolutionary War and in 1812

The First Cargo of Slaves landed in the Colonies in 1620.—Slave Representations in Congress.—Opposition to the Slave-Trade.—Crispus Attucks, the First Victim of the Revolutionary War.—Bancroft's Testimony.—Capture of Gen. Prescott.—Colored Men in the War of 1812.—Gen. Andrew Jackson on Negro Soldiers.

I now undertake to write a history of the part which the colored men took in the great American Rebellion. Previous to entering upon that subject, however, I may be pardoned for bringing before the reader the condition of the blacks previous to the breaking out of the war.

The Declaration of American Independence, made July 4, 1776, had scarcely been enunciated, and an organization of the government commenced, ere the people found themselves surrounded by new and trying difficulties, which, for a time, threatened to wreck the ship of state.

The forty-five slaves landed on the banks of the James River, in the colony of Virginia, from the coast of Africa, in 1620, had multiplied to several thousands, and were influencing the political, social, and religious institutions of the country. Brought into the colonies against their will; made the "hewers of wood and the drawers of water;" considered, in the light of law and public opinion, as mere chattels,—things to be bought and sold at the will of the owner; driven to their unrequited toil by unfeeling men, picked for the purpose from the lowest and most degraded of the uneducated whites, whose moral, social, and political degradation, by slavery, was equal to that of the slave,—the condition of the negro was indeed a sad one.

439

The history of this people, full of sorrow, blood, and tears, is full also of instruction for mankind. God has so ordered it that one class shall not degrade another, without becoming themselves contaminated. So with slavery in America. The institution bred in the master insulting arrogance, deteriorating sloth, pampered the loathsome lust it inflamed, until licentious luxury sapped the strength and rottened the virtue of the slave-owners of the South. Never were the institutions of a people, or the principles of liberty, put to such a severe test as those of the American Republic. The convention to frame the Constitution for the government of the United States had not organized before the slave-masters began to press the claims of their system upon the delegates. They wanted their property represented in the national Congress, and undue guarantees thrown around it; they wanted the African slave-trade made lawful, and their victims returned if they should attempt to escape; they begged that an article might be inserted in the Constitution, making it the duty of the General Government to put down the slaves if they should imitate their masters in striking a blow for freedom. They seemed afraid of the very evil they were clinging so closely to. "Thus conscience doth make cowards of us all."

In all this early difficulty, South Carolina took the lead against humanity, her delegates ever showing themselves the foes of freedom. Both in the Federal Convention to frame the Constitution, and in the State Conventions to ratify the same, it was admitted that the blacks had fought bravely against the British, and in favor of the American Republic; for the fact that a black man (Crispus Attucks) was the first to give his life at the commencement of the Revolution was still fresh in their minds. Eighteen years previous to the breaking out of the war, Attucks was held as a slave by Mr. William Brown of Framingham, Mass., and from whom he escaped about that time, taking up his residence in Boston. The Boston Massacre, March 5, 1770, may be regarded as the first act in the great drama of the American Revolution. "From that moment," said Daniel Webster, "we may date the severance of the British Empire." The presence of the British soldiers in King Street excited the patriotic indignation of the people. The whole community was stirred, and sage counsellors were deliberating and writing and talking about the public grievances. But it was not for "the wise and prudent" to be the first to *act* against the encroachments of arbitrary power. "A motley rabble of saucy boys, negroes and mullatoes, Irish Teagues, and outlandish Jack tars" (as John Adams described them in his plea in defence of soldiers) could not restrain their emotion, or stop to inquire if what they *must do* was according to the letter of any law. Led by Crispus Attucks, the mulatto slave, and shouting, "The way to get rid of these soldiers is to attack the main guard; strike at the root, this is the next," with more valor than discretion, they rushed to King Street, and were fired upon by Capt. Preston's Company. Crispus Attucks was the first to fall: he and Samuel Gray and Jonas Caldwell were killed on the spot. Samuel Maverick and Patrick Carr were mortally wounded.

The excitement which followed was intense. The bells of the town were rung. An impromptu town-meeting was held, and an immense assembly was gathered.

Three days after, on the 8th, a public funeral of the martyrs took place. The shops in Boston were closed; and all the bells of Boston and the neighboring towns were rung. It is said that a greater number of persons assembled on this occasion than were ever before gathered on this continent for a similar purpose. The body of Crispus Attucks, the mulatto slave, had been placed in Faneuil Hall, with that of Caldwell, both being strangers in the city. Maverick was buried from his mother's house, in Union Street; and Gray from his brother's in Royal Exchange Lane. The four hearses formed a junction in King Street: and there the procession marched in columns six deep, with a long file of coaches belonging to the most distinguished citizens, to the Middle Burying-ground, where the four victims were deposited in one grave, over which a stone was placed with this inscription:—

"Long as in Freedom's cause the wise contend,
Dear to your country shall your fame extend;
While to the world the lettered stone shall tell
Where Caldwell, Attucks, Gray, and Maverick fell."

The anniversary of this event was publicly commemorated in Boston, by an oration and other exercises, every year until after our national independence was achieved, when the Fourth of July was substituted for the Fifth of March as the more proper day for a general celebration. Not only was the event commemorated, but the martyrs who then gave up their lives were remembered and honored.

For half a century after the close of the war, the name of Crispus Attucks was honorably mentioned by the most noted men of the country who were not blinded by foolish prejudice. At the battle of Bunker Hill, Peter Salem, a negro, distinguished himself by shooting Major Pitcairn, who, in the midst of the battle, having passed the storm of fire without, mounting the redoubt, and waving his sword, cried to the "rebels" to surrender. The fall of Pitcairn ended the battle in favor of liberty.

A single passage from Mr. Bancroft's history will give a succinct and clear account of the condition of the army, in respect to colored soldiers, at the time of the battle of Bunker Hill:—

"Nor should history forget to record, that, as in the army at Cambridge, so also in this gallant band, the free negroes of the colony had their representatives. For the right of free negroes to bear arms in the public defence was, at that day, as little disputed in New England as their other rights. They took their place, not in a separate corps, but in the ranks with the white man; and their names may be read on the pension-rolls of the country, side by side with those of other soldiers of the Revolution."—*Bancroft's History of the United States*, vol. vii, p. 421.

The capture of Major-Gen. Prescott, of the British army, on the 9th of July, 1777, was an occasion of great joy throughout the country. Prince, the valiant negro who seized that officer, ought always to be remembered with honor for his important service. The exploit was much commended at the time, as its results were highly important; and Col. Barton, very properly, received from Congress the compliment of a sword for his ingenuity and bravery. . . .

There is abundant evidence of the fidelity and bravery of the colored patriots of Rhode Island during the whole war. Before they had been formed into a separate regiment, they had fought valiantly with the white soldiers at Red Bank and elsewhere. Their conduct at the "Battle of Rhode Island," on the 29th of August, 1778, entitles them to perpetual honor. That battle has been pronounced by military authorities to have been one of the best-fought battles of the Revolutionary War. Its success was owing, in a great degree, to the good fighting of the negro soldiers. Mr. Arnold, in his "History of Rhode Island," thus closes his account of it:—

"A third time the enemy, with desperate courage and increased strength, attempted to assail the redoubt, and would have carried it, but for the timely aid of two Continental battalions dispatched by Sullivan to support his almost exhausted troops. It was in repelling these furious onsets, that the newly raised black regiment, under Col. Greene, distinguished itself by deeds of desperate valor. Posted behind a thicket in the valley, they three times drove back the Hessians, who charged repeatedly down the hill to dislodge them; and so determined were the enemy in these successive charges, that, the day after the battle, the Hessian colonel, upon whom this duty had devolved, applied to exchange his command, and go to New York, because he dared not lead his regiment again to battle, lest his men should shoot him for having caused them so much loss."
—*Arnold's History of Rhode Island*, vol ii, pp. 427, 428. . . .

When Col Greene was surprised and murdered, near Points Bridge, New York, on the 14th of May, 1781, his colored soldiers heroically defended him till they were cut to pieces; and the enemy reached him over the dead bodies of his faithful negroes.

That large numbers of negroes were enrolled in the army, and served faithfully as soldiers during the whole period of the war of the Revolution, may be regarded as a well-established historical fact. And it should be borne in mind, that the enlistment was not confined, by any means, to those who had before enjoyed the privileges of free citizens. Very many slaves were offered to, and received by, the army, on the condition that they were to be emancipated, either at the time of enlisting, or when they had served out the term of their enlistment. The inconsistency of keeping in slavery any person who had taken up arms for the defence of our national liberty had led to the passing of an order forbidding "slaves," as such, to be received as soldiers.

Notes

1 In his journals, Charles Chesnutt dismisses Brown's later work as sloppy and mediocre: "March 17, Thursday. I have skimmed "The Negro in the Rebellion," by Dr. Brown, and it only strengthens me in my opinion, that the Negro is yet to become known who can write a good book. Dr. Brown's books are mere compilations, and, as Thos. Jefferson says of Phillis Wheatley[']s poems, "beneath the dignity of criticism." If they were not written by a colored man, they would not sell enough to pay for the printing. I read them merely for facts, but I could appreciate the facts better if they were well presented. The book reminds me of a gentleman in a dirty shirt. You are rather apt to doubt his gentility under such circumstances. I am sometimes doubtful of the facts for the same reason—they make but a shabby appearance." *The Journals of Charles W. Chesnutt*, Ed. Richard H. Brodhead. Duke University Press, 1993, p. 164.

2 2 Chron. xiv: 8–13.

3 Hawkins, in his work on Meroe, identifies Tirhakah with the priest Sethos, upon ground, we think, not tenable.

4 2 Kings, xvii: 4.

5 2 Kings, xix: 9.

6 Herod. iii: 114.

7 Herod iii: 21.

8 Iliad II: 423.

9 Iliad XXIII.

10 Chron. xiv: 9; xvi: 8; Isaiah xlv: 14; Jeremiah xlvi: 9; Josephus Aut. II; Heeren, vol. I: p. 290.

11 E. H. Sears, in the "Christian Examiner," July, 1846.

12 Josephus Aut., Vol. I: p. 8.

13 Smith on "The Complexion of the Human Species."

14 Pritchard.

15 "Tribute for the Negro," p. 59.

16 Pennington's Text Book, p. 96.

17 "Livingstone's Travels," p. 296.

18 Ibid, p. 364.

19 Heeren, Vol. I., p. 297.

20 Murray's "North America."

21 Pritchard.

22 Ibid.

23 Aeolian, lib. xii, cap. 36.

24 Pritchard.

25 "Livingstone's Travels," p. 366.

26 "Dublin University Magazine," Vol. IV., p. 653.

27 Prof. Blyden, in "Methodist Quarterly Review," June, 1871.

28 Dr. Livingstone.

29 Thau.

30 Brown's History of St. Domingo, Vol. I., p. 257.

31 Beard's Life of Touissant L' Ouverture

32 John Josselyn.

33 Joshua Coffin.

34 Bancroft's "History of the United States." Vol. VII. p. 421.

35 Moore's "Diary of the American Revolution." Vol. I. p. 468.

36 Niles' Register, Vol. VII., p. 205.

37 T. W. Higginson, in Atlantic Monthly, June, 1861.

Selected Letters

In *The Liberator,* July 12, 1850

To the Public.

As a paragraph which made its appearance a few weeks since[, i]n the New York Tribune, and has been extensively copied into other papers, charges me with deserting my wife, I feel myself called upon to make the following statement of facts:—

In the summer of 1834, the same year in which I made my escape from slavery, I unfortunately became acquainted with Miss Betsey Schooner, and after a very short acquaintance, we were married. Up to the time of our marriage, I was entirely unacquainted with the fact that Mrs. Brown's mother was living with a second husband, while her first was still alive, having never been divorced. Soon after, I was made acquainted with the fact that Mrs. Brown's only sister was a mother, without having been a wife. Still later, I learned that Mrs. Brown's eldest brother, John, was in the Auburn, N.Y. State prison, where he died.

Though thus mistaken in the character of the family from which I had selected a wife, still being devotedly attached to Mrs. Brown, and aware that one member of a family should not be blamed for the misconduct of the others, I loved my wife none the less for what I had learned in relation to her family. In the autumn of 1836, I removed to the city of Buffalo, where, with the exception of a short period, I resided until the summer of 1845. On my return from an anti-slavery tour in December, 1844, I was treated with any thing but kindness by Mrs. Brown, a change of which I tried in vain to find out the cause. During the month of March, 1845, I left home to attend some meetings in Genesee county, N.Y., intending, when I left, to be absent ten days; but, owing to ill-health, I returned four days earlier than I had anticipated. I arrived in Buffalo about 11 o'clock at night, and on entering our dwelling, discovered Mrs. Brown and an acquaintance of ours, Mr. James Garrett, in circumstances which filled me with the most painful suspicions. The next day, they attempted some explanations. These were not at all satisfactory; still, as I had always regarded Garrett as one of my best friends, as I was unwilling to believe that my wife had acted improperly farther than what I had seen, I let the matter drop, with the understanding that Garrett should no longer visit the house. I soon became satisfied, however, that he still visited my house in my absence. When I first charged Mrs. Brown with permitting him to visit the house, she denied it, but afterwards admitted it, giving as an excuse that he came to borrow my anti-slavery papers, which previous to this time, he had taken from my box in the post-office, with my consent. I was satisfied, however, that Garret knew when I was going into the country, and how long I would remain; and soon after, on my return home, after a short absence, I entered the house through the back way, and found Garrett there, and under circumstances of a still more revolting character than on a former occasion. This satisfied me, beyond the shadow of a doubt, that my worst apprehensions were too true, and I determined at the moment to make an exposition of the whole matter. But the entreaties of Mrs. Brown, the helpless condition of my children, and my infatuated attachment to my wife, induced me to forego the exposure.

I determined to leave Buffalo. I had thought of this previous to the discovery of the guilt of Mrs. Brown, and had gone so far as to get a house in Farmington, which was at that time unoccupied. But Mrs. Brown had so strenuously opposed our removal, that I had given up the idea. She now consented to leave Buffalo, if I would not make the matter public. About this time, I was called into the county of Ontario, to attend some meetings. Some two or three days after leaving home, and after a little more reflection upon what had occurred, I wrote to Mrs. Brown that I should not remove to Farmington, with the express purpose of giving up the house; but was surprised when I called upon the gentleman who had the charge of it, to hear that Mrs. Brown and the children were at the house of a friend of mine in Macedon, a short distance from where I then was. I said nothing about giving up the house, but sought ou[t] Mrs. Brown. The result was, that I adhered to my former resolution to remove from Buffalo. But Mrs. Brown must have one last look at Buffalo, and a last farewell with Garrett; and for this purpose she returned to the city, a distance of over one hundred miles, leaving her children behind. As she had left home without any excuse, not letting the lady, who resided in the other part of the house, know what she was leaving home for, she said on her return that I was ill, and had written for her. We soon returned to Farmington; but here Mrs. Brown was not satisfied, and during the winter of 1846, she determined to visit Buffalo again, even though she had to do it alone. The children were left at the house of a friend, and off Mrs. Brown started. I refused to accompany her.

After reaching Buffalo, she wrote to me, asking me to come to her, and saying that the people were talking about her, and that myself alone could put a stop to it by contradicting certain reports. Against the advice of the best of friends and my own judgment, I went to Buffalo. I found that her conduct had been so improper, and was so widely known, that though I at first did what I could to shield her, I become so disgusted with the position in which Mrs. Brown had placed me, that I left Buffalo, after being there two or three days, leaving her behind. She soon, however, returned to Farmington. We then had many conversations respecting a separation. In the spring of 1847, Mrs. Brown wrote to me, saying that she had made up her mind to leave Farmington, and that if I did not come and take the children, she would leave them with some of the neighbors. I immediately returned home, and in four days from that time I was on my way to the East with the children, while Mrs. Brown was on her way to the West. The separation was by mutual consent. Mrs. Brown went to Canada, thence to Detroit, where Garrett then resided. I heard but little of her until the month of July, 1848, when she made her appearance in Boston, where she brought with her a child. She stopped at the house of a friend of mine, where I called the next day to see her. She at first declined seeing me, but after much persuading, she agreed to see me upon condition that her child should not be brought into the room. I saw her, but did not see her child. She did not say a word about it. She stated that she wished to see the children which were at school in New Bedford, and that she was out of money. I furnished her with money, but I had scarcely left the house ere she commenced trying to poison the minds of the best of friends against me. Mrs. Brown went to New Bedford, and soon after wrote to me, saying she wanted to return to New York, and that she had not the means. I went to New Bedford a few days after, and furnished her with money. She started, as she then said, for Buffalo, but instead of going there, she went to Springfield, where she spared no pains in spreading injurious reports against me. From Springfield she came east again to Worcester, and thence returned again to New Bedford. In each of these places, she spent three or four weeks, using up the time in going among influential abolitionists, to prejudice them against me. Soon, letters were sent to the Secretary of the Massachusetts Anti-Slavery Society, of which I was that time an agent, complaining of my conduct to Mrs. Brown, and asking for my dismissal from the agency. During the whole of this time, Mrs. Brown was traveling solely at my expense. She soon wrote to some of my friends in Boston, complaining of my refusal to give her money, which I declined doing as soon as I became aware of her object.

About this time, the Board of Managers of the Massachusetts Anti-Slavery Society, anxious that nothing should be done to injure the cause of the slave, and wishing to retain no agents in their employ but those of untarnished character, appointed a committee to investigate the matter.

Before this Committee, Mrs. Brown at first declined to appear, though requested to bring any friend with her; but she was finally, with much persuasion, prevailed upon to come before them. The result of the investigation was, that I was retained as an agent; and to the Board of Managers of the Massachusetts Anti-Slavery Society I am indebted for valuable letters of introduction to the people of Great Britain. After the investigation was over, Mrs. Brown expressed a wish to return to Buffalo, where she left no stone unturned to damage me. She has said that she would travel over the entire country to injure me, and she has gone as far as her means would permit: and she finds fault with me for not furnishing her with money. Had Mrs. Brown wished, she could still have had a home with my children; but she left, it is well known, of her own accord. I have declined giving any further support to a woman whose own misconduct has alienated her from me forever. Whether I have done right in this matter or not, I leave to a candid and impartial public to judge. In looking back upon the former part of this transaction, I see many acts of mine which I regret. But to do otherwise, at the time, was beyond my power. My attachment to my wife was too great to allow me to do what I saw clearly to be a duty to myself and my children. I have been blamed by many for my long silence upon this subject, and even now I give this statement with great reluctance. Nothing but self-defence could possibly have induced me to pen this article.

William Wells Brown
London, June 1, 1850

In relation to the above statement, it is only necessary for us to add, that, without intending to decide on the truth of all the facts mentioned above,—the truth of many of which can be known only to the parties themselves,—we and our friends were satisfied, from the investigation we were able to make here, and from all we could gather of the opinions of those, in whose neighborhood Mr. and Mrs. Brown resided at the time alluded to, that there was nothing in his conduct toward his wife worthy of censure; but that, on the contrary, he had shown her great forbearance—had endeavored to do his duty as a husband and father, watchful for the best interests of his children, for whom his exertions were untiring; and that he was entitled to the sympathy of his friends in the painful circumstances in which he was placed. Most assuredly, no such recommendations as he carried with him to the friends of the anti-slavery cause in England would have been given by us or our associates here, if we and they had not cherished for him the warmest sympathy and the most cordial friendship, and reposed the most entire confidence in the integrity of his character.

In *Frederick Douglass' Paper,*
October 2, 1851

DEAR DOUGLASS:—I have just finished a short visit to the far famed city of Oxford, which has not unaptly been styled, the city of palaces.

Aside from this being one of the principal seats of learning in the world, it is distinguished alike for its religious, and political changes in times past. At one time it was the seat of popery; at another, the uncompromising enemy of Rome. Here the tyrant, Richard the Third, held his court, and when James the First, and his son Charles the First found their capital too hot to hold them, they removed to their loyal city of Oxford.

The writings of the great Republicans were here committed to the flames. At one time popery sent Protestants to the stake and faggot; at another, a papist King found no favor with the people. A noble monument now stands where Cranmer, Ridley, and Latimer, proclaimed their sentiments and faith, and sealed it with their blood. And we read upon the town treasurer's book,—for three loads of wood, one load of faggots, one post, two chains and staples, to burn Ridley and Latimer, L1 5s 2p.

Such is the information one gets by looking over the records of books written three centuries ago.

It was a beautiful day on which I arrived at Oxford, and instead of remaining in my hotel, I sallied forth to take a survey of the beauties of the city. I strolled into Christ Church Meadows, and there spent the evening in viewing the numerous halls of learning, which surrounds that splendid promenade.

And fine old buildings they are; centuries have rolled over many of them, hallowing the old walls and making them gray with age. They have been for ages the chosen homes of piety, and philosophy. Heroes and scholars, have gone forth from their studies here, into the great field of the world, to seek their fortunes, and to conquer and be conquered.

As I surveyed the exterior of the different Colleges, I could here and there see the reflection of the light from the window of some student, who was busy at his studies, or throwing away his time over some trashy novel, too many of which find their way into the trunks or carpet bags of the young man on setting out for College. As I looked upon the walls of these buildings, I thought as the rough stone is taken from the quarry to the finisher, there to be made into an ornament, so was the young mind brought here to be cultivated and developed.

Many a poor unobtrusive young man with the appearance of little or no ability, is here moulded into a hero, a scholar, a tyrant, or a friend of humanity.

I never look upon these monuments of education, without a feeling of regret, that so few of our own race can find a place within their walls.

And this being the fact, I see more and more the need of our people being encouraged to turn their attention more seriously to self-education, and thus to take a respectable position before the world, by virtue of their own cultivated minds, and moral standing.

Education, though obtained by a little at a time, and that, too, over the midnight lamp, will place its owner in a position to be respected by all, even though he be black.

I know that the obstacles which the laws of the land, and of society, places between the colored man and education in the United States, is very great, yet if one can break through these barriers, more can, and if our people would only place the right appreciation upon education, they would find these obstacles are easier to be overcome than appears at first sight. A young man once asked Carlyle, what was the secret of success. His reply was, "Energy; whatever you undertake, do it with all your might."

Had it not been for the possession of energy, I might now have been working as a servant for some brainless fellow who might be able to command my labour with his money, or I might have been yet toiling in chains and slavery. But thanks to energy, not only for my being to day in a land of freedom, but also for my dear girls being in one of the best Seminaries in France, instead of being in an American school, where the finger of scorn would be pointed at them, by those whose superiority rests entirely upon their having a whiter skin.

But I am straying too far from the purpose of this letter.

Oxford is indeed one of the finest located places in the Kingdom, and every inch of ground about it, seems hallowed by interesting associations.

The University founded by the good King Alfred, still throws its shadow upon the side walk; and the lapse of ten centuries seems to have made but little impression upon it. Other seats of learning may be entitled to our admiration, but Oxford claims our veneration. Although the lateness of the night compelled me to, yet I felt an unwillingness to tear myself from the scene of such surpassing interest. Few places in any country as noted as Oxford is, but that has some distinguished person residing within its precincts. And knowing that the city of palaces was not an exception to this rule, I resolved to see some of its Visions.

Here of course is the headquarters of the Bishop of Oxford, a son of the late William Wilberforce, Africa's noble champion.

I should have been glad to have seen this distinguished pillar of the Church, but I soon learned that the Bishop's residence was out of town, and that he seldom visited the city, except on business.

I then determined to see one, who, although, a lesser dignitary in the church, is nevertheless, scarcely less known than the Bishop of Oxford.

This was the Rev. Dr. Pusey, a divine whose name is known wherever the religion of Jesus is known and taught, and the acknowledged head of the Puseyites. On the second morning of my visit, I proceeded to Christ Church Chapel, where the Rev. Gentleman officiates.

Fortunately I had an opportunity of seeing the Dr., and following close in his footsteps to the church.

His personal appearance is anything but that of one who is the leader of a growing, and powerful party in the church.

He is rather under the middle size, and is round shouldered, or rather stoops. His profile is more striking than his front face, the nose being very large and prominent. As a matter of course, I expected to see a large nose, for all great men have them.

He has a thoughtful, and somewhat sullen brow, a firm, and somewhat pensive mouth, a cheek pale, thin, and deeply furrowed.

A monk fresh from the cloisters of Tintern Abby, in its proudest days, could scarcely have made a more ascetic and solemn appearance than did Dr. Pusey on this occasion.

He is not apparently above forty-five, or at most fifty years of age, and his whole aspect renders him an admirable study for an artist.

Dr. Pusey's style of preaching is cold and tame, and one looking at him would scarcely believe that such an uninteresting appearing man could cause such an eruption in the church as he has. I was glad to find that a colored young man was among the students at Oxford.

A few months since, I paid a visit to our countryman, Alexander Crummell, who is still pursuing his studies at Cambridge, a place, though far inferior to Oxford, as far as appearance is concerned, is said to be greatly its superior as a place of learning. In an hour's walk through the Strand, Regent, or Piccadilly streets in London, one may meet a half a dozen colored young men, who are inmates of the various Colleges in the metropolis. These are all signs of progress in the cause of the sons of Africa.

Then let our people take courage, and with that courage let them apply themselves to learning.

A determination to excel, is the secret road to greatness, and that is as open to the black man as the white.

It was that which has accomplished the mightiest and noblest triumphs in the intellectual and physical world. It was that which has made such rapid strides towards civilization, and broken the chains of ignorance, and superstition, which has so long fettered the human intellect.

It was determination which raised so many worthy individuals from the humble walks of society, and from poverty, and placed them in positions of trust and renown. It is no slight barrier that can effectually oppose the determination of the will; success must ultimately crown its efforts.

"The world shall hear of me," was the exclamation of one whose name has become as familiar as household words. A Toussaint, once laboured in the sugar field with his spelling book in his pocket, and the combined efforts of a nation to keep him in ignorance. His name is now recorded among the list of Statesmen of the past. A Soulouque was once a slave, and knew not how to read. He now sits upon the throne of an Empire.

In our own country, there are men who once held the plough, and that too without any compensation, that are now presiding at the editor's table.

It was determination that brought out the genius of a Franklin, a Fulton, and that has distinguished many of the American Statesmen, who but for their energy and determination would never have had a name beyond the precincts of their own homes.

It is not always those who have the best advantages, or the greatest talents, that eventually succeed in their undertakings, but it is those who strive with untiring diligence to remove all obstacles to success, and with unconquerable resolution to labour on until the rich reward of perseverance is within their grasp.

Then again let me say to our young men, Take courage, "There is a good time coming." The darkness of the night appears greatest, just before the dawn of day.

Yours, right truly,
W.W. BROWN.

In *Frederick Douglass' Paper*, March 16, 1855

(reprinted from the *Anti-Slavery Standard*)

TO FREDERICK DOUGLASS.

SIR: Had not your many changes and rechanges prepared me to be astonished at not[h]ing that you might say, or do, I would have been somewhat
surprised at [t]he attack made upon me by you, in your paper of the 2nd of
March. You commence by saying, "we do [regret t]hat he should feel
called upon to show his faithfulness to the American Anti-Slavery Society
by covering us with dishonor." Let me say to you, Frederick Douglass, that
my difference with you has not[h]ing whatever to do with the American
Anti-Slavery Society, and no one knows that better than yourself. And I
regard such an insinuation as fit only to come from one whose feelings are
entirely lost to all sense of shame. My charge against you is, that, just
before I left the United States for England, you wrote a private letter to a
distinguished Abolitionis[t] in Great Britain, injurious to me, and
intended to forestall my movements there. In a note which I forwarded to
you, to your address at Rochester on the 20th of January last, I gave you to
understand that I had been made aware of your having acted in that
underhand manner. The following is a part of the note I sent you more
than a month ago. "During my sojourn in England, and several months
after my arrival there, and while spending a few days with a friend of
yours, the post brought me a letter, which had been re-mailed in London,
and it proved to be from you, dated at New Bedford. After I had finished
reading the letter, your frien[d] seemed anxious to learn its contents. I
handed it to her, with the request that she would read it; your frien[d]
appeared much astonished at the kindness expressed by you to me, and
exclaimed, 'Douglass has done you a great injustice,' and immediately
revealed to me the contents of a letter which she had received from you,
some months before, and which was written a short time previous to my

departure from America. I need not say that the very unfavorable position in which your letter placed me before your friend, secured me for a cold reception at her hands. I need not name the lady; you know to whom I refer unless you wrote to more than one." Your attack upon me, in your paper of the 2nd inst., in which you ask for "facts," when my note containing the above had been in your possession more than a month, shows too well your wish to make a sneaking fling at me, instead of seeking for "facts," and acting the part of an honorable man. Why did you not give my note a place in your paper, and make such comments as you thought best? No, that would not have suited you. But, anxious to heap insult upon injury you resort to [t]he [m]ode most congenial to your feelings and sense of justice. Had I not thought it due to the public to state the above "facts," I would have treated your scurrilous paragraph with that silence and contempt that all such articles so justly deserve. However, no future insinuation of yours, no mater how false or unjust, shall provoke from me a reply.

WILLIAM WELLS BROWN.

In *The Christian Recorder*, January 22, 1874

The Colored Race. HOW IT MAY SECURE ITS OWN ADVANCE.

We can advance only by the adoption and deep inculcation of the principle that leads us to abstain from all intoxicants. This is a prerequisite for success in all the relations of life. For it must never be forgotten that whatever degree of exhilaration may be produced in a healthy person by the use of wine, it will most certainly be succeeded by a degree of our nervous depression proportioned to the amount of previous excitement. Hence the immoderate use of wine, it will most certainly be succeeded by a degree of our nervous depression proportioned to the amount of previous excitement. Hence the immoderate use of wine, or its habitual indulgence, debilities the brain and nervous system, paralyzes the intellectual powers, impairs the functions of the stomach, produces a perverted appetite for the renewal of the delirious beverage, or a morbid imagination, which destroys man's usefulness. The next important need with our people is the cultivation of habits of business. We have been so long a dependent race, so long looking to the whites as our leaders, and being content with doing the drudgery of life, that most who commence business for the themselves are likely to fail, because of want of a knowledge of what we undertake. As the education of a large percentage of the colored people is of a fragmentary character, having been gained by little and little here and there, and must necessarily be limited to a certain degree, we should use our spare hours in study and form association for moral, social and literary culture. We must aim to enlighten ourselves and to influence others to higher associations.

Our work lies primarily with the inward culture, at the springs and sources of individual life and character seeking everywhere to encourage, and assist to the fullest emancipation of the human mind from ignorance, inviting the largest liberty of thought and the utmost possible exaltation of life into approximation to the loftier standard of cultivated character. Feeling that the literature of our age is the reflection of the existing manners and modes of thought, ether realized and refined in the alembic of genius, we should give our principal encouragement to literature, bringing before our associations the importance of original essays, selected readings, and the cultivation of the musical talent. If we need any proof of the good that would accrue from such cultivation, we have only to look back and see the wonderful influence of Homer over the Greeks, of Virgil and Horace over the Romans, of Dante and Ariosto over the Italians, of Goethe and Schiller over the Germans, of Racine and Voltaire over the French, of Shakespeare and Milton over the English. The imaginative powers of these men, wrought into verse or prose, have been the theme of the king in his palace, the love[r] in his dreamy moods, the farmer in the harvest field, the mechanic in the workshop, the sailor on the high seas, and the prisoner in his gloomy cell.

Indeed, authors possess the most gifted and fertile mind who combine all the grace of style with rare, fascinating powers of language, eloquence, wit, humor, pathos, genius and learning. And to draw knowledge from such sources should be one of the highest aims of man. The better elements of society can only be brought together by some method like ours. The cultivation of the mind is the superstructure of the moral, social and religious character, which will follow us into our everyday life, and make us what God, intended us to be—the noblest instruments of His creative power. Our efforts should be to imbue our minds with broader and better views of science, literature and a nobleness of spirit that ignores petty aims of patriotism, glory, or mere personal aggrandizement. It is said, never a shadow falls that does not leave a permanent impress of its image, a monument of its passing presence. Every character is modified by association. Words, the image of ideas, are more impressive than shadows; actions, embodied thoughts, more enduring than ought material. Believing these truths, then, I say, for every thought expressed, ennobling in its tendency and elevating to Christian dignity and manly honor, God will reward us. Permanent success depends upon intrinsic worth. The best way to have a public character is to have a private one.

The great struggle for our elevation is now with ourselves. We may talk of Hannibal, Euclid, Philli[s] Wheatley, Benjami[n] Banneker and Toussaint L'Overture, but the world ask us for our men and women of the day. We cannot live upon the past[;] we must hew out a reputation that will stand the test, one that we have a legitimate right to. To do this we must imitate the best examples set us by the cultivated whites, and by so doing we will teach them that they can claim no superiority on account of race.

Teaching
William Wells Brown:
Four Versions
of an Anecdote

William Wells Brown borrowed—unabashedly—from his own work and the works of others in his fictional and humorous works. One particular anecdote of a sham dentist and a mistaken extraction appears in four works: Clotel *(1853),* The Escape *(1858),* Clotelle *(1865), and* My Southern Home *(1880). In the context of Brown's lengthy and occasionally tumultuous relationship with Frederick Douglass, it is tempting to read this compulsive retelling as allegorical.*

1. From *Clotel* (1853)

Sam's former master was a doctor, and had a large practice among his neighbours, doctoring both masters and slaves. When Sam was about fifteen years of age, his old master set him to grinding up the ointment, then to making pills. As the young student grew older and became more practiced in his profession, his services were of more importance to the doctor. The physician having a good business, and a large number of his patients being slaves, the most of whom had to call on the doctor when ill, he put Sam to bleeding, pulling teeth, and administering medicine to the slaves. Sam soon acquired the name amongst the slaves of the "Black Doctor." With this appellation he was delighted, and no regular physician could possibly have put on more airs than did the black doctor when his services were required. In bleeding, he must have more bandages, and rub and smack the arm more than the doctor would have thought of. We once saw Sam taking out a tooth for one of his patients, and nothing appeared more amusing. He got the poor fellow down on his back, and he got astraddle of the man's chest, and getting the turnkeys on the wrong tooth, he shut both eyes and pulled for his life. The poor man screamed as loud as he could, but to no purpose. Sam had him fast. After a great effort, out came the sound grinder, and the young doctor saw his mistake; but consoled himself with the idea that as the wrong tooth was out of the way, there was more room to get at the right one. Bleeding and a dose of calomel was always considered indispensable by the "Old Boss"; and, as a matter of course, Sam followed in his footsteps.

2. From *The Escape* (1858)

"What you come in dat door widout knockin' for?" exclaimed Cato.

Bill. "My toof ache so, I didn't tink to knock. Oh, my toof! my toof! Whar is de Doctor?"

Cato. "Here I is; don't you see me?"

Bill. "What! you de Doctor, you brack cuss! You looks like a doctor! Oh, my toof! my toof! Whar is de Doctor?"

Cato. "I tells you I is de doctor. Ef you don't believe me, ax dese men. I can pull your toof in a minnit."

Bill. "Well, den, pull it out. Oh, my toof! how it aches! Oh, my toof!" [Cato gets the rusty turnkeys.]

Cato. "Now lay down on your back."

Bill. "What for?"

Cato. "Dat's de way massa does."

Bill. "Oh, my toof! Well, den, come on." [Lies down. Cato gets astraddle of Bill's breast, puts the turnkeys on the wrong tooth, and pulls—Bill kicks and cries out]—["]Oh, do stop! Oh, oh, oh!["] [Cato pulls the wrong tooth—Bill jumps up.]

Cato. "Dar, now, I tole you I could pull your toof for you."

Bill. ["]Oh, dear me! Oh, it aches yet! Oh, me! Lor-e-massy! You dun pull de wrong toof. Drat your skin! ef I don't pay you for this, you brack cuss!["] [*They fight, and turn over table, chairs, and bench—Pete and Ned look on.*]

During the *melée*, Dr. Gaines entered the office, and unceremoniously went at them with his cane, giving both a sound drubbing before any explanation could be offered. As soon as he could get an opportunity, Cato said, "Oh, massa! He's to blame, sir, he's to blame. He struck me fuss."

Bill. "No, sir; he's to blame; he pull de wrong toof. Oh, my toof! oh, my toof!"

Dr. G. "Let me see your tooth. Open your mouth. As I live, you've taken out the wrong tooth. I am amazed. I'll whip you for this; I'll whip you well. You're a pretty doctor. Now, lie down, Bill, and let him take out the right tooth; and if he makes a mistake this time, I'll cowhide him well. Lie down, Bill." [Bill lies down, and Cato pulls the tooth.] "There, now, why didn't you do that in the first place?"

Cato. "He wouldn't hole still, sir."

Bill. "I did hole still."

Dr. G. "Now go home, boys; go home."

3. From *Clotelle* (1865)

The evening's entertainment concluded by Sam relating a little of his own experience while with his first master, in old Kentucky. This master was a doctor, and had a large practice among his neighbors, doctoring both masters and slaves. When Sam was about fifteen years old, his master set him to grinding up ointment and making pills. As the young student grew older and became more practiced in his profession, his services were of more importance to the doctor. The physician having a good business, and a large number of his patients being slaves,—the most of whom had to call on the doctor when ill,—he put Sam to bleeding, pulling teeth, and administering medicine to the slaves. Sam soon acquired the name among the slaves of the "Black Doctor." With this appellation he was delighted; and no regular physician could have put on more airs than did the black doctor when his services were required. In bleeding, he must have more bandages, and would rub and smack the arm more than the doctor would have thought of.

Sam was once seen taking out a tooth for one of his patients, and nothing appeared more amusing. He got the poor fellow down on his back, and then getting astride of his chest, he applied the turnkeys and pulled away for dear life. Unfortunately, he had got hold of the wrong tooth, and the poor man screamed as loud as he could; but it was to no purpose, for Sam had him fast, and after a pretty severe tussle out came the sound grinder. The young doctor now saw his mistake, but consoled himself with the thought that as the wrong tooth was out of the way, there was more room to get at the right one.

4. From *My Southern Home* (1880)

Just then, Mr. Parker's negro boy Bill, with his hand up to his mouth, and evidently in great pain, entered the office without giving the usual knock at the door, and which gave great offence to the new physician.

"What you come in dat door widout knockin' for?" exclaimed Cato.

Bill. "My toof ache so, I didn't tink to knock. Oh, my toof! my toof! Whar is de Doctor?"

Cato. "Here I is; don't you see me?"

Bill. "What! you de Doctor, you brack cuss! You looks like a doctor! Oh, my toof! my toof! Whar is de Doctor?"

Cato. "I tells you I is de doctor. Ef you don't believe me, ax dese men. I can pull your toof in a minnit."

Bill. "Well, den, pull it out. Oh, my toof! how it aches! Oh, my toof!" [Cato gets the rusty turnkeys.]

Cato. "Now lay down on your back."

Bill. "What for?"

Cato. "Dat's de way massa does."

Bill. "Oh, my toof! Well, den, come on." [Lies down. Cato gets astraddle of Bill's breast, puts the turnkeys on the wrong tooth, and pulls—Bill kicks and cries out]—["]Oh, do stop! Oh, oh, oh!["] [Cato pulls the wrong tooth—Bill jumps up.]

Cato. "Dar, now, I tole you I could pull your toof for you."

Bill. ["]Oh, dear me! Oh, it aches yet! Oh, me! Lor-e-massy! You dun pull de wrong toof. Drat your skin! ef I don't pay you for this, you brack cuss!["] [They fight, and turn over table, chairs, and bench—Pete and Ned look on.]

During the melée, Dr. Gaines entered the office, and unceremoniously went at them with his cane, giving both a sound drubbing before any explanation could be offered. As soon as he could get an opportunity, Cato said, "Oh, massa! He's to blame, sir, he's to blame. He struck me fuss."

Bill. "No, sir; he's to blame; he pull de wrong toof. Oh, my toof! oh, my toof!"

Dr. G. "Let me see your tooth. Open your mouth. As I live, you've taken out the wrong tooth. I am amazed. I'll whip you for this; I'll whip you well. You're a pretty doctor. Now, lie down, Bill, and let him take out the right tooth; and if he makes a mistake this time, I'll cowhide him well. Lie down, Bill." [Bill lies down, and Cato pulls the tooth.] "There, now, why didn't you do that in the first place?"

Cato. "He wouldn't hole still, sir."

Bill. "I did hole still."

Dr. G. "Now go home, boys; go home."

Bibliography

Allen, Alexandra. *Traveling Ladies*. London: Jupiter Press, 1980.

Andrews, William. *From Fugitive Slave to Free Man: The Autobiographies of William Wells Brown*. New York: New American Library, 1993.

Andrews, William, ed. *Journeys in New Worlds: Early American Women's Narratives*. Madison: University of Wisconsin Press, 1990.

Bardes, Barbara, and Suzanne Gossett. *Declarations of Independence: Women and Political Power in Nineteenth-Century American Fiction*. New Brunswick, N.J.: Rutgers University Press, 1990.

Barreca, Regina, ed. *Last Laughs: New Perspectives on Women and Comedy*. Philadelphia: Gordon and Breach, 1988.

Baym, Nina. "Melodramas of Beset Manhood: How Theories of American Fiction Exclude Women Authors." *American Quarterly* 33 (Summer 1981): 123–139.

Baym, Nina. *Woman's Fiction: A Guide to Novels by and about Women in America, 1820–70*. New York: Cornell University Press, 1978.

Bentley, Nancy. "Nathaniel Hawthorne and the Fetish of Race." In *The Ethnography of Manners: Hawthorne, James, Wharton*, pp. 24–67. New York: Cambridge University Press, 1995.

Berthold, Michael. "Cross-Dressing and Forgetfulness of Self in William Wells Brown's *Clotel*." *College Literature* 20, no. 3 (October 1993): 19–29.

Bone, Robert A. *The Negro Novel in America*. New Haven, Conn.: Yale University Press, 1965.

Buzard, James. *The Beaten Track: European Tourism, Literature, and the Ways to "Culture," 1800–1918*. Oxford: Clarendon Press, 1993.

Carlson, A. Cheree. "Limitations on the Comic Frame: Some Witty American Women of the Nineteenth Century." *Quarterly Journal of Speech* 74 (1988): 310–322.

Clinton, Catherine. *The Other Civil War: American Women in the Nineteenth Century.* New York: Farrar, Straus and Giroux, 1984.

Cott, Nancy F. *The Bonds of Womanhood: "Woman's Sphere" in New England, 1780–1835.* New Haven, Conn.: Yale University Press, 1977.

Coultrap-McQuin, Susan. *Doing Literary Business.* Chapel Hill: University of North Carolina Press, 1990.

Dorsey, Peter A. "De-Authorizing Slavery: Realism in Stowe's *Uncle Tom's Cabin* and Brown's *Clotel.*" *ESQ* 41, no. 4 (1995): 256–288.

Douglas, Ann. *The Feminization of American Culture.* New York: Knopf, 1977.

Ernest, John. *The Escape; or, A Leap for Freedom.* Knoxville: University of Tennessee Press, 2001.

Fabi, Giulia. "The 'Unguarded Expressions of the Feelings of the Negroes': Gender, Slave Resistance, and William Wells Brown's Revisions of *Clotel.*" *African-American Review* 27, no. 4 (Winter 1993): 639–654.

Farrison, William. *William Wells Brown: Author and Reformer.* Chicago: University of Chicago Press, 1969.

Fuller, Margaret. *At Home and Abroad; or, Things and Thoughts in American and Europe.* Edited by Arthur B. Fuller. Boston: Roberts Brothers, 1895.

Fuller, Margaret. *Summer on the Lakes, in 1843.* Boston: Little and Brown; New York: Charles S. Francis, 1844.

Genovese, Eugene D. *Roll, Jordan, Roll: The World the Slaves Made.* New York: Vintage, 1974.

Greenwood, Grace. *Haps and Mishaps of a Tour in Europe.* Boston: Ticknor, Reed, and Fields, 1854.

Harris, Susan K. *Nineteenth-Century American Women's Novels: Interpretive Strategies.* New York: Cambridge University Press, 1990.

Holley, Marietta. *Samantha among the Brethren.* New York: Funk and Wagnalls, 1890.

Holley, Marietta. *Samantha on the Race Problem* (1892). Upper Saddle River, N.J.: Literature House, 1969.

Irving, Washington. *The Alhambra*. 2 vols. Philadelphia: Carey & Lea, 1832.

Jackson, Blyden. "The First Negro Novelist." In *A History of Afro-American Literature*, vol. 1, pp. 326–332. Baton Rouge: Louisiana State University Press, 1989.

Kirkland, Caroline Stansbury. *Holidays Abroad; or, Europe from the West*. New York: Baker and Scribner, 1849.

Kolodny, Annette. *The Land before Her: Fantasy and Experience of the American Frontiers, 1630–1860*. Chapel Hill: University of North Carolina Press, 1984.

Kolodny, Annette. *The Lay of the Land: Metaphor as Experience and History in American Life and Letters*. Chapel Hill: University of North Carolina Press, 1975.

Levine, Robert S. "Commentary: Critical Disruptions." *American Literary History* 14, no. 3 (2002): 540–550.

Levine, Robert S., ed. *Clotel; or, The President's Daughter*. Bedford Cultural Edition. Boston: Bedford, 2000.

Lewis, Richard O. "Literary Conventions in the Novels of William Wells Brown." *College Language Association Journal* 29, no. 2 (December 1985): 129–156.

Loggins, Vernon. *The Negro Author: His Development in America to 1900*. New York: Columbia University Press, 1931.

Melville, Herman. *Typee*. New York: Wiley and Putnam, 1846.

Mills, Sara. *Discourses of Difference: An Analysis of Women's Travel Writing and Colonialism*. New York: Routledge, 1991.

Mitchell, Angelyn. "Her Side of His Story: A Feminist Analysis of Two Nineteenth-Century Antebellum Novels—William Wells Brown's *Clotel* and Harriet E. Wilson's *Our Nig*." *American Literary Realism* 24, no. 3 (Spring 1992): 7–21.

Moses, Wilson Jeremiah. *Alexander Crummell: A Study of Civilization and Discontent*. Amherst: University of Massachusetts Press, 1992.

Mulvey, Christopher. "The Fugitive Self and the New World of the North: William Wells Brown's Discovery of America." In *The Black Columbiad: Defining Moments in African American Literature and Culture*, edited by Werner Sollors and Maria Diedrich, pp. 99–111. Cambridge, Mass.: Harvard University Press, 1994.

Nelson, Dana. *National Manhood*. Durham, N.C.: Duke University Press, 1998.

Nelson, Dana. *The Word in Black and White: Reading Race in American Literature.* New York: Oxford University Press, 1992.

Pierson, Michael D. " 'Slavery Cannot Be Covered Up with Broadcloth or a Bandanna': The Evolution of White Abolitionist Attacks on the 'Patriarchal Institution.' " *Journal of the Early Republic* 25, no. 3 (2005): 383–415.

Pratt, Mary Louise. *Imperial Eyes: Travel Writing and Transculturation.* London: Routledge, 1992.

Ray, Angela G. *The Lyceum and Public Culture in the Nineteenth-Century United States.* East Lansing: Michigan State University Press, 2005.

Rosselot, Gerald S. "*Clotel,* a Black Romance." *College Language Association Journal* 23 (1980): 296–302.

Sedgwick, Catherine Maria. *Hope Leslie; or, Early Times in the Massachusetts.* 2 vols. New York: White, Gallaher, and White, 1827.

Sedgwick, Catherine Maria. *Letters from Abroad to Kindred at Home . . . by the Author of "Hope Leslie."* 2 vols. New York: Harper, 1841.

Sloss, Phyllis A. "Hierarchy, Irony, and the Thesis of Death in William Wells Brown's *Clotel; or, The President's Daughter.*" *Dissertation Abstracts International* 37 (1976): 974A.

Stowe, Harriet Beecher. *Sunny Memories of Foreign Lands.* 2 vols. Boston: Phillips, Sampson, 1854.

Tamarkin, Elisa. "Black Anglophilia; or, The Sociability of Antislavery." *American Literary History* 14, no. 3 (2002): 444–478.

Yellin, Jean F. *The Intricate Knot: The Negro in American Literature 1776–1863.* New York: New York University Press, 1971.

Yellin, Jean F. "Preface." *Clotel; or, the President's Daughter.* New York: Arno Press, 1969.

Index